Brief [Principles] of Macroeconomics: *a* GUIDED TOUR

Continued on next page

Brief Principles of
Macroeconomics

Sixth Edition

Brief Principles of

Macroeconomics

Sixth Edition

N. Gregory Mankiw
HARVARD UNIVERSITY

SOUTH-WESTERN
CENGAGE Learning™

Australia • Brazil • Japan • Korea • Mexico • Singapore • Spain • United Kingdom • United States

Brief Principles of Macroeconomics, 6E
N. Gregory Mankiw

Vice President of Editorial, Business:
 Jack W. Calhoun

Editor-in-Chief: Joseph Sabatino

Executive Editor: Mike Worls

Developmental Editor: Jane Tufts

Contributing Editors: Jennifer E. Thomas
 and Katie Trotta

Editorial Assistant: Allyn Bissmeyer

Senior Marketing Manager: John Carey

Associate Marketing Manager: Betty Jung

Senior Content Project Manager:
 Colleen A. Farmer

Media Editor: Sharon Morgan

Senior Frontlist Buyer, Manufacturing:
 Kevin Kluck

Senior Marketing Communications Manager:
 Sarah Greber

Production Service: Cadmus

Senior Art Director: Michelle Kunkler

Cover and Internal Designer: Ke Design

Internal Illustrations: Larry Moore

Cover Image: © Chalmers Bequest, Hackney
 Art Gallery, UK / Bridgeman Art Library
 International; © marc fischer / iStockphoto

Rights Acquisitions Specialist, Photos: John Hill

For product information and technology assistance, contact us at
Cengage Learning Customer & Sales Support, 1-800-354-9706

For permission to use material from this text or product, submit all requests online at **www.cengage.com/permissions**
Further permissions questions can be emailed to
permissionrequest@cengage.com

Exam*View*® is a registered trademark of eInstruction Corp. Windows is a registered trademark of the Microsoft Corporation used herein under license. Macintosh and Power Macintosh are registered trademarks of Apple Computer, Inc. used herein under license. © 2008 Cengage Learning. All Rights Reserved.

Library of Congress Control Number: 2010941872
Cengage Learning WebTutor™ is a trademark of Cengage Learning.

ISBN 13: 978-0-538-45307-3
ISBN 10: 0-538-45307-9

South-Western Cengage Learning
5191 Natorp Boulevard
Mason, OH 45040
USA

Cengage Learning products are represented in Canada by Nelson Education, Ltd.

For your course and learning solutions, visit **www.cengage.com**
Purchase any of our products at your local college store or at our preferred online store **www.cengageBrain.com**

Printed in the United States of America
1 2 3 4 5 6 7 14 13 12 11

To Catherine, Nicholas, and Peter,
my other contributions to the next generation

about the author

N. Gregory Mankiw is professor of economics at Harvard University. As a student, he studied economics at Princeton University and MIT. As a teacher, he has taught macroeconomics, micro-economics, statistics, and principles of economics. He even spent one summer long ago as a sailing instructor on Long Beach Island.

Professor Mankiw is a prolific writer and a regular participant in academic and policy debates. His work has been published in scholarly journals, such as the *American Economic Review, Journal of Political Economy*, and *Quarterly Journal of Economics*, and in more popular forums, such as *The New York Times* and *The Wall Street Journal*. He is also author of the best-selling intermediate-level text-book *Macroeconomics* (Worth Publishers). In addition to his teaching, research, and writing, Professor Mankiw has been a research associate of the National Bureau of Economic Research, an adviser to the Congressional Budget Office and the Federal Reserve Banks of Boston and New York, and a member of the ETS test development committee for the Advanced Placement exam in economics. From 2003 to 2005, he served as chairman of the President's Council of Economic Advisers.

Professor Mankiw lives in Wellesley, Massachusetts, with his wife, Deborah, three children, Catherine, Nicholas, and Peter, and their border terrier, Tobin.

brief contents

preface
to the instructor

During my twenty-year career as a student, the course that excited me most was the two-semester sequence on the principles of economics that I took during my freshman year in college. It is no exaggeration to say that it changed my life.

I had grown up in a family that often discussed politics over the dinner table. The pros and cons of various solutions to society's problems generated fervent debate. But in school, I had been drawn to the sciences. Whereas politics seemed vague, rambling, and subjective, science was analytic, systematic, and objective. While political debate continued without end, science made progress.

My freshman course on the principles of economics opened my eyes to a new way of thinking. Economics combines the virtues of politics and science. It is, truly, a social science. Its subject matter is society—how people choose to lead their lives and how they interact with one another—but it approaches the subject with the dispassion of a science. By bringing the methods of science to the questions of politics, economics tries to make progress on the challenges that all societies face.

I was drawn to write this book in the hope that I could convey some of the excitement about economics that I felt as a student in my first economics course. Economics is a subject in which a little knowledge goes a long way. (The same cannot be said, for instance, of the study of physics or the Japanese language.) Economists have a unique way of viewing the world, much of which can be taught in one or two semesters. My goal in this book is to transmit this way of thinking to the widest possible audience and to convince readers that it illuminates much about the world around them.

I believe that everyone should study the fundamental ideas that economics has to offer. One purpose of general education is to inform people about the world and thereby make them better citizens. The study of economics, as much as any discipline, serves this goal. Writing an economics textbook is, therefore, a great honor and a great responsibility. It is one way that economists can help promote better government and a more prosperous future. As the great economist Paul Samuelson put it, "I don't care who writes a nation's laws, or crafts its advanced treaties, if I can write its economics textbooks."

What's New in the Sixth Edition?

More of this book is devoted to applications—and less to formal economic theory—than is the case with many other books written for the principles course. Most chapters include case studies illustrating how the principles of economics are applied. In addition, "In The News" boxes offer excerpts from newspaper and magazine articles showing how economic ideas shed light on current issues facing society. After students finish their first course in economics, they should think about news stories from a new perspective and with greater insight.

The principles of economics are timeless, but the application of those principles changes over time as events unfold and as policymakers consider new initiatives.

To keep the study of economics fresh and relevant for each new cohort of students, teachers of economics must constantly update their courses. This is especially true today. Over the past few years, the economy experienced a major financial crisis and a deep economic downturn, the government and central bank took extraordinary steps to deal with these problems, and the nation elected a new president with an ambitious policy agenda. Students are eager to learn how to apply the ideas of economics to better understand these recent events.

This new edition contributes to that effort by including substantial new material, including dozens of new case studies and boxes. The new features in this edition are too numerous to list in their entirety, but here is a sample of the topics covered (and the chapters in which they occur):

- In 2008, oil prices skyrocketed, inducing a variety of expected and unexpected incentive effects. (Chapter 1)
- In 2009, President Obama moved into the White House. Chief economist Larry Summers summarized the president's economic vision. (Chapter 2)
- France's President Nicolas Sarkozy formed a commission, chaired by economist Joe Stiglitz, to examine whether GDP is a good measure of economic well-being. (Chapter 5)
- The financial system's ability to intermediate saving and investment was interrupted by a financial crisis. (Chapter 8)
- As unemployment rose, economists and policymakers reexamined the proper scope of unemployment insurance. (Chapter 10)
- Problems in the banking system highlighted the role of leverage and bank capital. (Chapter 11)
- The Federal Reserve introduced new tools for monetary policy, including the Term Auction Facility and interest on reserves. (Chapter 11)
- The U.S. economy experienced a deep recession in 2008 and 2009, with some parallels to the Great Depression. (Chapter 15)
- The Fed wrestled with the zero lower bound on interest rates. (Chapter 16)
- President Obama's stimulus bill reignited the debate over fiscal policy multipliers. (Chapter 16)
- Some economists suggested that the Fed should aim for somewhat higher inflation. (Chapter 17)

In addition to updating the book, I have refined its coverage and pedagogy with input from many users of the previous edition. There are numerous changes, large and small, aimed at making the book clearer and more student-friendly. For example, a poll of instructors has identified which end-of-chapters problems were most useful for homework assignments and in-class discussions. I have taken out less useful problems and have added many new ones.

All the changes that I made, and the many others that I considered, were evaluated in light of the benefits of brevity. Like most things that we study in economics, a student's time is a scarce resource. I always keep in mind a dictum from the great novelist Robertson Davies: "One of the most important things about writing is to boil it down and not bore the hell out of everybody."

How Is This Book Organized?

To write a brief and student-friendly book, I had to consider new ways to organize familiar material. What follows is a whirlwind tour of this text. The tour will, I hope, give instructors some sense of how the pieces fit together.

Introductory Material   Chapter 1, "Ten Principles of Economics," introduces students to the economist's view of the world. It previews some of the big ideas that recur throughout economics, such as opportunity cost, marginal decision making, the role of incentives, the gains from trade, and the efficiency of market allocations. Throughout the book, I refer regularly to the *Ten Principles of Economics* introduced in Chapter 1 to remind students that these ideas are the foundation for all economics.

Chapter 2, "Thinking Like an Economist," examines how economists approach their field of study. It discusses the role of assumptions in developing a theory and introduces the concept of an economic model. It also explores the role of economists in making policy. This chapter's appendix offers a brief refresher course on how graphs are used, as well as how they can be abused.

Chapter 3, "Interdependence and the Gains from Trade," presents the theory of comparative advantage. This theory explains why individuals trade with their neighbors, as well as why nations trade with other nations. Much of economics is about how market forces coordinate many individual production and consumption decisions. As a starting point for this analysis, students see in this chapter why specialization, interdependence, and trade can benefit everyone.

I next introduce the basic tools of supply and demand. Chapter 4, "The Market Forces of Supply and Demand," develops the supply curve, the demand curve, and the notion of market equilibrium. This microeconomic model is the starting point for much of macroeconomic theory.

Macroeconomics   My overall approach to teaching macroeconomics is to examine the economy in the long run (when prices are flexible) before examining the economy in the short run (when prices are sticky). I believe that this organization simplifies learning macroeconomics for several reasons. First, the classical assumption of price flexibility is more closely linked to the basic lessons of supply and demand, which students have already mastered. Second, the classical dichotomy allows the study of the long run to be broken up into several easily digested pieces. Third, because the business cycle represents a transitory deviation from the economy's long-run growth path, studying the transitory deviations is more natural after the long-run equilibrium is understood. Fourth, the macroeconomic theory of the long run is less controversial among economists than is the macroeconomic theory of the short run. For these reasons, most upper-level courses in macroeconomics now follow this long-run-before-short-run approach; my goal is to offer introductory students the same advantage.

I start the coverage of macroeconomics with issues of measurement. Chapter 5, "Measuring a Nation's Income," discusses the meaning of gross domestic product and related statistics from the national income accounts. Chapter 6, "Measuring the Cost of Living," examines the measurement and use of the consumer price index.

The next four chapters describe the behavior of the real economy in the long run. Chapter 7, "Production and Growth," examines the determinants of the large variation in living standards over time and across countries. Chapter 8, "Saving, Investment, and the Financial System," discusses the types of financial institutions in our economy and examines their role in allocating resources. Chapter 9, "The Basic Tools of Finance," introduces present value, risk management, and asset pricing. Chapter 10, "Unemployment," considers the long-run determinants of the unemployment rate, including job search, minimum-wage laws, the market power of unions, and efficiency wages.

Having described the long-run behavior of the real economy, the book then turns to the long-run behavior of money and prices. Chapter 11, "The Monetary

System," introduces the economist's concept of money and the role of the central bank in controlling the quantity of money. Chapter 12, "Money Growth and Inflation," develops the classical theory of inflation and discusses the costs that inflation imposes on a society.

The next two chapters present the macroeconomics of open economies, maintaining the long-run assumptions of price flexibility and full employment. Chapter 13, "Open-Economy Macroeconomics: Basic Concepts," explains the relationship among saving, investment, and the trade balance, the distinction between the nominal and real exchange rate, and the theory of purchasing-power parity. Chapter 14, "A Macroeconomic Theory of the Open Economy," presents a classical model of the international flow of goods and capital. The model sheds light on various issues, including the link between budget deficits and trade deficits and the macroeconomic effects of trade policies. Because instructors differ in their emphasis on this material, these chapters are written so they can be used in different ways. Some may choose to cover Chapter 13 but not Chapter 14; others may skip both chapters; and still others may choose to defer the analysis of open-economy macroeconomics until the end of their courses.

After developing the long-run theory of the economy in Chapters 7 through 14, the book turns to explaining short-run fluctuations around the long-run trend. Chapter 15, "Aggregate Demand and Aggregate Supply," begins with some facts about the business cycle and then introduces the model of aggregate demand and aggregate supply. Chapter 16, "The Influence of Monetary and Fiscal Policy on Aggregate Demand," explains how policymakers can use the tools at their disposal to shift the aggregate-demand curve. Chapter 17, "The Short-Run Trade-off between Inflation and Unemployment," explains why policymakers who control aggregate demand face a trade-off between inflation and unemployment. It examines why this trade-off exists in the short run, why it shifts over time, and why it does not exist in the long run.

The book concludes with Chapter 18, "Six Debates over Macroeconomic Policy." This capstone chapter considers six controversial issues facing policymakers: the proper degree of policy activism in response to the business cycle, the relative efficacy of government spending hikes and tax cuts to fight recessions, the choice between rules and discretion in the conduct of monetary policy, the desirability of reaching zero inflation, the importance of balancing the government's budget, and the need for tax reform to encourage saving. For each issue, the chapter presents both sides of the debate and encourages students to make their own judgments.

Learning Tools

The purpose of this book is to help students learn the fundamental lessons of economics and to show how they can apply these lessons to their lives and the world in which they live. Toward that end, I have used various learning tools that recur throughout the book.

Case Studies   Economic theory is useful and interesting only if it can be applied to understanding actual events and policies. This book, therefore, contains numerous case studies that apply the theory that has just been developed.

In The News Boxes   One benefit that students gain from studying economics is a new perspective and greater understanding about news from around the world. To highlight this benefit, I have included excerpts from many newspaper and magazine articles, some of which are opinion columns written by prominent economists. These articles, together with my brief introductions, show how basic economic theory can be applied. Most of these boxes are new to this edition.

FYI Boxes These boxes provide additional material "for your information." Some of them offer a glimpse into the history of economic thought. Others clarify technical issues. Still others discuss supplementary topics that instructors might choose either to discuss or skip in their lectures.

Definitions of Key Concepts When key concepts are introduced in the chapter, they are presented in **bold** typeface. In addition, their definitions are placed in the margins. This treatment should aid students in learning and reviewing the material.

Quick Quizzes After each major section, students are offered a Quick Quiz to check their comprehension of what they have just learned. If students cannot readily answer these quizzes, they should stop and reread material before continuing. The answers to all Quick Quizzes are available on the book's website.

Chapter Summaries Each chapter ends with a brief summary that reminds students of the most important lessons that they have just learned. Later in their study, it offers an efficient way to review for exams.

List of Key Concepts A list of key concepts at the end of each chapter offers students a way to test their understanding of the new terms that have been introduced. Page references are included so that students can review the terms they do not understand.

Questions for Review Located at the end of each chapter, questions for review cover the chapter's primary lessons. Students can use these questions to check their comprehension and prepare for exams.

Problems and Applications Each chapter also contains a variety of problems and applications that ask students to apply the material that they have learned. Some instructors may use these questions for homework assignments. Others may use them as a starting point for classroom discussions.

Alternative Versions of the Book

The book you are holding in your hand is one of five versions of this text that are available for introducing students to economics. South-Western/Cengage Learning and I offer this menu of books because instructors differ in how much time they have and what topics they choose to cover. Here is a brief description of each:

- *Principles of Economics*. This complete version of the book contains all 36 chapters. It is designed for two-semester introductory courses that cover both microeconomics and macroeconomics.
- *Principles of Microeconomics*. This version contains 22 chapters and is designed for one-semester courses in introductory microeconomics.
- *Principles of Macroeconomics*. This version contains 23 chapters and is designed for one-semester courses in introductory macroeconomics. It contains a full development of the theory of supply and demand.
- *Brief Principles of Macroeconomics*. This shortened macro version of 18 chapters contains only one chapter on the basics of supply and demand. It is designed for instructors who want to jump to the core topics of macroeconomics more quickly.
- *Essentials of Economics*. This version of the book contains 24 chapters. It is designed for one-semester survey courses that cover the basics of both microeconomics and macroeconomics.

The Five Versions of This Book

Chapter	Principles of Economics	Principles of Microeconomics	Principles of Macroeconomics	Brief Principles of Macroeconomics	Essentials of Economics
1. Ten Principles of Economics	X	X	X	X	X
2. Thinking Like an Economist	X	X	X	X	X
3. Interdependence and the Gains from Trade	X	X	X	X	X
4. The Market Forces of Supply and Demand	X	X	X	X	X
5. Elasticity and Its Application	X	X	X		X
6. Supply, Demand, and Government Policies	X	X	X		X
7. Consumers, Producers, and the Efficiency of Markets	X	X	X		X
8. Application: The Costs of Taxation	X	X	X		X
9. Application: International Trade	X	X	X		X
10. Externalities	X	X			X
11. Public Goods and Common Resources	X	X			X
12. The Design of the Tax System	X	X			
13. The Costs of Production	X	X			X
14. Firms in Competitive Markets	X	X			X
15. Monopoly	X	X			X
16. Monopolistic Competition	X	X			
17. Oligopoly	X	X			
18. The Markets for the Factors of Production	X	X			
19. Earnings and Discrimination	X	X			
20. Income Inequality and Poverty	X	X			
21. The Theory of Consumer Choice	X	X			
22. Frontiers of Microeconomics	X	X			
23. Measuring a Nation's Income	X		X	X	X
24. Measuring the Cost of Living	X		X	X	X
25. Production and Growth	X		X	X	X
26. Saving, Investment, and the Financial System	X		X	X	X
27. The Basic Tools of Finance	X		X	X	X
28. Unemployment	X		X	X	X
29. The Monetary System	X		X	X	X
30. Money Growth and Inflation	X		X	X	X
31. Open-Economy Macroeconomics: Basic Concepts	X		X	X	
32. A Macroeconomic Theory of the Open Economy	X		X	X	
33. Aggregate Demand and Aggregate Supply	X		X	X	X
34. The Influence of Monetary and Fiscal Policy on Aggregate Demand	X		X	X	X
35. The Short-Run Trade-off between Inflation and Unemployment	X		X	X	
36. Six Debates over Macroeconomic Policy	X		X	X	

Note: Chapter numbers refer to the complete book, *Principles of Economics.*

The accompanying table shows precisely which chapters are included in each book. Instructors who want more information about these alternative versions should contact their local South-Western/Cengage Learning representative.

Supplements
South-Western/Cengage Learning offers various supplements for instructors and students who use this book. These resources make teaching the principles of economics easy for the instructor and learning them easy for the student. David R. Hakes of the University of Northern Iowa, a dedicated teacher and economist, supervised the development of the supplements for this edition.

Translations and Adaptations
I am delighted that versions of this book are (or will soon be) available in many of the world's languages. Currently scheduled translations include Azeri, Chinese (in both standard and simplified characters), Croatian, Czech, Dutch, French, Georgian, German, Greek, Indonesian, Italian, Japanese, Korean, Macedonian, Montenegrin, Portuguese, Romanian, Russian, Serbian, and Spanish. In addition, adaptations of the book for Australian, Canadian, European, and New Zealand students are also available. Instructors who would like more information about these books should contact South-Western/Cengage Learning.

Acknowledgments
In writing this book, I benefited from the input of many talented people. Indeed, the list of people who have contributed to this project is so long, and their contributions so valuable, that it seems an injustice that only a single name appears on the cover.

Let me begin with my colleagues in the economics profession. The six editions of this text and its supplemental materials have benefited enormously from their input. In reviews and surveys, they have offered suggestions, identified challenges, and shared ideas from their own classroom experience. I am indebted to them for the perspectives they have brought to the text. Unfortunately, the list has become too long to thank those who contributed to previous editions, even though students reading the current edition are still benefiting from their insights.

Most important in this process have been Ron Cronovich (Carthage College) and David Hakes (University of Northern Iowa). Ron and David, both dedicated teachers, have served as reliable sounding boards for ideas and hardworking partners with me in putting together the superb package of supplements.

For this new edition, the following diary reviewers recorded their day-to-day experience over the course of a semester, offering detailed suggestions about how to improve the text.

Mark Abajian, *San Diego Mesa College*
Jennifer Bailly, *Long Beach City College*
J. Ulyses Balderas, *Sam Houston State University*
Antonio Bos, *Tusculum College*
Greg Brock, *Georgia Southern University*
Donna Bueckman, *University of Tennessee Knoxville*
Rita Callahan, *Keiser University*
Tina Collins, *San Joaquin Valley College*
Bob Holland, *Purdue University*
Tom Holmes, *University of Minnesota*
Simran Kahai, *John Carroll University*
Miles Kimball, *University of Michigan*
Jason C. Rudbeck, *University of Georgia*
Kent Zirlott, *University of Alabama Tuscaloosa*

The following reviewers of the fifth edition provided suggestions for refining the content, organization, and approach in the sixth.

Mark Abajian, *San Diego Mesa College*
Hamid Bastin, *Shippensburg University*
Laura Jean Bhadra, *Northern Virginia Community College*
Benjamin Blair, *Mississippi State University*
Lane Boyte, *Troy University*
Greg Brock, *Georgia Southern University*
Andrew Cassey, *Washington State University*
Joni Charles, *Texas State University - San Marcos*
Daren Conrad, *Bowie State University*
Diane de Freitas, *Fresno City College*
Veronika Dolar, *Cleveland State University*
Justin Dubas, *Texas Lutheran University*
Robert L Holland, *Purdue University*
Andres Jauregui, *Columbus State University*
Miles Kimball, *University of Michigan*
Andrew Kohen, *James Madison University*
Daniel Lee, *Shippensburg University*

David Lindauer, *Wellesley College*
Joshua Long, *Ivy Tech Community College*
James Makokha, *Collin College*
Jim McAndrew, *Luzerne County Community College*
William Mertens, *University of Colorado*
Cindy Munson, *Western Technical College*
David Mushinski, *Colorado State University*
Fola Odebunmi, *Cypress College*
Jeff Rubin, *Rutgers University, New Brunswick*
Lynda Rush, *California State Polytechnic University Pomona*
Naveen Sarna, *Northern Virginia Community College*
Jesse Schwartz, *Kennesaw State University*
Mark Showalter, *Brigham Young University*
Michael Tasto, *Southern New Hampshire University*

I received detailed feedback on specific elements in the text, including all end-of-chapter problems and applications, from the following instructors.

Mark Abajian, *San Diego Mesa College*
Afolabi Adebayo, *University of New Hampshire*
Mehdi Afiat, *College of Southern Nevada*
Douglas Agbetsiafa, *Indiana University South Bend*
Richard Agnello, *University of Delaware*
Henry Akian, *Gibbs College*
Constantine Alexandrakis, *Hofstra University*
Michelle Amaral, *University of the Pacific*
Shahina Amin, *University of Northern Iowa*
Larry Angel, *South Seattle Community College*
Kathleen Arano, *Fort Hays State University*

J. J. Arias, *Georgia College & State University*
Nestor Azcona, *Babson College*
Steve Balassi, *St. Mary's College/Napa Valley College*
Juventino Ulyses Balderas, *Sam Houston State University*
Tannista Banerjee, *Purdue University*
Jason Barr, *Rutgers University, Newark*
Alan Barreca, *Tulane University*
Hamid Bastin, *Shippensburg University*
Tammy Batson, *Northern Illinois University / Rock Valley College*
Carl Bauer, *Oakton Community College*
Klaus Becker, *Texas Tech University*
Robert Beekman, *University of Tampa*
Christian Beer, *Cape Fear Community College*
Gary Bennett, *State University of New York Fredonia*

Bettina Berch, *Borough of Manhattan Community College*

Thomas M. Beveridge, *Durham Technical Community College*

Abhijeet Bhattacharya, *Illinois Valley Community College*

Prasad Bidarkota, *Florida International University*

Jekab Bikis, *Dallas Baptist University*

Michael Bognanno, *Temple University*

Cecil Bohanon, *Ball State University*

Natalia Boliari, *Manhattan College*

Melanie Boyte, *Troy University*

Charles Braymen, *Kansas State*

William Brennan, *Minnesota State University at Mankato*

Greg Brock, *Georgia Southern University*

Ken Brown, *University of Northern Iowa*

Laura Bucila, *Texas Christian University*

Stan Buck, *Huntington University*

Donna Bueckman, *University of Tennessee Knoxville*

Joe Bunting, *St. Andrews Presbyterian College*

Rita Callahan, *Keiser University*

Michael G. Carew, *Baruch College*

John Carter, *Modesto Junior College*

Kalyan Chakraborty, *Emporia State University*

Henry Check, *Penn State University*

Xudong Chen, *Baldwin-Wallace College*

Clifton M. Chow, *Mass Bay Community College*

Tina Collins, *San Joaquin Valley College*

Valerie Collins, *Sheridan College*

Sarah Cosgrove, *University of Massachusetts Dartmouth*

Dana Costea, *Indiana University South Bend*

Maria DaCosta, *University of Wisconsin Eau Claire*

Mian Dai, *Drexel University*

Joel Dalafave, *Bucks County Community College*

Maylene Damoense, *Monash University South Africa*

Lorie Darche, *Southwest Florida College*

Diane de Freitas, *Fresno City College*

Ejigou Demissie, *University of Maryland Eastern Shore*

Richard DePolt, *Guilford Technical Community College*

Aaron Dighton, *University of Minnesota*

Veronika Dolar, *Cleveland State University*

Fisher Donna, *Georgia Southern University*

Harold Elder, *University of Alabama*

Jamie Emerson, *Salisbury University*

Elena Ermolenko, *Oakton Community College*

Pat Euzent, *University of Central Florida*

Yan Feng, *Hunter College, Queens College, CUNY*

Donna K. Fisher, *Georgia Southern University*

Paul Fisher, *Henry Ford Community College*

Fred Foldvary, *Santa Clara University*

Nikki Follis, *Chadron State College*

Kent Ford, *State University of New York / Onondaga Community College*

Ryan Ford, *Pasadena City College*

Timothy Ford, *California State University Sacramento*

Johanna Francis, *Fordham University*

Robert Francis, *Shoreline Community College*

Mark Frascatore, *Clarkson University*

David Furst, *University of South Florida*

Monica Galizzi, *University of Massachusetts Lowell*

Jean-Philippe Gervais, *North Carolina State University*

Dipak Ghosh, *Emporia State University*

Bill Goffe, *State University of New York Oswego*

Ryan Gorka, *University of Nebraska Lincoln*

Marshall Gramm, *Rhodes College*

Elias C. Grivoyannis, *Yeshiva University*

Eleanor Gubins, *Rosemont College*

Darrin Gulla, *University of Kentucky*

Karen Gulliver, *Argosy University*

Ranganai Gwati, *University of Washington Seattle*

Mike Haupert, *University of Wisconsin La Crosse*
L Jay Helms, *University of California Davis*
Dr. David Hennessy, *University of Dubuque*
Curry Hilton, *Guilford Technical Community College*
George Hoffer, *Virginia Commonwealth University*
Mark Holmes, *University of Waikato*
Carl Hooker, *Community College of Vermont*
Daniel Horton, *Cleveland State University*
Scott Houser, *Colorado School of the Mines*
Fanchang Huang, *Washington University in St Louis*
Gregory Hunter, *California State Polytechnic University Pomona*
Christopher Hyer, *University of New Mexico*
Leke Ijiyode, *St. Mary's University of Minnesota*
Chris Inama, *Golden Gate University*
Sarbaum Jeff, *University of North Carolina Greensboro*
Chad Jennings, *Tennessee Temple University*
Philipp Jonas, *Kalamazoo Valley Community College*
Robert Jones, *Rensselaer Polytechnic Institute*
Prathibha Joshi, *Gordon College*
James Jozefowicz, *Indiana University of Pennsylvania*
Mahbubul Kabir, *Lyon College*
Simran Kahai, *John Carroll University*
David Kalist, *Shippensburg University*
Camilla Kazimi, *St. Mary's College*
Chris Kelton, *Naval Postgraduate School*
Brian Kench, *University of Tampa*
Hyeongwoo Kim, *Auburn University*
Miles Kimball, *University of Michigan*
Alfreda L. King, *Lawson State Community College*
Elizabeth Knowles, *–Univeristy of Wisconsin La Crosse*
Fred Kolb, *University of Wisconsin Eau Claire*
Risa Kumazawa, *Duquesne University*

Sumner La Croix, *University of Hawaii*
Christopher Laincz, *Drexel University*
Ghislaine Lang, *San Jose State University*
Carolyn Langston, *South Arkansas Community College*
Richard Le, *Cosumnes River College*
Daniel Lee, *Shippensburg University*
Tom Lehman, *Indiana Wesleyan University*
Megan Leonard, *Hendrix College*
Larry Lichtenstein, *Canisius College*
Tad Lincoln, *Middlesex Community College*
David Linthicum, *Cecil College North East*
Sam Liu, *West Valley College*
Melody Lo, *University of Texas at San Antonio*
Volodymyr Logovskyy, *Georgia Institute of Technology*
Min Lu, *Robert Morris University*
Gennady Lyakir, *Champlain College*
Bruce Madariaga, *Montgomery Community College*
Brinda Mahalingam, *University of California Riverside*
Rubana Mahjabeen, *Truman State University*
Bahman Maneshni, *Paradise Valley Community College*
Denton Marks, *University of Wisconsin-Whitewater*
Timothy Mathews, *Kennesaw State University*
Frances Mc Donald, *Northern Virginia Community College*
Edward McGrath, *Holyoke Community College*
Shirley Ann Merchant, *George Washington University*
William Mertens, *University of Colorado*
Mitch Mitchell, *Bladen Community College*
Mitch Mitchell, *North Carolina Wesleyan*
Mike Mogavero, *University of Notre Dame*
Prof Ramesh Mohan, *Bryant University*
Daniel Monchuk, *University of Southern Mississippi*

Vasudeva Murthy, *Creighton University*

David Mushinsk, *Colorado State University*

Paula Nas, *University of Michigan Flint*

Russ Neal, *Collin County Community College*

Megumi Nishimura, *University of Colorado*

Peter Olson, *Indiana University*

Esen Onur, *California State University Sacramento*

Stephen Onyeiwu, *Allegheny College*

Margaret Oppenheimer, *DePaul University*

Glenda Orosco, *Oklahoma State University Institute of Technology*

David Ortmeyer, *Bentley University*

Thomas Owen, *College of the Redwoods*

Jan Palmer, *Ohio University*

Amar Parai, *State University of New York at Fredonia*

Nitin Paranjpe, *Wayne State and Oakland University*

Carl Parker, *Fort Hays State University*

Michael Petrack, *Oakland Community College*

Gyan Pradhan, *Eastern Kentucky University*

Michael Pries, *University of Notre Dame*

Joe Quinn, *Boston College*

Mahesh Ramachandran, *Clark University*

Ratha Ramoo, *Diablo Valley College*

Surekha Rao, *Indiana University Northwest*

Ryan Ratcliff, *University of San Diego*

Scott Redenius, *Brandeis University*

Susan Reilly, *Florida State College at Jacksonville*

Imke Reimers, *University of Minnesota*

Christopher Richardson, *Merrillville High School*

Art Riegal, *State University of New York Sullivan*

Richard Risinit, *Middlesex Community College*

Michael Rogers, *Albany State University*

Paul Roscelli, *Canada College*

Larry Ross, *University of Alaska Anchorage*

Jeff Rubin, *Rutgers University*

Allen Sanderson, *University of Chicago*

Jeff Sarbaum, *University of North Carolina Greensboro*

Dennis Shannon, *Southwestern Illinois College*

Xuguang Sheng, *State University of New York at Fredonia*

Mark Showalter, *Brigham Young University*

Johnny Shull, *Central Carolina Community College*

Suann Shumaker, *Las Positas Community College*

Jonathan Silberman, *Oakland University*

Steven Skinner, *Western Connecticut State University*

Catherine Skura, *Sandhills Community College*

Gary Smith, *D'Youville College*

Warren Smith, *Keiser University*

William Snyder, *Peru State College*

Ken Somppi, *Southern Union State Community College*

Dale Steinreich, *Drury University*

Liliana Stern, *Auburn University*

Derek Stimel, *Menlo College*

Carolyn Fabian Stumph, *Indiana University Purdue University Fort Wayne*

Bryce Sutton, *University of Alabama at Birmingham*

Justin Tapp, *Southwest Baptist University*

Dosse Toulaboe, *Fort Hays State University*

Richard Trainer, *State University of New York at Nassau*

Ngoc Bich Tran, *San Jacinto College*

Sandra Trejos, *Clarion University of Pennsylvania*

Julie Trivitt, *Arkansas Tech University*

Arja Turunen-Red, *University of New Orleans*

Diane Tyndall, *Craven Community College*

Kay Unger, *University of Montana*

Lee J. Van Scyoc, *University of Wisconsin Oshkosh*

Lisa Verissimo-Bates, *Foothill College*
Priti Verma, *Texas A&M University, Kingsville*
Patrick Walsh, *St. Michael's College*
Jing Wang, *Northeastern University*
Donald Waters, *Brayant and Stratton College, Virginia Beach, Virgina Campus*
Patrick Welle, *Bemidji State University*
Elizabeth Wheaton, *Southern Methodist University*
Luther White, *Central Carolina Community College*
Oxana Wieland, *University of Minnesota Crookston*
John Winters, *Auburn University at Montgomery*
Suzanne Wisniewski, *University of St. Thomas*
Patricia Wiswell, *Columbia-Greene Community College*
Mark Witte, *College of Charleston*
Louis A. Woods, *University of North Florida*
Guy Yamashiro, *California State University Long Beach*
Benhua Yang, *Stetson University*
Leslie Young, *Kilian Community College*
Karen Zempel, *Bryant and Stratton College*

The team of editors who worked on this book improved it tremendously. Jane Tufts, developmental editor, provided truly spectacular editing—as she always does. Mike Worls, economics executive editor, did a splendid job of overseeing the many people involved in such a large project. Jennifer Thomas (supervising developmental editor) and Katie Yanos (supervising developmental editor) were crucial in assembling an extensive and thoughtful group of reviewers to give me feedback on the previous edition, while putting together an excellent team to revise the supplements. Colleen Farmer, senior content project manager, and Malvine Litten, project manager, had the patience and dedication necessary to turn my manuscript into this book. Michelle Kunkler, senior art director, gave this book its clean, friendly look. Larry Moore, the illustrator, helped make the book more visually appealing and the economics in it less abstract. Sheryl Nelson, copyeditor, refined my prose, and Cindy Kerr, indexer, prepared a careful and thorough index. John Carey, senior marketing manager, worked long hours getting the word out to potential users of this book. The rest of the Cengage team was also consistently professional, enthusiastic, and dedicated: Allyn Bissmeyer, Darrell Frye, Sarah Greber, Betty Jung, Deepak Kumar, Kim Kusnerak, Sharon Morgan, Suellen Ruttkay, and Joe Sabatino.

I am grateful also to Stacy Carlson and Daniel Norris, two star Harvard undergraduates, who helped me refine the manuscript and check the page proofs for this edition. Josh Bookin, a former Advanced Placement economics teacher and recently an extraordinary section leader for Harvard's Ec 10, gave invaluable advice on some of the new material in this edition.

As always, I must thank my "in-house" editor Deborah Mankiw. As the first reader of most things I write, she continued to offer just the right mix of criticism and encouragement.

Finally, I would like to mention my three children Catherine, Nicholas, and Peter. Their contribution to this book was putting up with a father spending too many hours in his study. The four of us have much in common—not least of which is our love of ice cream (which becomes apparent in Chapter 4). Maybe sometime soon one of them will pick up my passion for economics as well.

N. Gregory Mankiw
December 2010

preface
to the student

"Economics is a study of mankind in the ordinary business of life." So wrote Alfred Marshall, the great 19th-century economist, in his textbook, *Principles of Economics*. Although we have learned much about the economy since Marshall's time, this definition of economics is as true today as it was in 1890, when the first edition of his text was published.

Why should you, as a student at the beginning of the 21st century, embark on the study of economics? There are three reasons.

The first reason to study economics is that it will help you understand the world in which you live. There are many questions about the economy that might spark your curiosity. Why are apartments so hard to find in New York City? Why do airlines charge less for a round-trip ticket if the traveler stays over a Saturday night? Why is Johnny Depp paid so much to star in movies? Why are living standards so meager in many African countries? Why do some countries have high rates of inflation while others have stable prices? Why are jobs easy to find in some years and hard to find in others? These are just a few of the questions that a course in economics will help you answer.

The second reason to study economics is that it will make you a more astute participant in the economy. As you go about your life, you make many economic decisions. While you are a student, you decide how many years to stay in school. Once you take a job, you decide how much of your income to spend, how much to save, and how to invest your savings. Someday you may find yourself running a small business or a large corporation, and you will decide what prices to charge for your products. The insights developed in the coming chapters will give you a new perspective on how best to make these decisions. Studying economics will not by itself make you rich, but it will give you some tools that may help in that endeavor.

The third reason to study economics is that it will give you a better understanding of both the potential and the limits of economic policy. Economic questions are always on the minds of policymakers in mayors' offices, governors' mansions, and the White House. What are the burdens associated with alternative forms of taxation? What are the effects of free trade with other countries? What is the best way to protect the environment? How does a government budget deficit affect the economy? As a voter, you help choose the policies that guide the allocation of society's resources. An understanding of economics will help you carry out that responsibility. And who knows: Perhaps someday you will end up as one of those policymakers yourself.

Thus, the principles of economics can be applied in many of life's situations. Whether the future finds you reading the newspaper, running a business, or sitting in the Oval Office, you will be glad that you studied economics.

N. Gregory Mankiw
December 2010

Experience
Mankiw

The Art of Instruction, The Power of Engagement, The Spark of Discovery

N. Gregory Mankiw's economics texts became best sellers after their introduction and they continue to be the most widely used texts in the world because a superb writer and economist understood that true learning is a collaborative effort and he created the right tools to make the process possible. The Mankiw family of texts stress the most important concepts without overwhelming students with an excess of detail—a formula widely imitated, but yet to be matched!

EXPERIENCE
The Art of Instruction. The Power of Engagement. The Spark of Discovery.
MANKIW

The Art of
Instruction

The art of teaching is the
art of **assisting discovery.**
– Mark Van Doren

EXPERIENCE PREMIUM TEACHING TOOLS

Teaching resources and ancillaries are one of the central features of the Mankiw experience. Mankiw is the only principles text that uses a team of instructor/ancillary preparers, many of whom have been involved since the first edition. No other publisher invests as heavily as we do to ensure that our materials are worthy of the effort that you put into teaching.

The Mankiw experience offers three choices of PowerPoint®:

Premium slides offer examples and classroom ideas that go beyond what is included in the book to enhance the value of classroom discussion; **Lecture** Slides cover the highlights from the book; **Exhibit** slides include the graphs and visuals directly from the book.

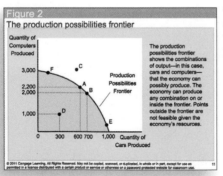

This slide example was taken from the Traditional Lecture PowerPoint Slides.

Test Bank
Over 7,800 Quality Test Questions

The Mankiw Test Bank consists of more than 250 questions per chapter. Every question has been checked to ensure the accuracy and clarity of the answer, and questions have been thoroughly revised to address the main text revisions. Included are true/false, multiple-choice, and short-answer questions that assess students' critical thinking skills. Easy, medium, and difficult questions outline the process that students must use to arrive at their answers: recall, application, and integration. Questions are organized by text section to help you pick and choose your selections with ease. All questions are tagged to AACSB learning standards so that student outcomes can be measured as needed by your department/university.

Instructor's Manual with Solutions Manual

Prepared by Linda S. Ghent, Eastern Illinois University, the sixth edition offers a detailed outline for each chapter of the text that provides learning objectives, identifies stumbling blocks that students may face and offers helpful teaching tips, and provides suggested in-classroom activities for a more "cooperative learning" experience. The manual also includes solutions to all end-of-chapter exercises, Quick Quizzes, Questions for Review, and Problems and Applications found in the text. It is also available online and on the Instructor's Resource CD.

Mankiw 6e Community Site

Visit Mankiw's community site for the 6th edition at **www.cengage.com/community/mankiw**. Developed to keep you tied to the pulse of economics, our community website takes your Mankiw Experience to a whole new level. This expansive resource enables you to access teaching resources, find the latest news updates, and learn more about what Mankiw 6e can do for you and your students!

The Power of Engagement

We learn best when we are engaged in the process of learning and effort is a function of success. No other publisher offers the range and quality of resources to engage students.

EXPERIENCE APLIA

Aplia™

Created by economist Paul Romer for his classroom, Aplia is the best selling online economics product. In fact, Aplia is the most successful and widely used homework solution in the Economics market. Aplia provides automatically graded assignments that were written to make the most of the web medium and contain detailed immediate explanations of every question. A digital edition of the complete Mankiw textbook is embedded in the Aplia course.

ApliaText

The Mankiw Aplia product is now available with ApliaText, a complete interactive digital edition of the text embedded right into the Aplia program. Unlike a static eBook, ApliaText engages students with the same style and feel of the Internet sites students visit with animated graphs, videos embedded within each chapter, and note-taking functionality.

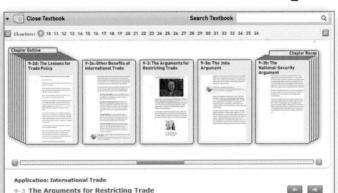

For complete details, visit **www.aplia.com.**

To see a demo of ApliaText with Mankiw, visit **www.cengage.com/economics/mankiw.**

EXPERIENCE ECONOMICS COURSEMATE

CourseMate

Economics CourseMate: Engaging, Trackable, Affordable

Economics CourseMate brings course concepts to life with interactive learning, study, and exam preparation tools that support the printed textbook. Watch student comprehension soar as your class works with the printed textbook and the text-specific website. Economics CourseMate goes beyond the book to deliver what you need!

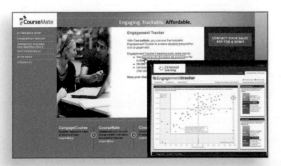

ENGAGEMENT TRACKER:
How do you know your students have read the material or viewed the resources you've assigned? Engagement Tracker assesses student preparation and engagement. Use the tracking tools to see progress for the class as a whole or for individual students. Identify students at risk early in the course. Uncover which concepts are most difficult for your class. Monitor time on task. Keep your students engaged.

INTERACTIVE TEACHING AND LEARNING TOOLS:
Economics CourseMate provides interactive teaching and learning tools including:
- Quizzes
- Flashcards
- Videos
- Graphing Tutorials
- News, Debates, and Data

INTERACTIVE EBOOK:
In addition to interactive teaching and learning tools, Economics CourseMate includes an interactive eBook. Students can take notes, highlight, search and interact with embedded media specific to their book.

Go to **login.cengage.com** to access these resources within CourseMate.

The Power of Engagement

EXPERIENCE THE WATCH

The Global Economic Watch

The Watch, a groundbreaking resource, stimulates discussion and understanding of the global downturn with easy-to-integrate teaching solutions:

- A content-rich blog of breaking news, expert analysis, and commentary—updated multiple times daily.
- A powerful real-time database of hundreds of relevant and vetted journal, newspaper, and periodical articles, videos, and podcasts—updated four times every day.
- A thorough overview and timeline of events leading up to the global economic crisis.
- Discussion and testing content, PowerPoint slides on key topics, sample syllabi, and other teaching resources.

For more information, visit **www.cengage.com/thewatch**.

EXPERIENCE CENGAGENOW

CengageNOW

Ensure that your students have the understanding of procedures and concepts they need to know with CengageNOW for Mankiw 6e. This integrated, online course management and learning system combines the best of current technology to save time in planning and managing your course and assignments. You can reinforce comprehension with customized student learning paths and efficiently test and automatically grade assignments with reports that correspond to AACSB standards. With CengageNOW, you'll find:

- End-of-chapter questions are included and can be assigned as homework.
- **A diagnostic Personalized Study Plan** identifies troublesome concepts for individual students and creates student-specific study plans for better class preparations and grades.
- All questions are **clearly identified by AACSB standards.**
- Access to EconApps, Graphing Workshop, Quizzes, Mankiw's Ten Principles of Economics Videos, Greg Mankiw Answers Key Questions Videos, Student PowerPoint handouts, and the Mankiw Blog Map.
- CengageNOW is compatible with your current Learning Management System, such as Blackboard® or WebTutor™.

Find out more at www.cengage.com/now.

The Spark of
Discovery

Greg Mankiw is one of the best writers in economics both for the academic audience and for the general public. Nobody illuminates and clarifies economics like **Mankiw**.

" A **mighty flame**
followeth a tiny spark."
– Dante

EXPERIENCE MANKIW: SUPERIOR WRITING AND CONTENT

Along with the crystal-clear writing style, this edition fully incorporates the most current information and analysis of the current economics environment.

- **Extensively updated coverage of areas impacted by the financial crisis**, including a discussion of the downturn in the chapter on "Aggregate Demand and Aggregate Supply" and an **expanded discussion of how the Fed influences the money supply** in the chapter on "The Influence of Monetary and Fiscal Policy on Aggregate Demand."

- **Updated coverage and examples reflecting current economic conditions** throughout, including the rise of long-term unemployment and the debate over fiscal policy multipliers.

- The final macroeconomic chapter now includes a new sixth topic covering spending increases versus tax cuts to fight recessions.

---

in the news

The Rise of Long-Term Unemployment

During the economic downturn of 2008 and 2009, the number of long-term unemployed reached historic highs.

Chronic Joblessness Bites Deep

By Sara Murray

Richard Moran, sitting in his garage in Ortonville, Mich., Tuesday, has been unemployed for two-and-a-half years after losing his job with Chrysler.

The job market is improving, but one statistic presents a stark reminder of the challenges that remain: Nearly half of the unemployed—45.9%—have been out of work longer than six months, more than at any time since the Labor Department began keeping track in 1948.

Source: *The Wall Street Journal*, June 2, 2010.

Even in the worst months of the early 1980s, when the jobless rate topped 10% for months on end, only about one in four of the unemployed was out of work for more than six months.

Overall, seven million Americans have been looking for work for 27 weeks or more, and most of them—4.7 million—have been out of work for a year or more.

Long-term unemployment has reached nearly every segment of the population, but some have been particularly hard-hit. The typical long-term unemployed worker is a white man with a high-school education or less. Older unemployed workers also tend to be out of work longer. Those between ages 65 and 69 who still wish to work have typically been jobless for 49.8 weeks.

The effects of long-term unemployment are likely to linger when the overall jobless rate falls toward normal, threatening to create a pool of nearly permanently unemployed workers, a condition once more common in Europe than in the U.S.

"The consequences are worse for those who can't find a job quickly," said Till Marco von Wachter, a Columbia University economist. They extend from atrophying skills to a higher likelihood of unhappiness and anxiety. Workers out of work for a long time tend to find it more difficult to find a job, and "the longer people are unemployed the more likely they are to eventually give up searching and thereby drop out of the labor force," Mr. von Wachter said.

unemployment rate never falls to zero; instead, it fluctuates around the natural rate of unemployment. To understand this natural rate, the remaining sections of this chapter examine the reasons actual labor markets depart from the ideal of full employment.

To preview our conclusions, we will find that there are four ways to explain unemployment in the long run. The first explanation is that it takes time for workers to search for the jobs that are best suited for them. The unemployment that results from the process of matching workers and jobs is sometimes called **frictional unemployment**, and it is often thought to explain relatively short spells of unemployment.

The next three explanations for unemployment suggest that the number of jobs available in some labor markets may be insufficient to give a job to everyone who wants one. This occurs when the quantity of labor supplied exceeds the quantity demanded. Unemployment of this sort is sometimes called

frictional unemployment
unemployment that results because it takes time for workers to search for the jobs that best suit their tastes and skills

The Spark of
Discovery

·········· in the **news**

> ### Bernanke on the Fed's Toolbox
During the financial crisis of 2008 and 2009, the Federal Reserve helped rescue a variety of banks and other financial institutions and, in the process, substantially expanded the quantity of bank reserves. Most of these newly created reserves were held as excess reserves by the banking system. In this article, the chairman of the Federal Reserve explains the Fed's plans to unwind the process in the aftermath of these events.

The Fed's Exit Strategy
BY BEN BERNANKE

The depth and breadth of the global recession has required a highly accommodative monetary policy. Since the onset of the financial crisis nearly two years ago, the Federal Reserve has reduced the interest-rate target for overnight lending between banks (the federal-funds rate) nearly to zero. We have also greatly expanded the size of the Fed's balance sheet through purchases of longer-term securities and through targeted lending programs aimed at restarting the flow of credit.

These actions have softened the economic impact of the financial crisis. They have also improved the functioning of key credit markets, including the markets for interbank lending, commercial paper, consumer and small-business credit, and residential mortgages.

My colleagues and I believe that accommodative policies will likely be warranted for an extended period. At some point, however, as economic recovery takes hold, we will need to tighten moneta... to prevent the emergence of an ... problem down the road. The Fede...

Fed Chairman Ben Bernanke

Market Committee, which is responsible for setting U.S. monetary policy, has devoted considerable time to issues relating to an exit strategy. We are confident we have the necessary tools to withdraw policy accommodation, when that becomes appropriate, in a smooth and timely manner.

The exit strategy is closely tied to the management of the Federal Reserve balance sheet. When the Fed makes loans or acquires securities, the funds enter the banking system and ultimately appear in the reserve accounts held at the Fed by banks and other depository institutions. These reserve balances now total about $800 billion, much

But as the economy recovers, banks should find more opportunities to lend out their reserves. That would produce faster growth in broad money (for example, M1 or M2) and easier credit conditions, which could ultimately result in inflationary pressures—unless we adopt countervailing policy measures. When the time comes to tighten monetary policy, we must either eliminate these large reserve balances or, if they remain, neutralize any potential undesired effects on the economy.

To some extent, reserves held by banks at the Fed will contract automatically, as improving financial conditions lead to reduced use of our short-term lending facilities, and ultimately to their wind down. Indeed, short-term credit extended by the Fed to financial institutions and other market participants has already fallen to less than $600 billion as of mid-July from about $1.5 trillion at the end of 2008. In addition, reserves could be reduced by about $100 billion to $200 billion each year over the next few years as securities held by the Fed mature or are prepaid. However,

---

- Dozens of **new applications throughout emphasize the real-world relevance of economics for today's students** through interesting articles, realistic case studies, and engaging problems. Many new *In The News, Case Study,* and *FYI* features reflect the most current data and news stories that keep students talking. A few examples of the new applications include:

  - In the News: The Economics of President Obama
  - In the News: Is the Efficient Markets Hypothesis Kaput?
  - In the News: Bernanke on the Fed's Toolbox
  - In the News: The Rise of Long-Term Unemployment
  - FYI: Financial Crises
  - In the News: How Much Do the Unemployed Respond to Incentives?
  - FYI: Hyperinflation in Zimbabwe
  - Case Study: The Recession of 2008–2009
  - FYI: Inflation Targeting

·········· in the **news**

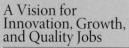

> ### The Economics of President Obama
Here is how Larry Summers, a chief economic adviser to Barack Obama, describes the president's policies.

A Vision for Innovation, Growth, and Quality Jobs
BY LAWRENCE H. SUMMERS

President Obama laid out his vision for innovation, growth, and quality jobs earlier today at Hudson Valley Community College. This President's plan is grounded not only in the American tradition of entrepreneurship, but also in the traditions of robust economic thought.

During the past two years, the ideas propounded by John Maynard Keynes have assumed greater importance than most people would have thought in the previous generation. As Keynes famously observed, during those rare times of deep financial and economic crisis, when the "invisible hand" Adam Smith talked about has temporarily ceased to function, there is a more urgent need for government to play an active role in restoring markets to their healthy function.

The wisdom of Keynesian policies has been confirmed by the performance of the economy over the past year. After the collapse of Lehman Brothers last September, government policy moved in a strongly activist direction.

As a result of those policies, our outlook today has shifted from rescue to recovery, from worrying about the very real prospect of depression to thinking about what kind of an expansion we want to have.

An important aspect of any economic expansion is the role innovation plays as

Federal Reserve, the institution that sets the nation's monetary policy, employs hundreds of economists to analyze economic developments in the United States and throughout the world.

PART I Introduction 1

PART II How Markets Work 63

PART III The Data of Macro-economics 89

PART V   Money and Prices in the Long Run   217

PART **VII** Short-Run
Economic
Fluctuations   317

PART **VIII** Final
Thoughts 409

PART I Introduction

Ten Principles of Economics

1

The word *economy* comes from the Greek word *oikonomos*, which means "one who manages a household." At first, this origin might seem peculiar. But in fact, households and economies have much in common.

A household faces many decisions. It must decide which members of the household do which tasks and what each member gets in return: Who cooks dinner? Who does the laundry? Who gets the extra dessert at dinner? Who gets to choose what TV show to watch? In short, the household must allocate its scarce resources among its various members, taking into account each member's abilities, efforts, and desires.

Like a household, a society faces many decisions. A society must find some way to decide what jobs will be done and who will do them. It needs some people to grow food, other people to make clothing, and still others to design computer software. Once society has allocated people (as well as land, buildings, and machines) to various jobs, it must also allocate the output of goods and services

3

they produce. It must decide who will eat caviar and who will eat potatoes. It must decide who will drive a Ferrari and who will take the bus.

scarcity
the limited nature of society's resources

The management of society's resources is important because resources are scarce. **Scarcity** means that society has limited resources and therefore cannot produce all the goods and services people wish to have. Just as each member of a household cannot get everything he or she wants, each individual in a society cannot attain the highest standard of living to which he or she might aspire.

economics
the study of how society manages its scarce resources

Economics is the study of how society manages its scarce resources. In most societies, resources are allocated not by an all-powerful dictator but through the combined actions of millions of households and firms. Economists therefore study how people make decisions: how much they work, what they buy, how much they save, and how they invest their savings. Economists also study how people interact with one another. For instance, they examine how the multitude of buyers and sellers of a good together determine the price at which the good is sold and the quantity that is sold. Finally, economists analyze forces and trends that affect the economy as a whole, including the growth in average income, the fraction of the population that cannot find work, and the rate at which prices are rising.

The study of economics has many facets, but it is unified by several central ideas. In this chapter, we look at *Ten Principles of Economics*. Don't worry if you don't understand them all at first or if you aren't completely convinced. We will explore these ideas more fully in later chapters. The ten principles are introduced here to give you an overview of what economics is all about. Consider this chapter a "preview of coming attractions."

How People Make Decisions

There is no mystery to what an economy is. Whether we are talking about the economy of Los Angeles, the United States, or the whole world, an economy is just a group of people dealing with one another as they go about their lives. Because the behavior of an economy reflects the behavior of the individuals who make up the economy, we begin our study of economics with four principles of individual decision making.

Principle 1: People Face Trade-offs

You may have heard the old saying, "There ain't no such thing as a free lunch." Grammar aside, there is much truth to this adage. To get one thing that we like, we usually have to give up another thing that we like. Making decisions requires trading off one goal against another.

Consider a student who must decide how to allocate her most valuable resource—her time. She can spend all her time studying economics, spend all of it studying psychology, or divide it between the two fields. For every hour she studies one subject, she gives up an hour she could have used studying the other. And for every hour she spends studying, she gives up an hour that she could have spent napping, bike riding, watching TV, or working at her part-time job for some extra spending money.

Or consider parents deciding how to spend their family income. They can buy food, clothing, or a family vacation. Or they can save some of the family income for retirement or the children's college education. When they choose to spend an extra dollar on one of these goods, they have one less dollar to spend on some other good.

When people are grouped into societies, they face different kinds of trade-offs. One classic trade-off is between "guns and butter." The more a society spends on national defense (guns) to protect its shores from foreign aggressors, the less it can spend on consumer goods (butter) to raise the standard of living at home. Also important in modern society is the trade-off between a clean environment and a high level of income. Laws that require firms to reduce pollution raise the cost of producing goods and services. Because of the higher costs, these firms end up earning smaller profits, paying lower wages, charging higher prices, or some combination of these three. Thus, while pollution regulations yield the benefit of a cleaner environment and the improved health that comes with it, the regulations come at the cost of reducing the incomes of the regulated firms' owners, workers, and customers.

Another trade-off society faces is between efficiency and equality. **Efficiency** means that society is getting the maximum benefits from its scarce resources. **Equality** means that those benefits are distributed uniformly among society's members. In other words, efficiency refers to the size of the economic pie, and equality refers to how the pie is divided into individual slices.

efficiency
the property of society getting the most it can from its scarce resources

equality
the property of distributing economic prosperity uniformly among the members of society

When government policies are designed, these two goals often conflict. Consider, for instance, policies aimed at equalizing the distribution of economic well-being. Some of these policies, such as the welfare system or unemployment insurance, try to help the members of society who are most in need. Others, such as the individual income tax, ask the financially successful to contribute more than others to support the government. While achieving greater equality, these policies reduce efficiency. When the government redistributes income from the rich to the poor, it reduces the reward for working hard; as a result, people work less and produce fewer goods and services. In other words, when the government tries to cut the economic pie into more equal slices, the pie gets smaller.

Recognizing that people face trade-offs does not by itself tell us what decisions they will or should make. A student should not abandon the study of psychology just because doing so would increase the time available for the study of economics. Society should not stop protecting the environment just because environmental regulations reduce our material standard of living. The poor should not be ignored just because helping them distorts work incentives. Nonetheless, people are likely to make good decisions only if they understand the options they have available. Our study of economics, therefore, starts by acknowledging life's trade-offs.

Principle 2: The Cost of Something Is What You Give Up to Get It

Because people face trade-offs, making decisions requires comparing the costs and benefits of alternative courses of action. In many cases, however, the cost of an action is not as obvious as it might first appear.

Consider the decision to go to college. The main benefits are intellectual enrichment and a lifetime of better job opportunities. But what are the costs? To answer this question, you might be tempted to add up the money you spend on tuition, books, room, and board. Yet this total does not truly represent what you give up to spend a year in college.

There are two problems with this calculation. First, it includes some things that are not really costs of going to college. Even if you quit school, you need a place to sleep and food to eat. Room and board are costs of going to college only to the extent that they are more expensive at college than elsewhere. Second, this calculation ignores the largest cost of going to college—your time. When you spend a year listening to lectures, reading textbooks, and writing papers, you cannot spend that time working at a job. For most students, the earnings given up to attend school are the largest single cost of their education.

opportunity cost
whatever must be given up to obtain some item

The **opportunity cost** of an item is what you give up to get that item. When making any decision, decision makers should be aware of the opportunity costs that accompany each possible action. In fact, they usually are. College athletes who can earn millions if they drop out of school and play professional sports are well aware that their opportunity cost of college is very high. It is not surprising that they often decide that the benefit of a college education is not worth the cost.

Principle 3: Rational People Think at the Margin

rational people
people who systematically and purposefully do the best they can to achieve their objectives

Economists normally assume that people are rational. **Rational people** systematically and purposefully do the best they can to achieve their objectives, given the available opportunities. As you study economics, you will encounter firms that decide how many workers to hire and how much of their product to manufacture and sell to maximize profits. You will also encounter individuals who decide how much time to spend working and what goods and services to buy with the resulting income to achieve the highest possible level of satisfaction.

Rational people know that decisions in life are rarely black and white but usually involve shades of gray. At dinnertime, the decision you face is not between fasting or eating like a pig but whether to take that extra spoonful of mashed potatoes. When exams roll around, your decision is not between blowing them off or studying 24 hours a day but whether to spend an extra hour reviewing your notes instead of watching TV. Economists use the term **marginal change** to describe a small incremental adjustment to an existing plan of action. Keep in mind that *margin* means "edge," so marginal changes are adjustments around the edges of what you are doing. Rational people often make decisions by comparing *marginal benefits* and *marginal costs*.

marginal change
a small incremental adjustment to a plan of action

For example, consider an airline deciding how much to charge passengers who fly standby. Suppose that flying a 200-seat plane across the United States costs the airline $100,000. In this case, the average cost of each seat is $100,000/200, which is $500. One might be tempted to conclude that the airline should never sell a ticket for less than $500. Actually, a rational airline can often find ways to raise its profits by thinking at the margin. Imagine that a plane is about to take off with ten empty seats, and a standby passenger waiting at the gate will pay $300 for a seat. Should the airline sell the ticket? Of course it should. If the plane has empty seats, the cost of adding one more passenger is tiny. Although the *average* cost of flying a passenger is $500, the *marginal* cost is merely the cost of the bag of peanuts and can of soda that the extra passenger will consume. As long as the standby passenger pays more than the marginal cost, selling the ticket is profitable.

Marginal decision making can help explain some otherwise puzzling economic phenomena. Here is a classic question: Why is water so cheap, while diamonds are so expensive? Humans need water to survive, while diamonds are unnecessary; but for some reason, people are willing to pay much more for a diamond than for a cup of water. The reason is that a person's willingness to pay for a good is based on the marginal benefit that an extra unit of the good would yield. The marginal benefit, in turn, depends on how many units a person already has. Water is essential, but the marginal benefit of an extra cup is small because water is plentiful. By contrast, no one needs diamonds to survive, but because diamonds are so rare, people consider the marginal benefit of an extra diamond to be large.

A rational decision maker takes an action if and only if the marginal benefit of the action exceeds the marginal cost. This principle can explain why airlines are willing to sell a ticket below average cost and why people are willing to pay more for diamonds than for water. It can take some time to get used to the logic of marginal thinking, but the study of economics will give you ample opportunity to practice.

Principle 4: People Respond to Incentives

An **incentive** is something that induces a person to act, such as the prospect of a punishment or a reward. Because rational people make decisions by comparing costs and benefits, they respond to incentives. You will see that incentives play a central role in the study of economics. One economist went so far as to suggest that the entire field could be summarized simply: "People respond to incentives. The rest is commentary."

incentive
something that induces a person to act

Incentives are crucial to analyzing how markets work. For example, when the price of an apple rises, people decide to eat fewer apples. At the same time, apple orchards decide to hire more workers and harvest more apples. In other words, a higher price in a market provides an incentive for buyers to consume less and an incentive for sellers to produce more. As we will see, the influence of prices on the behavior of consumers and producers is crucial for how a market economy allocates scarce resources.

Public policymakers should never forget about incentives: Many policies change the costs or benefits that people face and, therefore, alter their behavior. A tax on gasoline, for instance, encourages people to drive smaller, more fuel-efficient cars. That is one reason people drive smaller cars in Europe, where gasoline taxes are high, than in the United States, where gasoline taxes are low. A gasoline tax also encourages people to carpool, take public transportation, and live closer to where they work. If the tax were larger, more people would be driving hybrid cars, and if it were large enough, they would switch to electric cars.

When policymakers fail to consider how their policies affect incentives, they often end up with unintended consequences. For example, consider public policy regarding auto safety. Today, all cars have seat belts, but this was not true 50 years ago. In the 1960s, Ralph Nader's book *Unsafe at Any Speed* generated much public concern over auto safety. Congress responded with laws requiring seat belts as standard equipment on new cars.

How does a seat belt law affect auto safety? The direct effect is obvious: When a person wears a seat belt, the probability of surviving an auto accident rises. But that's not the end of the story because the law also affects behavior by altering incentives. The relevant behavior here is the speed and care with which drivers operate their cars. Driving slowly and carefully is costly because it uses the driver's time and energy. When deciding how safely to drive, rational people compare, perhaps unconsciously, the marginal benefit from safer driving to the marginal cost. As a result, they drive more slowly and carefully when the benefit of increased safety is high. For example, when road conditions are icy, people drive more attentively and at lower speeds than they do when road conditions are clear.

Consider how a seat belt law alters a driver's cost–benefit calculation. Seat belts make accidents less costly because they reduce the likelihood of injury or death. In other words, seat belts reduce the benefits of slow and careful driving. People respond to seat belts as they would to an improvement in road conditions—by driving faster and less carefully. The result of a seat belt law, therefore, is a larger number of accidents. The decline in safe driving has a clear, adverse impact on pedestrians, who are more likely to find themselves in an accident but (unlike the drivers) don't have the benefit of added protection.

At first, this discussion of incentives and seat belts might seem like idle speculation. Yet in a classic 1975 study, economist Sam Peltzman argued that auto-safety laws have had many of these effects. According to Peltzman's evidence, these laws produce both fewer deaths per accident and more accidents. He concluded that the net result is little change in the number of driver deaths and an increase in the number of pedestrian deaths.

Peltzman's analysis of auto safety is an offbeat and controversial example of the general principle that people respond to incentives. When analyzing any policy, we must consider not only the direct effects but also the less obvious indirect effects that work through incentives. If the policy changes incentives, it will cause people to alter their behavior.

CASE STUDY The Incentive Effects of Gasoline Prices

From 2005 to 2008 the price of oil in world oil markets skyrocketed, the result of limited supplies together with surging demand from robust world growth, especially in China. The price of gasoline in the United States rose from about $2 to about $4 a gallon. At the time, the news was filled with stories about how people responded to the increased incentive to conserve, sometimes in obvious ways, sometimes in less obvious ways.

Here is a sampling of various stories:

- "As Gas Prices Soar, Buyers Are Flocking to Small Cars"
- "As Gas Prices Climb, So Do Scooter Sales"
- "Gas Prices Knock Bicycles Sales, Repairs into Higher Gear"
- "Gas Prices Send Surge of Riders to Mass Transit"
- "Camel Demand Up as Oil Price Soars": Farmers in the Indian state of Rajasthan are rediscovering the humble camel. As the cost of running gas-guzzling tractors soars, even-toed ungulates are making a comeback.
- "The Airlines Are Suffering, But the Order Books of Boeing and Airbus Are Bulging": Demand for new, more fuel-efficient aircraft has never been greater. The latest versions of the Airbus A320 and Boeing 737, the single-aisle workhorses for which demand is strongest, are up to 40% cheaper to run than the vintage planes some American airlines still use.
- "Home Buying Practices Adjust to High Gas Prices": In his hunt for a new home, Demetrius Stroud crunched the numbers to find out that, with gas prices climbing, moving near an Amtrak station is the best thing for his wallet.
- "Gas Prices Drive Students to Online Courses": For Christy LaBadie, a sophomore at Northampton Community College, the 30-minute drive from her home to the Bethlehem, Pa., campus has become a financial hardship now that gasoline prices have soared to more than $4 a gallon. So this semester she decided to take an online course to save herself the trip—and the money.
- "Diddy Halts Private Jet Flights Over Fuel Prices": Fuel prices have grounded an unexpected frequent-flyer: Sean "Diddy" Combs. . . . The hip-hop mogul said he is now flying on commercial airlines instead of in private jets, which Combs said had previously cost him $200,000 and up for a roundtrip between New York and Los Angeles. "I'm actually flying commercial," Diddy said before walking onto an airplane, sitting in a first-class seat and flashing his boarding pass to the camera. "That's how high gas prices are."

Hip-hop mogul Sean "Diddy" Combs responds to incentives.

© AP PHOTO/STEPHAN SAVOIA

Many of these developments proved transitory. The economic downturn that began in 2008 and continued into 2009 reduced the world demand for oil, and the price of gasoline declined substantially. No word yet on whether Mr. Combs has returned to his private jet. ■

QUICK QUIZ *Describe an important trade-off you recently faced.* • *Give an example of some action that has both a monetary and nonmonetary opportunity cost.* • *Describe an incentive your parents offered to you in an effort to influence your behavior.*

in the news

> ### Incentive Pay

As this article illustrates, how people are paid affects their incentives and the decisions they make. (The article's author, by the way, subsequently became one of the chief economic advisers to President Barack Obama.)

Where the Buses Run on Time

BY AUSTAN GOOLSBEE

On a summer afternoon, the drive home from the University of Chicago to the north side of the city must be one of the most beautiful commutes in the world. On the left on Lake Shore Drive you pass Grant Park, some of the world's first skyscrapers, and the Sears Tower. On the right is the intense blue of Lake Michigan. But for all the beauty, the traffic can be hell. So, if you drive the route every day, you learn the shortcuts. You know that if it backs up from the Buckingham Fountain all the way to McCormick Place, you're better off taking the surface streets and getting back onto Lake Shore Drive a few miles north.

A lot of buses, however, wait in the traffic jams. I have always wondered about that: Why don't the bus drivers use the shortcuts? Surely they know about them—they drive the same route every day, and they probably avoid the traffic when they drive their own

cars. Buses don't stop on Lake Shore Drive, so they wouldn't strand anyone by detouring around the congestion. And when buses get delayed in heavy traffic, it wreaks havoc on the scheduled service. Instead of arriving once every 10 minutes, three buses come in at the same time after half an hour. That sort of bunching is the least efficient way to run a public transportation system. So, why not take the surface streets if that would keep the schedule properly spaced and on time?

You might think at first that the problem is that the drivers aren't paid enough to strategize. But Chicago bus drivers are the seventh-highest paid in the nation; full-timers earned more than $23 an hour, according to a November 2004 survey. The problem may have to do not with how much they are paid, but how they are paid. At least, that's the implication of a new study of Chilean bus drivers by Ryan Johnson and David Reiley of the University of Arizona and Juan Carlos Muñoz of Pontificia Universidad Católica de Chile.

Companies in Chile pay bus drivers one of two ways: either by the hour or by the passenger. Paying by the passenger leads to significantly shorter delays. Give them

incentives, and drivers start acting like regular people do. They take shortcuts when the traffic is bad. They take shorter meal breaks and bathroom breaks. They want to get on the road and pick up more passengers as quickly as they can. In short, their productivity increases….

Not everything about incentive pay is perfect, of course. When bus drivers start moving from place to place more quickly, they get in more accidents (just like the rest of us). Some passengers also complain that the rides make them nauseated because the drivers stomp on the gas as soon as the last passenger gets on the bus. Yet when given the choice, people overwhelmingly choose the bus companies that get them where they're going on time. More than 95 percent of the routes in Santiago use incentive pay.

Perhaps we should have known that incentive pay could increase bus driver productivity. After all, the taxis in Chicago take the shortcuts on Lake Shore Drive to avoid the traffic that buses just sit in. Since taxi drivers earn money for every trip they make, they want to get you home as quickly as possible so they can pick up somebody else.

Source: Slate.com, March 16, 2006.

How People Interact

The first four principles discussed how individuals make decisions. As we go about our lives, many of our decisions affect not only ourselves but other people as well. The next three principles concern how people interact with one another.

Principle 5: Trade Can Make Everyone Better Off

You may have heard on the news that the Japanese are our competitors in the world economy. In some ways, this is true because American and Japanese firms produce many of the same goods. Ford and Toyota compete for the same customers in the market for automobiles. Apple and Sony compete for the same customers in the market for digital music players.

Yet it is easy to be misled when thinking about competition among countries. Trade between the United States and Japan is not like a sports contest in which one side wins and the other side loses. In fact, the opposite is true: Trade between two countries can make each country better off.

To see why, consider how trade affects your family. When a member of your family looks for a job, he or she competes against members of other families who are looking for jobs. Families also compete against one another when they go shopping because each family wants to buy the best goods at the lowest prices. In a sense, each family in the economy is competing with all other families.

Despite this competition, your family would not be better off isolating itself from all other families. If it did, your family would need to grow its own food, make its own clothes, and build its own home. Clearly, your family gains much from its ability to trade with others. Trade allows each person to specialize in the activities he or she does best, whether it is farming, sewing, or home building. By trading with others, people can buy a greater variety of goods and services at lower cost.

Countries as well as families benefit from the ability to trade with one another. Trade allows countries to specialize in what they do best and to enjoy a greater variety of goods and services. The Japanese, as well as the French and the Egyptians and the Brazilians, are as much our partners in the world economy as they are our competitors.

THE WALL STREET JOURNAL

"For $5 a week you can watch baseball without being nagged to cut the grass!"

Principle 6: Markets Are Usually a Good Way to Organize Economic Activity

The collapse of communism in the Soviet Union and Eastern Europe in the 1980s may be the most important change in the world during the past half century. Communist countries worked on the premise that government officials were in the best position to allocate the economy's scarce resources. These central planners decided what goods and services were produced, how much was produced, and who produced and consumed these goods and services. The theory behind central planning was that only the government could organize economic activity in a way that promoted economic well-being for the country as a whole.

Most countries that once had centrally planned economies have abandoned the system and are instead developing market economies. In a **market economy**, the decisions of a central planner are replaced by the decisions of millions of firms and households. Firms decide whom to hire and what to make. Households decide which firms to work for and what to buy with their incomes. These firms

market economy

an economy that allocates resources through the decentralized decisions of many firms and households as they interact in markets for goods and services and households interact in the marketplace, where prices and self-interest guide their decisions.

At first glance, the success of market economies is puzzling. In a market economy, no one is looking out for the economic well-being of society as a whole. Free markets contain many buyers and sellers of numerous goods and services, and all of them are interested primarily in their own well-being. Yet despite decentralized decision making and self-interested decision makers, market economies have proven remarkably successful in organizing economic activity to promote overall economic well-being.

In his 1776 book *An Inquiry into the Nature and Causes of the Wealth of Nations*, economist Adam Smith made the most famous observation in all of economics: Households and firms interacting in markets act as if they are guided by an "invisible hand" that leads them to desirable market outcomes. One of our goals in this book is to understand how this invisible hand works its magic.

As you study economics, you will learn that prices are the instrument with which the invisible hand directs economic activity. In any market, buyers look at the price when determining how much to demand, and sellers look at the price when deciding how much to supply. As a result of the decisions that buyers and sellers make, market prices reflect both the value of a good to society and the cost to society of making the good. Smith's great insight was that prices adjust to guide these individual buyers and sellers to reach outcomes that, in many cases, maximize the well-being of society as a whole.

Smith's insight has an important corollary: When the government prevents prices from adjusting naturally to supply and demand, it impedes the invisible hand's ability to coordinate the decisions of the households and firms that make up the economy. This corollary explains why taxes adversely affect the allocation of resources, for they distort prices and thus the decisions of households and firms. It also explains the great harm caused by policies that directly control prices, such as rent control. And it explains the failure of communism. In communist countries, prices were not determined in the marketplace but were dictated by central planners. These planners lacked the necessary information about consumers' tastes and producers' costs, which in a market economy is reflected in prices. Central planners failed because they tried to run the economy with one hand tied behind their backs—the invisible hand of the marketplace.

Principle 7: Governments Can Sometimes Improve Market Outcomes

If the invisible hand of the market is so great, why do we need government? One purpose of studying economics is to refine your view about the proper role and scope of government policy.

One reason we need government is that the invisible hand can work its magic only if the government enforces the rules and maintains the institutions that are key to a market economy. Most important, market economies need institutions to enforce **property rights** so individuals can own and control scarce resources. A farmer won't grow food if he expects his crop to be stolen; a restaurant won't serve meals unless it is assured that customers will pay before they leave; and an entertainment company won't produce DVDs if too many potential customers avoid paying by making illegal copies. We all rely on government-provided police and courts to enforce our rights over the things we produce—and the invisible hand counts on our ability to enforce our rights.

property rights
the ability of an individual to own and exercise control over scarce resources

FYI

> ## Adam Smith and the Invisible Hand

It may be only a coincidence that Adam Smith's great book *The Wealth of Nations* was published in 1776, the exact year American revolutionaries signed the Declaration of Independence. But the two documents share a point of view that was prevalent at the time: Individuals are usually best left to their own devices, without the heavy hand of government guiding their actions. This political philosophy provides the intellectual basis for the market economy and for free society more generally.

Why do decentralized market economies work so well? Is it because people can be counted on to treat one another with love and kindness? Not at all. Here is Adam Smith's description of how people interact in a market economy:

> Man has almost constant occasion for the help of his brethren, and it is in vain for him to expect it from their benevolence only. He will be more likely to prevail if he can interest their self-love in his favour, and show them that it is for their own advantage to do for him what he requires of them. . . . Give me that which I want, and you shall have this which you want, is the meaning of every such offer; and it is in this manner that we obtain from one another the far greater part of those good offices which we stand in need of.

Adam Smith

> It is not from the benevolence of the butcher, the brewer, or the baker that we expect our dinner, but from their regard to their own interest. We address ourselves, not to their humanity but to their self-love, and never talk to them of our own necessities but of their advantages. Nobody but a beggar chooses to depend chiefly upon the benevolence of his fellow-citizens. . . .
>
> Every individual . . . neither intends to promote the public interest, nor knows how much he is promoting it. . . . He intends only his own gain, and he is in this, as in many other cases, led by an invisible hand to promote an end which was no part of his intention. Nor is it always the worse for the society that it was no part of it. By pursuing his own interest he frequently promotes that of the society more effectually than when he really intends to promote it.

Smith is saying that participants in the economy are motivated by self-interest and that the "invisible hand" of the marketplace guides this self-interest into promoting general economic well-being.

Many of Smith's insights remain at the center of modern economics. Our analysis in the coming chapters will allow us to express Smith's conclusions more precisely and to analyze more fully the strengths and weaknesses of the market's invisible hand.

market failure
a situation in which a market left on its own fails to allocate resources efficiently

externality
the impact of one person's actions on the well-being of a bystander

Yet there is another reason we need government: The invisible hand is powerful, but it is not omnipotent. There are two broad reasons for a government to intervene in the economy and change the allocation of resources that people would choose on their own: to promote efficiency or to promote equality. That is, most policies aim either to enlarge the economic pie or to change how the pie is divided.

Consider first the goal of efficiency. Although the invisible hand usually leads markets to allocate resources to maximize the size of the economic pie, this is not always the case. Economists use the term **market failure** to refer to a situation in which the market on its own fails to produce an efficient allocation of resources. As we will see, one possible cause of market failure is an **externality,** which is the impact of one person's actions on the well-being of a bystander. The classic example of an externality is pollution. Another possible cause of market failure is **market power,** which refers to the ability of a single person (or small group) to unduly influence market prices. For example, if everyone in town needs water but there is only one well, the owner of the well is not subject to the rigorous competition with which the invisible hand normally keeps self-interest in check. In the presence of externalities or market power, well-designed public policy can enhance economic efficiency.

Now consider the goal of equality. Even when the invisible hand is yielding efficient outcomes, it can nonetheless leave sizable disparities in economic well-being. A market economy rewards people according to their ability to produce things that other people are willing to pay for. The world's best basketball player earns more than the world's best chess player simply because people are willing to pay more to watch basketball than chess. The invisible hand does not ensure that everyone has sufficient food, decent clothing, and adequate health-care. This inequality may, depending on one's political philosophy, call for government intervention. In practice, many public policies, such as the income tax and the welfare system, aim to achieve a more equal distribution of economic well-being.

To say that the government *can* improve on market outcomes at times does not mean that it always *will.* Public policy is made not by angels but by a political process that is far from perfect. Sometimes policies are designed simply to reward the politically powerful. Sometimes they are made by well-intentioned leaders who are not fully informed. As you study economics, you will become a better judge of when a government policy is justifiable because it promotes efficiency or equality and when it is not.

QUICK QUIZ   *Why is a country better off not isolating itself from all other countries? • Why do we have markets, and, according to economists, what roles should government play in them?*

> **market power**
> the ability of a single economic actor (or small group of actors) to have a substantial influence on market prices

How the Economy as a Whole Works

We started by discussing how individuals make decisions and then looked at how people interact with one another. All these decisions and interactions together make up "the economy." The last three principles concern the workings of the economy as a whole.

Principle 8: A Country's Standard of Living Depends on Its Ability to Produce Goods and Services

The differences in living standards around the world are staggering. In 2008, the average American had an income of about $47,000. In the same year, the average Mexican earned about $10,000, and the average Nigerian earned only $1,400. Not surprisingly, this large variation in average income is reflected in various measures of the quality of life. Citizens of high-income countries have more TV sets, more cars, better nutrition, better healthcare, and a longer life expectancy than citizens of low-income countries.

Changes in living standards over time are also large. In the United States, incomes have historically grown about 2 percent per year (after adjusting for changes in the cost of living). At this rate, average income doubles every 35 years. Over the past century, average U.S. income has risen about eightfold.

What explains these large differences in living standards among countries and over time? The answer is surprisingly simple. Almost all variation in living standards is attributable to differences in countries' **productivity**—that is, the amount of goods and services produced from each unit of labor input. In nations where workers can produce a large quantity of goods and services per unit of time, most people enjoy a high standard of living; in nations where workers are less productive, most people endure a more meager existence. Similarly, the growth rate of a nation's productivity determines the growth rate of its average income.

The fundamental relationship between productivity and living standards is simple, but its implications are far-reaching. If productivity is the primary determinant of living standards, other explanations must be of secondary importance. For example, it might be tempting to credit labor unions or minimum-wage laws for the rise in living standards of American workers over the past century. Yet the real hero of American workers is their rising productivity. As another example, some commentators have claimed that increased competition from Japan and other countries explained the slow growth in U.S. incomes during the 1970s and 1980s. Yet the real villain was not competition from abroad but flagging productivity growth in the United States.

The relationship between productivity and living standards also has profound implications for public policy. When thinking about how any policy will affect living standards, the key question is how it will affect our ability to produce goods and services. To boost living standards, policymakers need to raise productivity by ensuring that workers are well educated, have the tools needed to produce goods and services, and have access to the best available technology.

productivity

the quantity of goods and services produced from each unit of labor input

. . . . in the news

> *Why You Should Study Economics*

In this excerpt from a commencement address, the former president of the Federal Reserve Bank of Dallas makes the case for studying economics

The Dismal Science? Hardly!

BY ROBERT D. MCTEER, JR.

My take on training in economics is that it becomes increasingly valuable as you move up the career ladder. I can't imagine a better major for corporate CEOs, congressmen, or American presidents. You've learned a systematic, disciplined way of thinking that will serve you well. By contrast, the economically challenged must be perplexed about how it is that economies work better the fewer people they have in charge. Who does the planning? Who makes decisions? Who decides what to produce?

For my money, Adam Smith's invisible hand is the most important thing you've learned by studying economics. You understand how we can each work for our own self-interest and still produce a desirable social outcome. You know how uncoordinated activity gets coordinated by the market to enhance the wealth of nations. You understand the magic of markets and the dangers of tampering with them too much. You know better what you first learned in kindergarten: that you shouldn't kill or cripple the goose that lays the golden eggs. . . .

Economics training will help you understand fallacies and unintended consequences.

Principle 9: Prices Rise When the Government Prints Too Much Money

In January 1921, a daily newspaper in Germany cost 0.30 marks. Less than two years later, in November 1922, the same newspaper cost 70,000,000 marks. All other prices in the economy rose by similar amounts. This episode is one of history's most spectacular examples of **inflation,** an increase in the overall level of prices in the economy.

Although the United States has never experienced inflation even close to that of Germany in the 1920s, inflation has at times been an economic problem. During the 1970s, for instance, when the overall level of prices more than doubled, President Gerald Ford called inflation "public enemy number one." By contrast, inflation in the first decade of the 21st century has run about 2½ percent per year; at this rate, it would take almost 30 years for prices to double. Because high inflation imposes various costs on society, keeping inflation at a low level is a goal of economic policymakers around the world.

What causes inflation? In almost all cases of large or persistent inflation, the culprit is growth in the quantity of money. When a government creates large quantities of the nation's money, the value of the money falls. In Germany in the early 1920s, when prices were on average tripling every month, the quantity of money was also tripling every month. Although less dramatic, the economic history of the United States points to a similar conclusion: The high inflation of the 1970s was associated with rapid growth in the quantity of money, and the low inflation of more recent experience was associated with slow growth in the quantity of money.

inflation

an increase in the overall level of prices in the economy

"Well it may have been 68 cents when you got in line, but it's 74 cents now!"

In fact, I am inclined to define economics as the study of how to anticipate unintended consequences. . . .

Little in the literature seems more relevant to contemporary economic debates than what usually is called the broken window fallacy. Whenever a government program is justified not on its merits but by the jobs it will create, remember the broken window: Some teenagers, being the little beasts that they are, toss a brick through a bakery window. A crowd gathers and laments, "What a shame." But before you know it, someone suggests a silver lining to the situation: Now the baker will have to spend money to have the window repaired. This will add to the income of the repairman, who will spend his additional income, which will add to another seller's income, and so on. You know the drill. The chain of spending will multiply and generate higher income and employment. If the broken window is large enough, it might produce an economic boom! . . .

Most voters fall for the broken window fallacy, but not economics majors. They will say, "Hey, wait a minute!" If the baker hadn't spent his money on window repair, he would have spent it on the new suit he was saving to buy. Then the tailor would have the new income to spend, and so on. The broken window didn't create net new spending; it just diverted spending from somewhere else. The broken window does not create new activity, just different activity. People see the activity that takes place. They don't see the activity that *would* have taken place.

The broken window fallacy is perpetuated in many forms. Whenever job creation or retention is the primary objective I call it the job-counting fallacy. Economics majors understand the non-intuitive reality that real progress comes from job destruction. It once took 90 percent of our population to grow our food. Now it takes 3 percent. Pardon me, Willie, but are we worse off because of the job losses in agriculture? The would-have-been farmers are now college professors and computer gurus. . . .

So instead of counting jobs, we should make every job count. We will occasionally hit a soft spot when we have a mismatch of supply and demand in the labor market. But that is temporary. Don't become a Luddite and destroy the machinery, or become a protectionist and try to grow bananas in New York City.

Source: *The Wall Street Journal*, June 4, 2003.

Principle 10: Society Faces a Short-Run Trade-off between Inflation and Unemployment

Although a higher level of prices is, in the long run, the primary effect of increasing the quantity of money, the short-run story is more complex and controversial. Most economists describe the short-run effects of monetary injections as follows:

- Increasing the amount of money in the economy stimulates the overall level of spending and thus the demand for goods and services.
- Higher demand may over time cause firms to raise their prices, but in the meantime, it also encourages them to hire more workers and produce a larger quantity of goods and services.
- More hiring means lower unemployment.

This line of reasoning leads to one final economy-wide trade-off: a short-run trade-off between inflation and unemployment.

Although some economists still question these ideas, most accept that society faces a short-run trade-off between inflation and unemployment. This simply means that, over a period of a year or two, many economic policies push inflation and unemployment in opposite directions. Policymakers face this trade-off regardless of whether inflation and unemployment both start out at high levels (as they did in the early 1980s), at low levels (as they did in the late 1990s), or someplace in between. This short-run trade-off plays a key role in the analysis of the **business cycle**—the irregular and largely unpredictable fluctuations in economic activity, as measured by the production of goods and services or the number of people employed.

Policymakers can exploit the short-run trade-off between inflation and unemployment using various policy instruments. By changing the amount that the government spends, the amount it taxes, and the amount of money it prints, policymakers can influence the overall demand for goods and services. Changes in demand in turn influence the combination of inflation and unemployment that the economy experiences in the short run. Because these instruments of economic policy are potentially so powerful, how policymakers should use these instruments to control the economy, if at all, is a subject of continuing debate.

This debate heated up in the early years of Barack Obama's presidency. In 2008 and 2009, the U.S. economy, as well as many other economies around the world, experienced a deep economic downturn. Problems in the financial system, caused by bad bets on the housing market, spilled over into the rest of the economy, causing incomes to fall and unemployment to soar. Policymakers responded in various ways to increase the overall demand for goods and services. President Obama's first major initiative was a stimulus package of reduced taxes and increased government spending. At the same time, the nation's central bank, the Federal Reserve, increased the supply of money. The goal of these policies was to reduce unemployment. Some feared, however, that these policies might over time lead to an excessive level of inflation.

QUICK QUIZ *List and briefly explain the three principles that describe how the economy as a whole works.*

business cycle

fluctuations in economic activity, such as employment and production

FYI

> ## How to Read This Book

Economics is fun, but it can also be hard to learn. My aim in writing this text is to make it as enjoyable and easy as possible. But you, the student, also have a role to play. Experience shows that if you are actively involved as you study this book, you will enjoy a better outcome both on your exams and in the years that follow. Here are a few tips about how best to read this book.

1. *Read before class.* Students do better when they read the relevant textbook chapter before attending a lecture. You will understand the lecture better, and your questions will be better focused on where you need extra help.

2. *Summarize, don't highlight.* Running a yellow marker over the text is too passive an activity to keep your mind engaged. Instead, when you come to the end of a section, take a minute and summarize what you just learned in your own words, writing your summary in the wide margins we've provided. When you've finished the chapter, compare your summaries with the one at the end of the chapter. Did you pick up the main points?

3. *Test yourself.* Throughout the book, Quick Quizzes offer instant feedback to find out if you've learned what you are supposed to. Take the opportunity to write down your answer, and then check it against the answers provided at this book's website. The quizzes are meant to test your basic comprehension. If your answer is incorrect, you probably need to review the section.

4. *Practice, practice, practice.* At the end of each chapter, Questions for Review test your understanding, and Problems and Applications ask you to apply and extend the material. Perhaps your instructor will assign some of these exercises as homework.

If so, do them. If not, do them anyway. The more you use your new knowledge, the more solid it becomes.

5. *Go online.* The publisher of this book maintains an extensive website to help you in your study of economics. It includes additional examples, applications, and problems, as well as quizzes so you can test yourself. Check it out. The website is www .cengage.com/economics/mankiw.

6. *Study in groups.* After you've read the book and worked problems on your own, get together with classmates to discuss the material. You will learn from each other—an example of the gains from trade.

7. *Teach someone.* As all teachers know, there is no better way to learn something than to teach it to someone else. Take the opportunity to teach new economic concepts to a study partner, a friend, a parent, or even a pet.

8. *Don't skip the real-world examples.* In the midst of all the numbers, graphs, and strange new words, it is easy to lose sight of what economics is all about. The Case Studies and In the News boxes sprinkled throughout this book should help remind you. They show how the theory is tied to events happening in all our lives.

9. *Apply economic thinking to your daily life.* Once you've read about how others apply economics to the real world, try it yourself! You can use economic analysis to better understand your own decisions, the economy around you, and the events you read about in the newspaper. The world may never look the same again.

Conclusion

You now have a taste of what economics is all about. In the coming chapters, we develop many specific insights about people, markets, and economies. Mastering these insights will take some effort, but it is not an overwhelming task. The field of economics is based on a few big ideas that can be applied in many different situations.

Throughout this book, we will refer back to the *Ten Principles of Economics* highlighted in this chapter and summarized in Table 1. Keep these building blocks in mind: Even the most sophisticated economic analysis is founded on the ten principles introduced here.

Table **1**

Ten Principles of Economics

How People Make Decisions
1: People Face Trade-offs
2: The Cost of Something Is What You Give Up to Get It
3: Rational People Think at the Margin
4: People Respond to Incentives

How People Interact
5: Trade Can Make Everyone Better Off
6: Markets Are Usually a Good Way to Organize Economic Activity
7: Governments Can Sometimes Improve Market Outcomes

How the Economy as a Whole Works
8: A Country's Standard of Living Depends on Its Ability to Produce Goods and Services
9: Prices Rise When the Government Prints Too Much Money
10: Society Faces a Short-Run Trade-off between Inflation and Unemployment

SUMMARY

- The fundamental lessons about individual decision making are that people face trade-offs among alternative goals, that the cost of any action is measured in terms of forgone opportunities, that rational people make decisions by comparing marginal costs and marginal benefits, and that people change their behavior in response to the incentives they face.

- The fundamental lessons about interactions among people are that trade and interdependence can be mutually beneficial, that markets are usually a good way of coordinating economic activity among people, and that the government can potentially improve market outcomes by remedying a market failure or by promoting greater economic equality.

- The fundamental lessons about the economy as a whole are that productivity is the ultimate source of living standards, that growth in the quantity of money is the ultimate source of inflation, and that society faces a short-run trade-off between inflation and unemployment.

KEY CONCEPTS

scarcity, *p. 4*
economics, *p. 4*
efficiency, *p. 5*
equality, *p. 5*
opportunity cost, *p. 6*
rational people, *p. 6*

marginal change, *p. 6*
incentive, *p. 7*
market economy, *p. 10*
property rights, *p. 11*
market failure, *p. 12*
externality, *p. 12*

market power, *p. 13*
productivity, *p. 14*
inflation, *p. 15*
business cycle, *p. 16*

QUESTIONS FOR REVIEW

1. Give three examples of important trade-offs that you face in your life.
2. What is the opportunity cost of seeing a movie?
3. Water is necessary for life. Is the marginal benefit of a glass of water large or small?
4. Why should policymakers think about incentives?

5. Why isn't trade among countries like a game with some winners and some losers?
6. What does the "invisible hand" of the market-place do?
7. Explain the two main causes of market failure and give an example of each.
8. Why is productivity important?
9. What is inflation and what causes it?
10. How are inflation and unemployment related in the short run?

PROBLEMS AND APPLICATIONS

1. Describe some of the trade-offs faced by each of the following:
   a. a family deciding whether to buy a new car
   b. a member of Congress deciding how much to spend on national parks
   c. a company president deciding whether to open a new factory
   d. a professor deciding how much to prepare for class
   e. a recent college graduate deciding whether to go to graduate school
2. You are trying to decide whether to take a vacation. Most of the costs of the vacation (air-fare, hotel, and forgone wages) are measured in dollars, but the benefits of the vacation are psychological. How can you compare the benefits to the costs?
3. You were planning to spend Saturday working at your part-time job, but a friend asks you to go skiing. What is the true cost of going skiing? Now suppose you had been planning to spend the day studying at the library. What is the cost of going skiing in this case? Explain.
4. You win $100 in a basketball pool. You have a choice between spending the money now or putting it away for a year in a bank account that pays 5 percent interest. What is the opportunity cost of spending the $100 now?
5. The company that you manage has invested $5 million in developing a new product, but the development is not quite finished. At a recent meeting, your salespeople report that the introduction of competing products has reduced the expected sales of your new product to $3 million. If it would cost $1 million to finish development and make the product, should you go ahead and do so? What is the most that you should pay to complete development?
6. The Social Security system provides income for people over age 65. If a recipient of Social

Security decides to work and earn some income, the amount he or she receives in Social Security benefits is typically reduced.
   a. How does the provision of Social Security affect people's incentive to save while working?
   b. How does the reduction in benefits associated with higher earnings affect people's incentive to work past age 65?
7. A 1996 bill reforming the federal government's antipoverty programs limited many welfare recipients to only two years of benefits.
   a. How does this change affect the incentives for working?
   b. How might this change represent a trade-off between equality and efficiency?
8. Your roommate is a better cook than you are, but you can clean more quickly than your roommate can. If your roommate did all the cooking and you did all the cleaning, would your chores take you more or less time than if you divided each task evenly? Give a similar example of how specialization and trade can make two countries both better off.
9. Explain whether each of the following government activities is motivated by a concern about equality or a concern about efficiency. In the case of efficiency, discuss the type of market failure involved.
   a. regulating cable TV prices
   b. providing some poor people with vouchers that can be used to buy food
   c. prohibiting smoking in public places
   d. breaking up Standard Oil (which once owned 90 percent of all oil refineries) into several smaller companies
   e. imposing higher personal income tax rates on people with higher incomes
   f. instituting laws against driving while intoxicated

10. Discuss each of the following statements from the standpoints of equality and efficiency.
    a. "Everyone in society should be guaranteed the best healthcare possible."
    b. "When workers are laid off, they should be able to collect unemployment benefits until they find a new job."

11. In what ways is your standard of living different from that of your parents or grandparents when they were your age? Why have these changes occurred?

12. Suppose Americans decide to save more of their incomes. If banks lend this extra saving to businesses, which use the funds to build new factories, how might this lead to faster growth in productivity? Who do you suppose benefits from the higher productivity? Is society getting a free lunch?

13. In 2010, President Barack Obama and Congress enacted a healthcare reform bill in the United States. Two goals of the bill were to provide more Americans with health insurance (via subsidies for lower-income households financed by taxes on higher-income households) and to reduce the cost of healthcare (via various reforms in how healthcare is provided).
    a. How do these goals relate to equality and efficiency?
    b. How might healthcare reform increase productivity in the United States?
    c. How might healthcare reform decrease productivity in the United States?

14. During the Revolutionary War, the American colonies could not raise enough tax revenue to fully fund the war effort; to make up this difference, the colonies decided to print more money. Printing money to cover expenditures is sometimes referred to as an "inflation tax." Who do you think is being "taxed" when more money is printed? Why?

15. Imagine that you are a policymaker trying to decide whether to reduce the rate of inflation. To make an intelligent decision, what would you need to know about inflation, unemployment, and the trade-off between them?

16. A policymaker is deciding how to finance the construction of a new airport. He can either pay for it by increasing citizens' taxes or by printing more money. What are some of the short-run and long-run consequences of each option?

For further information on topics in this chapter, additional problems, applications, examples, online quizzes, and more, please visit our website at www.cengage.com/economics/mankiw.

Thinking Like an Economist

2

E very field of study has its own language and its own way of thinking. Mathematicians talk about axioms, integrals, and vector spaces. Psychologists talk about ego, id, and cognitive dissonance. Lawyers talk about venue, torts, and promissory estoppel.

Economics is no different. Supply, demand, elasticity, comparative advantage, consumer surplus, deadweight loss—these terms are part of the economist's language. In the coming chapters, you will encounter many new terms and some familiar words that economists use in specialized ways. At first, this new language may seem needlessly arcane. But as you will see, its value lies in its ability to provide you with a new and useful way of thinking about the world in which you live.

The purpose of this book is to help you learn the economist's way of thinking. Just as you cannot become a mathematician, psychologist, or lawyer overnight, learning to think like an economist will take some time. Yet with a combination of theory, case studies, and examples of economics in the news, this book will give you ample opportunity to develop and practice this skill.

Before delving into the substance and details of economics, it is helpful to have an overview of how economists approach the world. This chapter discusses the field's methodology. What is distinctive about how economists confront a question? What does it mean to think like an economist?

The Economist as Scientist

"I'm a social scientist, Michael. That means I can't explain electricity or anything like that, but if you ever want to know about people, I'm your man."

Economists try to address their subject with a scientist's objectivity. They approach the study of the economy in much the same way a physicist approaches the study of matter and a biologist approaches the study of life: They devise theories, collect data, and then analyze these data in an attempt to verify or refute their theories.

To beginners, it can seem odd to claim that economics is a science. After all, economists do not work with test tubes or telescopes. The essence of science, however, is the *scientific method*—the dispassionate development and testing of theories about how the world works. This method of inquiry is as applicable to studying a nation's economy as it is to studying the earth's gravity or a species' evolution. As Albert Einstein once put it, "The whole of science is nothing more than the refinement of everyday thinking."

Although Einstein's comment is as true for social sciences such as economics as it is for natural sciences such as physics, most people are not accustomed to looking at society through the eyes of a scientist. Let's discuss some of the ways in which economists apply the logic of science to examine how an economy works.

The Scientific Method: Observation, Theory, and More Observation

Isaac Newton, the famous 17th-century scientist and mathematician, allegedly became intrigued one day when he saw an apple fall from a tree. This observation motivated Newton to develop a theory of gravity that applies not only to an apple falling to the earth but to any two objects in the universe. Subsequent testing of Newton's theory has shown that it works well in many circumstances (although, as Einstein would later emphasize, not in all circumstances). Because Newton's theory has been so successful at explaining observation, it is still taught in undergraduate physics courses around the world.

This interplay between theory and observation also occurs in the field of economics. An economist might live in a country experiencing rapidly increasing prices and be moved by this observation to develop a theory of inflation. The theory might assert that high inflation arises when the government prints too much money. To test this theory, the economist could collect and analyze data on prices and money from many different countries. If growth in the quantity of money were not at all related to the rate at which prices are rising, the economist would start to doubt the validity of this theory of inflation. If money growth and inflation were strongly correlated in international data, as in fact they are, the economist would become more confident in the theory.

Although economists use theory and observation like other scientists, they face an obstacle that makes their task especially challenging: In economics, conducting experiments is often difficult and sometimes impossible. Physicists studying gravity can drop many objects in their laboratories to generate data to test their theories. By contrast, economists studying inflation are not allowed to manipulate a nation's monetary policy simply to generate useful data. Economists, like astronomers and evolutionary biologists, usually have to make do with whatever data the world happens to give them.

To find a substitute for laboratory experiments, economists pay close attention to the natural experiments offered by history. When a war in the Middle East interrupts the flow of crude oil, for instance, oil prices skyrocket around the world. For consumers of oil and oil products, such an event depresses living standards. For economic policymakers, it poses a difficult choice about how best to respond. But for economic scientists, the event provides an opportunity to study the effects of a key natural resource on the world's economies. Throughout this book, therefore, we consider many historical episodes. These episodes are valuable to study because they give us insight into the economy of the past and, more important, because they allow us to illustrate and evaluate economic theories of the present.

The Role of Assumptions

If you ask a physicist how long it would take a marble to fall from the top of a ten-story building, she will likely answer the question by assuming that the marble falls in a vacuum. Of course, this assumption is false. In fact, the building is surrounded by air, which exerts friction on the falling marble and slows it down. Yet the physicist will point out that the friction on the marble is so small that its effect is negligible. Assuming the marble falls in a vacuum simplifies the problem without substantially affecting the answer.

Economists make assumptions for the same reason: Assumptions can simplify the complex world and make it easier to understand. To study the effects of international trade, for example, we might assume that the world consists of only two countries and that each country produces only two goods. In reality, there are numerous countries, each of which produces thousands of different types of goods. But by assuming two countries and two goods, we can focus our thinking on the essence of the problem. Once we understand international trade in this simplified imaginary world, we are in a better position to understand international trade in the more complex world in which we live.

The art in scientific thinking—whether in physics, biology, or economics—is deciding which assumptions to make. Suppose, for instance, that instead of dropping a marble from the top of the building, we were dropping a beachball of the same weight. Our physicist would realize that the assumption of no friction is less accurate in this case: Friction exerts a greater force on a beachball than on a marble because a beachball is much larger. The assumption that gravity works in a vacuum is reasonable for studying a falling marble but not for studying a falling beachball.

Similarly, economists use different assumptions to answer different questions. Suppose that we want to study what happens to the economy when the government changes the number of dollars in circulation. An important piece of this analysis, it turns out, is how prices respond. Many prices in the economy change infrequently; the newsstand prices of magazines, for instance, change only every few years. Knowing this fact may lead us to make different assumptions when studying the effects of the policy change over different time horizons. For studying the short-run effects of the policy, we may assume that prices do not change much. We may even make the extreme and artificial assumption that all prices are completely fixed. For studying the long-run effects of the policy, however, we may assume that all prices are completely flexible. Just as a physicist uses different assumptions when studying falling marbles and falling beachballs, economists use different assumptions when studying the short-run and long-run effects of a change in the quantity of money.

Economic Models

High school biology teachers teach basic anatomy with plastic replicas of the human body. These models have all the major organs: the heart, the liver, the kidneys, and so on. The models allow teachers to show their students very simply how the important parts of the body fit together. Because these plastic models are stylized and omit many details, no one would mistake one of them for a real person. Despite this lack of realism—indeed, because of this lack of realism—studying these models is useful for learning how the human body works.

Economists also use models to learn about the world, but instead of being made of plastic, they are most often composed of diagrams and equations. Like a biology teacher's plastic model, economic models omit many details to allow us to see what is truly important. Just as the biology teacher's model does not include all the body's muscles and capillaries, an economist's model does not include every feature of the economy.

As we use models to examine various economic issues throughout this book, you will see that all the models are built with assumptions. Just as a physicist begins the analysis of a falling marble by assuming away the existence of friction, economists assume away many of the details of the economy that are irrelevant for studying the question at hand. All models—in physics, biology, and economics—simplify reality to improve our understanding of it.

Our First Model: The Circular-Flow Diagram

The economy consists of millions of people engaged in many activities—buying, selling, working, hiring, manufacturing, and so on. To understand how the economy works, we must find some way to simplify our thinking about all these activities. In other words, we need a model that explains, in general terms, how the economy is organized and how participants in the economy interact with one another.

Figure 1 presents a visual model of the economy called a **circular-flow diagram.** In this model, the economy is simplified to include only two types of decision makers—firms and households. Firms produce goods and services using inputs, such as labor, land, and capital (buildings and machines). These inputs are called the *factors of production*. Households own the factors of production and consume all the goods and services that the firms produce.

Households and firms interact in two types of markets. In the *markets for goods and services*, households are buyers, and firms are sellers. In particular, households buy the output of goods and services that firms produce. In the *markets for the factors of production*, households are sellers, and firms are buyers. In these markets, households provide the inputs that firms use to produce goods and services. The circular-flow diagram offers a simple way of organizing the economic transactions that occur between households and firms in the economy.

The two loops of the circular-flow diagram are distinct but related. The inner loop represents the flows of inputs and outputs. The households sell the use of

circular-flow diagram

a visual model of the economy that shows how dollars flow through markets among households and firms

Figure 1

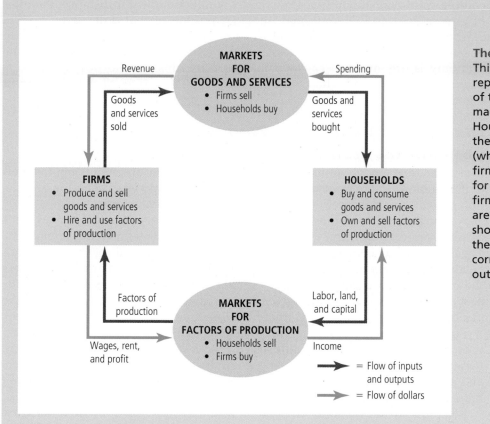

The Circular Flow
This diagram is a schematic representation of the organization of the economy. Decisions are made by households and firms. Households and firms interact in the markets for goods and services (where households are buyers and firms are sellers) and in the markets for the factors of production (where firms are buyers and households are sellers). The outer set of arrows shows the flow of dollars, and the inner set of arrows shows the corresponding flow of inputs and outputs.

their labor, land, and capital to the firms in the markets for the factors of production. The firms then use these factors to produce goods and services, which in turn are sold to households in the markets for goods and services. The outer loop of the diagram represents the corresponding flow of dollars. The households spend money to buy goods and services from the firms. The firms use some of the revenue from these sales to pay for the factors of production, such as the wages of their workers. What's left is the profit of the firm owners, who themselves are members of households.

Let's take a tour of the circular flow by following a dollar bill as it makes its way from person to person through the economy. Imagine that the dollar begins at a household, say, in your wallet. If you want to buy a cup of coffee, you take the dollar to one of the economy's markets for goods and services, such as your local Starbucks coffee shop. There, you spend it on your favorite drink. When the dollar moves into the Starbucks cash register, it becomes revenue for the firm. The dollar doesn't stay at Starbucks for long, however, because the firm uses it to buy inputs in the markets for the factors of production. Starbucks might use the dollar to pay rent to its landlord for the space it occupies or to pay the wages of its workers. In either case, the dollar enters the income of some household and, once again, is back in someone's wallet. At that point, the story of the economy's circular flow starts once again.

The circular-flow diagram in Figure 1 is a very simple model of the economy. It dispenses with details that, for some purposes, are significant. A more complex and realistic circular-flow model would include, for instance, the roles of government and international trade. (A portion of that dollar you gave to Starbucks might be used to pay taxes or to buy coffee beans from a farmer in Brazil.) Yet these details are not crucial for a basic understanding of how the economy is organized. Because of its simplicity, this circular-flow diagram is useful to keep in mind when thinking about how the pieces of the economy fit together.

Our Second Model: The Production Possibilities Frontier

Most economic models, unlike the circular-flow diagram, are built using the tools of mathematics. Here we use one of the simplest such models, called the production possibilities frontier, to illustrate some basic economic ideas.

Although real economies produce thousands of goods and services, let's assume an economy that produces only two goods—cars and computers. Together, the car industry and the computer industry use all of the economy's factors of production. The **production possibilities frontier** is a graph that shows the various combinations of output—in this case, cars and computers—that the economy can possibly produce given the available factors of production and the available production technology that firms use to turn these factors into output.

Figure 2 shows this economy's production possibilities frontier. If the economy uses all its resources in the car industry, it produces 1,000 cars and no computers. If it uses all its resources in the computer industry, it produces 3,000 computers and no cars. The two endpoints of the production possibilities frontier represent these extreme possibilities.

More likely, the economy divides its resources between the two industries, producing some cars and some computers. For example, it can produce 600 cars

production possibilities frontier
a graph that shows the combinations of output that the economy can possibly produce given the available factors of production and the available production technology

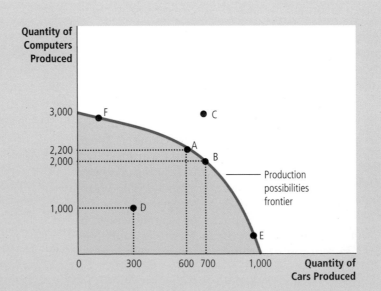

Figure 2

The Production Possibilities Frontier
The production possibilities frontier shows the combinations of output—in this case, cars and computers—that the economy can possibly produce. The economy can produce any combination on or inside the frontier. Points outside the frontier are not feasible given the economy's resources.

and 2,200 computers, shown in the figure by point A. Or, by moving some of the factors of production to the car industry from the computer industry, the economy can produce 700 cars and 2,000 computers, represented by point B.

Because resources are scarce, not every conceivable outcome is feasible. For example, no matter how resources are allocated between the two industries, the economy cannot produce the amount of cars and computers represented by point C. Given the technology available for manufacturing cars and computers, the economy does not have enough of the factors of production to support that level of output. With the resources it has, the economy can produce at any point on or inside the production possibilities frontier, but it cannot produce at points outside the frontier.

An outcome is said to be *efficient* if the economy is getting all it can from the scarce resources it has available. Points on (rather than inside) the production possibilities frontier represent efficient levels of production. When the economy is producing at such a point, say point A, there is no way to produce more of one good without producing less of the other. Point D represents an *inefficient* outcome. For some reason, perhaps widespread unemployment, the economy is producing less than it could from the resources it has available: It is producing only 300 cars and 1,000 computers. If the source of the inefficiency is eliminated, the economy can increase its production of both goods. For example, if the economy moves from point D to point A, its production of cars increases from 300 to 600, and its production of computers increases from 1,000 to 2,200.

One of the *Ten Principles of Economics* discussed in Chapter 1 is that people face trade-offs. The production possibilities frontier shows one trade-off that society faces. Once we have reached the efficient points on the frontier, the only way of producing more of one good is to produce less of the other. When the economy moves from point A to point B, for instance, society produces 100 more cars but at the expense of producing 200 fewer computers.

This trade-off helps us understand another of the *Ten Principles of Economics:* The cost of something is what you give up to get it. This is called the *opportunity cost.* The production possibilities frontier shows the opportunity cost of one good as measured in terms of the other good. When society moves from point A to point B, it gives up 200 computers to get 100 additional cars. That is, at point A, the opportunity cost of 100 cars is 200 computers. Put another way, the opportunity cost of each car is two computers. Notice that the opportunity cost of a car equals the slope of the production possibilities frontier. (If you don't recall what slope is, you can refresh your memory with the graphing appendix to this chapter.)

The opportunity cost of a car in terms of the number of computers is not constant in this economy but depends on how many cars and computers the economy is producing. This is reflected in the shape of the production possibilities frontier. Because the production possibilities frontier in Figure 2 is bowed outward, the opportunity cost of a car is highest when the economy is producing many cars and few computers, such as at point E, where the frontier is steep. When the economy is producing few cars and many computers, such as at point F, the frontier is flatter, and the opportunity cost of a car is lower.

Economists believe that production possibilities frontiers often have this bowed shape. When the economy is using most of its resources to make computers, such as at point F, the resources best suited to car production, such as skilled autoworkers, are being used in the computer industry. Because these workers probably aren't very good at making computers, the economy won't have to lose much computer production to increase car production by one unit. The opportunity cost of a car in terms of computers is small, and the frontier is relatively flat. By contrast, when the economy is using most of its resources to make cars, such as at point E, the resources best suited to making cars are already in the car industry. Producing an additional car means moving some of the best computer technicians out of the computer industry and making them autoworkers. As a result, producing an additional car will mean a substantial loss of computer output. The opportunity cost of a car is high, and the frontier is steep.

The production possibilities frontier shows the trade-off between the outputs of different goods at a given time, but the trade-off can change over time. For example, suppose a technological advance in the computer industry raises the number of computers that a worker can produce per week. This advance expands society's set of opportunities. For any given number of cars, the economy can make more computers. If the economy does not produce any computers, it can still produce 1,000 cars, so one endpoint of the frontier stays the same. But the rest of the production possibilities frontier shifts outward, as in Figure 3.

This figure illustrates economic growth. Society can move production from a point on the old frontier to a point on the new frontier. Which point it chooses depends on its preferences for the two goods. In this example, society moves from point A to point G, enjoying more computers (2,300 instead of 2,200) and more cars (650 instead of 600).

The production possibilities frontier simplifies a complex economy to highlight some basic but powerful ideas: scarcity, efficiency, trade-offs, opportunity cost,

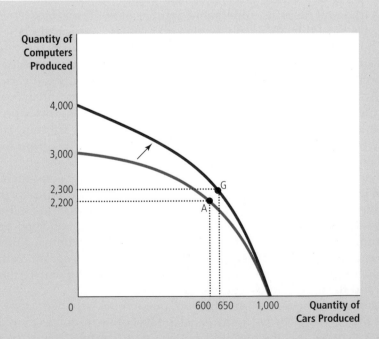

Figure 3

A Shift in the Production Possibilities Frontier
A technological advance in the computer industry enables the economy to produce more computers for any given number of cars. As a result, the production possibilities frontier shifts outward. If the economy moves from point A to point G, then the production of both cars and computers increases.

and economic growth. As you study economics, these ideas will recur in various forms. The production possibilities frontier offers one simple way of thinking about them.

Microeconomics and Macroeconomics

Many subjects are studied on various levels. Consider biology, for example. Molecular biologists study the chemical compounds that make up living things. Cellular biologists study cells, which are made up of many chemical compounds and, at the same time, are themselves the building blocks of living organisms. Evolutionary biologists study the many varieties of animals and plants and how species change gradually over the centuries.

Economics is also studied on various levels. We can study the decisions of individual households and firms. Or we can study the interaction of households and firms in markets for specific goods and services. Or we can study the operation of the economy as a whole, which is the sum of the activities of all these decision makers in all these markets.

The field of economics is traditionally divided into two broad subfields. **Microeconomics** is the study of how households and firms make decisions and how they interact in specific markets. **Macroeconomics** is the study of economywide phenomena. A microeconomist might study the effects of rent control on housing in New York City, the impact of foreign competition on the U.S. auto industry, or the effects of compulsory school attendance on workers' earnings. A macroeconomist might study the effects of borrowing by the federal government, the changes over time in the economy's rate of unemployment, or alternative policies to promote growth in national living standards.

Microeconomics and macroeconomics are closely intertwined. Because changes in the overall economy arise from the decisions of millions of individuals, it is impossible to understand macroeconomic developments without considering the associated microeconomic decisions. For example, a macroeconomist might study the effect of a federal income tax cut on the overall production of goods and services. But to analyze this issue, he or she must consider how the tax cut affects the decisions of households about how much to spend on goods and services.

Despite the inherent link between microeconomics and macroeconomics, the two fields are distinct. Because they address different questions, each field has its own set of models, which are often taught in separate courses.

microeconomics
the study of how households and firms make decisions and how they interact in markets

macroeconomics
the study of economywide phenomena, including inflation, unemployment, and economic growth

QUICK QUIZ   *In what sense is economics like a science? • Draw a production possibilities frontier for a society that produces food and clothing. Show an efficient point, an inefficient point, and an infeasible point. Show the effects of a drought. • Define* microeconomics *and* macroeconomics.

The Economist as Policy Adviser

Often, economists are asked to explain the causes of economic events. Why, for example, is unemployment higher for teenagers than for older workers? Sometimes, economists are asked to recommend policies to improve economic outcomes. What, for instance, should the government do to improve the economic

FYI

Who Studies Economics?

As a college student, you might be asking yourself: How many economics classes should I take? How useful will this stuff be to me later in life? Economics can seem abstract at first, but the field is fundamentally very practical, and the study of economics is useful in many different career paths. Here is a small sampling of some well-known people who majored in economics when they were in college.

George H. W. Bush	Former President of the United States
Donald Trump	Business and TV Mogul
Meg Whitman	Former Chief Executive Officer of eBay
Danny Glover	Actor
Barbara Boxer	U.S. Senator
John Elway	Former NFL Quarterback
Kofi Annan	Former Secretary General, United Nations
Ted Turner	Founder of CNN
Lionel Richie	Singer

Diane von Furstenberg	Fashion Designer
Michael Kinsley	Journalist
Ben Stein	Political Speechwriter, Journalist, and Actor
Cate Blanchett	Actor
Anthony Zinni	General (ret.), U.S. Marine Corps
Steve Ballmer	Chief Executive Officer, Microsoft
Arnold Schwarzenegger	Governor of California
Sandra Day-O'Connor	Former Supreme Court Justice
Scott Adams	Cartoonist for *Dilbert*
Mick Jagger	Singer for the Rolling Stones

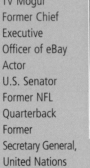

When asked in 2005 why The Rolling Stones were going on tour again, former economics major Mick Jagger replied, "Supply and demand." Keith Richards added, "If the demand's there, we'll supply."

Having studied at the London School of Economics may not help Mick Jagger hit the high notes, but it has probably given him some insight about how to invest the substantial sums he has earned during his rock 'n' roll career.

well-being of teenagers? When economists are trying to explain the world, they are scientists. When they are trying to help improve it, they are policy advisers.

Positive versus Normative Analysis

To help clarify the two roles that economists play, let's examine the use of language. Because scientists and policy advisers have different goals, they use language in different ways.

For example, suppose that two people are discussing minimum-wage laws. Here are two statements you might hear:

POLLY: Minimum-wage laws cause unemployment.
NORM: The government should raise the minimum wage.

Ignoring for now whether you agree with these statements, notice that Polly and Norm differ in what they are trying to do. Polly is speaking like a scientist: She is making a claim about how the world works. Norm is speaking like a policy adviser: He is making a claim about how he would like to change the world.

In general, statements about the world come in two types. One type, such as Polly's, is positive. **Positive statements** are descriptive. They make a claim about how the world *is*. A second type of statement, such as Norm's, is normative. **Normative statements** are prescriptive. They make a claim about how the world *ought to be*.

A key difference between positive and normative statements is how we judge their validity. We can, in principle, confirm or refute positive statements by examining evidence. An economist might evaluate Polly's statement by analyzing data on changes in minimum wages and changes in unemployment over time. By contrast, evaluating normative statements involves values as well as facts. Norm's statement cannot be judged using data alone. Deciding what is good or bad policy is not just a matter of science. It also involves our views on ethics, religion, and political philosophy.

Positive and normative statements are fundamentally different, but they are often intertwined in a person's set of beliefs. In particular, positive views about how the world works affect normative views about what policies are desirable. Polly's claim that the minimum wage causes unemployment, if true, might lead her to reject Norm's conclusion that the government should raise the minimum wage. Yet normative conclusions cannot come from positive analysis alone; they involve value judgments as well.

As you study economics, keep in mind the distinction between positive and normative statements because it will help you stay focused on the task at hand. Much of economics is positive: It just tries to explain how the economy works. Yet those who use economics often have normative goals: They want to learn how to improve the economy. When you hear economists making normative statements, you know they are speaking not as scientists but as policy advisers.

positive statements
claims that attempt to describe the world as it is

normative statements
claims that attempt to prescribe how the world should be

Economists in Washington

President Harry Truman once said that he wanted to find a one-armed economist. When he asked his economists for advice, they always answered, "On the one hand, . . . On the other hand, . . . "

Truman was right in realizing that economists' advice is not always straightforward. This tendency is rooted in one of the *Ten Principles of Economics*: People face trade-offs. Economists are aware that trade-offs are involved in most policy decisions. A policy might increase efficiency at the cost of equality. It might help future generations but hurt current generations. An economist who says that all policy decisions are easy is an economist not to be trusted.

Truman was not the only president who relied on the advice of economists. Since 1946, the president of the United States has received guidance from the Council of Economic Advisers, which consists of three members and a staff of a few dozen economists. The council, whose offices are just a few steps from the White House, has no duty other than to advise the president and to write the annual *Economic Report of the President*, which discusses recent developments in the economy and presents the council's analysis of current policy issues.

The president also receives input from economists in many administrative departments. Economists at the Office of Management and Budget help formulate spending plans and regulatory policies. Economists at the Department of the Treasury help design tax policy. Economists at the Department of Labor analyze data on workers and those looking for work to help formulate labor-market policies. Economists at the Department of Justice help enforce the nation's antitrust laws.

Economists are also found outside the administrative branch of government. To obtain independent evaluations of policy proposals, Congress relies on the advice of the Congressional Budget Office, which is staffed by economists. The

"Let's switch. I'll make the policy, you implement it, and he'll explain it."

. . . . in the news

> ## The Economics of President Obama

Here is how Larry Summers, a chief economic adviser to Barack Obama, describes the president's policies.

A Vision for Innovation, Growth, and Quality Jobs

BY LAWRENCE H. SUMMERS

President Obama laid out his vision for innovation, growth, and quality jobs earlier today at Hudson Valley Community College. Ths President's plan is grounded not only in the American tradition of entrepreneurship, but also in the traditions of robust economic thought.

During the past two years, the ideas propounded by John Maynard Keynes have assumed greater importance than most people would have thought in the previous generation. As Keynes famously observed, during those rare times of deep financial and economic crisis, when the "invisible hand" Adam Smith talked about has temporarily ceased to function, there is a more urgent need for government to play an active role in restoring markets to their healthy function.

The wisdom of Keynesian policies has been confirmed by the performance of the economy over the past year. After the collapse of Lehman Brothers last September, government policy moved in a strongly activist direction.

As a result of those policies, our outlook today has shifted from rescue to recovery, from worrying about the very real prospect of depression to thinking about what kind of an expansion we want to have.

An important aspect of any economic expansion is the role innovation plays as

Federal Reserve, the institution that sets the nation's monetary policy, employs hundreds of economists to analyze economic developments in the United States and throughout the world.

The influence of economists on policy goes beyond their role as advisers: Their research and writings often affect policy indirectly. Economist John Maynard Keynes offered this observation:

> The ideas of economists and political philosophers, both when they are right and when they are wrong, are more powerful than is commonly understood. Indeed, the world is ruled by little else. Practical men, who believe themselves to be quite exempt from intellectual influences, are usually the slaves of some defunct economist. Madmen in authority, who hear voices in the air, are distilling their frenzy from some academic scribbler of a few years back.

Although these words were written in 1935, they remain true. Indeed, the "academic scribbler" now influencing public policy is often Keynes himself.

Why Economists' Advice Is Not Always Followed

Any economist who advises presidents or other elected leaders knows that his or her recommendations are not always heeded. Frustrating as this can be, it is easy to understand. The process by which economic policy is actually made differs in many ways from the idealized policy process assumed in economics textbooks.

an engine of economic growth. In this regard, the most important economist of the twenty-first century might actually turn out to be not Smith or Keynes, but Joseph Schumpeter.

One of Schumpeter's most important contributions was the emphasis he placed on the tremendous power of innovation and entrepreneurial initiative to drive growth through a process he famously characterized as "creative destruction." His work captured not only an economic truth, but also the particular source of America's strength and dynamism.

One of the ways to view the trajectory of economic history is through the key technologies that have reverberated across the economy. In the nineteenth century, these included the transcontinental railroad, the telegraph, and the steam engine, among others. In the twentieth, the most powerful innovations included the automobile, the jet plane, and, over the last generation, information technology.

While we can't know exactly where the next great area of American innovation will be, we already see a number of prominent sectors where American entrepreneurs are unleashing explosive, innovative energy:

- In information technology, where tremendous potential remains for a range of applications to increase for years to come;
- In life-science technologies, where developments made at the National Institutes of Health and in research facilities around the country will have profound implications not just for human health, but also for the environment, agriculture, and a range of other areas that require technological creativity; and,
- In energy, where the combination of environmental and geopolitical imperatives have created the context for an enormously productive period in developing energy technologies as well.

Looking across the breadth of the U.S. economy, the prospects for transformational innovation to occur are enormous. But to ensure that the entrepreneurial spirit that Schumpeter recognized in the early twentieth century will continue to drive the American economy in the twenty-first century requires a role for government as well: to create an environment that is conducive to generating those developments.

Source: The White House Blog, September 21, 2009. http://www.whitehouse.gov/blog/A-Vision-for-Innovation-Growth-and-Quality-Jobs/

Throughout this text, whenever we discuss economic policy, we often focus on one question: What is the best policy for the government to pursue? We act as if policy were set by a benevolent king. Once the king figures out the right policy, he has no trouble putting his ideas into action.

In the real world, figuring out the right policy is only part of a leader's job, sometimes the easiest part. After a president hears from his economic advisers about what policy is best from their perspective, he turns to other advisers for related input. His communications advisers will tell him how best to explain the proposed policy to the public, and they will try to anticipate any misunderstandings that might make the challenge more difficult. His press advisers will tell him how the news media will report on his proposal and what opinions will likely be expressed on the nation's editorial pages. His legislative affairs advisers will tell him how Congress will view the proposal, what amendments members of Congress will suggest, and the likelihood that Congress will pass some version of the president's proposal into law. His political advisers will tell him which groups will organize to support or oppose the proposed policy, how this proposal will affect his standing among different groups in the electorate, and whether it will affect support for any of the president's other policy initiatives. After hearing and weighing all this advice, the president then decides how to proceed.

Making economic policy in a representative democracy is a messy affair—and there are often good reasons presidents (and other politicians) do not advance the policies that economists advocate. Economists offer crucial input into the policy process, but their advice is only one ingredient of a complex recipe.

QUICK QUIZ   *Give an example of a positive statement and an example of a normative statement that somehow relates to your daily life. • Name three parts of government that regularly rely on advice from economists.*

Why Economists Disagree

"If all economists were laid end to end, they would not reach a conclusion." This quip from George Bernard Shaw is revealing. Economists as a group are often criticized for giving conflicting advice to policymakers. President Ronald Reagan once joked that if the game Trivial Pursuit were designed for economists, it would have 100 questions and 3,000 answers.

Why do economists so often appear to give conflicting advice to policymakers? There are two basic reasons:

- Economists may disagree about the validity of alternative positive theories about how the world works.
- Economists may have different values and therefore different normative views about what policy should try to accomplish.

Let's discuss each of these reasons.

Differences in Scientific Judgments

Several centuries ago, astronomers debated whether the earth or the sun was at the center of the solar system. More recently, meteorologists have debated whether the earth is experiencing global warming and, if so, why. Science is a search for understanding about the world around us. It is not surprising that as the search continues, scientists can disagree about the direction in which truth lies.

Economists often disagree for the same reason. Economics is a young science, and there is still much to be learned. Economists sometimes disagree because they have different hunches about the validity of alternative theories or about the size of important parameters that measure how economic variables are related.

For example, economists disagree about whether the government should tax a household's income or its consumption (spending). Advocates of a switch from the current income tax to a consumption tax believe that the change would encourage households to save more because income that is saved would not be taxed. Higher saving, in turn, would free resources for capital accumulation, leading to more rapid growth in productivity and living standards. Advocates of the current income tax system believe that household saving would not respond much to a change in the tax laws. These two groups of economists hold different normative views about the tax system because they have different positive views about the responsiveness of saving to tax incentives.

Differences in Values

Suppose that Peter and Paula both take the same amount of water from the town well. To pay for maintaining the well, the town taxes its residents. Peter has income of $100,000 and is taxed $10,000, or 10 percent of his income. Paula has income of $20,000 and is taxed $4,000, or 20 percent of her income.

Is this policy fair? If not, who pays too much and who pays too little? Does it matter whether Paula's low income is due to a medical disability or to her decision to pursue an acting career? Does it matter whether Peter's high income is due to a large inheritance or to his willingness to work long hours at a dreary job?

These are difficult questions on which people are likely to disagree. If the town hired two experts to study how the town should tax its residents to pay for the well, we would not be surprised if they offered conflicting advice.

This simple example shows why economists sometimes disagree about public policy. As we learned earlier in our discussion of normative and positive analysis, policies cannot be judged on scientific grounds alone. Economists give conflicting advice sometimes because they have different values. Perfecting the science of economics will not tell us whether Peter or Paula pays too much.

Perception versus Reality

Because of differences in scientific judgments and differences in values, some disagreement among economists is inevitable. Yet one should not overstate the amount of disagreement. Economists agree with one another far more than is sometimes understood.

Table 1 contains 20 propositions about economic policy. In surveys of professional economists, these propositions were endorsed by an overwhelming majority of respondents. Most of these propositions would fail to command a similar consensus among the public.

The first proposition in the table is about rent control, a policy that sets a legal maximum on the amount landlords can charge for their apartments. Almost all economists believe that rent control adversely affects the availability and quality of housing and is a costly way of helping the neediest members of society. Nonetheless, many city governments ignore the advice of economists and place ceilings on the rents that landlords may charge their tenants.

The second proposition in the table concerns tariffs and import quotas, two policies that restrict trade among nations. For reasons we discuss more fully later in this text, almost all economists oppose such barriers to free trade. Nonetheless, over the years, presidents and Congress have chosen to restrict the import of certain goods.

Why do policies such as rent control and trade barriers persist if the experts are united in their opposition? It may be that the realities of the political process stand as immovable obstacles. But it also may be that economists have not yet convinced enough of the public that these policies are undesirable. One purpose of this book is to help you understand the economist's view of these and other subjects and, perhaps, to persuade you that it is the right one.

QUICK QUIZ   *Why might economic advisers to the president disagree about a question of policy?*

Let's Get Going

The first two chapters of this book have introduced you to the ideas and methods of economics. We are now ready to get to work. In the next chapter, we start learning in more detail the principles of economic behavior and economic policy.

As you proceed through this book, you will be asked to draw on many of your intellectual skills. You might find it helpful to keep in mind some advice from the great economist John Maynard Keynes:

Table **1**

Propositions about Which Most Economists Agree

Proposition (and percentage of economists who agree)

1. A ceiling on rents reduces the quantity and quality of housing available. (93%)
2. Tariffs and import quotas usually reduce general economic welfare. (93%)
3. Flexible and floating exchange rates offer an effective international monetary arrangement. (90%)
4. Fiscal policy (e.g., tax cut and/or government expenditure increase) has a significant stimulative impact on a less than fully employed economy. (90%)
5. The United States should not restrict employers from outsourcing work to foreign countries. (90%)
6. Economic growth in developed countries like the United States leads to greater levels of well-being. (88%)
7. The United States should eliminate agricultural subsidies. (85%)
8. An appropriately designed fiscal policy can increase the long-run rate of capital formation. (85%)
9. Local and state governments should eliminate subsidies to professional sports franchises. (85%)
10. If the federal budget is to be balanced, it should be done over the business cycle rather than yearly. (85%)
11. The gap between Social Security funds and expenditures will become unsustainably large within the next 50 years if current policies remain unchanged. (85%)
12. Cash payments increase the welfare of recipients to a greater degree than do transfers-in-kind of equal cash value. (84%)
13. A large federal budget deficit has an adverse effect on the economy. (83%)
14. The redistribution of income in the United State is a legitimate role for the government. (83%)
15. Inflation is caused primarily by too much growth in the money supply. (83%)
16. The United States should not ban genetically modified crops. (82%)
17. A minimum wage increases unemployment among young and unskilled workers. (79%)
18. The government should restructure the welfare system along the lines of a "negative income tax." (79%)
19. Effluent taxes and marketable pollution permits represent a better approach to pollution control than imposition of pollution ceilings. (78%)
20. Government subsidies on ethanol in the United States should be reduced or eliminated. (78%)

Source: Richard M. Alston, J. R. Kearl, and Michael B. Vaughn, "Is There Consensus among Economists in the 1990s?" *American Economic Review* (May 1992): 203–209; Dan Fuller and Doris Geide-Stevenson, "Consensus among Economists Revisited," *Journal of Economics Education* (Fall 2003): 369–387; Robert Whaples, "Do Economists Agree on Anything? Yes!" *Economists' Voice* (November 2006): 1–6; Robert Whaples, "The Policy Views of American Economic Association Members: The Results of a New Survey, *Econ Journal Watch* (September 2009): 337–348.

The study of economics does not seem to require any specialized gifts of an unusually high order. Is it not . . . a very easy subject compared with the higher branches of philosophy or pure science? An easy subject, at which very few excel! The paradox finds its explanation, perhaps, in that the master-economist must possess a rare *combination* of gifts. He must be mathematician, historian, statesman, philosopher—in some degree. He must understand symbols and speak in words. He must contemplate the particular in terms of the general, and touch abstract and concrete in the same flight of thought. He must study the present in the light of the past for the purposes of the future. No part of man's nature or his institutions must lie entirely outside his regard. He must be purposeful and disinterested in a simultaneous mood; as aloof and incorruptible as an artist, yet sometimes as near the earth as a politician.

It is a tall order. But with practice, you will become more and more accustomed to thinking like an economist.

in the news

> ### Environmental Economics
> *Some economists are helping to save the planet.*

Green Groups See Potent Tool in Economics

BY JESSICA E. VASCELLARO

Many economists dream of getting high-paying jobs on Wall Street, at prestigious think tanks and universities or at powerful government agencies like the Federal Reserve.

But a growing number are choosing to use their skills not to track inflation or interest rates but to rescue rivers and trees. These are the "green economists," more formally known as environmental economists, who use economic arguments and systems to persuade companies to clean up pollution and to help conserve natural areas.

Working at dozens of advocacy groups and a myriad of state and federal environmental agencies, they are helping to formulate the intellectual framework behind approaches to protecting endangered species, reducing pollution and preventing climate change. They also are becoming a link between left-leaning advocacy groups and the public and private sectors.

"In the past, many advocacy groups interpreted economics as how to make a profit or maximize income," says Lawrence Goulder, a professor of environmental and resource economics at Stanford University in Stanford, Calif. "More economists are

realizing that it offers a framework for resource allocation where resources are not only labor and capital but natural resources as well."

Environmental economists are on the payroll of government agencies (the Environmental Protection Agency had about 164 on staff in 2004, up 36% from 1995) and groups like the Wilderness Society, a Washington-based conservation group, which has four of them to work on projects such as assessing the economic impact of building off-road driving trails. Environmental Defense, also based in Washington, was one of the first environmental-advocacy groups to hire economists and now has about eight, who do such things as develop market incentives to address environmental problems like climate change and water shortages. . . .

"There used to be this idea that we shouldn't have to monetize the environment because it is invaluable," says Caroline Alkire, who in 1991 joined the Wilderness Society, an advocacy group in Washington, D.C., as one of the group's first economists. "But if we are going to engage in debate on the Hill about drilling in the Arctic we need to be able to combat the financial arguments. We have to play that card or we are going to lose."

The field of environmental economics began to take form in the 1960s when academics started to apply the tools of economics to the nascent green movement. The discipline grew more popular through-

out the 1980s when the Environmental Protection Agency adopted a system of tradable permits for phasing out leaded gasoline. It wasn't until the 1990 amendment to the Clean Air Act, however, that most environmentalists started to take economics seriously.

The amendment implemented a system of tradable allowances for acid rain, a program pushed by Environmental Defense. Under the law, plants that can reduce their emissions more cost-effectively may sell their allowances to more heavy polluters. Today, the program has exceeded its goal of reducing the amount of acid rain to half its 1980 level and is celebrated as evidence that markets can help achieve environmental goals.

Its success has convinced its former critics, who at the time contended that environmental regulation was a matter of ethics, not economics, and favored installing expensive acid rain removal technology in all power plants instead.

Greenpeace, the international environmental giant, was one of the leading opponents of the 1990 amendment. But Kert Davies, research director for Greenpeace USA, said its success and the lack of any significant action on climate policy throughout [the] early 1990s brought the organization around to the concept. "We now believe that [tradable permits] are the most straightforward system of reducing emissions and creating the incentives necessary for massive reductions."

Source: *The Wall Street Journal*, August 23, 2005.

SUMMARY

- Economists try to address their subject with a scientist's objectivity. Like all scientists, they make appropriate assumptions and build simplified models to understand the world around them. Two simple economic models are the circular-flow diagram and the production possibilities frontier.

- The field of economics is divided into two subfields: microeconomics and macroeconomics. Microeconomists study decision making by households and firms and the interaction among households and firms in the marketplace. Macroeconomists study the forces and trends that affect the economy as a whole.

- A positive statement is an assertion about how the world *is*. A normative statement is an assertion about how the world *ought to be*. When economists make normative statements, they are acting more as policy advisers than scientists.

- Economists who advise policymakers offer conflicting advice either because of differences in scientific judgments or because of differences in values. At other times, economists are united in the advice they offer, but policymakers may choose to ignore it.

KEY CONCEPTS

circular-flow diagram, *p. 24*
production possibilities
    frontier, *p. 26*

microeconomics, *p. 29*
macroeconomics, *p. 29*

positive statements, *p. 31*
normative statements, *p. 31*

QUESTIONS FOR REVIEW

1. How is economics a science?
2. Why do economists make assumptions?
3. Should an economic model describe reality exactly?
4. Name a way that your family interacts in the factor market and a way that it interacts in the product market.
5. Name one economic interaction that isn't covered by the simplified circular-flow diagram.
6. Draw and explain a production possibilities frontier for an economy that produces milk and cookies. What happens to this frontier if disease kills half of the economy's cows?
7. Use a production possibilities frontier to describe the idea of "efficiency."
8. What are the two subfields into which economics is divided? Explain what each subfield studies.
9. What is the difference between a positive and a normative statement? Give an example of each.
10. Why do economists sometimes offer conflicting advice to policymakers?

PROBLEMS AND APPLICATIONS

1. Draw a circular-flow diagram. Identify the parts of the model that correspond to the flow of goods and services and the flow of dollars for each of the following activities.
   a. Selena pays a storekeeper $1 for a quart of milk.
   b. Stuart earns $4.50 per hour working at a fast-food restaurant.
   c. Shanna spends $30 to get a haircut.
   d. Sally earns $10,000 from her 10 percent ownership of Acme Industrial.

2. Imagine a society that produces military goods and consumer goods, which we'll call "guns" and "butter."
   a. Draw a production possibilities frontier for guns and butter. Using the concept of opportunity cost, explain why it most likely has a bowed-out shape.
   b. Show a point that is impossible for the economy to achieve. Show a point that is feasible but inefficient.
   c. Imagine that the society has two political parties, called the Hawks (who want a strong military) and the Doves (who want a smaller military). Show a point on your production possibilities frontier that the Hawks might choose and a point the Doves might choose.
   d. Imagine that an aggressive neighboring country reduces the size of its military. As a result, both the Hawks and the Doves reduce their desired production of guns by the same amount. Which party would get the bigger "peace dividend," measured by the increase in butter production? Explain.

3. The first principle of economics discussed in Chapter 1 is that people face trade-offs. Use a production possibilities frontier to illustrate society's trade-off between two "goods"—a clean environment and the quantity of industrial output. What do you suppose determines the shape and position of the frontier? Show what happens to the frontier if engineers develop a new way of producing electricity that emits fewer pollutants.

4. An economy consists of three workers: Larry, Moe, and Curly. Each works ten hours a day and can produce two services: mowing lawns and washing cars. In an hour, Larry can either mow one lawn or wash one car; Moe can either mow one lawn or wash two cars; and Curly can either mow two lawns or wash one car.
   a. Calculate how much of each service is produced under the following circumstances, which we label A, B, C, and D:
      • All three spend all their time mowing lawns. (A)
      • All three spend all their time washing cars. (B)
      • All three spend half their time on each activity. (C)
      • Larry spends half his time on each activity, while Moe only washes cars and Curly only mows lawns. (D)
   b. Graph the production possibilities frontier for this economy. Using your answers to part (a), identify points A, B, C, and D on your graph.
   c. Explain why the production possibilities frontier has the shape it does.
   d. Are any of the allocations calculated in part (a) inefficient? Explain.

5. Classify the following topics as relating to microeconomics or macroeconomics.
   a. a family's decision about how much income to save
   b. the effect of government regulations on auto emissions
   c. the impact of higher national saving on economic growth
   d. a firm's decision about how many workers to hire
   e. the relationship between the inflation rate and changes in the quantity of money

6. Classify each of the following statements as positive or normative. Explain.
   a. Society faces a short-run trade-off between inflation and unemployment.
   b. A reduction in the rate of money growth will reduce the rate of inflation.
   c. The Federal Reserve should reduce the rate of money growth.
   d. Society ought to require welfare recipients to look for jobs.
   e. Lower tax rates encourage more work and more saving.

7. If you were president, would you be more interested in your economic advisers' positive views or their normative views? Why?

For further information on topics in this chapter, additional problems, applications, examples, online quizzes, and more, please visit our website at www.cengage.com/economics/mankiw.

Appendix

Graphing: A Brief Review

Many of the concepts that economists study can be expressed with numbers—the price of bananas, the quantity of bananas sold, the cost of growing bananas, and so on. Often, these economic variables are related to one another: When the price of bananas rises, people buy fewer bananas. One way of expressing the relationships among variables is with graphs.

Graphs serve two purposes. First, when developing economic theories, graphs offer a way to visually express ideas that might be less clear if described with equations or words. Second, when analyzing economic data, graphs provide a powerful way of finding and interpreting patterns. Whether we are working with theory or with data, graphs provide a lens through which a recognizable forest emerges from a multitude of trees.

Numerical information can be expressed graphically in many ways, just as there are many ways to express a thought in words. A good writer chooses words that will make an argument clear, a description pleasing, or a scene dramatic. An effective economist chooses the type of graph that best suits the purpose at hand.

In this appendix, we discuss how economists use graphs to study the mathematical relationships among variables. We also discuss some of the pitfalls that can arise in the use of graphical methods.

Graphs of a Single Variable

Three common graphs are shown in Figure A-1. The *pie chart* in panel (a) shows how total income in the United States is divided among the sources of income, including compensation of employees, corporate profits, and so on. A slice of the

Figure **A-1**

Types of Graphs

The pie chart in panel (a) shows how U.S. national income in 2008 was derived from various sources. The bar graph in panel (b) compares the 2008 average income in four countries. The time-series graph in panel (c) shows the productivity of labor in U.S. businesses from 1950 to 2000.

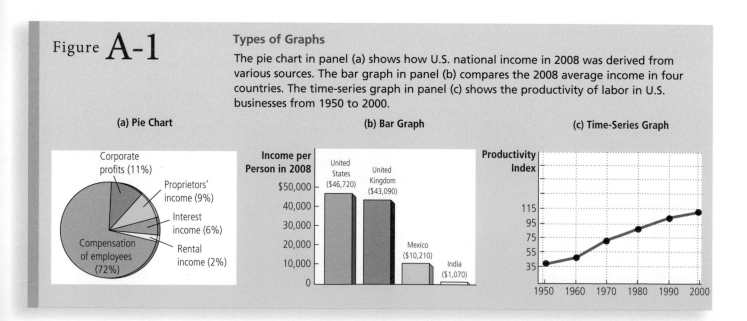

(a) Pie Chart

(b) Bar Graph

(c) Time-Series Graph

pie represents each source's share of the total. The *bar graph* in panel (b) compares income for four countries. The height of each bar represents the average income in each country. The *time-series graph* in panel (c) traces the rising productivity in the U.S. business sector over time. The height of the line shows output per hour in each year. You have probably seen similar graphs in newspapers and magazines.

Graphs of Two Variables: The Coordinate System

The three graphs in Figure A-1 are useful in showing how a variable changes over time or across individuals, but they are limited in how much they can tell us. These graphs display information only on a single variable. Economists are often concerned with the relationships between variables. Thus, they need to display two variables on a single graph. The *coordinate system* makes this possible.

Suppose you want to examine the relationship between study time and grade point average. For each student in your class, you could record a pair of numbers: hours per week spent studying and grade point average. These numbers could then be placed in parentheses as an *ordered pair* and appear as a single point on the graph. Albert E., for instance, is represented by the ordered pair (25 hours/week, 3.5 GPA), while his "what-me-worry?" classmate Alfred E. is represented by the ordered pair (5 hours/week, 2.0 GPA).

We can graph these ordered pairs on a two-dimensional grid. The first number in each ordered pair, called the *x-coordinate*, tells us the horizontal location of the point. The second number, called the *y-coordinate*, tells us the vertical location of the point. The point with both an *x*-coordinate and a *y*-coordinate of zero is known as the *origin*. The two coordinates in the ordered pair tell us where the point is located in relation to the origin: *x* units to the right of the origin and *y* units above it.

Figure A-2 graphs grade point average against study time for Albert E., Alfred E., and their classmates. This type of graph is called a *scatterplot* because it plots scattered points. Looking at this graph, we immediately notice that points farther

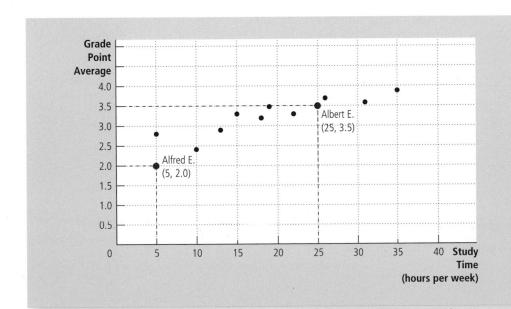

Figure A-2

Using the Coordinate System
Grade point average is measured on the vertical axis and study time on the horizontal axis. Albert E., Alfred E., and their classmates are represented by various points. We can see from the graph that students who study more tend to get higher grades.

to the right (indicating more study time) also tend to be higher (indicating a better grade point average). Because study time and grade point average typically move in the same direction, we say that these two variables have a *positive correlation*. By contrast, if we were to graph party time and grades, we would likely find that higher party time is associated with lower grades; because these variables typically move in opposite directions, we call this a *negative correlation*. In either case, the coordinate system makes the correlation between the two variables easy to see.

Curves in the Coordinate System

Students who study more do tend to get higher grades, but other factors also influence a student's grade. Previous preparation is an important factor, for instance, as are talent, attention from teachers, even eating a good breakfast. A scatterplot like Figure A-2 does not attempt to isolate the effect that studying has on grades from the effects of other variables. Often, however, economists prefer looking at how one variable affects another, holding everything else constant.

To see how this is done, let's consider one of the most important graphs in economics: the *demand curve*. The demand curve traces out the effect of a good's price on the quantity of the good consumers want to buy. Before showing a demand curve, however, consider Table A-1, which shows how the number of novels that Emma buys depends on her income and on the price of novels. When novels are cheap, Emma buys them in large quantities. As they become more expensive, she instead borrows books from the library or chooses to go to the movies rather than read. Similarly, at any given price, Emma buys more novels when she has a higher income. That is, when her income increases, she spends part of the additional income on novels and part on other goods.

We now have three variables—the price of novels, income, and the number of novels purchased—which are more than we can represent in two dimensions. To put the information from Table A-1 in graphical form, we need to hold one of the three variables constant and trace out the relationship between the other two. Because the demand curve represents the relationship between price and quantity demanded, we hold Emma's income constant and show how the number of novels she buys varies with the price of novels.

Suppose that Emma's income is $30,000 per year. If we place the number of novels Emma purchases on the *x*-axis and the price of novels on the *y*-axis, we

Table A-1

Novels Purchased by Emma
This table shows the number of novels Emma buys at various incomes and prices. For any given level of income, the data on price and quantity demanded can be graphed to produce Emma's demand curve for novels, as shown in Figures A-3 and A-4.

Price	For $20,000 Income:	For $30,000 Income:	For $40,000 Income:
$10	2 novels	5 novels	8 novels
9	6	9	12
8	10	13	16
7	14	17	20
6	18	21	24
5	22	25	28
	Demand curve, D_3	Demand curve, D_1	Demand curve, D_2

can graphically represent the middle column of Table A-1. When the points that represent these entries from the table—(5 novels, $10), (9 novels, $9), and so on—are connected, they form a line. This line, pictured in Figure A-3, is known as Emma's demand curve for novels; it tells us how many novels Emma purchases at any given price. The demand curve is downward sloping, indicating that a higher price reduces the quantity of novels demanded. Because the quantity of novels demanded and the price move in opposite directions, we say that the two variables are *negatively related*. (Conversely, when two variables move in the same direction, the curve relating them is upward sloping, and we say the variables are *positively related*.)

Now suppose that Emma's income rises to $40,000 per year. At any given price, Emma will purchase more novels than she did at her previous level of income. Just as earlier we drew Emma's demand curve for novels using the entries from the middle column of Table A-1, we now draw a new demand curve using the entries from the right column of the table. This new demand curve (curve D_2) is pictured alongside the old one (curve D_1) in Figure A-4; the new curve is a similar line drawn farther to the right. We therefore say that Emma's demand curve for novels *shifts* to the right when her income increases. Likewise, if Emma's income were to fall to $20,000 per year, she would buy fewer novels at any given price and her demand curve would shift to the left (to curve D_3).

In economics, it is important to distinguish between *movements along a curve* and *shifts of a curve*. As we can see from Figure A-3, if Emma earns $30,000 per year and novels cost $8 apiece, she will purchase 13 novels per year. If the price of novels falls to $7, Emma will increase her purchases of novels to 17 per year. The demand curve, however, stays fixed in the same place. Emma still buys the same

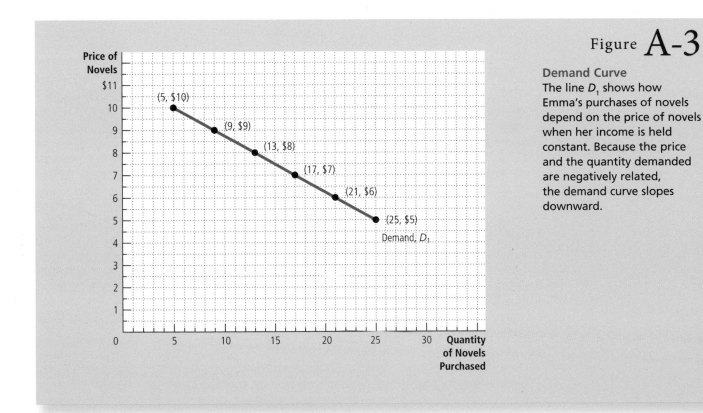

Figure A-3

Demand Curve
The line D_1 shows how Emma's purchases of novels depend on the price of novels when her income is held constant. Because the price and the quantity demanded are negatively related, the demand curve slopes downward.

Figure A-4

Shifting Demand Curves
The location of Emma's demand curve for novels depends on how much income she earns. The more she earns, the more novels she will purchase at any given price, and the farther to the right her demand curve will lie. Curve D_1 represents Emma's original demand curve when her income is $30,000 per year. If her income rises to $40,000 per year, her demand curve shifts to D_2. If her income falls to $20,000 per year, her demand curve shifts to D_3.

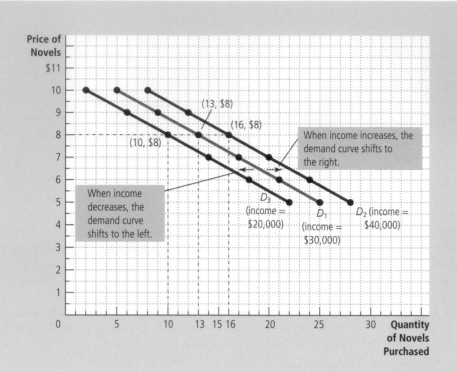

number of novels *at each price*, but as the price falls, she moves along her demand curve from left to right. By contrast, if the price of novels remains fixed at $8 but her income rises to $40,000, Emma increases her purchases of novels from 13 to 16 per year. Because Emma buys more novels *at each price*, her demand curve shifts out, as shown in Figure A-4.

There is a simple way to tell when it is necessary to shift a curve: *When a variable that is not named on either axis changes, the curve shifts.* Income is on neither the *x*-axis nor the *y*-axis of the graph, so when Emma's income changes, her demand curve must shift. The same is true for any change that affects Emma's purchasing habits besides a change in the price of novels. If, for instance, the public library closes and Emma must buy all the books she wants to read, she will demand more novels at each price, and her demand curve will shift to the right. Or if the price of movies falls and Emma spends more time at the movies and less time reading, she will demand fewer novels at each price, and her demand curve will shift to the left. By contrast, when a variable on an axis of the graph changes, the curve does not shift. We read the change as a movement along the curve.

Slope

One question we might want to ask about Emma is how much her purchasing habits respond to price. Look at the demand curve pictured in Figure A-5. If this curve is very steep, Emma purchases nearly the same number of novels regardless

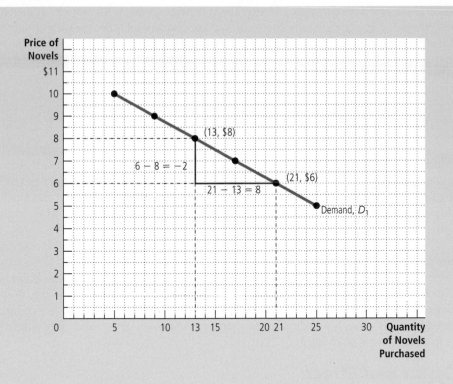

Calculating the Slope of a Line
To calculate the slope of the demand curve, we can look at the changes in the *x*- and *y*-coordinates as we move from the point (21 novels, $6) to the point (13 novels, $8). The slope of the line is the ratio of the change in the *y*-coordinate (−2) to the change in the *x*-coordinate (+8), which equals −¼

of whether they are cheap or expensive. If this curve is much flatter, the number of novels Emma purchases is more sensitive to changes in the price. To answer questions about how much one variable responds to changes in another variable, we can use the concept of *slope*.

The slope of a line is the ratio of the vertical distance covered to the horizontal distance covered as we move along the line. This definition is usually written out in mathematical symbols as follows:

$$\text{slope} = \frac{\Delta y}{\Delta x},$$

where the Greek letter Δ (delta) stands for the change in a variable. In other words, the slope of a line is equal to the "rise" (change in *y*) divided by the "run" (change in *x*). The slope will be a small positive number for a fairly flat upward-sloping line, a large positive number for a steep upward-sloping line, and a negative number for a downward-sloping line. A horizontal line has a slope of zero because in this case the *y*-variable never changes; a vertical line is said to have an infinite slope because the *y*-variable can take any value without the *x*-variable changing at all.

What is the slope of Emma's demand curve for novels? First of all, because the curve slopes down, we know the slope will be negative. To calculate a numerical value for the slope, we must choose two points on the line. With Emma's income at $30,000, she will purchase 21 novels at a price of $6 or 13 novels at a price of $8. When we apply the slope formula, we are concerned with the change between these two points; in other words, we are concerned with the difference between them, which lets us know that we will have to subtract one set of values from the other, as follows:

$$\text{slope} = \frac{\Delta y}{\Delta x} = \frac{\text{first } y\text{-coordinate} - \text{second } y\text{-coordinate}}{\text{first } x\text{-coordinate} - \text{second } x\text{-coordinate}} = \frac{6-8}{21-13} = \frac{-2}{8} = \frac{-1}{4}$$

Figure A-5 shows graphically how this calculation works. Try computing the slope of Emma's demand curve using two different points. You should get exactly the same result, $-\frac{1}{4}$. One of the properties of a straight line is that it has the same slope everywhere. This is not true of other types of curves, which are steeper in some places than in others.

The slope of Emma's demand curve tells us something about how responsive her purchases are to changes in the price. A small slope (a number close to zero) means that Emma's demand curve is relatively flat; in this case, she adjusts the number of novels she buys substantially in response to a price change. A larger slope (a number farther from zero) means that Emma's demand curve is relatively steep; in this case, she adjusts the number of novels she buys only slightly in response to a price change.

Cause and Effect

Economists often use graphs to advance an argument about how the economy works. In other words, they use graphs to argue about how one set of events *causes* another set of events. With a graph like the demand curve, there is no doubt about cause and effect. Because we are varying price and holding all other variables constant, we know that changes in the price of novels cause changes in the quantity Emma demands. Remember, however, that our demand curve came from a hypothetical example. When graphing data from the real world, it is often more difficult to establish how one variable affects another.

The first problem is that it is difficult to hold everything else constant when studying the relationship between two variables. If we are not able to hold other variables constant, we might decide that one variable on our graph is causing changes in the other variable when actually those changes are caused by a third *omitted variable* not pictured on the graph. Even if we have identified the correct

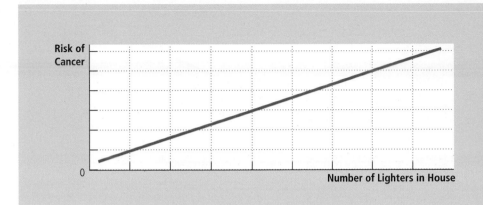

Figure A-6

Graph with an Omitted Variable The upward-sloping curve shows that members of households with more cigarette lighters are more likely to develop cancer. Yet we should not conclude that ownership of lighters causes cancer because the graph does not take into account the number of cigarettes smoked.

two variables to look at, we might run into a second problem—*reverse causality*. In other words, we might decide that A causes B when in fact B causes A. The omitted-variable and reverse-causality traps require us to proceed with caution when using graphs to draw conclusions about causes and effects.

Omitted Variables   To see how omitting a variable can lead to a deceptive graph, let's consider an example. Imagine that the government, spurred by public concern about the large number of deaths from cancer, commissions an exhaustive study from Big Brother Statistical Services, Inc. Big Brother examines many of the items found in people's homes to see which of them are associated with the risk of cancer. Big Brother reports a strong relationship between two variables: the number of cigarette lighters that a household owns and the probability that someone in the household will develop cancer. Figure A-6 shows this relationship.

What should we make of this result? Big Brother advises a quick policy response. It recommends that the government discourage the ownership of cigarette lighters by taxing their sale. It also recommends that the government require warning labels: "Big Brother has determined that this lighter is dangerous to your health."

In judging the validity of Big Brother's analysis, one question is paramount: Has Big Brother held constant every relevant variable except the one under consideration? If the answer is no, the results are suspect. An easy explanation for Figure A-6 is that people who own more cigarette lighters are more likely to smoke cigarettes and that cigarettes, not lighters, cause cancer. If Figure A-6 does not hold constant the amount of smoking, it does not tell us the true effect of owning a cigarette lighter.

This story illustrates an important principle: When you see a graph used to support an argument about cause and effect, it is important to ask whether the movements of an omitted variable could explain the results you see.

Reverse Causality   Economists can also make mistakes about causality by misreading its direction. To see how this is possible, suppose the Association of American Anarchists commissions a study of crime in America and arrives at

Figure A-7

Graph Suggesting Reverse Causality

The upward-sloping curve shows that cities with a higher concentration of police are more dangerous. Yet the graph does not tell us whether police cause crime or crime-plagued cities hire more police.

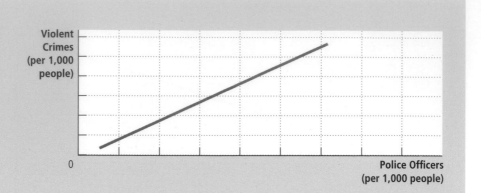

Figure A-7, which plots the number of violent crimes per thousand people in major cities against the number of police officers per thousand people. The anarchists note the curve's upward slope and argue that because police increase rather than decrease the amount of urban violence, law enforcement should be abolished.

If we could run a controlled experiment, we would avoid the danger of reverse causality. To run an experiment, we would set the number of police officers in different cities randomly and then examine the correlation between police and crime. Figure A-7, however, is not based on such an experiment. We simply observe that more dangerous cities have more police officers. The explanation for this may be that more dangerous cities hire more police. In other words, rather than police causing crime, crime may cause police. Nothing in the graph itself allows us to establish the direction of causality.

It might seem that an easy way to determine the direction of causality is to examine which variable moves first. If we see crime increase and then the police force expand, we reach one conclusion. If we see the police force expand and then crime increase, we reach the other. Yet there is also a flaw with this approach: Often, people change their behavior not in response to a change in their present conditions but in response to a change in their *expectations* of future conditions. A city that expects a major crime wave in the future, for instance, might hire more police now. This problem is even easier to see in the case of babies and minivans. Couples often buy a minivan in anticipation of the birth of a child. The minivan comes before the baby, but we wouldn't want to conclude that the sale of minivans causes the population to grow!

There is no complete set of rules that says when it is appropriate to draw causal conclusions from graphs. Yet just keeping in mind that cigarette lighters don't cause cancer (omitted variable) and minivans don't cause larger families (reverse causality) will keep you from falling for many faulty economic arguments.

Interdependence and the Gains from Trade

Consider your typical day. You wake up in the morning and pour yourself juice from oranges grown in Florida and coffee from beans grown in Brazil. Over breakfast, you watch a news program broadcast from New York on your television made in China. You get dressed in clothes made of cotton grown in Georgia and sewn in factories in Thailand. You drive to class in a car made of parts manufactured in more than a dozen countries around the world. Then you open up your economics textbook written by an author living in Massachusetts, published by a company located in Ohio, and printed on paper made from trees grown in Oregon.

Every day, you rely on many people, most of whom you have never met, to provide you with the goods and services that you enjoy. Such interdependence is possible because people trade with one another. Those people providing you goods and services are not acting out of generosity. Nor is some government agency directing them to satisfy your desires. Instead, people provide you and other consumers with the goods and services they produce because they get something in return.

In subsequent chapters, we examine how our economy coordinates the activities of millions of people with varying tastes and abilities. As a starting point for this analysis, here we consider the reasons for economic interdependence. One of the *Ten Principles of Economics* highlighted in Chapter 1 is that trade can make everyone better off. In this chapter, we examine this principle more closely. What exactly do people gain when they trade with one another? Why do people choose to become interdependent?

The answers to these questions are key to understanding the modern global economy. In most countries today, many goods and services consumed are imported from abroad, and many goods and services produced are exported to foreign customers. The analysis in this chapter explains interdependence not only among individuals but also among nations. As we will see, the gains from trade are much the same whether you are buying a haircut from your local barber or a T-shirt made by a worker on the other side of the globe.

A Parable for the Modern Economy

To understand why people choose to depend on others for goods and services and how this choice improves their lives, let's look at a simple economy. Imagine that there are two goods in the world: meat and potatoes. And there are two people in the world—a cattle rancher and a potato farmer—each of whom would like to eat both meat and potatoes.

The gains from trade are most obvious if the rancher can produce only meat and the farmer can produce only potatoes. In one scenario, the rancher and the farmer could choose to have nothing to do with each other. But after several months of eating beef roasted, boiled, broiled, and grilled, the rancher might decide that self-sufficiency is not all it's cracked up to be. The farmer, who has been eating potatoes mashed, fried, baked, and scalloped, would likely agree. It is easy to see that trade would allow them to enjoy greater variety: Each could then have a steak with a baked potato or a burger with fries.

Although this scene illustrates most simply how everyone can benefit from trade, the gains would be similar if the rancher and the farmer were each capable of producing the other good, but only at great cost. Suppose, for example, that the potato farmer is able to raise cattle and produce meat, but that he is not very good at it. Similarly, suppose that the cattle rancher is able to grow potatoes but that her land is not very well suited for it. In this case, the farmer and the rancher can each benefit by specializing in what he or she does best and then trading with the other.

The gains from trade are less obvious, however, when one person is better at producing *every* good. For example, suppose that the rancher is better at raising cattle *and* better at growing potatoes than the farmer. In this case, should the rancher choose to remain self-sufficient? Or is there still reason for her to trade with the farmer? To answer this question, we need to look more closely at the factors that affect such a decision.

Production Possibilities

Suppose that the farmer and the rancher each work 8 hours per day and can devote this time to growing potatoes, raising cattle, or a combination of the two.

The table in Figure 1 shows the amount of time each person requires to produce 1 ounce of each good. The farmer can produce an ounce of potatoes in 15 minutes and an ounce of meat in 60 minutes. The rancher, who is more productive in both activities, can produce an ounce of potatoes in 10 minutes and an ounce of meat in 20 minutes. The last two columns in the table show the amounts of meat or potatoes the farmer and rancher can produce if they work an 8-hour day producing only that good.

Panel (b) of Figure 1 illustrates the amounts of meat and potatoes that the farmer can produce. If the farmer devotes all 8 hours of his time to potatoes, he produces 32 ounces of potatoes (measured on the horizontal axis) and no meat. If he devotes all his time to meat, he produces 8 ounces of meat (measured on the vertical axis) and no potatoes. If the farmer divides his time equally between the two activities, spending 4 hours on each, he produces 16 ounces of potatoes and 4 ounces of meat. The figure shows these three possible outcomes and all others in between.

Panel (a) shows the production opportunities available to the farmer and the rancher. Panel (b) shows the combinations of meat and potatoes that the farmer can produce. Panel (c) shows the combinations of meat and potatoes that the rancher can produce. Both production possibilities frontiers are derived assuming that the farmer and rancher each work 8 hours per day. If there is no trade, each person's production possibilities frontier is also his or her consumption possibilities frontier.

Figure 1

The Production Possibilities Frontier

(a) Production Opportunities

	Minutes Needed to Make 1 Ounce of:		Amount Produced in 8 Hours	
	Meat	Potatoes	Meat	Potatoes
Farmer	60 min/oz	15 min/oz	8 oz	32 oz
Rancher	20 min/oz	10 min/oz	24 oz	48 oz

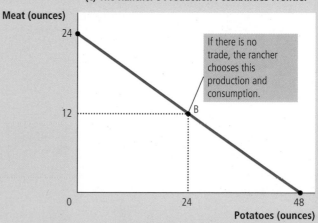

This graph is the farmer's production possibilities frontier. As we discussed in Chapter 2, a production possibilities frontier shows the various mixes of output that an economy can produce. It illustrates one of the *Ten Principles of Economics* in Chapter 1: People face trade-offs. Here the farmer faces a trade-off between producing meat and producing potatoes.

You may recall that the production possibilities frontier in Chapter 2 was drawn bowed out. In that case, the rate at which society could trade one good for the other depended on the amounts that were being produced. Here, however, the farmer's technology for producing meat and potatoes (as summarized in Figure 1) allows him to switch between the two goods at a constant rate. Whenever the farmer spends 1 hour less producing meat and 1 hour more producing potatoes, he reduces his output of meat by 1 ounce and raises his output of potatoes by 4 ounces—and this is true regardless of how much he is already producing. As a result, the production possibilities frontier is a straight line.

Panel (c) of Figure 1 shows the production possibilities frontier for the rancher. If the rancher devotes all 8 hours of her time to potatoes, she produces 48 ounces of potatoes and no meat. If she devotes all her time to meat, she produces 24 ounces of meat and no potatoes. If the rancher divides her time equally, spending 4 hours on each activity, she produces 24 ounces of potatoes and 12 ounces of meat. Once again, the production possibilities frontier shows all the possible outcomes.

If the farmer and rancher choose to be self-sufficient rather than trade with each other, then each consumes exactly what he or she produces. In this case, the production possibilities frontier is also the consumption possibilities frontier. That is, without trade, Figure 1 shows the possible combinations of meat and potatoes that the farmer and rancher can each produce and then consume.

These production possibilities frontiers are useful in showing the trade-offs that the farmer and rancher face, but they do not tell us what the farmer and rancher will actually choose to do. To determine their choices, we need to know the tastes of the farmer and the rancher. Let's suppose they choose the combinations identified by points A and B in Figure 1: The farmer produces and consumes 16 ounces of potatoes and 4 ounces of meat, while the rancher produces and consumes 24 ounces of potatoes and 12 ounces of meat.

Specialization and Trade

After several years of eating combination B, the rancher gets an idea and goes to talk to the farmer:

RANCHER: Farmer, my friend, have I got a deal for you! I know how to improve life for both of us. I think you should stop producing meat altogether and devote all your time to growing potatoes. According to my calculations, if you work 8 hours a day growing potatoes, you'll produce 32 ounces of potatoes. If you give me 15 of those 32 ounces, I'll give you 5 ounces of meat in return. In the end, you'll get to eat 17 ounces of potatoes and 5 ounces of meat every day, instead of the 16 ounces of potatoes and 4 ounces of meat you now get. If you go along with my plan, you'll have more of *both* foods. [To illustrate her point, the rancher shows the farmer panel (a) of Figure 2.]

FARMER: (sounding skeptical) That seems like a good deal for me. But I don't understand why you are offering it. If the deal is so good for me, it can't be good for you too.

RANCHER: Oh, but it is! Suppose I spend 6 hours a day raising cattle and 2 hours growing potatoes. Then I can produce 18 ounces of meat

The proposed trade between the farmer and the rancher offers each of them a combination of meat and potatoes that would be impossible in the absence of trade. In panel (a), the farmer gets to consume at point A* rather than point A. In panel (b), the rancher gets to consume at point B* rather than point B. Trade allows each to consume more meat and more potatoes.

Figure **2**

How Trade Expands the Set of Consumption Opportunities

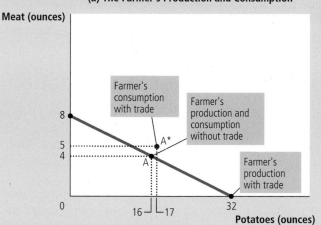

(a) The Farmer's Production and Consumption

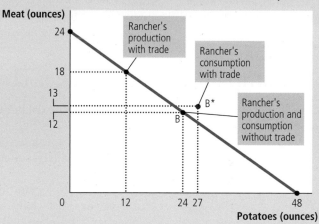

(b) The Rancher's Production and Consumption

(c) The Gains from Trade: A Summary

	Farmer		Rancher	
	Meat	Potatoes	Meat	Potatoes
Without Trade:				
Production and Consumption	4 oz	16 oz	12 oz	24 oz
With Trade:				
Production	0 oz	32 oz	18 oz	12 oz
Trade	Gets 5 oz	Gives 15 oz	Gives 5 oz	Gets 15 oz
Consumption	5 oz	17 oz	13 oz	27 oz
GAINS FROM TRADE:				
Increase in Consumption	+1 oz	+1 oz	+1 oz	+3 oz

and 12 ounces of potatoes. After I give you 5 ounces of my meat in exchange for 15 ounces of your potatoes, I'll end up with 13 ounces of meat and 27 ounces of potatoes, instead of the 12 ounces of meat and 24 ounces of potatoes that I now get. So I will also consume more of both foods than I do now. [She points out panel (b) of Figure 2.]

FARMER: I don't know. . . . This sounds too good to be true.

RANCHER: It's really not as complicated as it first seems. Here—I've summarized my proposal for you in a simple table. [The rancher shows the farmer a copy of the table at the bottom of Figure 2.]

FARMER: (after pausing to study the table) These calculations seem correct, but I am puzzled. How can this deal make us both better off?

RANCHER: We can both benefit because trade allows each of us to specialize in doing what we do best. You will spend more time growing potatoes and less time raising cattle. I will spend more time raising cattle and less time growing potatoes. As a result of specialization and trade, each of us can consume more meat and more potatoes without working any more hours.

QUICK QUIZ   *Draw an example of a production possibilities frontier for Robinson Crusoe, a shipwrecked sailor who spends his time gathering coconuts and catching fish. Does this frontier limit Crusoe's consumption of coconuts and fish if he lives by himself? Does he face the same limits if he can trade with natives on the island?*

Comparative Advantage: The Driving Force of Specialization

The rancher's explanation of the gains from trade, though correct, poses a puzzle: If the rancher is better at both raising cattle and growing potatoes, how can the farmer ever specialize in doing what he does best? The farmer doesn't seem to do anything best. To solve this puzzle, we need to look at the principle of *comparative advantage*.

As a first step in developing this principle, consider the following question: In our example, who can produce potatoes at a lower cost—the farmer or the rancher? There are two possible answers, and in these two answers lie the solution to our puzzle and the key to understanding the gains from trade.

Absolute Advantage

One way to answer the question about the cost of producing potatoes is to compare the inputs required by the two producers. Economists use the term **absolute advantage** when comparing the productivity of one person, firm, or nation to that of another. The producer that requires a smaller quantity of inputs to produce a good is said to have an absolute advantage in producing that good.

In our example, time is the only input, so we can determine absolute advantage by looking at how much time each type of production takes. The rancher has an absolute advantage both in producing meat and in producing potatoes because she requires less time than the farmer to produce a unit of either good. The rancher needs to input only 20 minutes to produce an ounce of meat, whereas the farmer needs 60 minutes. Similarly, the rancher needs only 10 minutes to produce an ounce of potatoes, whereas the farmer needs 15 minutes. Based on this information, we can conclude that the rancher has the lower cost of producing potatoes, if we measure cost by the quantity of inputs.

Opportunity Cost and Comparative Advantage

There is another way to look at the cost of producing potatoes. Rather than comparing inputs required, we can compare the opportunity costs. Recall from Chapter 1 that the **opportunity cost** of some item is what we give up to get that item. In our example, we assumed that the farmer and the rancher each spend 8 hours a day working. Time spent producing potatoes, therefore, takes away from time available for producing meat. When reallocating time between the two goods, the rancher and farmer give up units of one good to produce units of the other, thereby moving along the production possibilities frontier. The opportunity cost measures the trade-off between the two goods that each producer faces.

absolute advantage
the ability to produce a good using fewer inputs than another producer

opportunity cost
whatever must be given up to obtain some item

Table 1

The Opportunity Cost of Meat and Potatoes

	Opportunity Cost of:	
	1 oz of Meat	**1 oz of Potatoes**
Farmer	4 oz potatoes	¼ oz meat
Rancher	2 oz potatoes	½ oz meat

Let's first consider the rancher's opportunity cost. According to the table in panel (a) of Figure 1, producing 1 ounce of potatoes takes 10 minutes of work. When the rancher spends those 10 minutes producing potatoes, she spends 10 minutes less producing meat. Because the rancher needs 20 minutes to produce 1 ounce of meat, 10 minutes of work would yield ½ ounce of meat. Hence, the rancher's opportunity cost of producing 1 ounce of potatoes is ½ ounce of meat.

Now consider the farmer's opportunity cost. Producing 1 ounce of potatoes takes him 15 minutes. Because he needs 60 minutes to produce 1 ounce of meat, 15 minutes of work would yield ¼ ounce of meat. Hence, the farmer's opportunity cost of 1 ounce of potatoes is ¼ ounce of meat.

Table 1 shows the opportunity costs of meat and potatoes for the two producers. Notice that the opportunity cost of meat is the inverse of the opportunity cost of potatoes. Because 1 ounce of potatoes costs the rancher ½ ounce of meat, 1 ounce of meat costs the rancher 2 ounces of potatoes. Similarly, because 1 ounce of potatoes costs the farmer ¼ ounce of meat, 1 ounce of meat costs the farmer 4 ounces of potatoes.

Economists use the term **comparative advantage** when describing the opportunity cost of two producers. The producer who gives up less of other goods to produce Good X has the smaller opportunity cost of producing Good X and is said to have a comparative advantage in producing it. In our example, the farmer has a lower opportunity cost of producing potatoes than the rancher: An ounce of potatoes costs the farmer only ¼ ounce of meat, but it costs the rancher ½ ounce of meat. Conversely, the rancher has a lower opportunity cost of producing meat than the farmer: An ounce of meat costs the rancher 2 ounces of potatoes, but it costs the farmer 4 ounces of potatoes. Thus, the farmer has a comparative advantage in growing potatoes, and the rancher has a comparative advantage in producing meat.

Although it is possible for one person to have an absolute advantage in both goods (as the rancher does in our example), it is impossible for one person to have a comparative advantage in both goods. Because the opportunity cost of one good is the inverse of the opportunity cost of the other, if a person's opportunity cost of one good is relatively high, the opportunity cost of the other good must be relatively low. Comparative advantage reflects the relative opportunity cost. Unless two people have exactly the same opportunity cost, one person will have a comparative advantage in one good, and the other person will have a comparative advantage in the other good.

comparative advantage
the ability to produce a good at a lower opportunity cost than another producer

Comparative Advantage and Trade

The gains from specialization and trade are based not on absolute advantage but on comparative advantage. When each person specializes in producing the good for which he or she has a comparative advantage, total production in the economy rises. This increase in the size of the economic pie can be used to make everyone better off.

In our example, the farmer spends more time growing potatoes, and the rancher spends more time producing meat. As a result, the total production of potatoes rises from 40 to 44 ounces, and the total production of meat rises from 16 to 18 ounces. The farmer and rancher share the benefits of this increased production.

We can also look at the gains from trade in terms of the price that each party pays the other. Because the farmer and rancher have different opportunity costs, they can both get a bargain. That is, each benefits from trade by obtaining a good at a price that is lower than his or her opportunity cost of that good.

Consider the proposed deal from the viewpoint of the farmer. The farmer gets 5 ounces of meat in exchange for 15 ounces of potatoes. In other words, the farmer buys each ounce of meat for a price of 3 ounces of potatoes. This price of meat is lower than his opportunity cost for an ounce of meat, which is 4 ounces of potatoes. Thus, the farmer benefits from the deal because he gets to buy meat at a good price.

Now consider the deal from the rancher's viewpoint. The rancher buys 15 ounces of potatoes for a price of 5 ounces of meat. That is, the price of potatoes is ⅓ ounce of meat. This price of potatoes is lower than her opportunity cost of an ounce of potatoes, which is ½ ounce of meat. The rancher benefits because she gets to buy potatoes at a good price.

The moral of the story of the farmer and the rancher should now be clear: *Trade can benefit everyone in society because it allows people to specialize in activities in which they have a comparative advantage.*

The Price of the Trade

The principle of comparative advantage establishes that there are gains from specialization and trade, but it leaves open a couple of related questions: What determines the price at which trade takes place? How are the gains from trade shared between the trading parties? The precise answer to these questions is beyond the scope of this chapter, but we can state one general rule: *For both parties to gain from trade, the price at which they trade must lie between the two opportunity costs.*

In our example, the farmer and rancher agreed to trade at a rate of 3 ounces of potatoes for each ounce of meat. This price is between the rancher's opportunity cost (2 ounces of potatoes per ounce of meat) and the farmer's opportunity cost (4 ounces of potatoes per ounce of meat). The price need not be exactly in the middle for both parties to gain, but it must be somewhere between 2 and 4.

To see why the price has to be in this range, consider what would happen if it were not. If the price of meat were below 2 ounces of potatoes, both the farmer and the rancher would want to buy meat, because the price would be below their opportunity costs. Similarly, if the price of meat were above 4 ounces of potatoes, both would want to sell meat, because the price would be above their opportunity costs. But there are only two members of this economy. They cannot both be buyers of meat, nor can they both be sellers. Someone has to take the other side of the deal.

A mutually advantageous trade can be struck at a price between 2 and 4. In this price range, the rancher wants to sell meat to buy potatoes, and the farmer wants to sell potatoes to buy meat. Each party can buy a good at a price that is lower than his or her opportunity cost. In the end, both of them specialize in the good for which he or she has a comparative advantage and are, as a result, better off.

QUICK QUIZ *Robinson Crusoe can gather 10 coconuts or catch 1 fish per hour. His friend Friday can gather 30 coconuts or catch 2 fish per hour. What is Crusoe's opportunity cost of catching one fish? What is Friday's? Who has an absolute advantage in catching fish? Who has a comparative advantage in catching fish?*

FYI

> ## The Legacy of Adam Smith and David Ricardo

Economists have long understood the gains from trade. Here is how the great economist Adam Smith put the argument:

It is a maxim of every prudent master of a family, never to attempt to make at home what it will cost him more to make than to buy. The tailor does not attempt to make his own shoes, but buys them of the shoemaker. The shoemaker does not attempt to make his own clothes but employs a tailor. The farmer attempts to make neither the one nor the other, but employs those different artificers. All of them find it for their interest to employ their whole industry in a way in which they have some advantage over their neighbors, and to purchase with a part of its produce, or what is the same thing, with the price of part of it, whatever else they have occasion for.

This quotation is from Smith's 1776 book *An Inquiry into the Nature and Causes of the Wealth of Nations*, which was a landmark in the analysis of trade and economic interdependence.

Smith's book inspired David Ricardo, a millionaire stockbroker, to become an economist. In his 1817

book *Principles of Political Economy and Taxation*, Ricardo developed the principle of comparative advantage as we know it today. He considered an example with two goods (wine and cloth) and two countries (England and Portugal). He showed that both countries can gain by opening up trade and specializing based on comparative advantage.

Ricardo's theory is the starting point of modern international economics, but his defense of free trade was not a mere academic exercise. Ricardo put his beliefs to work as a member of the British Parliament, where he opposed the Corn Laws, which restricted the import of grain.

David Ricardo

The conclusions of Adam Smith and David Ricardo on the gains from trade have held up well over time. Although economists often disagree on questions of policy, they are united in their support of free trade. Moreover, the central argument for free trade has not changed much in the past two centuries. Even though the field of economics has broadened its scope and refined its theories since the time of Smith and Ricardo, economists' opposition to trade restrictions is still based largely on the principle of comparative advantage.

Applications of Comparative Advantage

The principle of comparative advantage explains interdependence and the gains from trade. Because interdependence is so prevalent in the modern world, the principle of comparative advantage has many applications. Here are two examples, one fanciful and one of great practical importance.

Should Tom Brady Mow His Own Lawn?

Tom Brady spends a lot of time running around on grass. One of the most talented football players of all time, he can throw a pass with a speed and accuracy that most casual athletes can only dream of. Most likely, he is talented at other physical activities as well. For example, let's imagine that Brady can mow his lawn faster than anyone else. But just because he *can* mow his lawn fast, does this mean he *should*?

To answer this question, we can use the concepts of opportunity cost and comparative advantage. Let's say that Brady can mow his lawn in 2 hours. In that

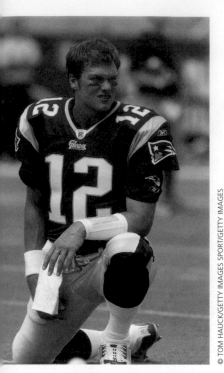

"They did a nice job mowing this grass."

imports
goods produced abroad and sold domestically

exports
goods produced domestically and sold abroad

same 2 hours, he could film a television commercial and earn $20,000. By contrast, Forrest Gump, the boy next door, can mow Brady's lawn in 4 hours. In that same 4 hours, Gump could work at McDonald's and earn $40.

In this example, Brady has an absolute advantage in mowing lawns because he can do the work with a lower input of time. Yet because Brady's opportunity cost of mowing the lawn is $20,000 and Gump's opportunity cost is only $40, Gump has a comparative advantage in mowing lawns.

The gains from trade in this example are tremendous. Rather than mowing his own lawn, Brady should make the commercial and hire Gump to mow the lawn. As long as Brady pays Gump more than $40 and less than $20,000, both of them are better off.

Should the United States Trade with Other Countries?

Just as individuals can benefit from specialization and trade with one another, as the farmer and rancher did, so can populations of people in different countries. Many of the goods that Americans enjoy are produced abroad, and many of the goods produced in the United States are sold abroad. Goods produced abroad and sold domestically are called **imports**. Goods produced domestically and sold abroad are called **exports**.

To see how countries can benefit from trade, suppose there are two countries, the United States and Japan, and two goods, food and cars. Imagine that the two countries produce cars equally well: An American worker and a Japanese worker can each produce one car per month. By contrast, because the United States has more and better land, it is better at producing food: A U.S. worker can produce 2 tons of food per month, whereas a Japanese worker can produce only 1 ton of food per month.

The principle of comparative advantage states that each good should be produced by the country that has the smaller opportunity cost of producing that good. Because the opportunity cost of a car is 2 tons of food in the United States but only 1 ton of food in Japan, Japan has a comparative advantage in producing cars. Japan should produce more cars than it wants for its own use and export some of them to the United States. Similarly, because the opportunity cost of a ton of food is 1 car in Japan but only ½ car in the United States, the United States has a comparative advantage in producing food. The United States should produce more food than it wants to consume and export some to Japan. Through specialization and trade, both countries can have more food and more cars.

In reality, of course, the issues involved in trade among nations are more complex than this example suggests. Most important among these issues is that each country has many citizens with different interests. International trade can make some individuals worse off, even as it makes the country as a whole better off. When the United States exports food and imports cars, the impact on an American farmer is not the same as the impact on an American autoworker. Yet, contrary to the opinions sometimes voiced by politicians and pundits, international trade is not like war, in which some countries win and others lose. Trade allows all countries to achieve greater prosperity.

QUICK QUIZ *Suppose that a skilled brain surgeon also happens to be the world's fastest typist. Should she do her own typing or hire a secretary? Explain.*

in the news

> ## The Changing Face of International Trade

A decade ago, no one would have asked which nation has a comparative advantage in slaying ogres. But technology is rapidly changing the goods and services that are traded across national borders.

Ogre to Slay? Outsource It to Chinese

BY DAVID BARBOZA

Fuzhou, China—One of China's newest factories operates here in the basement of an old warehouse. Posters of World of Warcraft and Magic Land hang above a corps of young people glued to their computer screens, pounding away at their keyboards in the latest hustle for money.

The people working at this clandestine locale are "gold farmers." Every day, in 12-hour shifts, they "play" computer games by killing onscreen monsters and winning battles, harvesting artificial gold coins and other virtual goods as rewards that, as it turns out, can be transformed into real cash.

That is because, from Seoul to San Francisco, affluent online gamers who lack the time and patience to work their way up to the higher levels of gamedom are willing to pay the young Chinese here to play the early rounds for them.

"For 12 hours a day, 7 days a week, my colleagues and I are killing monsters," said a 23-year-old gamer who works here in this makeshift factory and goes by the online code name Wandering. "I make about $250 a month, which is pretty good compared with the other jobs I've had. And I can play games all day."

He and his comrades have created yet another new business out of cheap Chinese labor. They are tapping into the fast-growing world of "massively multiplayer online games," which involve role playing and often revolve around fantasy or warfare in medieval kingdoms or distant galaxies. . . .

For the Chinese in game-playing factories like these, though, it is not all fun and games. These workers have strict quotas and are supervised by bosses who equip them with computers, software and Internet connections to thrash online trolls, gnomes and ogres.

As they grind through the games, they accumulate virtual currency that is valuable to game players around the world. The games allow players to trade currency to other players, who can then use it to buy better armor, amulets, magic spells and other accoutrements to climb to higher levels or create more powerful characters.

The Internet is now filled with classified advertisements from small companies—many of them here in China—auctioning for real money their powerful figures, called avatars. . . .

"It's unimaginable how big this is," says Chen Yu, 27, who employs 20 full-time gamers here in Fuzhou. "They say that in some of these popular games, 40 or 50 percent of the players are actually Chinese farmers."

Source: *New York Times,* December 9, 2005.

© MARK RALSTON/AFP/GETTY IMAGES

Conclusion

You should now understand more fully the benefits of living in an interdependent economy. When Americans buy tube socks from China, when residents of Maine drink orange juice from Florida, and when a homeowner hires the kid next door to mow the lawn, the same economic forces are at work. The principle of comparative advantage shows that trade can make everyone better off.

Having seen why interdependence is desirable, you might naturally ask how it is possible. How do free societies coordinate the diverse activities of all the people involved in their economies? What ensures that goods and services will get from those who should be producing them to those who should be consuming them? In a world with only two people, such as the rancher and the farmer, the answer is simple: These two people can bargain and allocate resources between themselves. In the real world with billions of people, the answer is less obvious. We take up this issue in the next chapter, where we see that free societies allocate resources through the market forces of supply and demand.

SUMMARY

- Each person consumes goods and services produced by many other people both in the United States and around the world. Interdependence and trade are desirable because they allow everyone to enjoy a greater quantity and variety of goods and services.

- There are two ways to compare the ability of two people in producing a good. The person who can produce the good with the smaller quantity of inputs is said to have an *absolute advantage* in producing the good. The person who has the

smaller opportunity cost of producing the good is said to have a *comparative advantage*. The gains from trade are based on comparative advantage, not absolute advantage.

- Trade makes everyone better off because it allows people to specialize in those activities in which they have a comparative advantage.

- The principle of comparative advantage applies to countries as well as to people. Economists use the principle of comparative advantage to advocate free trade among countries.

KEY CONCEPTS

absolute advantage, *p. 54*
opportunity cost, *p. 54*

comparative advantage, *p. 55*
imports, *p. 58*

exports, *p. 58*

QUESTIONS FOR REVIEW

1. Under what conditions is the production possibilities frontier linear rather than bowed out?
2. Explain how absolute advantage and comparative advantage differ.
3. Give an example in which one person has an absolute advantage in doing something but another person has a comparative advantage.
4. Is absolute advantage or comparative advantage more important for trade? Explain your

reasoning using the example in your answer to Question 3.
5. If two parties trade based on comparative advantage and both gain, in what range must the price of the trade lie?
6. Will a nation tend to export or import goods for which it has a comparative advantage? Explain.
7. Why do economists oppose policies that restrict trade among nations?

PROBLEMS AND APPLICATIONS

1. Maria can read 20 pages of economics in an hour. She can also read 50 pages of sociology in an hour. She spends 5 hours per day studying.
   a. Draw Maria's production possibilities frontier for reading economics and sociology.
   b. What is Maria's opportunity cost of reading 100 pages of sociology?

2. American and Japanese workers can each produce 4 cars a year. An American worker can produce 10 tons of grain a year, whereas a Japanese worker can produce 5 tons of grain a year. To keep things simple, assume that each country has 100 million workers.
   a. For this situation, construct a table analogous to the table in Figure 1.
   b. Graph the production possibilities frontier of the American and Japanese economies.
   c. For the United States, what is the opportunity cost of a car? Of grain? For Japan, what is the opportunity cost of a car? Of grain? Put this information in a table analogous to Table 1.
   d. Which country has an absolute advantage in producing cars? In producing grain?
   e. Which country has a comparative advantage in producing cars? In producing grain?
   f. Without trade, half of each country's workers produce cars and half produce grain. What quantities of cars and grain does each country produce?
   g. Starting from a position without trade, give an example in which trade makes each country better off.

3. Pat and Kris are roommates. They spend most of their time studying (of course), but they leave some time for their favorite activities: making pizza and brewing root beer. Pat takes 4 hours to brew a gallon of root beer and 2 hours to make a pizza. Kris takes 6 hours to brew a gallon of root beer and 4 hours to make a pizza.
   a. What is each roommate's opportunity cost of making a pizza? Who has the absolute advantage in making pizza? Who has the comparative advantage in making pizza?
   b. If Pat and Kris trade foods with each other, who will trade away pizza in exchange for root beer?
   c. The price of pizza can be expressed in terms of gallons of root beer. What is the highest price at which pizza can be traded that

would make both roommates better off? What is the lowest price? Explain.

4. Suppose that there are 10 million workers in Canada and that each of these workers can produce either 2 cars or 30 bushels of wheat in a year.
   a. What is the opportunity cost of producing a car in Canada? What is the opportunity cost of producing a bushel of wheat in Canada? Explain the relationship between the opportunity costs of the two goods.
   b. Draw Canada's production possibilities frontier. If Canada chooses to consume 10 million cars, how much wheat can it consume without trade? Label this point on the production possibilities frontier.
   c. Now suppose that the United States offers to buy 10 million cars from Canada in exchange for 20 bushels of wheat per car. If Canada continues to consume 10 million cars, how much wheat does this deal allow Canada to consume? Label this point on your diagram. Should Canada accept the deal?

5. England and Scotland both produce scones and sweaters. Suppose that an English worker can produce 50 scones per hour or 1 sweater per hour. Suppose that a Scottish worker can produce 40 scones per hour or 2 sweaters per hour.
   a. Which country has the absolute advantage in the production of each good? Which country has the comparative advantage?
   b. If England and Scotland decide to trade, which commodity will Scotland trade to England? Explain.
   c. If a Scottish worker could produce only 1 sweater per hour, would Scotland still gain from trade? Would England still gain from trade? Explain.

6. The following table describes the production possibilities of two cities in the country of Baseballia:

	Pairs of Red Socks per Worker per Hour	Pairs of White Socks per Worker per Hour
Boston	3	3
Chicago	2	1

   a. Without trade, what is the price of white socks (in terms of red socks) in Boston? What is the price in Chicago?
   b. Which city has an absolute advantage in the production of each color sock? Which city has

a comparative advantage in the production of each color sock?

c. If the cities trade with each other, which color sock will each export?

d. What is the range of prices at which trade can occur?

7. Suppose that in a year an American worker can produce 100 shirts or 20 computers, while a Chinese worker can produce 100 shirts or 10 computers.

a. Graph the production possibilities curve for the two countries. Suppose that without trade the workers in each country spend half their time producing each good. Identify this point in your graph.

b. If these countries were open to trade, which country would export shirts? Give a specific numerical example and show it on your graph. Which country would benefit from trade? Explain.

c. Explain at what price of computers (in terms of shirts) the two countries might trade.

d. Suppose that China catches up with American productivity so that a Chinese worker can produce 100 shirts or 20 computers. What pattern of trade would you predict now? How does this advance in Chinese productivity affect the economic well-being of the citizens of the two countries?

8. An average worker in Brazil can produce an ounce of soybeans in 20 minutes and an ounce of coffee in 60 minutes, while an average worker in Peru can produce an ounce of soybeans in 50 minutes and an ounce of coffee in 75 minutes.

a. Who has the absolute advantage in coffee? Explain.

b. Who has the comparative advantage in coffee? Explain.

c. If the two countries specialize and trade with each other, who will import coffee? Explain.

d. Assume that the two countries trade and that the country importing coffee trades 2 ounces of soybeans for 1 ounce of coffee. Explain why both countries will benefit from this trade.

9. Are the following statements true or false? Explain in each case.

a. "Two countries can achieve gains from trade even if one of the countries has an absolute advantage in the production of all goods."

b. "Certain very talented people have a comparative advantage in everything they do."

c. "If a certain trade is good for one person, it can't be good for the other one."

d. "If a certain trade is good for one person, it is always good for the other one."

e. "If trade is good for a country, it must be good for everyone in the country."

10. The United States exports corn and aircraft to the rest of the world, and it imports oil and clothing from the rest of the world. Do you think this pattern of trade is consistent with the principle of comparative advantage? Why or why not?

11. Bill and Hillary produce food and clothing. In an hour, Bill can produce 1 unit of food or 1 unit of clothing, while Hillary can produce 2 units of food or 3 units of clothing. They each work 10 hours a day.

a. Who has an absolute advantage in producing food? Who has an absolute advantage in producing clothing? Explain.

b. Who has a comparative advantage in producing food? Who has a comparative advantage in producing clothing? Explain.

c. Draw the production possibilities frontier for the household (that is, Bill and Hillary together) assuming that each spends the same number of hours each day as the other producing food and clothing.

d. Hillary suggests, instead, that she specialize in making clothing. That is, she will do all the clothing production for the family; however, if all her time is devoted to clothing and they still want more, then Bill can help with clothing production. What does the household production possibilities frontier look like now?

e. Bill suggests that Hillary specialize in producing food. That is, Hillary will do all the food production for the family; however, if all her time is devoted to food and they still want more, then Bill can help with food production. What does the household production possibilities frontier look like under Bill's proposal?

f. Comparing your answers to parts c, d, and e, which allocation of time makes the most sense? Relate your answer to the theory of comparative advantage.

For further information on topics in this chapter, additional problems, applications, examples, online quizzes, and more, please visit our website at www.cengage.com/economics/mankiw.

PART II | How Markets Work

The Market Forces of Supply and Demand

W
hen a cold snap hits Florida, the price of orange juice rises in supermarkets throughout the country. When the weather turns warm in New England every summer, the price of hotel rooms in the Caribbean plummets. When a war breaks out in the Middle East, the price of gasoline in the United States rises, and the price of a used Cadillac falls. What do these events have in common? They all show the workings of supply and demand.

Supply and *demand* are the two words economists use most often—and for good reason. Supply and demand are the forces that make market economies work. They determine the quantity of each good produced and the price at which it is sold. If you want to know how any event or policy will affect the economy, you must think first about how it will affect supply and demand.

This chapter introduces the theory of supply and demand. It considers how buyers and sellers behave and how they interact with one another. It shows how supply and demand determine prices in a market economy and how prices, in turn, allocate the economy's scarce resources.

Markets and Competition

The terms *supply* and *demand* refer to the behavior of people as they interact with one another in competitive markets. Before discussing how buyers and sellers behave, let's first consider more fully what we mean by the terms *market* and *competition*.

What Is a Market?

market
a group of buyers and sellers of a particular good or service

A **market** is a group of buyers and sellers of a particular good or service. The buyers as a group determine the demand for the product, and the sellers as a group determine the supply of the product.

Markets take many forms. Some markets are highly organized, such as the markets for many agricultural commodities. In these markets, buyers and sellers meet at a specific time and place, where an auctioneer helps set prices and arrange sales.

More often, markets are less organized. For example, consider the market for ice cream in a particular town. Buyers of ice cream do not meet together at any one time. The sellers of ice cream are in different locations and offer somewhat different products. There is no auctioneer calling out the price of ice cream. Each seller posts a price for an ice-cream cone, and each buyer decides how much ice cream to buy at each store. Nonetheless, these consumers and producers of ice cream are closely connected. The ice-cream buyers are choosing from the various ice-cream sellers to satisfy their cravings, and the ice-cream sellers are all trying to appeal to the same ice-cream buyers to make their businesses successful. Even though it is not as organized, the group of ice-cream buyers and ice-cream sellers forms a market.

What Is Competition?

The market for ice cream, like most markets in the economy, is highly competitive. Each buyer knows that there are several sellers from which to choose, and each seller is aware that his or her product is similar to that offered by other sellers. As a result, the price of ice cream and the quantity of ice cream sold are not determined by any single buyer or seller. Rather, price and quantity are determined by all buyers and sellers as they interact in the marketplace.

competitive market
a market in which there are many buyers and many sellers so that each has a negligible impact on the market price

Economists use the term **competitive market** to describe a market in which there are so many buyers and so many sellers that each has a negligible impact on the market price. Each seller of ice cream has limited control over the price because other sellers are offering similar products. A seller has little reason to charge less than the going price, and if he or she charges more, buyers will make their purchases elsewhere. Similarly, no single buyer of ice cream can influence the price of ice cream because each buyer purchases only a small amount.

In this chapter, we assume that markets are *perfectly competitive*. To reach this highest form of competition, a market must have two characteristics: (1) the goods offered for sale are all exactly the same, and (2) the buyers and sellers are so numerous that no single buyer or seller has any influence over the market price. Because buyers and sellers in perfectly competitive markets must accept the price the market determines, they are said to be *price takers*. At the market price, buyers can buy all they want, and sellers can sell all they want.

There are some markets in which the assumption of perfect competition applies perfectly. In the wheat market, for example, there are thousands of farmers who sell wheat and millions of consumers who use wheat and wheat products. Because no single buyer or seller can influence the price of wheat, each takes the price as given.

Not all goods and services, however, are sold in perfectly competitive markets. Some markets have only one seller, and this seller sets the price. Such a seller is called a *monopoly*. Your local cable television company, for instance, may be a monopoly. Residents of your town probably have only one cable company from which to buy this service. Still other markets fall between the extremes of perfect competition and monopoly.

Despite the diversity of market types we find in the world, assuming perfect competition is a useful simplification and, therefore, a natural place to start. Perfectly competitive markets are the easiest to analyze because everyone participating in the market takes the price as given by market conditions. Moreover, because some degree of competition is present in most markets, many of the lessons that we learn by studying supply and demand under perfect competition apply in more complicated markets as well.

QUICK QUIZ *What is a market? • What are the characteristics of a perfectly competitive market?*

Demand

We begin our study of markets by examining the behavior of buyers. To focus our thinking, let's keep in mind a particular good—ice cream.

The Demand Curve: The Relationship between Price and Quantity Demanded

The **quantity demanded** of any good is the amount of the good that buyers are willing and able to purchase. As we will see, many things determine the quantity demanded of any good, but in our analysis of how markets work, one determinant plays a central role—the price of the good. If the price of ice cream rose to $20 per scoop, you would buy less ice cream. You might buy frozen yogurt instead. If the price of ice cream fell to $0.20 per scoop, you would buy more. This relationship between price and quantity demanded is true for most goods in the economy and, in fact, is so pervasive that economists call it the **law of demand**: Other things equal, when the price of a good rises, the quantity demanded of the good falls, and when the price falls, the quantity demanded rises.

The table in Figure 1 shows how many ice-cream cones Catherine buys each month at different prices of ice cream. If ice cream is free, Catherine eats 12 cones per month. At $0.50 per cone, Catherine buys 10 cones each month. As the price rises further, she buys fewer and fewer cones. When the price reaches $3.00, Catherine doesn't buy any ice cream at all. This table is a **demand schedule**, a table that shows the relationship between the price of a good and the quantity demanded, holding constant everything else that influences how much of the good consumers want to buy.

quantity demanded
the amount of a good that buyers are willing and able to purchase

law of demand
the claim that, other things equal, the quantity demanded of a good falls when the price of the good rises

demand schedule
a table that shows the relationship between the price of a good and the quantity demanded

Figure 3

Shifts in the Demand Curve
Any change that raises the quantity that buyers wish to purchase at any given price shifts the demand curve to the right. Any change that lowers the quantity that buyers wish to purchase at any given price shifts the demand curve to the left.

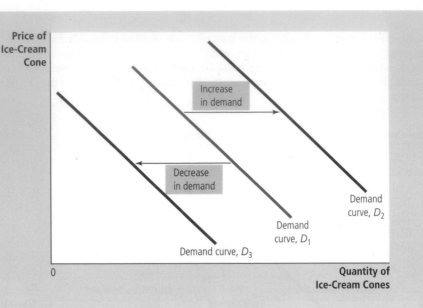

normal good
a good for which, other things equal, an increase in income leads to an increase in demand

inferior good
a good for which, other things equal, an increase in income leads to a decrease in demand

substitutes
two goods for which an increase in the price of one leads to an increase in the demand for the other

complements
two goods for which an increase in the price of one leads to a decrease in the demand for the other

Income   What would happen to your demand for ice cream if you lost your job one summer? Most likely, it would fall. A lower income means that you have less to spend in total, so you would have to spend less on some—and probably most—goods. If the demand for a good falls when income falls, the good is called a **normal good**.

Not all goods are normal goods. If the demand for a good rises when income falls, the good is called an **inferior good**. An example of an inferior good might be bus rides. As your income falls, you are less likely to buy a car or take a cab and more likely to ride a bus.

Prices of Related Goods   Suppose that the price of frozen yogurt falls. The law of demand says that you will buy more frozen yogurt. At the same time, you will probably buy less ice cream. Because ice cream and frozen yogurt are both cold, sweet, creamy desserts, they satisfy similar desires. When a fall in the price of one good reduces the demand for another good, the two goods are called **substitutes**. Substitutes are often pairs of goods that are used in place of each other, such as hot dogs and hamburgers, sweaters and sweatshirts, and movie tickets and DVD rentals.

Now suppose that the price of hot fudge falls. According to the law of demand, you will buy more hot fudge. Yet in this case, you will buy more ice cream as well because ice cream and hot fudge are often used together. When a fall in the price of one good raises the demand for another good, the two goods are called **complements**. Complements are often pairs of goods that are used together, such as gasoline and automobiles, computers and software, and peanut butter and jelly.

Tastes   The most obvious determinant of your demand is your tastes. If you like ice cream, you buy more of it. Economists normally do not try to explain people's tastes because tastes are based on historical and psychological forces that are beyond the realm of economics. Economists do, however, examine what happens when tastes change.

Expectations   Your expectations about the future may affect your demand for a good or service today. If you expect to earn a higher income next month, you may choose to save less now and spend more of your current income buying ice cream. If you expect the price of ice cream to fall tomorrow, you may be less willing to buy an ice-cream cone at today's price.

Number of Buyers   In addition to the preceding factors, which influence the behavior of individual buyers, market demand depends on the number of these buyers. If Peter were to join Catherine and Nicholas as another consumer of ice cream, the quantity demanded in the market would be higher at every price, and market demand would increase.

Summary   The demand curve shows what happens to the quantity demanded of a good when its price varies, holding constant all the other variables that influence buyers. When one of these other variables changes, the demand curve shifts. Table 1 lists the variables that influence how much consumers choose to buy of a good.

If you have trouble remembering whether you need to shift or move along the demand curve, it helps to recall a lesson from the appendix to Chapter 2. A curve shifts when there is a change in a relevant variable that is not measured on either axis. Because the price is on the vertical axis, a change in price represents a movement along the demand curve. By contrast, income, the prices of related goods, tastes, expectations, and the number of buyers are not measured on either axis, so a change in one of these variables shifts the demand curve.

Two Ways to Reduce the Quantity of Smoking Demanded

Public policymakers often want to reduce the amount that people smoke because of smoking's adverse health effects. There are two ways that policy can attempt to achieve this goal.

One way to reduce smoking is to shift the demand curve for cigarettes and other tobacco products. Public service announcements, mandatory health warnings on cigarette packages, and the prohibition of cigarette advertising on television are all policies aimed at reducing the quantity of cigarettes demanded at any given price. If successful, these policies shift the demand curve for cigarettes to the left, as in panel (a) of Figure 4.

What is the best way to stop this?

© ACESTOCK/ACE STOCK LIMITED/ALAMY

Table 1

Variable	A Change in This Variable . . .
Price of the good itself	Represents a movement along the demand curve
Income	Shifts the demand curve
Prices of related goods	Shifts the demand curve
Tastes	Shifts the demand curve
Expectations	Shifts the demand curve
Number of buyers	Shifts the demand curve

Variables That Influence Buyers
This table lists the variables that affect how much consumers choose to buy of any good. Notice the special role that the price of the good plays: A change in the good's price represents a movement along the demand curve, whereas a change in one of the other variables shifts the demand curve.

Figure 4

Shifts in the Demand Curve versus Movements along the Demand Curve

If warnings on cigarette packages convince smokers to smoke less, the demand curve for cigarettes shifts to the left. In panel (a), the demand curve shifts from D_1 to D_2. At a price of $2.00 per pack, the quantity demanded falls from 20 to 10 cigarettes per day, as reflected by the shift from point A to point B. By contrast, if a tax raises the price of cigarettes, the demand curve does not shift. Instead, we observe a movement to a different point on the demand curve. In panel (b), when the price rises from $2.00 to $4.00, the quantity demanded falls from 20 to 12 cigarettes per day, as reflected by the movement from point A to point C.

(a) A Shift in the Demand Curve

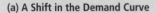

(b) A Movement along the Demand Curve

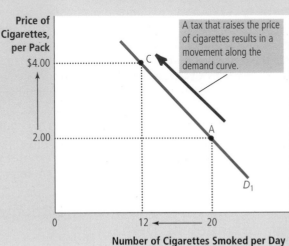

Alternatively, policymakers can try to raise the price of cigarettes. If the government taxes the manufacture of cigarettes, for example, cigarette companies pass much of this tax on to consumers in the form of higher prices. A higher price encourages smokers to reduce the numbers of cigarettes they smoke. In this case, the reduced amount of smoking does not represent a shift in the demand curve. Instead, it represents a movement along the same demand curve to a point with a higher price and lower quantity, as in panel (b) of Figure 4.

How much does the amount of smoking respond to changes in the price of cigarettes? Economists have attempted to answer this question by studying what happens when the tax on cigarettes changes. They have found that a 10 percent increase in the price causes a 4 percent reduction in the quantity demanded. Teenagers are found to be especially sensitive to the price of cigarettes: A 10 percent increase in the price causes a 12 percent drop in teenage smoking.

A related question is how the price of cigarettes affects the demand for illicit drugs, such as marijuana. Opponents of cigarette taxes often argue that tobacco and marijuana are substitutes so that high cigarette prices encourage marijuana use. By contrast, many experts on substance abuse view tobacco as a "gateway drug" leading the young to experiment with other harmful substances. Most studies of the data are consistent with this latter view: They find that lower cigarette prices are associated with greater use of marijuana. In other words, tobacco and marijuana appear to be complements rather than substitutes. ■

QUICK QUIZ   *Make up an example of a monthly demand schedule for pizza and graph the implied demand curve. • Give an example of something that would shift this demand curve, and briefly explain your reasoning. • Would a change in the price of pizza shift this demand curve?*

Supply

We now turn to the other side of the market and examine the behavior of sellers. Once again, to focus our thinking, let's consider the market for ice cream.

The Supply Curve: The Relationship between Price and Quantity Supplied

The **quantity supplied** of any good or service is the amount that sellers are willing and able to sell. There are many determinants of quantity supplied, but once again, price plays a special role in our analysis. When the price of ice cream is high, selling ice cream is profitable, and so the quantity supplied is large. Sellers of ice cream work long hours, buy many ice-cream machines, and hire many workers. By contrast, when the price of ice cream is low, the business is less profitable, so sellers produce less ice cream. At a low price, some sellers may even choose to shut down, and their quantity supplied falls to zero. This relationship between price and quantity supplied is called the **law of supply**: Other things equal, when the price of a good rises, the quantity supplied of the good also rises, and when the price falls, the quantity supplied falls as well.

The table in Figure 5 shows the quantity of ice-cream cones supplied each month by Ben, an ice-cream seller, at various prices of ice cream. At a price below $1.00, Ben does not supply any ice cream at all. As the price rises, he supplies a greater and greater quantity. This is the **supply schedule**, a table that shows the relationship between the price of a good and the quantity supplied, holding constant everything else that influences how much producers of the good want to sell.

The graph in Figure 5 uses the numbers from the table to illustrate the law of supply. The curve relating price and quantity supplied is called the **supply curve**. The supply curve slopes upward because, other things equal, a higher price means a greater quantity supplied.

Market Supply versus Individual Supply

Just as market demand is the sum of the demands of all buyers, market supply is the sum of the supplies of all sellers. The table in Figure 6 shows the supply schedules for the two ice-cream producers in the market—Ben and Jerry. At any price, Ben's supply schedule tells us the quantity of ice cream Ben supplies, and Jerry's supply schedule tells us the quantity of ice cream Jerry supplies. The market supply is the sum of the two individual supplies.

The graph in Figure 6 shows the supply curves that correspond to the supply schedules. As with demand curves, we sum the individual supply curves *horizontally* to obtain the market supply curve. That is, to find the total quantity supplied at any price, we add the individual quantities, which are found on the horizontal axis of the individual supply curves. The market supply curve shows how the

quantity supplied
the amount of a good that sellers are willing and able to sell

law of supply
the claim that, other things equal, the quantity supplied of a good rises when the price of the good rises

supply schedule
a table that shows the relationship between the price of a good and the quantity supplied

supply curve
a graph of the relationship between the price of a good and the quantity supplied

Figure 5

Ben's Supply Schedule and Supply Curve

The supply schedule is a table that shows the quantity supplied at each price. This supply curve, which graphs the supply schedule, illustrates how the quantity supplied of the good changes as its price varies. Because a higher price increases the quantity supplied, the supply curve slopes upward.

Price of Ice-Cream Cone	Quantity of Cones Supplied
$0.00	0 cones
0.50	0
1.00	1
1.50	2
2.00	3
2.50	4
3.00	5

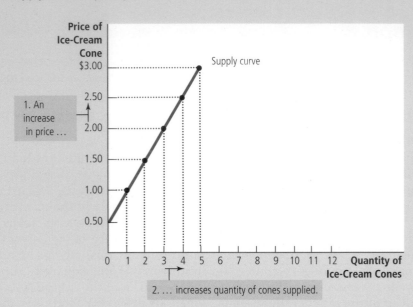

total quantity supplied varies as the price of the good varies, holding constant all the other factors beyond price that influence producers' decisions about how much to sell.

Shifts in the Supply Curve

Because the market supply curve holds other things constant, the curve shifts when one of the factors changes. For example, suppose the price of sugar falls. Sugar is an input into producing ice cream, so the fall in the price of sugar makes selling ice cream more profitable. This raises the supply of ice cream: At any given price, sellers are now willing to produce a larger quantity. The supply curve for ice cream shifts to the right.

Figure 7 illustrates shifts in supply. Any change that raises quantity supplied at every price, such as a fall in the price of sugar, shifts the supply curve to the right and is called an *increase in supply*. Similarly, any change that reduces the quantity supplied at every price shifts the supply curve to the left and is called a *decrease in supply*.

There are many variables that can shift the supply curve. Here are some of the most important.

Input Prices   To produce their output of ice cream, sellers use various inputs: cream, sugar, flavoring, ice-cream machines, the buildings in which the ice cream is made, and the labor of workers to mix the ingredients and operate the machines. When the price of one or more of these inputs rises, producing

The quantity supplied in a market is the sum of the quantities supplied by all the sellers at each price. Thus, the market supply curve is found by adding horizontally the individual supply curves. At a price of $2.00, Ben supplies 3 ice-cream cones, and Jerry supplies 4 ice-cream cones. The quantity supplied in the market at this price is 7 cones.

Figure 6

Market Supply as the Sum of Individual Supplies

Price of Ice-Cream Cone	Ben		Jerry		Market
$0.00	0	+	0	=	0 cones
0.50	0		0		0
1.00	1		0		1
1.50	2		2		4
2.00	3		4		7
2.50	4		6		10
3.00	5		8		13

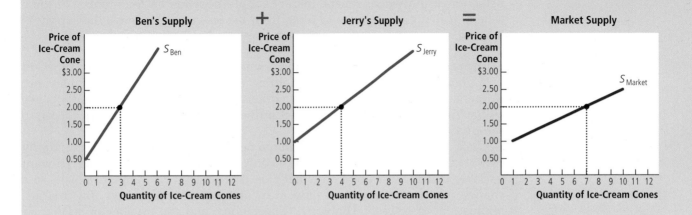

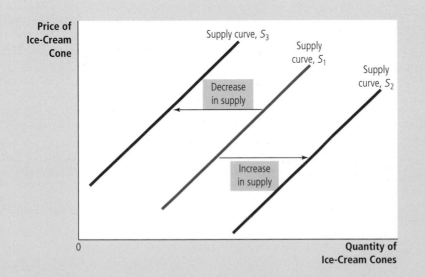

Figure 7

Shifts in the Supply Curve Any change that raises the quantity that sellers wish to produce at any given price shifts the supply curve to the right. Any change that lowers the quantity that sellers wish to produce at any given price shifts the supply curve to the left.

ice cream is less profitable, and firms supply less ice cream. If input prices rise substantially, a firm might shut down and supply no ice cream at all. Thus, the supply of a good is negatively related to the price of the inputs used to make the good.

Technology   The technology for turning inputs into ice cream is another determinant of supply. The invention of the mechanized ice-cream machine, for example, reduced the amount of labor necessary to make ice cream. By reducing firms' costs, the advance in technology raised the supply of ice cream.

Expectations   The amount of ice cream a firm supplies today may depend on its expectations about the future. For example, if a firm expects the price of ice cream to rise in the future, it will put some of its current production into storage and supply less to the market today.

Number of Sellers   In addition to the preceding factors, which influence the behavior of individual sellers, market supply depends on the number of these sellers. If Ben or Jerry were to retire from the ice-cream business, the supply in the market would fall.

Summary   The supply curve shows what happens to the quantity supplied of a good when its price varies, holding constant all the other variables that influence sellers. When one of these other variables changes, the supply curve shifts. Table 2 lists the variables that influence how much producers choose to sell of a good.

   Once again, to remember whether you need to shift or move along the supply curve, keep in mind that a curve shifts only when there is a change in a relevant variable that is not named on either axis. The price is on the vertical axis, so a change in price represents a movement along the supply curve. By contrast, because input prices, technology, expectations, and the number of sellers are not measured on either axis, a change in one of these variables shifts the supply curve.

QUICK QUIZ   *Make up an example of a monthly supply schedule for pizza and graph the implied supply curve. • Give an example of something that would shift this supply curve, and briefly explain your reasoning. • Would a change in the price of pizza shift this supply curve?*

Table 2

Variables That Influence Sellers
This table lists the variables that affect how much producers choose to sell of any good. Notice the special role that the price of the good plays: A change in the good's price represents a movement along the supply curve, whereas a change in one of the other variables shifts the supply curve.

Variable	A Change in This Variable . . .
Price of the good itself	Represents a movement along the supply curve
Input prices	Shifts the supply curve
Technology	Shifts the supply curve
Expectations	Shifts the supply curve
Number of sellers	Shifts the supply curve

Supply and Demand Together

Having analyzed supply and demand separately, we now combine them to see how they determine the price and quantity of a good sold in a market.

Equilibrium

Figure 8 shows the market supply curve and market demand curve together. Notice that there is one point at which the supply and demand curves intersect. This point is called the market's **equilibrium**. The price at this intersection is called the **equilibrium price**, and the quantity is called the **equilibrium quantity**. Here the equilibrium price is $2.00 per cone, and the equilibrium quantity is 7 ice-cream cones.

The dictionary defines the word *equilibrium* as a situation in which various forces are in balance—and this also describes a market's equilibrium. *At the equilibrium price, the quantity of the good that buyers are willing and able to buy exactly balances the quantity that sellers are willing and able to sell.* The equilibrium price is sometimes called the *market-clearing price* because, at this price, everyone in the market has been satisfied: Buyers have bought all they want to buy, and sellers have sold all they want to sell.

The actions of buyers and sellers naturally move markets toward the equilibrium of supply and demand. To see why, consider what happens when the market price is not equal to the equilibrium price.

Suppose first that the market price is above the equilibrium price, as in panel (a) of Figure 9. At a price of $2.50 per cone, the quantity of the good supplied (10 cones) exceeds the quantity demanded (4 cones). There is a **surplus** of the good: Suppliers are unable to sell all they want at the going price. A surplus is sometimes called a situation of *excess supply*. When there is a surplus in the ice-cream market, sellers of ice cream find their freezers increasingly full of ice cream they would like to sell

equilibrium
a situation in which the market price has reached the level at which quantity supplied equals quantity demanded

equilibrium price
the price that balances quantity supplied and quantity demanded

equilibrium quantity
the quantity supplied and the quantity demanded at the equilibrium price

surplus
a situation in which quantity supplied is greater than quantity demanded

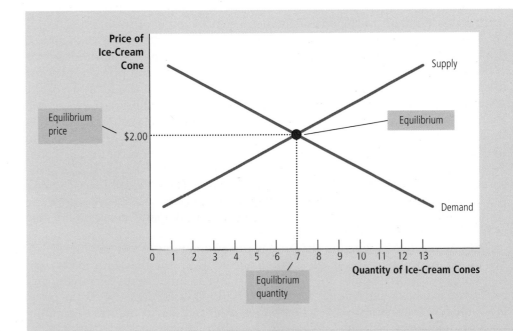

Figure **8**

The Equilibrium of Supply and Demand
The equilibrium is found where the supply and demand curves intersect. At the equilibrium price, the quantity supplied equals the quantity demanded. Here the equilibrium price is $2.00: At this price, 7 ice-cream cones are supplied, and 7 ice-cream cones are demanded.

Figure **9**

Markets Not in Equilibrium

In panel (a), there is a surplus. Because the market price of $2.50 is above the equilibrium price, the quantity supplied (10 cones) exceeds the quantity demanded (4 cones). Suppliers try to increase sales by cutting the price of a cone, and this moves the price toward its equilibrium level. In panel (b), there is a shortage. Because the market price of $1.50 is below the equilibrium price, the quantity demanded (10 cones) exceeds the quantity supplied (4 cones). With too many buyers chasing too few goods, suppliers can take advantage of the shortage by raising the price. Hence, in both cases, the price adjustment moves the market toward the equilibrium of supply and demand.

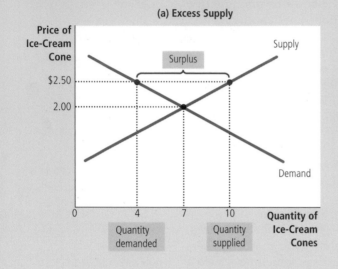
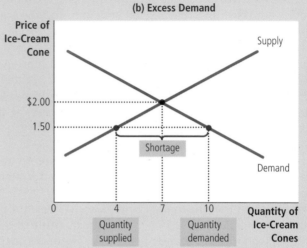

(a) Excess Supply

(b) Excess Demand

but cannot. They respond to the surplus by cutting their prices. Falling prices, in turn, increase the quantity demanded and decrease the quantity supplied. These changes represent movements *along* the supply and demand curves, not shifts in the curves. Prices continue to fall until the market reaches the equilibrium.

Suppose now that the market price is below the equilibrium price, as in panel (b) of Figure 9. In this case, the price is $1.50 per cone, and the quantity of the good demanded exceeds the quantity supplied. There is a **shortage** of the good: Demanders are unable to buy all they want at the going price. A shortage is sometimes called a situation of *excess demand*. When a shortage occurs in the ice-cream market, buyers have to wait in long lines for a chance to buy one of the few cones available. With too many buyers chasing too few goods, sellers can respond to the shortage by raising their prices without losing sales. These price increases cause the quantity demanded to fall and the quantity supplied to rise. Once again, these changes represent movements *along* the supply and demand curves, and they move the market toward the equilibrium.

Thus, regardless of whether the price starts off too high or too low, the activities of the many buyers and sellers automatically push the market price toward the equilibrium price. Once the market reaches its equilibrium, all buyers and sellers are satisfied, and there is no upward or downward pressure on the price. How quickly equilibrium is reached varies from market to market depending on how quickly prices adjust. In most free markets, surpluses and shortages are only temporary because prices eventually move toward their equilibrium levels.

shortage

a situation in which quantity demanded is greater than quantity supplied

Indeed, this phenomenon is so pervasive that it is called the **law of supply and demand**: The price of any good adjusts to bring the quantity supplied and quantity demanded for that good into balance.

Three Steps to Analyzing Changes in Equilibrium

So far, we have seen how supply and demand together determine a market's equilibrium, which in turn determines the price and quantity of the good that buyers purchase and sellers produce. The equilibrium price and quantity depend on the position of the supply and demand curves. When some event shifts one of these curves, the equilibrium in the market changes, resulting in a new price and a new quantity exchanged between buyers and sellers.

When analyzing how some event affects the equilibrium in a market, we proceed in three steps. First, we decide whether the event shifts the supply curve, the demand curve, or, in some cases, both curves. Second, we decide whether the curve shifts to the right or to the left. Third, we use the supply-and-demand diagram to compare the initial and the new equilibrium, which shows how the shift affects the equilibrium price and quantity. Table 3 summarizes these three steps. To see how this recipe is used, let's consider various events that might affect the market for ice cream.

Example: A Change in Market Equilibrium Due to a Shift in Demand

Suppose that one summer the weather is very hot. How does this event affect the market for ice cream? To answer this question, let's follow our three steps.

1. The hot weather affects the demand curve by changing people's taste for ice cream. That is, the weather changes the amount of ice cream that people want to buy at any given price. The supply curve is unchanged because the weather does not directly affect the firms that sell ice cream.
2. Because hot weather makes people want to eat more ice cream, the demand curve shifts to the right. Figure 10 shows this increase in demand as the shift in the demand curve from D_1 to D_2. This shift indicates that the quantity of ice cream demanded is higher at every price.
3. At the old price of $2, there is now an excess demand for ice cream, and this shortage induces firms to raise the price. As Figure 10 shows, the increase in demand raises the equilibrium price from $2.00 to $2.50 and the equilibrium quantity from 7 to 10 cones. In other words, the hot weather increases the price of ice cream and the quantity of ice cream sold.

Shifts in Curves versus Movements along Curves Notice that when hot weather increases the demand for ice cream and drives up the price, the quantity of ice cream that firms supply rises, even though the supply curve remains the

law of supply and demand

the claim that the price of any good adjusts to bring the quantity supplied and the quantity demanded for that good into balance

Table 3

Three Steps for Analyzing Changes in Equilibrium

1. Decide whether the event shifts the supply or demand curve (or perhaps both).
2. Decide in which direction the curve shifts.
3. Use the supply-and-demand diagram to see how the shift changes the equilibrium price and quantity.

Figure 10

How an Increase in Demand Affects the Equilibrium

An event that raises quantity demanded at any given price shifts the demand curve to the right. The equilibrium price and the equilibrium quantity both rise. Here an abnormally hot summer causes buyers to demand more ice cream. The demand curve shifts from D_1 to D_2, which causes the equilibrium price to rise from $2.00 to $2.50 and the equilibrium quantity to rise from 7 to 10 cones.

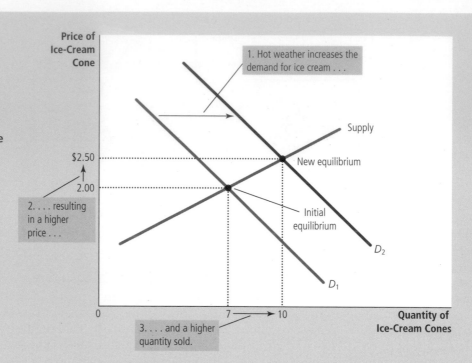

same. In this case, economists say there has been an increase in "quantity supplied" but no change in "supply."

Supply refers to the position of the supply curve, whereas the *quantity supplied* refers to the amount suppliers wish to sell. In this example, supply does not change because the weather does not alter firms' desire to sell at any given price. Instead, the hot weather alters consumers' desire to buy at any given price and thereby shifts the demand curve to the right. The increase in demand causes the equilibrium price to rise. When the price rises, the quantity supplied rises. This increase in quantity supplied is represented by the movement along the supply curve.

To summarize, a shift *in* the supply curve is called a "change in supply," and a shift *in* the demand curve is called a "change in demand." A movement *along* a fixed supply curve is called a "change in the quantity supplied," and a movement *along* a fixed demand curve is called a "change in the quantity demanded."

Example: A Change in Market Equilibrium Due to a Shift in Supply

Suppose that during another summer, a hurricane destroys part of the sugarcane crop and drives up the price of sugar. How does this event affect the market for ice cream? Once again, to answer this question, we follow our three steps.

1. The change in the price of sugar, an input for making ice cream, affects the supply curve. By raising the costs of production, it reduces the amount of ice cream that firms produce and sell at any given price. The demand curve does not change because the higher cost of inputs does not directly affect the amount of ice cream households wish to buy.
2. The supply curve shifts to the left because, at every price, the total amount that firms are willing and able to sell is reduced. Figure 11 illustrates this decrease in supply as a shift in the supply curve from S_1 to S_2.

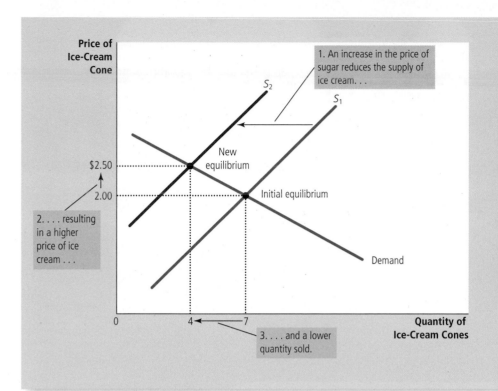

Figure **11**

How a Decrease in Supply Affects the Equilibrium
An event that reduces quantity supplied at any given price shifts the supply curve to the left. The equilibrium price rises, and the equilibrium quantity falls. Here an increase in the price of sugar (an input) causes sellers to supply less ice cream. The supply curve shifts from S_1 to S_2, which causes the equilibrium price of ice cream to rise from $2.00 to $2.50 and the equilibrium quantity to fall from 7 to 4 cones.

3. At the old price of $2, there is now an excess demand for ice cream, and this shortage causes firms to raise the price. As Figure 11 shows, the shift in the supply curve raises the equilibrium price from $2.00 to $2.50 and lowers the equilibrium quantity from 7 to 4 cones. As a result of the sugar price increase, the price of ice cream rises, and the quantity of ice cream sold falls.

Example: Shifts in Both Supply and Demand Now suppose that a heat wave and a hurricane occur during the same summer. To analyze this combination of events, we again follow our three steps.

1. We determine that both curves must shift. The hot weather affects the demand curve because it alters the amount of ice cream that households want to buy at any given price. At the same time, when the hurricane drives up sugar prices, it alters the supply curve for ice cream because it changes the amount of ice cream that firms want to sell at any given price.
2. The curves shift in the same directions as they did in our previous analysis: The demand curve shifts to the right, and the supply curve shifts to the left. Figure 12 illustrates these shifts.
3. As Figure 12 shows, two possible outcomes might result depending on the relative size of the demand and supply shifts. In both cases, the equilibrium price rises. In panel (a), where demand increases substantially while supply falls just a little, the equilibrium quantity also rises. By contrast, in panel (b), where supply falls substantially while demand rises just a little, the equilibrium quantity falls. Thus, these events certainly raise the price of ice cream, but their impact on the amount of ice cream sold is ambiguous (that is, it could go either way).

Figure **12**

A Shift in Both Supply and Demand

Here we observe a simultaneous increase in demand and decrease in supply. Two outcomes are possible. In panel (a), the equilibrium price rises from P_1 to P_2, and the equilibrium quantity rises from Q_1 to Q_2. In panel (b), the equilibrium price again rises from P_1 to P_2, but the equilibrium quantity falls from Q_1 to Q_2.

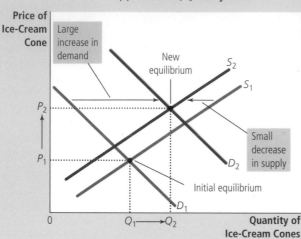

(a) Price Rises, Quantity Rises

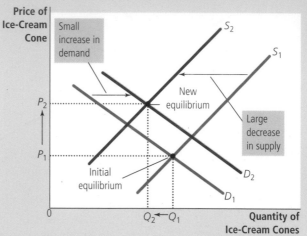

(b) Price Rises, Quantity Falls

···················· in the **news**

> ### Price Increases after Disasters

For several days in 2010, many towns around Boston found themselves without drinkable tap water. This increased the demand for bottled water, putting upward pressure on the price. While some policymakers cried foul, this opinion piece endorses the market's natural response.

What's Wrong with Price Gouging?

BY JEFF JACOBY

There wasn't much [Attorney General] Martha Coakley could do about the massive pipe break that left dozens of Greater Boston towns without clean drinking water over the weekend. So she kept herself busy instead lecturing vendors not to increase the price of the bottled water that tens of thousands of consumers were suddenly in a frenzy to buy.

"We have begun hearing anecdotal reports of the possible price gouging of store-bought water," Coakley announced Sunday. "Businesses and individuals cannot and should not take advantage of this public emergency to unfairly charge consumers . . . for water." Inspectors were being dispatched, "spot-checks" were being conducted, and "if we discover that businesses are engaging in price gouging," she warned, "we will take appropriate legal action."

Governor Deval Patrick got into the act, too. He ordered the state's Division of Standards to "closely monitor bottled water prices" in the area affected by the water emergency. "There is never an excuse for taking advantage of consumers," he intoned, "especially not during times like this."

It never fails. No sooner does some calamity trigger an urgent need for basic resources than self-righteous voices are raised to denounce the amazingly efficient system that stimulates suppliers to speed those resources to the people who need them. That system is the free market's price mechanism—the fluctuation of prices because of changes in supply and demand.

When the demand for bottled water goes through the roof—which is another way of saying that bottled water has become (relatively) scarce—the price of water quickly rises in response. That price spike may be annoying, but it's not nearly as annoying as being unable to find water for sale at any price.

	No Change in Supply	An Increase in Supply	A Decrease in Supply
No Change in Demand	*P* same *Q* same	*P* down *Q* up	*P* up *Q* down
An Increase in Demand	*P* up *Q* up	*P* ambiguous *Q* up	*P* up *Q* ambiguous
A Decrease in Demand	*P* down *Q* down	*P* down *Q* ambiguous	*P* ambiguous *Q* down

Table **4**

What Happens to Price and Quantity When Supply or Demand Shifts?
As a quick quiz, make sure you can explain at least a few of the entries in this table using a supply-and-demand diagram.

Summary We have just seen three examples of how to use supply and demand curves to analyze a change in equilibrium. Whenever an event shifts the supply curve, the demand curve, or perhaps both curves, you can use these tools to predict how the event will alter the price and quantity sold in equilibrium. Table 4 shows the predicted outcome for any combination of shifts in the two curves. To make sure you understand how to use the tools of supply and demand, pick a

Rising prices help keep limited quantities from vanishing today, while increasing the odds of fresh supplies arriving tomorrow.

It is easy to demonize vendors who charge what the market will bear following a catastrophe. "After storm come the vultures" *USA Today* memorably headlined a story about the price hikes that followed Hurricane Charley in Florida in 2004. Coakley hasn't called anybody a vulture, at least not yet, but her office has dedicated a telephone hotline and is encouraging the public to drop a dime on "price gougers."

Before you drop that dime, though, consider who really serves the public interest—the merchant who boosts his price during a crisis, or the merchant who refuses to?

A thought experiment: A massive pipe ruptures, tap water grows undrinkable, and consumers rush to buy bottled water from the only two vendors who sell it. Vendor A, not wanting to annoy the governor and attorney general, leaves the price of his water unchanged at 69 cents a bottle. Vendor B, who is more interested in doing business than truckling to politicians, more than quadruples his price to $2.99.

Source: *The Boston Globe*, May 4, 2010.

You don't need an economics textbook to know what happens next.

Customers descend on Vendor A in droves, loading up on his 69-cent water. Within hours his entire stock has been cleaned out, and subsequent customers are turned away empty-handed. At Vendor B's, on the other hand, sales of water are slower and there is a lot of grumbling about the high price. But even late-arriving customers are able to buy the water they need—and almost no one buys more than he truly *needs*.

A scarce resource.

When demand intensifies, prices rise. And as prices rise, suppliers work harder to meet demand. The same *Globe* story that reported yesterday on Coakley's "price-gouging" statement reported as well on the lengths to which bottlers and retailers were going to get more water into customers' hands.

"Suppliers worked overtime, pumping up production at regional bottling facilities and coordinating deliveries," reporter Erin Ailworth noted. Polar Beverages in Worcester, for example, "had emptied out its plant in the city last night and trucked in loads of water from its New York facility."

Letting prices rise freely isn't the only possible response to a sudden shortage. Government rationing is an option, and so are price controls—assuming you don't object to the inevitable corruption, long lines, and black market. Better by far to let prices rise and fall freely. That isn't "gouging," but plain good sense—and the best method yet devised for allocating goods and services among free men and women.

few entries in this table and make sure you can explain to yourself why the table contains the prediction it does.

QUICK QUIZ *On the appropriate diagram, show what happens to the market for pizza if the price of tomatoes rises. • On a separate diagram, show what happens to the market for pizza if the price of hamburgers falls.*

Conclusion: How Prices Allocate Resources

"Two dollars"

"—and seventy-five cents."

This chapter has analyzed supply and demand in a single market. Although our discussion has centered on the market for ice cream, the lessons learned here apply in most other markets as well. Whenever you go to a store to buy something, you are contributing to the demand for that item. Whenever you look for a job, you are contributing to the supply of labor services. Because supply and demand are such pervasive economic phenomena, the model of supply and demand is a powerful tool for analysis. We will be using this model repeatedly in the following chapters.

One of the *Ten Principles of Economics* discussed in Chapter 1 is that markets are usually a good way to organize economic activity. Although it is still too early to judge whether market outcomes are good or bad, in this chapter we have begun to see how markets work. In any economic system, scarce resources have to be allocated among competing uses. Market economies harness the forces of supply and demand to serve that end. Supply and demand together determine the prices of the economy's many different goods and services; prices in turn are the signals that guide the allocation of resources.

For example, consider the allocation of beachfront land. Because the amount of this land is limited, not everyone can enjoy the luxury of living by the beach. Who gets this resource? The answer is whoever is willing and able to pay the price. The price of beachfront land adjusts until the quantity of land demanded exactly balances the quantity supplied. Thus, in market economies, prices are the mechanism for rationing scarce resources.

Similarly, prices determine who produces each good and how much is produced. For instance, consider farming. Because we need food to survive, it is crucial that some people work on farms. What determines who is a farmer and who is not? In a free society, there is no government planning agency making this decision and ensuring an adequate supply of food. Instead, the allocation of workers to farms is based on the job decisions of millions of workers. This decentralized system works well because these decisions depend on prices. The prices of food and the wages of farmworkers (the price of their labor) adjust to ensure that enough people choose to be farmers.

If a person had never seen a market economy in action, the whole idea might seem preposterous. Economies are enormous groups of people engaged in a multitude of interdependent activities. What prevents decentralized decision making from degenerating into chaos? What coordinates the actions of the millions of people with their varying abilities and desires? What ensures that what needs to be done is in fact done? The answer, in a word, is *prices*. If an invisible hand guides market economies, as Adam Smith famously suggested, then the price system is the baton that the invisible hand uses to conduct the economic orchestra.

SUMMARY

- Economists use the model of supply and demand to analyze competitive markets. In a competitive market, there are many buyers and sellers, each of whom has little or no influence on the market price.

- The demand curve shows how the quantity of a good demanded depends on the price. According to the law of demand, as the price of a good falls, the quantity demanded rises. Therefore, the demand curve slopes downward.

- In addition to price, other determinants of how much consumers want to buy include income, the prices of substitutes and complements, tastes, expectations, and the number of buyers. If one of these factors changes, the demand curve shifts.

- The supply curve shows how the quantity of a good supplied depends on the price. According to the law of supply, as the price of a good rises, the quantity supplied rises. Therefore, the supply curve slopes upward.

- In addition to price, other determinants of how much producers want to sell include input prices, technology, expectations, and the number of sellers. If one of these factors changes, the supply curve shifts.

- The intersection of the supply and demand curves determines the market equilibrium. At the equilibrium price, the quantity demanded equals the quantity supplied.

- The behavior of buyers and sellers naturally drives markets toward their equilibrium. When the market price is above the equilibrium price, there is a surplus of the good, which causes the market price to fall. When the market price is below the equilibrium price, there is a shortage, which causes the market price to rise.

- To analyze how any event influences a market, we use the supply-and-demand diagram to examine how the event affects the equilibrium price and quantity. To do this, we follow three steps. First, we decide whether the event shifts the supply curve or the demand curve (or both). Second, we decide in which direction the curve shifts. Third, we compare the new equilibrium with the initial equilibrium.

- In market economies, prices are the signals that guide economic decisions and thereby allocate scarce resources. For every good in the economy, the price ensures that supply and demand are in balance. The equilibrium price then determines how much of the good buyers choose to consume and how much sellers choose to produce.

KEY CONCEPTS

market, *p. 66*
competitive market, *p. 66*
quantity demanded, *p. 67*
law of demand, *p. 67*
demand schedule, *p. 67*
demand curve, *p. 68*
normal good, *p. 70*

inferior good, *p. 70*
substitutes, *p. 70*
complements, *p. 70*
quantity supplied, *p. 73*
law of supply, *p. 73*
supply schedule, *p. 73*
supply curve, *p. 73*

equilibrium, *p. 77*
equilibrium price, *p. 77*
equilibrium quantity, *p. 77*
surplus, *p. 77*
shortage, *p. 78*
law of supply and
  demand, *p. 79*

QUESTIONS FOR REVIEW

1. What is a competitive market? Briefly describe a type of market that is not perfectly competitive.

2. What are the demand schedule and the demand curve, and how are they related? Why does the demand curve slope downward?

3. Does a change in consumers' tastes lead to a movement along the demand curve or a shift in the demand curve? Does a change in price lead to a movement along the demand curve or a shift in the demand curve?

4. Popeye's income declines, and as a result, he buys more spinach. Is spinach an inferior or a normal good? What happens to Popeye's demand curve for spinach?

5. What are the supply schedule and the supply curve, and how are they related? Why does the supply curve slope upward?

6. Does a change in producers' technology lead to a movement along the supply curve or a shift in the supply curve? Does a change in price lead to a movement along the supply curve or a shift in the supply curve?

7. Define the equilibrium of a market. Describe the forces that move a market toward its equilibrium.

8. Beer and pizza are complements because they are often enjoyed together. When the price of beer rises, what happens to the supply, demand, quantity supplied, quantity demanded, and the price in the market for pizza?

9. Describe the role of prices in market economies.

PROBLEMS AND APPLICATIONS

1. Explain each of the following statements using supply-and-demand diagrams.
   a. "When a cold snap hits Florida, the price of orange juice rises in supermarkets throughout the country."
   b. "When the weather turns warm in New England every summer, the price of hotel rooms in Caribbean resorts plummets."
   c. "When a war breaks out in the Middle East, the price of gasoline rises, and the price of a used Cadillac falls."

2. "An increase in the demand for notebooks raises the quantity of notebooks demanded but not the quantity supplied." Is this statement true or false? Explain.

3. Consider the market for minivans. For each of the events listed here, identify which of the determinants of demand or supply are affected. Also indicate whether demand or supply increases or decreases. Then draw a diagram to show the effect on the price and quantity of minivans.
   a. People decide to have more children.
   b. A strike by steelworkers raises steel prices.
   c. Engineers develop new automated machinery for the production of minivans.
   d. The price of sports utility vehicles rises.
   e. A stock-market crash lowers people's wealth.

4. Consider the markets for DVDs, TV screens, and tickets at movie theaters.
   a. For each pair, identify whether they are complements or substitutes:
      - DVDs and TV screens
      - DVDs and movie tickets
      - TV screens and movie tickets
   b. Suppose a technological advance reduces the cost of manufacturing TV screens. Draw a diagram to show what happens in the market for TV screens.
   c. Draw two more diagrams to show how the change in the market for TV screens affects the markets for DVDs and movie tickets.

5. Over the past 30 years, technological advances have reduced the cost of computer chips. How do you think this has affected the market for computers? For computer software? For typewriters?

6. Using supply-and-demand diagrams, show the effect of the following events on the market for sweatshirts.
   a. A hurricane in South Carolina damages the cotton crop.
   b. The price of leather jackets falls.
   c. All colleges require morning exercise in appropriate attire.
   d. New knitting machines are invented.

7. A survey shows an increase in drug use by young people. In the ensuing debate, two hypotheses are proposed:
   - Reduced police efforts have increased the availability of drugs on the street.
   - Cutbacks in education efforts have decreased awareness of the dangers of drug addiction.

a Use supply-and-demand diagrams to show how each of these hypotheses could lead to an increase in quantity of drugs consumed.

b How could information on what has happened to the price of drugs help us to distinguish between these explanations?

8. Suppose that in the year 2015 the number of births is temporarily high. How does this baby boom affect the price of babysitting services in 2020 and 2030? (Hint: 5-year-olds need babysitters, whereas 15-year-olds can be babysitters.)

9. Ketchup is a complement (as well as a condiment) for hot dogs. If the price of hot dogs rises, what happens to the market for ketchup? For tomatoes? For tomato juice? For orange juice?

10. The market for pizza has the following demand and supply schedules:

Price	Quantity Demanded	Quantity Supplied
$4	135 pizzas	26 pizzas
5	104	53
6	81	81
7	68	98
8	53	110
9	39	121

a. Graph the demand and supply curves. What is the equilibrium price and quantity in this market?

b. If the actual price in this market were *above* the equilibrium price, what would drive the market toward the equilibrium?

c. If the actual price in this market were *below* the equilibrium price, what would drive the market toward the equilibrium?

11. Consider the following events: Scientists reveal that consumption of oranges decreases the risk of diabetes, and at the same time, farmers use a new fertilizer that makes orange trees more productive. Illustrate and explain what effect these changes have on the equilibrium price and quantity of oranges.

12. Because bagels and cream cheese are often eaten together, they are complements.

a. We observe that both the equilibrium price of cream cheese and the equilibrium quantity of bagels have risen. What could be responsible for this pattern—a fall in the price of flour or a fall in the price of milk? Illustrate and explain your answer.

b. Suppose instead that the equilibrium price of cream cheese has risen but the equilibrium quantity of bagels has fallen. What could be responsible for this pattern—a rise in the price of flour or a rise in the price of milk? Illustrate and explain your answer.

13. Suppose that the price of basketball tickets at your college is determined by market forces. Currently, the demand and supply schedules are as follows:

Price	Quantity Demanded	Quantity Supplied
$4	10,000 tickets	8,000 tickets
8	8,000	8,000
12	6,000	8,000
16	4,000	8,000
20	2,000	8,000

a. Draw the demand and supply curves. What is unusual about this supply curve? Why might this be true?

b. What are the equilibrium price and quantity of tickets?

c. Your college plans to increase total enrollment next year by 5,000 students. The additional students will have the following demand schedule:

Price	Quantity Demanded
$4	4,000 tickets
8	3,000
12	2,000
16	1,000
20	0

Now add the old demand schedule and the demand schedule for the new students to calculate the new demand schedule for the entire college. What will be the new equilibrium price and quantity?

14. Market research has revealed the following information about the market for chocolate bars: The demand schedule can be represented by the equation $Q^D = 1{,}600 - 300P$, where Q^D is the quantity demanded and P is the price. The supply schedule can be represented by the equation $Q^S = 1{,}400 + 700P$, where Q^S is the quantity supplied. Calculate the equilibrium price and quantity in the market for chocolate bars.

For further information on topics in this chapter, additional problems, applications, examples, online quizzes, and more, please visit our website at www.cengage.com/economics/mankiw.

PART III The Data of Macroeconomics

Measuring a Nation's Income

5

When you finish school and start looking for a full-time job, your experience will, to a large extent, be shaped by prevailing economic conditions. In some years, firms throughout the economy are expanding their production of goods and services, employment is rising, and jobs are easy to find. In other years, firms are cutting back production, employment is declining, and finding a good job takes a long time. Not surprisingly, any college graduate would rather enter the labor force in a year of economic expansion than in a year of economic contraction.

Because the health of the overall economy profoundly affects all of us, changes in economic conditions are widely reported by the media. Indeed, it is hard to pick up a newspaper, check an online news service, or turn on the TV without seeing some newly reported statistic about the economy. The statistic might measure the total income of everyone in the economy (gross domestic product, or GDP), the rate at which average prices are rising or falling (inflation/deflation), the percentage of the labor force that is out of work (unemployment), total spending at stores (retail sales), or the imbalance of trade between the United States and the rest of the world (the trade deficit). All these statistics are *macroeconomic*. Rather than telling us about a particular household, firm, or market, they tell us something about the entire economy.

As you may recall from Chapter 2, economics is divided into two branches: microeconomics and macroeconomics. **Microeconomics** is the study of how individual households and firms make decisions and how they interact with one another in markets. **Macroeconomics** is the study of the economy as a whole. The goal of macroeconomics is to explain the economic changes that affect many households, firms, and markets simultaneously. Macroeconomists address diverse questions: Why is average income high in some countries while it is low in others? Why do prices sometimes rise rapidly while at other times they are more stable? Why do production and employment expand in some years and contract in others? What, if anything, can the government do to promote rapid growth in incomes, low inflation, and stable employment? These questions are all macroeconomic in nature because they concern the workings of the entire economy.

Because the economy as a whole is a collection of many households and many firms interacting in many markets, microeconomics and macroeconomics are closely linked. The basic tools of supply and demand, for instance, are as central to macroeconomic analysis as they are to microeconomic analysis. Yet studying the economy in its entirety raises some new and intriguing challenges.

In this and the next chapter, we discuss some of the data that economists and policymakers use to monitor the performance of the overall economy. These data reflect the economic changes that macroeconomists try to explain. This chapter considers *gross domestic product*, which measures the total income of a nation. GDP is the most closely watched economic statistic because it is thought to be the best single measure of a society's economic well-being.

microeconomics

the study of how households and firms make decisions and how they interact in markets

macroeconomics

the study of economy-wide phenomena, including inflation, unemployment, and economic growth

The Economy's Income and Expenditure

If you were to judge how a person is doing economically, you might first look at his or her income. A person with a high income can more easily afford life's necessities and luxuries. It is no surprise that people with higher incomes enjoy higher standards of living—better housing, better healthcare, fancier cars, more opulent vacations, and so on.

The same logic applies to a nation's overall economy. When judging whether the economy is doing well or poorly, it is natural to look at the total income that everyone in the economy is earning. That is the task of gross domestic product.

GDP measures two things at once: the total income of everyone in the economy and the total expenditure on the economy's output of goods and services. GDP can perform the trick of measuring both total income and total expenditure because these two things are really the same. *For an economy as a whole, income must equal expenditure.*

Why is this true? An economy's income is the same as its expenditure because every transaction has two parties: a buyer and a seller. Every dollar of spending by some buyer is a dollar of income for some seller. Suppose, for instance, that Karen pays Doug $100 to mow her lawn. In this case, Doug is a seller of a service, and Karen is a buyer. Doug earns $100, and Karen spends $100. Thus, the transaction

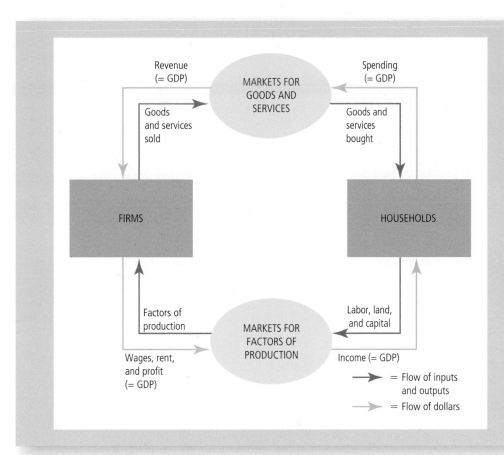

Figure 1

The Circular-Flow Diagram
Households buy goods and services from firms, and firms use their revenue from sales to pay wages to workers, rent to landowners, and profit to firm owners. GDP equals the total amount spent by households in the market for goods and services. It also equals the total wages, rent, and profit paid by firms in the markets for the factors of production.

contributes equally to the economy's income and to its expenditure. GDP, whether measured as total income or total expenditure, rises by $100.

Another way to see the equality of income and expenditure is with the circular-flow diagram in Figure 1. As you may recall from Chapter 2, this diagram describes all the transactions between households and firms in a simple economy. It simplifies matters by assuming that all goods and services are bought by households and that households spend all of their income. In this economy, when households buy goods and services from firms, these expenditures flow through the markets for goods and services. When the firms in turn use the money they receive from sales to pay workers' wages, landowners' rent, and firm owners' profit, this income flows through the markets for the factors of production. Money continuously flows from households to firms and then back to households.

GDP measures this flow of money. We can compute it for this economy in one of two ways: by adding up the total expenditure by households or by adding up the total income (wages, rent, and profit) paid by firms. Because all expenditure in the economy ends up as someone's income, GDP is the same regardless of how we compute it.

The actual economy is, of course, more complicated than the one illustrated in Figure 1. Households do not spend all of their income; they pay some of it to the government in taxes, and they save some for use in the future. In addition, households do not buy all goods and services produced in the economy; some goods and services are bought by governments, and some are bought by firms that plan to use them in the future to produce their own output. Yet the basic lesson remains the same: Regardless of whether a household, government, or firm buys a good or service, the transaction has a buyer and seller. Thus, for the economy as a whole, expenditure and income are always the same.

QUICK QUIZ   *What two things does gross domestic product measure? How can it measure two things at once?*

The Measurement of Gross Domestic Product

Having discussed the meaning of gross domestic product in general terms, let's be more precise about how this statistic is measured. Here is a definition of GDP that focuses on GDP as a measure of total expenditure:

gross domestic product (GDP)

the market value of all final goods and services produced within a country in a given period of time

- **Gross domestic product (GDP)** is the market value of all final goods and services produced within a country in a given period of time.

This definition might seem simple enough. But in fact, many subtle issues arise when computing an economy's GDP. Let's therefore consider each phrase in this definition with some care.

"GDP Is the Market Value . . ."

You have probably heard the adage, "You can't compare apples and oranges." Yet GDP does exactly that. GDP adds together many different kinds of products into a single measure of the value of economic activity. To do this, it uses market prices. Because market prices measure the amount people are willing to pay for different goods, they reflect the value of those goods. If the price of an apple is twice the price of an orange, then an apple contributes twice as much to GDP as does an orange.

". . . of All . . ."

GDP tries to be comprehensive. It includes all items produced in the economy and sold legally in markets. GDP measures the market value of not just apples and oranges but also pears and grapefruit, books and movies, haircuts and healthcare, and on and on.

GDP also includes the market value of the housing services provided by the economy's stock of housing. For rental housing, this value is easy to calculate—the rent equals both the tenant's expenditure and the landlord's income. Yet many people own the place where they live and, therefore, do not pay rent. The government includes this owner-occupied housing in GDP by estimating its rental value. In effect, GDP is based on the assumption that the owner is renting the house to himself. The imputed rent is included both in the homeowner's expenditure and in his income, so it adds to GDP.

There are some products, however, that GDP excludes because measuring them is so difficult. GDP excludes most items produced and sold illicitly, such as illegal drugs. It also excludes most items that are produced and consumed at home and, therefore, never enter the marketplace. Vegetables you buy at the grocery store are part of GDP; vegetables you grow in your garden are not.

These exclusions from GDP can at times lead to paradoxical results. For example, when Karen pays Doug to mow her lawn, that transaction is part of GDP. If

Karen were to marry Doug, the situation would change. Even though Doug may continue to mow Karen's lawn, the value of the mowing is now left out of GDP because Doug's service is no longer sold in a market. Thus, when Karen and Doug marry, GDP falls.

". . . Final . . ."

When International Paper makes paper, which Hallmark then uses to make a greeting card, the paper is called an *intermediate good*, and the card is called a *final good*. GDP includes only the value of final goods. This is done because the value of intermediate goods is already included in the prices of the final goods. Adding the market value of the paper to the market value of the card would be double counting. That is, it would (incorrectly) count the paper twice.

An important exception to this principle arises when an intermediate good is produced and, rather than being used, is added to a firm's inventory of goods for use or sale at a later date. In this case, the intermediate good is taken to be "final" for the moment, and its value as inventory investment is included as part of GDP. Thus, additions to inventory add to GDP, and when the goods in inventory are later used or sold, the reductions in inventory subtract from GDP.

". . . Goods and Services . . ."

GDP includes both tangible goods (food, clothing, cars) and intangible services (haircuts, housecleaning, doctor visits). When you buy a CD by your favorite band, you are buying a good, and the purchase price is part of GDP. When you pay to hear a concert by the same band, you are buying a service, and the ticket price is also part of GDP.

". . . Produced . . ."

GDP includes goods and services currently produced. It does not include transactions involving items produced in the past. When Ford produces and sells a new car, the value of the car is included in GDP. When one person sells a used car to another person, the value of the used car is not included in GDP.

". . . Within a Country . . ."

GDP measures the value of production within the geographic confines of a country. When a Canadian citizen works temporarily in the United States, her production is part of U.S. GDP. When an American citizen owns a factory in Haiti, the production at his factory is not part of U.S. GDP. (It is part of Haiti's GDP.) Thus, items are included in a nation's GDP if they are produced domestically, regardless of the nationality of the producer.

". . . In a Given Period of Time."

GDP measures the value of production that takes place within a specific interval of time. Usually, that interval is a year or a quarter (three months). GDP measures the economy's flow of income and expenditure during that interval.

When the government reports the GDP for a quarter, it usually presents GDP "at an annual rate." This means that the figure reported for quarterly GDP is the amount of income and expenditure during the quarter multiplied by 4. The government uses this convention so that quarterly and annual figures on GDP can be compared more easily.

In addition, when the government reports quarterly GDP, it presents the data after they have been modified by a statistical procedure called *seasonal adjustment*. The unadjusted data show clearly that the economy produces more goods and services during some times of year than during others. (As you might guess, December's holiday shopping season is a high point.) When monitoring the condition of the economy, economists and policymakers often want to look beyond these regular seasonal changes. Therefore, government statisticians adjust the quarterly data to take out the seasonal cycle. The GDP data reported in the news are always seasonally adjusted.

Now let's repeat the definition of GDP:

* Gross domestic product (GDP) is the market value of all final goods and services produced within a country in a given period of time.

This definition focuses on GDP as total expenditure in the economy. But don't forget that every dollar spent by a buyer of a good or service becomes a dollar of income to the seller of that good or service. Therefore, in addition to applying this definition, the government adds up total income in the economy. The two ways of calculating GDP give almost exactly the same answer. (Why "almost"? Although the two measures should be precisely the same, data sources are not perfect. The difference between the two calculations of GDP is called the *statistical discrepancy*.)

It should be apparent that GDP is a sophisticated measure of the value of economic activity. In advanced courses in macroeconomics, you will learn more about the subtleties that arise in its calculation. But even now you can see that each phrase in this definition is packed with meaning.

QUICK QUIZ *Which contributes more to GDP—the production of a pound of hamburger or the production of a pound of caviar? Why?*

The Components of GDP

Spending in the economy takes many forms. At any moment, the Smith family may be having lunch at Burger King; Ford may be building a car factory; the Navy may be procuring a submarine; and British Airways may be buying an airplane from Boeing. GDP includes all of these various forms of spending on domestically produced goods and services.

To understand how the economy is using its scarce resources, economists study the composition of GDP among various types of spending. To do this, GDP (which we denote as Y) is divided into four components: consumption (C), investment (I), government purchases (G), and net exports (NX):

$$Y = C + I + G + NX.$$

This equation is an *identity*—an equation that must be true because of how the variables in the equation are defined. In this case, because each dollar of expenditure included in GDP is placed into one of the four components of GDP, the total of the four components must be equal to GDP. Let's look at each of these four components more closely.

FYI

▶ Other Measures of Income

When the U.S. Department of Commerce computes the nation's GDP every three months, it also computes various other measures of income to get a more complete picture of what's happening in the economy. These other measures differ from GDP by excluding or including certain categories of income. What follows is a brief description of five of these income measures, ordered from largest to smallest.

- *Gross national product* (GNP) is the total income earned by a nation's permanent residents (called *nationals*). It differs from GDP by including income that our citizens earn abroad and excluding income that foreigners earn here. For example, when a Canadian citizen works temporarily in the United States, her production is part of U.S. GDP, but it is not part of U.S. GNP. (It is part of Canada's GNP.) For most countries, including the United States, domestic residents are responsible for most domestic production, so GDP and GNP are quite close.
- *Net national product* (NNP) is the total income of a nation's residents (GNP) minus losses from depreciation. *Depreciation* is the wear and tear on the economy's stock of equipment and structures, such as trucks rusting and computers becoming obsolete. In the national income accounts prepared by the Department of Commerce, depreciation is called the "consumption of fixed capital."
- *National income* is the total income earned by a nation's residents in the production of goods and services. It is almost identical

to net national product. These two measures differ because of the *statistical discrepancy* that arises from problems in data collection.
- *Personal income* is the income that households and noncorporate businesses receive. Unlike national income, it excludes *retained earnings*, which is income that corporations have earned but have not paid out to their owners. It also subtracts indirect business taxes (such as sales taxes), corporate income taxes, and contributions for social insurance (mostly Social Security taxes). In addition, personal income includes the interest income that households receive from their holdings of government debt and the income that households receive from government transfer programs, such as welfare and Social Security.
- *Disposable personal income* is the income that households and noncorporate businesses have left after satisfying all their obligations to the government. It equals personal income minus personal taxes and certain nontax payments (such as traffic tickets).

Although the various measures of income differ in detail, they almost always tell the same story about economic conditions. When GDP is growing rapidly, these other measures of income are usually growing rapidly. And when GDP is falling, these other measures are usually falling as well. For monitoring fluctuations in the overall economy, it does not matter much which measure of income we use.

Consumption

Consumption is spending by households on goods and services, with the exception of purchases of new housing. Goods include household spending on durable goods, such as automobiles and appliances, and nondurable goods, such as food and clothing. Services include such intangible items as haircuts and medical care. Household spending on education is also included in consumption of services (although one might argue that it would fit better in the next component).

Investment

Investment is the purchase of goods that will be used in the future to produce more goods and services. It is the sum of purchases of capital equipment, inventories,

consumption
spending by households on goods and services, with the exception of purchases of new housing

investment
spending on capital equipment, inventories, and structures, including household purchases of new housing

and structures. Investment in structures includes expenditure on new housing. By convention, the purchase of a new house is the one form of household spending categorized as investment rather than consumption.

As mentioned earlier in this chapter, the treatment of inventory accumulation is noteworthy. When Dell produces a computer and adds it to its inventory instead of selling it, Dell is assumed to have "purchased" the computer for itself. That is, the national income accountants treat the computer as part of Dell's investment spending. (If Dell later sells the computer out of inventory, Dell's inventory investment will then be negative, offsetting the positive expenditure of the buyer.) Inventories are treated this way because one aim of GDP is to measure the value of the economy's production, and goods added to inventory are part of that period's production.

Notice that GDP accounting uses the word *investment* differently from how you might hear the term in everyday conversation. When you hear the word *investment,* you might think of financial investments, such as stocks, bonds, and mutual funds—topics that we study later in this book. By contrast, because GDP measures expenditure on goods and services, here the word *investment* means purchases of goods (such as capital equipment, structures, and inventories) used to produce other goods.

Government Purchases

government purchases

spending on goods and services by local, state, and federal governments

Government purchases include spending on goods and services by local, state, and federal governments. It includes the salaries of government workers as well as expenditures on public works. Recently, the U.S. national income accounts have switched to the longer label *government consumption expenditure and gross investment,* but in this book, we will use the traditional and shorter term *government purchases.*

The meaning of government purchases requires a bit of clarification. When the government pays the salary of an Army general or a schoolteacher, that salary is part of government purchases. But when the government pays a Social Security benefit to a person who is elderly or an unemployment insurance benefit to a worker who was recently laid off, the story is very different: These are called *transfer payments* because they are not made in exchange for a currently produced good or service. Transfer payments alter household income, but they do not reflect the economy's production. (From a macroeconomic standpoint, transfer payments are like negative taxes.) Because GDP is intended to measure income from, and expenditure on, the production of goods and services, transfer payments are not counted as part of government purchases.

Net Exports

net exports

spending on domestically produced goods by foreigners (exports) minus spending on foreign goods by domestic residents (imports)

Net exports equal the foreign purchases of domestically produced goods (exports) minus the domestic purchases of foreign goods (imports). A domestic firm's sale to a buyer in another country, such as Boeing's sale of an airplane to British Airways, increases net exports.

The *net* in *net exports* refers to the fact that imports are subtracted from exports. This subtraction is made because other components of GDP include imports of goods and services. For example, suppose that a household buys a $30,000 car from Volvo, the Swedish carmaker. That transaction increases consumption by $30,000 because car purchases are part of consumer spending. It also reduces net exports by $30,000 because the car is an import. In other words, net exports

	Total (in billions of dollars)	Per Person (in dollars)	Percent of Total
Gross domestic product, Y	$14,259	$46,372	100%
Consumption, C	10,093	32,823	71
Investment, I	1,623	5,278	11
Government purchases, G	2,933	9,540	21
Net exports, NX	−390	−1,269	−3

Source: U.S. Department of Commerce. Parts may not sum to totals due to rounding.

Table 1

GDP and Its Components
This table shows total GDP for the U.S. economy in 2009 and the breakdown of GDP among its four components. When reading this table, recall the identity $Y = C + I + G + NX$.

include goods and services produced abroad (with a minus sign) because these goods and services are included in consumption, investment, and government purchases (with a plus sign). Thus, when a domestic household, firm, or government buys a good or service from abroad, the purchase reduces net exports, but because it also raises consumption, investment, or government purchases, it does not affect GDP.

CASE STUDY The Components of U.S. GDP

Table 1 shows the composition of U.S. GDP in 2009. In this year, the GDP of the United States was over $14 trillion. Dividing this number by the 2009 U.S. population of 307 million yields GDP per person (sometimes called GDP per capita). In 2009 the income and expenditure of the average American was $46,372.

Consumption made up 71 percent of GDP, or $32,823 per person. Investment was $5,278 per person. Government purchases were $9,540 per person. Net exports were –$1,269 per person. This number is negative because Americans spent more on foreign goods than foreigners spent on American goods.

These data come from the Bureau of Economic Analysis, the part of the U.S. Department of Commerce that produces the national income accounts. You can find more recent data on GDP at its website, http://www.bea.gov. ■

QUICK QUIZ   *List the four components of expenditure. Which is the largest?*

Real versus Nominal GDP

As we have seen, GDP measures the total spending on goods and services in all markets in the economy. If total spending rises from one year to the next, at least one of two things must be true: (1) the economy is producing a larger output of goods and services, or (2) goods and services are being sold at higher prices. When studying changes in the economy over time, economists want to separate these two effects. In particular, they want a measure of the total quantity of goods and services the economy is producing that is not affected by changes in the prices of those goods and services.

To do this, economists use a measure called *real GDP*. Real GDP answers a hypothetical question: What would be the value of the goods and services produced this year if we valued these goods and services at the prices that prevailed in some specific year in the past? By evaluating current production using prices that are fixed at past levels, real GDP shows how the economy's overall production of goods and services changes over time.

To see more precisely how real GDP is constructed, let's consider an example.

A Numerical Example

Table 2 shows some data for an economy that produces only two goods: hot dogs and hamburgers. The table shows the prices and quantities produced of the two goods in the years 2010, 2011, and 2012.

To compute total spending in this economy, we would multiply the quantities of hot dogs and hamburgers by their prices. In the year 2010, 100 hot dogs are sold at a price of $1 per hot dog, so expenditure on hot dogs equals $100. In the same year, 50 hamburgers are sold for $2 per hamburger, so expenditure on hamburgers also equals $100. Total expenditure in the economy—the sum of expenditure on hot dogs and expenditure on hamburgers—is $200. This amount, the production of goods and services valued at current prices, is called **nominal GDP**.

nominal GDP

the production of goods and services valued at current prices

The table shows the calculation of nominal GDP for these three years. Total spending rises from $200 in 2010 to $600 in 2011 and then to $1,200 in 2012. Part of this rise is attributable to the increase in the quantities of hot dogs and hamburgers, and part is attributable to the increase in the prices of hot dogs and hamburgers.

Table **2**

Real and Nominal GDP
This table shows how to calculate real GDP, nominal GDP, and the GDP deflator for a hypothetical economy that produces only hot dogs and hamburgers.

Prices and Quantities

Year	Price of Hot Dogs	Quantity of Hot Dogs	Price of Hamburgers	Quantity of Hamburgers
2010	$1	100	$2	50
2011	$2	150	$3	100
2012	$3	200	$4	150

Calculating Nominal GDP

2010	($1 per hot dog × 100 hot dogs) + ($2 per hamburger × 50 hamburgers) = $200
2011	($2 per hot dog × 150 hot dogs) + ($3 per hamburger × 100 hamburgers) = $600
2012	($3 per hot dog × 200 hot dogs) + ($4 per hamburger × 150 hamburgers) = $1,200

Calculating Real GDP (base year 2010)

2010	($1 per hot dog × 100 hot dogs) + ($2 per hamburger × 50 hamburgers) = $200
2011	($1 per hot dog × 150 hot dogs) + ($2 per hamburger × 100 hamburgers) = $350
2012	($1 per hot dog × 200 hot dogs) + ($2 per hamburger × 150 hamburgers) = $500

Calculating the GDP Deflator

2010	($200 / $200) × 100 = 100
2011	($600 / $350) × 100 = 171
2012	($1,200 / $500) × 100 = 240

To obtain a measure of the amount produced that is not affected by changes in prices, we use **real GDP**, which is the production of goods and services valued at constant prices. We calculate real GDP by first designating one year as a *base year*. We then use the prices of hot dogs and hamburgers in the base year to compute the value of goods and services in all the years. In other words, the prices in the base year provide the basis for comparing quantities in different years.

real GDP
the production of goods and services valued at constant prices

Suppose that we choose 2010 to be the base year in our example. We can then use the prices of hot dogs and hamburgers in 2010 to compute the value of goods and services produced in 2010, 2011, and 2012. Table 2 shows these calculations. To compute real GDP for 2010, we use the prices of hot dogs and hamburgers in 2010 (the base year) and the quantities of hot dogs and hamburgers produced in 2010. (Thus, for the base year, real GDP always equals nominal GDP.) To compute real GDP for 2011, we use the prices of hot dogs and hamburgers in 2010 (the base year) and the quantities of hot dogs and hamburgers produced in 2011. Similarly, to compute real GDP for 2012, we use the prices in 2010 and the quantities in 2012. When we find that real GDP has risen from $200 in 2010 to $350 in 2011 and then to $500 in 2012, we know that the increase is attributable to an increase in the quantities produced because the prices are being held fixed at base-year levels.

To sum up: *Nominal GDP uses current prices to place a value on the economy's production of goods and services. Real GDP uses constant base-year prices to place a value on the economy's production of goods and services.* Because real GDP is not affected by changes in prices, changes in real GDP reflect only changes in the amounts being produced. Thus, real GDP is a measure of the economy's production of goods and services.

Our goal in computing GDP is to gauge how well the overall economy is performing. Because real GDP measures the economy's production of goods and services, it reflects the economy's ability to satisfy people's needs and desires. Thus, real GDP is a better gauge of economic well-being than is nominal GDP. When economists talk about the economy's GDP, they usually mean real GDP rather than nominal GDP. And when they talk about growth in the economy, they measure that growth as the percentage change in real GDP from one period to another.

The GDP Deflator

As we have just seen, nominal GDP reflects both the quantities of goods and services the economy is producing and the prices of those goods and services. By contrast, by holding prices constant at base-year levels, real GDP reflects only the quantities produced. From these two statistics, we can compute a third, called the GDP deflator, which reflects only the prices of goods and services.

The **GDP deflator** is calculated as follows:

$$\text{GDP deflator} = \frac{\text{Nominal GDP}}{\text{Real GDP}} \times 100.$$

GDP deflator
a measure of the price level calculated as the ratio of nominal GDP to real GDP times 100

Because nominal GDP and real GDP must be the same in the base year, the GDP deflator for the base year always equals 100. The GDP deflator for subsequent years measures the change in nominal GDP from the base year that cannot be attributable to a change in real GDP.

The GDP deflator measures the current level of prices relative to the level of prices in the base year. To see why this is true, consider a couple of simple examples. First, imagine that the quantities produced in the economy rise over time but prices remain the same. In this case, both nominal and real GDP rise together, so the GDP deflator is constant. Now suppose, instead, that prices rise over time but the quantities produced stay the same. In this second case, nominal GDP rises but real GDP remains the same, so the GDP deflator rises as well. Notice that, in both cases, the GDP deflator reflects what's happening to prices, not quantities.

Let's now return to our numerical example in Table 2. The GDP deflator is computed at the bottom of the table. For year 2010, nominal GDP is $200, and real GDP is $200, so the GDP deflator is 100. (The deflator is always 100 in the base year.) For the year 2011, nominal GDP is $600, and real GDP is $350, so the GDP deflator is 171.

Economists use the term *inflation* to describe a situation in which the economy's overall price level is rising. The *inflation rate* is the percentage change in some measure of the price level from one period to the next. Using the GDP deflator, the inflation rate between two consecutive years is computed as follows:

$$\text{Inflation rate in year 2} = \frac{\text{GDP deflator in year 2} - \text{GDP deflator in year 1}}{\text{GDP deflator in year 1}} \times 100.$$

Because the GDP deflator rose in year 2011 from 100 to 171, the inflation rate is $100 \times (171 - 100)/100$, or 71 percent. In 2012, the GDP deflator rose to 240 from 171 the previous year, so the inflation rate is $100 \times (240 - 171)/171$, or 40 percent.

The GDP deflator is one measure that economists use to monitor the average level of prices in the economy and thus the rate of inflation. The GDP deflator gets its name because it can be used to take inflation out of nominal GDP—that is, to "deflate" nominal GDP for the rise that is due to increases in prices. We examine another measure of the economy's price level, called the consumer price index, in the next chapter, where we also describe the differences between the two measures.

 ## Real GDP over Recent History

Now that we know how real GDP is defined and measured, let's look at what this macroeconomic variable tells us about the recent history of the United States. Figure 2 shows quarterly data on real GDP for the U.S. economy since 1965.

The most obvious feature of these data is that real GDP grows over time. The real GDP of the U.S. economy in 2009 was almost four times its 1965 level. Put differently, the output of goods and services produced in the United States has grown on average about 3 percent per year. This continued growth in real GDP enables the typical American to enjoy greater economic prosperity than his or her parents and grandparents did.

A second feature of the GDP data is that growth is not steady. The upward climb of real GDP is occasionally interrupted by periods during which GDP declines, called *recessions*. Figure 2 marks recessions with shaded vertical bars. (There is no ironclad rule for when the official business cycle dating committee will declare that a recession has occurred, but an old rule of thumb is two consecutive quarters of falling real GDP.) Recessions are associated not only with lower

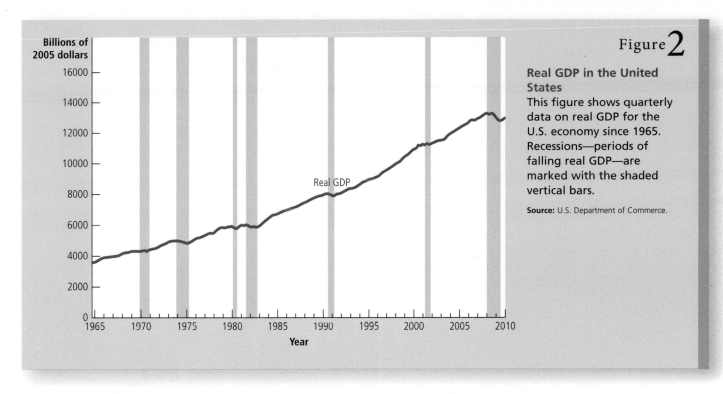

Billions of 2005 dollars

Figure 2

Real GDP in the United States
This figure shows quarterly data on real GDP for the U.S. economy since 1965. Recessions—periods of falling real GDP—are marked with the shaded vertical bars.

Source: U.S. Department of Commerce.

incomes but also with other forms of economic distress: rising unemployment, falling profits, increased bankruptcies, and so on.

Much of macroeconomics is aimed at explaining the long-run growth and short-run fluctuations in real GDP. As we will see in the coming chapters, we need different models for these two purposes. Because the short-run fluctuations represent deviations from the long-run trend, we first examine the behavior of key macroeconomic variables, including real GDP, in the long run. Then in later chapters, we build on this analysis to explain short-run fluctuations. ∎

QUICK QUIZ *Define* real GDP *and* nominal GDP. *Which is a better measure of economic well-being? Why?*

Is GDP a Good Measure of Economic Well-Being?

Earlier in this chapter, GDP was called the best single measure of the economic well-being of a society. Now that we know what GDP is, we can evaluate this claim.

As we have seen, GDP measures both the economy's total income and the economy's total expenditure on goods and services. Thus, GDP per person tells us the income and expenditure of the average person in the economy. Because most people would prefer to receive higher income and enjoy higher expenditure, GDP per person seems a natural measure of the economic well-being of the average individual.

Yet some people dispute the validity of GDP as a measure of well-being. When Senator Robert Kennedy was running for president in 1968, he gave a moving critique of such economic measures:

> [Gross domestic product] does not allow for the health of our children, the quality of their education, or the joy of their play. It does not include the beauty

of our poetry or the strength of our marriages, the intelligence of our public debate or the integrity of our public officials. It measures neither our courage, nor our wisdom, nor our devotion to our country. It measures everything, in short, except that which makes life worthwhile, and it can tell us everything about America except why we are proud that we are Americans.

Much of what Robert Kennedy said is correct. Why, then, do we care about GDP?

The answer is that a large GDP does in fact help us to lead a good life. GDP does not measure the health of our children, but nations with larger GDP can afford better healthcare for their children. GDP does not measure the quality of their education, but nations with larger GDP can afford better educational systems. GDP does not measure the beauty of our poetry, but nations with larger GDP can afford to teach more of their citizens to read and enjoy poetry. GDP does not take account of our intelligence, integrity, courage, wisdom,

· · · · · · · · · · · · · · · · · · in the news

> ### The Underground Economy

The gross domestic product misses many transactions that take place in the underground economy.

Searching for the Hidden Economy

BY DOUG CAMPBELL

ere is the brief, unremarkable story of how I recently came to participate in the underground economy:

Midafternoon on the iciest day this past winter, a man knocked at my front door. "Shovel your walk?" he asked. "Only $5."

Outside, it was a bone-chilling 15 degrees. "Sold," I said. A half-hour later I handed over a five-dollar bill and thanked him for saving me the trouble.

Officially, this was an unofficial trans-action—off the books, with no taxes paid or safety regulations followed. (At least, I assume this hired hand didn't bother to report that income or register

with the proper authorities.) As such, it was technically illegal. And, of course,

International Differences in the Underground Economy

Country	Underground Economy as a Percentage of GDP
Bolivia	68 percent
Zimbabwe	63
Peru	61
Thailand	54
Mexico	33
Argentina	29
Sweden	18
Australia	13
United Kingdom	12
Japan	11
Switzerland	9
United States	8

Source: Friedrich Schneider. Figures are for 2002.

it's the sort of thing that happens all the time.

The size of the official U.S. economy, as measured by Gross Domestic Product (GDP), was almost $12 trillion in 2004. Measurements of the unofficial economy—not including illegal activities like drug dealing and prostitution—differ substan-tially. But it's generally agreed to be signifi-cant, somewhere between 6 percent and 20 percent of GDP. At the midpoint, this would be about $1.5 trillion a year.

Broadly defined, the underground, gray, informal, or shadow economy involves oth-erwise legal transactions that go unreported or unrecorded. That's a wide net, capturing everything from babysitting fees, to barter-ing home repairs with a neighbor, to fail-ing to report pay from moonlighting gigs. The "underground" label tends to make it sound much more sinister than it really is.

or devotion to country, but all of these laudable attributes are easier to foster when people are less concerned about being able to afford the material necessities of life. In short, GDP does not directly measure those things that make life worthwhile, but it does measure our ability to obtain many of the inputs into a worthwhile life.

GDP is not, however, a perfect measure of well-being. Some things that contribute to a good life are left out of GDP. One is leisure. Suppose, for instance, that everyone in the economy suddenly started working every day of the week, rather than enjoying leisure on weekends. More goods and services would be produced, and GDP would rise. Yet despite the increase in GDP, we should not conclude that everyone would be better off. The loss from reduced leisure would offset the gain from producing and consuming a greater quantity of goods and services.

Criminal activities make up a large portion of what could be termed the total underground economy. Many studies have been done on the economics of drug dealing, prostitution, and gambling. But because money from crime is almost never recovered, many policymakers are more interested in portions of the underground economy that otherwise would be legal if not hidden from authorities. Things like shoveling walks.

Despite its intrigue, the informal economy's importance and consequences remain in debate. The reason: "You're trying to measure a phenomenon whose entire purpose is to hide itself from observation," says Ed Feige, an economist at the University of Wisconsin.

This uncertainty poses problems for policymakers. Without knowing the precise size, scope, and causes of the underground economy, how can they decide what—if anything—to do about it?

Was the man who shoveled my walk engaging in a socially positive or negative activity? Was I? Suffice it to say, some economists have dedicated their entire careers to answering questions about the underground economy—and still there is

A Shadowy Enterprise?

nothing close to a consensus about its size or description. . . .

Economists generally agree that the shadow economy is worse in developing nations, whose webs of bureaucratic red tape and corruption are notorious. For instance, [economist Friedrich] Schneider in 2003 published "shadow economy" estimates (defined broadly as all market-based, legal production of goods and services deliberately concealed from the authorities)

for countries including: Zimbabwe, estimated at a whopping 63.2 percent of GDP, Thailand's at 54.1 percent, and Bolivia's at 68.3 percent. Among former Soviet bloc nations, Georgia led the way with a 68 percent of GDP shadow economy, and together those nations had an average 40.1 percent of GDP underground. This contrasts with an average of 16.7 percent among Western nations. . . .

In his 2003 book, *Reefer Madness: Sex, Drugs and Cheap Labor in the American Black Market,* investigative writer Eric Schlosser invokes Adam Smith's "invisible hand" theory that men pursuing their own self-interest will generate benefits for society as a whole. This invisible hand has produced a fairly sizable underground economy, and we cannot understand our entire economic system without understanding how the hidden underbelly functions, too. "The underground is a good measure of the progress and the health of nations," Schlosser writes. "When much is wrong, much needs to be hidden." Schlosser's implication was that much is wrong in the United States. If he had taken a more global view, he might have decided relatively little is hidden here.

Source: "Region Focus," Federal Reserve Bank of Richmond, Spring 2005.

GDP reflects the factory's production, but not the harm that it inflicts on the environment.

Because GDP uses market prices to value goods and services, it excludes the value of almost all activity that takes place outside markets. In particular, GDP omits the value of goods and services produced at home. When a chef prepares a delicious meal and sells it at his restaurant, the value of that meal is part of GDP. But if the chef prepares the same meal for his family, the value he has added to the raw ingredients is left out of GDP. Similarly, child care provided in day-care centers is part of GDP, whereas child care by parents at home is not. Volunteer work also contributes to the well-being of those in society, but GDP does not reflect these contributions.

Another thing that GDP excludes is the quality of the environment. Imagine that the government eliminated all environmental regulations. Firms could then produce goods and services without considering the pollution they create, and GDP might rise. Yet well-being would most likely fall. The deterioration in the quality of air and water would more than offset the gains from greater production.

GDP also says nothing about the distribution of income. A society in which 100 people have annual incomes of $50,000 has GDP of $5 million and, not surprisingly, GDP per person of $50,000. So does a society in which 10 people

· in the news

> ### Beyond Gross Domestic Product

With the encouragement of the French president, some economists wonder whether we need better measures of economic well-being.

GDP Seen as Inadequate Measure of Economic Health

BY DAVID JOLLY

PARIS—President Nicolas Sarkozy told the French national statistics agency Monday to take greater account of factors like quality of life and the environment when measuring the country's economic health.

Mr. Sarkozy made the request after accepting a report from a panel of top economists he had charged with reviewing the adequacy of the current standard of fiscal well-being: gross domestic product.

The panel, chaired by two Nobel economists, Joseph E. Stiglitz of Columbia University and Amartya Sen of Harvard University, concluded that GDP was insufficient and that measures of sustainability and human well-being should be included.

An "excessive focus on GDP metrics" also contributed to the onset of the current financial crisis, according to the report. Policy makers cheered rising economic growth while other data, like those that showed the increasing and unsustainable indebtedness of households and businesses, were overlooked, the report found.

"The main message is to get away from GDP fetishism and to understand the

limits to it," Mr. Stiglitz said in an interview. "There are many aspects of our society that are not covered by GDP." ...

GDP is the measure of the market value of all the goods and services produced in the economy. Its development in the 1930s, when the U.S. government was looking for new tools to measure national income and output more accurately, has been described as one of the most important advances in macroeconomics.

However, there has long been criticism that, while it accurately captures the growth or contraction of the overall economy, it is a crude tool for describing social health.

The United States, for example, with the world's largest economy, naturally tops GDP rankings, but it ranks lower by other earn $500,000 and 90 suffer with nothing at all. Few people would look at those two situations and call them equivalent. GDP per person tells us what happens to the average person, but behind the average lies a large variety of personal experiences.

In the end, we can conclude that GDP is a good measure of economic well-being for most—but not all—purposes. It is important to keep in mind what GDP includes and what it leaves out.

CASE STUDY

International Differences in GDP and the Quality of Life

One way to gauge the usefulness of GDP as a measure of economic well-being is to examine international data. Rich and poor countries have vastly different levels of GDP per person. If a large GDP leads to a higher standard of living, then we should observe GDP to be strongly correlated with various measures of the quality of life. And, in fact, we do.

measures. The United Nations Development Program's human development index, which incorporates GDP as only one of a number of criteria, ranked Iceland, Norway and Canada the top three spots in 2008, with the United States a distant 15th. The human development indexes also seek to incorporate the value of a long and healthy life, access to knowledge and a decent standard of living.

As an alternative to the developed world's pursuit of GDP, the Himalayan kingdom of Bhutan has chosen to focus on "gross national happiness," complete with the 4 pillars, the 9 domains and the 72 indicators of happiness....

The Stiglitz commission report, known formally as "The Measurement of Economic Performance and Social Progress Revisited," said that one of the most glaring problems with using economic growth as a proxy for well-being was the fact that it excluded the damage to society and ultimately to the economy of environmentally non-sustainable activities.

For instance, "developing countries may be encouraged to allow a foreign mining company to develop a mine, even though the country receives low royalties, even though the environment may be degraded, and even though miners may be exposed to health hazards," the report says, "because by doing so GDP will be increased."

They also identify another problem with the reliance on GDP and other "standard" measures: the gap between what the numbers say and what people are actually experiencing. Over the course of recent decades, they note, GDP was rising in most of the world, even as the median disposable income—the income of the "representative individual"—was falling in many countries, meaning that a large share of the gains from economic growth ended up in the hands of the wealthy at the expense of the rest.

The specific recommendations include ensuring that GDP itself is measured the same in every country, as statistical agencies calculate it differently from one country to the next, leading in some cases, to large variations in the way government services

are valued. That has the potential to lead to policy mistakes, they warned.

"What we measure affects what we do; and if our measurements are flawed, decisions may be distorted," they wrote. "Policies should be aimed at increasing societal welfare, not GDP."

Economist Joe Stiglitz

Source: *New York Times,* September 15, 2009.

Table **3**

GDP and the Quality of Life

The table shows GDP per person and three other measures of the quality of life for twelve major countries.

Country	Real GDP per Person (2007)	Life Expectancy	Adult Literacy (% of population)	Internet Usage (% of population)
United States	$45,592	79 years	99%	63%
Germany	34,401	80	99	45
Japan	33,632	83	99	67
Russia	14, 690	66	99	15
Mexico	14,104	76	93	18
Brazil	9,567	72	90	19
China	5,383	73	93	9
Indonesia	3,843	71	92	7
India	2,753	63	66	3
Pakistan	2,496	66	54	7
Nigeria	1,969	48	72	4
Bangladesh	1,241	66	54	0.3

Source: *Human Development Report 2009,* United Nations. Data on real GDP, life expectancy, and literacy are for 2007. Data on Internet use is for 2005.

Table 3 shows twelve of the world's most populous countries ranked in order of GDP per person. The table also shows life expectancy (the expected life span at birth), literacy (the percentage of the adult population who can read), and Internet usage (the percentage of the population that regularly uses the Internet). These data show a clear pattern. In rich countries, such as the United States, Japan, and Germany, people can expect to live to about 80, almost all of the population can read, and a half to two-thirds of the population uses the Internet. In poor countries, such as Nigeria, Bangladesh, and Pakistan, people typically die 10 to 20 years earlier, a substantial share of the population is illiterate, and Internet usage is rare.

Data on other aspects of the quality of life tell a similar story. Countries with low GDP per person tend to have more infants with low birth weight, higher rates of infant mortality, higher rates of maternal mortality, higher rates of child malnutrition, and less common access to safe drinking water. In countries with low GDP per person, fewer school-age children are actually in school, and those who are in school must learn with fewer teachers per student. These countries also tend to have fewer televisions, fewer telephones, fewer paved roads, and fewer households with electricity. International data leave no doubt that a nation's GDP per person is closely associated with its citizens' standard of living. ∎

QUICK QUIZ   *Why should policymakers care about GDP?*

Conclusion

This chapter has discussed how economists measure the total income of a nation. Measurement is, of course, only a starting point. Much of macroeconomics is aimed at revealing the long-run and short-run determinants of a nation's gross domestic product. Why, for example, is GDP higher in the United States and Japan than in India and Nigeria? What can the governments of the poorest countries do to promote more rapid GDP growth? Why does GDP in the United States rise rapidly in some years and fall in others? What can U.S. policymakers do to reduce the severity of these fluctuations in GDP? These are the questions we will take up shortly.

At this point, it is important to acknowledge the significance of just measuring GDP. We all get some sense of how the economy is doing as we go about our lives. But the economists who study changes in the economy and the policymakers who formulate economic policies need more than this vague sense—they need concrete data on which to base their judgments. Quantifying the behavior of the economy with statistics such as GDP is, therefore, the first step to developing a science of macroeconomics.

SUMMARY

- Because every transaction has a buyer and a seller, the total expenditure in the economy must equal the total income in the economy.

- Gross domestic product (GDP) measures an economy's total expenditure on newly produced goods and services and the total income earned from the production of these goods and services. More precisely, GDP is the market value of all final goods and services produced within a country in a given period of time.

- GDP is divided among four components of expenditure: consumption, investment, government purchases, and net exports. Consumption includes spending on goods and services by households, with the exception of purchases of new housing. Investment includes spending on new equipment and structures, including households' purchases of new housing. Government purchases include spending on goods and services by local, state, and federal governments. Net exports equal the value of goods and services produced domestically and sold abroad (exports) minus the value of goods and services produced abroad and sold domestically (imports).

- Nominal GDP uses current prices to value the economy's production of goods and services. Real GDP uses constant base-year prices to value the economy's production of goods and services. The GDP deflator—calculated from the ratio of nominal to real GDP—measures the level of prices in the economy.

- GDP is a good measure of economic well-being because people prefer higher to lower incomes. But it is not a perfect measure of well-being. For example, GDP excludes the value of leisure and the value of a clean environment.

KEY CONCEPTS

microeconomics, *p. 92*
macroeconomics, *p. 92*
gross domestic product
    (GDP), *p. 94*

consumption, *p. 97*
investment, *p. 97*
government purchases, *p. 98*
net exports, *p. 98*

nominal GDP, *p. 100*
real GDP, *p. 101*
GDP deflator, *p. 101*

QUESTIONS FOR REVIEW

1. Explain why an economy's income must equal its expenditure.
2. Which contributes more to GDP—the production of an economy car or the production of a luxury car? Why?
3. A farmer sells wheat to a baker for $2. The baker uses the wheat to make bread, which is sold for $3. What is the total contribution of these transactions to GDP?
4. Many years ago, Peggy paid $500 to put together a record collection. Today, she sold her albums at a garage sale for $100. How does this sale affect current GDP?
5. List the four components of GDP. Give an example of each.

6. Why do economists use real GDP rather than nominal GDP to gauge economic well-being?
7. In the year 2010, the economy produces 100 loaves of bread that sell for $2 each. In the year 2011, the economy produces 200 loaves of bread that sell for $3 each. Calculate nominal GDP, real GDP, and the GDP deflator for each year. (Use 2010 as the base year.) By what percentage does each of these three statistics rise from one year to the next?
8. Why is it desirable for a country to have a large GDP? Give an example of something that would raise GDP and yet be undesirable.

PROBLEMS AND APPLICATIONS

1. What components of GDP (if any) would each of the following transactions affect? Explain.
   a. A family buys a new refrigerator.
   b. Aunt Jane buys a new house.
   c. Ford sells a Mustang from its inventory.
   d. You buy a pizza.
   e. California repaves Highway 101.
   f. Your parents buy a bottle of French wine.
   g. Honda expands its factory in Marysville, Ohio.
2. The government purchases component of GDP does not include spending on transfer payments such as Social Security. Thinking about the definition of GDP, explain why transfer payments are excluded.
3. As the chapter states, GDP does not include the value of used goods that are resold. Why would including such transactions make GDP a less informative measure of economic well-being?
4. Below are some data from the land of milk and honey.

Year	Price of Milk	Quantity of Milk	Price of Honey	Quantity of Honey
2010	$1	100 quarts	$2	50 quarts
2011	$1	200	$2	100
2012	$2	200	$4	100

   a. Compute nominal GDP, real GDP, and the GDP deflator for each year, using 2010 as the base year.
   b. Compute the percentage change in nominal GDP, real GDP, and the GDP deflator in 2011 and 2012 from the preceding year. For each year, identify the variable that does not change. Explain in words why your answer makes sense.
   c. Did economic well-being rise more in 2011 or 2012? Explain.
5. Consider an economy that produces only chocolate bars. In year 1, the quantity produced is 3 bars and the price is $4. In year 2, the quantity produced is 4 bars and the price is $5. In year 3, the quantity produced is 5 bars and the price is $6. Year 1 is the base year.
   a. What is nominal GDP for each of these three years?
   b. What is real GDP for each of these years?
   c. What is the GDP deflator for each of these years?
   d. What is the percentage growth rate of real GDP from year 2 to year 3?
   e. What is the inflation rate as measured by the GDP deflator from year 2 to year 3?
   f. In this one-good economy, how might you have answered parts (d) and (e) without first answering parts (b) and (c)?

6. Consider the following data on U.S. GDP:

Year	Nominal GDP (in billions of dollars)	GDP Deflator (base year 2005)
2009	14,256	109.8
1999	9,353	86.8

a. What was the growth rate of nominal GDP between 1999 and 2009? (Hint: The growth rate of a variable X over a N-year period is calculated as $100 \times [(X_{final}/X_{initial})^{1/N} - 1]$.)
b. What was the growth rate of the GDP deflator between 1999 and 2009?
c. What was real GDP in 1999 measured in 2005 prices?
d. What was real GDP in 2009 measured in 2005 prices?
e. What was the growth rate of real GDP between 1999 and 2009?
f. Was the growth rate of nominal GDP higher or lower than the growth rate of real GDP? Explain.

7. Revised estimates of U.S. GDP are usually released by the government near the end of each month. Find a newspaper article that reports on the most recent release, or read the news release yourself at http://www.bea.gov, the website of the U.S. Bureau of Economic Analysis. Discuss the recent changes in real and nominal GDP and in the components of GDP.

8. A farmer grows wheat, which he sells to a miller for $100. The miller turns the wheat into flour, which he sells to a baker for $150. The baker turns the wheat into bread, which he sells to consumers for $180. Consumers eat the bread.
a. What is GDP in this economy? Explain.
b. *Value added* is defined as the value of a producer's output minus the value of the intermediate goods that the producer buys to make the output. Assuming there are no intermediate goods beyond those described above, calculate the value added of each of the three producers.

c. What is total value added of the three producers in this economy? How does it compare to the economy's GDP? Does this example suggest another way of calculating GDP?

9. Goods and services that are not sold in markets, such as food produced and consumed at home, are generally not included in GDP. Can you think of how this might cause the numbers in the second column of Table 3 to be misleading in a comparison of the economic well-being of the United States and India? Explain.

10. The participation of women in the U.S. labor force has risen dramatically since 1970.
a. How do you think this rise affected GDP?
b. Now imagine a measure of well-being that includes time spent working in the home and taking leisure. How would the change in this measure of well-being compare to the change in GDP?
c. Can you think of other aspects of well-being that are associated with the rise in women's labor-force participation? Would it be practical to construct a measure of well-being that includes these aspects?

11. One day, Barry the Barber, Inc., collects $400 for haircuts. Over this day, his equipment depreciates in value by $50. Of the remaining $350, Barry sends $30 to the government in sales taxes, takes home $220 in wages, and retains $100 in his business to add new equipment in the future. From the $220 that Barry takes home, he pays $70 in income taxes. Based on this information, compute Barry's contribution to the following measures of income.
a. gross domestic product
b. net national product
c. national income
d. personal income
e. disposable personal income

For further information on topics in this chapter, additional problems, applications, examples, online quizzes, and more, please visit our website at www.cengage.com/economics/mankiw.

Measuring the Cost of Living

6

In 1931, as the U.S. economy was suffering through the Great Depression, the New York Yankees paid famed baseball player Babe Ruth a salary of $80,000. At the time, this pay was extraordinary, even among the stars of baseball. According to one story, a reporter asked Ruth whether he thought it was right that he made more than President Herbert Hoover, who had a salary of only $75,000. Ruth replied, "I had a better year."

In 2010, the median salary earned by a player on the New York Yankees was $5.5 million, and shortstop Alex Rodriguez was paid $33 million. At first, this fact might lead you to think that baseball has become vastly more lucrative over the past eight decades. But as everyone knows, the prices of goods and services have also risen. In 1931, a nickel would buy an ice-cream cone, and a quarter would buy a ticket at the local movie theater. Because prices were so much lower in Babe Ruth's day than they are today, it is not clear whether Ruth enjoyed a higher or lower standard of living than today's players.

In the preceding chapter, we looked at how economists use gross domestic product (GDP) to measure the quantity of goods and services that the economy is producing. This chapter examines how economists measure the overall cost of living. To compare Babe Ruth's salary of $80,000 to salaries from today, we need to find some way of turning dollar figures into meaningful measures of purchasing power. That is exactly the job of a statistic called the *consumer price index*. After seeing how the consumer price index is constructed, we discuss how we can use such a price index to compare dollar figures from different points in time.

The consumer price index is used to monitor changes in the cost of living over time. When the consumer price index rises, the typical family has to spend more money to maintain the same standard of living. Economists use the term *inflation* to describe a situation in which the economy's overall price level is rising. The *inflation rate* is the percentage change in the price level from the previous period. The preceding chapter showed how economists can measure inflation using the GDP deflator. The inflation rate you are likely to hear on the nightly news, however, is not calculated from this statistic. Because the consumer price index better reflects the goods and services bought by consumers, it is the more common gauge of inflation.

As we will see in the coming chapters, inflation is a closely watched aspect of macroeconomic performance and is a key variable guiding macroeconomic policy. This chapter provides the background for that analysis by showing how economists measure the inflation rate using the consumer price index and how this statistic can be used to compare dollar figures from different times.

The Consumer Price Index

consumer price index (CPI)

a measure of the overall cost of the goods and services bought by a typical consumer

The **consumer price index (CPI)** is a measure of the overall cost of the goods and services bought by a typical consumer. Each month, the Bureau of Labor Statistics (BLS), which is part of the Department of Labor, computes and reports the consumer price index. In this section, we discuss how the consumer price index is calculated and what problems arise in its measurement. We also consider how this index compares to the GDP deflator, another measure of the overall level of prices, which we examined in the preceding chapter.

How the Consumer Price Index Is Calculated

When the BLS calculates the consumer price index and the inflation rate, it uses data on the prices of thousands of goods and services. To see exactly how these statistics are constructed, let's consider a simple economy in which consumers buy only two goods: hot dogs and hamburgers. Table 1 shows the five steps that the BLS follows.

1. *Fix the basket*. Determine which prices are most important to the typical consumer. If the typical consumer buys more hot dogs than hamburgers, then the price of hot dogs is more important than the price of hamburgers and, therefore, should be given greater weight in measuring the cost of living. The BLS sets these weights by surveying consumers to find the basket of goods and services bought by the typical consumer. In the example in the table, the typical consumer buys a basket of 4 hot dogs and 2 hamburgers.
2. *Find the prices*. Find the prices of each of the goods and services in the basket at each point in time. The table shows the prices of hot dogs and hamburgers for three different years.

Table 1

Calculating the Consumer Price Index and the Inflation Rate: An Example
This table shows how to calculate the consumer price index and the inflation rate for a hypothetical economy in which consumers buy only hot dogs and hamburgers.

Step 1: Survey Consumers to Determine a Fixed Basket of Goods

Basket = 4 hot dogs, 2 hamburgers

Step 2: Find the Price of Each Good in Each Year

Year	Price of Hot Dogs	Price of Hamburgers
2010	$1	$2
2011	2	3
2012	3	4

Step 3: Compute the Cost of the Basket of Goods in Each Year

2010 ($1 per hot dog × 4 hot dogs) + ($2 per hamburger × 2 hamburgers) = $8 per basket
2011 ($2 per hot dog × 4 hot dogs) + ($3 per hamburger × 2 hamburgers) = $14 per basket
2012 ($3 per hot dog × 4 hot dogs) + ($4 per hamburger × 2 hamburgers) = $20 per basket

Step 4: Choose One Year as a Base Year (2010) and Compute the Consumer Price Index in Each Year

2010 ($8 / $8) × 100 = 100
2011 ($14 / $8) × 100 = 175
2012 ($20 / $8) × 100 = 250

Step 5: Use the Consumer Price Index to Compute the Inflation Rate from Previous Year

2011 (175 − 100) / 100 × 100 = 75%
2012 (250 − 175) / 175 × 100 = 43%

3. *Compute the basket's cost.* Use the data on prices to calculate the cost of the basket of goods and services at different times. The table shows this calculation for each of the three years. Notice that only the prices in this calculation change. By keeping the basket of goods the same (4 hot dogs and 2 hamburgers), we are isolating the effects of price changes from the effect of any quantity changes that might be occurring at the same time.

4. *Choose a base year and compute the index.* Designate one year as the base year, the benchmark against which other years are compared. (The choice of base year is arbitrary, as the index is used to measure *changes* in the cost of living.) Once the base year is chosen, the index is calculated as follows:

$$\text{Consumer price index} = \frac{\text{Price of basket of goods and services in current year}}{\text{Price of basket in base year}} \times 100.$$

That is, the price of the basket of goods and services in each year is divided by the price of the basket in the base year, and this ratio is then multiplied by 100. The resulting number is the consumer price index.

In the example in the table, 2010 is the base year. In this year, the basket of hot dogs and hamburgers costs $8. Therefore, the price of the basket in all years is divided by $8 and multiplied by 100. The consumer price index is

inflation rate

the percentage change in the price index from the preceding period

100 in 2010. (The index is always 100 in the base year.) The consumer price index is 175 in 2011. This means that the price of the basket in 2011 is 175 percent of its price in the base year. Put differently, a basket of goods that costs $100 in the base year costs $175 in 2011. Similarly, the consumer price index is 250 in 2012, indicating that the price level in 2012 is 250 percent of the price level in the base year.

5. *Compute the inflation rate.* Use the consumer price index to calculate the **inflation rate,** which is the percentage change in the price index from the preceding period. That is, the inflation rate between two consecutive years is computed as follows:

$$\text{Inflation rate in year 2} = \frac{\text{CPI in year 2} - \text{CPI in year 1}}{\text{CPI in year 1}} \times 100.$$

As shown at the bottom of Table 1, the inflation rate in our example is 75 percent in 2011 and 43 percent in 2012.

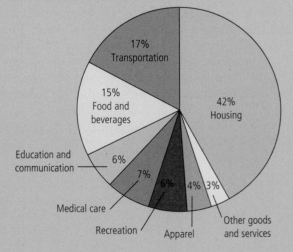

What Is in the CPI's Basket?

When constructing the consumer price index, the Bureau of Labor Statistics tries to include all the goods and services that the typical consumer buys. Moreover, it tries to weight these goods and services according to how much consumers buy of each item.

Figure 1 shows the breakdown of consumer spending into the major categories of goods and services. By far the largest category is housing, which makes up 42 percent of the typical consumer's budget. This category includes the cost of shelter (32 percent), fuel and other utilities (5 percent), and household furnishings and operation (5 percent). The next largest category, at 17 percent, is transportation, which includes spending on cars, gasoline, buses, subways, and so on. The next category, at 15 percent, is food and beverages; this includes food at home (8 percent), food away from home (6 percent), and alcoholic beverages (1 percent). Next are medical care, recreation, and education and communication, each at about 6 percent. This last category includes, for example, college tuition and personal computers. Apparel, which includes clothing, footwear, and jewelry, makes up 4 percent of the typical consumer's budget.

Also included in the figure, at 3 percent of spending, is a category for other goods and services. This is a catchall for consumer purchases (such as cigarettes, haircuts, and funeral expenses) that do not naturally fit into the other categories.

Figure 1

The Typical Basket of Goods and Services
This figure shows how the typical consumer divides spending among various categories of goods and services. The Bureau of Labor Statistics calls each percentage the "relative importance" of the category.

Source: Bureau of Labor Statistics.

Although this example simplifies the real world by including only two goods, it shows how the BLS computes the consumer price index and the inflation rate. The BLS collects and processes data on the prices of thousands of goods and services every month and, by following the five foregoing steps, determines how quickly the cost of living for the typical consumer is rising. When the BLS makes its monthly announcement of the consumer price index, you can usually hear the number on the evening television news or see it in the next day's newspaper.

In addition to the consumer price index for the overall economy, the BLS calculates several other price indexes. It reports the index for specific metropolitan areas within the country (such as Boston, New York, and Los Angeles) and for some narrow categories of goods and services (such as food, clothing, and energy). It also calculates the **producer price index** (PPI), which measures the cost of a basket of goods and services bought by firms rather than consumers. Because firms eventually pass on their costs to consumers in the form of higher consumer prices, changes in the producer price index are often thought to be useful in predicting changes in the consumer price index.

producer price index

a measure of the cost of a basket of goods and services bought by firms

Problems in Measuring the Cost of Living

The goal of the consumer price index is to measure changes in the cost of living. In other words, the consumer price index tries to gauge how much incomes must rise to maintain a constant standard of living. The consumer price index, however, is not a perfect measure of the cost of living. Three problems with the index are widely acknowledged but difficult to solve.

The first problem is called *substitution bias*. When prices change from one year to the next, they do not all change proportionately: Some prices rise more than others. Consumers respond to these differing price changes by buying less of the goods whose prices have risen by relatively large amounts and by buying more of the goods whose prices have risen less or perhaps even have fallen. That is, consumers substitute toward goods that have become relatively less expensive. If a price index is computed assuming a fixed basket of goods, it ignores the possibility of consumer substitution and, therefore, overstates the increase in the cost of living from one year to the next.

Let's consider a simple example. Imagine that in the base year, apples are cheaper than pears, so consumers buy more apples than pears. When the BLS constructs the basket of goods, it will include more apples than pears. Suppose that next year pears are cheaper than apples. Consumers will naturally respond to the price changes by buying more pears and fewer apples. Yet when computing the consumer price index, the BLS uses a fixed basket, which in essence assumes that consumers continue buying the now expensive apples in the same quantities as before. For this reason, the index will measure a much larger increase in the cost of living than consumers actually experience.

The second problem with the consumer price index is the *introduction of new goods*. When a new good is introduced, consumers have more variety from which to choose, and this in turn reduces the cost of maintaining the same level of economic well-being. To see why, consider a hypothetical situation: Suppose you could choose between a $100 gift certificate at a large store that offered a wide array of goods and a $100 gift certificate at a small store with the same prices but a more limited selection. Which would you prefer? Most people would pick the store with greater variety. In essence, the increased set of possible choices makes each dollar more valuable. The same is true with the evolution of the economy over time: As new goods are introduced, consumers have more choices, and each dollar is worth more. Yet because the consumer price index is based on a fixed basket of goods and services, it does not reflect the increase in the value of the dollar that arises from the introduction of new goods.

Again, let's consider an example. When video cassette recorders (VCRs) were introduced in the late 1970s, consumers were able to watch their favorite movies at home. Although not a perfect substitute for a first-run movie on a large screen, an old movie in the comfort of your family room was a new option that increased consumers' set of opportunities. For any given number of dollars, the introduction of the VCR made people better off; conversely, achieving the same level of economic well-being required a smaller number of dollars. A perfect cost-of-living

in the news

Shopping for the CPI

Behind every macroeconomic statistic are thousands of individual pieces of data on the economy. This classic article follows one of the economists who collect these data.

In the Field with the Price Indexers

BY ROBERT D. HERSHEY, JR.

WILMINGTON, Del.—Her thick blue binder in hand, Diane Balaguer strides purposefully through the department store in the Concord Mall north of town. She checks the price of a women's pullover (short sleeve, solid color, no design), eyes a Hastings & Smith polo shirt, notes the seasonal absence of men's turtlenecks and then confronts the day's first challenge to statistical perfection.

Ms. Balaguer shakes her head slightly as she regards a rack of Towne raincoats, a style in the London Fog line (tagged at the same $99.90 as the month before). She considers Towne to be of slightly, almost imperceptibly, lesser quality than the Severn line (costing about twice as much) that they

replaced this year. It's a matter of things like stitching and buttons.

Earlier this spring she had informed specialists in Washington of this not uncommon situation but they overruled her suggestion that she substitute another product. Thus do tiny imprecisions creep unavoidably into the Consumer Price Index, the most widely used inflation measure, one directly affecting the incomes of more than 70 million Americans, Federal income-tax brackets and the cost of school lunches.

"It's not a black-and-white sort of determination," Ms. Balaguer said. "Even though we ask very specific questions to try to get very specific answers, it takes a great deal of judgment."

When the price index is announced monthly by the Labor Department, the figure has the Olympian air common to Government statistics. But a day spent with Ms. Balaguer gives a vivid illustration of the

messiness inherent in the immense task of monitoring changes in a $7 trillion economy. In any given month, she and several hundred counterparts around the country check the cost of 90,000 items—ranging from catfish fillets to time spent in a hospital recovery room. . . .

A trained economist who both supervises data collection and often goes on the road herself, Ms. Balaguer expresses no opinion about the debate over the price index.

The system takes account of the possibility of human error or subversion—cross-checks of other data collectors' work is standard procedure. "We're taking our best shot," said Patrick C. Jackman, the index's chief day-to-day overseer in Washington. "I don't think we're picking up many bad quotes."

Drawing on an annual Government survey of what people are buying, and at what index would have reflected the introduction of the VCR with a decrease in the cost of living. The consumer price index, however, did not decrease in response to the introduction of the VCR. Eventually, the BLS did revise the basket of goods to include VCRs, and subsequently, the index reflected changes in VCR prices. But the reduction in the cost of living associated with the initial introduction of the VCR never showed up in the index.

The third problem with the consumer price index is *unmeasured quality change*. If the quality of a good deteriorates from one year to the next while its price remains the same, the value of a dollar falls, because you are getting a lesser good for the same amount of money. Similarly, if the quality rises from one year to the next, the value of a dollar rises. The BLS does its best to account for quality change. When the quality of a good in the basket changes—for example, when a car model has more horsepower or gets better gas mileage from one year to the

kinds of outlets, headquarters tells the field staff what items to price. The findings are shipped by courier to Washington, where they are run through the mill to be sure they make sense. Because the bureau promises its respondents confidentiality, it insists that none of the 10 outlets Ms. Balaguer visits be identified by name. But she did disclose not only how prices in May compared with April's, but also explained in detail how to handle such vexations as discontinued products, clearance sales and what to do in those rare cases when she suspects somebody of giving wrong prices.

One of the day's most complicated readings came at a garden shop just across the state line in Pennsylvania where, after finding 3 1/2-inch barrel cactus and 16-inch Boston ferns unchanged in price (at $4 and $25, respectively) Ms. Balaguer found that the requisite flower seeds, black-eyed susans, were no longer being stocked.

After being told this was not just a temporary situation, Ms. Balaguer's solution was to find a substitute seed in the same product line to enter into the system on the spot. With the aid of a table in her binder that produces random numbers and with some rapid-fire pointing at rows of seed packets, the answer emerged in less than a

minute. From now on, she declared, "we'll use pampas grass" in the index.

Not every hurdle was so quickly overcome. She spent a sizable chunk of her 20-minute session with a hospital administrator to figure out how to adjust for a confusing reconfiguration of recovery-room charges that effectively halved the price.

"You have to be able to ask questions, to be a sort of Sherlock Holmes," Ms. Balaguer said.

Ms. Balaguer's stop at a beer distributor to check one-liter bottles of Canada Dry seltzer caused some embarrassment when she questioned the assertion of Richard Gropper, a proprietor, that the price was 84 cents. After she observed that this would mean a 9-cent

rise from April he realized his mistake, adding that he was glad to help with the index since he periodically used it to adjust the rent of tenants in the doughnut shop next door.

The hardest items to price, Ms. Balaguer said, are electricity and natural gas, information the bureau gets directly from utilities in statistically awkward form. Children's meals and meals in Chinese restaurants also pose problems, even with menus to work from, because they tend to include beverages for which separate prices are required, Ms. Balaguer said.

Housing, which accounts for 41 percent of the urban consumer index, is surveyed by periodically questioning homeowners and renters. For both groups, the question is the same: What is the monthly rental value of the property? When necessary, such as when a house is vacant, she and her staff ask real estate brokers and neighbors to get housing data, Ms. Balaguer said.

Some surveyers might be bothered by one potentially onerous job restriction. But not Ms. Balaguer.

"We never carry purses because we're not allowed to shop while we work," she said. "Actually," she added, noting that she had originally worked in retailing, "I hate to shop."

Source: *New York Times*, June 20, 1995.

© ALEXANDER WALTER/STONE/GETTY IMAGES

next—the Bureau adjusts the price of the good to account for the quality change. It is, in essence, trying to compute the price of a basket of goods of constant quality. Despite these efforts, changes in quality remain a problem because quality is so hard to measure.

There is still much debate among economists about how severe these measurement problems are and what should be done about them. Several studies written during the 1990s concluded that the consumer price index overstated inflation by about 1 percentage point per year. In response to this criticism, the BLS adopted several technical changes to improve the CPI, and many economists believe the bias is now only about half as large as it once was. The issue is important because many government programs use the consumer price index to adjust for changes in the overall level of prices. Recipients of Social Security, for instance, get annual increases in benefits that are tied to the consumer price index. Some economists have suggested modifying these programs to correct for the measurement problems by, for instance, reducing the magnitude of the automatic benefit increases.

The GDP Deflator versus the Consumer Price Index

In the preceding chapter, we examined another measure of the overall level of prices in the economy—the GDP deflator. The GDP deflator is the ratio of nominal GDP to real GDP. Because nominal GDP is current output valued at current prices and real GDP is current output valued at base-year prices, the GDP deflator reflects the current level of prices relative to the level of prices in the base year.

Economists and policymakers monitor both the GDP deflator and the consumer price index to gauge how quickly prices are rising. Usually, these two statistics tell a similar story. Yet two important differences can cause them to diverge.

The first difference is that the GDP deflator reflects the prices of all goods and services *produced domestically,* whereas the consumer price index reflects the prices of all goods and services *bought by consumers.* For example, suppose that the price of an airplane produced by Boeing and sold to the Air Force rises. Even though the plane is part of GDP, it is not part of the basket of goods and services bought by a typical consumer. Thus, the price increase shows up in the GDP deflator but not in the consumer price index.

As another example, suppose that Volvo raises the price of its cars. Because Volvos are made in Sweden, the car is not part of U.S. GDP. But U.S. consumers buy Volvos, so the car is part of the typical consumer's basket of goods. Hence, a price increase in an imported consumption good, such as a Volvo, shows up in the consumer price index but not in the GDP deflator.

This first difference between the consumer price index and the GDP deflator is particularly important when the price of oil changes. Although the United States does produce some oil, much of the oil we use is imported. As a result, oil and oil products such as gasoline and heating oil are a much larger share of consumer spending than of GDP. When the price of oil rises, the consumer price index rises by much more than does the GDP deflator.

The second and subtler difference between the GDP deflator and the consumer price index concerns how various prices are weighted to yield a single number for the overall level of prices. The consumer price index compares the price of a *fixed* basket of goods and services to the price of the basket in the base year. Only occasionally does the Bureau of Labor Statistics change the basket of goods. By contrast, the GDP deflator compares the price of *currently produced* goods and services to the price of the same goods and services in the base year. Thus, the

THE WALL STREET JOURNAL

|AUDIO - VIDEO|

"*The price may seem a little high, but you have to remember that's in today's dollars.*"

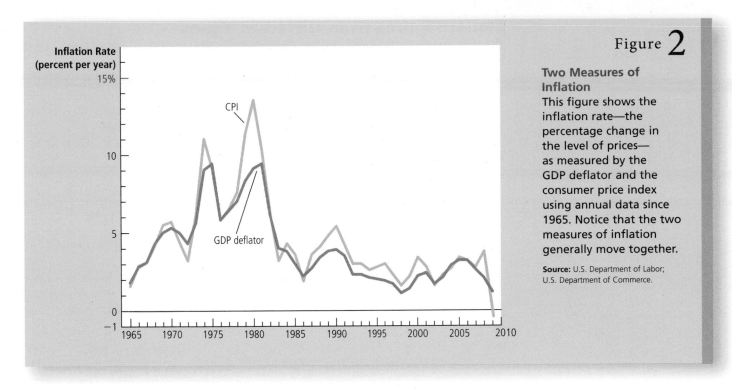

Figure **2**

Two Measures of Inflation
This figure shows the inflation rate—the percentage change in the level of prices— as measured by the GDP deflator and the consumer price index using annual data since 1965. Notice that the two measures of inflation generally move together.

Source: U.S. Department of Labor; U.S. Department of Commerce.

group of goods and services used to compute the GDP deflator changes automatically over time. This difference is not important when all prices are changing proportionately. But if the prices of different goods and services are changing by varying amounts, the way we weight the various prices matters for the overall inflation rate.

Figure 2 shows the inflation rate as measured by both the GDP deflator and the consumer price index for each year since 1965. You can see that sometimes the two measures diverge. When they do diverge, it is possible to go behind these numbers and explain the divergence with the two differences we have discussed. For example, in 1979 and 1980, CPI inflation spiked up more than the GDP deflator largely because oil prices more than doubled during these two years. Yet divergence between these two measures is the exception rather than the rule. In the 1970s, both the GDP deflator and the consumer price index show high rates of inflation. In the late 1980s, 1990s, and the first decade of the 2000s, both measures show low rates of inflation.

QUICK QUIZ   *Explain briefly what the consumer price index measures and how it is constructed. • Identify one reason why the CPI is an imperfect measure of the cost of living.*

Correcting Economic Variables for the Effects of Inflation

The purpose of measuring the overall level of prices in the economy is to allow us to compare dollar figures from different times. Now that we know how price indexes are calculated, let's see how we might use such an index to compare a dollar figure from the past to a dollar figure in the present.

Dollar Figures from Different Times

We first return to the issue of Babe Ruth's salary. Was his salary of $80,000 in 1931 high or low compared to the salaries of today's players?

To answer this question, we need to know the level of prices in 1931 and the level of prices today. Part of the increase in baseball salaries compensates players for higher prices today. To compare Ruth's salary to those of today's players, we need to inflate Ruth's salary to turn 1931 dollars into today's dollars.

The formula for turning dollar figures from year T into today's dollars is the following:

$$\text{Amount in today's dollars} = \text{Amount in year } T \text{ dollars} \times \frac{\text{Price level today}}{\text{Price level in year } T}.$$

A price index such as the consumer price index measures the price level and thus determines the size of the inflation correction.

Let's apply this formula to Ruth's salary. Government statistics show a consumer price index of 15.2 for 1931 and 214.5 for 2009. Thus, the overall level of prices has risen by a factor of 14.1 (which equals 214.5/15.2). We can use these numbers to measure Ruth's salary in 2009 dollars, as follows:

$$\text{Salary in 2009 dollars} = \text{Salary in 1931 dollars} \times \frac{\text{Price level in 2009}}{\text{Price level in 1931}}$$

$$= \$80,000 \times \frac{214.5}{15.2}$$

$$= \$1,128,947$$

We find that Babe Ruth's 1931 salary is equivalent to a salary today of over $1 million. That is a good income, but it is less than a quarter of the median Yankee salary today and only 3 percent of what the Yankees pay A-Rod. Various forces, including overall economic growth and the increasing income shares earned by superstars, have substantially raised the living standards of the best athletes.

Let's also examine President Hoover's 1931 salary of $75,000. To translate that figure into 2009 dollars, we again multiply the ratio of the price levels in the two years. We find that Hoover's salary is equivalent to $75,000 × (214.5/15.2), or $1,058,388, in 2009 dollars. This is well above President Barack Obama's salary of $400,000. It seems that President Hoover did have a pretty good year after all.

Indexation

As we have just seen, price indexes are used to correct for the effects of inflation when comparing dollar figures from different times. This type of correction shows up in many places in the economy. When some dollar amount is automatically corrected for changes in the price level by law or contract, the amount is said to be **indexed** for inflation.

indexation
the automatic correction by law or contract of a dollar amount for the effects of inflation

For example, many long-term contracts between firms and unions include partial or complete indexation of the wage to the consumer price index. Such a provision is called a *cost-of-living allowance*, or COLA. A COLA automatically raises the wage when the consumer price index rises.

Indexation is also a feature of many laws. Social Security benefits, for example, are adjusted every year to compensate the elderly for increases in prices. The brackets

FYI

> ## Mr. Index Goes to Hollywood

What is the most popular movie of all time? The answer might surprise you.

Movie popularity is usually gauged by box office receipts. By that measure, *Avatar* is the number 1 movie of all time with domestic receipts of $749 million, followed by *Titanic* ($601 million) and *The Dark Knight* ($533 million). But this ranking ignores an obvious but important fact: Prices, including those of movie tickets, have been rising over time. Inflation gives an advantage to newer films.

When we correct box office receipts for the effects of inflation, the story is very

"I see you don't like the effects of inflation."

different. The number 1 movie is now *Gone with the Wind* ($1,606 million), followed by *Star Wars* ($1,416 million) and *The Sound*

of *Music* ($1,132 million). *Avatar* falls to number 14.

Gone with the Wind was released in 1939, before everyone had televisions in their homes. In the 1930s, about 90 million Americans went to the cinema each week, compared to about 25 million today. But the movies from that era don't show up in conventional popularity rankings because ticket prices were only a quarter. And indeed, in the ranking based on nominal box office receipts, *Gone with the Wind* does not make the top 50 films. Scarlett and Rhett fare a lot better once we correct for the effects of inflation.

of the federal income tax—the income levels at which the tax rates change—are also indexed for inflation. There are, however, many ways in which the tax system is not indexed for inflation, even when perhaps it should be. We discuss these issues more fully when we discuss the costs of inflation later in this book.

Real and Nominal Interest Rates

Correcting economic variables for the effects of inflation is particularly important, and somewhat tricky, when we look at data on interest rates. The very concept of an interest rate necessarily involves comparing amounts of money at different points in time. When you deposit your savings in a bank account, you give the bank some money now, and the bank returns your deposit with interest in the future. Similarly, when you borrow from a bank, you get some money now, but you will have to repay the loan with interest in the future. In both cases, to fully understand the deal between you and the bank, it is crucial to acknowledge that future dollars could have a different value than today's dollars. That is, you have to correct for the effects of inflation.

Let's consider an example. Suppose Sally Saver deposits $1,000 in a bank account that pays an annual interest rate of 10 percent. A year later, after Sally has accumulated $100 in interest, she withdraws her $1,100. Is Sally $100 richer than she was when she made the deposit a year earlier?

The answer depends on what we mean by "richer." Sally does have $100 more than she had before. In other words, the number of dollars in her possession has risen by 10 percent. But Sally does not care about the amount of money itself: She cares about what she can buy with it. If prices have risen while her money was in the bank, each dollar now buys less than it did a year ago. In this case, her purchasing power—the amount of goods and services she can buy—has not risen by 10 percent.

To keep things simple, let's suppose that Sally is a movie fan and buys only DVDs. When Sally made her deposit, a DVD at her local movie store cost $10. Her deposit of $1,000 was equivalent to 100 DVDs. A year later, after getting her 10 percent interest, she has $1,100. How many DVDs can she buy now? It depends on what has happened to the price of a DVD. Here are some examples:

- Zero inflation: If the price of a DVD remains at $10, the amount she can buy has risen from 100 to 110 DVDs. The 10 percent increase in the number of dollars means a 10 percent increase in her purchasing power.
- Six percent inflation: If the price of a DVD rises from $10 to $10.60, then the number of DVDs she can buy has risen from 100 to approximately 104. Her purchasing power has increased by about 4 percent.
- Ten percent inflation: If the price of a DVD rises from $10 to $11, she can still buy only 100 DVDs. Even though Sally's dollar wealth has risen, her purchasing power is the same as it was a year earlier.
- Twelve percent inflation: If the price of a DVD increases from $10 to $11.20, the number of DVDs she can buy has fallen from 100 to approximately 98. Even with her greater number of dollars, her purchasing power has decreased by about 2 percent.

And if Sally were living in an economy with deflation—falling prices—another possibility could arise:

- Two percent deflation: If the price of a DVD falls from $10 to $9.80, then the number of DVDs she can buy rises from 100 to approximately 112. Her purchasing power increases by about 12 percent.

These examples show that the higher the rate of inflation, the smaller the increase in Sally's purchasing power. If the rate of inflation exceeds the rate of interest, her purchasing power actually falls. And if there is deflation (that is, a negative rate of inflation), her purchasing power rises by more than the rate of interest.

To understand how much a person earns in a savings account, we need to consider both the interest rate and the change in the prices. The interest rate that measures the change in dollar amounts is called the **nominal interest rate,** and the interest rate corrected for inflation is called the **real interest rate.** The nominal interest rate, the real interest rate, and inflation are related approximately as follows:

$$\text{Real interest rate} = \text{Nominal interest rate} - \text{Inflation rate}.$$

The real interest rate is the difference between the nominal interest rate and the rate of inflation. The nominal interest rate tells you how fast the number of dollars in your bank account rises over time, while the real interest rate tells you how fast the purchasing power of your bank account rises over time.

nominal interest rate

the interest rate as usually reported without a correction for the effects of inflation

real interest rate

the interest rate corrected for the effects of inflation

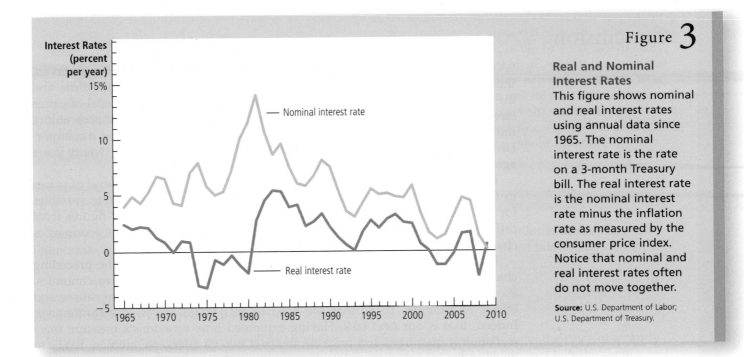

Figure **3**

**Real and Nominal
Interest Rates**
This figure shows nominal
and real interest rates
using annual data since
1965. The nominal
interest rate is the rate
on a 3-month Treasury
bill. The real interest rate
is the nominal interest
rate minus the inflation
rate as measured by the
consumer price index.
Notice that nominal and
real interest rates often
do not move together.

Source: U.S. Department of Labor;
U.S. Department of Treasury.

Interest Rates in the U.S. Economy

Figure 3 shows real and nominal interest rates in the U.S. economy since 1965. The nominal interest rate in this figure is the rate on 3-month Treasury bills (although data on other interest rates would be similar). The real interest rate is computed by subtracting the rate of inflation from this nominal interest rate. Here the inflation rate is measured as the percentage change in the consumer price index.

One feature of this figure is that the nominal interest rate almost always exceeds the real interest rate. This reflects the fact that the U.S. economy has experienced rising consumer prices in almost every year during this period. By contrast, if you look at data for the U.S. economy during the late 19th century or for the Japanese economy in some recent years, you will find periods of deflation. During deflation, the real interest rate exceeds the nominal interest rate.

The figure also shows that because inflation is variable, real and nominal interest rates do not always move together. For example, in the late 1970s, nominal interest rates were high. But because inflation was very high, real interest rates were low. Indeed, during much of the 1970s, real interest rates were negative, for inflation eroded people's savings more quickly than nominal interest payments increased them. By contrast, in the late 1990s, nominal interest rates were lower than they had been two decades earlier. But because inflation was much lower, real interest rates were higher. In the coming chapters, we will examine the economic forces that determine both real and nominal interest rates. ■

QUICK QUIZ *Henry Ford paid his workers $5 a day in 1914. If the consumer price index was 10 in 1914 and 218 in 2010, how much is the Ford paycheck worth in 2010 dollars?*

Production and Growth

7

When you travel around the world, you see tremendous variation in the standard of living. The average income in a rich country, such as the United States, Japan, or Germany, is more than ten times the average income in a poor country, such as India, Indonesia, or Nigeria. These large differences in income are reflected in large differences in the quality of life. People in richer countries have better nutrition, safer housing, better healthcare, and longer life expectancy as well as more automobiles, more telephones, and more televisions.

Even within a country, there are large changes in the standard of living over time. In the United States over the past century, average income as measured by real GDP per person has grown by about 2 percent per year. Although 2 percent might seem small, this rate of growth implies that average income doubles every 35 years. Because of this growth, average income today is about eight times the average income a century ago. As a result, the typical American enjoys much greater economic prosperity than did his or her parents, grandparents, and great-grandparents.

Growth rates vary substantially from country to country. In recent history, some East Asian countries, such as Singapore, South Korea, and Taiwan, have experienced economic growth of about 7 percent per year; at this rate, average income doubles every 10 years. Over the past two decades, China has enjoyed an even higher rate of growth—about 12 percent per year, according to some estimates. A country experiencing such rapid growth can, in one generation, go from being among the poorest in the world to being among the richest. By contrast, in some African countries, such as Chad, Gabon, and Senegal, average income has been stagnant for many years.

What explains these diverse experiences? How can rich countries maintain their high standard of living? What policies should poor countries pursue to promote more rapid growth and join the developed world? These are among the most important questions in macroeconomics. As the Nobel-Prize-winning economist Robert Lucas put it, "The consequences for human welfare in questions like these are simply staggering: Once one starts to think about them, it is hard to think about anything else."

In the previous two chapters, we discussed how economists measure macroeconomic quantities and prices. We can now begin to study the forces that determine these variables. As we have seen, an economy's gross domestic product (GDP) measures both the total income earned in the economy and the total expenditure on the economy's output of goods and services. The level of real GDP is a good gauge of economic prosperity, and the growth of real GDP is a good gauge of economic progress. In this chapter we focus on the long-run determinants of the level and growth of real GDP. Later in this book, we study the short-run fluctuations of real GDP around its long-run trend.

We proceed here in three steps. First, we examine international data on real GDP per person. These data will give you some sense of how much the level and growth of living standards vary around the world. Second, we examine the role of *productivity*—the amount of goods and services produced for each hour of a worker's time. In particular, we see that a nation's standard of living is determined by the productivity of its workers, and we consider the factors that determine a nation's productivity. Third, we consider the link between productivity and the economic policies that a nation pursues.

Economic Growth around the World

As a starting point for our study of long-run growth, let's look at the experiences of some of the world's economies. Table 1 shows data on real GDP per person for thirteen countries. For each country, the data cover more than a century of history. The first and second columns of the table present the countries and time periods. (The time periods differ somewhat from country to country because of differences in data availability.) The third and fourth columns show estimates of real GDP per person about a century ago and for a recent year.

The data on real GDP per person show that living standards vary widely from country to country. Income per person in the United States, for instance, is about eight times that in China and about sixteen times that in India. The poorest countries have average levels of income not seen in the developed world for many decades. The typical citizen of India in 2008 had less real income than the typical resident of England in 1870. The typical person in Bangladesh in 2008 had about two-thirds the real income of a typical American a century ago.

The last column of the table shows each country's growth rate. The growth rate measures how rapidly real GDP per person grew in the typical year. In the United States, for example, where real GDP per person was $4,007 in 1870 and $46,970 in

Table 1

The Variety of Growth Experiences

Country	Period	Real GDP per Person at Beginning of Period*	Real GDP per Person at End of Period*	Growth Rate (per year)
Japan	1890–2008	$1,504	$35,220	2.71%
Brazil	1900–2008	779	10,070	2.40
Mexico	1900–2008	1,159	14,270	2.35
Germany	1870–2008	2,184	35,940	2.05
Canada	1870–2008	2,375	36,220	1.99
China	1900–2008	716	6,020	1.99
United States	1870–2008	4,007	46,970	1.80
Argentina	1900–2008	2,293	14,020	1.69
United Kingdom	1870–2008	4,808	36,130	1.47
India	1900–2008	675	2,960	1.38
Indonesia	1900–2008	891	3,830	1.36
Pakistan	1900–2008	737	2,700	1.21
Bangladesh	1900–2008	623	1,440	0.78

*Real GDP is measured in 2008 dollars.
Source: Robert J. Barro and Xavier Sala-i-Martin, *Economic Growth* (New York: McGraw-Hill, 1995), tables 10.2 and 10.3; *World Development Report 2010*, Table 1; and author's calculations.

2008, the growth rate was 1.80 percent per year. This means that if real GDP per person, beginning at $4,007, were to increase by 1.80 percent for each of 138 years, it would end up at $46,970. Of course, real GDP per person did not actually rise exactly 1.80 percent every year: Some years it rose by more, other years it rose by less, and in still other years it fell. The growth rate of 1.80 percent per year ignores short-run fluctuations around the long-run trend and represents an average rate of growth for real GDP per person over many years.

The countries in Table 1 are ordered by their growth rate from the most to the least rapid. Japan tops the list, with a growth rate of 2.71 percent per year. A hundred years ago, Japan was not a rich country. Japan's average income was only somewhat higher than Mexico's, and it was well behind Argentina's. The standard of living in Japan in 1890 was less than half of that in India today. But because of its spectacular growth, Japan is now an economic superpower, with average income more than twice that of Mexico and Argentina and similar to Germany, Canada, and the United Kingdom. At the bottom of the list of countries are Pakistan and Bangladesh, which have experienced growth of less than 1.3 percent per year over the past century. As a result, the typical resident of these countries continues to live in abject poverty.

Because of differences in growth rates, the ranking of countries by income changes substantially over time. As we have seen, Japan is a country that has risen relative to others. One country that has fallen behind is the United Kingdom. In 1870, the United Kingdom was the richest country in the world, with average income about 20 percent higher than that of the United States and more than twice Canada's. Today, average income in the United Kingdom is 20 percent below that of the United States and similar to Canada's.

These data show that the world's richest countries have no guarantee they will stay the richest and that the world's poorest countries are not doomed forever to remain in poverty. But what explains these changes over time? Why do some countries zoom ahead while others lag behind? These are precisely the questions that we take up next.

FYI

> ## A Picture Is Worth a Thousand Statistics

George Bernard Shaw once said, "The sign of a truly educated man is to be deeply moved by statistics." Most of us, however, have trouble being deeply moved by data on GDP—until we see what these statistics represent.

The three photos on these pages show a typical family from each of three countries—the United Kingdom, Mexico, and Mali. Each family was photographed outside their home, together with all their material possessions.

These nations have very different standards of living, as judged by these photos, GDP, or other statistics.

- The United Kingdom is an advanced economy. In 2008, its GDP per person was $36,130. A negligible share of the population lives in extreme poverty, defined here as less than $2 a day. Educational attainment is high: Among children of high school age, 91 percent are in school. Residents of the United Kingdom can expect to enjoy a long life: The probability of a person surviving to age 65 is 85 percent for men and 91 percent for women.

- Mexico is a middle-income country. In 2008, its GDP per person was $14,270. About 5 percent of the population lives on less than $2 a day. Among children of high school age, 71 percent are in school. The probability of a person surviving to age 65 is 78 percent for men and 86 percent for women.

- Mali is a poor country. In 2008, its GDP per person was only $1,090. Extreme poverty is the norm: More than three-quarters of the population lives on less than $2 per day. Educational attainment in Mali is low: Among children of high school age, only 29 percent are in school. And life is often cut short: The probability of a person surviving to age 65 is only 38 percent for men and 42 percent for women.

Economists who study economic growth try to understand what causes such large differences in the standard of living.

A Typical Family in the United Kingdom

A Typical Family in Mexico

A Typical Family in Mali

FYI

> ### Are You Richer Than the Richest American?

American Heritage magazine once published a list of the richest Americans of all time. The number 1 spot went to John D. Rockefeller, the oil entrepreneur who lived from 1839 to 1937. According to the magazine's calculations, his wealth would today be the equivalent of about $200 billion, almost four times that of Bill Gates, the software entrepreneur who is today's richest American.

Despite his great wealth, Rockefeller did not enjoy many of the conveniences that we now take for granted. He couldn't watch television, play video games, surf the Internet, or send e-mail. During the heat of summer, he couldn't cool his home with air conditioning. For much of his life, he couldn't travel by car or plane, and he couldn't use a telephone to call friends or family. If he became ill, he couldn't take advantage of many medicines, such as antibiotics, that doctors today routinely use to prolong and enhance life.

John D. Rockefeller

Now consider: How much money would someone have to pay you to give up for the rest of your life all the modern conveniences that Rockefeller lived without? Would you do it for $200 billion? Perhaps not. And if you wouldn't, is it fair to say that you are better off than John D. Rockefeller, allegedly the richest American ever?

The preceding chapter discussed how standard price indexes, which are used to compare sums of money from different points in time, fail to fully reflect the introduction of new goods in the economy. As a result, the rate of inflation is overestimated. The flip side of this observation is that the rate of real economic growth is underestimated. Pondering Rockefeller's life shows how significant this problem might be. Because of tremendous technological advances, the average American today is arguably "richer" than the richest American a century ago, even if that fact is lost in standard economic statistics.

QUICK QUIZ   *What is the approximate growth rate of real GDP per person in the United States? Name a country that has had faster growth and a country that has had slower growth.*

Productivity: Its Role and Determinants

Explaining the large variation in living standards around the world is, in one sense, very easy. As we will see, the explanation can be summarized in a single word—*productivity*. But in another sense, the international variation is deeply puzzling. To explain why incomes are so much higher in some countries than in others, we must look at the many factors that determine a nation's productivity.

Why Productivity Is So Important

Let's begin our study of productivity and economic growth by developing a simple model based loosely on Daniel Defoe's famous novel *Robinson Crusoe* about a sailor stranded on a desert island. Because Crusoe lives alone, he catches his own fish, grows his own vegetables, and makes his own clothes. We can think of Crusoe's activities—his production and consumption of fish, vegetables, and clothing—as a simple economy. By examining Crusoe's economy, we can learn some lessons that also apply to more complex and realistic economies.

What determines Crusoe's standard of living? In a word, **productivity,** the quantity of goods and services produced from each unit of labor input. If Crusoe is good at catching fish, growing vegetables, and making clothes, he lives well. If he is bad at doing these things, he lives poorly. Because Crusoe gets to consume only what he produces, his living standard is tied to his productivity.

In the case of Crusoe's economy, it is easy to see that productivity is the key determinant of living standards and that growth in productivity is the key determinant of growth in living standards. The more fish Crusoe can catch per hour, the more he eats at dinner. If Crusoe finds a better place to catch fish, his productivity rises. This increase in productivity makes Crusoe better off: He can eat the extra fish, or he can spend less time fishing and devote more time to making other goods he enjoys.

Productivity's key role in determining living standards is as true for nations as it is for stranded sailors. Recall that an economy's gross domestic product (GDP) measures two things at once: the total income earned by everyone in the economy and the total expenditure on the economy's output of goods and services. GDP can measure these two things simultaneously because, for the economy as a whole, they must be equal. Put simply, an economy's income is the economy's output.

Like Crusoe, a nation can enjoy a high standard of living only if it can produce a large quantity of goods and services. Americans live better than Nigerians because American workers are more productive than Nigerian workers. The Japanese have enjoyed more rapid growth in living standards than Argentineans because Japanese workers have experienced more rapid growth in productivity. Indeed, one of the *Ten Principles of Economics* in Chapter 1 is that a country's standard of living depends on its ability to produce goods and services.

Hence, to understand the large differences in living standards we observe across countries or over time, we must focus on the production of goods and services. But seeing the link between living standards and productivity is only the first step. It leads naturally to the next question: Why are some economies so much better at producing goods and services than others?

How Productivity Is Determined

Although productivity is uniquely important in determining Robinson Crusoe's standard of living, many factors determine Crusoe's productivity. Crusoe will be better at catching fish, for instance, if he has more fishing poles, if he has been trained in the best fishing techniques, if his island has a plentiful fish supply, or if he invents a better fishing lure. Each of these determinants of Crusoe's productivity—which we can call *physical capital, human capital, natural resources,* and *technological knowledge*—has a counterpart in more complex and realistic economies. Let's consider each factor in turn.

Physical Capital per Worker Workers are more productive if they have tools with which to work. The stock of equipment and structures used to produce goods and services is called **physical capital,** or just *capital.* For example, when woodworkers make furniture, they use saws, lathes, and drill presses. More tools allow the woodworkers to produce their output more quickly and more accurately: A worker with only basic hand tools can make less furniture each week than a worker with sophisticated and specialized woodworking equipment.

As you may recall, the inputs used to produce goods and services—labor, capital, and so on—are called the *factors of production.* An important feature of capital is that it is a *produced* factor of production. That is, capital is an input into the production process that in the past was an output from the production process. The

productivity
the quantity of goods and services produced from each unit of labor input

physical capital
the stock of equipment and structures that are used to produce goods and services

woodworker uses a lathe to make the leg of a table. Earlier, the lathe itself was the output of a firm that manufactures lathes. The lathe manufacturer in turn used other equipment to make its product. Thus, capital is a factor of production used to produce all kinds of goods and services, including more capital.

Human Capital per Worker   A second determinant of productivity is human capital. **Human capital** is the economist's term for the knowledge and skills that workers acquire through education, training, and experience. Human capital includes the skills accumulated in early childhood programs, grade school, high school, college, and on-the-job training for adults in the labor force.

Education, training, and experience are less tangible than lathes, bulldozers, and buildings, but human capital is like physical capital in many ways. Like physical capital, human capital raises a nation's ability to produce goods and services. Also like physical capital, human capital is a produced factor of production. Producing human capital requires inputs in the form of teachers, libraries, and student time. Indeed, students can be viewed as "workers" who have the important job of producing the human capital that will be used in future production.

Natural Resources per Worker   A third determinant of productivity is **natural resources.** Natural resources are inputs into production that are provided by nature, such as land, rivers, and mineral deposits. Natural resources take two forms: renewable and nonrenewable. A forest is an example of a renewable resource. When one tree is cut down, a seedling can be planted in its place to be harvested in the future. Oil is an example of a nonrenewable resource. Because oil is produced by nature over many millions of years, there is only a limited supply. Once the supply of oil is depleted, it is impossible to create more.

Differences in natural resources are responsible for some of the differences in standards of living around the world. The historical success of the United States was driven in part by the large supply of land well suited for agriculture. Today, some countries in the Middle East, such as Kuwait and Saudi Arabia, are rich simply because they happen to be on top of some of the largest pools of oil in the world.

Although natural resources can be important, they are not necessary for an economy to be highly productive in producing goods and services. Japan, for instance, is one of the richest countries in the world, despite having few natural resources. International trade makes Japan's success possible. Japan imports many of the natural resources it needs, such as oil, and exports its manufactured goods to economies rich in natural resources.

Technological Knowledge   A fourth determinant of productivity is **technological knowledge**—the understanding of the best ways to produce goods and services. A hundred years ago, most Americans worked on farms because farm technology required a high input of labor to feed the entire population. Today, thanks to advances in farming technology, a small fraction of the population can produce enough food to feed the entire country. This technological change made labor available to produce other goods and services.

Technological knowledge takes many forms. Some technology is common knowledge—after one person uses it, everyone becomes aware of it. For example, once Henry Ford successfully introduced production in assembly lines, other carmakers quickly followed suit. Other technology is proprietary—it is known only by the company that discovers it. Only the Coca-Cola Company, for instance, knows the secret recipe for making its famous soft drink. Still other technology is proprietary for a short time. When a pharmaceutical company discovers a new

human capital
the knowledge and skills that workers acquire through education, training, and experience

natural resources
the inputs into the production of goods and services that are provided by nature, such as land, rivers, and mineral deposits

technological knowledge
society's understanding of the best ways to produce goods and services

FYI

The Production Function

Economists often use a *production function* to describe the relationship between the quantity of inputs used in production and the quantity of output from production. For example, suppose Y denotes the quantity of output, L the quantity of labor, K the quantity of physical capital, H the quantity of human capital, and N the quantity of natural resources. Then we might write

$$Y = A \, F(L, K, H, N),$$

where $F(\;)$ is a function that shows how the inputs are combined to produce output. A is a variable that reflects the available production technology. As technology improves, A rises, so the economy produces more output from any given combination of inputs.

Many production functions have a property called *constant returns to scale*. If a production function has constant returns to scale, then doubling all inputs causes the amount of output to double as well. Mathematically, we write that a production function has constant returns to scale if, for any positive number x,

$$xY = A \, F(xL, xK, xH, xN).$$

A doubling of all inputs would be represented in this equation by $x = 2$. The right side shows the inputs doubling, and the left side shows output doubling.

Production functions with constant returns to scale have an interesting and useful implication. To see this implication, it will prove instructive to set $x = 1/L$. Then the preceding equation becomes

$$Y/L = A \, F(1, K/L, H/L, N/L).$$

Notice that Y/L is output per worker, which is a measure of productivity. This equation says that labor productivity depends on physical capital per worker (K/L), human capital per worker (H/L), and natural resources per worker (N/L). Productivity also depends on the state of technology, as reflected by the variable A. Thus, this equation provides a mathematical summary of the four determinants of productivity we have just discussed.

---

drug, the patent system gives that company a temporary right to be its exclusive manufacturer. When the patent expires, however, other companies are allowed to make the drug. All these forms of technological knowledge are important for the economy's production of goods and services.

It is worthwhile to distinguish between technological knowledge and human capital. Although they are closely related, there is an important difference. Technological knowledge refers to society's understanding about how the world works. Human capital refers to the resources expended transmitting this understanding to the labor force. To use a relevant metaphor, knowledge is the quality of society's textbooks, whereas human capital is the amount of time that the population has devoted to reading them. Workers' productivity depends on both.

Are Natural Resources a Limit to Growth?

Today, the world's population is almost 7 billion, more than four times what it was a century ago. At the same time, many people are enjoying a much higher standard of living than did their great-grandparents. A perennial debate concerns whether this growth in population and living standards can continue in the future.

Many commentators have argued that natural resources will eventually limit how much the world's economies can grow. At first, this argument might seem hard to ignore. If the world has only a fixed supply of nonrenewable natural resources, how can population, production, and living standards continue to grow over time? Eventually, won't supplies of oil and minerals start to run out? When these shortages start to occur, won't they stop economic growth and, perhaps, even force living standards to fall?

Despite the apparent appeal of such arguments, most economists are less concerned about such limits to growth than one might guess. They argue that technological progress often yields ways to avoid these limits. If we compare the economy today to the economy of the past, we see various ways in which the use of natural resources has improved. Modern cars have better gas mileage. New houses have better insulation and require less energy to heat and cool them. More efficient oil rigs waste less oil in the process of extraction. Recycling allows some nonrenewable resources to be reused. The development of alternative fuels, such as ethanol instead of gasoline, allows us to substitute renewable for nonrenewable resources.

Sixty years ago, some conservationists were concerned about the excessive use of tin and copper. At the time, these were crucial commodities: Tin was used to make many food containers, and copper was used to make telephone wire. Some people advocated mandatory recycling and rationing of tin and copper so that supplies would be available for future generations. Today, however, plastic has replaced tin as a material for making many food containers, and phone calls often travel over fiber-optic cables, which are made from sand. Technological progress has made once crucial natural resources less necessary.

But are all these efforts enough to permit continued economic growth? One way to answer this question is to look at the prices of natural resources. In a market economy, scarcity is reflected in market prices. If the world were running out of natural resources, then the prices of those resources would be rising over time. But in fact, the opposite is more often true. Natural resource prices exhibit substantial short-run fluctuations, but over long spans of time, the prices of most natural resources (adjusted for overall inflation) are stable or falling. It appears that our ability to conserve these resources is growing more rapidly than their supplies are dwindling. Market prices give no reason to believe that natural resources are a limit to economic growth. ■

QUICK QUIZ   *List and describe four determinants of a country's productivity.*

Economic Growth and Public Policy

So far, we have determined that a society's standard of living depends on its ability to produce goods and services and that its productivity in turn depends on physical capital per worker, human capital per worker, natural resources per worker, and technological knowledge. Let's now turn to the question faced by policymakers around the world: What can government policy do to raise productivity and living standards?

Saving and Investment

Because capital is a produced factor of production, a society can change the amount of capital it has. If today the economy produces a large quantity of new capital goods, then tomorrow it will have a larger stock of capital and be able to produce more goods and services. Thus, one way to raise future productivity is to invest more current resources in the production of capital.

One of the *Ten Principles of Economics* presented in Chapter 1 is that people face trade-offs. This principle is especially important when considering the accumulation of capital. Because resources are scarce, devoting more resources to producing capital requires devoting fewer resources to producing goods and services for current consumption. That is, for society to invest more in capital, it must consume less and save more of its current income. The growth that arises from capital accumulation is not a free lunch: It requires that society sacrifice consumption of goods and services in the present to enjoy higher consumption in the future.

The next chapter examines in more detail how the economy's financial markets coordinate saving and investment. It also examines how government policies influence the amount of saving and investment that takes place. At this point, it is important to note that encouraging saving and investment is one way that a government can encourage growth and, in the long run, raise the economy's standard of living.

Diminishing Returns and the Catch-Up Effect

Suppose that a government pursues policies that raise the nation's saving rate—the percentage of GDP devoted to saving rather than consumption. What happens? With the nation saving more, fewer resources are needed to make consumption goods, and more resources are available to make capital goods. As a result, the capital stock increases, leading to rising productivity and more rapid growth in GDP. But how long does this higher rate of growth last? Assuming that the saving rate remains at its new higher level, does the growth rate of GDP stay high indefinitely or only for a period of time?

The traditional view of the production process is that capital is subject to **diminishing returns:** As the stock of capital rises, the extra output produced from an additional unit of capital falls. In other words, when workers already have a large quantity of capital to use in producing goods and services, giving them an additional unit of capital increases their productivity only slightly. This is illustrated in Figure 1, which shows how the amount of capital per worker determines the amount of output per worker, holding constant all the other determinants of output.

Because of diminishing returns, an increase in the saving rate leads to higher growth only for a while. As the higher saving rate allows more capital to be accumulated, the benefits from additional capital become smaller over time, and so growth slows down. *In the long run, the higher saving rate leads to a higher level of productivity and income but not to higher growth in these variables.* Reaching this long run, however, can take quite a while. According to studies of international data on economic growth, increasing the saving rate can lead to substantially higher growth for a period of several decades.

The diminishing returns to capital has another important implication: Other things equal, it is easier for a country to grow fast if it starts out relatively poor. This effect of initial conditions on subsequent growth is sometimes called the **catch-up effect.** In poor countries, workers lack even the most rudimentary tools and, as a result, have low productivity. Small amounts of capital investment would substantially raise these workers' productivity. By contrast, workers in rich countries have large amounts of capital with which to work, and this partly

diminishing returns
the property whereby the benefit from an extra unit of an input declines as the quantity of the input increases

catch-up effect
the property whereby countries that start off poor tend to grow more rapidly than countries that start off rich

Figure **1**

Illustrating the Production Function
This figure shows how the amount of capital per worker influences the amount of output per worker. Other determinants of output, including human capital, natural resources, and technology, are held constant. The curve becomes flatter as the amount of capital increases because of diminishing returns to capital.

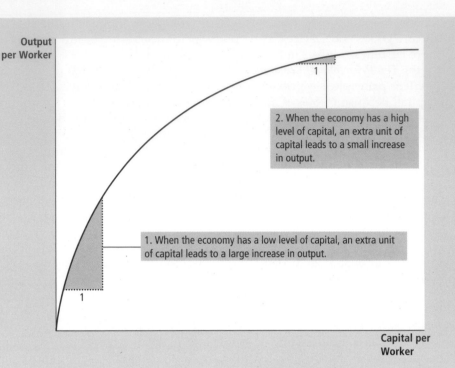

explains their high productivity. Yet with the amount of capital per worker already so high, additional capital investment has a relatively small effect on productivity. Studies of international data on economic growth confirm this catch-up effect: Controlling for other variables, such as the percentage of GDP devoted to investment, poor countries tend to grow at faster rates than rich countries.

This catch-up effect can help explain some otherwise puzzling facts. Here's an example: From 1960 to 1990, the United States and South Korea devoted a similar share of GDP to investment. Yet over this time, the United States experienced only mediocre growth of about 2 percent, while South Korea experienced spectacular growth of more than 6 percent. The explanation is the catch-up effect. In 1960, South Korea had GDP per person less than one-tenth the U.S. level, in part because previous investment had been so low. With a small initial capital stock, the benefits to capital accumulation were much greater in South Korea, and this gave South Korea a higher subsequent growth rate.

This catch-up effect shows up in other aspects of life. When a school gives an end-of-year award to the "Most Improved" student, that student is usually one who began the year with relatively poor performance. Students who began the year not studying find improvement easier than students who always worked hard. Note that it is good to be "Most Improved," given the starting point, but it is even better to be "Best Student." Similarly, economic growth over the last several decades has been much more rapid in South Korea than in the United States, but GDP per person is still higher in the United States.

Investment from Abroad

So far, we have discussed how policies aimed at increasing a country's saving rate can increase investment and, thereby, long-term economic growth. Yet saving by domestic residents is not the only way for a country to invest in new capital. The other way is investment by foreigners.

Investment from abroad takes several forms. Ford Motor Company might build a car factory in Mexico. A capital investment that is owned and operated by a foreign entity is called *foreign direct investment*. Alternatively, an American might buy stock in a Mexican corporation (that is, buy a share in the ownership of the corporation); the Mexican corporation can use the proceeds from the stock sale to build a new factory. An investment that is financed with foreign money but operated by domestic residents is called *foreign portfolio investment*. In both cases, Americans provide the resources necessary to increase the stock of capital in Mexico. That is, American saving is being used to finance Mexican investment.

When foreigners invest in a country, they do so because they expect to earn a return on their investment. Ford's car factory increases the Mexican capital stock and, therefore, increases Mexican productivity and Mexican GDP. Yet Ford takes some of this additional income back to the United States in the form of profit. Similarly, when an American investor buys Mexican stock, the investor has a right to a portion of the profit that the Mexican corporation earns.

Investment from abroad, therefore, does not have the same effect on all measures of economic prosperity. Recall that gross domestic product (GDP) is the income earned within a country by both residents and nonresidents, whereas gross national product (GNP) is the income earned by residents of a country both at home and abroad. When Ford opens its car factory in Mexico, some of the income the factory generates accrues to people who do not live in Mexico. As a result, foreign investment in Mexico raises the income of Mexicans (measured by GNP) by less than it raises the production in Mexico (measured by GDP).

Nonetheless, investment from abroad is one way for a country to grow. Even though some of the benefits from this investment flow back to the foreign owners, this investment does increase the economy's stock of capital, leading to higher productivity and higher wages. Moreover, investment from abroad is one way for poor countries to learn the state-of-the-art technologies developed and used in richer countries. For these reasons, many economists who advise governments in less developed economies advocate policies that encourage investment from abroad. Often, this means removing restrictions that governments have imposed on foreign ownership of domestic capital.

An organization that tries to encourage the flow of capital to poor countries is the World Bank. This international organization obtains funds from the world's advanced countries, such as the United States, and uses these resources to make loans to less developed countries so that they can invest in roads, sewer systems, schools, and other types of capital. It also offers the countries advice about how the funds might best be used. The World Bank, together with its sister organization, the International Monetary Fund, was set up after World War II. One lesson from the war was that economic distress often leads to political turmoil, international tensions, and military conflict. Thus, every country has an interest in promoting economic prosperity around the world. The World Bank and the International Monetary Fund were established to achieve that common goal.

Education

Education—investment in human capital—is at least as important as investment in physical capital for a country's long-run economic success. In the United States, each year of schooling has historically raised a person's wage by an average of about 10 percent. In less developed countries, where human capital is especially scarce, the gap between the wages of educated and uneducated workers is even larger. Thus, one way government policy can enhance the standard of living is to provide good schools and to encourage the population to take advantage of them.

Investment in human capital, like investment in physical capital, has an opportunity cost. When students are in school, they forgo the wages they could have earned as members of the labor force. In less developed countries, children often drop out of school at an early age, even though the benefit of additional schooling is very high, simply because their labor is needed to help support the family.

Some economists have argued that human capital is particularly important for economic growth because human capital conveys positive externalities. An *externality* is the effect of one person's actions on the well-being of a bystander. An educated person, for instance, might generate new ideas about how best to produce goods and services. If these ideas enter society's pool of knowledge so that everyone can use them, then the ideas are an external benefit of education. In this case, the return to schooling for society is even greater than the return for the individual. This argument would justify the large subsidies to human-capital investment that we observe in the form of public education.

One problem facing some poor countries is the *brain drain*—the emigration of many of the most highly educated workers to rich countries, where these workers can enjoy a higher standard of living. If human capital does have positive externalities, then this brain drain makes those people left behind poorer than they otherwise would be. This problem offers policymakers a dilemma. On the one hand, the United States and other rich countries have the best systems of higher education, and it would seem natural for poor countries to send their best students abroad to earn higher degrees. On the other hand, those students who have spent time abroad may choose not to return home, and this brain drain will reduce the poor nation's stock of human capital even further.

Health and Nutrition

The term *human capital* usually refers to education, but it can also be used to describe another type of investment in people: expenditures that lead to a healthier population. Other things equal, healthier workers are more productive. The right investments in the health of the population provide one way for a nation to increase productivity and raise living standards.

Economic historian Robert Fogel has suggested that a significant factor in long-run economic growth is improved health from better nutrition. He estimates that in Great Britain in 1780, about one in five people were so malnourished that they were incapable of manual labor. Among those who could work, insufficient caloric intake substantially reduced the work effort they could put forth. As nutrition improved, so did workers' productivity.

Fogel studies these historical trends in part by looking at the height of the population. Short stature can be an indicator of malnutrition, especially during gestation and the early years of life. Fogel finds that as nations develop economically, people eat more, and the population gets taller. From 1775 to 1975, the average caloric intake in Great Britain rose by 26 percent, and the height of the average man rose by 3.6 inches. Similarly, during the spectacular economic growth in South Korea from 1962 to 1995, caloric consumption rose by 44 percent, and average male height rose by 2 inches. Of course, a person's height is determined by a combination of genetic predisposition and environment. But because the genetic makeup of a population is slow to change, such increases in average

in the news

> ## Promoting Human Capital

Because human capital is a key to economic growth, some developing countries give parents an immediate financial incentive to keep their children in school.

Brazil Pays Parents to Help Poor Be Pupils, Not Wage Earners

By Celia W. Dugger

Vandelson Andrade, 13, often used to skip school to work 12-hour days on the small, graceful fishing boats that sail from the picturesque harbor here. His meager earnings helped pay for rice and beans for his desperately poor family.

But this year he qualified for a small monthly cash payment from the government that his mother receives on the condition that he shows up in the classroom.

"I can't skip school anymore," said Vandelson, whose hand-me-down pants were so big that the crotch ended at his knees and the legs bunched up around his ankles. "If I miss one more day, my mother won't get the money."

This year, Vandelson will finally pass the fourth grade on his third try—a small victory

Vandelson Andrade, student

in a new breed of social program that is spreading swiftly across Latin America. It is a developing-country version of American welfare reform: to break the cycle of poverty, the government gives the poor small cash payments in exchange for keeping their children in school and taking them for regular medical checkups.

"I think these programs are as close as you can come to a magic bullet in development," said Nancy Birdsall, president of the Center for Global Development, a nonprofit research group in Washington. "They're creating an

incentive for families to invest in their own children's futures. Every decade or so, we see something that can really make a difference, and this is one of those things." . . .

Antônio Souza, 48, and Maria Torres, 37, are raising seven children in a mud hut a couple of hills away from Ms. Andrade. Every member of the family is sinewy and lean. The parents cannot remember the last time the family ate meat or vegetables. But their grant of $27 a month makes it possible to buy rice, sugar, pasta and oil.

Mr. Souza and Ms. Torres, illiterate believers in the power of education, have always sent their children to school. "If they don't study, they'll turn into dummies like me," said their father, whose weathered, deeply creased face broke into a wide smile as he surveyed his bright-eyed daughters, Ana Paula, 11, and Daniele, 8, among them. "All I can do is work in the fields."

His wife said proudly: "There are fathers who don't want their children to go to school. But this man here has done everything he could to send his children to school."

Source: *New York Times*, January 3, 2004.

height are most likely due to changes in the environment—nutrition being the obvious explanation.

Moreover, studies have found that height is an indicator of productivity. Looking at data on a large number of workers at a point in time, researchers have found that taller workers tend to earn more. Because wages reflect a worker's productivity, this finding suggests that taller workers tend to be more productive. The effect of height on wages is especially pronounced in poorer countries, where malnutrition is a bigger risk.

Fogel won the Nobel Prize in Economics in 1993 for his work in economic history, which includes not only his studies of nutrition but also his studies of American slavery and the role of railroads in the development of the American economy. In the lecture he gave when he was awarded the prize, he surveyed the evidence on health and economic growth. He concluded that "improved gross nutrition accounts for roughly 30 percent of the growth of per capita income in Britain between 1790 and 1980."

Today, malnutrition is fortunately rare in developed nations such as Great Britain and the United States. (Obesity is a more widespread problem.) But for people in developing nations, poor health and inadequate nutrition remain obstacles to higher productivity and improved living standards. The United Nations estimates that almost a third of the population in sub-Saharan Africa is undernourished.

The causal link between health and wealth runs in both directions. Poor countries are poor in part because their populations are not healthy, and their populations are not healthy in part because they are poor and cannot afford adequate healthcare and nutrition. It is a vicious circle. But this fact opens the possibility of a virtuous circle: Policies that lead to more rapid economic growth would naturally improve health outcomes, which in turn would further promote economic growth.

Property Rights and Political Stability

Another way policymakers can foster economic growth is by protecting property rights and promoting political stability. This issue goes to the very heart of how market economies work.

Production in market economies arises from the interactions of millions of individuals and firms. When you buy a car, for instance, you are buying the output of a car dealer, a car manufacturer, a steel company, an iron ore mining company, and so on. This division of production among many firms allows the economy's factors of production to be used as effectively as possible. To achieve this outcome, the economy has to coordinate transactions among these firms, as well as between firms and consumers. Market economies achieve this coordination through market prices. That is, market prices are the instrument with which the invisible hand of the marketplace brings supply and demand into balance in each of the many thousands of markets that make up the economy.

An important prerequisite for the price system to work is an economy-wide respect for *property rights*. Property rights refer to the ability of people to exercise authority over the resources they own. A mining company will not make the effort to mine iron ore if it expects the ore to be stolen. The company mines the ore only if it is confident that it will benefit from the ore's subsequent sale. For this reason, courts serve an important role in a market economy: They enforce property rights. Through the criminal justice system, the courts discourage direct theft. In addition, through the civil justice system, the courts ensure that buyers and sellers live up to their contracts.

Those of us in developed countries tend to take property rights for granted, but those living in less developed countries understand that a lack of property rights can be a major problem. In many countries, the system of justice does not work well. Contracts are hard to enforce, and fraud often goes unpunished. In more extreme cases, the government not only fails to enforce property rights but actually infringes upon them. To do business in some countries, firms are expected to bribe government officials. Such corruption impedes the coordinating power of markets. It also discourages domestic saving and investment from abroad.

One threat to property rights is political instability. When revolutions and coups are common, there is doubt about whether property rights will be respected in the future. If a revolutionary government might confiscate the capital of some businesses, as was often true after communist revolutions, domestic residents have less incentive to save, invest, and start new businesses. At the same time, foreigners have less incentive to invest in the country. Even the threat of revolution can act to depress a nation's standard of living.

Thus, economic prosperity depends in part on political prosperity. A country with an efficient court system, honest government officials, and a stable constitution will enjoy a higher economic standard of living than a country with a poor court system, corrupt officials, and frequent revolutions and coups.

Free Trade

Some of the world's poorest countries have tried to achieve more rapid economic growth by pursuing *inward-oriented policies*. These policies attempt to increase productivity and living standards within the country by avoiding interaction with the rest of the world. Domestic firms often advance the infant-industry argument, claiming they need protection from foreign competition to thrive and grow. Together with a general distrust of foreigners, this argument has at times led policymakers in less developed countries to impose tariffs and other trade restrictions.

Most economists today believe that poor countries are better off pursuing *outward-oriented policies* that integrate these countries into the world economy. International trade in goods and services can improve the economic well-being of a country's citizens. Trade is, in some ways, a type of technology. When a country exports wheat and imports textiles, the country benefits as if it had invented a technology for turning wheat into textiles. A country that eliminates trade restrictions will, therefore, experience the same kind of economic growth that would occur after a major technological advance.

The adverse impact of inward orientation becomes clear when one considers the small size of many less developed economies. The total GDP of Argentina, for instance, is about that of Philadelphia. Imagine what would happen if the Philadelphia city council were to prohibit city residents from trading with people living outside the city limits. Without being able to take advantage of the gains from trade, Philadelphia would need to produce all the goods it consumes. It would also have to produce all its own capital goods, rather than importing state-of-the-art equipment from other cities. Living standards in Philadelphia would fall immediately, and the problem would likely only get worse over time. This is precisely what happened when Argentina pursued inward-oriented policies throughout much of the 20th century. In contrast, countries that pursued outward-oriented policies, such as South Korea, Singapore, and Taiwan, enjoyed high rates of economic growth.

The amount that a nation trades with others is determined not only by government policy but also by geography. Countries with natural seaports find trade easier than countries without this resource. It is not a coincidence that many of the world's major cities, such as New York, San Francisco, and Hong Kong, are located next to oceans. Similarly, because landlocked countries find international trade more difficult, they tend to have lower levels of income than countries with easy access to the world's waterways. For example, countries with more than 80 percent of their population living within 100 kilometers of a coast have an average GDP per person about four times as large as countries with less than 20 percent of their population living near a coast. The critical importance of access to the sea helps explain why the African continent, which contains many landlocked countries, is so poor.

Research and Development

The primary reason that living standards are higher today than they were a century ago is that technological knowledge has advanced. The telephone, the transistor, the computer, and the internal combustion engine are among the thousands of innovations that have improved the ability to produce goods and services.

Most technological advances come from private research by firms and individual inventors, but there is also a public interest in promoting these efforts. To a large extent, knowledge is a *public good:* That is, once one person discovers an idea, the idea enters society's pool of knowledge, and other people can freely use it. Just as government has a role in providing a public good such as national defense, it also has a role in encouraging the research and development of new technologies.

The U.S. government has long played a role in the creation and dissemination of technological knowledge. A century ago, the government sponsored research about farming methods and advised farmers how best to use their land. More recently, the U.S. government, through the Air Force and NASA, has supported aerospace research; as a result, the United States is a leading maker of rockets and planes. The government continues to encourage advances in knowledge with research grants from the National Science Foundation and the National Institutes of Health and with tax breaks for firms engaging in research and development.

Yet another way in which government policy encourages research is through the patent system. When a person or firm invents a new product, such as a new drug, the inventor can apply for a patent. If the product is deemed truly original, the government awards the patent, which gives the inventor the exclusive right to make the product for a specified number of years. In essence, the patent gives the inventor a property right over his invention, turning his new idea from a public good into a private good. By allowing inventors to profit from their inventions—even if only temporarily—the patent system enhances the incentive for individuals and firms to engage in research.

Population Growth

Economists and other social scientists have long debated how population affects a society. The most direct effect is on the size of the labor force: A large population means more workers to produce goods and services. The tremendous size of the Chinese population is one reason China is such an important player in the world economy.

At the same time, however, a large population means more people to consume those goods and services. So while a large population means a larger total output of goods and services, it need not mean a higher standard of living for a typical citizen. Indeed, both large and small nations are found at all levels of economic development.

Beyond these obvious effects of population size, population growth interacts with the other factors of production in ways that are more subtle and open to debate.

Stretching Natural Resources Thomas Robert Malthus (1766–1834), an English minister and early economic thinker, is famous for his book called *An Essay on the Principle of Population as It Affects the Future Improvement of Society.* In it, he offered what may be history's most chilling forecast. Malthus argued that an ever-increasing population would continually strain society's ability to provide for itself. As a result, mankind was doomed to forever live in poverty.

Malthus's logic was simple. He began by noting that "food is necessary to the existence of man" and that "the passion between the sexes is necessary and will remain nearly in its present state." He concluded that "the power of population is infinitely greater than the power in the earth to produce subsistence for man." According to Malthus, the only check on population growth was "misery and vice." Attempts by charities or governments to alleviate poverty were counter-productive, he argued, because they merely allowed the poor to have more children, placing even greater strains on society's productive capabilities.

Malthus may have correctly described the world at the time when he lived, but fortunately, his dire forecast was far off the mark. The world population has increased about sixfold over the past two centuries, but living standards around the world are on average much higher. As a result of economic growth, chronic hunger and malnutrition are less common now than they were in Malthus's day. Modern famines occur from time to time but are more often the result of an unequal income distribution or political instability than inadequate food production.

Where did Malthus go wrong? As we discussed in a case study earlier in this chapter, growth in human ingenuity has offset the effects of a larger population. Pesticides, fertilizers, mechanized farm equipment, new crop varieties, and other technological advances that Malthus never imagined have allowed each farmer to feed ever greater numbers of people. Even with more mouths to feed, fewer farmers are necessary because each farmer is much more productive.

Thomas Robert Malthus

Diluting the Capital Stock Whereas Malthus worried about the effects of population on the use of natural resources, some modern theories of economic growth emphasize its effects on capital accumulation. According to these theories, high population growth reduces GDP per worker because rapid growth in the number of workers forces the capital stock to be spread more thinly. In other words, when population growth is rapid, each worker is equipped with less capital. A smaller quantity of capital per worker leads to lower productivity and lower GDP per worker.

This problem is most apparent in the case of human capital. Countries with high population growth have large numbers of school-age children. This places a larger burden on the educational system. It is not surprising, therefore, that educational attainment tends to be low in countries with high population growth.

The differences in population growth around the world are large. In developed countries, such as the United States and those in Western Europe, the population has risen only about 1 percent per year in recent decades and is expected to rise even more slowly in the future. By contrast, in many poor African countries, population grows at about 3 percent per year. At this rate, the population doubles every 23 years. This rapid population growth makes it harder to provide workers with the tools and skills they need to achieve high levels of productivity.

Rapid population growth is not the main reason that less developed countries are poor, but some analysts believe that reducing the rate of population growth would help these countries raise their standards of living. In some countries, this goal is accomplished directly with laws that regulate the number of children families may have. China, for instance, allows only one child per family; couples who violate this rule are subject to substantial fines. In countries with greater freedom, the goal of reduced population growth is accomplished less directly by increasing awareness of birth control techniques.

Another way in which a country can influence population growth is to apply one of the *Ten Principles of Economics:* People respond to incentives. Bearing a child, like any decision, has an opportunity cost. When the opportunity cost rises, people will choose to have smaller families. In particular, women with the opportunity to receive a good education and desirable employment tend to want fewer

in the news

> One Economist's Answer

MIT economist Daron Acemoglu considers why some nations thrive while others do not.

What Makes a Nation Rich?

BY DARON ACEMOGLU

We are the rich, the haves, the developed. And most of the rest—in Africa, South Asia, and South America, the Somalias and Bolivias and Bangladeshes of the world—are the nots. It's always been this way, a globe divided by wealth and poverty, health and sickness, food and famine, though the extent of inequality across nations today is unprecedented: The average citizen of the United States is ten times as prosperous as the average Guatemalan, more than twenty times as prosperous as the average North Korean, and more than forty times as prosperous as those living in Mali, Ethiopia, Congo, or Sierra Leone.

The question social scientists have unsuccessfully wrestled with for centuries is, Why? But the question they should have been asking is, How? Because inequality is not predetermined. Nations are not like children—they are not born rich or poor. Their governments make them that way.

You can chart the search for a theory of inequality to the French political philosopher Montesquieu, who in the mid-eighteenth century came up with a very simple explanation: People in hot places are inherently lazy. Other no less sweeping explanations soon followed: Could it be that Max Weber's Protestant work ethic is the true driver of economic success? Or perhaps the richest countries are those that were former British colonies? Or maybe it's as simple as tracing which nations have the largest populations of European descent? The problem with all of these theories is that while they superficially fit some specific cases, others radically disprove them.

It's the same with the theories put forth today. Economist Jeffrey Sachs, director of Columbia University's Earth Institute, attributes the relative success of nations to geography and weather: In the poorest parts of the world, he argues, nutrient-starved tropical soil makes agriculture a challenge, and tropical climates foment disease, particularly malaria. Perhaps if we were to fix these problems, teach the citizens of these nations better farming techniques, eliminate malaria, or at the very least equip them with artemisinin to fight this deadly disease, we could eliminate poverty. Or better yet, perhaps we just move these people and abandon their inhospitable land altogether.

Jared Diamond, the famous ecologist and best-selling author, has a different theory: The origin of world inequality stems from the historical endowment of plant and animal species and the advancement of technology. In Diamond's telling, the cultures that first learned to plant crops were the first to learn how to use a plow, and thus were first to adopt other technologies, the engine of every successful economy. Perhaps then the solution to world inequality rests in technology—wiring the developing world with Internet and cell phones.

And yet while Sachs and Diamond offer good insight into certain aspects of poverty, they share something in common with Montesquieu and others who followed: They ignore incentives. People need incentives to invest and prosper; they need to know that if they work hard, they can make money and actually keep that money. And the key to ensuring those incentives is sound institutions—the rule of law and security and a governing system that offers opportunities to achieve and innovate. That's what determines the haves from the have-nots—not geography or weather or technology or disease or ethnicity.

Put simply: Fix incentives and you will fix poverty. And if you wish to fix institutions, you have to fix governments.

How do we know that institutions are so central to the wealth and poverty of nations? Start in Nogales, a city cut in half

children than those with fewer opportunities outside the home. Hence, policies that foster equal treatment of women may be one way for less developed economies to reduce the rate of population growth and, perhaps, raise their standards of living.

by the Mexican-American border fence. There is no difference in geography between the two halves of Nogales. The weather is the same. The winds are the same, as are the soils. The types of diseases prevalent in the area given its geography and climate are the same, as is the ethnic, cultural, and linguistic background of the residents. By logic, both sides of the city should be identical economically.

And yet they are far from the same.

On one side of the border fence, in Santa Cruz County, Arizona, the median household income is $30,000. A few feet away, it's $10,000. On one side, most of the teenagers are in public high school, and the majority of the adults are high school graduates. On the other side, few of the residents have gone to high school, let alone college. Those in Arizona enjoy relatively good health and Medicare for those over sixty-five, not to mention an efficient road network, electricity, telephone service, and a dependable sewage and public-health system. None of those things are a given across the border. There, the roads are bad, the infant-mortality rate high, electricity and phone service expensive and spotty.

The key difference is that those on the north side of the border enjoy law and order and dependable government services—they can go about their daily activities and jobs without fear for their life or safety or property rights. On the other side, the inhabitants have institutions that perpetuate crime, graft, and insecurity.

Nogales may be the most obvious example, but it's far from the only one. Take Singapore, a once-impoverished tropical island that became the richest nation in Asia after British colonialists enshrined property

rights and encouraged trade. Or China, where decades of stagnation and famine were reversed only after Deng Xiaoping began introducing private-property rights in agriculture, and later in industry. Or Botswana, whose economy has flourished over the past forty years while the rest of Africa has withered, thanks to strong tribal institutions and farsighted nation building by its early elected leaders.

Now look at the economic and political failures. You can begin in Sierra Leone, where a lack of functioning institutions and an overabundance of diamonds have fueled decades of civil war and strife and corruption that continue unchecked today. Or take communist North Korea, a geographical, ethnic, and cultural mirror of its capitalist neighbor to the south, yet ten times poorer. Or Egypt, cradle of one of the world's great civilizations yet stagnant

Daron Acemoglu

economically ever since its colonization by the Ottomans and then the Europeans, only made worse by its post-independence governments, which have restricted all economic activities and markets. In fact, the theory can be used to shed light on the patterns of inequality for much of the world.

If we know why nations are poor, the resulting question is what can we do to help them. Our ability to impose institutions from the outside is limited, as the recent U.S. experiences in Afghanistan and Iraq demonstrate. But we are not helpless, and in many instances, there is a lot to be done. Even the most repressed citizens of the world will stand up to tyrants when given the opportunity. We saw this recently in Iran and a few years ago in Ukraine during the Orange Revolution.

The U.S. must not take a passive role in encouraging these types of movements. Our foreign policy should encourage them by punishing repressive regimes through trade embargoes and diplomacy.... At the microlevel, we can help foreign citizens by educating them and arming them with the modern tools of activism, most notably the Internet, and perhaps even encryption technology and cell-phone platforms that can evade firewalls and censorship put in place by repressive governments, such as those in China or Iran, that fear the power of information.

There's no doubt that erasing global inequality, which has been with us for millennia and has expanded to unprecedented levels over the past century and a half, won't be easy. But by accepting the role of failed governments and institutions in causing poverty, we have a fighting chance of reversing it.

Source: *Esquire*, November 18, 2009.

Promoting Technological Progress Rapid population growth may depress economic prosperity by reducing the amount of capital each worker has, but it may also have some benefits. Some economists have suggested that world population growth has been an engine of technological progress and economic prosperity. The mechanism is simple: If there are more people, then there are more scientists, inventors, and engineers to contribute to technological advance, which benefits everyone.

Economist Michael Kremer has provided some support for this hypothesis in an article titled "Population Growth and Technological Change: One Million B.C. to 1990," which was published in the *Quarterly Journal of Economics* in 1993. Kremer begins by noting that over the broad span of human history, world growth rates have increased with world population. For example, world growth was more rapid when the world population was 1 billion (which occurred around the year 1800) than when the population was only 100 million (around 500 B.C.). This fact is consistent with the hypothesis that a larger population induces more technological progress.

Kremer's second piece of evidence comes from comparing regions of the world. The melting of the polar icecaps at the end of the Ice Age around 10,000 B.C. flooded the land bridges and separated the world into several distinct regions that could not communicate with one another for thousands of years. If technological progress is more rapid when there are more people to discover things, then larger regions should have experienced more rapid growth.

According to Kremer, that is exactly what happened. The most successful region of the world in 1500 (when Columbus reestablished technological contact) comprised the "Old World" civilizations of the large Eurasia-Africa region. Next in technological development were the Aztec and Mayan civilizations in the Americas, followed by the hunter-gatherers of Australia, and then the primitive people of Tasmania, who lacked even fire-making and most stone and bone tools.

The smallest isolated region was Flinders Island, a tiny island between Tasmania and Australia. With the smallest population, Flinders Island had the fewest opportunities for technological advance and, indeed, seemed to regress. Around 3000 B.C., human society on Flinders Island died out completely. A large population, Kremer concludes, is a prerequisite for technological advance.

QUICK QUIZ   *Describe three ways a government policymaker can try to raise the growth in living standards in a society. Are there any drawbacks to these policies?*

Conclusion: The Importance of Long-Run Growth

In this chapter, we have discussed what determines the standard of living in a nation and how policymakers can endeavor to raise the standard of living through policies that promote economic growth. Most of this chapter is summarized in one of the *Ten Principles of Economics:* A country's standard of living depends on its ability to produce goods and services. Policymakers who want to encourage growth in living standards must aim to increase their nation's productive ability by encouraging rapid accumulation of the factors of production and ensuring that these factors are employed as effectively as possible.

Economists differ in their views of the role of government in promoting economic growth. At the very least, government can lend support to the invisible hand by maintaining property rights and political stability. More controversial is whether government should target and subsidize specific industries that might be especially important for technological progress. There is no doubt that these issues are among the most important in economics. The success of one generation's policymakers in learning and heeding the fundamental lessons about economic growth determines what kind of world the next generation will inherit.

SUMMARY

- Economic prosperity, as measured by GDP per person, varies substantially around the world. The average income in the world's richest countries is more than ten times that in the world's poorest countries. Because growth rates of real GDP also vary substantially, the relative positions of countries can change dramatically over time.

- The standard of living in an economy depends on the economy's ability to produce goods and services. Productivity, in turn, depends on the physical capital, human capital, natural resources, and technological knowledge available to workers.

- Government policies can try to influence the economy's growth rate in many ways: by encouraging saving and investment, encouraging investment from abroad, fostering education, promoting good health, maintaining property rights and political stability, allowing free trade, and promoting the research and development of new technologies.

- The accumulation of capital is subject to diminishing returns: The more capital an economy has, the less additional output the economy gets from an extra unit of capital. As a result, while higher saving leads to higher growth for a period of time, growth eventually slows down as capital, productivity, and income rise. Also because of diminishing returns, the return to capital is especially high in poor countries. Other things equal, these countries can grow faster because of the catch-up effect.

- Population growth has a variety of effects on economic growth. On the one hand, more rapid population growth may lower productivity by stretching the supply of natural resources and by reducing the amount of capital available for each worker. On the other hand, a larger population may enhance the rate of technological progress because there are more scientists and engineers.

KEY CONCEPTS

productivity, *p. 137*
physical capital, *p. 137*
human capital, *p. 138*

natural resources, *p. 138*
technological
  knowledge, *p. 138*

diminishing returns, *p. 141*
catch-up effect, *p. 141*

QUESTIONS FOR REVIEW

1. What does the level of a nation's GDP measure? What does the growth rate of GDP measure? Would you rather live in a nation with a high level of GDP and a low growth rate or in a nation with a low level of GDP and a high growth rate?
2. List and describe four determinants of productivity.
3. In what way is a college degree a form of capital?
4. Explain how higher saving leads to a higher standard of living. What might deter a policymaker from trying to raise the rate of saving?
5. Does a higher rate of saving lead to higher growth temporarily or indefinitely?
6. Why would removing a trade restriction, such as a tariff, lead to more rapid economic growth?
7. How does the rate of population growth influence the level of GDP per person?
8. Describe two ways the U.S. government tries to encourage advances in technological knowledge.

PROBLEMS AND APPLICATIONS

1. Most countries, including the United States, import substantial amounts of goods and services from other countries. Yet the chapter says that a nation can enjoy a high standard of living only if it can produce a large quantity of goods and services itself. Can you reconcile these two facts?

2. Suppose that society decided to reduce consumption and increase investment.
   a. How would this change affect economic growth?
   b. What groups in society would benefit from this change? What groups might be hurt?

3. Societies choose what share of their resources to devote to consumption and what share to devote to investment. Some of these decisions involve private spending; others involve government spending.
   a. Describe some forms of private spending that represent consumption and some forms that represent investment. The national income accounts include tuition as a part of consumer spending. In your opinion, are the resources you devote to your education a form of consumption or a form of investment?
   b. Describe some forms of government spending that represent consumption and some forms that represent investment. In your opinion, should we view government spending on health programs as a form of consumption or investment? Would you distinguish between health programs for the young and health programs for the elderly?

4. What is the opportunity cost of investing in capital? Do you think a country can "overinvest" in capital? What is the opportunity cost of investing in human capital? Do you think a country can "overinvest" in human capital? Explain.

5. Suppose that an auto company owned entirely by German citizens opens a new factory in South Carolina.
   a. What sort of foreign investment would this represent?
   b. What would be the effect of this investment on U.S. GDP? Would the effect on U.S. GNP be larger or smaller?

6. In the 1990s and the first decade of the 2000s, investors from the Asian economies of Japan and China made significant direct and portfolio investments in the United States. At the time, many Americans were unhappy that this investment was occurring.
   a. In what way was it better for the United States to receive this foreign investment than not to receive it?
   b. In what way would it have been better still for Americans to have made this investment?

7. In many developing nations, young women have lower enrollment rates in secondary school than do young men. Describe several ways in which greater educational opportunities for young women could lead to faster economic growth in these countries.

8. International data show a positive correlation between income per person and the health of the population.
   a. Explain how higher income might cause better health outcomes.
   b. Explain how better health outcomes might cause higher income.
   c. How might the relative importance of your two hypotheses be relevant for public policy?

9. International data show a positive correlation between political stability and economic growth.
   a. Through what mechanism could political stability lead to strong economic growth?
   b. Through what mechanism could strong economic growth lead to political stability?

10. From 1950 to 2000, manufacturing employment as a percentage of total employment in the U.S. economy fell from 28 percent to 13 percent. At the same time, manufacturing output experienced slightly more rapid growth than the overall economy.
    a. What do these facts say about growth in labor productivity (defined as output per worker) in manufacturing?
    b. In your opinion, should policymakers be concerned about the decline in the share of manufacturing employment? Explain.

For further information on topics in this chapter, additional problems, applications, examples, online quizzes, and more, please visit our website at www .cengage.com/economics/mankiw.

Saving, Investment, and the Financial System

8

I
magine that you have just graduated from college (with a degree in economics, of course) and you decide to start your own business—an economic forecasting firm. Before you make any money selling your forecasts, you have to incur substantial costs to set up your business. You have to buy computers with which to make your forecasts, as well as desks, chairs, and filing cabinets to furnish your new office. Each of these items is a type of capital that your firm will use to produce and sell its services.

How do you obtain the funds to invest in these capital goods? Perhaps you are able to pay for them out of your past savings. More likely, however, like most entrepreneurs, you do not have enough money of your own to finance the start of your business. As a result, you have to get the money you need from other sources.

There are various ways to finance these capital investments. You could borrow the money, perhaps from a bank or from a friend or relative. In this case, you would promise not only to return the money at a later date but also to pay interest for the use of the money. Alternatively, you could convince someone to provide the money you need for your business in exchange for a share of your future profits, whatever they might happen to be. In either case, your investment in computers and office equipment is being financed by someone else's saving.

financial system

the group of institutions in the economy that help to match one person's saving with another person's investment

The **financial system** consists of the institutions that help to match one person's saving with another person's investment. As we discussed in the previous chapter, saving and investment are key ingredients to long-run economic growth: When a country saves a large portion of its GDP, more resources are available for investment in capital, and higher capital raises a country's productivity and living standard. The previous chapter, however, did not explain how the economy coordinates saving and investment. At any time, some people want to save some of their income for the future, and others want to borrow to finance investments in new and growing businesses. What brings these two groups of people together? What ensures that the supply of funds from those who want to save balances the demand for funds from those who want to invest?

This chapter examines how the financial system works. First, we discuss the large variety of institutions that make up the financial system in our economy. Second, we discuss the relationship between the financial system and some key macroeconomic variables—notably saving and investment. Third, we develop a model of the supply and demand for funds in financial markets. In the model, the interest rate is the price that adjusts to balance supply and demand. The model shows how various government policies affect the interest rate and, thereby, society's allocation of scarce resources.

Financial Institutions in the U.S. Economy

At the broadest level, the financial system moves the economy's scarce resources from savers (people who spend less than they earn) to borrowers (people who spend more than they earn). Savers save for various reasons—to put a child through college in several years or to retire comfortably in several decades. Similarly, borrowers borrow for various reasons—to buy a house in which to live or to start a business with which to make a living. Savers supply their money to the financial system with the expectation that they will get it back with interest at a later date. Borrowers demand money from the financial system with the knowledge that they will be required to pay it back with interest at a later date.

The financial system is made up of various financial institutions that help coordinate savers and borrowers. As a prelude to analyzing the economic forces that drive the financial system, let's discuss the most important of these institutions. Financial institutions can be grouped into two categories: financial markets and financial intermediaries. We consider each category in turn.

Financial Markets

financial markets

financial institutions through which savers can directly provide funds to borrowers

Financial markets are the institutions through which a person who wants to save can directly supply funds to a person who wants to borrow. The two most important financial markets in our economy are the bond market and the stock market.

bond

a certificate of indebtedness

The Bond Market   When Intel, the giant maker of computer chips, wants to borrow to finance construction of a new factory, it can borrow directly from the public. It does this by selling bonds. A **bond** is a certificate of indebtedness that specifies the obligations of the borrower to the holder of the bond. Put simply, a bond is an IOU. It identifies the time at which the loan will be repaid, called the *date of maturity,* and the rate of interest that will be paid periodically until the loan matures. The buyer of a bond gives his or her money to Intel in exchange for this promise of interest and eventual repayment of the amount borrowed (called the *principal*). The buyer can hold the bond until maturity or can sell the bond at an earlier date to someone else.

There are literally millions of different bonds in the U.S. economy. When large corporations, the federal government, or state and local governments need to borrow to finance the purchase of a new factory, a new jet fighter, or a new school, they usually do so by issuing bonds. If you look at *The Wall Street Journal* or the business section of your local newspaper, you will find a listing of the prices and interest rates on some of the most important bond issues. These bonds differ according to three significant characteristics.

The first characteristic is a bond's *term*—the length of time until the bond matures. Some bonds have short terms, such as a few months, while others have terms as long as thirty years. (The British government has even issued a bond that never matures, called a *perpetuity*. This bond pays interest forever, but the principal is never repaid.) The interest rate on a bond depends, in part, on its term. Long-term bonds are riskier than short-term bonds because holders of long-term bonds have to wait longer for repayment of principal. If a holder of a long-term bond needs his money earlier than the distant date of maturity, he has no choice but to sell the bond to someone else, perhaps at a reduced price. To compensate for this risk, long-term bonds usually pay higher interest rates than short-term bonds.

The second important characteristic of a bond is its *credit risk*—the probability that the borrower will fail to pay some of the interest or principal. Such a failure to pay is called a *default*. Borrowers can (and sometimes do) default on their loans by declaring bankruptcy. When bond buyers perceive that the probability of default is high, they demand a higher interest rate to compensate them for this risk. Because the U.S. government is considered a safe credit risk, government bonds tend to pay low interest rates. By contrast, financially shaky corporations raise money by issuing *junk bonds,* which pay very high interest rates. Buyers of bonds can judge credit risk by checking with various private agencies, such as Standard & Poor's, which rate the credit risk of different bonds.

The third important characteristic of a bond is its *tax treatment*—the way the tax laws treat the interest earned on the bond. The interest on most bonds is taxable income; that is, the bond owner has to pay a portion of the interest in income taxes. By contrast, when state and local governments issue bonds, called *municipal bonds,* the bond owners are not required to pay federal income tax on the interest income. Because of this tax advantage, bonds issued by state and local governments typically pay a lower interest rate than bonds issued by corporations or the federal government.

The Stock Market Another way for Intel to raise funds to build a new semiconductor factory is to sell stock in the company. **Stock** represents ownership in a firm and is, therefore, a claim to the profits that the firm makes. For example, if Intel sells a total of 1,000,000 shares of stock, then each share represents ownership of 1/1,000,000 of the business.

stock
a claim to partial ownership in a firm

The sale of stock to raise money is called *equity finance,* whereas the sale of bonds is called *debt finance*. Although corporations use both equity and debt finance to raise money for new investments, stocks and bonds are very different. The owner of shares of Intel stock is a part owner of Intel, while the owner of an Intel bond is a creditor of the corporation. If Intel is very profitable, the stockholders enjoy the benefits of these profits, whereas the bondholders get only the interest on their bonds. And if Intel runs into financial difficulty, the bondholders are paid what they are due before stockholders receive anything at all. Compared to bonds, stocks offer the holder both higher risk and potentially higher return.

After a corporation issues stock by selling shares to the public, these shares trade among stockholders on organized stock exchanges. In these transactions, the corporation itself receives no money when its stock changes hands. The most important stock exchanges in the U.S. economy are the New York Stock Exchange, the American Stock Exchange, and the NASDAQ (National Association of Securities Dealers Automated Quotation system). Most of the world's countries have their own stock exchanges on which the shares of local companies trade.

The prices at which shares trade on stock exchanges are determined by the supply of and demand for the stock in these companies. Because stock represents ownership in a corporation, the demand for a stock (and thus its price) reflects people's perception of the corporation's future profitability. When people become optimistic about a company's future, they raise their demand for its stock and thereby bid up the price of a share of stock. Conversely, when people come to expect a company to have little profit or even losses, the price of a share falls.

Various stock indexes are available to monitor the overall level of stock prices. A *stock index* is computed as an average of a group of stock prices. The most famous stock index is the Dow Jones Industrial Average, which has been computed regularly since 1896. It is now based on the prices of the stocks of thirty major U.S. companies, such as General Electric, Microsoft, Coca-Cola, Walt Disney Company, AT&T, and IBM. Another well-known stock index is the Standard & Poor's 500 Index, which is based on the prices of the stocks of 500 major companies. Because stock prices reflect expected profitability, these stock indexes are watched closely as possible indicators of future economic conditions.

Financial Intermediaries

financial intermediaries

financial institutions through which savers can indirectly provide funds to borrowers

Financial intermediaries are financial institutions through which savers can indirectly provide funds to borrowers. The term *intermediary* reflects the role of these institutions in standing between savers and borrowers. Here we consider two of the most important financial intermediaries: banks and mutual funds.

Banks   If the owner of a small grocery store wants to finance an expansion of his business, he probably takes a strategy quite different from that of Intel. Unlike Intel, a small grocer would find it difficult to raise funds in the bond and stock markets. Most buyers of stocks and bonds prefer to buy those issued by larger, more familiar companies. The small grocer, therefore, most likely finances his business expansion with a loan from a local bank.

Banks are the financial intermediaries with which people are most familiar. A primary job of banks is to take in deposits from people who want to save and use these deposits to make loans to people who want to borrow. Banks pay depositors interest on their deposits and charge borrowers slightly higher interest on their loans. The difference between these rates of interest covers the banks' costs and returns some profit to the owners of the banks.

Besides being financial intermediaries, banks play a second important role in the economy: They facilitate purchases of goods and services by allowing people to write checks against their deposits and to access those deposits with debit cards.

FYI

> ## Key Numbers for Stock Watchers

When following the stock of any company, you should keep an eye on three key numbers. These numbers are reported on the financial pages of some newspapers, and you can easily obtain them from online news services:

- **Price.** The single most important piece of information about a stock is the price of a share. News services usually present several prices. The "last" or "closing" price is the price of the last transaction that occurred before the stock exchange closed in its most recent day of trading. A news service may also give the "high" and "low" prices over the past day of trading and, sometimes, over the past year as well. It may also report the change from the previous day's closing price.

- **Dividend.** Corporations pay out some of their profits to their stockholders; this amount is called the *dividend.* (Profits not paid out are called *retained earnings* and are used by the corporation for additional investment.) News services often report the dividend paid over the previous year for each share of stock. They sometimes report the *dividend yield,* which is the dividend expressed as a percentage of the stock's price.

- **Price-earnings ratio.** A corporation's earnings, or accounting profit, is the amount of revenue it receives for the sale of its products minus its costs of production as measured by its accountants. *Earnings per share* is the company's total earnings divided by the number of shares of stock outstanding. The *price-earnings ratio,* often called the P/E, is the price of a corporation's stock divided by the amount the corporation earned per share over the past year. Historically, the typical price-earnings ratio is about 15. A higher P/E indicates that a corporation's stock is expensive relative to its recent earnings; this might indicate either that people expect earnings to rise in the future or that the stock is overvalued. Conversely, a lower P/E indicates that a corporation's stock is cheap relative to its recent earnings; this might indicate either that people expect earnings to fall or that the stock is undervalued.

Why do news services report all these data? Many people who invest their savings in stock follow these numbers closely when deciding which stocks to buy and sell. By contrast, other stockholders follow a buy-and-hold strategy: They buy the stock of well-run companies, hold it for long periods of time, and do not respond to the daily fluctuations.

In other words, banks help create a special asset that people can use as a *medium of exchange.* A medium of exchange is an item that people can easily use to engage in transactions. A bank's role in providing a medium of exchange distinguishes it from many other financial institutions. Stocks and bonds, like bank deposits, are a possible *store of value* for the wealth that people have accumulated in past saving, but access to this wealth is not as easy, cheap, and immediate as just writing a check or using a debit card. For now, we ignore this second role of banks, but we will return to it when we discuss the monetary system later in the book.

Mutual Funds   A financial intermediary of increasing importance in the U.S. economy is the mutual fund. A **mutual fund** is an institution that sells shares to the public and uses the proceeds to buy a selection, or *portfolio,* of various types of stocks, bonds, or both stocks and bonds. The shareholder of the mutual fund accepts all the risk and return associated with the portfolio. If the value of the portfolio rises, the shareholder benefits; if the value of the portfolio falls, the shareholder suffers the loss.

The primary advantage of mutual funds is that they allow people with small amounts of money to diversify their holdings. Buyers of stocks and bonds are

mutual fund
an institution that sells shares to the public and uses the proceeds to buy a portfolio of stocks and bonds

ARLO AND JANIS by Jimmy Johnson

well advised to heed the adage: Don't put all your eggs in one basket. Because the value of any single stock or bond is tied to the fortunes of one company, holding a single kind of stock or bond is very risky. By contrast, people who hold a diverse portfolio of stocks and bonds face less risk because they have only a small stake in each company. Mutual funds make this diversification easy. With only a few hundred dollars, a person can buy shares in a mutual fund and, indirectly, become the part owner or creditor of hundreds of major companies. For this service, the company operating the mutual fund charges shareholders a fee, usually between 0.5 and 2.0 percent of assets each year.

A second advantage claimed by mutual fund companies is that mutual funds give ordinary people access to the skills of professional money managers. The managers of most mutual funds pay close attention to the developments and prospects of the companies in which they buy stock. These managers buy the stock of companies they view as having a profitable future and sell the stock of companies with less promising prospects. This professional management, it is argued, should increase the return that mutual fund depositors earn on their savings.

Financial economists, however, are often skeptical of this second argument. With thousands of money managers paying close attention to each company's prospects, the price of a company's stock is usually a good reflection of the company's true value. As a result, it is hard to "beat the market" by buying good stocks and selling bad ones. In fact, mutual funds called *index funds,* which buy all the stocks in a given stock index, perform somewhat better on average than mutual funds that take advantage of active trading by professional money managers. The explanation for the superior performance of index funds is that they keep costs low by buying and selling very rarely and by not having to pay the salaries of the professional money managers.

Summing Up

The U.S. economy contains a large variety of financial institutions. In addition to the bond market, the stock market, banks, and mutual funds, there are also pension funds, credit unions, insurance companies, and even the local loan shark. These institutions differ in many ways. When analyzing the macroeconomic role of the financial system, however, it is more important to keep in mind the similarity of these institutions than the differences. These financial institutions all serve the same goal: directing the resources of savers into the hands of borrowers.

QUICK QUIZ   *What is stock? What is a bond? How are they different? How are they similar?*

FYI

> Financial Crises

In 2008 and 2009, the U.S. economy and many other major economies around the world experienced a financial crisis, which in turn led to a deep downturn in economic activity. We will examine these events in detail later in this book, but here we can outline the key elements of financial crises.

The first element of a financial crisis is a large decline in some asset prices. In 2008 and 2009, that asset was real estate. The price of housing, after experiencing a boom earlier in the decade, fell by about 30 percent over just a few years. Such a large decline in real estate prices had not been seen in the United States since the 1930s.

The second element of a financial crisis is insolvencies at financial institutions. In 2008 and 2009, many banks and other financial firms had in effect placed bets on real estate prices by holding mortgages backed by that real estate. When house prices fell, large numbers of homeowners stopped repaying their loans. These defaults pushed several financial institutions toward bankruptcy.

The third element of a financial crisis is a decline in confidence in financial institutions. While some deposits in banks are insured by government policies, not all are. As insolvencies mounted, every financial institution became a possible candidate for the next bankruptcy. Individuals and firms with uninsured deposits in those institutions pulled out their money. Facing a rash of withdrawals,

banks started selling off assets (sometimes at reduced "fire-sale" prices), and they cut back on new lending.

The fourth element of a financial crisis is a credit crunch. With many financial institutions facing difficulties, would-be borrowers had trouble getting loans, even if they had profitable investment projects. In essence, the financial system had trouble performing its normal function of directing the resources of savers into the hands of borrowers with the best investment opportunities.

The fifth element of a financial crisis is an economic downturn. With people unable to obtain financing for new investment projects, the overall demand for goods and services declined. As a result, for reasons we discuss more fully later in the book, national income fell and unemployment rose.

The sixth and final element of a financial crisis is a vicious circle. The economic downturn reduced the profitability of many companies and the value of many assets. Thus, we returned to step one, and the problems in the financial system and the economic downturn reinforced each other.

Financial crises, such as that of 2008 and 2009, can have severe consequences. Fortunately, they do end. Financial institutions eventually get back on their feet, perhaps with some help from government policy, and they return to their normal function of financial intermediation.

Saving and Investment in the National Income Accounts

Events that occur within the financial system are central to understanding developments in the overall economy. As we have just seen, the institutions that make up this system—the bond market, the stock market, banks, and mutual funds— have the role of coordinating the economy's saving and investment. And as we saw in the previous chapter, saving and investment are important determinants of long-run growth in GDP and living standards. As a result, macroeconomists need to understand how financial markets work and how various events and policies affect them.

As a starting point for an analysis of financial markets, we discuss in this section the key macroeconomic variables that measure activity in these markets. Our emphasis here is not on behavior but on accounting. *Accounting* refers to how various numbers are defined and added up. A personal accountant might help an individual add up her income and expenses. A national income accountant does the same thing for the economy as a whole. The national income accounts include, in particular, GDP and the many related statistics.

The rules of national income accounting include several important identities. Recall that an *identity* is an equation that must be true because of the way the variables in the equation are defined. Identities are useful to keep in mind, for they clarify how different variables are related to one another. Here we consider some accounting identities that shed light on the macroeconomic role of financial markets.

Some Important Identities

Recall that gross domestic product (GDP) is both total income in an economy and the total expenditure on the economy's output of goods and services. GDP (denoted as Y) is divided into four components of expenditure: consumption (C), investment (I), government purchases (G), and net exports (NX). We write

$$Y = C + I + G + NX.$$

This equation is an identity because every dollar of expenditure that shows up on the left side also shows up in one of the four components on the right side. Because of the way each of the variables is defined and measured, this equation must always hold.

In this chapter, we simplify our analysis by assuming that the economy we are examining is closed. A *closed economy* is one that does not interact with other economies. In particular, a closed economy does not engage in international trade in goods and services, nor does it engage in international borrowing and lending. Actual economies are *open economies*—that is, they interact with other economies around the world. Nonetheless, assuming a closed economy is a useful simplification with which we can learn some lessons that apply to all economies. Moreover, this assumption applies perfectly to the world economy (for interplanetary trade is not yet common).

Because a closed economy does not engage in international trade, imports and exports are exactly zero. Therefore, net exports (NX) are also zero. In this case, we can write

$$Y = C + I + G.$$

This equation states that GDP is the sum of consumption, investment, and government purchases. Each unit of output sold in a closed economy is consumed, invested, or bought by the government.

To see what this identity can tell us about financial markets, subtract C and G from both sides of this equation. We obtain

$$Y - C - G = I.$$

national saving (saving)

the total income in the economy that remains after paying for consumption and government purchases

The left side of this equation ($Y - C - G$) is the total income in the economy that remains after paying for consumption and government purchases: This amount is called **national saving**, or just **saving**, and is denoted S. Substituting S for $Y - C - G$, we can write the last equation as

$$S = I.$$

This equation states that saving equals investment.

To understand the meaning of national saving, it is helpful to manipulate the definition a bit more. Let T denote the amount that the government collects from households in taxes minus the amount it pays back to households in the form of transfer payments (such as Social Security and welfare). We can then write national saving in either of two ways:

$$S = Y - C - G$$

or

$$S = (Y - T - C) + (T - G).$$

These equations are the same because the two Ts in the second equation cancel each other, but each reveals a different way of thinking about national saving. In particular, the second equation separates national saving into two pieces: private saving $(Y - T - C)$ and public saving $(T - G)$.

Consider each of these two pieces. **Private saving** is the amount of income that households have left after paying their taxes and paying for their consumption. In particular, because households receive income of Y, pay taxes of T, and spend C on consumption, private saving is $Y - T - C$. **Public saving** is the amount of tax revenue that the government has left after paying for its spending. The government receives T in tax revenue and spends G on goods and services. If T exceeds G, the government runs a **budget surplus** because it receives more money than it spends. This surplus of $T - G$ represents public saving. If the government spends more than it receives in tax revenue, then G is larger than T. In this case, the government runs a **budget deficit,** and public saving $T - G$ is a negative number.

Now consider how these accounting identities are related to financial markets. The equation $S = I$ reveals an important fact: *For the economy as a whole, saving must be equal to investment.* Yet this fact raises some important questions: What mechanisms lie behind this identity? What coordinates those people who are deciding how much to save and those people who are deciding how much to invest? The answer is the financial system. The bond market, the stock market, banks, mutual funds, and other financial markets and intermediaries stand between the two sides of the $S = I$ equation. They take in the nation's saving and direct it to the nation's investment.

The Meaning of Saving and Investment

The terms *saving* and *investment* can sometimes be confusing. Most people use these terms casually and sometimes interchangeably. By contrast, the macroeconomists who put together the national income accounts use these terms carefully and distinctly.

Consider an example. Suppose that Larry earns more than he spends and deposits his unspent income in a bank or uses it to buy some stock or a bond from a corporation. Because Larry's income exceeds his consumption, he adds to the nation's saving. Larry might think of himself as "investing" his money, but a macroeconomist would call Larry's act saving rather than investment.

In the language of macroeconomics, investment refers to the purchase of new capital, such as equipment or buildings. When Moe borrows from the bank to build himself a new house, he adds to the nation's investment. (Remember, the purchase of a new house is the one form of household spending that is investment rather than consumption.) Similarly, when the Curly Corporation sells some stock and uses the proceeds to build a new factory, it also adds to the nation's investment.

private saving
the income that households have left after paying for taxes and consumption

public saving
the tax revenue that the government has left after paying for its spending

budget surplus
an excess of tax revenue over government spending

budget deficit
a shortfall of tax revenue from government spending

Although the accounting identity $S = I$ shows that saving and investment are equal for the economy as a whole, this does not have to be true for every individual household or firm. Larry's saving can be greater than his investment, and he can deposit the excess in a bank. Moe's saving can be less than his investment, and he can borrow the shortfall from a bank. Banks and other financial institutions make these individual differences between saving and investment possible by allowing one person's saving to finance another person's investment.

QUICK QUIZ   *Define* private saving, public saving, national saving, *and* investment. *How are they related?*

The Market for Loanable Funds

Having discussed some of the important financial institutions in our economy and the macroeconomic role of these institutions, we are ready to build a model of financial markets. Our purpose in building this model is to explain how financial markets coordinate the economy's saving and investment. The model also gives us a tool with which we can analyze various government policies that influence saving and investment.

To keep things simple, we assume that the economy has only one financial market, called the **market for loanable funds**. All savers go to this market to deposit their saving, and all borrowers go to this market to take out their loans. Thus, the term *loanable funds* refers to all income that people have chosen to save and lend out, rather than use for their own consumption, and to the amount that investors have chosen to borrow to fund new investment projects. In the market for loanable funds, there is one interest rate, which is both the return to saving and the cost of borrowing.

The assumption of a single financial market, of course, is not literally true. As we have seen, the economy has many types of financial institutions. But as we discussed in Chapter 2, the art in building an economic model is simplifying the world in order to explain it. For our purposes here, we can ignore the diversity of financial institutions and assume that the economy has a single financial market.

market for loanable funds

the market in which those who want to save supply funds and those who want to borrow to invest demand funds

Supply and Demand for Loanable Funds

The economy's market for loanable funds, like other markets in the economy, is governed by supply and demand. To understand how the market for loanable funds operates, therefore, we first look at the sources of supply and demand in that market.

The supply of loanable funds comes from people who have some extra income they want to save and lend out. This lending can occur directly, such as when a household buys a bond from a firm, or it can occur indirectly, such as when a household makes a deposit in a bank, which in turn uses the funds to make loans. In both cases, *saving is the source of the supply of loanable funds.*

The demand for loanable funds comes from households and firms who wish to borrow to make investments. This demand includes families taking out mortgages to buy new homes. It also includes firms borrowing to buy new equipment or build factories. In both cases, *investment is the source of the demand for loanable funds.*

The interest rate is the price of a loan. It represents the amount that borrowers pay for loans and the amount that lenders receive on their saving. Because a high

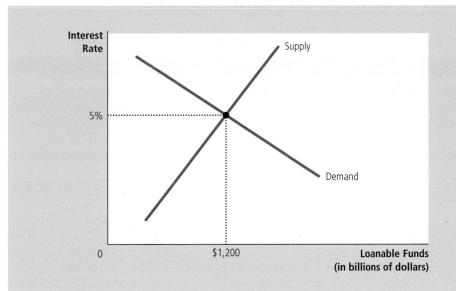

Figure **1**

The Market for Loanable Funds
The interest rate in the economy
adjusts to balance the supply and
demand for loanable funds. The
supply of loanable funds comes
from national saving, including
both private saving and public
saving. The demand for loanable
funds comes from firms and
households that want to borrow
for purposes of investment. Here
the equilibrium interest rate is
5 percent, and $1,200 billion of
loanable funds are supplied and
demanded.

interest rate makes borrowing more expensive, the quantity of loanable funds
demanded falls as the interest rate rises. Similarly, because a high interest rate
makes saving more attractive, the quantity of loanable funds supplied rises as the
interest rate rises. In other words, the demand curve for loanable funds slopes
downward, and the supply curve for loanable funds slopes upward.

Figure 1 shows the interest rate that balances the supply and demand for loanable funds. In the equilibrium shown, the interest rate is 5 percent, and the quantity
of loanable funds demanded and the quantity of loanable funds supplied both
equal $1,200 billion.

The adjustment of the interest rate to the equilibrium level occurs for the usual
reasons. If the interest rate were lower than the equilibrium level, the quantity
of loanable funds supplied would be less than the quantity of loanable funds
demanded. The resulting shortage of loanable funds would encourage lenders
to raise the interest rate they charge. A higher interest rate would encourage saving (thereby increasing the quantity of loanable funds supplied) and discourage
borrowing for investment (thereby decreasing the quantity of loanable funds
demanded). Conversely, if the interest rate were higher than the equilibrium
level, the quantity of loanable funds supplied would exceed the quantity of loanable funds demanded. As lenders competed for the scarce borrowers, interest rates
would be driven down. In this way, the interest rate approaches the equilibrium
level at which the supply and demand for loanable funds exactly balance.

Recall that economists distinguish between the real interest rate and the
nominal interest rate. The nominal interest rate is the interest rate as usually
reported—the monetary return to saving and the monetary cost of borrowing. The
real interest rate is the nominal interest rate corrected for inflation; it equals the
nominal interest rate minus the inflation rate. Because inflation erodes the value
of money over time, the real interest rate more accurately reflects the real return
to saving and the real cost of borrowing. Therefore, the supply and demand for
loanable funds depend on the real (rather than nominal) interest rate, and the
equilibrium in Figure 1 should be interpreted as determining the real interest rate

in the economy. For the rest of this chapter, when you see the term *interest rate,* you should remember that we are talking about the real interest rate.

This model of the supply and demand for loanable funds shows that financial markets work much like other markets in the economy. In the market for milk, for instance, the price of milk adjusts so that the quantity of milk supplied balances the quantity of milk demanded. In this way, the invisible hand coordinates the behavior of dairy farmers and the behavior of milk drinkers. Once we realize that saving represents the supply of loanable funds and investment represents the demand, we can see how the invisible hand coordinates saving and investment. When the interest rate adjusts to balance supply and demand in the market for loanable funds, it coordinates the behavior of people who want to save (the suppliers of loanable funds) and the behavior of people who want to invest (the demanders of loanable funds).

We can now use this analysis of the market for loanable funds to examine various government policies that affect the economy's saving and investment. Because this model is just supply and demand in a particular market, we analyze any policy using the three steps discussed in Chapter 4. First, we decide whether the policy shifts the supply curve or the demand curve. Second, we determine the direction of the shift. Third, we use the supply-and-demand diagram to see how the equilibrium changes.

Policy 1: Saving Incentives

American families save a smaller fraction of their incomes than their counterparts in many other countries, such as Japan and Germany. Although the reasons for these international differences are unclear, many U.S. policymakers view the low level of U.S. saving as a major problem. One of the *Ten Principles of Economics* in Chapter 1 is that a country's standard of living depends on its ability to produce goods and services. And as we discussed in the preceding chapter, saving is an important long-run determinant of a nation's productivity. If the United States could somehow raise its saving rate to the level that prevails in other countries, the growth rate of GDP would increase, and over time, U.S. citizens would enjoy a higher standard of living.

Another of the *Ten Principles of Economics* is that people respond to incentives. Many economists have used this principle to suggest that the low saving rate in the United States is at least partly attributable to tax laws that discourage saving. The U.S. federal government, as well as many state governments, collects revenue by taxing income, including interest and dividend income. To see the effects of this policy, consider a 25-year-old who saves $1,000 and buys a 30-year bond that pays an interest rate of 9 percent. In the absence of taxes, the $1,000 grows to $13,268 when the individual reaches age 55. Yet if that interest is taxed at a rate of, say, 33 percent, then the after-tax interest rate is only 6 percent. In this case, the $1,000 grows to only $5,743 after 30 years. The tax on interest income substantially reduces the future payoff from current saving and, as a result, reduces the incentive for people to save.

In response to this problem, many economists and lawmakers have proposed reforming the tax code to encourage greater saving. For example, one proposal is to expand eligibility for special accounts, such as Individual Retirement Accounts, that allow people to shelter some of their saving from taxation. Let's consider the effect of such a saving incentive on the market for loanable funds, as illustrated in Figure 2. We analyze this policy following our three steps.

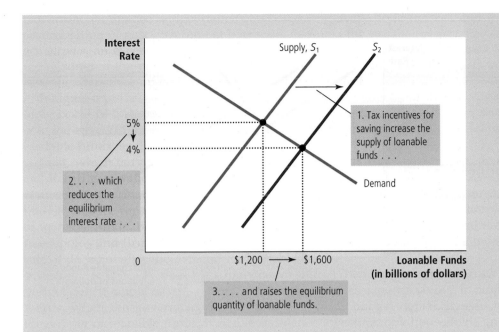

Figure **2**

Saving Incentives Increase the Supply of Loanable Funds
A change in the tax laws to encourage Americans to save more would shift the supply of loanable funds to the right from S_1 to S_2. As a result, the equilibrium interest rate would fall, and the lower interest rate would stimulate investment. Here the equilibrium interest rate falls from 5 percent to 4 percent, and the equilibrium quantity of loanable funds saved and invested rises from $1,200 billion to $1,600 billion.

First, which curve would this policy affect? Because the tax change would alter the incentive for households to save *at any given interest rate*, it would affect the quantity of loanable funds supplied at each interest rate. Thus, the supply of loanable funds would shift. The demand for loanable funds would remain the same because the tax change would not directly affect the amount that borrowers want to borrow at any given interest rate.

Second, which way would the supply curve shift? Because saving would be taxed less heavily than under current law, households would increase their saving by consuming a smaller fraction of their income. Households would use this additional saving to increase their deposits in banks or to buy more bonds. The supply of loanable funds would increase, and the supply curve would shift to the right from S_1 to S_2, as shown in Figure 2.

Finally, we can compare the old and new equilibria. In the figure, the increased supply of loanable funds reduces the interest rate from 5 percent to 4 percent. The lower interest rate raises the quantity of loanable funds demanded from $1,200 billion to $1,600 billion. That is, the shift in the supply curve moves the market equilibrium along the demand curve. With a lower cost of borrowing, households and firms are motivated to borrow more to finance greater investment. Thus, *if a reform of the tax laws encouraged greater saving, the result would be lower interest rates and greater investment.*

This analysis of the effects of increased saving is widely accepted among economists, but there is less consensus about what kinds of tax changes should be enacted. Many economists endorse tax reform aimed at increasing saving to stimulate investment and growth. Yet others are skeptical that these tax changes would have much effect on national saving. These skeptics also doubt the equity of the proposed reforms. They argue that, in many cases, the benefits of the tax changes would accrue primarily to the wealthy, who are least in need of tax relief.

crowding out

a decrease in investment that results from government borrowing

Third, we can compare the old and new equilibria. In the figure, when the budget deficit reduces the supply of loanable funds, the interest rate rises from 5 percent to 6 percent. This higher interest rate then alters the behavior of the households and firms that participate in the loan market. In particular, many demanders of loanable funds are discouraged by the higher interest rate. Fewer families buy new homes, and fewer firms choose to build new factories. The fall in investment because of government borrowing is called **crowding out** and is represented in the figure by the movement along the demand curve from a quantity of $1,200 billion in loanable funds to a quantity of $800 billion. That is, when the government borrows to finance its budget deficit, it crowds out private borrowers who are trying to finance investment.

Thus, the most basic lesson about budget deficits follows directly from their effects on the supply and demand for loanable funds: *When the government reduces national saving by running a budget deficit, the interest rate rises, and investment falls.* Because investment is important for long-run economic growth, government budget deficits reduce the economy's growth rate.

Why, you might ask, does a budget deficit affect the supply of loanable funds, rather than the demand for them? After all, the government finances a budget deficit by selling bonds, thereby borrowing from the private sector. Why does increased borrowing from the government shift the supply curve, while increased borrowing by private investors shifts the demand curve? To answer this question, we need to examine more precisely the meaning of "loanable funds." The model as presented here takes this term to mean the *flow of resources available to fund private investment*; thus, a government budget deficit reduces the supply of loanable funds. If, instead, we had defined the term "loanable funds" to mean the *flow of resources available from private saving,* then the government budget deficit would increase demand rather than reduce supply. Changing the interpretation of the term would cause a semantic change in how we described the model, but the bottom line from the analysis would be the same: In either case, a budget deficit increases the interest rate, thereby crowding out private borrowers who are relying on financial markets to fund private investment projects.

Now that we understand the impact of budget deficits, we can turn the analysis around and see that government budget surpluses have the opposite effects. When government collects more in tax revenue than it spends, it saves the difference by retiring some of the outstanding government debt. This budget surplus, or public saving, contributes to national saving. Thus, *a budget surplus increases the supply of loanable funds, reduces the interest rate, and stimulates investment.* Higher investment, in turn, means greater capital accumulation and more rapid economic growth.

CASE STUDY The History of U.S. Government Debt

How indebted is the U.S. government? The answer to this question varies substantially over time. Figure 5 shows the debt of the U.S. federal government expressed as a percentage of U.S. GDP. It shows that the government debt has fluctuated from zero in 1836 to 107 percent of GDP in 1945.

The behavior of the debt-GDP ratio is one gauge of what's happening with the government's finances. Because GDP is a rough measure of the government's tax base, a declining debt-GDP ratio indicates that the government indebtedness is

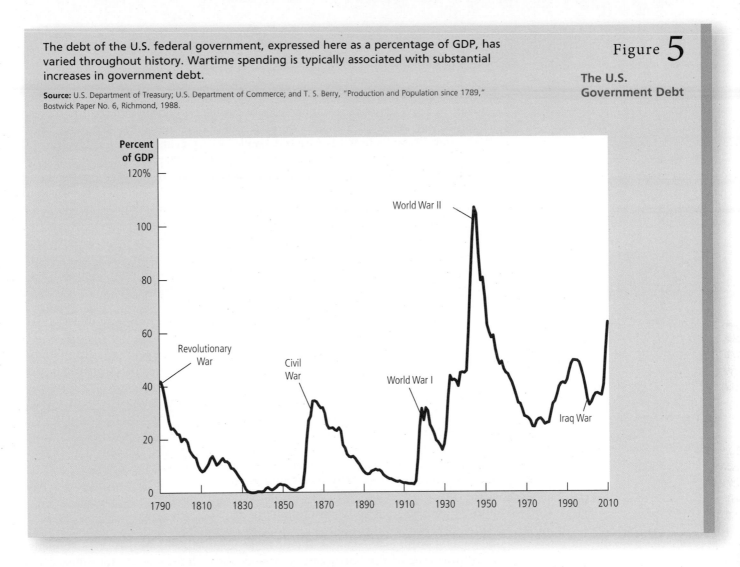

The debt of the U.S. federal government, expressed here as a percentage of GDP, has varied throughout history. Wartime spending is typically associated with substantial increases in government debt.

Source: U.S. Department of Treasury; U.S. Department of Commerce; and T. S. Berry, "Production and Population since 1789," Bostwick Paper No. 6, Richmond, 1988.

Figure **5**

The U.S. Government Debt

shrinking relative to its ability to raise tax revenue. This suggests that the government is, in some sense, living within its means. By contrast, a rising debt-GDP ratio means that the government indebtedness is increasing relative to its ability to raise tax revenue. It is often interpreted as meaning that fiscal policy—government spending and taxes—cannot be sustained forever at current levels.

Throughout history, the primary cause of fluctuations in government debt is war. When wars occur, government spending on national defense rises substantially to pay for soldiers and military equipment. Taxes sometimes rise as well but typically by much less than the increase in spending. The result is a budget deficit and increasing government debt. When the war is over, government spending declines, and the debt-GDP ratio starts declining as well.

There are two reasons to believe that debt financing of war is an appropriate policy. First, it allows the government to keep tax rates smooth over time. Without debt financing, tax rates would have to rise sharply during wars, and this would cause a substantial decline in economic efficiency. Second, debt financing of wars shifts part of the cost of wars to future generations, who will have to pay off the government debt. This is arguably a fair distribution of the burden, for future generations get some of the benefit when one generation fights a war to defend the nation against foreign aggressors.

One large increase in government debt that cannot be explained by war is the increase that occurred beginning around 1980. When President Ronald Reagan took office in 1981, he was committed to smaller government and lower taxes. Yet he found cutting government spending to be more difficult politically than cutting taxes. The result was the beginning of a period of large budget deficits that continued not only through Reagan's time in office but also for many years thereafter. As a result, government debt rose from 26 percent of GDP in 1980 to 50 percent of GDP in 1993.

As we discussed earlier, government budget deficits reduce national saving, investment, and long-run economic growth, and this is precisely why the rise in government debt during the 1980s troubled many economists and policymakers. When Bill Clinton moved into the Oval Office in 1993, deficit reduction was his first major goal. Similarly, when the Republicans took control of Congress in 1995, deficit reduction was high on their legislative agenda. Both of these efforts substantially reduced the size of the government budget deficit, and it eventually turned into a surplus. As a result, by the late 1990s, the debt-GDP ratio was declining.

The debt-GDP ratio started rising again during the first few years of the George W. Bush presidency, as the budget surplus turned into a budget deficit. There were three reasons for this change. First, President Bush signed into law several major tax cuts, which he had promised during the 2000 presidential campaign. Second, in 2001, the economy experienced a *recession* (a reduction in economic activity), which automatically decreased tax revenue and increased government spending. Third, spending on homeland security following the September 11, 2001 attacks and the subsequent wars in Iraq and Afghanistan led to increases in government spending.

Truly dramatic increase in the debt-GDP ratio started occurring in 2008, as the economy experienced a financial crisis and a deep recession (a topic we will be addressing more fully in coming chapters). The recession automatically increased the budget deficit, and several policy measures passed by the Bush and Obama administrations aimed at combating the recession reduced tax revenue and increased government spending even more. In 2009 and 2010, the federal government's budget deficit was about 10 percent of GDP, the largest deficits since World War II. The borrowing to finance these deficits led to the substantial increase in the debt-GDP ratio shown in the figure. Putting the federal budget back on a sustainable path with a stable or declining debt-GDP ratio is one of the great policy challenges facing future generations of policymakers. ■

QUICK QUIZ   *If more Americans adopted a "live for today" approach to life, how would this affect saving, investment, and the interest rate?*

Conclusion

"Neither a borrower nor a lender be," Polonius advises his son in Shakespeare's *Hamlet*. If everyone followed this advice, this chapter would have been unnecessary.

Few economists would agree with Polonius. In our economy, people borrow and lend often, and usually for good reason. You may borrow one day to start your own business or to buy a home. And people may lend to you in the hope that the interest you pay will allow them to enjoy a more prosperous retirement. The financial system has the job of coordinating all this borrowing and lending activity.

In many ways, financial markets are like other markets in the economy. The price of loanable funds—the interest rate—is governed by the forces of supply and demand, just as other prices in the economy are. And we can analyze shifts in supply or demand in financial markets as we do in other markets. One of the *Ten Principles of Economics* introduced in Chapter 1 is that markets are usually a good way to organize economic activity. This principle applies to financial markets as well. When financial markets bring the supply and demand for loanable funds into balance, they help allocate the economy's scarce resources to their most efficient use.

In one way, however, financial markets are special. Financial markets, unlike most other markets, serve the important role of linking the present and the future. Those who supply loanable funds—savers—do so because they want to convert some of their current income into future purchasing power. Those who demand loanable funds—borrowers—do so because they want to invest today in order to have additional capital in the future to produce goods and services. Thus, well-functioning financial markets are important not only for current generations but also for future generations who will inherit many of the resulting benefits.

SUMMARY

- The U.S. financial system is made up of many types of financial institutions, such as the bond market, the stock market, banks, and mutual funds. All these institutions act to direct the resources of households that want to save some of their income into the hands of households and firms that want to borrow.

- National income accounting identities reveal some important relationships among macroeconomic variables. In particular, for a closed economy, national saving must equal investment. Financial institutions are the mechanism through which the economy matches one person's saving with another person's investment.

- The interest rate is determined by the supply and demand for loanable funds. The supply

of loanable funds comes from households that want to save some of their income and lend it out. The demand for loanable funds comes from households and firms that want to borrow for investment. To analyze how any policy or event affects the interest rate, one must consider how it affects the supply and demand for loanable funds.

- National saving equals private saving plus public saving. A government budget deficit represents negative public saving and, therefore, reduces national saving and the supply of loanable funds available to finance investment. When a government budget deficit crowds out investment, it reduces the growth of productivity and GDP.

KEY CONCEPTS

QUESTIONS FOR REVIEW

1. What is the role of the financial system? Name and describe two markets that are part of the financial system in the U.S. economy. Name and describe two financial intermediaries.
2. Why is it important for people who own stocks and bonds to diversify their holdings? What type of financial institution makes diversification easier?
3. What is national saving? What is private saving? What is public saving? How are these three variables related?

4. What is investment? How is it related to national saving?
5. Describe a change in the tax code that might increase private saving. If this policy were implemented, how would it affect the market for loanable funds?
6. What is a government budget deficit? How does it affect interest rates, investment, and economic growth?

PROBLEMS AND APPLICATIONS

1. For each of the following pairs, which bond would you expect to pay a higher interest rate? Explain.
   a. a bond of the U.S. government or a bond of an East European government
   b. a bond that repays the principal in year 2015 or a bond that repays the principal in year 2040
   c. a bond from Coca-Cola or a bond from a software company you run in your garage
   d. a bond issued by the federal government or a bond issued by New York State
2. Many workers hold large amounts of stock issued by the firms at which they work. Why do you suppose companies encourage this behavior? Why might a person *not* want to hold stock in the company where he works?
3. Explain the difference between saving and investment as defined by a macroeconomist. Which of the following situations represent investment? Saving? Explain.
   a. Your family takes out a mortgage and buys a new house.
   b. You use your $200 paycheck to buy stock in AT&T.
   c. Your roommate earns $100 and deposits it in her account at a bank.
   d. You borrow $1,000 from a bank to buy a car to use in your pizza delivery business.
4. Suppose GDP is $8 trillion, taxes are $1.5 trillion, private saving is $0.5 trillion, and public saving is $0.2 trillion. Assuming this economy

is closed, calculate consumption, government purchases, national saving, and investment.
5. Economists in Funlandia, a closed economy, have collected the following information about the economy for a particular year:

$$Y = 10,000$$
$$C = 6,000$$
$$T = 1,500$$
$$G = 1,700$$

The economists also estimate that the investment function is:

$$I = 3,300 - 100\,r,$$

where r is the country's real interest rate, expressed as a percentage. Calculate private saving, public saving, national saving, investment, and the equilibrium real interest rate.
6. Suppose that Intel is considering building a new chip-making factory.
   a. Assuming that Intel needs to borrow money in the bond market, why would an increase in interest rates affect Intel's decision about whether to build the factory?
   b. If Intel has enough of its own funds to finance the new factory without borrowing, would an increase in interest rates still affect Intel's decision about whether to build the factory? Explain.
7. Three students have each saved $1,000. Each has an investment opportunity in which he or

she can invest up to $2,000. Here are the rates of return on the students' investment projects:

Harry	5 percent
Ron	8 percent
Hermione	20 percent

   a. If borrowing and lending is prohibited, so each student uses only his or her saving to finance his or her own investment project, how much will each student have a year later when the project pays its return?
   b. Now suppose their school opens up a market for loanable funds in which students can borrow and lend among themselves at an interest rate r. What would determine whether a student would choose to be a borrower or lender in this market?
   c. Among these three students, what would be the quantity of loanable funds supplied and quantity demanded at an interest rate of 7 percent? At 10 percent?
   d. At what interest rate would the loanable funds market among these three students be in equilibrium? At this interest rate, which student(s) would borrow, and which student(s) would lend?
   e. At the equilibrium interest rate, how much does each student have a year later after the investment projects pay their return and loans have been repaid? Compare your answers to those you gave in part (a). Who benefits from the existence of the loanable funds market—the borrowers or the lenders? Is anyone worse off?
8. Suppose the government borrows $20 billion more next year than this year.
   a. Use a supply-and-demand diagram to analyze this policy. Does the interest rate rise or fall?
   b. What happens to investment? To private saving? To public saving? To national saving? Compare the size of the changes to the $20 billion of extra government borrowing.
   c. How does the elasticity of supply of loanable funds affect the size of these changes?

   d. How does the elasticity of demand for loanable funds affect the size of these changes?
   e. Suppose households believe that greater government borrowing today implies higher taxes to pay off the government debt in the future. What does this belief do to private saving and the supply of loanable funds today? Does it increase or decrease the effects you discussed in parts (a) and (b)?
9. In the summer of 2010, Congress passed a far-reaching financial reform to prevent another financial crisis like the one experienced in 2008–2009. Consider the following possibilities:
   a. Suppose that, by requiring firms to comply with strict regulations, the bill increases the costs of investment. On a well-labeled graph, show the consequences of the bill on the market for loanable funds. Be sure to specify changes in the equilibrium interest rate and level of saving and investment. What are the effects of the bill on long-run economic growth?
   b. Suppose, on the other hand, that by effectively regulating the financial system, the bill increases savers' confidence in the financial system. Show the consequences of the policy in this situation on a new graph, again noting changes in the equilibrium interest rate and level of saving and investment. Again evaluate the effects on long-run growth.
10. This chapter explains that investment can be increased both by reducing taxes on private saving and by reducing the government budget deficit.
   a. Why is it difficult to implement both of these policies at the same time?
   b. What would you need to know about private saving to judge which of these two policies would be a more effective way to raise investment?

For further information on topics in this chapter, additional problems, applications, examples, quizzes, and more, please visit our website, www.cengage.com/economics/mankiw.

The Basic Tools of Finance

S ometime in your life, you will have to deal with the economy's financial system. You will deposit your savings in a bank account, or you will take out a mortgage to buy a house. After you have a job, you will decide whether to invest the funds in your retirement account in stocks, bonds, or other financial instruments. If you try to put together your own portfolio, you will have to decide between buying stocks in established companies such as General Electric or newer ones such as Google. And whenever you watch the evening news, you will hear reports about whether the stock market is up or down, together with the often feeble attempts to explain why the market behaves as it does.

If you reflect for a moment on the many financial decisions you will make during your life, you will see two related elements in almost all of them: time and risk. As we saw in the preceding two chapters, the financial system coordinates the economy's saving and investment, which in turn are crucial determinants of economic growth. Most fundamentally, the financial system concerns decisions and actions we undertake today that will affect our lives in the future. But the future is unknown. When a person decides to allocate some saving, or a firm decides to undertake an investment, the decision is based on a guess about the likely result. The actual result, however, could end up being very different from what was expected.

This chapter introduces some tools that help us understand the decisions that people make as they participate in financial markets. The field of **finance** develops these tools in great detail, and you may choose to take courses that focus on this topic. But because the financial system is so important to the functioning of the economy, many of the basic insights of finance are central to understanding how the economy works. The tools of finance may also help you think through some of the decisions that you will make in your own life.

This chapter takes up three topics. First, we discuss how to compare sums of money at different points in time. Second, we discuss how to manage risk. Third, we build on our analysis of time and risk to examine what determines the value of an asset, such as a share of stock.

finance
the field that studies how people make decisions regarding the allocation of resources over time and the handling of risk

Present Value: Measuring the Time Value of Money

Imagine that someone offers to give you $100 today or $100 in 10 years. Which would you choose? This is an easy question. Getting $100 today is better because you can always deposit the money in a bank, still have it in 10 years, and earn interest on the $100 along the way. The lesson: Money today is more valuable than the same amount of money in the future.

Now consider a harder question: Imagine that someone offers you $100 today or $200 in 10 years. Which would you choose? To answer this question, you need some way to compare sums of money from different points in time. Economists do this with a concept called present value. The **present value** of any future sum of money is the amount today that would be needed, at current interest rates, to produce that future sum.

To learn how to use the concept of present value, let's work through a couple of simple examples:

Question: If you put $100 in a bank account today, how much will it be worth in N years? That is, what will be the **future value** of this $100?

Answer: Let's use r to denote the interest rate expressed in decimal form (so an interest rate of 5 percent means $r = 0.05$). Suppose that interest is paid annually and that the interest paid remains in the bank account to earn more interest—a process called **compounding.** Then the $100 will become

present value
the amount of money today that would be needed, using prevailing interest rates, to produce a given future amount of money

future value
the amount of money in the future that an amount of money today will yield, given prevailing interest rates

compounding
the accumulation of a sum of money in, say, a bank account, where the interest earned remains in the account to earn additional interest in the future

$(1 + r) \times \$100$	after 1 year,
$(1 + r) \times (1 + r) \times \$100 = (1 + r)^2 \times \$100$	after 2 years,
$(1 + r) \times (1 + r) \times (1 + r) \times \$100 = (1 + r)^3 \times \$100$	after 3 years, . . .
$(1 + r)^N \times \$100$	after N years.

For example, if we are investing at an interest rate of 5 percent for 10 years, then the future value of the $100 will be $(1.05)^{10} \times \$100$, which is $163.

Question: Now suppose you are going to be paid $200 in N years. What is the *present value* of this future payment? That is, how much would you have to deposit in a bank right now to yield $200 in N years?

Answer: To answer this question, just turn the previous answer on its head. In the last question, we computed a future value from a present value by *multiplying* by the factor $(1 + r)^N$. To compute a present value from a future value, we *divide* by the factor $(1 + r)^N$. Thus, the present value of $200 in N years is $200/(1 + r)^N$. If that amount is deposited in a bank today, after N years it would become $(1 + r)^N \times [$200/(1 + r)^N]$, which is $200. For instance, if the interest rate is 5 percent, the present value of $200 in 10 years is $200/(1.05)^{10}$, which is $123. This means that $123 deposited today in a bank account that earned 5 percent would produce $200 after 10 years.

This illustrates the general formula:

- If r is the interest rate, then an amount X to be received in N years has a present value of $X/(1 + r)^N$.

Because the possibility of earning interest reduces the present value below the amount X, the process of finding a present value of a future sum of money is called *discounting*. This formula shows precisely how much future sums should be discounted.

Let's now return to our earlier question: Should you choose $100 today or $200 in 10 years? We can infer from our calculation of present value that if the interest rate is 5 percent, you should prefer the $200 in 10 years. The future $200 has a present value of $123, which is greater than $100. You are better off waiting for the future sum.

Notice that the answer to our question depends on the interest rate. If the interest rate were 8 percent, then the $200 in 10 years would have a present value of $200/(1.08)^{10}$, which is only $93. In this case, you should take the $100 today. Why should the interest rate matter for your choice? The answer is that the higher the interest rate, the more you can earn by depositing your money in a bank, so the more attractive getting $100 today becomes.

The concept of present value is useful in many applications, including the decisions that companies face when evaluating investment projects. For instance, imagine that General Motors is thinking about building a new factory. Suppose that the factory will cost $100 million today and will yield the company $200 million in 10 years. Should General Motors undertake the project? You can see that this decision is exactly like the one we have been studying. To make its decision, the company will compare the present value of the $200 million return to the $100 million cost.

The company's decision, therefore, will depend on the interest rate. If the interest rate is 5 percent, then the present value of the $200 million return from the factory is $123 million, and the company will choose to pay the $100 million cost. By contrast, if the interest rate is 8 percent, then the present value of the return is only $93 million, and the company will decide to forgo the project. Thus, the concept of present value helps explain why investment—and thus the quantity of loanable funds demanded—declines when the interest rate rises.

Here is another application of present value: Suppose you win a million-dollar lottery and are given a choice between $20,000 a year for 50 years (totaling $1,000,000) or an immediate payment of $400,000. Which would you choose? To make the right choice, you need to calculate the present value of the stream of payments. Let's suppose the interest rate is 7 percent. After performing 50 calculations similar to those above (one calculation for each payment) and adding up the results, you would learn that the present value of this million-dollar prize at a 7 percent interest rate is only $276,000. You are better off picking the immediate

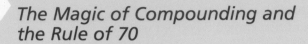

FYI

> ### The Magic of Compounding and the Rule of 70

Suppose you observe that one country has an average growth rate of 1 percent per year, while another has an average growth rate of 3 percent per year. At first, this might not seem like a big deal. What difference can 2 percent make?

The answer is: a big difference. Growth rates that seem small when written in percentage terms are large after they are compounded for many years.

Consider an example. Suppose that two college graduates—Finn and Quinn—both take their first jobs at the age of 22 earning $30,000 a year. Finn lives in an economy where all incomes grow at 1 percent per year, while Quinn lives in one where incomes grow at 3 percent per year. Straightforward calculations show what happens. Forty years later, when both are 62 years old, Finn earns $45,000 a year, while Quinn earns $98,000. Because of that difference of 2 percentage points in the growth rate, Quinn's salary is more than twice Finn's.

An old rule of thumb, called the *rule of 70*, is helpful in understanding growth rates and the effects of compounding. According to the rule of 70, if some variable grows at a rate of *x* percent per year, then

that variable doubles in approximately 70/*x* years. In Finn's economy, incomes grow at 1 percent per year, so it takes about 70 years for incomes to double. In Quinn's economy, incomes grow at 3 percent per year, so it takes about 70/3, or 23, years for incomes to double.

The rule of 70 applies not only to a growing economy but also to a growing savings account. Here is an example: In 1791, Ben Franklin died and left $5,000 to be invested for a period of 200 years to benefit medical students and scientific research. If this money had earned 7 percent per year (which would, in fact, have been possible to do), the investment would have doubled in value every 10 years. Over 200 years, it would have doubled 20 times. At the end of 200 years of compounding, the investment would have been worth $2^{20} \times \$5,000$, which is about $5 billion. (In fact, Franklin's $5,000 grew to only $2 million over 200 years because some of the money was spent along the way.)

As these examples show, growth rates and interest rates compounded over many years can lead to some spectacular results. That is probably why Albert Einstein once called compounding "the greatest mathematical discovery of all time."

payment of $400,000. The million dollars may seem like more money, but the future cash flows, once discounted to the present, are worth far less.

QUICK QUIZ   *The interest rate is 7 percent. What is the present value of $150 to be received in 10 years?*

Managing Risk

Life is full of gambles. When you go skiing, you risk breaking your leg in a fall. When you drive to work, you risk a car accident. When you put some of your savings in the stock market, you risk a fall in stock prices. The rational response to this risk is not necessarily to avoid it at any cost but to take it into account in your decision making. Let's consider how a person might do that.

Risk Aversion

risk aversion
a dislike of uncertainty

Most people are **risk averse.** This means more than that people dislike bad things happening to them. It means that they dislike bad things more than they like comparable good things.

For example, suppose a friend offers you the following opportunity. He will toss a coin. If it comes up heads, he will pay you $1,000. But if it comes up tails, you will have to pay him $1,000. Would you accept the bargain? You wouldn't if you were risk averse. For a risk-averse person, the pain of losing the $1,000 would exceed the pleasure from winning $1,000.

Economists have developed models of risk aversion using the concept of *utility,* which is a person's subjective measure of well-being or satisfaction. Every level of wealth provides a certain amount of utility, as shown by the utility function in Figure 1. But the function exhibits the property of diminishing marginal utility: The more wealth a person has, the less utility he gets from an additional dollar. Thus, in the figure, the utility function gets flatter as wealth increases. Because of diminishing marginal utility, the utility lost from losing the $1,000 bet is more than the utility gained from winning it. As a result, people are risk averse.

Risk aversion provides the starting point for explaining various things we observe in the economy. Let's consider three of them: insurance, diversification, and the risk-return trade-off.

The Markets for Insurance

One way to deal with risk is to buy insurance. The general feature of insurance contracts is that a person facing a risk pays a fee to an insurance company, which in return agrees to accept all or part of the risk. There are many types of insurance. Car insurance covers the risk of your being in an auto accident, fire insurance covers the risk that your house will burn down, health insurance covers the risk that you might need expensive medical treatment, and life insurance covers the risk that you will die and leave your family without your income. There is also insurance against the risk of living too long: For a fee paid today, an insurance company will pay you an *annuity*—a regular income every year until you die.

In a sense, every insurance contract is a gamble. It is possible that you will not be in an auto accident, that your house will not burn down, and that you will not need expensive medical treatment. In most years, you will pay the insurance company the premium and get nothing in return except peace of mind. Indeed, the insurance company is counting on the fact that most people will not make claims on their policies; otherwise, it couldn't pay out the large claims to the unlucky few and still stay in business.

From the standpoint of the economy as a whole, the role of insurance is not to eliminate the risks inherent in life but to spread them around more efficiently.

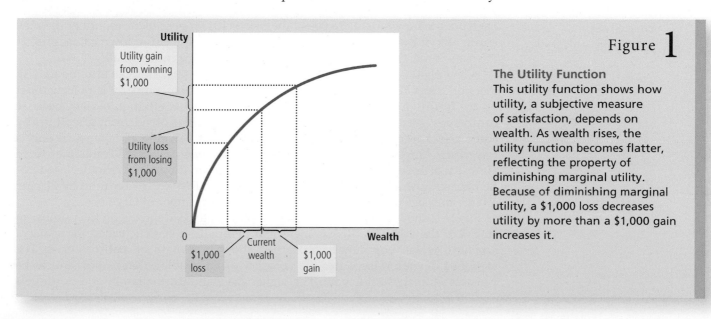

Figure 1

The Utility Function
This utility function shows how utility, a subjective measure of satisfaction, depends on wealth. As wealth rises, the utility function becomes flatter, reflecting the property of diminishing marginal utility. Because of diminishing marginal utility, a $1,000 loss decreases utility by more than a $1,000 gain increases it.

Consider fire insurance, for instance. Owning fire insurance does not reduce the risk of losing your home in a fire. But if that unlucky event occurs, the insurance company compensates you. The risk, rather than being borne by you alone, is shared among the thousands of insurance-company shareholders. Because people are risk averse, it is easier for 10,000 people to bear 1/10,000 of the risk than for one person to bear the entire risk himself.

The markets for insurance suffer from two types of problems that impede their ability to spread risk. One problem is *adverse selection:* A high-risk person is more likely to apply for insurance than a low-risk person because a high-risk person would benefit more from insurance protection. A second problem is *moral hazard:* After people buy insurance, they have less incentive to be careful about their risky behavior because the insurance company will cover much of the resulting losses. Insurance companies are aware of these problems, but they cannot fully guard against them. An insurance company cannot perfectly distinguish between high-risk and low-risk customers, and it cannot monitor all of its customers' risky behavior. The price of insurance reflects the actual risks that the insurance company will face after the insurance is bought. The high price of insurance is why some people, especially those who know themselves to be low-risk, decide against buying it and, instead, endure some of life's uncertainty on their own.

Diversification of Firm-Specific Risk

In 2002, Enron, a large and once widely respected company, went bankrupt amid accusations of fraud and accounting irregularities. Several of the company's top executives were prosecuted and ended up going to prison. The saddest part of the story, however, involved thousands of lower-level employees. Not only did they lose their jobs, but many lost their life savings as well. The employees had about two-thirds of their retirement funds in Enron stock, which became worthless.

If there is one piece of practical advice that finance offers to risk-averse people, it is this: "Don't put all your eggs in one basket." You may have heard this before, but finance has turned this folk wisdom into a science. It goes by the name **diversification.**

diversification

the reduction of risk achieved by replacing a single risk with a large number of smaller, unrelated risks

The market for insurance is one example of diversification. Imagine a town with 10,000 homeowners, each facing the risk of a house fire. If someone starts an insurance company and each person in town becomes both a shareholder and a policyholder of the company, they all reduce their risk through diversification. Each person now faces 1/10,000 of the risk of 10,000 possible fires, rather than the entire risk of a single fire in his own home. Unless the entire town catches fire at the same time, the downside that each person faces is much smaller.

When people use their savings to buy financial assets, they can also reduce risk through diversification. A person who buys stock in a company is placing a bet on the future profitability of that company. That bet is often quite risky because companies' fortunes are hard to predict. Microsoft evolved from a start-up by some geeky teenagers to one of the world's most valuable companies in only a few years; Enron went from one of the world's most respected companies to an almost worthless one in only a few months. Fortunately, a shareholder need not tie his own fortune to that of any single company. Risk can be reduced by placing a large number of small bets, rather than a small number of large ones.

Figure 2 shows how the risk of a portfolio of stocks depends on the number of stocks in the portfolio. Risk is measured here with a statistic called the *standard deviation,* which you may have learned about in a math or statistics class. The standard deviation measures the volatility of a variable—that is, how much the variable is likely to fluctuate. The higher the standard deviation of a portfolio's

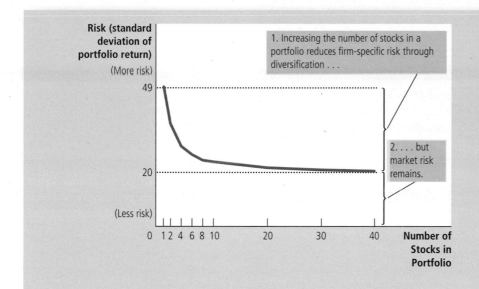

Risk (standard deviation of portfolio return)

(More risk)

1. Increasing the number of stocks in a portfolio reduces firm-specific risk through diversification . . .

2. . . . but market risk remains.

(Less risk)

49

20

0 1 2 4 6 8 10   20   30   40   **Number of Stocks in Portfolio**

Figure **2**

Diversification Reduces Risk
This figure shows how the risk of a portfolio, measured here with a statistic called the *standard deviation,* depends on the number of stocks in the portfolio. The investor is assumed to put an equal percentage of his portfolio in each of the stocks. Increasing the number of stocks reduces, but does not eliminate, the amount of risk in a stock portfolio.

Source: Adapted from Meir Statman, "How Many Stocks Make a Diversified Portfolio?" *Journal of Financial and Quantitative Analysis* 22 (September 1987): 353–364.

return, the more volatile its return is likely to be, and the riskier it is that someone holding the portfolio will fail to get the return that he or she expected.

The figure shows that the risk of a stock portfolio falls substantially as the number of stocks increases. For a portfolio with a single stock, the standard deviation is 49 percent. Going from 1 stock to 10 stocks eliminates about half the risk. Going from 10 to 20 stocks reduces the risk by another 13 percent. As the number of stocks continues to increase, risk continues to fall, although the reductions in risk after 20 or 30 stocks are small.

Notice that it is impossible to eliminate all risk by increasing the number of stocks in the portfolio. Diversification can eliminate **firm-specific risk**—the uncertainty associated with the specific companies. But diversification cannot eliminate **market risk**—the uncertainty associated with the entire economy, which affects all companies traded on the stock market. For example, when the economy goes into a recession, most companies experience falling sales, reduced profit, and low stock returns. Diversification reduces the risk of holding stocks, but it does not eliminate it.

firm-specific risk
risk that affects only a single company

market risk
risk that affects all companies in the stock market

The Trade-off between Risk and Return

One of the *Ten Principles of Economics* in Chapter 1 is that people face trade-offs. The trade-off that is most relevant for understanding financial decisions is the trade-off between risk and return.

As we have seen, there are risks inherent in holding stocks, even in a diversified portfolio. But risk-averse people are willing to accept this uncertainty because they are compensated for doing so. Historically, stocks have offered much higher rates of return than alternative financial assets, such as bonds and bank savings accounts. Over the past two centuries, stocks offered an average real return of about 8 percent per year, while short-term government bonds paid a real return of only 3 percent per year.

When deciding how to allocate their savings, people have to decide how much risk they are willing to undertake to earn a higher return. For example, consider a person choosing how to allocate his portfolio between two asset classes:

- The first asset class is a diversified group of risky stocks, with an average return of 8 percent and a standard deviation of 20 percent. (You may recall from a math or statistics class that a normal random variable stays within two standard deviations of its average about 95 percent of the time. Thus, while actual returns are centered around 8 percent, they typically vary from a gain of 48 percent to a loss of 32 percent.)
- The second asset class is a safe alternative, with a return of 3 percent and a standard deviation of zero. The safe alternative can be either a bank savings account or a government bond.

Figure 3 illustrates the trade-off between risk and return. Each point in this figure represents a particular allocation of a portfolio between risky stocks and the safe asset. The figure shows that the more the individual puts into stocks, the greater is both the risk and the return.

Acknowledging the risk-return trade-off does not, by itself, tell us what a person should do. The choice of a particular combination of risk and return depends on a person's risk aversion, which reflects a person's own preferences. But it is important for stockholders to recognize that the higher average return that they enjoy comes at the price of higher risk.

QUICK QUIZ *Describe three ways that a risk-averse person might reduce the risk he faces.*

Asset Valuation

Now that we have developed a basic understanding of the two building blocks of finance—time and risk—let's apply this knowledge. This section considers a simple question: What determines the price of a share of stock? Like most prices, the answer is supply and demand. But that is not the end of the story. To understand stock prices, we need to think more deeply about what determines a person's willingness to pay for a share of stock.

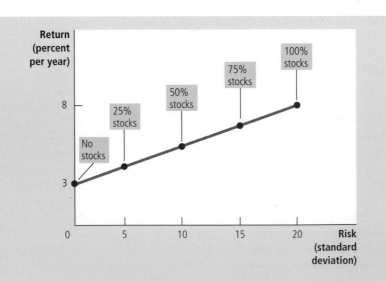

Figure **3**

The Trade-off between Risk and Return
When people increase the percentage of their savings that they have invested in stocks, they increase the average return they can expect to earn, but they also increase the risks they face.

Fundamental Analysis

Let's imagine that you have decided to put 60 percent of your savings into stock, and to achieve diversification, you have decided to buy twenty different stocks. If you open up the newspaper, you will find thousands of stocks listed. How should you pick the twenty for your portfolio?

When you buy stock, you are buying shares in a business. To decide which businesses you want to own, it is natural to consider two things: the value of that share of the business and the price at which the shares are being sold. If the price is less than the value, the stock is said to be *undervalued*. If the price is more than the value, the stock is said to be *overvalued*. If the price and the value are equal, the stock is said to be *fairly valued*. When choosing twenty stocks for your portfolio, you should prefer undervalued stocks. In these cases, you are getting a bargain by paying less than the business is worth.

This is easier said than done. Learning the price is easy: You can just look it up in the newspaper. Determining the value of the business is the hard part. The term **fundamental analysis** refers to the detailed analysis of a company to estimate its value. Many Wall Street firms hire stock analysts to conduct such fundamental analysis and offer advice about which stocks to buy.

fundamental analysis
the study of a company's accounting statements and future prospects to determine its value

The value of a stock to a stockholder is what he gets out of owning it, which includes the present value of the stream of dividend payments and the final sale price. Recall that *dividends* are the cash payments that a company makes to its shareholders. A company's ability to pay dividends, as well as the value of the stock when the stockholder sells his shares, depends on the company's ability to earn profits. Its profitability, in turn, depends on a large number of factors: the demand for its product, how much competition it faces, how much capital it has in place, whether its workers are unionized, how loyal its customers are, what kinds of government regulations and taxes it faces, and so on. The goal of fundamental analysis is to take all these factors into account to determine how much a share of stock in the company is worth.

If you want to rely on fundamental analysis to pick a stock portfolio, there are three ways to do it. One way is to do all the necessary research yourself, such as by reading through companies' annual reports. A second way is to rely on the advice of Wall Street analysts. A third way is to buy a mutual fund, which has a manager who conducts fundamental analysis and makes the decision for you.

The Efficient Markets Hypothesis

There is another way to choose twenty stocks for your portfolio: Pick them randomly by, for instance, putting the stock pages on your bulletin board and throwing darts at the page. This may sound crazy, but there is reason to believe that it won't lead you too far astray. That reason is called the **efficient markets hypothesis.**

efficient markets hypothesis
the theory that asset prices reflect all publicly available information about the value of an asset

To understand this theory, the starting point is to acknowledge that each company listed on a major stock exchange is followed closely by many money managers, such as the individuals who run mutual funds. Every day, these managers monitor news stories and conduct fundamental analysis to try to determine the stock's value. Their job is to buy a stock when its price falls below its fundamental value and to sell it when its price rises above its fundamental value.

The second piece to the efficient markets hypothesis is that the equilibrium of supply and demand sets the market price. This means that, at the market price, the number of shares being offered for sale exactly equals the number of shares that people want to buy. In other words, at the market price, the number of people who think the stock is overvalued exactly balances the number of people who

in the news

A Cartoonist's Guide to Stock Picking

The creator of the comic strip Dilbert *(who was an economics major in college) offers some financial advice.*

Betting on the Bad Guys

BY SCOTT ADAMS

When I heard that BP was destroying a big portion of Earth, with no serious discussion of cutting their dividend, I had two thoughts: 1) I hate them, and 2) This would be an excellent time to buy their stock. And so I did. Although I should have waited a week.

People ask me how it feels to take the side of moral bankruptcy. Answer: Pretty good! Thanks for asking. How's it feel to be a disgruntled victim?

I have a theory that you should invest in the companies that you hate the most. The usual reason for hating a company is that the company is so powerful it can make you balance your wallet on your nose while you beg for their product. Oil companies such as BP don't actually make you beg for oil, but I think we all realize that they could. It's implied in the price of gas.

I hate BP, but I admire them too, in the same way I respect the work ethic of serial killers. I remember the day I learned that BP was using a submarine . . . with a web cam . . . a mile under the sea . . . to feed live video of their disaster to the world. My mind screamed "STOP TRYING TO MAKE ME LOVE YOU! MUST . . . THINK . . . OF DEAD BIRDS TO MAINTAIN ANGER!" The geeky side of me has a bit of a crush on them, but I still hate them for turning Florida into a dip stick. . . .

Perhaps you think it's absurd to invest in companies just because you hate them. But let's compare my method to all of the other ways you could decide where to invest.

Technical Analysis

Technical analysis involves studying graphs of stock movement over time as a way to predict future moves. It's a widely used method on Wall Street, and it has exactly the same scientific validity as pretending

---

informational efficiency

the description of asset prices that rationally reflect all available information

random walk

the path of a variable whose changes are impossible to predict

think it's undervalued. As judged by the typical person in the market, all stocks are fairly valued all the time.

According to this theory, the stock market exhibits **informational efficiency:** It reflects all available information about the value of the asset. Stock prices change when information changes. When good news about the company's prospects becomes public, the value and the stock price both rise. When the company's prospects deteriorate, the value and price both fall. But at any moment in time, the market price is the best guess of the company's value based on available information.

One implication of the efficient markets hypothesis is that stock prices should follow a **random walk.** This means that the changes in stock prices are impossible to predict from available information. If, based on publicly available information, a person could predict that a stock price would rise by 10 percent tomorrow, then the stock market must be failing to incorporate that information today. According to this theory, the only thing that can move stock prices is news that changes the market's perception of the company's value. But news must be unpredictable—otherwise, it wouldn't really be news. For the same reason, changes in stock prices should be unpredictable.

If the efficient markets hypothesis is correct, then there is little point in spending many hours studying the business page to decide which twenty stocks to add to your portfolio. If prices reflect all available information, no stock is a better buy than any other. The best you can do is buy a diversified portfolio.

you are a witch and forecasting market moves from chicken droppings.

Investing in Well-Managed Companies

When companies make money, we assume they are well-managed. That perception is reinforced by the CEOs of those companies who are happy to tell you all the clever things they did to make it happen. The problem with relying on this source of information is that CEOs are highly skilled in a special form of lying called leadership. Leadership involves convincing employees and investors that the CEO has something called a vision, a type of optimistic hallucination that can come true only in an environment in which the CEO is massively overcompensated and the employees have learned to be less selfish.

Track Record

Perhaps you can safely invest in companies that have a long track record of being profitable. That sounds safe and reasonable, right? The problem is that every investment

expert knows two truths about investing: 1) Past performance is no indication of future performance. 2) You need to consider a company's track record.

Right, yes, those are opposites. And it's pretty much all that anyone knows about investing. An investment professional can argue for any sort of investment decision by selectively ignoring either point 1 or 2. And for that you will pay the investment professional 1% to 2% of your portfolio value annually, no matter the performance.

Invest in Companies You Love

Instead of investing in companies you hate, as I have suggested, perhaps you could invest in companies you love. I once hired professional money managers at Wells Fargo to do essentially that for me. As part of their service they promised to listen to the dopey-happy hallucinations of professional liars (CEOs) and be gullible on my behalf. The pros at Wells Fargo bought for my portfolio Enron, WorldCom, and a number of other much-loved companies that soon went out of business. For that, I hate Wells

Fargo. But I sure wish I had bought stock in Wells Fargo at the time I hated them the most, because Wells Fargo itself performed great. See how this works?

Do Your Own Research

I didn't let Wells Fargo manage my entire portfolio, thanks to my native distrust of all humanity. For the other half of my portfolio I did my own research. (Imagine a field of red flags, all wildly waving. I didn't notice them.) My favorite investment was in a company I absolutely loved. I loved their business model. I loved their mission. I loved how they planned to make our daily lives easier. They were simply adorable as they struggled to change an entrenched industry. Their leaders reported that the company had finally turned cash positive in one key area, thus validating their business model, and proving that the future was rosy. I doubled down. The company was Webvan, may it rest in peace.

(This would be a good time to remind you not to make investment decisions based on the wisdom of cartoonists.)

Source: *The Wall Street Journal*, June 5, 2010.

CASE STUDY Random Walks and Index Funds

The efficient markets hypothesis is a theory about how financial markets work. The theory is probably not completely true: As we discuss in the next section, there is reason to doubt that stockholders are always rational and that stock prices are informationally efficient at every moment. Nonetheless, the efficient markets hypothesis does much better as a description of the world than you might think.

There is much evidence that stock prices, even if not exactly a random walk, are very close to it. For example, you might be tempted to buy stocks that have recently risen and avoid stocks that have recently fallen (or perhaps just the opposite). But statistical studies have shown that following such trends (or bucking them) fails to outperform the market. The correlation between how well a stock does one year and how well it does the following year is almost exactly zero.

Some of the best evidence in favor of the efficient markets hypothesis comes from the performance of index funds. An index fund is a mutual fund that buys all the stocks in a given stock index. The performance of these funds can be compared with that of actively managed mutual funds, where a professional portfolio manager picks stocks based on extensive research and alleged expertise. In

essence, an index fund buys all stocks, whereas active funds are supposed to buy only the best stocks.

In practice, active managers usually fail to beat index funds. For example, in the fifteen years ending June 2010, 75 percent of stock mutual funds performed worse than a broadly based index fund holding all stocks traded on U.S. stock exchanges. Over this period, the average annual return on stock funds fell short of the return on the index fund by 1.25 percentage points. Most active portfolio managers failed to beat the market because they trade more frequently, incurring

in the news

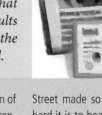

> ### Is the Efficient Markets Hypothesis Kaput?

In 2008 and 2009, the U.S. economy experienced a financial crisis that started with a substantial decline in house prices and widespread defaults on mortgages. Some observers say the crisis should cause us to reject the efficient market hypothesis. Economist Jeremy Siegel is not convinced.

Efficient Market Theory and the Crisis

BY JEREMY SIEGEL

Financial journalist and best-selling author Roger Lowenstein didn't mince words in a piece for the *Washington Post* this summer: "The upside of the current Great Recession is that it could drive a stake through the heart of the academic nostrum known as the efficient-market hypothesis." In a similar vein, the highly respected money manager and financial analyst Jeremy Grantham wrote in his quarterly letter last January: "The incredibly inaccurate efficient market theory [caused] a lethally dangerous combination of asset bubbles, lax controls, pernicious incentives and wickedly complicated instruments [that] led to our current plight."

But is the Efficient Market Hypothesis (EMH) really responsible for the current crisis? The answer is no. The EMH, originally put forth by Eugene Fama of the University of Chicago in the 1960s, states that the prices of securities reflect all known information that impacts their value. The hypothesis does not claim that the market price is always right. On the contrary, it implies that the prices in the market are mostly wrong, but at any given moment it is not at all easy to say whether they are too high or too low. The fact that the best and brightest on Wall Street made so many mistakes shows how hard it is to beat the market.

This does not mean the EMH can be used as an excuse by the CEOs of the failed financial firms or by the regulators who did not see the risks that subprime mortgage-backed securities posed to the financial stability of the economy. Regulators wrongly believed that financial firms were offsetting their credit risks, while the banks and credit rating agencies were fooled by faulty models that underestimated the risk in real estate.

After the 1982 recession, the U.S. and world economies entered into a long period where the fluctuations in variables such as gross domestic product, industrial production, and employment were significantly more trading costs, and because they charge greater fees as compensation for their alleged expertise.

What about the 25 percent of managers who did beat the market? Perhaps they are smarter than average, or perhaps they were luckier. If you have 5,000 people flipping coins ten times, on average about five will flip ten heads; these five might claim an exceptional coin-flipping skill, but they would have trouble replicating the feat. Similarly, studies have shown that mutual fund managers with a history of superior performance usually fail to maintain it in subsequent periods.

The Wall Street Journal published an example of this phenomenon on January 3, 2008. The paper reported that of the many thousands of mutual funds sold to the public, only thirty-one beat the Standard & Poor's 500 index in each of the eight years from 1999 to 2006. A skeptic of the efficient markets hypothesis might think that, subsequently, these highly performing funds would offer a better-than-average place to invest. In 2007, however, only fourteen of these thirty-one outperformed the index—about what would be expected from sheer chance. Exceptional past performance appears to give little reason to expect future success.

The efficient markets hypothesis says that it is impossible to beat the market. The accumulation of many studies in financial markets confirms that beating the market is, at best, extremely difficult. Even if the efficient markets hypothesis is not an exact description of the world, it contains a large element of truth. ■

lower than they had been since World War II. Economists called this period the "Great Moderation" and attributed the increased stability to better monetary policy, a larger service sector and better inventory control, among other factors.

The economic response to the Great Moderation was predictable: risk premiums shrank and individuals and firms took on more leverage. Housing prices were boosted by historically low nominal and real interest rates and the development of the securitized subprime lending market.

According to data collected by Prof. Robert Shiller of Yale University, in the 61 years from 1945 through 2006 the maximum cumulative decline in the average price of homes was 2.84% in 1991. If this low volatility of home prices persisted into the future, a mortgage security composed of a nationally diversified portfolio of loans comprising the first 80% of a home's value would have never come close to defaulting. The credit quality of home buyers was secondary because it was thought that underlying collateral—the home—could always cover the principal in the event

the homeowner defaulted. These models led credit agencies to rate these subprime mortgages as "investment grade."

But this assessment was faulty. From 2000 through 2006, national home prices rose by 88.7%, far more than the 17.5% gain in the consumer price index or the paltry 1% rise in median household income. Never before have home prices jumped that far ahead of prices and incomes.

This should have sent up red flags and cast doubts on using models that looked only at historical declines to judge future risk. But these flags were ignored as Wall Street was reaping large profits bundling and selling the securities while Congress was happy that more Americans could enjoy the "American Dream" of home ownership. Indeed, through government-sponsored enterprises such as Fannie Mae and Freddie Mac, Washington helped fuel the subprime boom.

Neither the rating agencies' mistakes nor the overleveraging by the financial firms in the subprime securities is the fault of the Efficient Market Hypothesis. The fact that the yields on these mortgages were high despite their investment-grade rating

indicated that the market was rightly suspicious of the quality of the securities, and this should have served as a warning to prospective buyers.

With few exceptions (Goldman Sachs being one), financial firms ignored these warnings. CEOs failed to exercise their authority to monitor overall risk of the firm and instead put their faith in technicians whose narrow models could not capture the big picture. . . .

Our crisis wasn't due to blind faith in the Efficient Market Hypothesis. The fact that risk premiums were low does not mean they were nonexistent and that market prices were right. Despite the recent recession, the Great Moderation is real and our economy is inherently more stable.

But this does not mean that risks have disappeared. To use an analogy, the fact that automobiles today are safer than they were years ago does not mean that you can drive at 120 mph. A small bump on the road, perhaps insignificant at lower speeds, will easily flip the best-engineered car. Our financial firms drove too fast, our central bank failed to stop them, and the housing deflation crashed the banks and the economy.

Source: *The Wall Street Journal,* October 28, 2009.

Market Irrationality

The efficient markets hypothesis assumes that people buying and selling stock rationally process the information they have about the stock's underlying value. But is the stock market really that rational? Or do stock prices sometimes deviate from reasonable expectations of their true value?

There is a long tradition suggesting that fluctuations in stock prices are partly psychological. In the 1930s, economist John Maynard Keynes suggested that asset markets are driven by the "animal spirits" of investors—irrational waves of optimism and pessimism. In the 1990s, as the stock market soared to new heights, Fed Chairman Alan Greenspan questioned whether the boom reflected "irrational exuberance." Stock prices did subsequently fall, but whether the exuberance of the 1990s was irrational given the information available at the time remains debatable. Whenever the price of an asset rises above what appears to be its fundamental value, the market is said to be experiencing a *speculative bubble*.

The possibility of speculative bubbles in the stock market arises in part because the value of the stock to a stockholder depends not only on the stream of dividend payments but also on the final sale price. Thus, a person might be willing to pay more than a stock is worth today if she expects another person to pay even more for it tomorrow. When you evaluate a stock, you have to estimate not only the value of the business but also what other people will think the business is worth in the future.

There is much debate among economists about the frequency and importance of departures from rational pricing. Believers in market irrationality point out (correctly) that the stock market often moves in ways that are hard to explain on the basis of news that might alter a rational valuation. Believers in the efficient markets hypothesis point out (correctly) that it is impossible to know the correct, rational valuation of a company, so one should not quickly jump to the conclusion that any particular valuation is irrational. Moreover, if the market were irrational, a rational person should be able to take advantage of this fact; yet as the previous case study discussed, beating the market is nearly impossible.

QUICK QUIZ Fortune *magazine regularly publishes a list of the "most respected" companies. According to the efficient markets hypothesis, if you restrict your stock portfolio to these companies, will you earn a better than average return? Explain.*

Conclusion

This chapter has developed some of the basic tools that people should (and often do) use as they make financial decisions. The concept of present value reminds us that a dollar in the future is less valuable than a dollar today, and it gives us a way to compare sums of money at different points in time. The theory of risk management reminds us that the future is uncertain and that risk-averse people can take precautions to guard against this uncertainty. The study of asset valuation tells us that the stock price of any company should reflect its expected future profitability.

Although most of the tools of finance are well established, there is more controversy about the validity of the efficient markets hypothesis and whether stock prices are, in practice, rational estimates of a company's true worth. Rational or not, the large movements in stock prices that we observe have important macroeconomic implications. Stock market fluctuations often go hand in hand with fluctuations in the economy more broadly. We revisit the stock market when we study economic fluctuations later in the book.

SUMMARY

- Because savings can earn interest, a sum of money today is more valuable than the same sum of money in the future. A person can compare sums from different times using the concept of present value. The present value of any future sum is the amount that would be needed today, given prevailing interest rates, to produce that future sum.

- Because of diminishing marginal utility, most people are risk averse. Risk-averse people can reduce risk by buying insurance, diversifying their holdings, and choosing a portfolio with lower risk and lower return.

- The value of an asset equals the present value of the cash flows the owner will receive. For a share of stock, these cash flows include the stream of dividends and the final sale price. According to the efficient markets hypothesis, financial markets process available information rationally, so a stock price always equals the best estimate of the value of the underlying business. Some economists question the efficient markets hypothesis, however, and believe that irrational psychological factors also influence asset prices.

KEY CONCEPTS

finance, *p. 178*
present value, *p. 178*
future value, *p. 178*
compounding, *p. 178*

risk aversion, *p. 180*
diversification, *p. 182*
firm-specific risk, *p. 183*
market risk, *p. 183*

fundamental analysis, *p. 185*
efficient markets hypothesis, *p. 185*
informational efficiency, *p. 186*
random walk, *p. 186*

QUESTIONS FOR REVIEW

1. The interest rate is 7 percent. Use the concept of present value to compare $200 to be received in 10 years and $300 to be received in 20 years.
2. What benefit do people get from the market for insurance? What two problems impede the insurance company from working perfectly?
3. What is diversification? Does a stockholder get more diversification going from 1 to 10 stocks or going from 100 to 120 stocks?

4. Comparing stocks and government bonds, which has more risk? Which pays a higher average return?
5. What factors should a stock analyst think about in determining the value of a share of stock?
6. Describe the efficient markets hypothesis and give a piece of evidence consistent with this hypothesis.
7. Explain the view of those economists who are skeptical of the efficient markets hypothesis.

PROBLEMS AND APPLICATIONS

1. According to an old myth, Native Americans sold the island of Manhattan about 400 years ago for $24. If they had invested this amount at an interest rate of 7 percent per year, how much would they have today?
2. A company has an investment project that would cost $10 million today and yield a payoff of $15 million in 4 years.

a. Should the firm undertake the project if the interest rate is 11 percent? 10 percent? 9 percent? 8 percent?
b. Can you figure out the exact cutoff for the interest rate between profitability and nonprofitability?
3. Bond A pays $8,000 in 20 years. Bond B pays $8,000 in 40 years. (To keep things simple,

assume these are zero-coupon bonds, which means the $8,000 is the only payment the bond holder receives.)

a. If the interest rate is 3.5 percent, what is the value of each bond today? Which bond is worth more? Why? (Hint: You can use a calculator, but the rule of 70 should make the calculation easy.)

b. If the interest rate increases to 7 percent, what is the value of each bond? Which bond has a larger *percentage* change in value?

c. Based on the example above, complete the two blanks in this sentence: "The value of a bond [rises/falls] when the interest rate increases, and bonds with a longer time to maturity are [more/less] sensitive to changes in the interest rate."

4. Your bank account pays an interest rate of 8 percent. You are considering buying a share of stock in XYZ Corporation for $110. After 1, 2, and 3 years, it will pay a dividend of $5. You expect to sell the stock after 3 years for $120. Is XYZ a good investment? Support your answer with calculations.

5. For each of the following kinds of insurance, give an example of behavior that can be called *moral hazard* and another example of behavior that can be called *adverse selection*.
   a. health insurance
   b. car insurance

6. Which kind of stock would you expect to pay the higher average return: stock in an industry that is very sensitive to economic conditions (such as an automaker) or stock in an industry that is relatively insensitive to economic conditions (such as a water company)? Why?

7. A company faces two kinds of risk. A firm-specific risk is that a competitor might enter its market and take some of its customers. A market risk is that the economy might enter a recession, reducing sales. Which of these two risks would more likely cause the company's shareholders to demand a higher return? Why?

8. You have two roommates who invest in the stock market.

a. One roommate says that he buys stock only in companies that everyone believes will experience big increases in profits in the future. How do you suppose the price-earnings ratio of these companies compares to the price-earnings ratio of other companies? What might be the disadvantage of buying stock in these companies?

b. Another roommate says he only buys stock in companies that are cheap, which he measures by a low price-earnings ratio. How do you suppose the earnings prospects of these companies compare to those of other companies? What might be the disadvantage of buying stock in these companies?

9. When company executives buy and sell stock based on private information they obtain as part of their jobs, they are engaged in *insider trading*.
   a. Give an example of inside information that might be useful for buying or selling stock.
   b. Those who trade stocks based on inside information usually earn very high rates of return. Does this fact violate the efficient markets hypothesis?
   c. Insider trading is illegal. Why do you suppose that is?

10. Jamal has a utility function $U = W^{1/2}$, where W is his wealth in millions of dollars (which determines how much he gets to buy and consume over his lifetime) and U is the utility he obtains.
   a. Graph Jamal's utility function. Is he risk averse? Explain.
   b. In the final stage of a game show, the host offers Jamal a choice between (A) $4 million for sure, or (B) a gamble that pays $1 million with probability 0.6 and $9 million with probability 0.4. Should Jamal pick A or B? Explain you reasoning with appropriate calculations. (Hint: The expected value of a random variable is the weighted average of the possible outcomes, where the probabilities are the weights.)

For further information on topics in this chapter, additional problems, applications, examples, online quizzes, and more, please visit our website at www .cengage.com/economics/mankiw.

Unemployment

Losing a job can be the most distressing economic event in a person's life. Most people rely on their labor earnings to maintain their standard of living, and many people also get a sense of personal accomplishment from working. A job loss means a lower living standard in the present, anxiety about the future, and reduced self-esteem. It is not surprising, therefore, that politicians campaigning for office often speak about how their proposed policies will help create jobs.

In previous chapters, we have seen some of the forces that determine the level and growth of a country's standard of living. A country that saves and invests a high fraction of its income, for instance, enjoys more rapid growth in its capital stock and GDP than a similar country that saves and invests less. An even more obvious determinant of a country's standard of living is the amount of unemployment it typically experiences. People who would like to work but cannot find a job are not contributing to the economy's production of goods and services. Although some degree of unemployment is inevitable in a complex economy with thousands of firms and millions of workers, the amount of unemployment varies substantially over time and across countries. When a country keeps its workers as fully employed as possible, it achieves a higher level of GDP than it would if it left many of its workers standing idle.

This chapter begins our study of unemployment. The problem of unemployment is usefully divided into two categories: the long-run problem and the short-run problem. The economy's *natural rate of unemployment* refers to the amount of unemployment that the economy normally experiences. *Cyclical unemployment* refers to the year-to-year fluctuations in unemployment around its natural rate, and it is closely associated with the short-run ups and downs of economic activity. Cyclical unemployment has its own explanation, which we defer until we study short-run economic fluctuations later in this book. In this chapter, we discuss the determinants of an economy's natural rate of unemployment. As we will see, the designation *natural* does not imply that this rate of unemployment is desirable. Nor does it imply that it is constant over time or impervious to economic policy. It merely means that this unemployment does not go away on its own even in the long run.

We begin the chapter by looking at some of the relevant facts that describe unemployment. In particular, we examine three questions: How does the government measure the economy's rate of unemployment? What problems arise in interpreting the unemployment data? How long are the unemployed typically without work?

We then turn to the reasons economies always experience some unemployment and the ways in which policymakers can help the unemployed. We discuss four explanations for the economy's natural rate of unemployment: job search, minimum-wage laws, unions, and efficiency wages. As we will see, long-run unemployment does not arise from a single problem that has a single solution. Instead, it reflects a variety of related problems. As a result, there is no easy way for policymakers to reduce the economy's natural rate of unemployment and, at the same time, to alleviate the hardships experienced by the unemployed.

Identifying Unemployment

Let's start by examining more precisely what the term *unemployment* means.

How Is Unemployment Measured?

Measuring unemployment is the job of the Bureau of Labor Statistics (BLS), which is part of the Department of Labor. Every month, the BLS produces data on unemployment and on other aspects of the labor market, including types of employment, length of the average workweek, and the duration of unemployment. These data come from a regular survey of about 60,000 households, called the Current Population Survey.

Based on the answers to survey questions, the BLS places each adult (age 16 and older) of each surveyed household into one of three categories:

• *Employed:* This category includes those who worked as paid employees, worked in their own business, or worked as unpaid workers in a family member's business. Both full-time and part-time workers are counted. This category also includes those who were not working but who had jobs from which they were temporarily absent because of, for example, vacation, illness, or bad weather.

- *Unemployed:* This category includes those who were not employed, were available for work, and had tried to find employment during the previous four weeks. It also includes those waiting to be recalled to a job from which they had been laid off.
- *Not in the labor force:* This category includes those who fit neither of the first two categories, such as a full-time student, homemaker, or retiree.

Figure 1 shows the breakdown into these categories for 2009.

Once the BLS has placed all the individuals covered by the survey in a category, it computes various statistics to summarize the state of the labor market. The BLS defines the **labor force** as the sum of the employed and the unemployed:

$$\text{Labor force} = \text{Number of employed} + \text{Number of unemployed}.$$

The BLS defines the **unemployment rate** as the percentage of the labor force that is unemployed:

$$\text{Unemployment rate} = \frac{\text{Number of unemployed}}{\text{Labor force}} \times 100.$$

The BLS computes unemployment rates for the entire adult population and for more narrowly defined groups such as blacks, whites, men, women, and so on.

The BLS uses the same survey to produce data on labor-force participation. The **labor-force participation rate** measures the percentage of the total adult population of the United States that is in the labor force:

$$\text{Labor-force participation rate} = \frac{\text{Labor force}}{\text{Adult population}} \times 100.$$

labor force
the total number of workers, including both the employed and the unemployed

unemployment rate
the percentage of the labor force that is unemployed

labor-force participation rate
the percentage of the adult population that is in the labor force

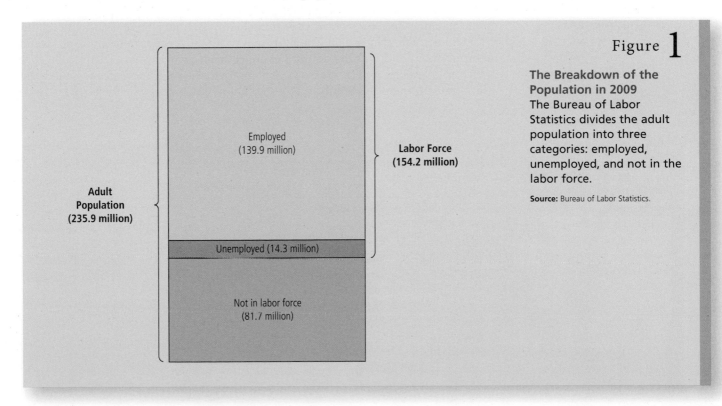

Figure **1**

The Breakdown of the Population in 2009
The Bureau of Labor Statistics divides the adult population into three categories: employed, unemployed, and not in the labor force.

Source: Bureau of Labor Statistics.

This statistic tells us the fraction of the population that has chosen to participate in the labor market. The labor-force participation rate, like the unemployment rate, is computed for both the entire adult population and more specific groups.

To see how these data are computed, consider the figures for 2009. In that year, 139.9 million people were employed, and 14.3 million people were unemployed. The labor force was

$$\text{Labor force} = 139.9 + 14.3 = 154.2 \text{ million.}$$

The unemployment rate was

$$\text{Unemployment rate} = (14.3 \,/\, 154.2) \times 100 = 9.3 \text{ percent.}$$

Because the adult population was 235.9 million, the labor-force participation rate was

$$\text{Labor-force participation rate} = (154.2 \,/\, 235.9) \times 100 = 65.4 \text{ percent.}$$

Hence, in 2009, almost two-thirds of the U.S. adult population were participating in the labor market, and 9.3 percent of those labor-market participants were without work.

Table 1 shows the statistics on unemployment and labor-force participation for various groups within the U.S. population. Three comparisons are most apparent. First, women ages 20 and older have lower rates of labor-force participation than men, but once in the labor force, women have somewhat lower rates of unemployment. Second, blacks ages 20 and older have similar rates of labor-force participation as whites, but they have much higher rates of unemployment. Third, teenagers have lower rates of labor-force participation and much higher rates of unemployment than older workers. More generally, these data show that labor-market experiences vary widely among groups within the economy.

The BLS data on the labor market also allow economists and policymakers to monitor changes in the economy over time. Figure 2 shows the unemployment rate in the United States since 1960. The figure shows that the economy always has some unemployment and that the amount changes from year to year. The normal rate of unemployment around which the unemployment rate fluctuates is called the **natural rate of unemployment**, and the deviation of unemployment from its natural

natural rate of unemployment
the normal rate of unemployment around which the unemployment rate fluctuates

Table **1**

The Labor-Market Experiences of Various Demographic Groups
This table shows the unemployment rate and the labor-force participation rate of various groups in the U.S. population for 2009.

Source: Bureau of Labor Statistics.

Demographic Group	Unemployment Rate	Labor-Force Participation Rate
Adults (ages 20 and older)		
White, male	8.8%	75.3%
White, female	6.8	60.4
Black, male	16.3	69.6
Black, female	11.5	63.4
Teenagers (ages 16–19)		
White, male	25.2	40.3
White, female	18.4	40.9
Black, male	46.0	26.4
Black, female	33.4	27.9

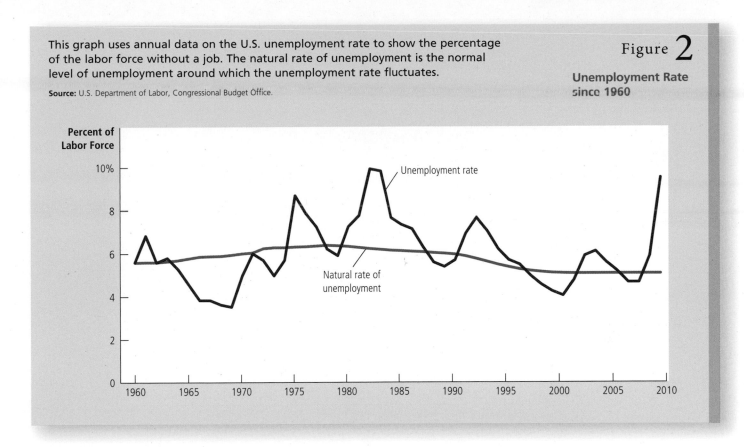

This graph uses annual data on the U.S. unemployment rate to show the percentage of the labor force without a job. The natural rate of unemployment is the normal level of unemployment around which the unemployment rate fluctuates.

Source: U.S. Department of Labor, Congressional Budget Office.

Figure **2**

Unemployment Rate since 1960

rate is called **cyclical unemployment**. The natural rate of unemployment shown in the figure is a series estimated by economists at the Congressional Budget Office. For 2009, they estimated a natural rate of 5.0 percent, far below the actual unemployment rate of 9.3 percent. Later in this book, we discuss short-run economic fluctuations, including the year-to-year fluctuations in unemployment around its natural rate. In the rest of this chapter, however, we ignore the short-run fluctuations and examine why there is always some unemployment in market economies.

cyclical unemployment
the deviation of unemployment from its natural rate

Labor-Force Participation of Men and Women in the U.S. Economy

Women's role in American society has changed dramatically over the past century. Social commentators have pointed to many causes for this change. In part, it is attributable to new technologies, such as the washing machine, clothes dryer, refrigerator, freezer, and dishwasher, which have reduced the amount of time required to complete routine household tasks. In part, it is attributable to improved birth control, which has reduced the number of children born to the typical family. This change in women's role is also partly attributable to changing political and social attitudes, which in turn may have been facilitated by the advances in technology and birth control. Together these developments have had a profound impact on society in general and on the economy in particular.

Nowhere is that impact more obvious than in data on labor-force participation. Figure 3 shows the labor-force participation rates of men and women in the

Labor-Force Participation
Rates for Men and Women
since 1950

This figure shows the percentage of adult men and women who are members of the
labor force. It shows that over the past several decades, women have entered the
labor force, and men have left it.

Source: U.S. Department of Labor.

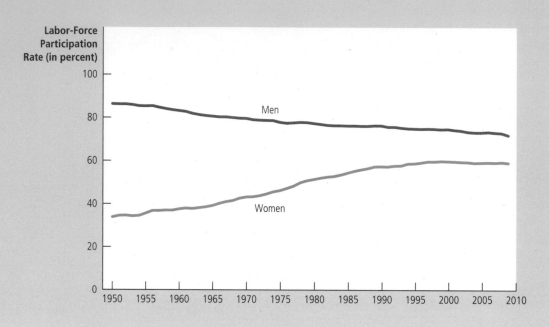

United States since 1950. Just after World War II, men and women had very different roles in society. Only 33 percent of women were working or looking for work, in contrast to 87 percent of men. Over the past several decades, the difference between the participation rates of men and women has gradually diminished, as growing numbers of women have entered the labor force and some men have left it. Data for 2009 show that 59 percent of women were in the labor force, in contrast to 72 percent of men. As measured by labor-force participation, men and women are now playing a more equal role in the economy.

The increase in women's labor-force participation is easy to understand, but the fall in men's may seem puzzling. There are several reasons for this decline. First, young men now stay in school longer than their fathers and grandfathers did. Second, older men now retire earlier and live longer. Third, with more women employed, more fathers now stay at home to raise their children. Full-time students, retirees, and stay-at-home dads are all counted as being out of the labor force. ■

Does the Unemployment Rate Measure What We Want It To?

Measuring the amount of unemployment in the economy might seem a straightforward task, but it is not. While it is easy to distinguish between a person with a full-time job and a person who is not working at all, it is much harder to distinguish between a person who is unemployed and a person who is not in the labor force.

Movements into and out of the labor force are, in fact, common. More than one-third of the unemployed are recent entrants into the labor force. These entrants include young workers looking for their first jobs. They also include, in greater numbers, older workers who had previously left the labor force but have now returned to look for work. Moreover, not all unemployment ends with the job seeker finding a job. Almost half of all spells of unemployment end when the unemployed person leaves the labor force.

Because people move into and out of the labor force so often, statistics on unemployment are difficult to interpret. On the one hand, some of those who report being unemployed may not, in fact, be trying hard to find a job. They may be calling themselves unemployed because they want to qualify for a government program that financially assists the unemployed or because they are actually working but paid "under the table" to avoid taxes on their earnings. It may be more realistic to view these individuals as out of the labor force or, in some cases, employed. On the other hand, some of those who report being out of the labor force may want to work. These individuals may have tried to find a job and may have given up after an unsuccessful search. Such individuals, called **discouraged workers**, do not show up in unemployment statistics, even though they are truly workers without jobs.

Because of these and other problems, the BLS calculates several other measures of labor underutilization, in addition to the official unemployment rate. These alternative measures are presented in Table 2. In the end, it is best to view the official unemployment rate as a useful but imperfect measure of joblessness.

discouraged workers
individuals who would like to work but have given up looking for a job

Table **2**

Alternative Measures of Labor Underutilization
The table shows various measures of joblessness for the U.S. economy. The data are for April 2010.

Source: U.S. Department of Labor.

Measure and Description	Rate
U-1 Persons unemployed fifteen weeks or longer, as a percent of the civilian labor force (includes only very long-term unemployed)	5.8%
U-2 Job losers and persons who have completed temporary jobs, as a percent of the civilian labor force (excludes job leavers)	6.0
U-3 Total unemployed, as a percent of the civilian labor force (official unemployment rate)	9.9
U-4 Total unemployed, plus discouraged workers, as a percent of the civilian labor force plus discouraged workers	10.6
U-5 Total unemployed plus all marginally attached workers, as a percent of the civilian labor force plus all marginally attached workers	11.3
U-6 Total unemployed, plus all marginally attached workers, plus total employed part-time for economic reasons, as a percent of the civilian labor force plus all marginally attached workers	17.1

Note: The Bureau of Labor Statistics defines terms as follows:
- *Marginally attached workers* are persons who currently are neither working nor looking for work but indicate that they want and are available for a job and have looked for work sometime in the recent past.
- *Discouraged workers* are marginally attached workers who have given a job-market-related reason for not currently looking for a job.
- *Persons employed part-time for economic reasons* are those who want and are available for full-time work but have had to settle for a part-time schedule.

How Long Are the Unemployed without Work?

In judging how serious the problem of unemployment is, one question to consider is whether unemployment is typically a short-term or long-term condition. If unemployment is short term, one might conclude that it is not a big problem. Workers may require a few weeks between jobs to find the openings that best suit their tastes and skills. Yet if unemployment is long term, one might conclude that it is a serious problem. Workers unemployed for many months are more likely to suffer economic and psychological hardship.

Because the duration of unemployment can affect our view about how big a problem unemployment is, economists have devoted much energy to studying data on the duration of unemployment spells. In this work, they have uncovered a result that is important, subtle, and seemingly contradictory: *Most spells of unemployment are short, and most unemployment observed at any given time is long-term.*

To see how this statement can be true, consider an example. Suppose that you visited the government's unemployment office every week for a year to survey the unemployed. Each week you find that there are four unemployed workers. Three of these workers are the same individuals for the whole year, while the fourth person changes every week. Based on this experience, would you say that unemployment is typically short-term or long-term?

Some simple calculations help answer this question. In this example, you meet a total of 55 unemployed people over the course of a year; 52 of them are unemployed for one week, and 3 are unemployed for the full year. This means that 52/55, or 95 percent, of unemployment spells end in one week. Yet whenever you walk into the unemployment office, three of the four people you meet will be unemployed for the entire year. So, even though 95 percent of unemployment spells end in one week, 75 percent of the unemployment observed at any moment is attributable to those individuals who are unemployed for a full year. In this example, as in the world, most spells of unemployment are short, and most unemployment observed at any given time is long-term.

This subtle conclusion implies that economists and policymakers must be careful when interpreting data on unemployment and when designing policies to help the unemployed. Most people who become unemployed will soon find jobs. Yet most of the economy's unemployment problem is attributable to the relatively few workers who are jobless for long periods of time.

Why Are There Always Some People Unemployed?

We have discussed how the government measures the amount of unemployment, the problems that arise in interpreting unemployment statistics, and the findings of labor economists on the duration of unemployment. You should now have a good idea about what unemployment is.

This discussion, however, has not explained why economies experience unemployment. In most markets in the economy, prices adjust to bring quantity supplied and quantity demanded into balance. In an ideal labor market, wages would adjust to balance the quantity of labor supplied and the quantity of labor demanded. This adjustment of wages would ensure that all workers are always fully employed.

Of course, reality does not resemble this ideal. There are always some workers without jobs, even when the overall economy is doing well. In other words, the

· · · · · · · · · · · · · in the **news**

> ## The Rise of Long-Term Unemployment

During the economic downturn of 2008 and 2009, the number of long-term unemployed reached historic highs.

Chronic Joblessness Bites Deep

BY SARA MURRAY

ichard Moran, sitting in his garage in Ortonville, Mich., Tuesday, has been unemployed for two-and-a-half years after losing his job with Chrysler.

The job market is improving, but one statistic presents a stark reminder of the challenges that remain: Nearly half of the unemployed—45.9%—have been out of work longer than six months, more than at any time since the Labor Department began keeping track in 1948.

Source: *The Wall Street Journal,* June 2, 2010.

Even in the worst months of the early 1980s, when the jobless rate topped 10% for months on end, only about one in four of the unemployed was out of work for more than six months.

Overall, seven million Americans have been looking for work for 27 weeks or more, and most of them—4.7 million—have been out of work for a year or more.

Long-term unemployment has reached nearly every segment of the population, but some have been particularly hard-hit. The typical long-term unemployed worker is a white man with a high-school education or less. Older unemployed workers also tend to be out of work longer. Those between ages 65 and 69 who still wish to work have typically been jobless for 49.8 weeks.

The effects of long-term unemployment are likely to linger when the overall jobless rate falls toward normal, threatening to create a pool of nearly permanently unemployed workers, a condition once more common in Europe than in the U.S.

"The consequences are worse for those who can't find a job quickly," said Till Marco von Wachter, a Columbia University economist. They extend from atrophying skills to a higher likelihood of unhappiness and anxiety. Workers out of work for a long time tend to find it more difficult to find a job, and "the longer people are unemployed the more likely they are to eventually give up searching and thereby drop out of the labor force," Mr. von Wachter said.

unemployment rate never falls to zero; instead, it fluctuates around the natural rate of unemployment. To understand this natural rate, the remaining sections of this chapter examine the reasons actual labor markets depart from the ideal of full employment.

To preview our conclusions, we will find that there are four ways to explain unemployment in the long run. The first explanation is that it takes time for workers to search for the jobs that are best suited for them. The unemployment that results from the process of matching workers and jobs is sometimes called **frictional unemployment**, and it is often thought to explain relatively short spells of unemployment.

The next three explanations for unemployment suggest that the number of jobs available in some labor markets may be insufficient to give a job to everyone who wants one. This occurs when the quantity of labor supplied exceeds the quantity demanded. Unemployment of this sort is sometimes called

frictional unemployment
unemployment that results because it takes time for workers to search for the jobs that best suit their tastes and skills

FYI

> ## The Jobs Number

When the Bureau of Labor Statistics announces the unemployment rate at the beginning of every month, it also announces the number of jobs the economy has gained or lost. As an indicator of short-run economic trends, the jobs number gets as much attention as the unemployment rate.

Where does the jobs number come from? You might guess that it comes from the same survey of 60,000 households that yields the unemployment rate. And indeed the household survey does produce data on total employment. The jobs number that gets the most attention, however, comes from a separate survey of 160,000 business establishments, which have over 40 million workers on their payrolls. The results from the establishment survey are announced at the same time as the results from the household survey.

Both surveys yield information about total employment, but the results are not always the same. One reason is that the establishment survey has a larger sample, which makes it more reliable. Another reason is that the surveys are not measuring exactly the same thing. For example, a person who has two part-time jobs in different companies would be counted as one employed person in the household survey but as two jobs in the establishment survey. As another example, a person running his own small business would be counted as employed in the household survey but would not show up at all in the establishment survey, because the establishment survey counts only employees on a business payroll.

The establishment survey is closely watched for its data on jobs, but it says nothing about unemployment. To measure the number of unemployed, we need to know how many people without jobs are trying to find them. The household survey is the only source of that information.

structural unemployment

unemployment that results because the number of jobs available in some labor markets is insufficient to provide a job for everyone who wants one

structural unemployment, and it is often thought to explain longer spells of unemployment. As we will see, this kind of unemployment results when wages are, for some reason, set above the level that brings supply and demand into equilibrium. We will examine three possible reasons for an above-equilibrium wage: minimum-wage laws, unions, and efficiency wages.

QUICK QUIZ   *How is the unemployment rate measured? • How might the unemployment rate overstate the amount of joblessness? How might it understate the amount of joblessness?*

Job Search

job search

the process by which workers find appropriate jobs given their tastes and skills

One reason economies always experience some unemployment is job search. **Job search** is the process of matching workers with appropriate jobs. If all workers and all jobs were the same, so that all workers were equally well suited for all jobs, job search would not be a problem. Laid-off workers would quickly find new jobs that were well suited for them. But in fact, workers differ in their tastes and skills, jobs differ in their attributes, and information about job candidates and job vacancies is disseminated slowly among the many firms and households in the economy.

Why Some Frictional Unemployment Is Inevitable

Frictional unemployment is often the result of changes in the demand for labor among different firms. When consumers decide that they prefer Dell to Apple computers, Dell increases employment, and Apple lays off workers. The former Apple workers must now search for new jobs, and Dell must decide which new workers to hire for the various jobs that have opened up. The result of this transition is a period of unemployment.

Similarly, because different regions of the country produce different goods, employment can rise in one region while falling in another. Consider, for instance, what happens when the world price of oil falls. Oil-producing firms in Alaska respond to the lower price by cutting back on production and employment. At the same time, cheaper gasoline stimulates car sales, so auto-producing firms in Michigan raise production and employment. Just the opposite happens when the world price of oil rises. Changes in the composition of demand among industries or regions are called *sectoral shifts*. Because it takes time for workers to search for jobs in the new sectors, sectoral shifts temporarily cause unemployment.

Frictional unemployment is inevitable simply because the economy is always changing. A century ago, the four industries with the largest employment in the United States were cotton goods, woolen goods, men's clothing, and lumber. Today, the four largest industries are autos, aircraft, communications, and electrical components. As this transition took place, jobs were created in some firms and destroyed in others. The result of this process has been higher productivity and higher living standards. But along the way, workers in declining industries found themselves out of work and searching for new jobs.

Data show that at least 10 percent of U.S. manufacturing jobs are destroyed every year. In addition, more than 3 percent of workers leave their jobs in a typical month, sometimes because they realize that the jobs are not a good match for their tastes and skills. Many of these workers, especially younger ones, find new jobs at higher wages. This churning of the labor force is normal in a well-functioning and dynamic market economy, but the result is some amount of frictional unemployment.

Public Policy and Job Search

Even if some frictional unemployment is inevitable, the precise amount is not. The faster information spreads about job openings and worker availability, the more rapidly the economy can match workers and firms. The Internet, for instance, may help facilitate job search and reduce frictional unemployment. In addition, public policy may play a role. If policy can reduce the time it takes unemployed workers to find new jobs, it can reduce the economy's natural rate of unemployment.

Government programs try to facilitate job search in various ways. One way is through government-run employment agencies, which give out information about job vacancies. Another way is through public training programs, which aim to ease workers' transition from declining to growing industries and to help disadvantaged groups escape poverty. Advocates of these programs believe that they make the economy operate more efficiently by keeping the labor force more fully employed and that they reduce the inequities inherent in a constantly changing market economy.

Critics of these programs question whether the government should get involved with the process of job search. They argue that it is better to let the private market match workers and jobs. In fact, most job search in our economy takes place without intervention by the government. Newspaper ads, Internet job sites, college placement offices, headhunters, and word of mouth all help spread information about job openings and job candidates. Similarly, much worker education is done privately, either through schools or through on-the-job training. These critics contend that the government is no better—and most likely worse—at disseminating the right information to the right workers and deciding what kinds of worker training would be most valuable. They claim that these decisions are best made privately by workers and employers.

unemployment insurance

a government program that partially protects workers' incomes when they become unemployed

Unemployment Insurance

One government program that increases the amount of frictional unemployment, without intending to do so, is **unemployment insurance**. This program is designed to offer workers partial protection against job loss. The unemployed

in the news

> ### How Much Do the Unemployed Respond to Incentives?

During the economic downturn of 2008 and 2009, economists and policymakers wrestled with the question of how much the unemployment-insurance system was affecting the behavior of unemployed workers.

Long Recession Ignites Debate on Jobless Benefits

By Sara Murray

Management Recruiters of Sacramento, Calif., says it recently had a tough time filling six engineering positions at an Oregon manufacturer paying $60,000 a year—and suspects long-term jobless benefits were part of the hitch.

"We called several engineers that were unemployed," says Karl Dinse, a managing partner at the recruiting firm. "They said, nah, you know, if it were paying $80,000 I'd think about it." Some candidates suggested he call them back when their benefits were scheduled to run out, he says.

Rick Jewell has a different take on extended jobless benefits: He didn't want to be on the dole, but had no alternative. He has been out of work since he lost his $12-an-hour job driving a forklift for a cosmetics company in Greenwood, Ind., in December 2008. He collected $315 a week in benefits until early June—when Congress declined to renew the law that gave workers in Indiana and some other states up to 99 weeks of assistance.

"I am tired of sitting at home. I am tired of not being the breadwinner," says Mr. Jewell, who says he looks for work every day. He and his wife now rely on her $480 a week job as a distribution supervisor at the same cosmetics company.

In the long recession and the lackluster recovery, the government expanded unemployment payments more than at any time since the benefits were rolled out in the 1930s. And workers have gone jobless for longer than any time since official tallies began in 1967.

Politicians and economists are now in a fierce debate that could have big consequences for the jobless: Did more-generous unemployment benefits prompt jobless workers to be pickier in their searches? Or was the program a prudent response to the worst recession in generations? . . .

Economists have argued for years about the extent to which government benefits prolong unemployment—and possibly augment the overall jobless rate. Most believe that expanding benefits does discourage some unemployed people from looking for work or taking available jobs. But they disagree on how acute that effect is, particularly at a time when jobs are scarce.

who quit their jobs, were fired for cause, or just entered the labor force are not eligible. Benefits are paid only to the unemployed who were laid off because their previous employers no longer needed their skills. The terms of the program vary over time and across states, but a typical worker covered by unemployment insurance in the United States receives 50 percent of his or her former wages for twenty-six weeks.

While unemployment insurance reduces the hardship of unemployment, it also increases the amount of unemployment. The explanation is based on one of the *Ten Principles of Economics* in Chapter 1: People respond to incentives. Because unemployment benefits stop when a worker takes a new job, the unemployed devote less effort to job search and are more likely to turn down unattractive job offers. In addition, because unemployment insurance makes unemployment

"Given the current economic situation I doubt that effect is very large," says Harvard University economist Raj Chetty. "I think people will take whatever job they can get."

Economists on the right see a danger to prolonging benefits. "I don't think anybody's getting rich off of unemployment, and I'm not saying people are lazy," says Michael Tanner of the Cato Institute, a libertarian think tank in Washington, D.C. "The fact is, when you have a check coming in, even if it's a fairly low check, you're less motivated to either look for work or accept less optimal jobs."

The recent recession was unusual in almost every respect. Compared to other post-World War II recessions, it was deeper, longer and put more people out of work. A year after the economy began growing, unemployment is still a very high 9.5%. Nearly half the jobless—6.8 million total— have been out of work for more than six months, and 4.3 million of those have been without work for more than a year. The typical unemployed person has been out of the job market for a median of 25.5 weeks.

The government response was also unusual, and not just in the big bank bailout. In normal times, the unemployed are offered up to 26 weeks of benefits, largely financed by a tax on employers. In recessions, state and federal governments often jointly finance up to an additional 20 weeks

Broader Coverage
Percent of all unemployed collecting jobless benefits

Source: Labor Dept.

in hard-hit states. In this recession, Congress added up to another 53 weeks of federally funded benefits; in the deep crisis of the 1980s, the maximum total never exceeded 55 weeks.

The unemployment compensation system, created in 1935, was designed to tide workers over during periods of temporary unemployment. Benefits are based on a worker's prior wages; the average is $310 a week. Only workers who have lost a job through no fault of their own are eligible. Those who quit or who are new to the work force don't qualify. They must reapply weekly or biweekly, depending on the state, and indicate that they are looking for work.

In the 1980s, only half of all unemployed received benefits. In the first quarter of 2010, 69% of the unemployed did. That's partly because the benefits lasted so much longer, economists say. It's also because Washington gave states incentives to extend benefits to workers looking for part-time jobs and those who enrolled in training programs.

A variety of studies suggest that adding another 53 weeks of benefits increases the time the average worker is jobless by between 4.2 and 10.6 weeks. The higher estimates are based on studies conducted decades ago when layoffs were often temporary; in this recession, many unemployed workers will never return to their old positions. . . . In a recession such as this one— with five unemployed workers for every job opening—it's not clear whether the old academic findings apply.

In his scholarly past, Lawrence Summers, now Mr. Obama's economic guru, wrote in 1993 that "government assistance programs contribute to long-term unemployment . . . by providing an incentive, and the means, not to work." When an April *Wall Street Journal* editorial described his position, Mr. Summers fired back in a letter to the editor: "In the wake of the worst economic crisis in eight decades . . . there can be no doubt that the overwhelming cause of unemployment is economic distress, not the existence of unemployment insurance."

Source: *The Wall Street Journal*, July 7, 2010.

less onerous, workers are less likely to seek guarantees of job security when they negotiate with employers over the terms of employment.

Many studies by labor economists have examined the incentive effects of unemployment insurance. One study examined an experiment run by the state of Illinois in 1985. When unemployed workers applied to collect unemployment insurance benefits, the state randomly selected some of them and offered each a $500 bonus if they found new jobs within eleven weeks. This group was then compared to a control group not offered the incentive. The average spell of unemployment for the group offered the bonus was 7 percent shorter than the average spell for the control group. This experiment shows that the design of the unemployment insurance system influences the effort that the unemployed devote to job search.

Several other studies examined search effort by following a group of workers over time. Unemployment insurance benefits, rather than lasting forever, usually run out after six months or one year. These studies found that when the unemployed become ineligible for benefits, the probability of their finding a new job rises markedly. Thus, receiving unemployment insurance benefits does reduce the search effort of the unemployed.

Even though unemployment insurance reduces search effort and raises unemployment, we should not necessarily conclude that the policy is bad. The program does achieve its primary goal of reducing the income uncertainty that workers face. In addition, when workers turn down unattractive job offers, they have the opportunity to look for jobs that better suit their tastes and skills. Some economists argue that unemployment insurance improves the ability of the economy to match each worker with the most appropriate job.

The study of unemployment insurance shows that the unemployment rate is an imperfect measure of a nation's overall level of economic well-being. Most economists agree that eliminating unemployment insurance would reduce the amount of unemployment in the economy. Yet economists disagree on whether economic well-being would be enhanced or diminished by this change in policy.

QUICK QUIZ *How would an increase in the world price of oil affect the amount of frictional unemployment? Is this unemployment undesirable? What public policies might affect the amount of unemployment caused by this price change?*

Minimum-Wage Laws

Having seen how frictional unemployment results from the process of matching workers and jobs, let's now examine how structural unemployment results when the number of jobs is insufficient for the number of workers.

To understand structural unemployment, we begin by reviewing how minimum-wage laws can cause unemployment. Although minimum wages are not the predominant reason for unemployment in our economy, they have an important effect on certain groups with particularly high unemployment rates. Moreover, the analysis of minimum wages is a natural place to start because, as we will see, it can be used to understand some of the other reasons for structural unemployment.

Figure 4 reviews the basic economics of a minimum wage. When a minimum-wage law forces the wage to remain above the level that balances supply and demand, it raises the quantity of labor supplied and reduces the quantity of labor demanded

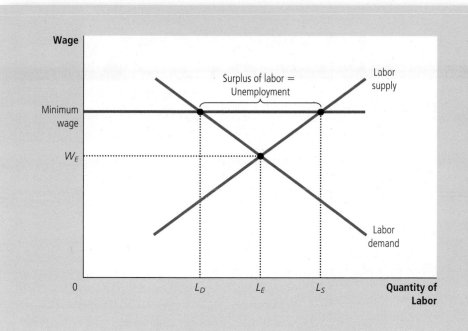

Figure 4

Unemployment from a Wage above the Equilibrium Level In this labor market, the wage at which supply and demand balance is W_E. At this equilibrium wage, the quantity of labor supplied and the quantity of labor demanded both equal L_E. By contrast, if the wage is forced to remain above the equilibrium level, perhaps because of a minimum-wage law, the quantity of labor supplied rises to L_S, and the quantity of labor demanded falls to L_D. The resulting surplus of labor, $L_s - L_D$, represents unemployment.

compared to the equilibrium level. There is a surplus of labor. Because there are more workers willing to work than there are jobs, some workers are unemployed.

While minimum-wage laws are one reason unemployment exists in the U.S. economy, they do not affect everyone. The vast majority of workers have wages well above the legal minimum, so the law does not prevent most wages from adjusting to balance supply and demand. Minimum-wage laws matter most for the least skilled and least experienced members of the labor force, such as teenagers. Their equilibrium wages tend to be low and, therefore, are more likely to fall below the legal minimum. It is only among these workers that minimum-wage laws explain the existence of unemployment.

Figure 4 is drawn to show the effects of a minimum-wage law, but it also illustrates a more general lesson: *If the wage is kept above the equilibrium level for any reason, the result is unemployment.* Minimum-wage laws are just one reason wages may be "too high." In the remaining two sections of this chapter, we consider two other reasons wages may be kept above the equilibrium level: unions and efficiency wages. The basic economics of unemployment in these cases is the same as that shown in Figure 4, but these explanations of unemployment can apply to many more of the economy's workers.

At this point, however, we should stop and notice that the structural unemployment that arises from an above-equilibrium wage is, in an important sense, different from the frictional unemployment that arises from the process of job search. The need for job search is not due to the failure of wages to balance labor supply and labor demand. When job search is the explanation for unemployment, workers are *searching* for the jobs that best suit their tastes and skills. By contrast, when the wage is above the equilibrium level, the quantity of labor supplied exceeds the quantity of labor demanded, and workers are unemployed because they are *waiting* for jobs to open up.

FYI

Who Earns the Minimum Wage?

In 2010, the Department of Labor released a study of which workers reported earnings at or below the minimum wage in 2009, when, in July, the minimum wage was raised from $6.55 to $7.25 per hour. (A reported wage below the minimum is possible because some workers are exempt from the statute, because enforcement is imperfect, and because some workers round down when reporting their wages on surveys.) Here is a summary of the findings:

- Of those workers paid an hourly rate, about 4 percent of men and 6 percent of women reported wages at or below the prevailing federal minimum.
- Minimum-wage workers tend to be young. About half of all hourly paid workers earning the minimum wage or less were under age 25, and about one-fourth were age 16–19. Among employed teenagers, 19 percent earned the minimum wage or less, compared with 3 percent of workers age 25 and older.
- Minimum-wage workers tend to be less educated. Among hourly paid workers age 16 and older, about 10 percent of those without

a high school diploma earned the minimum wage or less, compared with about 4 percent of those who earned a high school diploma (but did not attend college) and about 3 percent for those who had obtained a college degree.

- Minimum-wage workers are more likely to be working part time. Among part-time workers (those who usually work less than 35 hours per week), 11 percent were paid the minimum wage or less, compared to 2 percent of full-time workers.
- The industry with the highest proportion of workers with reported hourly wages at or below the minimum wage was leisure and hospitality (21 percent). About one-half of all workers paid at or below the minimum wage were employed in this industry, primarily in food services and drinking establishments. For many of these workers, tips supplement the hourly wages received.
- The proportion of hourly paid workers earning the prevailing federal minimum wage or less has trended downward since 1979, when data collection first began on a regular basis.

QUICK QUIZ *Draw the supply curve and the demand curve for a labor market in which the wage is fixed above the equilibrium level. Show the quantity of labor supplied, the quantity demanded, and the amount of unemployment.*

Unions and Collective Bargaining

union

a worker association that bargains with employers over wages, benefits, and working conditions

A **union** is a worker association that bargains with employers over wages, benefits, and working conditions. Only 12 percent of U.S. workers now belong to unions, but unions played a much larger role in the U.S. labor market in the past. In the 1940s and 1950s, when union membership was at its peak, about a third of the U.S. labor force was unionized.

Moreover, for a variety of historical reasons, unions continue to play a large role in many European countries. In Belgium, Norway, and Sweden, for instance, more than half of workers belong to unions. In France and Germany, a majority of workers have wages set by collective bargaining by law, even though only some of these workers are themselves union members. In these cases, wages are not determined by the equilibrium of supply and demand in competitive labor markets.

The Economics of Unions

A union is a type of cartel. Like any cartel, a union is a group of sellers acting together in the hope of exerting their joint market power. Most workers in the U.S. economy discuss their wages, benefits, and working conditions with their employers as individuals. By contrast, workers in a union do so as a group. The process by which unions and firms agree on the terms of employment is called **collective bargaining**.

When a union bargains with a firm, it asks for higher wages, better benefits, and better working conditions than the firm would offer in the absence of a union. If the union and the firm do not reach agreement, the union can organize a withdrawal of labor from the firm, called a **strike**. Because a strike reduces production, sales, and profit, a firm facing a strike threat is likely to agree to pay higher wages than it otherwise would. Economists who study the effects of unions typically find that union workers earn about 10 to 20 percent more than similar workers who do not belong to unions.

When a union raises the wage above the equilibrium level, it raises the quantity of labor supplied and reduces the quantity of labor demanded, resulting in unemployment. Workers who remain employed at the higher wage are better off, but those who were previously employed and are now unemployed are worse off. Indeed, unions are often thought to cause conflict between different groups of workers—between the *insiders* who benefit from high union wages and the *outsiders* who do not get the union jobs.

The outsiders can respond to their status in one of two ways. Some of them remain unemployed and wait for the chance to become insiders and earn the high union wage. Others take jobs in firms that are not unionized. Thus, when unions raise wages in one part of the economy, the supply of labor increases in other parts of the economy. This increase in labor supply, in turn, reduces wages in industries that are not unionized. In other words, workers in unions reap the benefit of collective bargaining, while workers not in unions bear some of the cost.

The role of unions in the economy depends in part on the laws that govern union organization and collective bargaining. Normally, explicit agreements among members of a cartel are illegal. When firms selling similar products agree to set high prices, the agreement is considered a "conspiracy in restraint of trade," and the government prosecutes the firms in civil and criminal court for violating the antitrust laws. By contrast, unions are exempt from these laws. The policymakers who wrote the antitrust laws believed that workers needed greater market power as they bargained with employers. Indeed, various laws are designed to encourage the formation of unions. In particular, the Wagner Act of 1935 prevents employers from interfering when workers try to organize unions and requires employers to bargain with unions in good faith. The National Labor Relations Board (NLRB) is the government agency that enforces workers' right to unionize.

Legislation affecting the market power of unions is a perennial topic of political debate. State lawmakers sometimes debate *right-to-work laws,* which give workers in a unionized firm the right to choose whether to join the union. In the absence of such laws, unions can insist during collective bargaining that firms make union membership a requirement for employment. At times, lawmakers in Washington have debated a proposed law that would prevent firms from hiring permanent replacements for workers who are on strike. This law would make strikes more costly for firms, thereby increasing the market power of unions. These and similar policy decisions will help determine the future of the union movement.

collective bargaining
the process by which unions and firms agree on the terms of employment

strike
the organized withdrawal of labor from a firm by a union

"Gentlemen, nothing stands in the way of a final accord except that management wants profit maximization and the union wants more moola."

Are Unions Good or Bad for the Economy?

Economists disagree about whether unions are good or bad for the economy as a whole. Let's consider both sides of the debate.

Critics argue that unions are merely a type of cartel. When unions raise wages above the level that would prevail in competitive markets, they reduce the quantity of labor demanded, cause some workers to be unemployed, and reduce the wages in the rest of the economy. The resulting allocation of labor is, critics argue, both inefficient and inequitable. It is inefficient because high union wages reduce employment in unionized firms below the efficient, competitive level. It is inequitable because some workers benefit at the expense of other workers.

Advocates contend that unions are a necessary antidote to the market power of the firms that hire workers. The extreme case of this market power is the "company town," where a single firm does most of the hiring in a geographical region. In a company town, if workers do not accept the wages and working conditions that the firm offers, they have little choice but to move or stop working. In the absence of a union, therefore, the firm could use its market power to pay lower wages and offer worse working conditions than would prevail if it had to compete with other firms for the same workers. In this case, a union may balance the firm's market power and protect the workers from being at the mercy of the firm's owners.

Advocates of unions also claim that unions are important for helping firms respond efficiently to workers' concerns. Whenever a worker takes a job, the worker and the firm must agree on many attributes of the job in addition to the wage: hours of work, overtime, vacations, sick leave, health benefits, promotion schedules, job security, and so on. By representing workers' views on these issues, unions allow firms to provide the right mix of job attributes. Even if unions have the adverse effect of pushing wages above the equilibrium level and causing unemployment, they have the benefit of helping firms keep a happy and productive workforce.

In the end, there is no consensus among economists about whether unions are good or bad for the economy. Like many institutions, their influence is probably beneficial in some circumstances and adverse in others.

QUICK QUIZ   *How does a union in the auto industry affect wages and employment at General Motors and Ford? How does it affect wages and employment in other industries?*

The Theory of Efficiency Wages

efficiency wages
above-equilibrium wages paid by firms to increase worker productivity

A fourth reason economies always experience some unemployment—in addition to job search, minimum-wage laws, and unions—is suggested by the theory of **efficiency wages**. According to this theory, firms operate more efficiently if wages are above the equilibrium level. Therefore, it may be profitable for firms to keep wages high even in the presence of a surplus of labor.

In some ways, the unemployment that arises from efficiency wages is similar to the unemployment that arises from minimum-wage laws and unions. In all three cases, unemployment is the result of wages above the level that balances the quantity of labor supplied and the quantity of labor demanded. Yet there is also an important difference. Minimum-wage laws and unions prevent firms from lowering wages in the presence of a surplus of workers. Efficiency-wage theory states that such a constraint on firms is unnecessary in many cases because firms may be better off keeping wages above the equilibrium level.

Why should firms want to keep wages high? This decision may seem odd at first, for wages are a large part of firms' costs. Normally, we expect profit-maximizing firms to want to keep costs—and therefore wages—as low as possible. The novel insight of efficiency-wage theory is that paying high wages might be profitable because they might raise the efficiency of a firm's workers.

There are several types of efficiency-wage theory. Each type suggests a different explanation for why firms may want to pay high wages. Let's now consider four of these types.

Worker Health

The first and simplest type of efficiency-wage theory emphasizes the link between wages and worker health. Better paid workers eat a more nutritious diet, and workers who eat a better diet are healthier and more productive. A firm may find it more profitable to pay high wages and have healthy, productive workers than to pay lower wages and have less healthy, less productive workers.

This type of efficiency-wage theory can be relevant for explaining unemployment in less developed countries where inadequate nutrition can be a problem. In these countries, firms may fear that cutting wages would, in fact, adversely influence their workers' health and productivity. In other words, nutrition concerns may explain why firms may maintain above-equilibrium wages despite a surplus of labor. Worker health concerns are far less relevant for firms in rich countries such as the United States, where the equilibrium wages for most workers are well above the level needed for an adequate diet.

Worker Turnover

A second type of efficiency-wage theory emphasizes the link between wages and worker turnover. Workers quit jobs for many reasons: to take jobs in other firms, to move to other parts of the country, to leave the labor force, and so on. The frequency with which they quit depends on the entire set of incentives they face, including the benefits of leaving and the benefits of staying. The more a firm pays its workers, the less often its workers will choose to leave. Thus, a firm can reduce turnover among its workers by paying them a high wage.

Why do firms care about turnover? The reason is that it is costly for firms to hire and train new workers. Moreover, even after they are trained, newly hired workers are not as productive as experienced workers. Firms with higher turnover, therefore, will tend to have higher production costs. Firms may find it profitable to pay wages above the equilibrium level to reduce worker turnover.

Worker Quality

A third type of efficiency-wage theory emphasizes the link between wages and worker quality. All firms want workers who are talented, and they try to pick the best applicants to fill job openings. But because firms cannot perfectly gauge the quality of applicants, hiring has a degree of randomness to it. When a firm pays a high wage, it attracts a better pool of workers to apply for its jobs and thereby increases the quality of its workforce. If the firm responded to a surplus of labor by reducing the wage, the most competent applicants—who are more likely to have better alternative opportunities than less competent applicants—may choose not to apply. If this influence of the wage on worker quality is strong enough, it may be profitable for the firm to pay a wage above the level that balances supply and demand.

will accept the money . . . and so on. To the restaurateur and to other people in our society, your cash or check represents a claim to goods and services in the future.

The social custom of using money for transactions is extraordinarily useful in a large, complex society. Imagine, for a moment, that there was no item in the economy widely accepted in exchange for goods and services. People would have to rely on *barter*—the exchange of one good or service for another—to obtain the things they need. To get your restaurant meal, for instance, you would have to offer the restaurateur something of immediate value. You could offer to wash some dishes, clean his car, or give him your family's secret recipe for meat loaf. An economy that relies on barter will have trouble allocating its scarce resources efficiently. In such an economy, trade is said to require the *double coincidence of wants*—the unlikely occurrence that two people each have a good or service that the other wants.

The existence of money makes trade easier. The restaurateur does not care whether you can produce a valuable good or service for him. He is happy to accept your money, knowing that other people will do the same for him. Such a convention allows trade to be roundabout. The restaurateur accepts your money and uses it to pay his chef; the chef uses her paycheck to send her child to day care; the day care center uses this tuition to pay a teacher; and the teacher hires you to mow his lawn. As money flows from person to person in the economy, it facilitates production and trade, thereby allowing each person to specialize in what he or she does best and raising everyone's standard of living.

In this chapter, we begin to examine the role of money in the economy. We discuss what money is, the various forms that money takes, how the banking system helps create money, and how the government controls the quantity of money in circulation. Because money is so important in the economy, we devote much effort in the rest of this book to learning how changes in the quantity of money affect various economic variables, including inflation, interest rates, production, and employment. Consistent with our long-run focus in the previous four chapters, in the next chapter we examine the long-run effects of changes in the quantity of money. The short-run effects of monetary changes are a more complex topic, which we take up later in the book. This chapter provides the background for all of this further analysis.

The Meaning of Money

What is money? This might seem like an odd question. When you read that billionaire Bill Gates has a lot of money, you know what that means: He is so rich that he can buy almost anything he wants. In this sense, the term *money* is used to mean *wealth*.

money
the set of assets in an economy that people regularly use to buy goods and services from other people

Economists, however, use the word in a more specific sense: **Money** is the set of assets in the economy that people regularly use to buy goods and services from each other. The cash in your wallet is money because you can use it to buy a meal at a restaurant or a shirt at a clothing store. By contrast, if you happened to own a large share of Microsoft Corporation, as Bill Gates does, you would be wealthy, but this asset is not considered a form of money. You could not buy a meal or a shirt with this wealth without first obtaining some cash. According to the economist's definition, money includes only those few types of wealth that are regularly accepted by sellers in exchange for goods and services.

The Functions of Money

Money has three functions in the economy: It is a *medium of exchange*, a *unit of account*, and a *store of value*. These three functions together distinguish money from other assets in the economy, such as stocks, bonds, real estate, art, and even baseball cards. Let's examine each of these functions of money in turn.

A **medium of exchange** is an item that buyers give to sellers when they purchase goods and services. When you buy a shirt at a clothing store, the store gives you the shirt, and you give the store your money. This transfer of money from buyer to seller allows the transaction to take place. When you walk into a store, you are confident that the store will accept your money for the items it is selling because money is the commonly accepted medium of exchange.

A **unit of account** is the yardstick people use to post prices and record debts. When you go shopping, you might observe that a shirt costs $30 and a hamburger costs $3. Even though it would be accurate to say that the price of a shirt is 10 hamburgers and the price of a hamburger is $\frac{1}{10}$ of a shirt, prices are never quoted in this way. Similarly, if you take out a loan from a bank, the size of your future loan repayments will be measured in dollars, not in a quantity of goods and services. When we want to measure and record economic value, we use money as the unit of account.

A **store of value** is an item that people can use to transfer purchasing power from the present to the future. When a seller accepts money today in exchange for a good or service, that seller can hold the money and become a buyer of another good or service at another time. Money is not the only store of value in the economy: A person can also transfer purchasing power from the present to the future by holding nonmonetary assets such as stocks and bonds. The term *wealth* is used to refer to the total of all stores of value, including both money and nonmonetary assets.

Economists use the term **liquidity** to describe the ease with which an asset can be converted into the economy's medium of exchange. Because money is the economy's medium of exchange, it is the most liquid asset available. Other assets vary widely in their liquidity. Most stocks and bonds can be sold easily with small cost, so they are relatively liquid assets. By contrast, selling a house, a Rembrandt painting, or a 1948 Joe DiMaggio baseball card requires more time and effort, so these assets are less liquid.

When people decide in what form to hold their wealth, they have to balance the liquidity of each possible asset against the asset's usefulness as a store of value. Money is the most liquid asset, but it is far from perfect as a store of value. When prices rise, the value of money falls. In other words, when goods and services become more expensive, each dollar in your wallet can buy less. This link between the price level and the value of money is key to understanding how money affects the economy, a topic we start to explore in the next chapter.

The Kinds of Money

When money takes the form of a commodity with intrinsic value, it is called **commodity money**. The term *intrinsic value* means that the item would have value even if it were not used as money. One example of commodity money is gold. Gold has intrinsic value because it is used in industry and in the making of jewelry. Although today we no longer use gold as money, historically gold has been a common form of money because it is relatively easy to carry, measure, and verify for impurities. When an economy uses gold as money (or uses paper money that is convertible into gold on demand), it is said to be operating under a *gold standard*.

---

medium of exchange
an item that buyers give to sellers when they want to purchase goods and services

unit of account
the yardstick people use to post prices and record debts

store of value
an item that people can use to transfer purchasing power from the present to the future

liquidity
the ease with which an asset can be converted into the economy's medium of exchange

commodity money
money that takes the form of a commodity with intrinsic value

Another example of commodity money is cigarettes. In prisoner-of-war camps during World War II, prisoners traded goods and services with one another using cigarettes as the store of value, unit of account, and medium of exchange. Similarly, as the Soviet Union was breaking up in the late 1980s, cigarettes started replacing the ruble as the preferred currency in Moscow. In both cases, even non-smokers were happy to accept cigarettes in an exchange, knowing that they could use the cigarettes to buy other goods and services.

fiat money

money without intrinsic value that is used as money because of government decree

Money without intrinsic value is called **fiat money**. A *fiat* is an order or decree, and fiat money is established as money by government decree. For example, compare the paper dollars in your wallet (printed by the U.S. government) and the paper dollars from a game of Monopoly (printed by the Parker Brothers game company). Why can you use the first to pay your bill at a restaurant but not the second? The answer is that the U.S. government has decreed its dollars to be valid money. Each paper dollar in your wallet reads: "This note is legal tender for all debts, public and private."

Although the government is central to establishing and regulating a system of fiat money (by prosecuting counterfeiters, for example), other factors are also required for the success of such a monetary system. To a large extent, the acceptance of fiat money depends as much on expectations and social convention as on government decree. The Soviet government in the 1980s never abandoned the ruble as the official currency. Yet the people of Moscow preferred to accept cigarettes (or even American dollars) in exchange for goods and services because they were more confident that these alternative monies would be accepted by others in the future.

in the news

> ### Mackereleconomics

Money evolves naturally to facilitate exchange, even in prisons.

Packs of Fish Catch on as Currency

BY JUSTIN SCHECK

When Larry Levine helped prepare divorce papers for a client a few years ago, he got paid in mackerel. Once the case ended, he says, "I had a stack of macks."

Mr. Levine and his client were prisoners in California's Lompoc Federal Correctional Complex. Like other federal inmates around the country, they found a can of mackerel—the "mack" in prison lingo—was the standard currency.

"It's the coin of the realm," says Mark Bailey, who paid Mr. Levine in fish. Mr. Bailey was serving a two-year tax-fraud sentence in connection with a chain of strip clubs he owned. Mr. Levine was serving a nine-year term for drug dealing. Mr. Levine says he used his macks to get his beard trimmed, his clothes pressed and his shoes shined by other prisoners. "A haircut is two macks," he says,

as an expected tip for inmates who work in the prison barber shop.

There's been a mackerel economy in federal prisons since about 2004, former inmates and some prison consultants say. That's when federal prisons prohibited smoking and, by default, the cigarette pack, which was the earlier gold standard.

Prisoners need a proxy for the dollar because they're not allowed to possess cash. Money they get from prison jobs (which pay a maximum of 40 cents an hour,

Money in the U.S. Economy

As we will see, the quantity of money circulating in the economy, called the *money stock*, has a powerful influence on many economic variables. But before we consider why that is true, we need to ask a preliminary question: What is the quantity of money? In particular, suppose you were given the task of measuring how much money there is in the U.S. economy. What would you include in your measure?

The most obvious asset to include is **currency**—the paper bills and coins in the hands of the public. Currency is clearly the most widely accepted medium of exchange in our economy. There is no doubt that it is part of the money stock.

Yet currency is not the only asset that you can use to buy goods and services. Many stores also accept personal checks. Wealth held in your checking account is almost as convenient for buying things as wealth held in your wallet. To measure the money stock, therefore, you might want to include **demand deposits**—balances in bank accounts that depositors can access on demand simply by writing a check or swiping a debit card at a store.

Once you start to consider balances in checking accounts as part of the money stock, you are led to consider the large variety of other accounts that people hold at banks and other financial institutions. Bank depositors usually cannot write checks against the balances in their savings accounts, but they can easily transfer funds from savings into checking accounts. In addition, depositors in money market mutual funds can often write checks against their balances. Thus, these other accounts should plausibly be part of the U.S. money stock.

currency
the paper bills and coins in the hands of the public

demand deposits
balances in bank accounts that depositors can access on demand by writing a check

---

according to the Federal Bureau of Prisons) or family members goes into commissary accounts that let them buy things such as food and toiletries. After the smokes disappeared, inmates turned to other items on the commissary menu to use as currency.

Books of stamps were one easy alternative. "It was like half a book for a piece of fruit," says Tony Serra, a well-known San Francisco criminal-defense attorney who last year finished nine months in Lompoc on tax charges. Elsewhere in the West, prisoners use PowerBars or cans of tuna, says Ed Bales, a consultant who advises people who are headed to prison. But in much of the federal prison system, he says, mackerel has become the currency of choice.

Mackerel supplier Global Source Marketing Inc. says demand from prisons has grown since 2004. In recent years, demand has switched from cans—which wardens don't like because inmates can turn them into makeshift knives—to plastic-and-foil pouches of mackerel fillets, says Jon Linder, a vice president at supplier Power Commissary Inc., in Bohemia, N.Y.

Mackerel is hot in prisons in the U.S., but not so much anywhere else, says Mark Muntz, president of Global Source, which imports fillets of the oily, dark-fleshed fish from Asian canneries. Mr. Muntz says he's tried marketing mackerel to discount retailers. "We've even tried 99-cent stores," he says. "It never has done very well at all, regardless of the retailer, but it's very popular in the prisons."

Mr. Muntz says he sold more than $1 million of mackerel for federal prison commissaries last year. It accounted for about half his commissary sales, he says, outstripping the canned tuna, crab, chicken and oysters he offers.

Unlike those more expensive delicacies, former prisoners say, the mack is a good stand-in for the greenback because each can (or pouch) costs about $1 and few—other than weight-lifters craving protein—want to eat it.

So inmates stash macks in lockers provided by the prison and use them to buy goods, including illicit ones such as stolen food and home-brewed "prison hooch," as well as services, such as shoeshines and cell cleaning.

"When I grow up, I am going to be a medium of exchange, unit of account, and store of value."

Source: *The Wall Street Journal*, October 2, 2008.

FYI

❯ Why Credit Cards Aren't Money

It might seem natural to include credit cards as part of the economy's stock of money. After all, people use credit cards to make many of their purchases. Aren't credit cards, therefore, a medium of exchange?

At first this argument may seem persuasive, but credit cards are excluded from all measures of the quantity of money. The reason is that credit cards are not really a method of payment but a method of *deferring* payment. When you buy a meal with a credit card, the bank that issued the card pays the restaurant what it is due. At a later date, you will have to repay the bank (perhaps with interest). When the time comes to pay your credit card bill, you will probably do so by writing a check against your checking account. The balance in this checking account is part of the economy's stock of money.

Notice that credit cards are very different from debit cards, which automatically withdraw funds from a bank account to pay for items bought. Rather than allowing the user to postpone payment for a purchase, a debit card allows the user immediate access to deposits in a bank account. In this sense, a debit card is more similar to a check than to a credit card. The account balances that lie behind debit cards are included in measures of the quantity of money.

Even though credit cards are not considered a form of money, they are nonetheless important for analyzing the monetary system. People who have credit cards can pay many of their bills together at the end of the month, rather than sporadically as they make purchases. As a result, people who have credit cards probably hold less money on average than people who do not have credit cards. Thus, the introduction and increased popularity of credit cards may reduce the amount of money that people choose to hold.

In a complex economy such as ours, it is not easy to draw a line between assets that can be called "money" and assets that cannot. The coins in your pocket clearly are part of the money stock, and the Empire State Building clearly is not, but there are many assets in between these extremes for which the choice is less clear. Because different analysts can reasonably disagree about where to draw the dividing line between monetary and nonmonetary assets, various measures of the money stock are available for the U.S. economy. Figure 1 shows the two most commonly used, designated M1 and M2. M2 includes more assets in its measure of money than does M1.

For our purposes in this book, we need not dwell on the differences between the various measures of money. None of our discussion will hinge on the distinction between M1 and M2. The important point is that the money stock for the U.S. economy includes not just currency but also deposits in banks and other financial institutions that can be readily accessed and used to buy goods and services.

 ## Where Is All the Currency?

One puzzle about the money stock of the U.S. economy concerns the amount of currency. At the end of 2009, there was $862 billion of currency outstanding. To put this number in perspective, we can divide it by 236 million, the number of

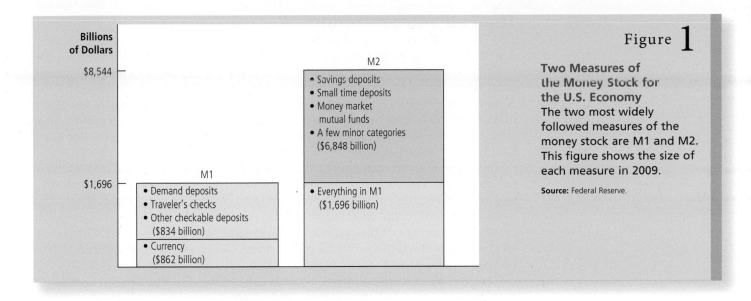

Figure 1

Two Measures of the Money Stock for the U.S. Economy
The two most widely followed measures of the money stock are M1 and M2. This figure shows the size of each measure in 2009.

Source: Federal Reserve.

adults (age 16 and older) in the United States. This calculation implies that the average adult holds about $3,653 of currency. Most people are surprised to learn that our economy has so much currency because they carry far less than this in their wallets.

Who is holding all this currency? No one knows for sure, but there are two plausible explanations.

The first explanation is that much of the currency is held abroad. In foreign countries without a stable monetary system, people often prefer U.S. dollars to domestic assets. It is, in fact, not unusual to see U.S. dollars used overseas as the medium of exchange, unit of account, and store of value.

The second explanation is that much of the currency is held by drug dealers, tax evaders, and other criminals. For most people in the U.S. economy, currency is not a particularly good way to hold wealth. Not only can currency be lost or stolen, but it also does not earn interest, whereas a bank deposit does. Thus, most people hold only small amounts of currency. By contrast, criminals may avoid putting their wealth in banks because a bank deposit gives police a paper trail they can use to trace illegal activities. For criminals, currency may be the best store of value available. ■

QUICK QUIZ   *List and describe the three functions of money.*

The Federal Reserve System

Whenever an economy uses a system of fiat money, as the U.S. economy does, some agency must be responsible for regulating the system. In the United States, that agency is the **Federal Reserve**, often simply called the **Fed**. If you look at the top of a dollar bill, you will see that it is called a "Federal Reserve Note." The Fed is an example of a **central bank**—an institution designed to oversee the banking system and regulate the quantity of money in the economy. Other major central banks around the world include the Bank of England, the Bank of Japan, and the European Central Bank.

Federal Reserve (Fed)
the central bank of the United States

central bank
an institution designed to oversee the banking system and regulate the quantity of money in the economy

The Fed's Organization

The Federal Reserve was created in 1913 after a series of bank failures in 1907 convinced Congress that the United States needed a central bank to ensure the health of the nation's banking system. Today, the Fed is run by its board of governors, which has seven members appointed by the president and confirmed by the Senate. The governors have fourteen-year terms. Just as federal judges are given lifetime appointments to insulate them from politics, Fed governors are given long terms to give them independence from short-term political pressures when they formulate monetary policy.

Among the seven members of the board of governors, the most important is the chairman. The chairman directs the Fed staff, presides over board meetings, and testifies regularly about Fed policy in front of congressional committees. The president appoints the chairman to a four-year term. As this book was going to press, the chairman of the Fed was Ben Bernanke, a former economics professor who was appointed to the Fed job by President George W. Bush in 2005 and reappointed by President Barack Obama in 2009.

The Federal Reserve System is made up of the Federal Reserve Board in Washington, D.C., and twelve regional Federal Reserve Banks located in major cities around the country. The presidents of the regional banks are chosen by each bank's board of directors, whose members are typically drawn from the region's banking and business community.

The Fed has two related jobs. The first is to regulate banks and ensure the health of the banking system. This task is largely the responsibility of the regional Federal Reserve Banks. In particular, the Fed monitors each bank's financial condition and facilitates bank transactions by clearing checks. It also acts as a bank's bank. That is, the Fed makes loans to banks when banks themselves want to borrow. When financially troubled banks find themselves short of cash, the Fed acts as a *lender of last resort*—a lender to those who cannot borrow anywhere else—to maintain stability in the overall banking system.

money supply
the quantity of money available in the economy

monetary policy
the setting of the money supply by policymakers in the central bank

The Fed's second and more important job is to control the quantity of money that is made available in the economy, called the **money supply**. Decisions by policymakers concerning the money supply constitute **monetary policy.** At the Federal Reserve, monetary policy is made by the Federal Open Market Committee (FOMC). The FOMC meets about every six weeks in Washington, D.C., to discuss the condition of the economy and consider changes in monetary policy.

The Federal Open Market Committee

The Federal Open Market Committee is made up of the seven members of the board of governors and five of the twelve regional bank presidents. All twelve regional presidents attend each FOMC meeting, but only five get to vote. The five with voting rights rotate among the twelve regional presidents over time. The president of the New York Fed always gets a vote, however, because New York is the traditional financial center of the U.S. economy and because all Fed purchases and sales of government bonds are conducted at the New York Fed's trading desk.

Through the decisions of the FOMC, the Fed has the power to increase or decrease the number of dollars in the economy. In simple metaphorical terms, you can imagine the Fed printing dollar bills and dropping them around the country by helicopter. Similarly, you can imagine the Fed using a giant vacuum cleaner to suck dollar bills out of people's wallets. Although in practice the Fed's methods for changing the money supply are more complex and subtle than this, the helicopter-vacuum metaphor is a good first step to understanding the meaning of monetary policy.

Later in this chapter, we discuss how the Fed actually changes the money supply, but it is worth noting here that the Fed's primary tool is the *open-market operation*—the purchase and sale of U.S. government bonds. (Recall that a U.S. government bond is a certificate of indebtedness of the federal government.) If the FOMC decides to increase the money supply, the Fed creates dollars and uses them to buy government bonds from the public in the nation's bond markets. After the purchase, these dollars are in the hands of the public. Thus, an open-market purchase of bonds by the Fed increases the money supply. Conversely, if the FOMC decides to decrease the money supply, the Fed sells government bonds from its portfolio to the public in the nation's bond markets. After the sale, the dollars it receives for the bonds are out of the hands of the public. Thus, an open-market sale of bonds by the Fed decreases the money supply.

Central banks are important institutions because changes in the money supply can profoundly affect the economy. One of the *Ten Principles of Economics* in Chapter 1 is that prices rise when the government prints too much money. Another of the *Ten Principles of Economics* is that society faces a short-run trade-off between inflation and unemployment. The power of the Fed rests on these principles. For reasons we discuss more fully in the coming chapters, the Fed's policy decisions have an important influence on the economy's rate of inflation in the long run and the economy's employment and production in the short run. Indeed, the chairman of the Federal Reserve has been called the second most powerful person in the United States.

QUICK QUIZ   *What are the primary responsibilities of the Federal Reserve? If the Fed wants to increase the supply of money, how does it usually do so?*

Banks and the Money Supply

So far, we have introduced the concept of "money" and discussed how the Federal Reserve controls the supply of money by buying and selling government bonds in open-market operations. Although this explanation of the money supply is correct, it is not complete. In particular, it omits the central role that banks play in the monetary system.

Recall that the amount of money you hold includes both currency (the bills in your wallet and coins in your pocket) and demand deposits (the balance in your checking account). Because demand deposits are held in banks, the behavior of banks can influence the quantity of demand deposits in the economy and, therefore, the money supply. This section examines how banks affect the money supply and, in doing so, how they complicate the Fed's job of controlling the money supply.

"I've heard a lot about money, and now I'd like to try some."

The Simple Case of 100-Percent-Reserve Banking

To see how banks influence the money supply, let's first imagine a world without any banks at all. In this simple world, currency is the only form of money. To be concrete, let's suppose that the total quantity of currency is $100. The supply of money is, therefore, $100.

Now suppose that someone opens a bank, appropriately called First National Bank. First National Bank is only a depository institution—that is, it accepts deposits but does not make loans. The purpose of the bank is to give depositors a safe place to keep their money. Whenever a person deposits some money, the bank keeps the money in its vault until the depositor withdraws it, writes a check, or uses a debit card to access his or her balance. Deposits that banks have received but have not loaned out are called **reserves**. In this imaginary economy, all deposits are held as reserves, so this system is called *100-percent-reserve banking*.

reserves

deposits that banks have received but have not loaned out

We can express the financial position of First National Bank with a *T-account*, which is a simplified accounting statement that shows changes in a bank's assets and liabilities. Here is the T-account for First National Bank if the economy's entire $100 of money is deposited in the bank:

First National Bank

Assets		Liabilities	
Reserves	$100.00	Deposits	$100.00

On the left side of the T-account are the bank's assets of $100 (the reserves it holds in its vaults). On the right side are the bank's liabilities of $100 (the amount it owes to its depositors). Because the assets and liabilities of First National Bank exactly balance, this accounting statement is sometimes called a *balance sheet*.

Now consider the money supply in this imaginary economy. Before First National Bank opens, the money supply is the $100 of currency that people are holding. After the bank opens and people deposit their currency, the money supply is the $100 of demand deposits. (There is no longer any currency outstanding, for it is all in the bank vault.) Each deposit in the bank reduces currency and raises demand deposits by exactly the same amount, leaving the money supply unchanged. Thus, *if banks hold all deposits in reserve, banks do not influence the supply of money*.

Money Creation with Fractional-Reserve Banking

Eventually, the bankers at First National Bank may start to reconsider their policy of 100-percent-reserve banking. Leaving all that money idle in their vaults seems unnecessary. Why not lend some of it out and earn a profit by charging interest on the loans? Families buying houses, firms building new factories, and students paying for college would all be happy to pay interest to borrow some of that money for a while. First National Bank has to keep some reserves so that currency is available if depositors want to make withdrawals. But if the flow of new deposits is roughly the same as the flow of withdrawals, First National needs to keep only a fraction of its deposits in reserve. Thus, First National adopts a system called **fractional-reserve banking.**

fractional-reserve banking

a banking system in which banks hold only a fraction of deposits as reserves

The fraction of total deposits that a bank holds as reserves is called the **reserve ratio.** This ratio is determined by a combination of government regulation and bank policy. As we discuss more fully later in the chapter, the Fed sets a minimum amount of reserves that banks must hold, called a *reserve requirement*. In addition, banks may hold reserves above the legal minimum, called *excess reserves*, so they can be more confident that they will not run short of cash. For our purpose here, we take the reserve ratio as given to examine how fractional-reserve banking influences the money supply.

reserve ratio

the fraction of deposits that banks hold as reserves

Let's suppose that First National has a reserve ratio of 1/10, or 10 percent. This means that it keeps 10 percent of its deposits in reserve and loans out the rest. Now let's look again at the bank's T-account:

First National Bank

Assets		Liabilities	
Reserves	$10.00	Deposits	$100.00
Loans	90.00		

First National still has $100 in liabilities because making the loans did not alter the bank's obligation to its depositors. But now the bank has two kinds of assets: It has $10 of reserves in its vault, and it has loans of $90. (These loans are liabilities of the people taking out the loans, but they are assets of the bank making the loans because the borrowers will later repay the bank.) In total, First National's assets still equal its liabilities.

Once again consider the supply of money in the economy. Before First National makes any loans, the money supply is the $100 of deposits in the bank. Yet when First National makes these loans, the money supply increases. The depositors still have demand deposits totaling $100, but now the borrowers hold $90 in currency. The money supply (which equals currency plus demand deposits) equals $190. Thus, *when banks hold only a fraction of deposits in reserve, banks create money.*

At first, this creation of money by fractional-reserve banking may seem too good to be true: It appears that the bank has created money out of thin air. To make this creation of money seem less miraculous, note that when First National Bank loans out some of its reserves and creates money, it does not create any wealth. Loans from First National give the borrowers some currency and thus the ability to buy goods and services. Yet the borrowers are also taking on debts, so the loans do not make them any richer. In other words, as a bank creates the asset of money, it also creates a corresponding liability for those who borrowed the created money. At the end of this process of money creation, the economy is more liquid in the sense that there is more of the medium of exchange, but the economy is no wealthier than before.

The Money Multiplier

The creation of money does not stop with First National Bank. Suppose the borrower from First National uses the $90 to buy something from someone who then deposits the currency in Second National Bank. Here is the T-account for Second National Bank:

Second National Bank

Assets		Liabilities	
Reserves	$ 9.00	Deposits	$90.00
Loans	81.00		

After the deposit, this bank has liabilities of $90. If Second National also has a reserve ratio of 10 percent, it keeps assets of $9 in reserve and makes $81 in loans. In this way, Second National Bank creates an additional $81 of money. If this $81 is eventually deposited in Third National Bank, which also has a reserve ratio of 10 percent, this bank keeps $8.10 in reserve and makes $72.90 in loans. Here is the T-account for Third National Bank:

Third National Bank

Assets		Liabilities	
Reserves	$ 8.10	Deposits	$81.00
Loans	72.90		

The process goes on and on. Each time that money is deposited and a bank loan is made, more money is created.

How much money is eventually created in this economy? Let's add it up:

Original deposit	= $100.00
First National lending	= $ 90.00 [= .9 × $100.00]
Second National lending	= $ 81.00 [= .9 × $90.00]
Third National lending	= $ 72.90 [= .9 × $81.00]
•	•
•	•
•	•
Total money supply	= $1,000.00

It turns out that even though this process of money creation can continue forever, it does not create an infinite amount of money. If you laboriously add the infinite sequence of numbers in the preceding example, you find the $100 of reserves generates $1,000 of money. The amount of money the banking system generates with each dollar of reserves is called the **money multiplier.** In this imaginary economy, where the $100 of reserves generates $1,000 of money, the money multiplier is 10.

money multiplier
the amount of money the banking system generates with each dollar of reserves

What determines the size of the money multiplier? It turns out that the answer is simple: *The money multiplier is the reciprocal of the reserve ratio.* If R is the reserve ratio for all banks in the economy, then each dollar of reserves generates $1/R$ dollars of money. In our example, $R = 1/10$, so the money multiplier is 10.

This reciprocal formula for the money multiplier makes sense. If a bank holds $1,000 in deposits, then a reserve ratio of $1/10$ (10 percent) means that the bank must hold $100 in reserves. The money multiplier just turns this idea around: If the banking system as a whole holds a total of $100 in reserves, it can have only $1,000 in deposits. In other words, if R is the ratio of reserves to deposits at each bank (that is, the reserve ratio), then the ratio of deposits to reserves in the banking system (that is, the money multiplier) must be $1/R$.

This formula shows how the amount of money banks create depends on the reserve ratio. If the reserve ratio were only $1/20$ (5 percent), then the banking system would have 20 times as much in deposits as in reserves, implying a money multiplier of 20. Each dollar of reserves would generate $20 of money. Similarly, if the reserve ratio were $1/4$ (25 percent), deposits would be 4 times reserves, the money multiplier would be 4, and each dollar of reserves would generate $4 of money. Thus, *the higher the reserve ratio, the less of each deposit banks loan out, and the smaller the money multiplier.* In the special case of 100-percent-reserve banking, the reserve ratio is 1, the money multiplier is 1, and banks do not make loans or create money.

Bank Capital, Leverage, and the Financial Crisis of 2008–2009

In the previous sections, we have seen a very simplified explanation of how banks work. The reality of modern banking, however, is a bit more complicated, and this complex reality played a leading role in the financial crisis of 2008 and 2009. Before looking at that crisis, we need to learn a bit more about how banks actually function.

In the bank balance sheets you have seen so far, a bank accepts deposits and uses those deposits either to make loans or to hold reserves. More realistically, a bank gets financial resources not only from accepting deposits but also, like other companies, from issuing equity and debt. The resources that a bank obtains from issuing equity to its owners are called **bank capital**. A bank uses these financial resources in various ways to generate profit for its owners. It not only makes loans and holds reserves but also buys financial securities, such as stocks and bonds.

Here is a more realistic example of a bank's balance sheet:

bank capital
the resources a bank's owners have put into the institution

More Realistic National Bank

Assets		Liabilities and Owners' Equity	
Reserves	$200	Deposits	$800
Loans	700	Debt	150
Securities	100	Capital (owners' equity)	50

On the right side of this balance sheet are the bank's liabilities and capital (also known as *owners' equity*). This bank obtained $50 of resources from its owners. It also took in $800 of deposits and issued $150 of debt. The total of $1,000 was put to use in three ways; these are listed on the left side of the balance sheet, which shows the bank's assets. This bank held $200 in reserves, made $700 in bank loans, and used $100 to buy financial securities, such as government or corporate bonds. The bank decides how to allocate its resources among asset classes based on their risk and return, as well as on any regulations (such as reserve requirements) that restrict the bank's choices.

By the rules of accounting, the reserves, loans, and securities on the left side of the balance sheet must always equal, in total, the deposits, debt, and capital on the right side of the balance sheet. There is no magic in this equality. It occurs because the value of the owners' equity is, by definition, the value of the bank's assets (reserves, loans, and securities) minus the value of its liabilities (deposits and debt). Therefore, the left and right hand sides of the balance sheet always sum to the same total.

Many businesses in the economy rely on **leverage**, the use of borrowed money to supplement existing funds for investment purposes. Indeed, whenever anyone uses debt to finance an investment project, he is applying leverage. Leverage is particularly important for banks, however, because borrowing and lending are at the heart of what they do. To fully understand banking, therefore, it is crucial to understand how leverage works.

The **leverage ratio** is the ratio of the bank's total assets to bank capital. In this example, the leverage ratio is $1,000/$50, or 20. A leverage ratio of 20 means that

leverage
the use of borrowed money to supplement existing funds for purposes of investment

leverage ratio
the ratio of assets to bank capital

for every dollar of capital that the bank owners have contributed, the bank has $20 of assets. Of the $20 of assets, $19 are financed with borrowed money—either by taking in deposits or issuing debt.

You may have learned in a science class that a lever can amplify a force: A boulder that you cannot move with your arms alone will move more easily if you use a lever. A similar result occurs with bank leverage. To see how this works, let's continue with this numerical example. Suppose that the bank's assets were to rise in value by 5 percent because, say, some of the securities the bank was holding rose in price. Then the $1,000 of assets would now be worth $1,050. Because the depositors and debt holders are still owed $950, the bank capital rises from $50 to $100. Thus, when the leverage rate is 20, a 5-percent increase in the value of assets increases the owners' equity by 100 percent.

The same principle works on the downside, but with troubling consequences. Suppose that some people who borrowed from the bank default on their loans, reducing the value of the bank's assets by 5 percent, to $950. Because the depositors and debt holders have the legal right to be paid before the bank owners, the value of the owners' equity falls to zero. Thus, when the leverage ratio is 20, a 5-percent fall in the value of the bank assets leads to a 100-percent fall in bank capital. If the value of assets were to fall by more than 5 percent, the bank's assets would fall below its liabilities. In this case, the bank would be *insolvent*, and it would be unable to pay off its debt holders and depositors in full.

capital requirement
a government regulation specifying a minimum amount of bank capital

Bank regulators require banks to hold a certain amount of capital. The goal of such a **capital requirement** is to ensure that banks will be able to pay off their depositors (without having to resort to government-provided deposit insurance funds). The amount of capital required depends on the kind of assets a bank holds. If the bank holds safe assets such as government bonds, regulators require less capital than if the bank holds risky assets such as loans to borrowers whose credit is of dubious quality.

In 2008 and 2009, many banks found themselves with too little capital after they had incurred losses on some of their assets—specifically, mortgage loans and securities backed by mortgage loans. The shortage of capital induced the banks to reduce their lending, a phenomenon sometimes called a *credit crunch*, which in turn contributed to a severe downturn in economic activity. (This event is discussed more fully in Chapter 15.) To address this problem, the U.S. Treasury, working together with the Federal Reserve, put many billions of dollars of public funds into the banking system to increase the amount of bank capital. As a result, it temporarily made the U.S. taxpayer a part owner of many banks. The goal of this unusual policy was to recapitalize the banking system so that bank lending could return to a more normal level, which in fact occurred by late 2009.

The Fed's Tools of Monetary Control

As we have already discussed, the Federal Reserve is responsible for controlling the supply of money in the economy. Now that we understand how banking works, we are in a better position to understand how the Fed carries out this job. Because banks create money in a system of fractional-reserve banking, the Fed's control of the money supply is indirect. When the Fed decides to change the money supply, it must consider how its actions will work through the banking system.

The Fed has a variety of tools in its monetary toolbox. We can group those tools into two groups: those that influence the quantity of reserves and those that influence the reserve ratio and thereby the money multiplier.

How the Fed Influences the Quantity of Reserves

The first way the Fed can change the money supply is by changing the quantity of reserves. The Fed alters the quantity of reserves in the economy either by buying or selling bonds in open-market operations or by making loans to banks (or by some combination of the two). Let's consider each of these in turn.

Open-Market Operations   As we noted earlier, the Fed conducts **open-market operations** when it buys or sells government bonds. To increase the money supply, the Fed instructs its bond traders at the New York Fed to buy bonds from the public in the nation's bond markets. The dollars the Fed pays for the bonds increase the number of dollars in the economy. Some of these new dollars are held as currency, and some are deposited in banks. Each new dollar held as currency increases the money supply by exactly $1. Each new dollar deposited in a bank increases the money supply by more than a dollar because it increases reserves and, thereby, the amount of money that the banking system can create.

To reduce the money supply, the Fed does just the opposite: It sells government bonds to the public in the nation's bond markets. The public pays for these bonds with its holdings of currency and bank deposits, directly reducing the amount of money in circulation. In addition, as people make withdrawals from banks to buy these bonds from the Fed, banks find themselves with a smaller quantity of reserves. In response, banks reduce the amount of lending, and the process of money creation reverses itself.

Open-market operations are easy to conduct. In fact, the Fed's purchases and sales of government bonds in the nation's bond markets are similar to the transactions that any individual might undertake for his own portfolio. (Of course, when an individual buys or sells a bond, money changes hands, but the amount of money in circulation remains the same.) In addition, the Fed can use open-market operations to change the money supply by a small or large amount on any day without major changes in laws or bank regulations. Therefore, open-market operations are the tool of monetary policy that the Fed uses most often.

Fed Lending to Banks   The Fed can also increase the quantity of reserves in the economy by lending reserves to banks. Banks borrow from the Fed when they feel they do not have enough reserves on hand, either to satisfy bank regulators, meet depositor withdrawals, make new loans, or for some other business reason.

There are various ways banks can borrow from the Fed. Traditionally, banks borrow from the Fed's *discount window* and pay an interest rate on that loan called the **discount rate**. When the Fed makes such a loan to a bank, the banking system has more reserves than it otherwise would, and these additional reserves allow the banking system to create more money.

The Fed can alter the money supply by changing the discount rate. A higher discount rate discourages banks from borrowing reserves from the Fed. Thus, an increase in the discount rate reduces the quantity of reserves in the banking system, which in turn reduces the money supply. Conversely, a lower discount rate encourages banks to borrow from the Fed, increasing the quantity of reserves and the money supply.

open-market operations
the purchase and sale of U.S. government bonds by the Fed

discount rate
the interest rate on the loans that the Fed makes to banks

In recent years, the Federal Reserve has set up new mechanisms for banks to borrow from the Fed. For example, under the *Term Auction Facility*, the Fed sets a quantity of funds it wants to lend to banks, and eligible banks then bid to borrow those funds. The loans go to the highest eligible bidders—that is, to the banks that have acceptable collateral and are offering to pay the highest interest rate. Unlike at the discount window, where the Fed sets the price of a loan and the banks determine the quantity of borrowing, at the Term Auction Facility the Fed sets the quantity of borrowing and competitive bidding among banks determines the price. The more funds the Fed makes available through this and similar facilities, the greater the quantity of reserves and the larger the money supply.

The Fed uses such lending not only to control the money supply but also to help financial institutions when they are in trouble. For example, when the stock market crashed by 22 percent on October 19, 1987, many Wall Street brokerage firms found themselves temporarily in need of funds to finance the high volume of stock trading. The next morning, before the stock market opened, Fed Chairman Alan Greenspan announced the Fed's "readiness to serve as a source of liquidity to support the economic and financial system." Many economists believe that Greenspan's reaction to the stock crash was an important reason it had few repercussions.

Similarly, in 2008 and 2009, a fall in housing prices throughout the United States led to a sharp rise in the number of homeowners defaulting on their mortgage loans, and many financial institutions holding those mortgages ran into trouble. In an attempt to prevent these events from having broader economic ramifications, the Fed provided many billions of dollars of loans to financial institutions in distress.

How the Fed Influences the Reserve Ratio

In addition to influencing the quantity of reserves, the Fed changes the money supply by influencing the reserve ratio and thereby the money multiplier. The Fed can influence the reserve ratio either through regulating the quantity of reserves banks must hold or through the interest rate that the Fed pays banks on their reserves. Again, we consider each of these monetary policy tools in turn.

reserve requirements

regulations on the minimum amount of reserves that banks must hold against deposits

Reserve Requirements   One way the Fed can influence the reserve ratio is by altering **reserve requirements**, the regulations that set the minimum amount of reserves that banks must hold against their deposits. Reserve requirements influence how much money the banking system can create with each dollar of reserves. An increase in reserve requirements means that banks must hold more reserves and, therefore, can loan out less of each dollar that is deposited. As a result, an increase in reserve requirements raises the reserve ratio, lowers the money multiplier, and decreases the money supply. Conversely, a decrease in reserve requirements lowers the reserve ratio, raises the money multiplier, and increases the money supply.

The Fed uses changes in reserve requirements only rarely because these changes disrupt the business of banking. When the Fed increases reserve requirements, for instance, some banks find themselves short of reserves, even though they have seen no change in deposits. As a result, they have to curtail lending until they build their level of reserves to the new required level. Moreover, in recent years, this particular tool has become less effective because many banks hold excess reserves (that is, more reserves than are required).

Paying Interest on Reserves Traditionally, banks did not earn any interest on the reserves they held. In October 2008, however, the Fed began paying *interest on reserves*. That is, when a bank holds reserves on deposit at the Fed, the Fed now pays the bank interest on those deposits. This change gives the Fed another tool with which to influence the economy. The higher the interest rate on reserves, the more reserves banks will choose to hold. Thus, an increase in the interest rate on reserves will tend to increase the reserve ratio, lower the money multiplier, and lower the money supply. Because the Fed has paid interest on reserves for a relatively short time, it is not yet clear how important this new instrument will be in the conduct of monetary policy.

Problems in Controlling the Money Supply

The Fed's various tools—open-market operations, bank lending, reserve requirements, and interest on reserves—have powerful effects on the money supply. Yet the Fed's control of the money supply is not precise. The Fed must wrestle with two problems, each of which arises because much of the money supply is created by our system of fractional-reserve banking.

The first problem is that the Fed does not control the amount of money that households choose to hold as deposits in banks. The more money households deposit, the more reserves banks have, and the more money the banking system can create. The less money households deposit, the less reserves banks have, and the less money the banking system can create. To see why this is a problem, suppose that one day people begin to lose confidence in the banking system and, therefore, decide to withdraw deposits and hold more currency. When this happens, the banking system loses reserves and creates less money. The money supply falls, even without any Fed action.

The second problem of monetary control is that the Fed does not control the amount that bankers choose to lend. When money is deposited in a bank, it creates more money only when the bank loans it out. Because banks can choose to hold excess reserves instead, the Fed cannot be sure how much money the banking system will create. For instance, suppose that one day bankers become more cautious about economic conditions and decide to make fewer loans and hold greater reserves. In this case, the banking system creates less money than it otherwise would. Because of the bankers' decision, the money supply falls.

Hence, in a system of fractional-reserve banking, the amount of money in the economy depends in part on the behavior of depositors and bankers. Because the Fed cannot control or perfectly predict this behavior, it cannot perfectly control the money supply. Yet if the Fed is vigilant, these problems need not be large. The Fed collects data on deposits and reserves from banks every week, so it is quickly aware of any changes in depositor or banker behavior. It can, therefore, respond to these changes and keep the money supply close to whatever level it chooses.

Bank Runs and the Money Supply

Most likely you have never witnessed a bank run in real life, but you may have seen one depicted in movies such as *Mary Poppins* or *It's a Wonderful Life*. A bank run occurs when depositors suspect that a bank may go bankrupt and, therefore, "run" to the bank to withdraw their deposits. The United States has not seen a major bank run in recent history, but in the United Kingdom, a bank called Northern Rock experienced a run in 2007 and, as a result, was eventually taken over by the government.

Bank runs are a problem for banks under fractional-reserve banking. Because a bank holds only a fraction of its deposits in reserve, it cannot satisfy withdrawal requests from all depositors. Even if the bank is in fact *solvent* (meaning that its assets exceed its liabilities), it will not have enough cash on hand to allow all depositors immediate access to all of their money. When a run occurs, the bank is forced to close its doors until some bank loans are repaid or until some lender of last resort (such as the Fed) provides it with the currency it needs to satisfy depositors.

Bank runs complicate the control of the money supply. An important example of this problem occurred during the Great Depression in the early 1930s. After a wave of bank runs and bank closings, households and bankers became more cautious. Households withdrew their deposits from banks, preferring to hold their money in the form of currency. This decision reversed the process of money creation, as bankers responded to falling reserves by reducing bank loans. At the same time, bankers increased their reserve ratios so that they would have enough cash on hand to meet their depositors' demands in any future bank runs. The higher reserve ratio reduced the money multiplier, which further reduced the money supply. From 1929 to 1933, the money supply fell by 28 percent, without the Federal Reserve taking any deliberate contractionary action. Many economists point to this massive fall in the money supply to explain the high unemployment and falling prices that prevailed during this period. (In future chapters, we examine the mechanisms by which changes in the money supply affect unemployment and prices.)

Today, bank runs are not a major problem for the U.S. banking system or the Fed. The federal government now guarantees the safety of deposits at most banks, primarily through the Federal Deposit Insurance Corporation (FDIC). Depositors do not run on their banks because they are confident that, even if their bank goes bankrupt, the FDIC will make good on the deposits. The policy of government deposit insurance has costs: Bankers whose deposits are guaranteed may have too little incentive to avoid bad risks when making loans. But one benefit of deposit insurance is a more stable banking system. As a result, most people see bank runs only in the movies. ■

A not-so-wonderful bank run

© RKO/THE KOBAL COLLECTION/PICTURE DESK

The Federal Funds Rate

If you read about U.S. monetary policy in the newspaper, you will find much discussion of the federal funds rate. This raises several questions:

Q: What is the federal funds rate?

A: The **federal funds rate** is the short-term interest rate that banks charge one another for loans. If one bank finds itself short of reserves while another

federal funds rate

the interest rate at which banks make overnight loans to one another bank has excess reserves, the second bank can lend some reserves to the first. The loans are temporary—typically overnight. The price of the loan is the federal funds rate.

Q: How is the federal funds rate different from the discount rate?

A: The discount rate is the interest rate banks pay to borrow directly from the Federal Reserve through the discount window. Borrowing reserves from another bank in the federal funds market is an alternative to borrowing reserves from the Fed, and a bank short of reserves will typically do whichever is cheaper. In practice, the discount rate and the federal funds rate move closely together.

Q: Does the federal funds rate matter only for banks?

A: Not at all. While only banks borrow directly in the federal funds market, the economic impact of this market is much broader. Because different parts of the financial system are highly interconnected, interest rates on different kinds of loans are strongly correlated with one another. So when the federal funds rate rises or falls, other interest rates often move in the same direction.

Q: What does the Federal Reserve have to do with the federal funds rate?

A: In recent years, the Federal Reserve has set a target goal for the federal funds rate. When the Federal Open Market Committee meets approximately every six weeks, it decides whether to raise or lower that target.

Q: How can the Fed make the federal funds rate hit the target it sets?

A: Although the actual federal funds rate is set by supply and demand in the market for loans among banks, the Fed can use open-market operations to influence that market. For example, when the Fed buys bonds in open-market operations, it injects reserves into the banking system. With more reserves in the system, fewer banks find themselves in need of borrowing reserves to meet reserve requirements. The fall in demand for borrowing reserves decreases the price of such borrowing, which is the federal funds rate. Conversely, when the Fed sells bonds and withdraws reserves from the banking system, more banks find themselves short of reserves, and they bid up the price of borrowing reserves. Thus, open-market purchases lower the federal funds rate, and open-market sales raise the federal funds rate.

Q: But don't these open-market operations affect the money supply?

A: Yes, absolutely. When the Fed announces a change in the federal funds rate, it is committing itself to the open-market operations necessary to make that change happen, and these open-market operations will alter the supply of money. Decisions by the FOMC to change the target for the federal funds rate are also decisions to change the money supply. They are two sides of the same coin. Other things equal, a decrease in the target for the federal funds rate means an expansion in the money supply, and an increase in the target for the federal funds rate means a contraction in the money supply.

QUICK QUIZ   *Describe how banks create money. • If the Fed wanted to use all three of its policy tools to decrease the money supply, what would it do?*

in the news

> ## Bernanke on the Fed's Toolbox

During the financial crisis of 2008 and 2009, the Federal Reserve helped rescue a variety of banks and other financial institutions and, in the process, substantially expanded the quantity of bank reserves. Most of these newly created reserves were held as excess reserves by the banking system. In this article, the chairman of the Federal Reserve explains the Fed's plans to unwind the process in the aftermath of these events.

The Fed's Exit Strategy

By Ben Bernanke

Fed Chairman Ben Bernanke

The depth and breadth of the global recession has required a highly accommodative monetary policy. Since the onset of the financial crisis nearly two years ago, the Federal Reserve has reduced the interest-rate target for overnight lending between banks (the federal-funds rate) nearly to zero. We have also greatly expanded the size of the Fed's balance sheet through purchases of longer-term securities and through targeted lending programs aimed at restarting the flow of credit.

These actions have softened the economic impact of the financial crisis. They have also improved the functioning of key credit markets, including the markets for interbank lending, commercial paper, consumer and small-business credit, and residential mortgages.

My colleagues and I believe that accommodative policies will likely be warranted for an extended period. At some point, however, as economic recovery takes hold, we will need to tighten monetary policy to prevent the emergence of an inflation problem down the road. The Federal Open Market Committee, which is responsible for setting U.S. monetary policy, has devoted considerable time to issues relating to an exit strategy. We are confident we have the necessary tools to withdraw policy accommodation, when that becomes appropriate, in a smooth and timely manner.

The exit strategy is closely tied to the management of the Federal Reserve balance sheet. When the Fed makes loans or acquires securities, the funds enter the banking system and ultimately appear in the reserve accounts held at the Fed by banks and other depository institutions. These reserve balances now total about $800 billion, much more than normal. And given the current economic conditions, banks have generally held their reserves as balances at the Fed.

But as the economy recovers, banks should find more opportunities to lend out their reserves. That would produce faster growth in broad money (for example, M1 or M2) and easier credit conditions, which could ultimately result in inflationary pressures—unless we adopt countervailing policy measures. When the time comes to tighten monetary policy, we must either eliminate these large reserve balances or, if they remain, neutralize any potential undesired effects on the economy.

To some extent, reserves held by banks at the Fed will contract automatically, as improving financial conditions lead to reduced use of our short-term lending facilities, and ultimately to their wind down. Indeed, short-term credit extended by the Fed to financial institutions and other market participants has already fallen to less than $600 billion as of mid-July from about $1.5 trillion at the end of 2008. In addition, reserves could be reduced by about $100 billion to $200 billion each year over the next few years as securities held by the Fed mature or are prepaid. However, reserves likely would remain quite high for several years unless additional policies are undertaken.

Even if our balance sheet stays large for a while, we have two broad means of tightening monetary policy at the appropriate time: paying interest on reserve balances and taking various actions that reduce the stock of reserves. We could use either of these approaches alone; however, to ensure effectiveness, we likely would use both in combination.

Congress granted us authority last fall to pay interest on balances held by banks at the Fed. Currently, we pay banks an interest rate of 0.25%. When the time comes to tighten policy, we can raise the rate paid on reserve balances as we increase our target for the federal funds rate.

Banks generally will not lend funds in the money market at an interest rate lower than the rate they can earn risk-free at the Federal Reserve. Moreover, they should compete to borrow any funds that are offered in private markets at rates below the interest rate on reserve balances because, by so doing, they can earn a spread without risk.

Thus the interest rate that the Fed pays should tend to put a floor under short-term market rates, including our policy target, the federal-funds rate. Raising the rate paid on reserve balances also discourages excessive growth in money or credit, because banks will not want to lend out their reserves at rates below what they can earn at the Fed.

Considerable international experience suggests that paying interest on reserves effectively manages short-term market rates. For example, the European Central Bank allows banks to place excess reserves in an interest-paying deposit facility. Even as that central bank's liquidity-operations substantially increased its balance sheet, the overnight interbank rate remained at or above its deposit rate. In addition, the Bank of Japan and the Bank of Canada have also used their ability to pay interest on reserves to maintain a floor under short-term market rates.

Despite this logic and experience, the federal-funds rate has dipped somewhat below the rate paid by the Fed, especially in October and November 2008, when the Fed first began to pay interest on reserves. This pattern partly reflected temporary factors, such as banks' inexperience with the new system.

However, this pattern appears also to have resulted from the fact that some large lenders in the federal-funds market, notably government-sponsored enterprises such as Fannie Mae and Freddie Mac, are ineligible to receive interest on balances held at the Fed, and thus they have an incentive to lend in that market at rates below what the Fed pays banks.

Under more normal financial conditions, the willingness of banks to engage in the simple arbitrage noted above will tend to limit the gap between the federal-funds rate and the rate the Fed pays on reserves. If that gap persists, the problem can be addressed by supplementing payment of interest on reserves with steps to reduce reserves and drain excess liquidity from markets—the second means of tightening monetary policy. Here are four options for doing this.

First, the Federal Reserve could drain bank reserves and reduce the excess liquidity at other institutions by arranging large-scale reverse repurchase agreements with financial market participants, including banks, government-sponsored enterprises and other institutions. Reverse repurchase agreements involve the sale by the Fed of securities from its portfolio with an agreement to buy the securities back at a slightly higher price at a later date.

Second, the Treasury could sell bills and deposit the proceeds with the Federal Reserve. When purchasers pay for the securities, the Treasury's account at the Federal Reserve rises and reserve balances decline.

The Treasury has been conducting such operations since last fall under its Supplementary Financing Program. Although the Treasury's operations are helpful, to protect the independence of monetary policy, we must take care to ensure that we can achieve our policy objectives without reliance on the Treasury.

Third, using the authority Congress gave us to pay interest on banks' balances at the Fed, we can offer term deposits to banks—analogous to the certificates of deposit that banks offer their customers. Bank funds held in term deposits at the Fed would not be available for the federal funds market.

Fourth, if necessary, the Fed could reduce reserves by selling a portion of its holdings of long-term securities into the open market.

Each of these policies would help to raise short-term interest rates and limit the growth of broad measures of money and credit, thereby tightening monetary policy.

Overall, the Federal Reserve has many effective tools to tighten monetary policy when the economic outlook requires us to do so. As my colleagues and I have stated, however, economic conditions are not likely to warrant tighter monetary policy for an extended period. We will calibrate the timing and pace of any future tightening, together with the mix of tools to best foster our dual objectives of maximum employment and price stability.

Source: *The Wall Street Journal,* July 21, 2009.

Conclusion

Some years ago, a book made the best-seller list with the title *Secrets of the Temple: How the Federal Reserve Runs the Country*. Although no doubt an exaggeration, this title did highlight the important role of the monetary system in our daily lives. Whenever we buy or sell anything, we are relying on the extraordinarily useful social convention called "money." Now that we know what money is and what determines its supply, we can discuss how changes in the quantity of money affect the economy. We begin to address that topic in the next chapter.

SUMMARY

- The term *money* refers to assets that people regularly use to buy goods and services.

- Money serves three functions. As a medium of exchange, it provides the item used to make transactions. As a unit of account, it provides the way in which prices and other economic values are recorded. As a store of value, it provides a way of transferring purchasing power from the present to the future.

- Commodity money, such as gold, is money that has intrinsic value: It would be valued even if it were not used as money. Fiat money, such as paper dollars, is money without intrinsic value: It would be worthless if it were not used as money.

- In the U.S. economy, money takes the form of currency and various types of bank deposits, such as checking accounts.

- The Federal Reserve, the central bank of the United States, is responsible for regulating the U.S. monetary system. The Fed chairman is appointed by the president and confirmed by Congress every four years. The chairman is the lead member of the Federal Open Market Committee, which meets about every six weeks to consider changes in monetary policy.

- Bank depositors provide resources to banks by depositing their funds into bank accounts. These deposits are part of a bank's liabilities. Bank owners also provide resources (called bank capital) for the bank. Because of leverage (the use of borrowed funds for investment), a small change in the value of a bank's assets can lead to a large change in the value of the bank's capital. To protect depositors, bank regulators require banks to hold a certain minimum amount of capital.

- The Fed controls the money supply primarily through open-market operations: The purchase of government bonds increases the money supply, and the sale of government bonds decreases the money supply. The Fed also uses other tools to control the money supply. It can expand the money supply by decreasing the discount rate, increasing its lending to banks, lowering reserve requirements, or decreasing the interest rate on reserves. It can contract the money supply by increasing the discount rate, decreasing its lending to banks, raising reserve requirements, or increasing the interest rate on reserves.

- When individuals deposit money in banks and banks loan out some of these deposits, the quantity of money in the economy increases. Because the banking system influences the money supply in this way, the Fed's control of the money supply is imperfect.

- The Federal Reserve has in recent years set monetary policy by choosing a target for the federal funds rate, a short-term interest rate at which banks make loans to one another. As the Fed achieves its target, it adjusts the money supply.

KEY CONCEPTS

money, *p. 220*
medium of exchange, *p. 221*
unit of account, *p. 221*
store of value, *p. 221*
liquidity, *p. 221*
commodity money, *p. 221*
fiat money, *p. 222*
currency, *p. 223*
demand deposits, *p. 223*

Federal Reserve (Fed), *p. 225*
central bank, *p. 225*
money supply, *p. 226*
monetary policy, *p. 226*
reserves, *p. 228*
fractional-reserve banking, *p. 228*
reserve ratio, *p. 228*
money multiplier, *p. 230*
bank capital, *p. 231*

leverage, *p. 231*
leverage ratio, *p. 231*
capital requirement, *p. 232*
open-market operations, *p. 233*
discount rate, *p. 233*
reserve requirements, *p. 234*
federal funds rate, *p. 236*

QUESTIONS FOR REVIEW

1. What distinguishes money from other assets in the economy?
2. What is commodity money? What is fiat money? Which kind do we use?
3. What are demand deposits and why should they be included in the stock of money?
4. Who is responsible for setting monetary policy in the United States? How is this group chosen?
5. If the Fed wants to increase the money supply with open-market operations, what does it do?
6. Why don't banks hold 100 percent reserves? How is the amount of reserves banks hold related to the amount of money the banking system creates?

7. Bank A has a leverage ratio of 10, while Bank B has a leverage ratio of 20. Similar losses on bank loans at the two banks cause the value of their assets to fall by 7 percent. Which bank shows a larger change in bank capital? Does either bank remain solvent? Explain.
8. What is the discount rate? What happens to the money supply when the Fed raises the discount rate?
9. What are reserve requirements? What happens to the money supply when the Fed raises reserve requirements?
10. Why can't the Fed control the money supply perfectly?

PROBLEMS AND APPLICATIONS

1. Which of the following are money in the U.S. economy? Which are not? Explain your answers by discussing each of the three functions of money.
   a. a U.S. penny
   b. a Mexican peso
   c. a Picasso painting
   d. a plastic credit card
2. Your uncle repays a $100 loan from Tenth National Bank (TNB) by writing a $100 check from his TNB checking account. Use T-accounts to show the effect of this transaction on your uncle and on TNB. Has your uncle's wealth changed? Explain.
3. Beleaguered State Bank (BSB) holds $250 million in deposits and maintains a reserve ratio of 10 percent.

a. Show a T-account for BSB.
b. Now suppose that BSB's largest depositor withdraws $10 million in cash from her account. If BSB decides to restore its reserve ratio by reducing the amount of loans outstanding, show its new T-account.
c. Explain what effect BSB's action will have on other banks.
d. Why might it be difficult for BSB to take the action described in part (b)? Discuss another way for BSB to return to its original reserve ratio.
4. You take $100 you had kept under your mattress and deposit it in your bank account. If this $100 stays in the banking system as reserves and if banks hold reserves equal to 10 percent

of deposits, by how much does the total amount of deposits in the banking system increase? By how much does the money supply increase?

5. Happy Bank starts with $200 in bank capital. It then takes in $800 in deposits. It keeps 12.5 percent (1/8th) of deposits in reserve. It uses the rest of its assets to make bank loans.
   a. Show the balance sheet of Happy Bank.
   b. What is Happy Bank's leverage ratio?
   c. Suppose that 10 percent of the borrowers from Happy Bank default and these bank loans become worthless. Show the bank's new balance sheet.
   d. By what percentage do the bank's total assets decline? By what percentage does the bank's capital decline? Which change is larger? Why?

6. The Federal Reserve conducts a $10 million open-market purchase of government bonds. If the required reserve ratio is 10 percent, what is the largest possible increase in the money supply that could result? Explain. What is the smallest possible increase? Explain.

7. Assume that the reserve requirement is 5 percent. All other things equal, will the money supply expand more if the Federal Reserve buys $2,000 worth of bonds or if someone deposits in a bank $2,000 that he had been hiding in his cookie jar? If one creates more, how much more does it create? Support your thinking.

8. Suppose that the T-account for First National Bank is as follows:

Assets		Liabilities	
Reserves	$100,000	Deposits	$500,000
Loans	400,000		

   a. If the Fed requires banks to hold 5 percent of deposits as reserves, how much in excess reserves does First National now hold?
   b. Assume that all other banks hold only the required amount of reserves. If First National decides to reduce its reserves to only the required amount, by how much would the economy's money supply increase?

9. Suppose that the reserve requirement for checking deposits is 10 percent and that banks do not hold any excess reserves.
   a. If the Fed sells $1 million of government bonds, what is the effect on the economy's reserves and money supply?

b. Now suppose the Fed lowers the reserve requirement to 5 percent, but banks choose to hold another 5 percent of deposits as excess reserves. Why might banks do so? What is the overall change in the money multiplier and the money supply as a result of these actions?

10. Assume that the banking system has total reserves of $100 billion. Assume also that required reserves are 10 percent of checking deposits and that banks hold no excess reserves and households hold no currency.
   a. What is the money multiplier? What is the money supply?
   b. If the Fed now raises required reserves to 20 percent of deposits, what are the changes in reserves and in the money supply?

11. Assume that the reserve requirement is 20 percent. Also assume that banks do not hold excess reserves and there is no cash held by the public. The Federal Reserve decides that it wants to expand the money supply by $40 million dollars.
   a. If the Fed is using open-market operations, will it buy or sell bonds?
   b. What quantity of bonds does the Fed need to buy or sell to accomplish the goal? Explain your reasoning.

12. The economy of Elmendyn contains 2,000 $1 bills.
   a. If people hold all money as currency, what is the quantity of money?
   b. If people hold all money as demand deposits and banks maintain 100 percent reserves, what is the quantity of money?
   c. If people hold equal amounts of currency and demand deposits and banks maintain 100 percent reserves, what is the quantity of money?
   d. If people hold all money as demand deposits and banks maintain a reserve ratio of 10 percent, what is the quantity of money?
   e. If people hold equal amounts of currency and demand deposits and banks maintain a reserve ratio of 10 percent, what is the quantity of money?

For further information on topics in this chapter, additional problems, applications, examples, online quizzes, and more, please visit our website at www .cengage.com/economics/mankiw.

Money Growth
and Inflation

12

Today, if you want to buy an ice-cream cone, you need at least a couple of dollars, but that has not always been the case. In the 1930s, my grandmother ran a sweet shop in Trenton, New Jersey, where she sold ice-cream cones in two sizes. A cone with a small scoop of ice cream cost three cents. Hungry customers could buy a large scoop for a nickel.

You may not be surprised at the increase in the price of ice cream. In our economy, most prices tend to rise over time. This increase in the overall level of prices is called *inflation*. Earlier in the book, we examined how economists measure the inflation rate as the percentage change in the consumer price index (CPI), the GDP deflator, or some other index of the overall price level. These price indexes show that, over the past 70 years, prices have risen on average about 4 percent per year. Accumulated over so many years, a 4 percent annual inflation rate leads to a sixteenfold increase in the price level.

Inflation may seem natural and inevitable to a person who grew up in the United States during recent decades, but in fact, it is not inevitable at all. There were long periods in the 19th century during which most prices fell—a phenomenon called *deflation*. The average level of prices in the U.S. economy was 23 percent lower in 1896 than in 1880, and this deflation was a major issue in the presidential election of 1896. Farmers, who had accumulated large debts, suffered when the fall in crop prices reduced their incomes and thus their ability to pay off their debts. They advocated government policies to reverse the deflation.

Although inflation has been the norm in more recent history, there has been substantial variation in the rate at which prices rise. During the 1990s, prices rose at an average rate of about 2 percent per year. By contrast, in the 1970s, prices rose by 7 percent per year, which meant a doubling of the price level over the decade. The public often views such high rates of inflation as a major economic problem. In fact, when President Jimmy Carter ran for reelection in 1980, challenger Ronald Reagan pointed to high inflation as one of the failures of Carter's economic policy.

International data show an even broader range of inflation experiences. In 2009, while the U.S. inflation rate was about 2 percent, inflation was –1.7 percent in Japan, 9 percent in Russia, and 25 percent in Venezuela. And even the high inflation rates in Russia and Venezuela are moderate by some standards. In February 2008, the central bank of Zimbabwe announced the inflation rate in its economy had reached 24,000 percent; some independent estimates put the figure even higher. An extraordinarily high rate of inflation such as this is called *hyperinflation*.

What determines whether an economy experiences inflation and, if so, how much? This chapter answers this question by developing the *quantity theory of money*. Chapter 1 summarized this theory as one of the *Ten Principles of Economics*: Prices rise when the government prints too much money. This insight has a long and venerable tradition among economists. The quantity theory was discussed by the famous 18th-century philosopher and economist David Hume and was advocated more recently by the prominent economist Milton Friedman. This theory can explain moderate inflations, such as those we have experienced in the United States, as well as hyperinflations.

After developing a theory of inflation, we turn to a related question: Why is inflation a problem? At first glance, the answer to this question may seem obvious: Inflation is a problem because people don't like it. In the 1970s, when the United States experienced a relatively high rate of inflation, opinion polls placed inflation as the most important issue facing the nation. President Ford echoed this sentiment in 1974 when he called inflation "public enemy number one." Ford wore a "WIN" button on his lapel—for Whip Inflation Now.

But what, exactly, are the costs that inflation imposes on a society? The answer may surprise you. Identifying the various costs of inflation is not as straightforward as it first appears. As a result, although all economists decry hyperinflation, some economists argue that the costs of moderate inflation are not nearly as large as the public believes.

The Classical Theory of Inflation

We begin our study of inflation by developing the quantity theory of money. This theory is often called "classical" because it was developed by some of the earliest economic thinkers. Most economists today rely on this theory to explain the long-run determinants of the price level and the inflation rate.

The Level of Prices and the Value of Money

Suppose we observe over some period of time the price of an ice-cream cone rising from a nickel to a dollar. What conclusion should we draw from the fact that people are willing to give up so much more money in exchange for a cone? It is possible that people have come to enjoy ice cream more (perhaps because some chemist has developed a miraculous new flavor). Yet that is probably not the case. It is more likely that people's enjoyment of ice cream has stayed roughly the same and that, over time, the money used to buy ice cream has become less valuable. Indeed, the first insight about inflation is that it is more about the value of money than about the value of goods.

This insight helps point the way toward a theory of inflation. When the consumer price index and other measures of the price level rise, commentators are often tempted to look at the many individual prices that make up these price indexes: "The CPI rose by 3 percent last month, led by a 20 percent rise in the price of coffee and a 30 percent rise in the price of heating oil." Although this approach does contain some interesting information about what's happening in the economy, it also misses a key point: Inflation is an economy-wide phenomenon that concerns, first and foremost, the value of the economy's medium of exchange.

The economy's overall price level can be viewed in two ways. So far, we have viewed the price level as the price of a basket of goods and services. When the price level rises, people have to pay more for the goods and services they buy. Alternatively, we can view the price level as a measure of the value of money. A rise in the price level means a lower value of money because each dollar in your wallet now buys a smaller quantity of goods and services.

It may help to express these ideas mathematically. Suppose P is the price level as measured, for instance, by the consumer price index or the GDP deflator. Then P measures the number of dollars needed to buy a basket of goods and services. Now turn this idea around: The quantity of goods and services that can be bought with \$1 equals $1/P$. In other words, if P is the price of goods and services measured in terms of money, $1/P$ is the value of money measured in terms of goods and services.

This mathematics is simplest to understand in an economy that produces only a single good, say, ice-cream cones. In that case, P would be the price of a cone. When the price of a cone (P) is \$2, then the value of a dollar ($1/P$) is half a cone. When the price (P) rises to \$3, the value of a dollar ($1/P$) falls to a third of a cone. The actual economy produces thousands of goods and services, so we use a price index rather than the price of a single good. But the logic remains the same: When the overall price level rises, the value of money falls.

Money Supply, Money Demand, and Monetary Equilibrium

What determines the value of money? The answer to this question, like many in economics, is supply and demand. Just as the supply and demand for bananas determines the price of bananas, the supply and demand for money determines the value of money. Thus, our next step in developing the quantity theory of money is to consider the determinants of money supply and money demand.

First consider money supply. In the preceding chapter, we discussed how the Federal Reserve, together with the banking system, determines the supply of money. When the Fed sells bonds in open-market operations, it receives dollars

"So what's it going to be? The same size as last year or the same price as last year?"

in exchange and contracts the money supply. When the Fed buys government bonds, it pays out dollars and expands the money supply. In addition, if any of these dollars are deposited in banks which hold some as reserves and loan out the rest, the money multiplier swings into action, and these open-market operations can have an even greater effect on the money supply. For our purposes in this chapter, we ignore the complications introduced by the banking system and simply take the quantity of money supplied as a policy variable that the Fed controls.

Now consider money demand. Most fundamentally, the demand for money reflects how much wealth people want to hold in liquid form. Many factors influence the quantity of money demanded. The amount of currency that people hold in their wallets, for instance, depends on how much they rely on credit cards and on whether an automatic teller machine is easy to find. And as we will emphasize in Chapter 16, the quantity of money demanded depends on the interest rate that a person could earn by using the money to buy an interest-bearing bond rather than leaving it in a wallet or low-interest checking account.

Although many variables affect the demand for money, one variable stands out in importance: the average level of prices in the economy. People hold money because it is the medium of exchange. Unlike other assets, such as bonds or stocks, people can use money to buy the goods and services on their shopping lists. How much money they choose to hold for this purpose depends on the prices of those goods and services. The higher prices are, the more money the typical transaction requires, and the more money people will choose to hold in their wallets and checking accounts. That is, a higher price level (a lower value of money) increases the quantity of money demanded.

What ensures that the quantity of money the Fed supplies balances the quantity of money people demand? The answer, it turns out, depends on the time horizon being considered. Later in this book, we examine the short-run answer and learn that interest rates play a key role. In the long run, however, the answer is different and much simpler. *In the long run, the overall level of prices adjusts to the level at which the demand for money equals the supply.* If the price level is above the equilibrium level, people will want to hold more money than the Fed has created, so the price level must fall to balance supply and demand. If the price level is below the equilibrium level, people will want to hold less money than the Fed has created, and the price level must rise to balance supply and demand. At the equilibrium price level, the quantity of money that people want to hold exactly balances the quantity of money supplied by the Fed.

Figure 1 illustrates these ideas. The horizontal axis of this graph shows the quantity of money. The left vertical axis shows the value of money $1/P$, and the right vertical axis shows the price level P. Notice that the price-level axis on the right is inverted: A low price level is shown near the top of this axis, and a high price level is shown near the bottom. This inverted axis illustrates that when the value of money is high (as shown near the top of the left axis), the price level is low (as shown near the top of the right axis).

The two curves in this figure are the supply and demand curves for money. The supply curve is vertical because the Fed has fixed the quantity of money available. The demand curve for money is downward sloping, indicating that when the value of money is low (and the price level is high), people demand a larger quantity of it to buy goods and services. At the equilibrium, shown in the figure as point A, the quantity of money demanded balances the quantity of money supplied. This equilibrium of money supply and money demand determines the value of money and the price level.

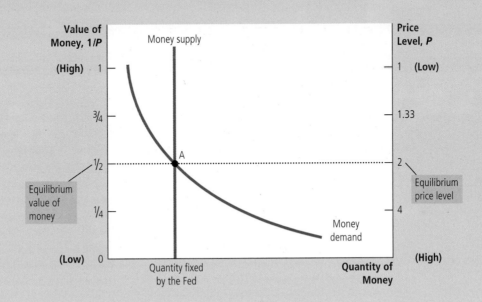

The horizontal axis shows the quantity of money. The left vertical axis shows the value of money, and the right vertical axis shows the price level. The supply curve for money is vertical because the quantity of money supplied is fixed by the Fed. The demand curve for money is downward sloping because people want to hold a larger quantity of money when each dollar buys less. At the equilibrium, point A, the value of money (on the left axis) and the price level (on the right axis) have adjusted to bring the quantity of money supplied and the quantity of money demanded into balance.

Figure 1

How the Supply and Demand for Money Determine the Equilibrium Price Level

The Effects of a Monetary Injection

Let's now consider the effects of a change in monetary policy. To do so, imagine that the economy is in equilibrium and then, suddenly, the Fed doubles the supply of money by printing some dollar bills and dropping them around the country from helicopters. (Or less dramatically and more realistically, the Fed could inject money into the economy by buying some government bonds from the public in open-market operations.) What happens after such a monetary injection? How does the new equilibrium compare to the old one?

Figure 2 shows what happens. The monetary injection shifts the supply curve to the right from MS_1 to MS_2, and the equilibrium moves from point A to point B. As a result, the value of money (shown on the left axis) decreases from ½ to ¼, and the equilibrium price level (shown on the right axis) increases from 2 to 4. In other words, when an increase in the money supply makes dollars more plentiful, the result is an increase in the price level that makes each dollar less valuable.

This explanation of how the price level is determined and why it might change over time is called the **quantity theory of money.** According to the quantity theory, the quantity of money available in an economy determines the value of money, and growth in the quantity of money is the primary cause of inflation. As

quantity theory of money

a theory asserting that the quantity of money available determines the price level and that the growth rate in the quantity of money available determines the inflation rate

Figure 2

An Increase in the Money Supply

When the Fed increases the supply of money, the money supply curve shifts from MS_1 to MS_2. The value of money (on the left axis) and the price level (on the right axis) adjust to bring supply and demand back into balance. The equilibrium moves from point A to point B. Thus, when an increase in the money supply makes dollars more plentiful, the price level increases, making each dollar less valuable.

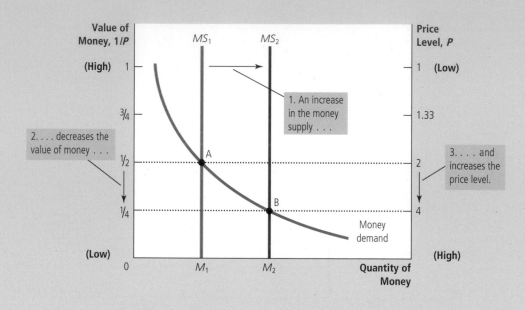

economist Milton Friedman once put it, "Inflation is always and everywhere a monetary phenomenon."

A Brief Look at the Adjustment Process

So far, we have compared the old equilibrium and the new equilibrium after an injection of money. How does the economy move from the old to the new equilibrium? A complete answer to this question requires an understanding of short-run fluctuations in the economy, which we examine later in this book. Here, we briefly consider the adjustment process that occurs after a change in the money supply.

The immediate effect of a monetary injection is to create an excess supply of money. Before the injection, the economy was in equilibrium (point A in Figure 2). At the prevailing price level, people had exactly as much money as they wanted. But after the helicopters drop the new money and people pick it up off the streets, people have more dollars in their wallets than they want. At the prevailing price level, the quantity of money supplied now exceeds the quantity demanded.

People try to get rid of this excess supply of money in various ways. They might use it to buy goods and services. Or they might use this excess money to make loans to others by buying bonds or by depositing the money in a bank savings account. These loans allow other people to buy goods and services. In either case, the injection of money increases the demand for goods and services.

The economy's ability to supply goods and services, however, has not changed. As we saw in the chapter on production and growth, the economy's output of goods and services is determined by the available labor, physical capital, human capital, natural resources, and technological knowledge. None of these is altered by the injection of money.

Thus, the greater demand for goods and services causes the prices of goods and services to increase. The increase in the price level, in turn, increases the quantity of money demanded because people are using more dollars for every transaction. Eventually, the economy reaches a new equilibrium (point B in Figure 2) at which the quantity of money demanded again equals the quantity of money supplied. In this way, the overall price level for goods and services adjusts to bring money supply and money demand into balance.

The Classical Dichotomy and Monetary Neutrality

We have seen how changes in the money supply lead to changes in the average level of prices of goods and services. How do monetary changes affect other economic variables, such as production, employment, real wages, and real interest rates? This question has long intrigued economists, including David Hume in the 18th century.

Hume and his contemporaries suggested that economic variables should be divided into two groups. The first group consists of **nominal variables**—variables measured in monetary units. The second group consists of **real variables**—variables measured in physical units. For example, the income of corn farmers is a nominal variable because it is measured in dollars, whereas the quantity of corn they produce is a real variable because it is measured in bushels. Nominal GDP is a nominal variable because it measures the dollar value of the economy's output of goods and services; real GDP is a real variable because it measures the total quantity of goods and services produced and is not influenced by the current prices of those goods and services. The separation of real and nominal variables is now called the **classical dichotomy.** (A *dichotomy* is a division into two groups, and *classical* refers to the earlier economic thinkers.)

Applying the classical dichotomy is tricky when we turn to prices. Most prices are quoted in units of money and, therefore, are nominal variables. When we say that the price of corn is $2 a bushel or that the price of wheat is $1 a bushel, both prices are nominal variables. But what about a *relative* price—the price of one thing compared to another? In our example, we could say that the price of a bushel of corn is 2 bushels of wheat. This relative price is not measured in terms of money. When comparing the prices of any two goods, the dollar signs cancel, and the resulting number is measured in physical units. Thus, while dollar prices are nominal variables, relative prices are real variables.

This lesson has many applications. For instance, the real wage (the dollar wage adjusted for inflation) is a real variable because it measures the rate at which people exchange goods and services for a unit of labor. Similarly, the real interest rate (the nominal interest rate adjusted for inflation) is a real variable because it measures the rate at which people exchange goods and services today for goods and services in the future.

Why separate variables into these groups? The classical dichotomy is useful because different forces influence real and nominal variables. According to classical analysis, nominal variables are influenced by developments in the economy's monetary system, whereas money is largely irrelevant for explaining real variables.

This idea was implicit in our discussion of the real economy in the long run. In previous chapters, we examined how real GDP, saving, investment, real interest rates, and unemployment are determined without mentioning the existence of money. In that analysis, the economy's production of goods and services depends

nominal variables
variables measured in monetary units

real variables
variables measured in physical units

classical dichotomy
the theoretical separation of nominal and real variables

on productivity and factor supplies, the real interest rate balances the supply and demand for loanable funds, the real wage balances the supply and demand for labor, and unemployment results when the real wage is for some reason kept above its equilibrium level. These conclusions have nothing to do with the quantity of money supplied.

Changes in the supply of money, according to classical analysis, affect nominal variables but not real ones. When the central bank doubles the money supply, the price level doubles, the dollar wage doubles, and all other dollar values double. Real variables, such as production, employment, real wages, and real interest rates, are unchanged. The irrelevance of monetary changes for real variables is called **monetary neutrality.**

An analogy helps explain monetary neutrality. As the unit of account, money is the yardstick we use to measure economic transactions. When a central bank doubles the money supply, all prices double, and the value of the unit of account falls by half. A similar change would occur if the government were to reduce the length of the yard from 36 to 18 inches: With the new unit of measurement, all *measured* distances (nominal variables) would double, but the *actual* distances (real variables) would remain the same. The dollar, like the yard, is merely a unit of measurement, so a change in its value should not have real effects.

Is monetary neutrality realistic? Not completely. A change in the length of the yard from 36 to 18 inches would not matter in the long run, but in the short run, it would lead to confusion and mistakes. Similarly, most economists today believe that over short periods of time—within the span of a year or two—monetary changes affect real variables. Hume himself also doubted that monetary neutrality would apply in the short run. (We will study short-run nonneutrality later in the book, and this topic will help explain why the Fed changes the money supply over time.)

Yet classical analysis is right about the economy in the long run. Over the course of a decade, monetary changes have significant effects on nominal variables (such as the price level) but only negligible effects on real variables (such as real GDP). When studying long-run changes in the economy, the neutrality of money offers a good description of how the world works.

monetary neutrality

the proposition that changes in the money supply do not affect real variables

Velocity and the Quantity Equation

We can obtain another perspective on the quantity theory of money by considering the following question: How many times per year is the typical dollar bill used to pay for a newly produced good or service? The answer to this question is given by a variable called the **velocity of money.** In physics, the term *velocity* refers to the speed at which an object travels. In economics, the velocity of money refers to the speed at which the typical dollar bill travels around the economy from wallet to wallet.

To calculate the velocity of money, we divide the nominal value of output (nominal GDP) by the quantity of money. If P is the price level (the GDP deflator), Y the quantity of output (real GDP), and M the quantity of money, then velocity is

$$V = (P \times Y) / M.$$

To see why this makes sense, imagine a simple economy that produces only pizza. Suppose that the economy produces 100 pizzas in a year, that a pizza sells for $10, and that the quantity of money in the economy is $50. Then the velocity of money is

$$V = (\$10 \times 100) / \$50$$

$$= 20.$$

velocity of money

the rate at which money changes hands

In this economy, people spend a total of $1,000 per year on pizza. For this $1,000 of spending to take place with only $50 of money, each dollar bill must change hands on average 20 times per year.

With slight algebraic rearrangement, this equation can be rewritten as

$$M \times V = P \times Y.$$

This equation states that the quantity of money (M) times the velocity of money (V) equals the price of output (P) times the amount of output (Y). It is called the **quantity equation** because it relates the quantity of money (M) to the nominal value of output ($P \times Y$). The quantity equation shows that an increase in the quantity of money in an economy must be reflected in one of the other three variables: The price level must rise, the quantity of output must rise, or the velocity of money must fall.

In many cases, it turns out that the velocity of money is relatively stable. For example, Figure 3 shows nominal GDP, the quantity of money (as measured by M2), and the velocity of money for the U.S. economy since 1960. During the period, the money supply and nominal GDP both increased more than twentyfold. By contrast, the velocity of money, although not exactly constant, has not changed dramatically. Thus, for some purposes, the assumption of constant velocity may be a good approximation.

quantity equation
the equation $M \times V = P \times Y$, which relates the quantity of money, the velocity of money, and the dollar value of the economy's output of goods and services

---

This figure shows the nominal value of output as measured by nominal GDP, the quantity of money as measured by M2, and the velocity of money as measured by their ratio. For comparability, all three series have been scaled to equal 100 in 1960. Notice that nominal GDP and the quantity of money have grown dramatically over this period, while velocity has been relatively stable.

Figure **3**

Nominal GDP, the Quantity of Money, and the Velocity of Money

Source: U.S. Department of Commerce; Federal Reserve Board.

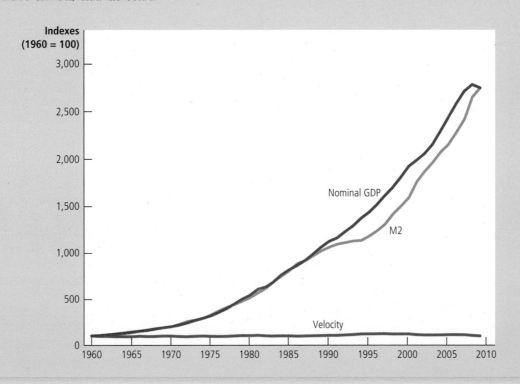

We now have all the elements necessary to explain the equilibrium price level and inflation rate. Here they are:

1. The velocity of money is relatively stable over time.
2. Because velocity is stable, when the central bank changes the quantity of money (M), it causes proportionate changes in the nominal value of output ($P \times Y$).
3. The economy's output of goods and services (Y) is primarily determined by factor supplies (labor, physical capital, human capital, and natural resources) and the available production technology. In particular, because money is neutral, money does not affect output.
4. With output (Y) determined by factor supplies and technology, when the central bank alters the money supply (M) and induces proportional changes in the nominal value of output ($P \times Y$), these changes are reflected in changes in the price level (P).
5. Therefore, when the central bank increases the money supply rapidly, the result is a high rate of inflation.

These five steps are the essence of the quantity theory of money.

Money and Prices during Four Hyperinflations

Although earthquakes can wreak havoc on a society, they have the beneficial by-product of providing much useful data for seismologists. These data can shed light on alternative theories and, thereby, help society predict and deal with future threats. Similarly, hyperinflations offer monetary economists a natural experiment they can use to study the effects of money on the economy.

Hyperinflations are interesting in part because the changes in the money supply and price level are so large. Indeed, hyperinflation is generally defined as inflation that exceeds 50 percent *per month*. This means that the price level increases more than a hundredfold over the course of a year.

The data on hyperinflation show a clear link between the quantity of money and the price level. Figure 4 graphs data from four classic hyperinflations that occurred during the 1920s in Austria, Hungary, Germany, and Poland. Each graph shows the quantity of money in the economy and an index of the price level. The slope of the money line represents the rate at which the quantity of money was growing, and the slope of the price line represents the inflation rate. The steeper the lines, the higher the rates of money growth or inflation.

Notice that in each graph the quantity of money and the price level are almost parallel. In each instance, growth in the quantity of money is moderate at first and so is inflation. But over time, the quantity of money in the economy starts growing faster and faster. At about the same time, inflation also takes off. Then when the quantity of money stabilizes, the price level stabilizes as well. These episodes illustrate well one of the *Ten Principles of Economics*: Prices rise when the government prints too much money. ■

The Inflation Tax

If inflation is so easy to explain, why do countries experience hyperinflation? That is, why do the central banks of these countries choose to print so much money that its value is certain to fall rapidly over time?

This figure shows the quantity of money and the price level during four hyperinflations. (Note that these variables are graphed on *logarithmic* scales. This means that equal vertical distances on the graph represent equal *percentage* changes in the variable.) In each case, the quantity of money and the price level move closely together. The strong association between these two variables is consistent with the quantity theory of money, which states that growth in the money supply is the primary cause of inflation.

Source: Adapted from Thomas J. Sargent, "The End of Four Big Inflations," in Robert Hall, ed., *Inflation* (Chicago: University of Chicago Press, 1983), pp. 41–93.

Figure 4

Money and Prices during Four Hyperinflations

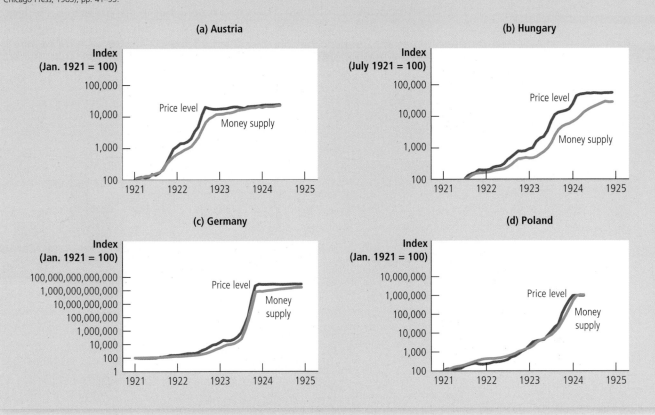

The answer is that the governments of these countries are using money creation as a way to pay for their spending. When the government wants to build roads, pay salaries to its soldiers, or give transfer payments to the poor or elderly, it first has to raise the necessary funds. Normally, the government does this by levying taxes, such as income and sales taxes, and by borrowing from the public by selling government bonds. Yet the government can also pay for spending simply by printing the money it needs.

When the government raises revenue by printing money, it is said to levy an **inflation tax.** The inflation tax is not exactly like other taxes, however, because no one receives a bill from the government for this tax. Instead, the inflation tax is subtler. When the government prints money, the price level rises, and the dollars in your wallet are less valuable. Thus, *the inflation tax is like a tax on everyone who holds money*.

The importance of the inflation tax varies from country to country and over time. In the United States in recent years, the inflation tax has been a trivial

inflation tax
the revenue the government raises by creating money

source of revenue: It has accounted for less than 3 percent of government revenue. During the 1770s, however, the Continental Congress of the fledgling United States relied heavily on the inflation tax to pay for military spending. Because the new government had a limited ability to raise funds through regular taxes or borrowing, printing dollars was the easiest way to pay the American soldiers. As the quantity theory predicts, the result was a high rate of inflation: Prices measured in terms of the continental dollar rose more than a hundredfold over a few years.

Almost all hyperinflations follow the same pattern as the hyperinflation during the American Revolution. The government has high spending, inadequate tax revenue, and limited ability to borrow. As a result, it turns to the printing press to pay for its spending. The massive increases in the quantity of money lead to massive inflation. The inflation ends when the government institutes fiscal reforms—such as cuts in government spending—that eliminate the need for the inflation tax.

FYI

❯ Hyperinflation in Zimbabwe

During the decade of the 2000s, the nation of Zimbabwe experienced one of history's most extreme examples of hyperinflation. In many ways, the story is common: Large government budget deficits led to the creation of large quantities of money and high rates of inflation. The hyperinflation ended in April 2009 when the Zimbabwe central bank stopped printing the Zimbabwe dollar, and the nation started using foreign currencies such as the U.S. dollar and the South African rand as the medium of exchange.

Estimates vary about how high inflation in Zimbabwe got, but the magnitude of the problem is well documented by the denomination of the notes being issued by the central bank. Before the hyperinflation started, the Zimbabwe dollar was worth a bit more than one U.S. dollar, so the denominations of the paper currency were similar to those one would find in the United States. A person might carry, for example, a ten-dollar note in his or her wallet. In January 2008, however, after years of high inflation, the Reserve Bank of Zimbabwe issued a note worth 10 million Zimbabwe dollars, which was then equivalent to about four U.S. dollars. But even that did not prove to be large enough. A year later, the central bank announced it would issue notes worth 10 trillion Zimbabwe dollars, then worth about three U.S. dollars.

As prices rose and the central bank printed ever larger denominations of money, the older, smaller denomination currency lost value and became almost worthless. One indication of this phenomenon can be found on this sign from a public restroom in Zimbabwe:

> **TOILET PAPER O N L Y**
> **TO BE USED IN THIS TOILET**
> **NO CARDBOARD**
> **NO CLOTH**
> **NO ZIM DOLLARS**
> **NO NEWSPAPER**

The Fisher Effect

According to the principle of monetary neutrality, an increase in the rate of money growth raises the rate of inflation but does not affect any real variable. An important application of this principle concerns the effect of money on interest rates. Interest rates are important variables for macroeconomists to understand because they link the economy of the present and the economy of the future through their effects on saving and investment.

To understand the relationship between money, inflation, and interest rates, recall the distinction between the nominal interest rate and the real interest rate. The *nominal interest rate* is the interest rate you hear about at your bank. If you have a savings account, for instance, the nominal interest rate tells you how fast the number of dollars in your account will rise over time. The *real interest rate* corrects the nominal interest rate for the effect of inflation to tell you how fast the purchasing power of your savings account will rise over time. The real interest rate is the nominal interest rate minus the inflation rate:

Real interest rate = Nominal interest rate − Inflation rate.

For example, if the bank posts a nominal interest rate of 7 percent per year and the inflation rate is 3 percent per year, then the real value of the deposits grows by 4 percent per year.

We can rewrite this equation to show that the nominal interest rate is the sum of the real interest rate and the inflation rate:

Nominal interest rate = Real interest rate + Inflation rate.

This way of looking at the nominal interest rate is useful because different economic forces determine each of the two terms on the right side of this equation. As we discussed earlier in the book, the supply and demand for loanable funds determine the real interest rate. And according to the quantity theory of money, growth in the money supply determines the inflation rate.

Let's now consider how the growth in the money supply affects interest rates. In the long run over which money is neutral, a change in money growth should not affect the real interest rate. The real interest rate is, after all, a real variable. For the real interest rate not to be affected, the nominal interest rate must adjust one-for-one to changes in the inflation rate. Thus, *when the Fed increases the rate of money growth, the long-run result is both a higher inflation rate and a higher nominal interest rate*. This adjustment of the nominal interest rate to the inflation rate is called the **Fisher effect,** after economist Irving Fisher (1867–1947), who first studied it.

Keep in mind that our analysis of the Fisher effect has maintained a long-run perspective. The Fisher effect need not hold in the short run because inflation may be unanticipated. A nominal interest rate is a payment on a loan, and it is typically set when the loan is first made. If a jump in inflation catches the borrower and lender by surprise, the nominal interest rate they agreed on will fail to reflect the higher inflation. But if inflation remains high, people will eventually come to expect it, and loan agreements will reflect this expectation. To be precise, therefore, the Fisher effect states that the nominal interest rate adjusts to expected inflation. Expected inflation moves with actual inflation in the long run, but that is not necessarily true in the short run.

The Fisher effect is crucial for understanding changes over time in the nominal interest rate. Figure 5 shows the nominal interest rate and the inflation rate in the U.S. economy since 1960. The close association between these two variables is clear. The nominal interest rate rose from the early 1960s through the 1970s because inflation

Fisher effect
the one-for-one adjustment of the nominal interest rate to the inflation rate

Figure **5**

The Nominal Interest Rate and the Inflation Rate

This figure uses annual data since 1960 to show the nominal interest rate on three-month Treasury bills and the inflation rate as measured by the consumer price index. The close association between these two variables is evidence for the Fisher effect: When the inflation rate rises, so does the nominal interest rate.

Source: U.S. Department of Treasury; U.S. Department of Labor.

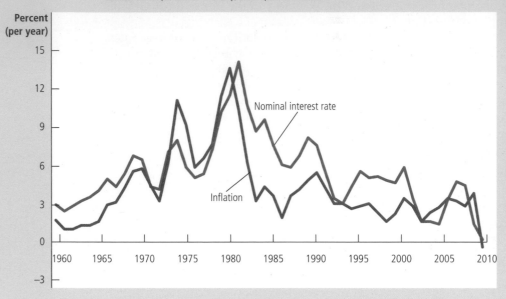

was also rising during this time. Similarly, the nominal interest rate fell from the early 1980s through the 1990s because the Fed got inflation under control.

QUICK QUIZ   *The government of a country increases the growth rate of the money supply from 5 percent per year to 50 percent per year. What happens to prices? What happens to nominal interest rates? Why might the government be doing this?*

The Costs of Inflation

In the late 1970s, when the U.S. inflation rate reached about 10 percent per year, inflation dominated debates over economic policy. And even though inflation has been low over the past decade, it remains a closely watched macroeconomic variable. One study found that *inflation* is the economic term mentioned most often in U.S. newspapers (far ahead of second-place finisher *unemployment* and third-place finisher *productivity*).

   Inflation is closely watched and widely discussed because it is thought to be a serious economic problem. But is that true? And if so, why?

A Fall in Purchasing Power? The Inflation Fallacy

If you ask the typical person why inflation is bad, he will tell you that the answer is obvious: Inflation robs him of the purchasing power of his hard-earned dollars.

When prices rise, each dollar of income buys fewer goods and services. Thus, it might seem that inflation directly lowers living standards.

Yet further thought reveals a fallacy in this answer. When prices rise, buyers of goods and services pay more for what they buy. At the same time, however, sellers of goods and services get more for what they sell. Because most people earn their incomes by selling their services, such as their labor, inflation in incomes goes hand in hand with inflation in prices. Thus, *inflation does not in itself reduce people's real purchasing power.*

People believe the inflation fallacy because they do not appreciate the principle of monetary neutrality. A worker who receives an annual raise of 10 percent tends to view that raise as a reward for her own talent and effort. When an inflation rate of 6 percent reduces the real value of that raise to only 4 percent, the worker might feel that she has been cheated of what is rightfully her due. In fact, as we discussed in the chapter on production and growth, real incomes are determined by real variables, such as physical capital, human capital, natural resources, and the available production technology. Nominal incomes are determined by those factors and the overall price level. If the Fed were to lower the inflation rate from 6 percent to zero, our worker's annual raise would fall from 10 percent to 4 percent. She might feel less robbed by inflation, but her real income would not rise more quickly.

If nominal incomes tend to keep pace with rising prices, why then is inflation a problem? It turns out that there is no single answer to this question. Instead, economists have identified several costs of inflation. Each of these costs shows some way in which persistent growth in the money supply does, in fact, have some effect on real variables.

Shoeleather Costs

As we have discussed, inflation is like a tax on the holders of money. The tax itself is not a cost to society: It is only a transfer of resources from households to the government. Yet most taxes give people an incentive to alter their behavior to avoid paying the tax, and this distortion of incentives causes deadweight losses for society as a whole. Like other taxes, the inflation tax also causes deadweight losses because people waste scarce resources trying to avoid it.

How can a person avoid paying the inflation tax? Because inflation erodes the real value of the money in your wallet, you can avoid the inflation tax by holding less money. One way to do this is to go to the bank more often. For example, rather than withdrawing $200 every four weeks, you might withdraw $50 once a week. By making more frequent trips to the bank, you can keep more of your wealth in your interest-bearing savings account and less in your wallet, where inflation erodes its value.

The cost of reducing your money holdings is called the **shoeleather cost** of inflation because making more frequent trips to the bank causes your shoes to wear out more quickly. Of course, this term is not to be taken literally: The actual cost of reducing your money holdings is not the wear and tear on your shoes but the time and convenience you must sacrifice to keep less money on hand than you would if there were no inflation.

shoeleather costs
the resources wasted when inflation encourages people to reduce their money holdings

The shoeleather costs of inflation may seem trivial. And in fact, they are in the U.S. economy, which has had only moderate inflation in recent years. But this cost is magnified in countries experiencing hyperinflation. Here is a description of one person's experience in Bolivia during its hyperinflation (as reported in the August 13, 1985, issue of *The Wall Street Journal*):

When Edgar Miranda gets his monthly teacher's pay of 25 million pesos, he hasn't a moment to lose. Every hour, pesos drop in value. So, while his wife rushes to market to lay in a month's supply of rice and noodles, he is off with the rest of the pesos to change them into black-market dollars.

Mr. Miranda is practicing the First Rule of Survival amid the most out-of-control inflation in the world today. Bolivia is a case study of how runaway inflation undermines a society. Price increases are so huge that the figures build up almost beyond comprehension. In one six-month period, for example, prices soared at an annual rate of 38,000 percent. By official count, however, last year's inflation reached 2,000 percent, and this year's is expected to hit 8,000 percent—though other estimates range many times higher. In any event, Bolivia's rate dwarfs Israel's 370 percent and Argentina's 1,100 percent—two other cases of severe inflation.

It is easier to comprehend what happens to the thirty-eight-year-old Mr. Miranda's pay if he doesn't quickly change it into dollars. The day he was paid 25 million pesos, a dollar cost 500,000 pesos. So he received $50. Just days later, with the rate at 900,000 pesos, he would have received $27.

As this story shows, the shoeleather costs of inflation can be substantial. With the high inflation rate, Mr. Miranda does not have the luxury of holding the local money as a store of value. Instead, he is forced to convert his pesos quickly into goods or into U.S. dollars, which offer a more stable store of value. The time and effort that Mr. Miranda expends to reduce his money holdings are a waste of resources. If the monetary authority pursued a low-inflation policy, Mr. Miranda would be happy to hold pesos, and he could put his time and effort to more productive use. In fact, shortly after this article was written, the Bolivian inflation rate was reduced substantially with more restrictive monetary policy.

Menu Costs

Most firms do not change the prices of their products every day. Instead, firms often announce prices and leave them unchanged for weeks, months, or even years. One survey found that the typical U.S. firm changes its prices about once a year.

menu costs

the costs of changing prices

Firms change prices infrequently because there are costs of changing prices. Costs of price adjustment are called **menu costs,** a term derived from a restaurant's cost of printing a new menu. Menu costs include the cost of deciding on new prices, the cost of printing new price lists and catalogs, the cost of sending these new price lists and catalogs to dealers and customers, the cost of advertising the new prices, and even the cost of dealing with customer annoyance over price changes.

Inflation increases the menu costs that firms must bear. In the current U.S. economy, with its low inflation rate, annual price adjustment is an appropriate business strategy for many firms. But when high inflation makes firms' costs rise rapidly, annual price adjustment is impractical. During hyperinflations, for example, firms must change their prices daily or even more often just to keep up with all the other prices in the economy.

Relative-Price Variability and the Misallocation of Resources

Suppose that the Eatabit Eatery prints a new menu with new prices every January and then leaves its prices unchanged for the rest of the year. If there is no inflation,

Eatabit's relative prices—the prices of its meals compared to other prices in the economy—would be constant over the course of the year. By contrast, if the inflation rate is 12 percent per year, Eatabit's relative prices will automatically fall by 1 percent each month. The restaurant's relative prices will be high in the early months of the year, just after it has printed a new menu, and low in the later months. And the higher the inflation rate, the greater is this automatic variability. Thus, because prices change only once in a while, inflation causes relative prices to vary more than they otherwise would.

Why does this matter? The reason is that market economies rely on relative prices to allocate scarce resources. Consumers decide what to buy by comparing the quality and prices of various goods and services. Through these decisions, they determine how the scarce factors of production are allocated among industries and firms. When inflation distorts relative prices, consumer decisions are distorted, and markets are less able to allocate resources to their best use.

Inflation-Induced Tax Distortions

Almost all taxes distort incentives, cause people to alter their behavior, and lead to a less efficient allocation of the economy's resources. Many taxes, however, become even more problematic in the presence of inflation. The reason is that lawmakers often fail to take inflation into account when writing the tax laws. Economists who have studied the tax code conclude that inflation tends to raise the tax burden on income earned from savings.

One example of how inflation discourages saving is the tax treatment of *capital gains*—the profits made by selling an asset for more than its purchase price. Suppose that in 1980 you used some of your savings to buy stock in Microsoft Corporation for $10 and that in 2010 you sold the stock for $50. According to the tax law, you have earned a capital gain of $40, which you must include in your income when computing how much income tax you owe. But suppose the overall price level doubled from 1980 to 2010. In this case, the $10 you invested in 1980 is equivalent (in terms of purchasing power) to $20 in 2010. When you sell your stock for $50, you have a real gain (an increase in purchasing power) of only $30. The tax code, however, does not take account of inflation and assesses you a tax on a gain of $40. Thus, inflation exaggerates the size of capital gains and inadvertently increases the tax burden on this type of income.

Another example is the tax treatment of interest income. The income tax treats the *nominal* interest earned on savings as income, even though part of the nominal interest rate merely compensates for inflation. To see the effects of this policy, consider the numerical example in Table 1. The table compares two economies, both of which tax interest income at a rate of 25 percent. In Economy A, inflation is zero, and the nominal and real interest rates are both 4 percent. In this case, the 25 percent tax on interest income reduces the real interest rate from 4 percent to 3 percent. In Economy B, the real interest rate is again 4 percent, but the inflation rate is 8 percent. As a result of the Fisher effect, the nominal interest rate is 12 percent. Because the income tax treats this entire 12 percent interest as income, the government takes 25 percent of it, leaving an after-tax nominal interest rate of only 9 percent and an after-tax real interest rate of only 1 percent. In this case, the 25 percent tax on interest income reduces the real interest rate from 4 percent to 1 percent. Because the after-tax real interest rate provides the incentive to save, saving is much less attractive in the economy with inflation (Economy B) than in the economy with stable prices (Economy A).

Table 1

How Inflation Raises the Tax Burden on Saving

In the presence of zero inflation, a 25 percent tax on interest income reduces the real interest rate from 4 percent to 3 percent. In the presence of 8 percent inflation, the same tax reduces the real interest rate from 4 percent to 1 percent.

	Economy A (price stability)	Economy B (inflation)
Real interest rate	4%	4%
Inflation rate	0	8
Nominal interest rate (real interest rate + inflation rate)	4	12
Reduced interest due to 25 percent tax (0.25 × nominal interest rate)	1	3
After-tax nominal interest rate (0.75 × nominal interest rate)	3	9
After-tax real interest rate (after-tax nominal interest rate − inflation rate)	3	1

The taxes on nominal capital gains and on nominal interest income are two examples of how the tax code interacts with inflation. There are many others. Because of these inflation-induced tax changes, higher inflation tends to discourage people from saving. Recall that the economy's saving provides the resources for investment, which in turn is a key ingredient to long-run economic growth. Thus, when inflation raises the tax burden on saving, it tends to depress the economy's long-run growth rate. There is, however, no consensus among economists about the size of this effect.

One solution to this problem, other than eliminating inflation, is to index the tax system. That is, the tax laws could be rewritten to take account of the effects of inflation. In the case of capital gains, for example, the tax code could adjust the purchase price using a price index and assess the tax only on the real gain. In the case of interest income, the government could tax only real interest income by excluding that portion of the interest income that merely compensates for inflation. To some extent, the tax laws have moved in the direction of indexation. For example, the income levels at which income tax rates change are adjusted automatically each year based on changes in the consumer price index. Yet many other aspects of the tax laws—such as the tax treatment of capital gains and interest income—are not indexed.

In an ideal world, the tax laws would be written so that inflation would not alter anyone's real tax liability. In the world in which we live, however, tax laws are far from perfect. More complete indexation would probably be desirable, but it would further complicate a tax code that many people already consider too complex.

Confusion and Inconvenience

Imagine that we took a poll and asked people the following question: "This year the yard is 36 inches. How long do you think it should be next year?" Assuming we could get people to take us seriously, they would tell us that the yard should stay the same length—36 inches. Anything else would just complicate life needlessly.

What does this finding have to do with inflation? Recall that money, as the economy's unit of account, is what we use to quote prices and record debts. In other words, money is the yardstick with which we measure economic transactions. The job of the Federal Reserve is a bit like the job of the Bureau of Standards—to ensure the reliability of a commonly used unit of measurement. When the Fed increases the money supply and creates inflation, it erodes the real value of the unit of account.

It is difficult to judge the costs of the confusion and inconvenience that arise from inflation. Earlier, we discussed how the tax code incorrectly measures real incomes in the presence of inflation. Similarly, accountants incorrectly measure firms' earnings when prices are rising over time. Because inflation causes dollars at different times to have different real values, computing a firm's profit—the difference between its revenue and costs—is more complicated in an economy with inflation. Therefore, to some extent, inflation makes investors less able to sort successful from unsuccessful firms, which in turn impedes financial markets in their role of allocating the economy's saving to alternative types of investment.

A Special Cost of Unexpected Inflation: Arbitrary Redistributions of Wealth

So far, the costs of inflation we have discussed occur even if inflation is steady and predictable. Inflation has an additional cost, however, when it comes as a surprise. Unexpected inflation redistributes wealth among the population in a way that has nothing to do with either merit or need. These redistributions occur because many loans in the economy are specified in terms of the unit of account—money.

Consider an example. Suppose that Sam Student takes out a $20,000 loan at a 7 percent interest rate from Bigbank to attend college. In 10 years, the loan will come due. After his debt has compounded for 10 years at 7 percent, Sam will owe Bigbank $40,000. The real value of this debt will depend on inflation over the decade. If Sam is lucky, the economy will have a hyperinflation. In this case, wages and prices will rise so high that Sam will be able to pay the $40,000 debt out of pocket change. By contrast, if the economy goes through a major deflation, then wages and prices will fall, and Sam will find the $40,000 debt a greater burden than he anticipated.

This example shows that unexpected changes in prices redistribute wealth among debtors and creditors. A hyperinflation enriches Sam at the expense of Bigbank because it diminishes the real value of the debt; Sam can repay the loan in less valuable dollars than he anticipated. Deflation enriches Bigbank at Sam's expense because it increases the real value of the debt; in this case, Sam has to repay the loan in more valuable dollars than he anticipated. If inflation were predictable, then Bigbank and Sam could take inflation into account when setting the nominal interest rate. (Recall the Fisher effect.) But if inflation is hard to predict, it imposes risk on Sam and Bigbank that both would prefer to avoid.

This cost of unexpected inflation is important to consider together with another fact: Inflation is especially volatile and uncertain when the average rate of inflation is high. This is seen most simply by examining the experience of different countries. Countries with low average inflation, such as Germany in the late 20th century, tend to have stable inflation. Countries with high average inflation, such as many countries in Latin America, tend to have unstable inflation. There are no known examples of economies with high, stable inflation. This relationship between the level and volatility of inflation points to another cost of inflation. If a country pursues a high-inflation monetary policy, it will have to bear not only the costs of high expected inflation but also the arbitrary redistributions of wealth associated with unexpected inflation.

Inflation Is Bad, But Deflation May Be Worse

In recent U.S. history, inflation has been the norm. But the level of prices has fallen at times, such as during the late nineteenth century and early 1930s. Moreover, Japan has experienced declines in its overall price level in recent years. So as we conclude our discussion of the costs of inflation, we should briefly consider the costs of deflation as well.

Some economists have suggested that a small and predictable amount of deflation may be desirable. Milton Friedman pointed out that deflation would lower the nominal interest rate (recall the Fisher effect) and that a lower nominal interest rate would reduce the cost of holding money. The shoeleather costs of holding money would, he argued, be minimized by a nominal interest rate close to zero, which in turn would require deflation equal to the real interest rate. This prescription for moderate deflation is called the *Friedman rule*.

Yet there are also costs of deflation. Some of these mirror the costs of inflation. For example, just as a rising price level induces menu costs and relative-price variability, so does a falling price level. Moreover, in practice, deflation is rarely as steady and predictable as Friedman recommended. More often, it comes as a surprise, resulting in the redistribution of wealth toward creditors and away from debtors. Because debtors are often poorer, these redistributions in wealth are particularly pernicious.

Perhaps most important, deflation often arises because of broader macroeconomic difficulties. As we will see in future chapters, falling prices result when some event, such as a monetary contraction, reduces the overall demand for goods and services in the economy. This fall in aggregate demand can lead to falling incomes and rising unemployment. In other words, deflation is often a symptom of deeper economic problems.

The Wizard of Oz and the Free-Silver Debate

As a child, you probably saw the movie *The Wizard of Oz*, based on a children's book written in 1900. The movie and book tell the story of a young girl, Dorothy, who finds herself lost in a strange land far from home. You probably did not know, however, that the story is actually an allegory about U.S. monetary policy in the late 19th century.

From 1880 to 1896, the price level in the U.S. economy fell by 23 percent. Because this event was unanticipated, it led to a major redistribution of wealth. Most farmers in the western part of the country were debtors. Their creditors were the bankers in the east. When the price level fell, it caused the real value of these debts to rise, which enriched the banks at the expense of the farmers.

According to Populist politicians of the time, the solution to the farmers' problem was the free coinage of silver. During this period, the United States was operating with a gold standard. The quantity of gold determined the money supply and, thereby, the price level. The free-silver advocates wanted silver, as well as gold, to be used as money. If adopted, this proposal would have increased the money supply, pushed up the price level, and reduced the real burden of the farmers' debts.

The debate over silver was heated, and it was central to the politics of the 1890s. A common election slogan of the Populists was "We Are Mortgaged. All but Our Votes." One prominent advocate of free silver was William Jennings Bryan, the Democratic nominee for president in 1896. He is remembered in part for a speech at the Democratic Party's nominating convention in which he said, "You shall not press down upon the brow of labor this crown of thorns. You shall not crucify mankind upon a cross of gold." Rarely since then have politicians waxed so poetic about alternative approaches to monetary policy. Nonetheless, Bryan lost the election to Republican William McKinley, and the United States remained on the gold standard.

L. Frank Baum, author of the book *The Wonderful Wizard of Oz,* was a midwestern journalist. When he sat down to write a story for children, he made the characters represent protagonists in the major political battle of his time. Here is how economic historian Hugh Rockoff, writing in the *Journal of Political Economy* in 1990, interprets the story:

DOROTHY:	Traditional American values
TOTO:	Prohibitionist party, also called the Teetotalers
SCARECROW:	Farmers
TIN WOODSMAN:	Industrial workers
COWARDLY LION:	William Jennings Bryan
MUNCHKINS:	Citizens of the East
WICKED WITCH OF THE EAST:	Grover Cleveland
WICKED WITCH OF THE WEST:	William McKinley
WIZARD:	Marcus Alonzo Hanna, chairman of the Republican Party
OZ:	Abbreviation for ounce of gold
YELLOW BRICK ROAD:	Gold standard

An early debate over monetary policy

In the end of Baum's story, Dorothy does find her way home, but it is not by just following the yellow brick road. After a long and perilous journey, she learns that the wizard is incapable of helping her or her friends. Instead, Dorothy finally discovers the magical power of her *silver* slippers. (When the book was made into a movie in 1939, Dorothy's slippers were changed from silver to ruby. The Hollywood filmmakers were more interested in showing off the new technology of Technicolor than in telling a story about 19th-century monetary policy.)

The Populists lost the debate over the free coinage of silver, but they eventually got the monetary expansion and inflation that they wanted. In 1898, prospectors discovered gold near the Klondike River in the Canadian Yukon. Increased supplies of gold also arrived from the mines of South Africa. As a result, the money supply and the price level started to rise in the United States and in other countries operating on the gold standard. Within fifteen years, prices in the United States were back to the levels that had prevailed in the 1880s, and farmers were better able to handle their debts. ■

QUICK QUIZ   *List and describe six costs of inflation.*

- A government can pay for some of its spending simply by printing money. When countries rely heavily on this "inflation tax," the result is hyperinflation.

- One application of the principle of monetary neutrality is the Fisher effect. According to the Fisher effect, when the inflation rate rises, the nominal interest rate rises by the same amount so that the real interest rate remains the same.

- Many people think that inflation makes them poorer because it raises the cost of what they buy. This view is a fallacy, however, because inflation also raises nominal incomes.

- Economists have identified six costs of inflation: shoeleather costs associated with reduced money holdings, menu costs associated with more frequent adjustment of prices, increased variability of relative prices, unintended changes in tax liabilities due to nonindexation of the tax code, confusion and inconvenience resulting from a changing unit of account, and arbitrary redistributions of wealth between debtors and creditors. Many of these costs are large during hyperinflation, but the size of these costs for moderate inflation is less clear.

KEY CONCEPTS

quantity theory of money, *p. 247*   monetary neutrality, *p. 250*   Fisher effect, *p. 255*
nominal variables, *p. 249*   velocity of money, *p. 250*   shoeleather costs, *p. 257*
real variables, *p. 249*   quantity equation, *p. 251*   menu costs, *p. 258*
classical dichotomy, *p. 249*   inflation tax, *p. 253*

QUESTIONS FOR REVIEW

1. Explain how an increase in the price level affects the real value of money.
2. According to the quantity theory of money, what is the effect of an increase in the quantity of money?
3. Explain the difference between nominal and real variables and give two examples of each. According to the principle of monetary neutrality, which variables are affected by changes in the quantity of money?
4. In what sense is inflation like a tax? How does thinking about inflation as a tax help explain hyperinflation?
5. According to the Fisher effect, how does an increase in the inflation rate affect the real interest rate and the nominal interest rate?
6. What are the costs of inflation? Which of these costs do you think are most important for the U.S. economy?
7. If inflation is less than expected, who benefits—debtors or creditors? Explain.

PROBLEMS AND APPLICATIONS

1. Suppose that this year's money supply is $500 billion, nominal GDP is $10 trillion, and real GDP is $5 trillion.
   a. What is the price level? What is the velocity of money?
   b. Suppose that velocity is constant and the economy's output of goods and services rises by 5 percent each year. What will

   happen to nominal GDP and the price level next year if the Fed keeps the money supply constant?
   c. What money supply should the Fed set next year if it wants to keep the price level stable?
   d. What money supply should the Fed set next year if it wants inflation of 10 percent?

2. Suppose that changes in bank regulations expand the availability of credit cards so that people need to hold less cash.
   a. How does this event affect the demand for money?
   b. If the Fed does not respond to this event, what will happen to the price level?
   c. If the Fed wants to keep the price level stable, what should it do?
3. It is sometimes suggested that the Federal Reserve should try to achieve zero inflation. If we assume that velocity is constant, does this zero-inflation goal require that the rate of money growth equal zero? If yes, explain why. If no, explain what the rate of money growth should equal.
4. Suppose that a country's inflation rate increases sharply. What happens to the inflation tax on the holders of money? Why is wealth that is held in savings accounts *not* subject to a change in the inflation tax? Can you think of any way holders of savings accounts are hurt by the increase in the inflation rate?
5. Hyperinflations are extremely rare in countries whose central banks are independent of the rest of the government. Why might this be so?
6. Let's consider the effects of inflation in an economy composed of only two people: Bob, a bean farmer, and Rita, a rice farmer. Bob and Rita both always consume equal amounts of rice and beans. In 2010, the price of beans was $1, and the price of rice was $3.
   a. Suppose that in 2011 the price of beans was $2 and the price of rice was $6. What was inflation? Was Bob better off, worse off, or unaffected by the changes in prices? What about Rita?
   b. Now suppose that in 2011 the price of beans was $2 and the price of rice was $4. What was inflation? Was Bob better off, worse off, or unaffected by the changes in prices? What about Rita?
   c. Finally, suppose that in 2011 the price of beans was $2 and the price of rice was $1.50. What was inflation? Was Bob better off, worse off, or unaffected by the changes in prices? What about Rita?
   d. What matters more to Bob and Rita—the overall inflation rate or the relative price of rice and beans?
7. If the tax rate is 40 percent, compute the before-tax real interest rate and the after-tax real interest rate in each of the following cases.
   a. The nominal interest rate is 10 percent, and the inflation rate is 5 percent.
   b. The nominal interest rate is 6 percent, and the inflation rate is 2 percent.
   c. The nominal interest rate is 4 percent, and the inflation rate is 1 percent.
8. What are your shoeleather costs of going to the bank? How might you measure these costs in dollars? How do you think the shoeleather costs of your college president differ from your own?
9. Recall that money serves three functions in the economy. What are those functions? How does inflation affect the ability of money to serve each of these functions?
10. Suppose that people expect inflation to equal 3 percent, but in fact, prices rise by 5 percent. Describe how this unexpectedly high inflation rate would help or hurt the following:
    a. the government
    b. a homeowner with a fixed-rate mortgage
    c. a union worker in the second year of a labor contract
    d. a college that has invested some of its endowment in government bonds
11. Explain one harm associated with unexpected inflation that is *not* associated with expected inflation. Then explain one harm associated with both expected and unexpected inflation.
12. Explain whether the following statements are true, false, or uncertain.
    a. "Inflation hurts borrowers and helps lenders, because borrowers must pay a higher rate of interest."
    b. "If prices change in a way that leaves the overall price level unchanged, then no one is made better or worse off."
    c. "Inflation does not reduce the purchasing power of most workers."

For further information on topics in this chapter, additional problems, applications, examples, online quizzes, and more, please visit our website at www.cengage.com/economics/mankiw.

PART **VI** The Macroeconomics
of Open Economies

Open-Economy Macroeconomics: Basic Concepts

13

When you decide to buy a car, you may compare the latest models offered by Ford and Toyota. When you take your next vacation, you may consider spending it on a beach in Florida or in Mexico. When you start saving for your retirement, you may choose between a mutual fund that buys stock in U.S. companies and one that buys stock in foreign companies. In all these cases, you are participating not just in the U.S. economy but in economies around the world.

Openness to international trade yields clear benefits: Trade allows people to produce what they produce best and to consume the great variety of goods and services produced around the world. Indeed, one of the *Ten Principles of Economics* highlighted in Chapter 1 is that trade can make everyone better off. International trade can raise living standards in all countries by allowing each country to specialize in producing those goods and services in which it has a comparative advantage.

So far, our development of macroeconomics has largely ignored the economy's interaction with other economies around the world. For most questions in macroeconomics, international issues are peripheral. For instance, when we discussed the natural rate of unemployment and the causes of inflation, the effects of international trade could safely be ignored. Indeed, to keep their models simple, macroeconomists often assume a **closed economy**—an economy that does not interact with other economies.

Yet new macroeconomic issues arise in an **open econom**y—an economy that interacts freely with other economies around the world. This chapter and the next, therefore, provide an introduction to open-economy macroeconomics. We begin in this chapter by discussing the key macroeconomic variables that describe an open economy's interactions in world markets. You may have noticed mention of these variables—exports, imports, the trade balance, and exchange rates—when reading news reports or watching the nightly news. Our first job is to understand what these data mean. In the next chapter, we develop a model to explain how these variables are determined and how they are affected by various government policies.

closed economy

an economy that does not interact with other economies in the world

open economy

an economy that interacts freely with other economies around the world

The International Flows of Goods and Capital

An open economy interacts with other economies in two ways: It buys and sells goods and services in world product markets, and it buys and sells capital assets such as stocks and bonds in world financial markets. Here we discuss these two activities and the close relationship between them.

The Flow of Goods: Exports, Imports, and Net Exports

Exports are domestically produced goods and services that are sold abroad, and **imports** are foreign-produced goods and services that are sold domestically. When Boeing, the U.S. aircraft manufacturer, builds a plane and sells it to Air France, the sale is an export for the United States and an import for France. When Volvo, the Swedish car manufacturer, makes a car and sells it to a U.S. resident, the sale is an import for the United States and an export for Sweden.

The **net exports** of any country are the difference between the value of its exports and the value of its imports:

$$\text{Net exports} = \text{Value of country's exports} - \text{Value of country's imports}.$$

The Boeing sale raises U.S. net exports, and the Volvo sale reduces U.S. net exports. Because net exports tell us whether a country is, in total, a seller or a buyer in world markets for goods and services, net exports are also called the **trade balance**. If net exports are positive, exports are greater than imports, indicating that the country sells more goods and services abroad than it buys from other countries. In this case, the country is said to run a **trade surplus**. If net exports are negative, exports are less than imports, indicating that the country sells fewer goods and services abroad than it buys from other countries. In this

exports

goods and services that are produced domestically and sold abroad

imports

goods and services that are produced abroad and sold domestically

net exports

the value of a nation's exports minus the value of its imports; also called the trade balance

trade balance

the value of a nation's exports minus the value of its imports; also called net exports

trade surplus

an excess of exports over imports

case, the country is said to run a **trade deficit.** If net exports are zero, its exports and imports are exactly equal, and the country is said to have **balanced trade.**

In the next chapter, we develop a theory that explains an economy's trade balance, but even at this early stage, it is easy to think of many factors that might influence a country's exports, imports, and net exports. Those factors include the following:

- The tastes of consumers for domestic and foreign goods
- The prices of goods at home and abroad
- The exchange rates at which people can use domestic currency to buy foreign currencies
- The incomes of consumers at home and abroad
- The cost of transporting goods from country to country
- Government policies toward international trade

As these variables change, so does the amount of international trade.

 The Increasing Openness of the U.S. Economy

One dramatic change in the U.S. economy over the past six decades has been the increasing importance of international trade and finance. This change is illustrated in Figure 1, which shows the total value of goods and services exported to other countries and imported from other countries expressed as a percentage of gross domestic product. In the 1950s, imports and exports of goods and services were typically between 4 and 5 percent of GDP. In recent years, they have been more than twice that level. The trading partners of the United States include a diverse group of countries. As of 2009, the largest trading partner, as measured by imports and exports combined, was Canada, followed by China, Mexico, Japan, Germany, and the United Kingdom.

trade deficit
an excess of imports over exports

balanced trade
a situation in which exports equal imports

"But we're not just talking about buying a car—we're talking about confronting this country's trade deficit with Japan."

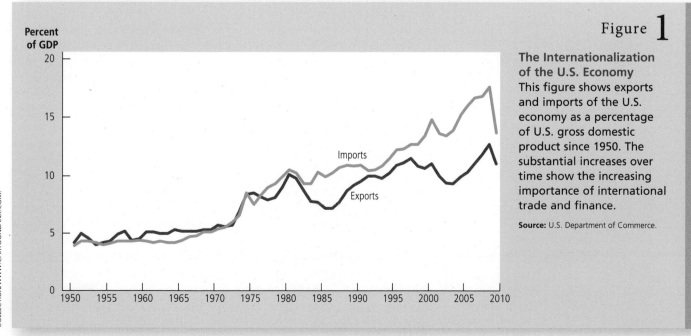

Percent of GDP

Figure **1**

The Internationalization of the U.S. Economy
This figure shows exports and imports of the U.S. economy as a percentage of U.S. gross domestic product since 1950. The substantial increases over time show the increasing importance of international trade and finance.

Source: U.S. Department of Commerce.

The increase in international trade over the past several decades is partly due to improvements in transportation. In 1950, the average merchant ship carried less than 10,000 tons of cargo; today, many ships carry more than 100,000 tons. The long-distance jet was introduced in 1958, and the wide-body jet in 1967, making air transport far cheaper than it had been. Because of these developments, goods that once had to be produced locally can now be traded around the world. Cut flowers grown in Israel are flown to the United States to be sold. Fresh fruits and vegetables that can grow only in summer can now be consumed in winter as well because they can be shipped to the United States from countries in the Southern Hemisphere.

The increase in international trade has also been influenced by advances in telecommunications, which have allowed businesses to reach overseas customers more easily. For example, the first transatlantic telephone cable was not laid until

in the news

> Breaking Up the Chain of Production

Some goods are manufactured not in one country but in many.

An iPod Has Global Value. Ask the (Many) Countries That Make It.

BY HAL R. VARIAN

Who makes the Apple iPod? Here's a hint: It is not Apple. The company outsources the entire manufacture of the device to a number of Asian enterprises, among them Asustek, Inventec Appliances and Foxconn.

But this list of companies isn't a satisfactory answer either: They only do final assembly. What about the 451 parts that go into the iPod? Where are they made and by whom?

Three researchers at the University of California, Irvine—Greg Linden, Kenneth L. Kraemer, and Jason Dedrick—applied some investigative cost accounting to this question, using a report from Portelligent Inc. that examined all the parts that went into the iPod.

Their study, sponsored by the Sloan Foundation, offers a fascinating illustration of the complexity of the global economy, and how difficult it is to understand that complexity by using only conventional trade statistics.

The retail value of the 30-gigabyte video iPod that the authors examined was $299. The most expensive component in it was the hard drive, which was manufactured by Toshiba and costs about $73. The next most costly components were the display module (about $20), the video/multimedia processor chip ($8) and the controller chip ($5). They estimated that the final assembly, done in China, cost only about $4 a unit.

One approach to tracing supply chain geography might be to attribute the cost of each component to the country of origin of its maker. So $73 of the cost of the iPod would be attributed to Japan since Toshiba is a Japanese company, and the $13 cost of the two chips would be attributed to the United States, since the suppliers, Broadcom and PortalPlayer, are American companies, and so on.

But this method hides some of the most important details. Toshiba may be a Japanese company, but it makes most of its hard drives in the Philippines and China. So perhaps we should also allocate part of the cost of that hard drive to one of those countries. The same problem arises regarding the Broadcom chips, with most of them manufactured in Taiwan. So how can one distribute the costs of the iPod components across the countries where they are manufactured in a meaningful way?

1956. As recently as 1966, the technology allowed only 138 simultaneous conversations between North America and Europe. Today, communications satellites permit more than 1 million conversations to occur at the same time.

Technological progress has also fostered international trade by changing the kinds of goods that economies produce. When bulky raw materials (such as steel) and perishable goods (such as foodstuffs) were a large part of the world's output, transporting goods was often costly and sometimes impossible. By contrast, goods produced with modern technology are often light and easy to transport. Consumer electronics, for instance, have low weight for every dollar of value, which makes them easy to produce in one country and sell in another. An even more extreme example is the film industry. Once a studio in Hollywood makes a movie, it can send copies of the film around the world at almost zero cost. And indeed, movies are a major export of the United States.

To answer this question, let us look at the production process as a sequence of steps, each possibly performed by a different company operating in a different country. At each step, inputs like computer chips and a bare circuit board are converted into outputs like an assembled circuit board. The difference between the cost of the inputs and the value of the outputs is the "value added" at that step, which can then be attributed to the country where that value was added.

The profit margin on generic parts like nuts and bolts is very low, since these items are produced in intensely competitive industries and can be manufactured anywhere. Hence, they add little to the final value of the iPod. More specialized parts, like the hard drives and controller chips, have much higher value added.

According to the authors' estimates, the $73 Toshiba hard drive in the iPod contains about $54 in parts and labor. So the value that Toshiba added to the hard drive was $19 plus its own direct labor costs. This $19 is attributed to Japan since Toshiba is a Japanese company.

Continuing in this way, the researchers examined the major components of the iPod and tried to calculate the value added

at different stages of the production process and then assigned that value added to the country where the value was created. This isn't an easy task, but even based on their initial examination, it is quite clear that the largest share of the value added in the iPod goes to enterprises in the United States, particularly for units sold here.

The researchers estimated that $163 of the iPod's $299 retail value in the United States was captured by American companies and workers, breaking it down to $75 for distribution and retail costs, $80 to Apple, and $8 to various domestic component makers. Japan contributed about $26 to the value added (mostly via the Toshiba disk drive), while Korea contributed less than $1.

The unaccounted-for parts and labor costs involved in making the iPod came to about $110. The authors hope to assign those labor costs to the appropriate countries, but as the

hard drive example illustrates, that's not so easy to do.

This value added calculation illustrates the futility of summarizing such a complex manufacturing process by using conventional trade statistics. Even though Chinese workers contribute only about 1 percent of the value of the iPod, the export of a finished iPod to the United States directly contributes about $150 to our bilateral trade deficit with the Chinese.

Ultimately, there is no simple answer to who makes the iPod or where it is made. The iPod, like many other products, is made in several countries by dozens of companies, with each stage of production contributing a different amount to the final value.

The real value of the iPod doesn't lie in its parts or even in putting those parts together. The bulk of the iPod's value is in the conception and design of the iPod. That is why Apple gets $80 for each of these video iPods it sells, which is by far the largest piece of value added in the entire supply chain.

Those clever folks at Apple figured out how to combine 451 mostly generic parts into a valuable product. They may not make the iPod, but they created it. In the end, that's what really matters.

Source: *New York Times,* June 28, 2007.

AP PHOTO/PAUL SAKUMA

The government's trade policies have also been a factor in increasing international trade. As we discussed earlier in this book, economists have long believed that free trade between countries is mutually beneficial. Over time, most policymakers around the world have come to accept these conclusions. International agreements, such as the North American Free Trade Agreement (NAFTA) and the General Agreement on Tariffs and Trade (GATT), have gradually lowered tariffs, import quotas, and other trade barriers. The pattern of increasing trade illustrated in Figure 1 is a phenomenon that most economists and policymakers endorse and encourage. ∎

The Flow of Financial Resources: Net Capital Outflow

So far, we have been discussing how residents of an open economy participate in world markets for goods and services. In addition, residents of an open economy participate in world financial markets. A U.S. resident with $20,000 could use that money to buy a car from Toyota, or he could instead use that money to buy stock in the Toyota Corporation. The first transaction would represent a flow of goods, whereas the second would represent a flow of capital.

net capital outflow

the purchase of foreign assets by domestic residents minus the purchase of domestic assets by foreigners

The term **net capital outflow** refers to the difference between the purchase of foreign assets by domestic residents and the purchase of domestic assets by foreigners:

Net capital outflow = Purchase of foreign assets by domestic residents
− Purchase of domestic assets by foreigners.

When a U.S. resident buys stock in Telmex, the Mexican telecommunications company, the purchase increases the first term on the right side of this equation and, therefore, increases U.S. net capital outflow. When a Japanese resident buys a bond issued by the U.S. government, the purchase increases the second term on the right side of this equation and, therefore, decreases U.S. net capital outflow.

The flow of capital between the U.S. economy and the rest of the world takes two forms. If McDonald's opens up a fast-food outlet in Russia, that is an example of *foreign direct investment*. Alternatively, if an American buys stock in a Russian corporation, that is an example of *foreign portfolio investment*. In the first case, the American owner (McDonald's Corporation) actively manages the investment, whereas in the second case, the American owner (the stockholder) has a more passive role. In both cases, U.S. residents are buying assets located in another country, so both purchases increase U.S. net capital outflow.

The net capital outflow (sometimes called *net foreign investment*) can be either positive or negative. When it is positive, domestic residents are buying more foreign assets than foreigners are buying domestic assets. Capital is said to be flowing out of the country. When the net capital outflow is negative, domestic residents are buying less foreign assets than foreigners are buying domestic assets. Capital is said to be flowing into the country. That is, when net capital outflow is negative, a country is experiencing a capital inflow.

We develop a theory to explain net capital outflow in the next chapter. Here let's consider briefly some of the more important variables that influence net capital outflow:

- The real interest rates paid on foreign assets
- The real interest rates paid on domestic assets
- The perceived economic and political risks of holding assets abroad
- The government policies that affect foreign ownership of domestic assets

For example, consider U.S. investors deciding whether to buy Mexican government bonds or U.S. government bonds. (Recall that a bond is, in effect, an IOU of the issuer.) To make this decision, U.S. investors compare the real interest rates offered on the two bonds. The higher a bond's real interest rate, the more attractive it is. While making this comparison, however, U.S. investors must also take into account the risk that one of these governments might default on its debt (that is, not pay interest or principal when it is due), as well as any restrictions that the Mexican government has imposed, or might impose in the future, on foreign investors in Mexico.

The Equality of Net Exports and Net Capital Outflow

We have seen that an open economy interacts with the rest of the world in two ways—in world markets for goods and services and in world financial markets. Net exports and net capital outflow each measure a type of imbalance in these markets. Net exports measure an imbalance between a country's exports and its imports. Net capital outflow measures an imbalance between the amount of foreign assets bought by domestic residents and the amount of domestic assets bought by foreigners.

An important but subtle fact of accounting states that, for an economy as a whole, net capital outflow (*NCO*) must always equal net exports (*NX*):

$$NCO = NX.$$

This equation holds because every transaction that affects one side of this equation affects the other side by exactly the same amount. This equation is an *identity*—an equation that must hold because of the way the variables in the equation are defined and measured.

To see why this accounting identity is true, let's consider an example. Imagine that you are a computer programmer residing in the United States. One day, you write some software and sell it to a Japanese consumer for 10,000 yen. The sale of software is an export of the United States, so it increases U.S. net exports. What else happens to ensure that this identity holds? The answer depends on what you do with the 10,000 yen you are paid.

First, let's suppose that you simply stuff the yen in your mattress. (We might say you have a yen for yen.) In this case, you are using some of your income to invest in the Japanese economy. That is, a domestic resident (you) has acquired a foreign asset (the Japanese currency). The increase in U.S. net exports is matched by an increase in the U.S. net capital outflow.

More realistically, however, if you want to invest in the Japanese economy, you won't do so by holding on to Japanese currency. More likely, you would use the 10,000 yen to buy stock in a Japanese corporation, or you might buy a Japanese government bond. Yet the result of your decision is much the same: A domestic resident ends up acquiring a foreign asset. The increase in U.S. net capital outflow (the purchase of the Japanese stock or bond) exactly equals the increase in U.S. net exports (the sale of software).

Let's now change the example. Suppose that instead of using the 10,000 yen to buy a Japanese asset, you use it to buy a good made in Japan, such as a Nintendo Wii. As a result of the Wii purchase, U.S. imports increase. The software export and the Wii import represent balanced trade. Because exports and imports increase by the same amount, net exports are unchanged. In this case, no American ends up acquiring a foreign asset and no foreigner ends up acquiring a U.S. asset, so there is also no impact on U.S. net capital outflow.

A final possibility is that you go to a local bank to exchange your 10,000 yen for U.S. dollars. But this doesn't change the situation because the bank now has to do something with the 10,000 yen. It can buy Japanese assets (a U.S. net capital outflow); it can buy a Japanese good (a U.S. import); or it can sell the yen to another American who wants to make such a transaction. In the end, U.S. net exports must equal U.S. net capital outflow.

This example all started when a U.S. programmer sold some software abroad, but the story is much the same when Americans buy goods and services from other countries. For example, if Walmart buys $50 million of clothing from China and sells it to American consumers, something must happen to that $50 million. One possibility is that China could use the $50 million to invest in the U.S. economy. This capital inflow from China might take the form of Chinese purchases of U.S. government bonds. In this case, the sale of the clothing reduces U.S. net exports, and the sale of bonds reduces U.S. net capital outflow. Alternatively, China could use the $50 million to buy a plane from Boeing, the U.S. aircraft manufacturer. In this case, the U.S. import of clothing balances the U.S. export of aircraft, so net exports and net capital outflow are both unchanged. In all cases, the transaction has the same effect on net exports and net capital outflow.

We can summarize these conclusions for the economy as a whole.

- When a nation is running a trade surplus ($NX > 0$), it is selling more goods and services to foreigners than it is buying from them. What is it doing with the foreign currency it receives from the net sale of goods and services abroad? It must be using it to buy foreign assets. Capital is flowing out of the country ($NCO > 0$).
- When a nation is running a trade deficit ($NX < 0$), it is buying more goods and services from foreigners than it is selling to them. How is it financing the net purchase of these goods and services in world markets? It must be selling assets abroad. Capital is flowing into the country ($NCO < 0$).

The international flow of goods and services and the international flow of capital are two sides of the same coin.

Saving, Investment, and Their Relationship to the International Flows

A nation's saving and investment are crucial to its long-run economic growth. As we have seen earlier in this book, saving and investment are equal in a closed economy. But matters are not as simple in an open economy. Let's now consider how saving and investment are related to the international flows of goods and capital as measured by net exports and net capital outflow.

As you may recall, the term *net exports* appeared earlier in the book when we discussed the components of gross domestic product. The economy's gross domestic product (Y) is divided among four components: consumption (C), investment (I), government purchases (G), and net exports (NX). We write this as

$$Y = C + I + G + NX.$$

Total expenditure on the economy's output of goods and services is the sum of expenditure on consumption, investment, government purchases, and net exports. Because each dollar of expenditure is placed into one of these four components, this equation is an accounting identity: It must be true because of the way the variables are defined and measured.

Recall that national saving is the income of the nation that is left after paying for current consumption and government purchases. National saving (S) equals $Y - C - G$. If we rearrange the equation to reflect this fact, we obtain

$$Y - C - G = I + NX$$
$$S = I + NX.$$

Because net exports (NX) also equal net capital outflow (NCO), we can write this equation as

$$S = I + NCO$$

$$\text{Saving} = \frac{\text{Domestic}}{\text{investment}} + \frac{\text{Net capital}}{\text{outflow}}.$$

This equation shows that a nation's saving must equal its domestic investment plus its net capital outflow. In other words, when U.S. citizens save a dollar of their income for the future, that dollar can be used to finance accumulation of domestic capital or it can be used to finance the purchase of capital abroad.

This equation should look somewhat familiar. Earlier in the book, when we analyzed the role of the financial system, we considered this identity for the special case of a closed economy. In a closed economy, net capital outflow is zero $(NCO = 0)$, so saving equals investment $(S = I)$. By contrast, an open economy has two uses for its saving: domestic investment and net capital outflow.

As before, we can view the financial system as standing between the two sides of this identity. For example, suppose the Smith family decides to save some of its income for retirement. This decision contributes to national saving, the left side of our equation. If the Smiths deposit their saving in a mutual fund, the mutual fund may use some of the deposit to buy stock issued by General Motors, which uses the proceeds to build a factory in Ohio. In addition, the mutual fund may use some of the Smiths' deposit to buy stock issued by Toyota, which uses the proceeds to build a factory in Osaka. These transactions show up on the right side of the equation. From the standpoint of U.S. accounting, the General Motors expenditure on a new factory is domestic investment, and the purchase of Toyota stock by a U.S. resident is net capital outflow. Thus, all saving in the U.S. economy shows up as investment in the U.S. economy or as U.S. net capital outflow.

The bottom line is that saving, investment, and international capital flows are inextricably linked. When a nation's saving exceeds its domestic investment, its net capital outflow is positive, indicating that the nation is using some of its saving to buy assets abroad. When a nation's domestic investment exceeds its saving, its net capital outflow is negative, indicating that foreigners are financing some of this investment by purchasing domestic assets.

Summing Up

Table 1 summarizes many of the ideas presented so far in this chapter. It describes the three possibilities for an open economy: a country with a trade deficit, a country with balanced trade, and a country with a trade surplus.

Consider first a country with a trade surplus. By definition, a trade surplus means that the value of exports exceeds the value of imports. Because net exports are exports minus imports, net exports NX are greater than zero. As a result, income $Y = C + I + G + NX$ must be greater than domestic spending $C + I + G$. But if income Y is more than spending $C + I + G$, then saving $S = Y - C - G$ must be more than investment I. Because the country is saving more than it is investing,

Table 1			
International Flows of Goods and Capital: Summary This table shows the three possible outcomes for an open economy.	**Trade Deficit**	**Balanced Trade**	**Trade Surplus**
	Exports < Imports	Exports = Imports	Exports > Imports
	Net Exports < 0	Net Exports = 0	Net Exports > 0
	$Y < C + I + G$	$Y = C + I + G$	$Y > C + I + G$
	Saving < Investment	Saving = Investment	Saving > Investment
	Net Capital Outflow < 0	Net Capital Outflow = 0	Net Capital Outflow > 0

it must be sending some of its saving abroad. That is, the net capital outflow must be greater than zero.

The converse logic applies to a country with a trade deficit (such as the U.S. economy in recent years). By definition, a trade deficit means that the value of exports is less than the value of imports. Because net exports are exports minus imports, net exports NX are negative. Thus, income $Y = C + I + G + NX$ must be less than domestic spending $C + I + G$. But if income Y is less than spending $C + I + G$, then saving $S = Y - C - G$ must be less than investment I. Because the country is investing more than it is saving, it must be financing some domestic investment by selling assets abroad. That is, the net capital outflow must be negative.

A country with balanced trade is between these cases. Exports equal imports, so net exports are zero. Income equals domestic spending, and saving equals investment. The net capital outflow equals zero.

Is the U.S. Trade Deficit a National Problem?

You may have heard the press call the United States "the world's largest debtor." The nation earned that description by borrowing heavily in world financial markets during the past three decades to finance large trade deficits. Why did the United States do this, and should this event give Americans reason to worry?

To answer these questions, let's see what the macroeconomic accounting identities tell us about the U.S. economy. Panel (a) of Figure 2 shows national saving and domestic investment as a percentage of GDP since 1960. Panel (b) shows net capital outflow (that is, the trade balance) as a percentage of GDP. Notice that, as the identities require, net capital outflow always equals national saving minus domestic investment.

The figure shows a dramatic change beginning in the early 1980s. Before 1980, national saving and domestic investment were close, and so net capital outflow was small. Yet after 1980, national saving fell substantially below investment, and net capital outflow became a large negative number. That is, there was a capital inflow: Foreigners were buying more capital assets in the United States than Americans were buying abroad. The United States was going into debt.

History shows that changes in capital flows arise sometimes from changes in saving and sometimes from changes in investment. From 1980 to 1987, the flow of capital into the United States went from 0.5 to 3.1 percent of GDP. This 2.6 percentage point change is largely attributable to a fall in saving of 3.2 percentage points. This decline in national saving, in turn, is often explained by the decline in public saving—that is, the increase in the government budget deficit.

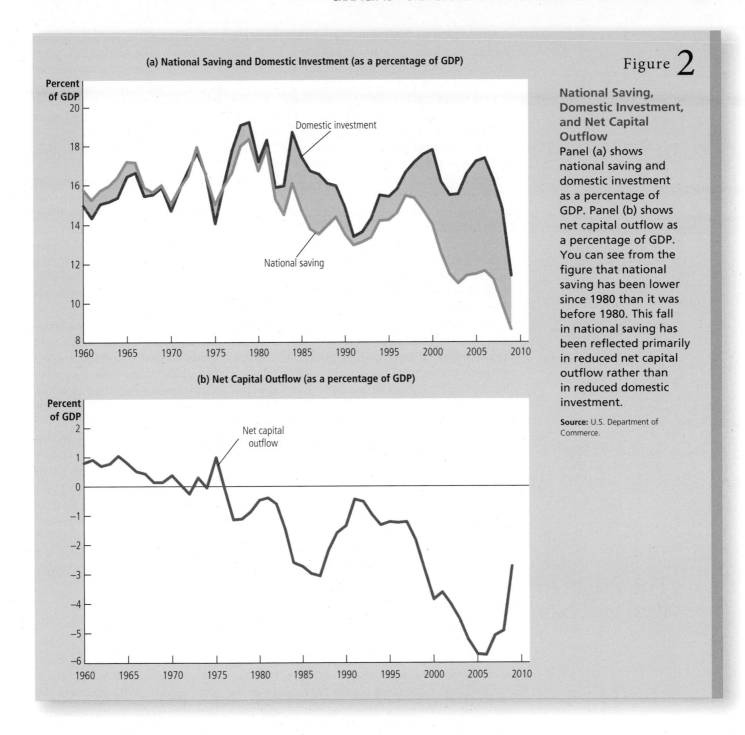

(a) National Saving and Domestic Investment (as a percentage of GDP)

Percent of GDP

Domestic investment

National saving

(b) Net Capital Outflow (as a percentage of GDP)

Percent of GDP

Net capital outflow

Figure **2**

National Saving, Domestic Investment, and Net Capital Outflow
Panel (a) shows national saving and domestic investment as a percentage of GDP. Panel (b) shows net capital outflow as a percentage of GDP. You can see from the figure that national saving has been lower since 1980 than it was before 1980. This fall in national saving has been reflected primarily in reduced net capital outflow rather than in reduced domestic investment.

Source: U.S. Department of Commerce.

A different story explains the events of the following decade. From 1991 to 2000, the capital flow into the United States went from 0.5 to 3.9 percent of GDP. None of this 3.4 percentage point change is attributable to a decline in saving; in fact, saving increased over this time, as the government's budget switched from deficit to surplus. But investment went from 13.4 to 17.7 percent of GDP, as the economy enjoyed a boom in information technology and many firms were eager to make these high-tech investments.

From 2000 to 2006, the capital flow into the United States increased further, reaching a record 5.7 percent of GDP. The investment boom abated after 2000, but once again, the federal government started running budget deficits, and national saving fell to extraordinarily low levels by historical standards.

This trend has reversed somewhat in recent years. From 2007 to 2009, the trade deficit shrank as the economy experienced a substantial decline in housing prices and a deep recession, both of which led to a dramatic fall in investment.

Are these trade deficits a problem for the U.S. economy? To answer this question, it is important to keep an eye on the nation's saving and investment.

Consider first a trade deficit induced by a fall in saving, as occurred during the 1980s and the early 2000s. Lower saving means that the nation is putting away less of its income to provide for its future. Once national saving has fallen, however, there is no reason to deplore the resulting trade deficits. If national saving fell without inducing a trade deficit, investment in the United States would have to fall. This fall in investment, in turn, would adversely affect the growth in the capital stock, labor productivity, and real wages. In other words, given that U.S. saving has declined, it is better to have foreigners invest in the U.S. economy than no one at all.

Now consider a trade deficit induced by an investment boom, such as the trade deficits of the 1990s. In this case, the economy is borrowing from abroad to finance the purchase of new capital goods. If this additional capital provides a good return in the form of higher production of goods and services, then the economy should be able to handle the debts that are being accumulated. On the other hand, if the investment projects fail to yield the expected returns, the debts will look less desirable, at least with the benefit of hindsight.

There is no simple and correct answer to the question posed in the title to this case study. Just as an individual can go into debt in either a prudent or a profligate manner, so can a nation. The trade deficit is not a problem in itself, but sometimes it can be a symptom of a problem. ■

QUICK QUIZ *Define* net exports *and* net capital outflow. *Explain how they are related.*

The Prices for International Transactions: Real and Nominal Exchange Rates

So far, we have discussed measures of the flow of goods and services and the flow of capital across a nation's border. In addition to these quantity variables, macroeconomists also study variables that measure the prices at which these international transactions take place. Just as the price in any market serves the important role of coordinating buyers and sellers in that market, international prices help coordinate the decisions of consumers and producers as they interact in world markets. Here we discuss the two most important international prices: the nominal and real exchange rates.

nominal exchange rate

the rate at which a person can trade the currency of one country for the currency of another

Nominal Exchange Rates

The **nominal exchange rate** is the rate at which a person can trade the currency of one country for the currency of another. For example, if you go to a bank, you might see a posted exchange rate of 80 yen per dollar. If you give the bank one

U.S. dollar, it will give you 80 Japanese yen; and if you give the bank 80 Japanese yen, it will give you one U.S. dollar. (In actuality, the bank will post slightly different prices for buying and selling yen. The difference gives the bank some profit for offering this service. For our purposes here, we can ignore these differences.)

An exchange rate can always be expressed in two ways. If the exchange rate is 80 yen per dollar, it is also $1/80$ (= 0.0125) dollar per yen. Throughout this book, we always express the nominal exchange rate as units of foreign currency per U.S. dollar, such as 80 yen per dollar.

If the exchange rate changes so that a dollar buys more foreign currency, that change is called an **appreciation** of the dollar. If the exchange rate changes so that a dollar buys less foreign currency, that change is called a **depreciation** of the dollar.

appreciation

an increase in the value of a currency as measured by the amount of foreign currency it can buy

depreciation

a decrease in the value of a currency as measured by the amount of foreign currency it can buy

FYI

The Euro

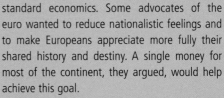

You may have once heard of, or perhaps even seen, currencies such as the French franc, the German mark, or the Italian lira. These types of money no longer exist. During the 1990s, many European nations decided to give up their national currencies and use a common currency called the *euro*. The euro started circulating on January 1, 2002. Monetary policy for the euro area is now set by the European Central Bank (ECB), with representatives from all of the participating countries. The ECB issues the euro and controls the supply of this money, much as the Federal Reserve controls the supply of dollars in the U.S. economy.

Why did these countries adopt a common currency? One benefit of a common currency is that it makes trade easier. Imagine that each of the fifty U.S. states had a different currency. Every time you crossed a state border, you would need to change your money and perform the kind of exchange-rate calculations discussed in the text. This would be inconvenient, and it might deter you from buying goods and services outside your own state. The countries of Europe decided that as their economies became more integrated, it would be better to avoid this inconvenience.

To some extent, the adoption of a common currency in Europe was a political decision based on concerns beyond the scope of

standard economics. Some advocates of the euro wanted to reduce nationalistic feelings and to make Europeans appreciate more fully their shared history and destiny. A single money for most of the continent, they argued, would help achieve this goal.

There are, however, costs of choosing a common currency. If the nations of Europe have only one money, they can have only one monetary policy. If they disagree about what monetary policy is best, they will have to reach some kind of agreement, rather than each going its own way. Because adopting a single money has both benefits and costs, there is debate among economists about whether Europe's adoption of the euro was a good decision.

In 2010, the euro question heated up as several European nations dealt with a variety of economic difficulties. Greece, in particular, had run up a large government debt and found itself facing possible default. As a result, it had to raise taxes and cut back government spending substantially. Some observers suggested that dealing with these problems would have been easier if the government had an additional tool—a national monetary policy. The possibility of Greece's leaving the euro area and reintroducing its own currency was even discussed. As this book was going to press, however, that outcome looked unlikely.

For example, when the exchange rate rises from 80 to 90 yen per dollar, the dollar is said to appreciate. At the same time, because a Japanese yen now buys less of the U.S. currency, the yen is said to depreciate. When the exchange rate falls from 80 to 70 yen per dollar, the dollar is said to depreciate, and the yen is said to appreciate.

At times, you may have heard the media report that the dollar is either "strong" or "weak." These descriptions usually refer to recent changes in the nominal exchange rate. When a currency appreciates, it is said to *strengthen* because it can then buy more foreign currency. Similarly, when a currency depreciates, it is said to *weaken*.

For any country, there are many nominal exchange rates. The U.S. dollar can be used to buy Japanese yen, British pounds, Mexican pesos, and so on. When economists study changes in the exchange rate, they often use indexes that average these many exchange rates. Just as the consumer price index turns the many prices in the economy into a single measure of the price level, an exchange rate index turns these many exchange rates into a single measure of the international value of a currency. So when economists talk about the dollar appreciating or depreciating, they often are referring to an exchange rate index that takes into account many individual exchange rates.

Real Exchange Rates

real exchange rate

the rate at which a person can trade the goods and services of one country for the goods and services of another

The **real exchange rate** is the rate at which a person can trade the goods and services of one country for the goods and services of another. For example, if you go shopping and find that a pound of Swiss cheese is twice as expensive as a pound of American cheese, the real exchange rate is ½ pound of Swiss cheese per pound of American cheese. Notice that, like the nominal exchange rate, we express the real exchange rate as units of the foreign item per unit of the domestic item. But in this instance, the item is a good rather than a currency.

Real and nominal exchange rates are closely related. To see how, consider an example. Suppose that a bushel of American rice sells for $100, and a bushel of Japanese rice sells for 16,000 yen. What is the real exchange rate between American and Japanese rice? To answer this question, we must first use the nominal exchange rate to convert the prices into a common currency. If the nominal exchange rate is 80 yen per dollar, then a price for American rice of $100 per bushel is equivalent to 8,000 yen per bushel. American rice is half as expensive as Japanese rice. The real exchange rate is ½ bushel of Japanese rice per bushel of American rice.

We can summarize this calculation for the real exchange rate with the following formula:

$$\text{Real exchange rate} = \frac{\text{Nominal exchange rate} \times \text{Domestic price}}{\text{Foreign price}}.$$

Using the numbers in our example, the formula applies as follows:

$$\text{Real exchange rate} = \frac{(80 \text{ yen/dollar}) \times (\$100/\text{bushel of American rice})}{16{,}000 \text{ yen/bushel of Japanese rice}}$$

$$= \frac{8000 \text{ yen/bushel of American rice}}{16{,}000 \text{ yen/bushel of Japanese rice}}$$

$$= \text{½ bushel of Japanese rice/bushel of American rice.}$$

Thus, the real exchange rate depends on the nominal exchange rate and on the prices of goods in the two countries measured in the local currencies.

Why does the real exchange rate matter? As you might guess, the real exchange rate is a key determinant of how much a country exports and imports. When Uncle Ben's, Inc., is deciding whether to buy U.S. rice or Japanese rice to put into its boxes, for example, it will ask which rice is cheaper. The real exchange rate gives the answer. As another example, imagine that you are deciding whether to take a seaside vacation in Miami, Florida, or in Cancún, Mexico. You might ask your travel agent the price of a hotel room in Miami (measured in dollars), the price of a hotel room in Cancún (measured in pesos), and the exchange rate between pesos and dollars. If you decide where to vacation by comparing costs, you are basing your decision on the real exchange rate.

When studying an economy as a whole, macroeconomists focus on overall prices rather than the prices of individual items. That is, to measure the real exchange rate, they use price indexes, such as the consumer price index, which measure the price of a basket of goods and services. By using a price index for a U.S. basket (P), a price index for a foreign basket (P^*), and the nominal exchange rate between the U.S. dollar and foreign currencies (e), we can compute the overall real exchange rate between the United States and other countries as follows:

$$\text{Real exchange rate} = (e \times P)/P^*.$$

This real exchange rate measures the price of a basket of goods and services available domestically relative to a basket of goods and services available abroad.

As we examine more fully in the next chapter, a country's real exchange rate is a key determinant of its net exports of goods and services. A depreciation (fall) in the U.S. real exchange rate means that U.S. goods have become cheaper relative to foreign goods. This change encourages consumers both at home and abroad to buy more U.S. goods and fewer goods from other countries. As a result, U.S. exports rise, and U.S. imports fall; both of these changes raise U.S. net exports. Conversely, an appreciation (rise) in the U.S. real exchange rate means that U.S. goods have become more expensive compared to foreign goods, so U.S. net exports fall.

QUICK QUIZ *Define nominal exchange rate and real exchange rate, and explain how they are related. • If the nominal exchange rate goes from 100 to 120 yen per dollar, has the dollar appreciated or depreciated?*

A First Theory of Exchange-Rate Determination: Purchasing-Power Parity

Exchange rates vary substantially over time. In 1970, a U.S. dollar could be used to buy 3.65 German marks or 627 Italian lira. In 1998, as both Germany and Italy were getting ready to adopt the euro as their common currency, a U.S. dollar bought 1.76 German marks or 1,737 Italian lira. In other words, over this period, the value of the dollar fell by more than half compared to the mark, while it more than doubled compared to the lira.

What explains these large and opposite changes? Economists have developed many models to explain how exchange rates are determined, each emphasizing just some of the many forces at work. Here we develop the simplest theory of

purchasing-power parity

a theory of exchange rates whereby a unit of any given currency should be able to buy the same quantity of goods in all countries

exchange rates, called **purchasing-power parity**. This theory states that a unit of any given currency should be able to buy the same quantity of goods in all countries. Many economists believe that purchasing-power parity describes the forces that determine exchange rates in the long run. We now consider the logic on which this long-run theory of exchange rates is based, as well as the theory's implications and limitations.

The Basic Logic of Purchasing-Power Parity

The theory of purchasing-power parity is based on a principle called the *law of one price*. This law asserts that a good must sell for the same price in all locations. Otherwise, there would be opportunities for profit left unexploited. For example, suppose that coffee beans sold for less in Seattle than in Boston. A person could buy coffee in Seattle for, say, $4 a pound and then sell it in Boston for $5 a pound, making a profit of $1 per pound from the difference in price. The process of taking advantage of price differences for the same item in different markets is called *arbitrage*. In our example, as people took advantage of this arbitrage opportunity, they would increase the demand for coffee in Seattle and increase the supply in Boston. The price of coffee would rise in Seattle (in response to greater demand) and fall in Boston (in response to greater supply). This process would continue until, eventually, the prices were the same in the two markets.

Now consider how the law of one price applies to the international marketplace. If a dollar (or any other currency) could buy more coffee in the United States than in Japan, international traders could profit by buying coffee in the United States and selling it in Japan. This export of coffee from the United States to Japan would drive up the U.S. price of coffee and drive down the Japanese price. Conversely, if a dollar could buy more coffee in Japan than in the United States, traders could buy coffee in Japan and sell it in the United States. This import of coffee into the United States from Japan would drive down the U.S. price of coffee and drive up the Japanese price. In the end, the law of one price tells us that a dollar must buy the same amount of coffee in all countries.

This logic leads us to the theory of purchasing-power parity. According to this theory, a currency must have the same purchasing power in all countries. That is, a U.S. dollar must buy the same quantity of goods in the United States and Japan, and a Japanese yen must buy the same quantity of goods in Japan and the United States. Indeed, the name of this theory describes it well. *Parity* means equality, and *purchasing power* refers to the value of money in terms of the quantity of goods it can buy. *Purchasing-power parity* states that a unit of a currency must have the same real value in every country.

Implications of Purchasing-Power Parity

What does the theory of purchasing-power parity say about exchange rates? It tells us that the nominal exchange rate between the currencies of two countries depends on the price levels in those countries. If a dollar buys the same quantity of goods in the United States (where prices are measured in dollars) as in Japan (where prices are measured in yen), then the number of yen per dollar must reflect the prices of goods in the United States and Japan. For example, if a pound of coffee costs 500 yen in Japan and $5 in the United States, then the nominal exchange rate must be 100 yen per dollar (500 yen/$5 = 100 yen per dollar). Otherwise, the purchasing power of the dollar would not be the same in the two countries.

To see more fully how this works, it is helpful to use just a bit of mathematics. Suppose that P is the price of a basket of goods in the United States (measured in dollars), P^* is the price of a basket of goods in Japan (measured in yen), and e is the nominal exchange rate (the number of yen a dollar can buy). Now consider the quantity of goods a dollar can buy at home and abroad. At home, the price level is P, so the purchasing power of $1 at home is $1/P$. That is, a dollar can buy $1/P$ quantity of goods. Abroad, a dollar can be exchanged into e units of foreign currency, which in turn have purchasing power e/P^*. For the purchasing power of a dollar to be the same in the two countries, it must be the case that

$$1/P = e/P^*.$$

With rearrangement, this equation becomes

$$1 = eP/P^*.$$

Notice that the left side of this equation is a constant, and the right side is the real exchange rate. Thus, *if the purchasing power of the dollar is always the same at home and abroad, then the real exchange rate—the relative price of domestic and foreign goods—cannot change.*

To see the implication of this analysis for the nominal exchange rate, we can rearrange the last equation to solve for the nominal exchange rate:

$$e = P^*/P.$$

That is, the nominal exchange rate equals the ratio of the foreign price level (measured in units of the foreign currency) to the domestic price level (measured in units of the domestic currency). *According to the theory of purchasing-power parity, the nominal exchange rate between the currencies of two countries must reflect the price levels in those countries.*

A key implication of this theory is that nominal exchange rates change when price levels change. As we saw in the preceding chapter, the price level in any country adjusts to bring the quantity of money supplied and the quantity of money demanded into balance. Because the nominal exchange rate depends on the price levels, it also depends on the money supply and money demand in each country. When a central bank in any country increases the money supply and causes the price level to rise, it also causes that country's currency to depreciate relative to other currencies in the world. In other words, *when the central bank prints large quantities of money, that money loses value both in terms of the goods and services it can buy and in terms of the amount of other currencies it can buy.*

We can now answer the question that began this section: Why did the U.S. dollar lose value compared to the German mark and gain value compared to the Italian lira? The answer is that Germany pursued a less inflationary monetary policy than the United States, and Italy pursued a more inflationary monetary policy. From 1970 to 1998, inflation in the United States was 5.3 percent per year. By contrast, inflation was 3.5 percent in Germany and 9.6 percent in Italy. As U.S. prices rose relative to German prices, the value of the dollar fell relative to the mark. Similarly, as U.S. prices fell relative to Italian prices, the value of the dollar rose relative to the lira.

Germany and Italy now have a common currency—the euro. This means that the two countries share a single monetary policy and that the inflation rates in the two countries will be closely linked. But the historical lessons of the lira and the mark will apply to the euro as well. Whether the U.S. dollar buys more or fewer euros twenty years from now than it does today depends on whether the European Central Bank produces more or less inflation in Europe than the Federal Reserve does in the United States.

CASE STUDY   The Nominal Exchange Rate during a Hyperinflation

Macroeconomists can only rarely conduct controlled experiments. Most often, they must glean what they can from the natural experiments that history gives them. One natural experiment is hyperinflation—the high inflation that arises when a government turns to the printing press to pay for large amounts of government spending. Because hyperinflations are so extreme, they illustrate some basic economic principles with clarity.

Consider the German hyperinflation of the early 1920s. Figure 3 shows the German money supply, the German price level, and the nominal exchange rate (measured as U.S. cents per German mark) for that period. Notice that these series move closely together. When the supply of money starts growing quickly, the price level also takes off, and the German mark depreciates. When the money supply stabilizes, so do the price level and the exchange rate.

The pattern shown in this figure appears during every hyperinflation. It leaves no doubt that there is a fundamental link among money, prices, and the nominal

---

Figure **3**

Money, Prices, and the Nominal Exchange Rate during the German Hyperinflation

This figure shows the money supply, the price level, and the nominal exchange rate (measured as U.S. cents per mark) for the German hyperinflation from January 1921 to December 1924. Notice how similarly these three variables move. When the quantity of money started growing quickly, the price level followed, and the mark depreciated relative to the dollar. When the German central bank stabilized the money supply, the price level and exchange rate stabilized as well.

Source: Adapted from Thomas J. Sargent, "The End of Four Big Inflations," in Robert Hall, ed., *Inflation* (Chicago: University of Chicago Press, 1983), pp. 41–93.

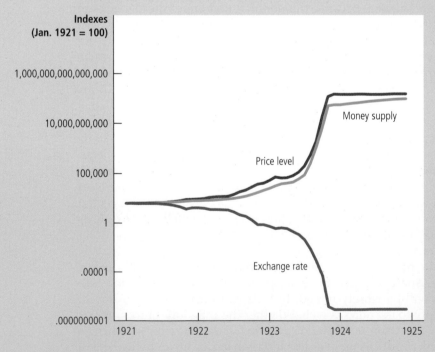

exchange rate. The quantity theory of money discussed in the previous chapter explains how the money supply affects the price level. The theory of purchasing-power parity discussed here explains how the price level affects the nominal exchange rate. ■

Limitations of Purchasing-Power Parity

Purchasing-power parity provides a simple model of how exchange rates are determined. For understanding many economic phenomena, the theory works well. In particular, it can explain many long-term trends, such as the depreciation of the U.S. dollar against the German mark and the appreciation of the U.S. dollar against the Italian lira. It can also explain the major changes in exchange rates that occur during hyperinflations.

Yet the theory of purchasing-power parity is not completely accurate. That is, exchange rates do not always move to ensure that a dollar has the same real value in all countries all the time. There are two reasons the theory of purchasing-power parity does not always hold in practice.

The first reason is that many goods are not easily traded. Imagine, for instance, that haircuts are more expensive in Paris than in New York. International travelers might avoid getting their haircuts in Paris, and some haircutters might move from New York to Paris. Yet such arbitrage would be too limited to eliminate the differences in prices. Thus, the deviation from purchasing-power parity might persist, and a dollar (or euro) would continue to buy less of a haircut in Paris than in New York.

The second reason that purchasing-power parity does not always hold is that even tradable goods are not always perfect substitutes when they are produced in different countries. For example, some consumers prefer German cars, and others prefer American cars. Moreover, consumer tastes can change over time. If German cars suddenly become more popular, the increase in demand will drive up the price of German cars compared to American cars. Despite this difference in prices in the two markets, there might be no opportunity for profitable arbitrage because consumers do not view the two cars as equivalent.

Thus, both because some goods are not tradable and because some tradable goods are not perfect substitutes with their foreign counterparts, purchasing-power parity is not a perfect theory of exchange-rate determination. For these reasons, real exchange rates fluctuate over time. Nonetheless, the theory of purchasing-power parity does provide a useful first step in understanding exchange rates. The basic logic is persuasive: As the real exchange rate drifts from the level predicted by purchasing-power parity, people have greater incentive to move goods across national borders. Even if the forces of purchasing-power parity do not completely fix the real exchange rate, they provide a reason to expect that changes in the real exchange rate are most often small or temporary. As a result, large and persistent movements in nominal exchange rates typically reflect changes in price levels at home and abroad.

 CASE STUDY   The Hamburger Standard

When economists apply the theory of purchasing-power parity to explain exchange rates, they need data on the prices of a basket of goods available in different countries. One analysis of this sort is conducted by *The Economist*, an

You can find a Big Mac almost anywhere you look.

international newsmagazine. The magazine occasionally collects data on a basket of goods consisting of "two all-beef patties, special sauce, lettuce, cheese, pickles, onions, on a sesame seed bun." It's called the "Big Mac" and is sold by McDonald's around the world.

Once we have the prices of Big Macs in two countries denominated in the local currencies, we can compute the exchange rate predicted by the theory of purchasing-power parity. The predicted exchange rate is the one that makes the cost of the Big Mac the same in the two countries. For instance, if the price of a Big Mac is $3 in the United States and 300 yen in Japan, purchasing-power parity would predict an exchange rate of 100 yen per dollar.

How well does purchasing-power parity work when applied using Big Mac prices? Here are some examples from July 2009, when the price of a Big Mac was $3.57 in the United States:

Country	Price of a Big Mac	Predicted Exchange Rate	Actual Exchange Rate
Indonesia	20,900 rupiah	5,854 rupiah/$	10,200 rupiah/$
South Korea	3,400 won	952 won/$	1315 won/$
Japan	320 yen	89.6 yen/$	92.6 yen/$
Sweden	39 krona	10.9 krona/$	7.9 krona/$
Mexico	33 pesos	9.2 pesos/$	13.8 pesos/$
Euro area	3.31 euros	0.93 euros/$	0.72 euros/$
Britain	2.29 pounds	0.64 pound/$	0.62 pound/$

You can see that the predicted and actual exchange rates are not exactly the same. After all, international arbitrage in Big Macs is not easy. Yet the two exchange rates are usually in the same ballpark. Purchasing-power parity is not a precise theory of exchange rates, but it often provides a reasonable first approximation. ■

QUICK QUIZ   *Over the past twenty years, Mexico has had high inflation, and Japan has had low inflation. What do you predict has happened to the number of Mexican pesos a person can buy with a Japanese yen?*

Conclusion

The purpose of this chapter has been to develop some basic concepts that macroeconomists use to study open economies. You should now understand how a nation's trade balance is related to the international flow of capital and how national saving can differ from domestic investment in an open economy. You should understand that when a nation is running a trade surplus, it must be sending capital abroad, and that when it is running a trade deficit, it must be experiencing a capital inflow. You should also understand the meaning of the nominal and real exchange rates, as well as the implications and limitations of purchasing-power parity as a theory of how exchange rates are determined.

The macroeconomic variables defined here offer a starting point for analyzing an open economy's interactions with the rest of the world. In the next chapter, we develop a model that can explain what determines these variables. We can then discuss how various events and policies affect a country's trade balance and the rate at which nations make exchanges in world markets.

SUMMARY

- Net exports are the value of domestic goods and services sold abroad (exports) minus the value of foreign goods and services sold domestically (imports). Net capital outflow is the acquisition of foreign assets by domestic residents (capital outflow) minus the acquisition of domestic assets by foreigners (capital inflow). Because every international transaction involves an exchange of an asset for a good or service, an economy's net capital outflow always equals its net exports.

- An economy's saving can be used either to finance investment at home or to buy assets abroad. Thus, national saving equals domestic investment plus net capital outflow.

- The nominal exchange rate is the relative price of the currency of two countries, and the real exchange rate is the relative price of the goods and services of two countries. When the nominal exchange rate changes so that each dollar buys more foreign currency, the dollar is said to *appreciate* or *strengthen*. When the nominal exchange rate changes so that each dollar buys less foreign currency, the dollar is said to *depreciate* or *weaken*.

- According to the theory of purchasing-power parity, a dollar (or a unit of any other currency) should be able to buy the same quantity of goods in all countries. This theory implies that the nominal exchange rate between the currencies of two countries should reflect the price levels in those countries. As a result, countries with relatively high inflation should have depreciating currencies, and countries with relatively low inflation should have appreciating currencies.

KEY CONCEPTS

closed economy, *p. 272*
open economy, *p. 272*
exports, *p. 272*
imports, *p. 272*
net exports, *p. 272*

trade balance, *p. 272*
trade surplus, *p. 272*
trade deficit, *p. 273*
balanced trade, *p. 273*
net capital outflow, *p. 276*

nominal exchange rate, *p. 282*
appreciation, *p. 283*
depreciation, *p. 283*
real exchange rate, *p. 284*
purchasing-power parity, *p. 286*

QUESTIONS FOR REVIEW

1. Define *net exports* and *net capital outflow*. Explain how and why they are related.
2. Explain the relationship among saving, investment, and net capital outflow.
3. If a Japanese car costs 500,000 yen, a similar American car costs $10,000, and a dollar can buy 100 yen, what are the nominal and real exchange rates?
4. Describe the economic logic behind the theory of purchasing-power parity.
5. If the Fed started printing large quantities of U.S. dollars, what would happen to the number of Japanese yen a dollar could buy? Why?

PROBLEMS AND APPLICATIONS

1. How would the following transactions affect U.S. exports, imports, and net exports?
   a. An American art professor spends the summer touring museums in Europe.
   b. Students in Paris flock to see the latest movie from Hollywood.
   c. Your uncle buys a new Volvo.
   d. The student bookstore at Oxford University in England sells a pair of Levi's 501 jeans.
   e. A Canadian citizen shops at a store in northern Vermont to avoid Canadian sales taxes.

2. Would each of the following transactions be included in net exports or net capital outflow? Be sure to say whether it would represent an increase or a decrease in that variable.
   a. An American buys a Sony TV.
   b. An American buys a share of Sony stock.
   c. The Sony pension fund buys a bond from the U.S. Treasury.
   d. A worker at a Sony plant in Japan buys some Georgia peaches from an American farmer.

3. Describe the difference between foreign direct investment and foreign portfolio investment. Who is more likely to engage in foreign direct investment—a corporation or an individual investor? Who is more likely to engage in foreign portfolio investment?

4. How would the following transactions affect U.S. net capital outflow? Also, state whether each involves direct investment or portfolio investment.
   a. An American cellular phone company establishes an office in the Czech Republic.
   b. Harrods of London sells stock to the General Electric pension fund.
   c. Honda expands its factory in Marysville, Ohio.
   d. A Fidelity mutual fund sells its Volkswagen stock to a French investor.

5. The business section of most major newspapers contains a table showing U.S. exchange rates. Find such a table in a paper or online and use it to answer the following questions.
   a. Does this table show nominal or real exchange rates? Explain.
   b. What are the exchange rates between the United States and Canada and between the United States and Japan? Calculate the exchange rate between Canada and Japan.
   c. If U.S. inflation exceeds Japanese inflation over the next year, would you expect the U.S. dollar to appreciate or depreciate relative to the Japanese yen?

6. Would each of the following groups be happy or unhappy if the U.S. dollar appreciated? Explain.
   a. Dutch pension funds holding U.S. government bonds
   b. U.S. manufacturing industries
   c. Australian tourists planning a trip to the United States
   d. An American firm trying to purchase property overseas

7. What is happening to the U.S. real exchange rate in each of the following situations? Explain.
   a. The U.S. nominal exchange rate is unchanged, but prices rise faster in the United States than abroad.
   b. The U.S. nominal exchange rate is unchanged, but prices rise faster abroad than in the United States.
   c. The U.S. nominal exchange rate declines, and prices are unchanged in the United States and abroad.
   d. The U.S. nominal exchange rate declines, and prices rise faster abroad than in the United States.

8. A can of soda costs $0.75 in the United States and 12 pesos in Mexico. What would the peso-dollar exchange rate be if purchasing-power parity holds? If a monetary expansion caused all prices in Mexico to double, so that soda rose to 24 pesos, what would happen to the peso-dollar exchange rate?

9. Assume that American rice sells for $100 per bushel, Japanese rice sells for 16,000 yen per bushel, and the nominal exchange rate is 80 yen per dollar.
   a. Explain how you could make a profit from this situation. What would be your profit per bushel of rice? If other people exploit the same opportunity, what would happen to the price of rice in Japan and the price of rice in the United States?
   b. Suppose that rice is the only commodity in the world. What would happen to the real exchange rate between the United States and Japan?

10. A case study in the chapter analyzed purchasing-power parity for several countries using the price of Big Macs. Here are data for a few more countries:

Country	Price of a Big Mac	Predicted Exchange Rate	Actual Exchange Rate
Chile	1,750 pesos	_____ pesos/$	549 pesos/$
Hungary	720 forints	_____ forints/$	199 forints/$
Czech Republic	67.9 korunas	_____ korunas/$	18.7 korunas/$
Brazil	8.03 real	_____ real/$	2.00 real/$
Canada	3.89 C$	_____ C$/$	1.16 C$/$

   a. For each country, compute the predicted exchange rate of the local currency per U.S. dollar. (Recall that the U.S. price of a Big Mac was $3.57.)

b. According to purchasing-power parity, what is the predicted exchange rate between the Hungarian forint and the Canadian dollar? What is the actual exchange rate?

c. How well does the theory of purchasing-power parity explain exchange rates?

11. Purchasing-power parity holds between the nations of Ectenia and Wiknam, where the only commodity is Spam.

a. In 2000 a can of Spam costs 2 dollars in Ectenia and 6 pesos in Wiknam. What is the exchange rate between Ectenian dollars and Wiknamian pesos?

b. Over the next 20 years, inflation is 3.5 percent per year in Ectenia and 7 percent per year in Wiknam. What will happen over this period to the price of Spam and the exchange rate? (Hint: Recall the rule of 70 from Chapter 9.)

c. Which of these two nations will likely have a higher nominal interest rate? Why?

d. A friend of yours suggests a get-rich-quick scheme: Borrow from the nation with the lower nominal interest rate, invest in the nation with the higher nominal interest rate, and profit from the interest-rate differential. Do you see any potential problems with this idea? Explain.

For further information on topics in this chapter, additional problems, applications, examples, online quizzes, and more, please visit our website at www .cengage.com/economics/mankiw.

A Macroeconomic Theory of the Open Economy

14

Over the past three decades, the United States has persistently imported more goods and services than it has exported. That is, U.S. net exports have been negative. While economists debate whether these trade deficits are a problem for the U.S. economy, the nation's business community often has a strong opinion. Many business leaders claim that the trade deficits reflect unfair competition: Foreign firms are allowed to sell their products in U.S. markets, they contend, while foreign governments impede U.S. firms from selling U.S. products abroad.

Imagine that you are the president and you want to end these trade deficits. What should you do? Should you try to limit imports, perhaps by imposing a quota on textiles from China or cars from Japan? Or should you try to influence the nation's trade deficit in some other way?

To understand the factors that determine a country's trade balance and how government policies can affect it, we need a macroeconomic theory that explains how an open economy works. The preceding chapter introduced some of the key macroeconomic variables that describe an economy's relationship with other economies, including net exports, net capital outflow, and the real and nominal exchange rates. This chapter develops a model that identifies the forces that determine these variables and shows how these variables are related to one another.

To develop this macroeconomic model of an open economy, we build on our previous analysis in two ways. First, the model takes the economy's GDP as given. We assume that the economy's output of goods and services, as measured by real GDP, is determined by the supplies of the factors of production and by the available production technology that turns these inputs into output. Second, the model takes the economy's price level as given. We assume that the price level adjusts to bring the supply and demand for money into balance. In other words, this chapter takes as a starting point the lessons learned in previous chapters about the determination of the economy's output and price level.

The goal of the model in this chapter is to highlight the forces that determine the economy's trade balance and exchange rate. In one sense, the model is simple: It applies the tools of supply and demand to an open economy. Yet the model is also more complicated than others we have seen because it involves looking simultaneously at two related markets: the market for loanable funds and the market for foreign-currency exchange. After we develop this model of the open economy, we use it to examine how various events and policies affect the economy's trade balance and exchange rate. We will then be able to determine the government policies that are most likely to reverse the trade deficits that the U.S. economy has experienced over the past three decades.

Supply and Demand for Loanable Funds and for Foreign-Currency Exchange

To understand the forces at work in an open economy, we focus on supply and demand in two markets. The first is the market for loanable funds, which coordinates the economy's saving, investment, and flow of loanable funds abroad (called the net capital outflow). The second is the market for foreign-currency exchange, which coordinates people who want to exchange the domestic currency for the currency of other countries. In this section, we discuss supply and demand in each of these markets. In the next section, we put these markets together to explain the overall equilibrium for an open economy.

The Market for Loanable Funds

When we first analyzed the role of the financial system in Chapter 8, we made the simplifying assumption that the financial system consists of only one market, called the *market for loanable funds*. All savers go to this market to deposit their saving, and all borrowers go to this market to get their loans. In this market, there is one interest rate, which is both the return to saving and the cost of borrowing.

To understand the market for loanable funds in an open economy, the place to start is the identity discussed in the preceding chapter:

$$S = I + NCO$$

$$\text{Saving} = \frac{\text{Domestic}}{\text{investment}} + \frac{\text{Net capital}}{\text{outflow}}.$$

Whenever a nation saves a dollar of its income, it can use that dollar to finance the purchase of domestic capital or to finance the purchase of an asset abroad. The two sides of this identity represent the two sides of the market for loanable funds. The supply of loanable funds comes from national saving (S), and the demand for loanable funds comes from domestic investment (I) and net capital outflow (NCO).

Loanable funds should be interpreted as the domestically generated flow of resources available for capital accumulation. The purchase of a capital asset adds to the demand for loanable funds, regardless of whether that asset is located at home (I) or abroad (NCO). Because net capital outflow can be either positive or negative, it can either add to or subtract from the demand for loanable funds that arises from domestic investment. When NCO > 0, the country is experiencing a net outflow of capital; the net purchase of capital overseas adds to the demand for domestically generated loanable funds. When NCO < 0, the country is experiencing a net inflow of capital; the capital resources coming from abroad reduce the demand for domestically generated loanable funds.

As we learned in our earlier discussion of the market for loanable funds, the quantity of loanable funds supplied and the quantity of loanable funds demanded depend on the real interest rate. A higher real interest rate encourages people to save and, therefore, raises the quantity of loanable funds supplied. A higher interest rate also makes borrowing to finance capital projects more costly; thus, it discourages investment and reduces the quantity of loanable funds demanded.

In addition to influencing national saving and domestic investment, the real interest rate in a country affects that country's net capital outflow. To see why, consider two mutual funds—one in the United States and one in Germany—deciding whether to buy a U.S. government bond or a German government bond. The mutual fund manager would make this decision in part by comparing the real interest rates in the United States and Germany. When the U.S. real interest rate rises, the U.S. bond becomes more attractive to both mutual funds. Thus, an increase in the U.S. real interest rate discourages Americans from buying foreign assets and encourages foreigners to buy U.S. assets. For both reasons, a high U.S. real interest rate reduces U.S. net capital outflow.

We represent the market for loanable funds on the familiar supply-and-demand diagram in Figure 1. As in our earlier analysis of the financial system, the supply curve slopes upward because a higher interest rate increases the quantity of loanable funds supplied, and the demand curve slopes downward because a higher interest rate decreases the quantity of loanable funds demanded. Unlike the situation in our previous discussion, however, the demand side of the market now represents the behavior of both domestic investment and net capital outflow. That is, in an open economy, the demand for loanable funds comes not only from those who want loanable funds to buy domestic capital goods but also from those who want loanable funds to buy foreign assets.

The interest rate adjusts to bring the supply and demand for loanable funds into balance. If the interest rate were below the equilibrium level, the quantity of loanable funds supplied would be less than the quantity demanded. The resulting

Our third and final step is to compare the old and new equilibria. Panel (a) shows the impact of a U.S. budget deficit on the U.S. market for loanable funds. With fewer funds available for borrowers in U.S. financial markets, the interest rate rises from r_1 to r_2 to balance supply and demand. Faced with a higher interest rate, borrowers in the market for loanable funds choose to borrow less. This change is represented in the figure as the movement from point A to point B along the demand curve for loanable funds. In particular, households and firms reduce their purchases of capital goods. As in a closed economy, budget deficits crowd out domestic investment.

In an open economy, however, the reduced supply of loanable funds has additional effects. Panel (b) shows that the increase in the interest rate from r_1 to r_2 reduces net capital outflow. [This fall in net capital outflow is also part of the decrease in the quantity of loanable funds demanded in the movement from point A to point B in panel (a).] Because saving kept at home now earns higher rates of return, investing abroad is less attractive, and domestic residents buy fewer foreign assets. Higher interest rates also attract foreign investors, who want to earn the higher returns on U.S. assets. Thus, when budget deficits raise interest rates, both domestic and foreign behavior cause U.S. net capital outflow to fall.

Panel (c) shows how budget deficits affect the market for foreign-currency exchange. Because net capital outflow is reduced, people need less foreign currency to buy foreign assets and, therefore, supply fewer dollars in the market for foreign-currency exchange. The supply curve for dollars shifts leftward from S_1 to S_2. The reduced supply of dollars causes the real exchange rate to appreciate from E_1 to E_2. That is, the dollar becomes more valuable compared to foreign currencies. This appreciation, in turn, makes U.S. goods more expensive compared to foreign goods. Because people both at home and abroad switch their purchases away from the more expensive U.S. goods, exports from the United States fall, and imports into the United States rise. For both reasons, U.S. net exports fall. Hence, *in an open economy, government budget deficits raise real interest rates, crowd out domestic investment, cause the currency to appreciate, and push the trade balance toward deficit.*

An important example of this lesson occurred in the United States in the 1980s. Shortly after Ronald Reagan was elected president in 1980, the fiscal policy of the U.S. federal government changed dramatically. The president and Congress enacted large cuts in taxes, but they did not cut government spending by nearly as much, so the result was a large budget deficit. Our model of the open economy predicts that such a policy should lead to a trade deficit, and in fact it did, as we saw in a case study in the preceding chapter. Because the budget deficit and trade deficit during this period were so closely related in both theory and practice, they were nicknamed the *twin deficits*. We should not, however, view these twins as identical, for many factors beyond fiscal policy can influence the trade deficit.

Trade Policy

trade policy
a government policy that directly influences the quantity of goods and services that a country imports or exports

A **trade policy** is a government policy that directly influences the quantity of goods and services that a country imports or exports. Trade policy takes various forms, usually with the purpose of supporting a particular domestic industry. One common trade policy is a *tariff*, a tax on imported goods. Another is an *import quota*, a limit on the quantity of a good produced abroad that can be sold domestically. Trade policies are common throughout the world, although sometimes they are disguised. For example, the U.S. government has sometimes pressured Japanese automakers to reduce the number of cars they sell in the United States. These so-called voluntary export restrictions are not really voluntary and, in essence, are a form of import quota.

Let's consider the macroeconomic impact of trade policy. Suppose that the U.S. auto industry, concerned about competition from Japanese automakers, convinces the U.S. government to impose a quota on the number of cars that can be imported from Japan. In making their case, lobbyists for the auto industry assert that the trade restriction would shrink the size of the U.S. trade deficit. Are they right? Our model, as illustrated in Figure 6, offers an answer.

The first step in analyzing the trade policy is to determine which curve shifts. The initial impact of the import restriction is, not surprisingly, on imports. Because

When the U.S. government imposes a quota on the import of Japanese cars, nothing happens in the market for loanable funds in panel (a) or to net capital outflow in panel (b). The only effect is a rise in net exports (exports minus imports) for any given real exchange rate. As a result, the demand for dollars in the market for foreign-currency exchange rises, as shown by the shift from D_1 to D_2 in panel (c). This increase in the demand for dollars causes the value of the dollar to appreciate from E_1 to E_2. This appreciation of the dollar tends to reduce net exports, offsetting the direct effect of the import quota on the trade balance.

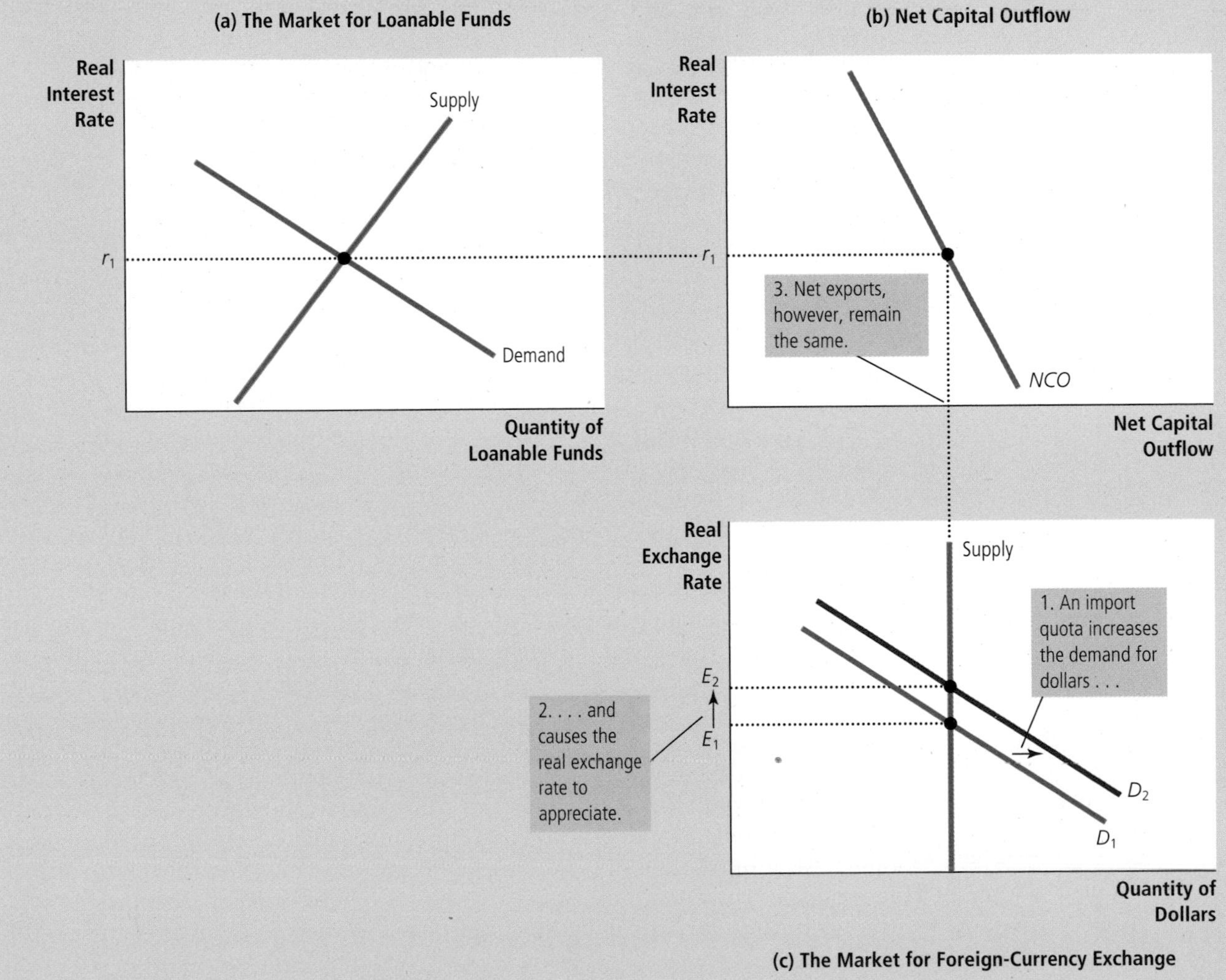

Figure 6

The Effects of an Import Quota

net exports equal exports minus imports, the policy also affects net exports. And because net exports are the source of demand for dollars in the market for foreign-currency exchange, the policy affects the demand curve in this market.

The second step is to determine which way this demand curve shifts. Because the quota restricts the number of Japanese cars sold in the United States, it reduces imports at any given real exchange rate. Net exports, which equal exports minus imports, will therefore *rise* for any given real exchange rate. Because foreigners need dollars to buy U.S. net exports, there is an increased demand for dollars in the market for foreign-currency exchange. This increase in the demand for dollars is shown in panel (c) of Figure 6 as the shift from D_1 to D_2.

The third step is to compare the old and new equilibria. As we can see in panel (c), the increase in the demand for dollars causes the real exchange rate to appreciate from E_1 to E_2. Because nothing has happened in the market for loanable funds in panel (a), there is no change in the real interest rate. Because there is no change in the real interest rate, there is also no change in net capital outflow, shown in panel (b). And because there is no change in net capital outflow, there can be no change in net exports, even though the import quota has reduced imports.

It might seem puzzling that net exports stay the same while imports fall. This puzzle is resolved by noting the change in the real exchange rate: When the dollar appreciates in value in the market for foreign-currency exchange, domestic goods become more expensive relative to foreign goods. This appreciation encourages imports and discourages exports, and both of these changes work to offset the direct increase in net exports due to the import quota. In the end, an import quota reduces both imports and exports, but net exports (exports minus imports) are unchanged.

We have thus come to a surprising implication: *Trade policies do not affect the trade balance*. That is, policies that directly influence exports or imports do not alter net exports. This conclusion seems less surprising if one recalls the accounting identity:

$$NX = NCO = S - I.$$

Net exports equal net capital outflow, which equals national saving minus domestic investment. Trade policies do not alter the trade balance because they do not alter national saving or domestic investment. For given levels of national saving and domestic investment, the real exchange rate adjusts to keep the trade balance the same, regardless of the trade policies the government puts in place.

Although trade policies do not affect a country's overall trade balance, these policies do affect specific firms, industries, and countries. When the U.S. government imposes an import quota on Japanese cars, General Motors has less competition from abroad and will sell more cars. At the same time, because the dollar has appreciated in value, Boeing, the U.S. aircraft maker, will find it harder to compete with Airbus, the European aircraft maker. U.S. exports of aircraft will fall, and U.S. imports of aircraft will rise. In this case, the import quota on Japanese cars will increase net exports of cars and decrease net exports of planes. In addition, it will increase net exports from the United States to Japan and decrease net exports from the United States to Europe. The overall trade balance of the U.S. economy, however, stays the same.

The effects of trade policies are, therefore, more microeconomic than macroeconomic. Although advocates of trade policies sometimes claim (incorrectly) that these policies can alter a country's trade balance, they are usually more motivated by concerns about particular firms or industries. One should not be surprised, for instance, to hear an executive from General Motors advocating import quotas for Japanese cars. Economists usually oppose such trade policies. Free trade allows economies to specialize in doing what they do best, making residents of all countries better off. Trade restrictions interfere with these gains from trade and, thus, reduce overall economic well-being.

Political Instability and Capital Flight

In 1994, political instability in Mexico, including the assassination of a prominent political leader, made world financial markets nervous. People began to view Mexico as a much less stable country than they had previously thought. They decided to pull some of their assets out of Mexico to move these funds to the United States and other "safe havens." Such a large and sudden movement of funds out of a country is called **capital flight.** To see the implications of capital flight for the Mexican economy, we again follow our three steps for analyzing a change in equilibrium, but this time, we apply our model of the open economy from the perspective of Mexico rather than the United States.

capital flight
a large and sudden reduction in the demand for assets located in a country

Consider first which curves in our model capital flight affects. When investors around the world observe political problems in Mexico, they decide to sell some of their Mexican assets and use the proceeds to buy U.S. assets. This act increases Mexican net capital outflow and, therefore, affects both markets in our model. Most obviously, it affects the net-capital-outflow curve, and this in turn influences the supply of pesos in the market for foreign-currency exchange. In addition, because the demand for loanable funds comes from both domestic investment and net capital outflow, capital flight affects the demand curve in the market for loanable funds.

Now consider which way these curves shift. When net capital outflow increases, there is greater demand for loanable funds to finance these purchases of capital assets abroad. Thus, as panel (a) of Figure 7 shows, the demand curve for loanable funds shifts to the right from D_1 to D_2. In addition, because net capital outflow is higher for any interest rate, the net-capital-outflow curve also shifts to the right from NCO_1 to NCO_2, as in panel (b).

To see the effects of capital flight on the Mexican economy, we compare the old and new equilibria. Panel (a) of Figure 7 shows that the increased demand for loanable funds causes the interest rate in Mexico to rise from r_1 to r_2. Panel (b) shows that Mexican net capital outflow increases. (Although the rise in the interest rate does make Mexican assets more attractive, this only partly offsets the impact of capital flight on net capital outflow.) Panel (c) shows that the increase in net capital outflow raises the supply of pesos in the market for foreign-currency exchange from S_1 to S_2. That is, as people try to get out of Mexican assets, there is a large supply of pesos to be converted into dollars. This increase in supply causes the peso to depreciate from E_1 to E_2. Thus, *capital flight from Mexico increases Mexican interest rates and decreases the value of the Mexican peso in the market for foreign-currency exchange.* This is exactly what was observed in 1994. From November 1994 to March 1995, the interest rate on short-term Mexican government bonds rose from 14 percent to 70 percent, and the peso depreciated in value from 29 to 15 U.S. cents per peso.

These price changes that result from capital flight influence some key macroeconomic quantities. The depreciation of the currency makes exports cheaper and imports more expensive, pushing the trade balance toward surplus. At the same time, the increase in the interest rate reduces domestic investment, which slows capital accumulation and economic growth.

Capital flight has its largest impact on the country from which capital is fleeing, but it also affects other countries. When capital flows out of Mexico into the United States, for instance, it has the opposite effect on the U.S. economy as it has

c. How will this change in the capital stock affect the Canadian labor market? Does this U.S. investment in Canada make Canadian workers better off or worse off?

d. Do you think this will make U.S. workers better off or worse off? Can you think of any reason the impact on U.S. citizens generally may be different from the impact on U.S. workers?

For further information on topics in this chapter, additional problems, applications, examples, online quizzes, and more, please visit our website at www.cengage.com/economics/mankiw.

PART **VII** Short-Run Economic Fluctuations

Aggregate Demand
and Aggregate Supply

15

Economic activity fluctuates from year to year. In most years, the production of goods and services rises. Because of increases in the labor force, increases in the capital stock, and advances in technological knowledge, the economy can produce more and more over time. This growth allows everyone to enjoy a higher standard of living. On average over the past half century, the production of the U.S. economy as measured by real GDP has grown by about 3 percent per year.

In some years, however, the economy experiences contraction rather than growth. Firms find themselves unable to sell all the goods and services they have to offer, so they cut back on production. Workers are laid off, unemployment rises, and factories are left idle. With the economy producing fewer goods and services, real GDP and other measures of income fall. Such a period of falling incomes and rising unemployment is called a **recession** if it is relatively mild and a **depression** if it is more severe.

recession
a period of declining real incomes and rising unemployment

depression
a severe recession

319

An example of such a downturn occurred in 2008 and 2009. From the fourth quarter of 2007 to the second quarter of 2009, real GDP for the U.S. economy fell by 4 percent. The rate of unemployment rose from 4.4 percent in May 2007 to 10.1 percent in October 2009—the highest level in more than a quarter century. Not surprisingly, students graduating during this time found that desirable jobs were hard to find.

What causes short-run fluctuations in economic activity? What, if anything, can public policy do to prevent periods of falling incomes and rising unemployment? When recessions and depressions occur, how can policymakers reduce their length and severity? These are the questions we take up now.

The variables that we study are largely those we have already seen in previous chapters. They include GDP, unemployment, interest rates, and the price level. Also familiar are the policy instruments of government spending, taxes, and the money supply. What differs from our earlier analysis is the time horizon. So far, our goal has been to explain the behavior of these variables in the long run. Our goal now is to explain their short-run deviations from long-run trends. In other words, instead of focusing on the forces that explain economic growth from generation to generation, we are now interested in the forces that explain economic fluctuations from year to year.

There remains some debate among economists about how best to analyze short-run fluctuations, but most economists use the *model of aggregate demand and aggregate supply*. Learning how to use this model for analyzing the short-run effects of various events and policies is the primary task ahead. This chapter introduces the model's two pieces: the aggregate-demand curve and the aggregate-supply curve. Before turning to the model, however, let's look at some of the key facts that describe the ups and downs of the economy.

Three Key Facts about Economic Fluctuations

Short-run fluctuations in economic activity have occurred in all countries throughout history. As a starting point for understanding these year-to-year fluctuations, let's discuss some of their most important properties.

Fact 1: Economic Fluctuations Are Irregular and Unpredictable

Fluctuations in the economy are often called *the business cycle*. As this term suggests, economic fluctuations correspond to changes in business conditions. When real GDP grows rapidly, business is good. During such periods of economic expansion, most firms find that customers are plentiful and that profits are growing. When real GDP falls during recessions, businesses have trouble. During such periods of economic contraction, most firms experience declining sales and dwindling profits.

The term *business cycle* is somewhat misleading because it suggests that economic fluctuations follow a regular, predictable pattern. In fact, economic fluctuations are not at all regular, and they are almost impossible to predict with much accuracy. Panel (a) of Figure 1 shows the real GDP of the U.S. economy since 1965. The shaded areas represent times of recession. As the figure shows, recessions do not come at regular intervals. Sometimes recessions are close together, such as the recessions of 1980 and 1982. Sometimes the economy goes many years without a recession. The longest period in U.S. history without a recession was the economic expansion from 1991 to 2001.

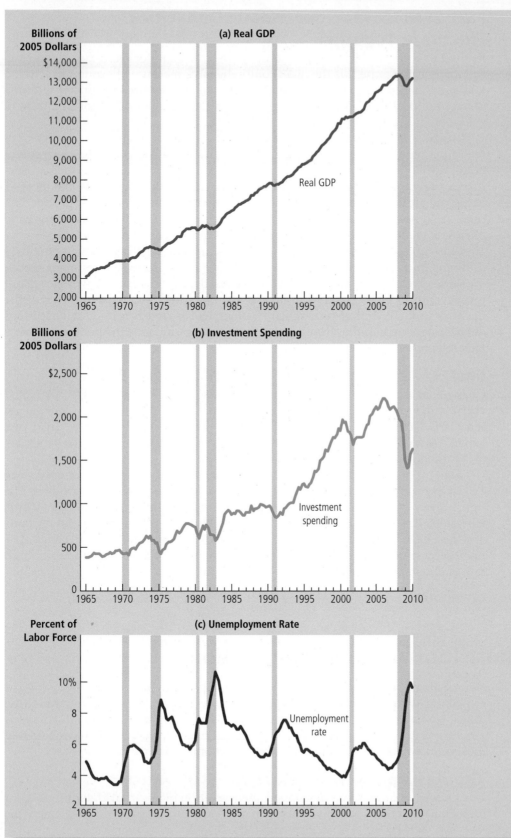

(a) Real GDP

(b) Investment Spending

(c) Unemployment Rate

Figure 1

A Look at Short-Run Economic Fluctuations

This figure shows real GDP in panel (a), investment spending in panel (b), and unemployment in panel (c) for the U.S. economy using quarterly data since 1965. Recessions are shown as the shaded areas. Notice that real GDP and investment spending decline during recessions, while unemployment rises.

Source: U.S. Department of Commerce; U.S. Department of Labor.

Fact 2: Most Macroeconomic Quantities Fluctuate Together

Real GDP is the variable most commonly used to monitor short-run changes in the economy because it is the most comprehensive measure of economic activity. Real GDP measures the value of all final goods and services produced within a given period of time. It also measures the total income (adjusted for inflation) of everyone in the economy.

It turns out, however, that for monitoring short-run fluctuations, it does not really matter which measure of economic activity one looks at. Most macroeconomic variables that measure some type of income, spending, or production fluctuate closely together. When real GDP falls in a recession, so do personal income, corporate profits, consumer spending, investment spending, industrial production, retail sales, home sales, auto sales, and so on. Because recessions are economy-wide phenomena, they show up in many sources of macroeconomic data.

Although many macroeconomic variables fluctuate together, they fluctuate by different amounts. In particular, as panel (b) of Figure 1 shows, investment spending varies greatly over the business cycle. Even though investment averages about one-seventh of GDP, declines in investment account for about two-thirds of the declines in GDP during recessions. In other words, when economic conditions deteriorate, much of the decline is attributable to reductions in spending on new factories, housing, and inventories.

"You're fired. Pass it on."

Fact 3: As Output Falls, Unemployment Rises

Changes in the economy's output of goods and services are strongly correlated with changes in the economy's utilization of its labor force. In other words, when real GDP declines, the rate of unemployment rises. This fact is hardly surprising: When firms choose to produce a smaller quantity of goods and services, they lay off workers, expanding the pool of unemployed.

Panel (c) of Figure 1 shows the unemployment rate in the U.S. economy since 1965. Once again, the shaded areas in the figure indicate periods of recession. The figure shows clearly the impact of recessions on unemployment. In each of the recessions, the unemployment rate rises substantially. When the recession ends and real GDP starts to expand, the unemployment rate gradually declines. The unemployment rate never approaches zero; instead, it fluctuates around its natural rate of about 5 or 6 percent.

QUICK QUIZ *List and discuss three key facts about economic fluctuations.*

Explaining Short-Run Economic Fluctuations

Describing what happens to economies as they fluctuate over time is easy. Explaining what causes these fluctuations is more difficult. Indeed, compared to the topics we have studied in previous chapters, the theory of economic fluctuations remains controversial. In this and the next two chapters, we develop the model that most economists use to explain short-run fluctuations in economic activity.

The Assumptions of Classical Economics

In previous chapters, we developed theories to explain what determines most important macroeconomic variables in the long run. Chapter 7 explained the level and growth of productivity and real GDP. Chapters 8 and 9 explained how the financial system works and how the real interest rate adjusts to balance saving and investment. Chapter 10 explained why there is always some unemployment in the economy. Chapters 11 and 12 explained the monetary system and how changes in the money supply affect the price level, the inflation rate, and the nominal interest rate. Chapters 13 and 14 extended this analysis to open economies to explain the trade balance and the exchange rate.

All of this previous analysis was based on two related ideas: the classical dichotomy and monetary neutrality. Recall that the classical dichotomy is the separation of variables into real variables (those that measure quantities or relative prices) and nominal variables (those measured in terms of money). According to classical macroeconomic theory, changes in the money supply affect nominal variables but not real variables. As a result of this monetary neutrality, Chapters 7 through 10 were able to examine the determinants of real variables (real GDP, the real interest rate, and unemployment) without introducing nominal variables (the money supply and the price level).

In a sense, money does not matter in a classical world. If the quantity of money in the economy were to double, everything would cost twice as much, and everyone's income would be twice as high. But so what? The change would be *nominal* (by the standard meaning of "nearly insignificant"). The things that people *really* care about—whether they have a job, how many goods and services they can afford, and so on—would be exactly the same.

This classical view is sometimes described by the saying, "Money is a veil." That is, nominal variables may be the first things we see when we observe an economy because economic variables are often expressed in units of money. But what's important are the real variables and the economic forces that determine them. According to classical theory, to understand these real variables, we need to look behind the veil.

The Reality of Short-Run Fluctuations

Do these assumptions of classical macroeconomic theory apply to the world in which we live? The answer to this question is of central importance to understanding how the economy works. *Most economists believe that classical theory describes the world in the long run but not in the short run.*

Consider again the impact of money on the economy. Most economists believe that, beyond a period of several years, changes in the money supply affect prices and other nominal variables but do not affect real GDP, unemployment, or other real variables—just as classical theory says. When studying year-to-year changes in the economy, however, the assumption of monetary neutrality is no longer appropriate. In the short run, real and nominal variables are highly intertwined, and changes in the money supply can temporarily push real GDP away from its long-run trend.

Even the classical economists themselves, such as David Hume, realized that classical economic theory did not hold in the short run. From his vantage point in 18th-century England, Hume observed that when the money supply expanded after gold discoveries, it took some time for prices to rise, and in the meantime, the economy enjoyed higher employment and production.

To understand how the economy works in the short run, we need a new model. This new model can be built using many of the tools we developed

in the news

> ### The Social Influences of Economic Downturns

The U.S. economy experienced a deep recession in 2008 and 2009, from which the economy was just beginning to recover as this book went to press. This event led some observers to ask how such events affect society more broadly.

Recession Can Change a Way of Life

BY TYLER COWEN

As job losses mount and bailout costs run into the trillions, the social costs of the economic downturn become clearer. The primary question, to be sure, is what can be done to shorten or alleviate these bad times. But there is also a broader set of questions about how this downturn is changing our lives, in ways beyond strict economics.

All recessions have cultural and social effects, but in major downturns the changes can be profound. The Great Depression, for example, may be regarded as a social and

cultural era as well as an economic one. And the current crisis is also likely to enact changes in various areas, from our entertainment habits to our health.

First, consider entertainment. Many studies have shown that when a job is harder to find or less lucrative, people spend more time on self-improvement and relatively inexpensive amusements. During the Depression of the 1930s, that meant listening to the radio and playing parlor and board games, sometimes in lieu of a glamorous night on the town. These stay-at-home tendencies persisted through at least the 1950s.

In today's recession, we can also expect to turn to less expensive activities—and maybe to keep those habits for years. They

may take the form of greater interest in free content on the Internet and the simple pleasures of a daily walk, instead of expensive vacations and N.B.A. box seats.

In any recession, the poor suffer the most pain. But in cultural influence, it may well be the rich who lose the most in the current crisis. This downturn is bringing a larger-than-usual decline in consumption by the wealthy.

The shift has been documented by Jonathan A. Parker and Annette Vissing-Jorgenson, finance professors at Northwestern University, in their recent paper, "Who Bears Aggregate Fluctuations and How? Estimates and Implications for Consumption Inequality." Of course, people who held much wealth in real estate or stocks have taken heavy losses. But most important, the

---

in previous chapters, but it must abandon the classical dichotomy and the neutrality of money. We can no longer separate our analysis of real variables such as output and employment from our analysis of nominal variables such as money and the price level. Our new model focuses on how real and nominal variables interact.

The Model of Aggregate Demand and Aggregate Supply

Our model of short-run economic fluctuations focuses on the behavior of two variables. The first variable is the economy's output of goods and services, as measured by real GDP. The second is the average level of prices, as measured by the CPI or the GDP deflator. Notice that output is a real variable, whereas the price level is a nominal variable. By focusing on the relationship between these two variables, we are departing from the classical assumption that real and nominal variables can be studied separately.

paper says, the labor incomes of high earners have declined more than in past recessions, as seen in the financial sector.

Popular culture's catering to the wealthy may also decline in this downturn. We can expect a shift away from the lionizing of fancy restaurants, for example, and toward more use of public libraries. Such changes tend to occur in downturns, but this time they may be especially pronounced.

Recessions and depressions, of course, are not good for mental health. But it is less widely known that in the United States and other affluent countries, physical health seems to improve, on average, during a downturn. Sure, it's stressful to miss a paycheck, but eliminating the stresses of a job may have some beneficial effects. Perhaps more important, people may take fewer car trips, thus lowering the risk of accidents, and spend less on alcohol and tobacco. They also have more time for exercise and sleep, and tend to choose home cooking over fast food.

In a 2003 paper, "Healthy Living in Hard Times," Christopher J. Ruhm, an economist at the University of North Carolina at Greensboro, found that the death rate falls as unemployment rises. In the United States, he found, a 1 percent increase in the unemployment rate, on average, decreases the death rate by 0.5 percent.

David Potts studied the social history of Australia in the 1930s in his 2006 book, "The Myth of the Great Depression." Australia's suicide rate spiked in 1930, but overall health improved and death rates declined; after 1930, suicide rates declined as well.

While he found in interviews that many people reminisced fondly about those depression years, we shouldn't rush to conclude that depressions are happy times.

Many of their reports are likely illusory, as documented by the Harvard psychologist Daniel Gilbert in his best-selling book "Stumbling on Happiness." According to Professor Gilbert, people often have rosy memories of very trying periods, which may include extreme poverty or fighting in a war.

In today's context, we are also suffering fear and anxiety for the rather dubious consolation of having some interesting memories for the distant future.

But this downturn will likely mean a more prudent generation to come. That is implied by the work of two professors, Ulrike Malmendier of the University of California, Berkeley, and Stefan Nagel of the Stanford Business School, in a 2007 paper, "Depression Babies: Do Macroeconomic Experiences Affect Risk-Taking?"

A generation that grows up in a period of low stock returns is likely to take an unusually cautious approach to investing, even decades later, the paper found. Similarly, a generation that grows up with high inflation will be more cautious about buying bonds decades later.

In other words, today's teenagers stand less chance of making foolish decisions in the stock market down the road. They are likely to forgo some good business opportunities, but also to make fewer mistakes.

When all is said and done, something terrible has happened in the United States economy, and no one should wish for such an event. But a deeper look at the downturn, and the social changes it is bringing, shows a more complex picture.

In addition to trying to get out of the recession—our first priority—many of us will be making do with less and relying more on ourselves and our families. The social changes may well be the next big story of this recession.

Source: *New York Times,* February 1, 2009.

We analyze fluctuations in the economy as a whole with the **model of aggregate demand and aggregate supply,** which is illustrated in Figure 2. On the vertical axis is the overall price level in the economy. On the horizontal axis is the overall quantity of goods and services produced in the economy. The **aggregate-demand curve** shows the quantity of goods and services that households, firms, the government, and customers abroad want to buy at each price level. The **aggregate-supply curve** shows the quantity of goods and services that firms produce and sell at each price level. According to this model, the price level and the quantity of output adjust to bring aggregate demand and aggregate supply into balance.

It is tempting to view the model of aggregate demand and aggregate supply as nothing more than a large version of the model of market demand and market supply introduced in Chapter 4. In fact, this model is quite different. When we consider demand and supply in a specific market—ice cream, for instance—the behavior of buyers and sellers depends on the ability of resources to move from one market to another. When the price of ice cream rises, the quantity demanded falls because buyers will use their incomes to buy products other than ice cream.

model of aggregate demand and aggregate supply

the model that most economists use to explain short-run fluctuations in economic activity around its long-run trend

aggregate-demand curve

a curve that shows the quantity of goods and services that households, firms, the government, and customers abroad want to buy at each price level

Figure **2**

Aggregate Demand and Aggregate Supply
Economists use the model of aggregate demand and aggregate supply to analyze economic fluctuations. On the vertical axis is the overall level of prices. On the horizontal axis is the economy's total output of goods and services. Output and the price level adjust to the point at which the aggregate-supply and aggregate-demand curves intersect.

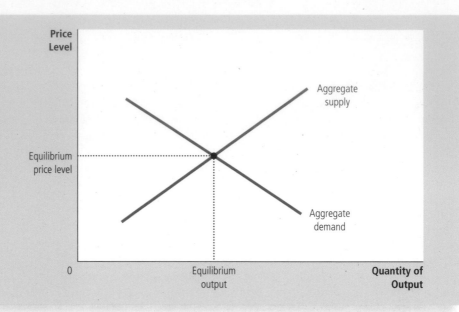

aggregate-supply curve

a curve that shows the quantity of goods and services that firms choose to produce and sell at each price level

Similarly, a higher price of ice cream raises the quantity supplied because firms that produce ice cream can increase production by hiring workers away from other parts of the economy. This *microeconomic* substitution from one market to another is impossible for the economy as a whole. After all, the quantity that our model is trying to explain—real GDP—measures the *total* quantity of goods and services produced by *all* firms in *all* markets. To understand why the aggregate-demand curve is downward sloping and why the aggregate-supply curve is upward sloping, we need a *macroeconomic* theory that explains the total quantity of goods and services demanded and the total quantity of goods and services supplied. Developing such a theory is our next task.

QUICK QUIZ   *How does the economy's behavior in the short run differ from its behavior in the long run? • Draw the model of aggregate demand and aggregate supply. What variables are on the two axes?*

The Aggregate-Demand Curve

The aggregate-demand curve tells us the quantity of all goods and services demanded in the economy at any given price level. As Figure 3 illustrates, the aggregate-demand curve is downward sloping. This means that, other things equal, a decrease in the economy's overall level of prices (from, say, P_1 to P_2) raises the quantity of goods and services demanded (from Y_1 to Y_2). Conversely, an increase in the price level reduces the quantity of goods and services demanded.

Why the Aggregate-Demand Curve Slopes Downward

Why does a change in the price level move the quantity of goods and services demanded in the opposite direction? To answer this question, it is useful to recall

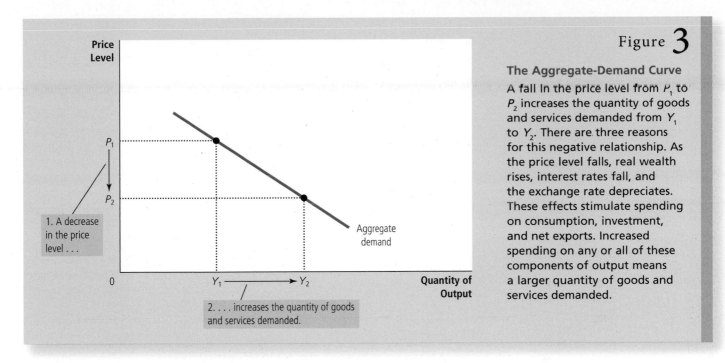

Figure 3

The Aggregate-Demand Curve

A fall in the price level from P_1 to P_2 increases the quantity of goods and services demanded from Y_1 to Y_2. There are three reasons for this negative relationship. As the price level falls, real wealth rises, interest rates fall, and the exchange rate depreciates. These effects stimulate spending on consumption, investment, and net exports. Increased spending on any or all of these components of output means a larger quantity of goods and services demanded.

that an economy's GDP (which we denote as Y) is the sum of its consumption (C), investment (I), government purchases (G), and net exports (NX):

$$Y = C + I + G + NX.$$

Each of these four components contributes to the aggregate demand for goods and services. For now, we assume that government spending is fixed by policy. The other three components of spending—consumption, investment, and net exports—depend on economic conditions and, in particular, on the price level. Therefore, to understand the downward slope of the aggregate-demand curve, we must examine how the price level affects the quantity of goods and services demanded for consumption, investment, and net exports.

The Price Level and Consumption: The Wealth Effect Consider the money that you hold in your wallet and your bank account. The nominal value of this money is fixed: One dollar is always worth one dollar. Yet the *real* value of a dollar is not fixed. If a candy bar costs one dollar, then a dollar is worth one candy bar. If the price of a candy bar falls to 50 cents, then one dollar is worth two candy bars. Thus, when the price level falls, the dollars you are holding rise in value, which increases your real wealth and your ability to buy goods and services.

This logic gives us the first reason the aggregate demand curve is downward sloping. *A decrease in the price level raises the real value of money and makes consumers wealthier, which in turn encourages them to spend more. The increase in consumer spending means a larger quantity of goods and services demanded. Conversely, an increase in the price level reduces the real value of money and makes consumers poorer, which in turn reduces consumer spending and the quantity of goods and services demanded.*

The Price Level and Investment: The Interest-Rate Effect The price level is one determinant of the quantity of money demanded. When the price level is lower, households need to hold less money to buy the goods and services they want. Therefore, when the price level falls, households try to reduce their holdings of money by lending some of it out. For instance, a household might use its excess money to buy interest-bearing bonds. Or it might deposit its excess money in an interest-bearing savings account, and the bank would use these funds to make more loans. In either case, as households try to convert some of their money into interest-bearing assets, they drive down interest rates. (The next chapter analyzes this process in more detail.)

Interest rates, in turn, affect spending on goods and services. Because a lower interest rate makes borrowing less expensive, it encourages firms to borrow more to invest in new plants and equipment, and it encourages households to borrow more to invest in new housing. (A lower interest rate might also stimulate consumer spending, especially spending on large durable purchases such as cars, which are often bought on credit.) Thus, a lower interest rate increases the quantity of goods and services demanded.

This logic gives us a second reason the aggregate demand curve is downward sloping. *A lower price level reduces the interest rate, encourages greater spending on investment goods, and thereby increases the quantity of goods and services demanded. Conversely, a higher price level raises the interest rate, discourages investment spending, and decreases the quantity of goods and services demanded.*

The Price Level and Net Exports: The Exchange-Rate Effect   As we have just discussed, a lower price level in the United States lowers the U.S. interest rate. In response to the lower interest rate, some U.S. investors will seek higher returns by investing abroad. For instance, as the interest rate on U.S. government bonds falls, a mutual fund might sell U.S. government bonds to buy German government bonds. As the mutual fund tries to convert its dollars into euros to buy the German bonds, it increases the supply of dollars in the market for foreign-currency exchange.

The increased supply of dollars to be turned into euros causes the dollar to depreciate relative to the euro. This leads to a change in the real exchange rate—the relative price of domestic and foreign goods. Because each dollar buys fewer units of foreign currencies, foreign goods become more expensive relative to domestic goods.

The change in relative prices affects spending, both at home and abroad. Because foreign goods are now more expensive, Americans buy less from other countries, causing U.S. imports of goods and services to decrease. At the same time, because U.S. goods are now cheaper, foreigners buy more from the United States, so U.S. exports increase. Net exports equal exports minus imports, so both of these changes cause U.S. net exports to increase. Thus, the fall in the real exchange value of the dollar leads to an increase in the quantity of goods and services demanded.

This logic yields a third reason the aggregate demand curve is downward sloping. *When a fall in the U.S. price level causes U.S. interest rates to fall, the real value of the dollar declines in foreign exchange markets. This depreciation stimulates U.S. net exports and thereby increases the quantity of goods and services demanded. Conversely, when the U.S. price level rises and causes U.S. interest rates to rise, the real value of the dollar increases, and this appreciation reduces U.S. net exports and the quantity of goods and services demanded.*

Summing Up   There are three distinct but related reasons a fall in the price level increases the quantity of goods and services demanded:

1. Consumers are wealthier, which stimulates the demand for consumption goods.
2. Interest rates fall, which stimulates the demand for investment goods.
3. The currency depreciates, which stimulates the demand for net exports.

The same three effects work in reverse: When the price level rises, decreased wealth depresses consumer spending, higher interest rates depress investment spending, and a currency appreciation depresses net exports.

Here is a thought experiment to hone your intuition about these effects. Imagine that one day you wake up and notice that, for some mysterious reason, the prices of all goods and services have fallen by half, so the dollars you are holding are worth twice as much. In real terms, you now have twice as much money as you had when you went to bed the night before. What would you do with the extra money? You could spend it at your favorite restaurant, increasing consumer spending. You could lend it out (by buying a bond or depositing it in your bank), reducing interest rates and increasing investment spending. Or you could invest it overseas (by buying shares in an international mutual fund), reducing the real exchange value of the dollar and increasing net exports. Whichever of these three responses you choose, the fall in the price level leads to an increase in the quantity of goods and services demanded. This is what the downward slope of the aggregate-demand curve represents.

It is important to keep in mind that the aggregate-demand curve (like all demand curves) is drawn holding "other things equal." In particular, our three explanations of the downward-sloping aggregate-demand curve assume that the money supply is fixed. That is, we have been considering how a change in the price level affects the demand for goods and services, holding the amount of money in the economy constant. As we will see, a change in the quantity of money shifts the aggregate-demand curve. At this point, just keep in mind that the aggregate-demand curve is drawn for a given quantity of the money supply.

Why the Aggregate-Demand Curve Might Shift

The downward slope of the aggregate-demand curve shows that a fall in the price level raises the overall quantity of goods and services demanded. Many other factors, however, affect the quantity of goods and services demanded at a given price level. When one of these other factors changes, the quantity of goods and services demanded at every price level changes, and the aggregate-demand curve shifts.

Let's consider some examples of events that shift aggregate demand. We can categorize them according to which component of spending is most directly affected.

Shifts Arising from Changes in Consumption Suppose Americans suddenly become more concerned about saving for retirement and, as a result, reduce their current consumption. Because the quantity of goods and services demanded at any price level is lower, the aggregate-demand curve shifts to the left. Conversely, imagine that a stock-market boom makes people wealthier and less concerned about saving. The resulting increase in consumer spending means a greater quantity of goods and services demanded at any given price level, so the aggregate-demand curve shifts to the right.

Thus, any event that changes how much people want to consume at a given price level shifts the aggregate-demand curve. One policy variable that has this effect is the level of taxation. When the government cuts taxes, it encourages people to spend more, so the aggregate-demand curve shifts to the right. When the government raises taxes, people cut back on their spending, and the aggregate-demand curve shifts to the left.

Shifts Arising from Changes in Investment Any event that changes how much firms want to invest at a given price level also shifts the aggregate-demand curve. For instance, imagine that the computer industry introduces a faster line of computers, and many firms decide to invest in new computer systems. Because the quantity of goods and services demanded at any price level is higher, the aggregate-demand curve shifts to the right. Conversely, if firms become pessimistic about future business conditions, they may cut back on investment spending, shifting the aggregate-demand curve to the left.

Tax policy can also influence aggregate demand through investment. For example, an investment tax credit (a tax rebate tied to a firm's investment spending) increases the quantity of investment goods that firms demand at any given interest rate and therefore shifts the aggregate-demand curve to the right. The repeal of an investment tax credit reduces investment and shifts the aggregate-demand curve to the left.

Another policy variable that can influence investment and aggregate demand is the money supply. As we discuss more fully in the next chapter, an increase in the money supply lowers the interest rate in the short run. This decrease in the interest rate makes borrowing less costly, which stimulates investment spending and thereby shifts the aggregate-demand curve to the right. Conversely, a decrease in the money supply raises the interest rate, discourages investment spending, and thereby shifts the aggregate-demand curve to the left. Many economists believe that throughout U.S. history, changes in monetary policy have been an important source of shifts in aggregate demand.

Shifts Arising from Changes in Government Purchases   The most direct way that policymakers shift the aggregate-demand curve is through government purchases. For example, suppose Congress decides to reduce purchases of new weapons systems. Because the quantity of goods and services demanded at any price level is lower, the aggregate-demand curve shifts to the left. Conversely, if state governments start building more highways, the result is a greater quantity of goods and services demanded at any price level, so the aggregate-demand curve shifts to the right.

Shifts Arising from Changes in Net Exports   Any event that changes net exports for a given price level also shifts aggregate demand. For instance, when Europe experiences a recession, it buys fewer goods from the United States. This reduces U.S. net exports at every price level and shifts the aggregate-demand curve for the U.S. economy to the left. When Europe recovers from its recession, it starts buying U.S. goods again, and the aggregate-demand curve shifts to the right.

Net exports can also change because international speculators cause movements in the exchange rate. Suppose, for instance, that these speculators lose confidence in foreign economies and want to move some of their wealth into the U.S. economy. In doing so, they bid up the value of the U.S. dollar in the foreign exchange market. This appreciation of the dollar makes U.S. goods more expensive compared to foreign goods, which depresses net exports and shifts the aggregate-demand curve to the left. Conversely, speculation that causes a depreciation of the dollar stimulates net exports and shifts the aggregate-demand curve to the right.

Summing Up   In the next chapter, we analyze the aggregate-demand curve in more detail. There we examine more precisely how the tools of monetary and fiscal policy can shift aggregate demand and whether policymakers should use these tools for that purpose. At this point, however, you should have some idea about why the aggregate-demand curve slopes downward and what kinds of events and policies can shift this curve. Table 1 summarizes what we have learned so far.

Table 1

The Aggregate-Demand Curve: Summary

Why Does the Aggregate-Demand Curve Slope Downward?

1. *The Wealth Effect:* A lower price level increases real wealth, which stimulates spending on consumption.
2. *The Interest-Rate Effect:* A lower price level reduces the interest rate, which stimulates spending on investment.
3. *The Exchange-Rate Effect:* A lower price level causes the real exchange rate to depreciate, which stimulates spending on net exports.

Why Might the Aggregate-Demand Curve Shift?

1. *Shifts Arising from Changes in Consumption:* An event that makes consumers spend more at a given price level (a tax cut, a stock-market boom) shifts the aggregate-demand curve to the right. An event that makes consumers spend less at a given price level (a tax hike, a stock-market decline) shifts the aggregate-demand curve to the left.
2. *Shifts Arising from Changes in Investment:* An event that makes firms invest more at a given price level (optimism about the future, a fall in interest rates due to an increase in the money supply) shifts the aggregate-demand curve to the right. An event that makes firms invest less at a given price level (pessimism about the future, a rise in interest rates due to a decrease in the money supply) shifts the aggregate-demand curve to the left.
3. *Shifts Arising from Changes in Government Purchases:* An increase in government purchases of goods and services (greater spending on defense or highway construction) shifts the aggregate-demand curve to the right. A decrease in government purchases on goods and services (a cutback in defense or highway spending) shifts the aggregate-demand curve to the left.
4. *Shifts Arising from Changes in Net Exports:* An event that raises spending on net exports at a given price level (a boom overseas, speculation that causes an exchange-rate depreciation) shifts the aggregate-demand curve to the right. An event that reduces spending on net exports at a given price level (a recession overseas, speculation that causes an exchange-rate appreciation) shifts the aggregate-demand curve to the left.

QUICK QUIZ *Explain the three reasons the aggregate-demand curve slopes downward • Give an example of an event that would shift the aggregate-demand curve. Which way would this event shift the curve?*

The Aggregate-Supply Curve

The aggregate-supply curve tells us the total quantity of goods and services that firms produce and sell at any given price level. Unlike the aggregate-demand curve, which is always downward sloping, the aggregate-supply curve shows a relationship that depends crucially on the time horizon examined. *In the long run, the aggregate-supply curve is vertical, whereas in the short run, the aggregate-supply curve is upward sloping.* To understand short-run economic fluctuations, and how the short-run behavior of the economy deviates from its long-run behavior, we need to examine both the long-run aggregate-supply curve and the short-run aggregate-supply curve.

Why the Aggregate-Supply Curve Is Vertical in the Long Run

What determines the quantity of goods and services supplied in the long run? We implicitly answered this question earlier in the book when we analyzed the process of economic growth. *In the long run, an economy's production of goods and services (its real GDP) depends on its supplies of labor, capital, and natural resources and on the available technology used to turn these factors of production into goods and services.*

When we analyzed these forces that govern long-run growth, we did not need to make any reference to the overall level of prices. We examined the price level in a separate chapter, where we saw that it was determined by the quantity of money. We learned that if two economies were identical except that one had twice as much money in circulation as the other, the price level would be twice as high in the economy with more money. But since the amount of money does not affect technology or the supplies of labor, capital, and natural resources, the output of goods and services in the two economies would be the same.

Because the price level does not affect the long-run determinants of real GDP, the long-run aggregate-supply curve is vertical, as in Figure 4. In other words, in the long run, the economy's labor, capital, natural resources, and technology determine the total quantity of goods and services supplied, and this quantity supplied is the same regardless of what the price level happens to be.

The vertical long-run aggregate-supply curve is a graphical representation of the classical dichotomy and monetary neutrality. As we have already discussed, classical macroeconomic theory is based on the assumption that real variables do not depend on nominal variables. The long-run aggregate-supply curve is consistent with this idea because it implies that the quantity of output (a real variable) does not depend on the level of prices (a nominal variable). As noted earlier, most economists believe this principle works well when studying the economy over a period of many years but not when studying year-to-year changes. Thus, the aggregate-supply curve is vertical only in the long run.

Why the Long-Run Aggregate-Supply Curve Might Shift

Because classical macroeconomic theory predicts the quantity of goods and services produced by an economy in the long run, it also explains the position of the

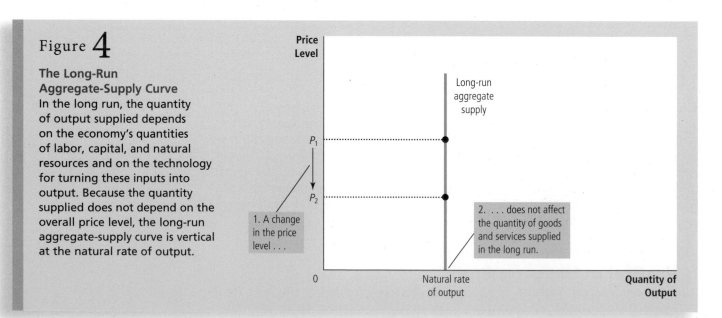

Figure 4

The Long-Run Aggregate-Supply Curve
In the long run, the quantity of output supplied depends on the economy's quantities of labor, capital, and natural resources and on the technology for turning these inputs into output. Because the quantity supplied does not depend on the overall price level, the long-run aggregate-supply curve is vertical at the natural rate of output.

Price Level

Long-run aggregate supply

P_1

P_2

1. A change in the price level . . .

2. . . . does not affect the quantity of goods and services supplied in the long run.

0   Natural rate of output   Quantity of Output

long-run aggregate-supply curve. The long-run level of production is sometimes called *potential output* or *full-employment output*. To be more precise, we call it the **natural rate of output** because it shows what the economy produces when unemployment is at its natural, or normal, rate. The natural rate of output is the level of production toward which the economy gravitates in the long run.

Any change in the economy that alters the natural rate of output shifts the long-run aggregate-supply curve. Because output in the classical model depends on labor, capital, natural resources, and technological knowledge, we can categorize shifts in the long-run aggregate-supply curve as arising from these four sources.

Shifts Arising from Changes in Labor Imagine that an economy experiences an increase in immigration. Because there would be a greater number of workers, the quantity of goods and services supplied would increase. As a result, the long-run aggregate-supply curve would shift to the right. Conversely, if many workers left the economy to go abroad, the long-run aggregate-supply curve would shift to the left.

The position of the long-run aggregate-supply curve also depends on the natural rate of unemployment, so any change in the natural rate of unemployment shifts the long-run aggregate-supply curve. For example, if Congress were to raise the minimum wage substantially, the natural rate of unemployment would rise, and the economy would produce a smaller quantity of goods and services. As a result, the long-run aggregate-supply curve would shift to the left. Conversely, if a reform of the unemployment insurance system were to encourage unemployed workers to search harder for new jobs, the natural rate of unemployment would fall, and the long-run aggregate-supply curve would shift to the right.

Shifts Arising from Changes in Capital An increase in the economy's capital stock increases productivity and, thereby, the quantity of goods and services supplied. As a result, the long-run aggregate-supply curve shifts to the right. Conversely, a decrease in the economy's capital stock decreases productivity and the quantity of goods and services supplied, shifting the long-run aggregate-supply curve to the left.

Notice that the same logic applies regardless of whether we are discussing physical capital such as machines and factories or human capital such as college degrees. An increase in either type of capital will raise the economy's ability to produce goods and services and, thus, shift the long-run aggregate-supply curve to the right.

Shifts Arising from Changes in Natural Resources An economy's production depends on its natural resources, including its land, minerals, and weather. The discovery of a new mineral deposit shifts the long-run aggregate-supply curve to the right. A change in weather patterns that makes farming more difficult shifts the long-run aggregate-supply curve to the left.

In many countries, important natural resources are imported. A change in the availability of these resources can also shift the aggregate-supply curve. As we discuss later in this chapter, events occurring in the world oil market have historically been an important source of shifts in aggregate supply for the United States and other oil-importing nations.

Shifts Arising from Changes in Technological Knowledge Perhaps the most important reason that the economy today produces more than it did a generation ago is that our technological knowledge has advanced. The invention of the computer, for instance, has allowed us to produce more goods and services from any given

natural rate of output

the production of goods and services that an economy achieves in the long run when unemployment is at its normal rate amounts of labor, capital, and natural resources. As computer use has spread throughout the economy, it has shifted the long-run aggregate-supply curve to the right.

Although not literally technological, many other events act like changes in technology. For instance, opening up international trade has effects similar to inventing new production processes because it allows a country to specialize in higher-productivity industries; therefore, it also shifts the long-run aggregate-supply curve to the right. Conversely, if the government passes new regulations preventing firms from using some production methods, perhaps to address worker safety or environmental concerns, the result would be a leftward shift in the long-run aggregate-supply curve.

Summing Up   Because the long-run aggregate-supply curve reflects the classical model of the economy we developed in previous chapters, it provides a new way to describe our earlier analysis. Any policy or event that raised real GDP in previous chapters can now be described as increasing the quantity of goods and services supplied and shifting the long-run aggregate-supply curve to the right. Any policy or event that lowered real GDP in previous chapters can now be described as decreasing the quantity of goods and services supplied and shifting the long-run aggregate-supply curve to the left.

Using Aggregate Demand and Aggregate Supply to Depict Long-Run Growth and Inflation

Having introduced the economy's aggregate-demand curve and the long-run aggregate-supply curve, we now have a new way to describe the economy's long-run trends. Figure 5 illustrates the changes that occur in an economy from decade to decade. Notice that both curves are shifting. Although many forces influence the economy in the long run and can in theory cause such shifts, the two most important forces in practice are technology and monetary policy. Technological progress enhances an economy's ability to produce goods and services, and the resulting increases in output are reflected in continual shifts of the long-run aggregate-supply curve to the right. At the same time, because the Fed increases the money supply over time, the aggregate-demand curve also shifts to the right. As the figure illustrates, the result is continuing growth in output (as shown by increasing Y) and continuing inflation (as shown by increasing P). This is just another way of representing the classical analysis of growth and inflation we conducted in earlier chapters.

The purpose of developing the model of aggregate demand and aggregate supply, however, is not to dress our previous long-run conclusions in new clothing. Instead, it is to provide a framework for short-run analysis, as we will see in a moment. As we develop the short-run model, we keep the analysis simple by not showing the continuing growth and inflation depicted by the shifts in Figure 5. But always remember that long-run trends are the background upon which short-run fluctuations are superimposed. *Short-run fluctuations in output and the price level should be viewed as deviations from the continuing long-run trends of output growth and inflation.*

Why the Aggregate-Supply Curve Slopes Upward in the Short Run

The key difference between the economy in the short run and in the long run is the behavior of aggregate supply. The long-run aggregate-supply curve is vertical because, in the long run, the overall level of prices does not affect the economy's ability to produce goods and services. By contrast, in the short run, the price

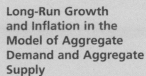

As the economy becomes better able to produce goods and services over time, primarily because of technological progress, the long-run aggregate-supply curve shifts to the right. At the same time, as the Fed increases the money supply, the aggregate-demand curve also shifts to the right. In this figure, output grows from Y_{1990} to Y_{2000} and then to Y_{2010}, and the price level rises from P_{1990} to P_{2000} and then to P_{2010}. Thus, the model of aggregate demand and aggregate supply offers a new way to describe the classical analysis of growth and inflation.

Figure 5

Long-Run Growth and Inflation in the Model of Aggregate Demand and Aggregate Supply

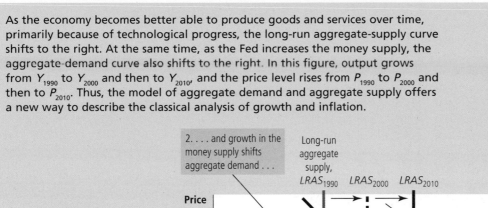

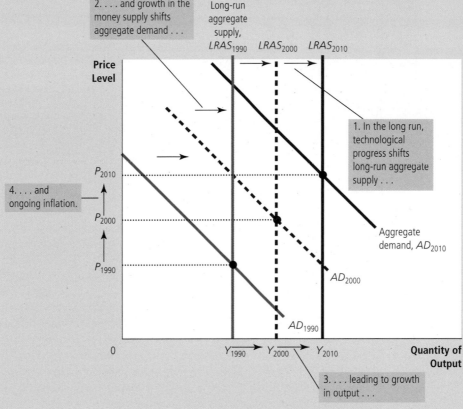

level *does* affect the economy's output. That is, over a period of a year or two, an increase in the overall level of prices in the economy tends to raise the quantity of goods and services supplied, and a decrease in the level of prices tends to reduce the quantity of goods and services supplied. As a result, the short-run aggregate-supply curve is upward sloping, as shown in Figure 6.

Why do changes in the price level affect output in the short run? Macroeconomists have proposed three theories for the upward slope of the short-run aggregate-supply curve. In each theory, a specific market imperfection causes the supply side of the economy to behave differently in the short run than it does in the long run. The following theories differ in their details, but they share a common theme: *The quantity of output supplied deviates from its long-run, or natural, level when the actual price level in the economy deviates from the price level that people expected to prevail.* When the price level rises above the level that people expected, output rises above its natural rate, and when the price level falls below the expected level, output falls below its natural rate.

Figure

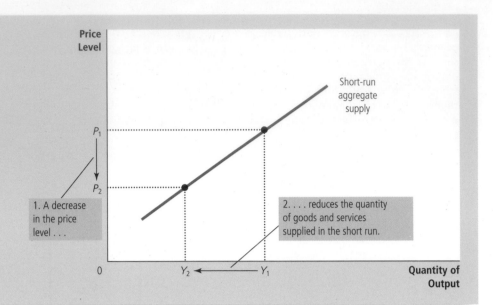

The Short-Run Aggregate-Supply Curve
In the short run, a fall in the price level from P_1 to P_2 reduces the quantity of output supplied from Y_1 to Y_2. This positive relationship could be due to sticky wages, sticky prices, or misperceptions. Over time, wages, prices, and perceptions adjust, so this positive relationship is only temporary.

The Sticky-Wage Theory   The first explanation of the upward slope of the short-run aggregate-supply curve is the sticky-wage theory. This theory is the simplest of the three approaches to aggregate supply, and some economists believe it highlights the most important reason why the economy in the short run differs from the economy in the long run. Therefore, it is the theory of short-run aggregate supply that we emphasize in this book.

According to this theory, the short-run aggregate-supply curve slopes upward because nominal wages are slow to adjust to changing economic conditions. In other words, wages are "sticky" in the short run. To some extent, the slow adjustment of nominal wages is attributable to long-term contracts between workers and firms that fix nominal wages, sometimes for as long as three years. In addition, this prolonged adjustment may be attributable to slowly changing social norms and notions of fairness that influence wage setting.

An example helps explain how sticky nominal wages can result in a short-run aggregate-supply curve that slopes upward. Imagine that a year ago a firm expected the price level today to be 100, and based on this expectation, it signed a contract with its workers agreeing to pay them, say, $20 an hour. In fact, the price level, P, turns out to be only 95. Because prices have fallen below expectations, the firm gets 5 percent less than expected for each unit of its product that it sells. The cost of labor used to make the output, however, is stuck at $20 per hour. Production is now less profitable, so the firm hires fewer workers and reduces the quantity of output supplied. Over time, the labor contract will expire, and the firm can renegotiate with its workers for a lower wage (which they may accept because prices are lower), but in the meantime, employment and production will remain below their long-run levels.

The same logic works in reverse. Suppose the price level turns out to be 105, and the wage remains stuck at $20. The firm sees that the amount it is paid for each unit sold is up by 5 percent, while its labor costs are not. In response, it hires more workers and increases the quantity supplied. Eventually, the workers will demand higher nominal wages to compensate for the higher price level, but for a while, the firm can take advantage of the profit opportunity by increasing employment and the quantity of output supplied above their long-run levels.

In short, according to the sticky-wage theory, the short-run aggregate-supply curve is upward sloping because nominal wages are based on expected prices and do not respond immediately when the actual price level turns out to be different from what was expected. This stickiness of wages gives firms an incentive to produce less output when the price level turns out lower than expected and to produce more when the price level turns out higher than expected.

The Sticky-Price Theory   Some economists have advocated another approach to explaining the upward slope of the short-run aggregate-supply curve, called the sticky-price theory. As we just discussed, the sticky-wage theory emphasizes that nominal wages adjust slowly over time. The sticky-price theory emphasizes that the prices of some goods and services also adjust sluggishly in response to changing economic conditions. This slow adjustment of prices occurs in part because there are costs to adjusting prices, called *menu costs*. These menu costs include the cost of printing and distributing catalogs and the time required to change price tags. As a result of these costs, prices as well as wages may be sticky in the short run.

To see how sticky prices explain the aggregate-supply curve's upward slope, suppose that each firm in the economy announces its prices in advance based on the economic conditions it expects to prevail over the coming year. Suppose further that after prices are announced, the economy experiences an unexpected contraction in the money supply, which (as we have learned) will reduce the overall price level in the long run. Although some firms can reduce their prices immediately in response to an unexpected change in economic conditions, other firms may not want to incur additional menu costs. As a result, they may temporarily lag behind in reducing their prices. Because these lagging firms have prices that are too high, their sales decline. Declining sales, in turn, cause these firms to cut back on production and employment. In other words, because not all prices adjust instantly to changing economic conditions, an unexpected fall in the price level leaves some firms with higher-than-desired prices, and these higher-than-desired prices depress sales and induce firms to reduce the quantity of goods and services they produce.

The same reasoning applies when the money supply and price level turn out to be above what firms expected when they originally set their prices. While some firms raise their prices immediately in response to the new economic environment, other firms lag behind, keeping their prices at the lower-than-desired levels. These low prices attract customers, which induces these firms to increase employment and production. Thus, during the time these lagging firms are operating with outdated prices, there is a positive association between the overall price level and the quantity of output. This positive association is represented by the upward slope of the short-run aggregate-supply curve.

The Misperceptions Theory   A third approach to explaining the upward slope of the short-run aggregate-supply curve is the misperceptions theory. According to this theory, changes in the overall price level can temporarily mislead suppliers about what is happening in the individual markets in which they sell their output. As a result of these short-run misperceptions, suppliers respond to changes in the level of prices, and this response leads to an upward-sloping aggregate-supply curve.

To see how this might work, suppose the overall price level falls below the level that suppliers expected. When suppliers see the prices of their products fall, they may mistakenly believe that their *relative* prices have fallen; that is, they may believe that their prices have fallen compared to other prices in the economy. For example, wheat farmers may notice a fall in the price of wheat before they notice a fall in the prices of the many items they buy as consumers. They may infer from this observation that the reward to producing wheat is temporarily low, and they may respond by reducing the quantity of wheat they supply. Similarly, workers may notice a fall in their nominal wages before they notice that the prices of the goods they buy are also falling. They may infer that the reward for working is temporarily low and respond by reducing the quantity of labor they supply. In both cases, a lower price level causes misperceptions about relative prices, and these misperceptions induce suppliers to respond to the lower price level by decreasing the quantity of goods and services supplied.

Similar misperceptions arise when the price level is above what was expected. Suppliers of goods and services may notice the price of their output rising and infer, mistakenly, that their relative prices are rising. They would conclude that it is a good time to produce. Until their misperceptions are corrected, they respond to the higher price level by increasing the quantity of goods and services supplied. This behavior results in a short-run aggregate-supply curve that slopes upward.

Summing Up   There are three alternative explanations for the upward slope of the short-run aggregate-supply curve: (1) sticky wages, (2) sticky prices, and (3) misperceptions about relative prices. Economists debate which of these theories is correct, and it is very possible each contains an element of truth. For our purposes in this book, the similarities of the theories are more important than the differences. All three theories suggest that output deviates in the short run from its long-run level (the natural rate) when the actual price level deviates from the price level that people had expected to prevail. We can express this mathematically as follows:

$$
\begin{array}{ccc}
\text{Quantity} & & \text{Natural} \\
\text{of output} \;=\; & \text{rate of} & +\; a \left(\begin{array}{ccc} \text{Actual} & & \text{Expected} \\ \text{price} & - & \text{price} \\ \text{level} & & \text{level} \end{array} \right) \\
\text{supplied} & \text{output} &
\end{array}
$$

where a is a number that determines how much output responds to unexpected changes in the price level.

Notice that each of the three theories of short-run aggregate supply emphasizes a problem that is likely to be temporary. Whether the upward slope of the aggregate-supply curve is attributable to sticky wages, sticky prices, or misperceptions, these conditions will not persist forever. Over time, nominal wages will become unstuck, prices will become unstuck, and misperceptions about relative prices will be corrected. In the long run, it is reasonable to assume that wages and prices are flexible rather than sticky and that people are not confused about relative prices. Thus, while we have several good theories to explain why the short-run aggregate-supply curve is upward sloping, they are all consistent with a long-run aggregate-supply curve that is vertical.

Why the Short-Run Aggregate-Supply Curve Might Shift

The short-run aggregate-supply curve tells us the quantity of goods and services supplied in the short run for any given level of prices. This curve is similar to the long-run aggregate-supply curve, but it is upward sloping rather than vertical because of sticky wages, sticky prices, and misperceptions. Thus, when thinking about what shifts the short-run aggregate-supply curve, we have to consider all those variables that shift the long-run aggregate-supply curve plus a new variable—the expected price level—that influences the wages that are stuck, the prices that are stuck, and the perceptions about relative prices that may be flawed.

Let's start with what we know about the long-run aggregate-supply curve. As we discussed earlier, shifts in the long-run aggregate-supply curve normally arise from changes in labor, capital, natural resources, or technological knowledge. These same variables shift the short-run aggregate-supply curve. For example, when an increase in the economy's capital stock increases productivity, the economy is able to produce more output, so both the long-run and short-run aggregate-supply curves shift to the right. When an increase in the minimum wage raises the natural rate of unemployment, the economy has fewer employed workers and thus produces less output, so both the long-run and short-run aggregate-supply curves shift to the left.

The important new variable that affects the position of the short-run aggregate-supply curve is the price level that people expected to prevail. As we have discussed, the quantity of goods and services supplied depends, in the short run, on sticky wages, sticky prices, and misperceptions. Yet wages, prices, and perceptions are set based on the expected price level. So when people change their expectations of the price level, the short-run aggregate-supply curve shifts.

To make this idea more concrete, let's consider a specific theory of aggregate supply—the sticky-wage theory. According to this theory, when workers and firms expect the price level to be high, they are more likely to reach a bargain with a high level of nominal wages. High wages raise firms' costs, and for any given actual price level, higher costs reduce the quantity of goods and services supplied. Thus, when the expected price level rises, wages are higher, costs increase, and firms produce a smaller quantity of goods and services at any given actual price level. Thus, the short-run aggregate-supply curve shifts to the left. Conversely, when the expected price level falls, wages are lower, costs decline, firms increase output at any given price level, and the short-run aggregate-supply curve shifts to the right.

A similar logic applies in each theory of aggregate supply. The general lesson is the following: *An increase in the expected price level reduces the quantity of goods and services supplied and shifts the short-run aggregate-supply curve to the left. A decrease in the expected price level raises the quantity of goods and services supplied and shifts the short-run aggregate-supply curve to the right.* As we will see in the next section, the influence of expectations on the position of the short-run aggregate-supply curve plays a key role in explaining how the economy makes the transition from the short run to the long run. In the short run, expectations are fixed, and the economy finds itself at the intersection of the aggregate-demand curve and the short-run aggregate-supply curve. In the long run, if people observe that the price level is different from what they expected, their expectations adjust, and the short-run aggregate-supply curve shifts. This shift ensures that the economy eventually finds itself at the intersection of the aggregate-demand curve and the long-run aggregate-supply curve.

You should now have some understanding about why the short-run aggregate-supply curve slopes upward and what events and policies can cause this curve to shift. Table 2 summarizes our discussion.

QUICK QUIZ *Explain why the long-run aggregate-supply curve is vertical.* • *Explain three theories for why the short-run aggregate-supply curve is upward sloping.* • *What variables shift both the long-run and short-run aggregate-supply curves?* • *What variable shifts the short-run aggregate-supply curve but not the long-run aggregate-supply curve?*

Table 2

The Short-Run Aggregate-Supply Curve: Summary

Why Does the Short-Run Aggregate-Supply Curve Slope Upward?

1. *The Sticky-Wage Theory:* An unexpectedly low price level raises the real wage, which causes firms to hire fewer workers and produce a smaller quantity of goods and services.
2. *The Sticky-Price Theory:* An unexpectedly low price level leaves some firms with higher-than-desired prices, which depresses their sales and leads them to cut back production.
3. *The Misperceptions Theory:* An unexpectedly low price level leads some suppliers to think their relative prices have fallen, which induces a fall in production.

Why Might the Short-Run Aggregate-Supply Curve Shift?

1. *Shifts Arising from Changes in Labor:* An increase in the quantity of labor available (perhaps due to a fall in the natural rate of unemployment) shifts the aggregate-supply curve to the right. A decrease in the quantity of labor available (perhaps due to a rise in the natural rate of unemployment) shifts the aggregate-supply curve to the left.
2. *Shifts Arising from Changes in Capital:* An increase in physical or human capital shifts the aggregate-supply curve to the right. A decrease in physical or human capital shifts the aggregate-supply curve to the left.
3. *Shifts Arising from Changes in Natural Resources:* An increase in the availability of natural resources shifts the aggregate-supply curve to the right. A decrease in the availability of natural resources shifts the aggregate-supply curve to the left.
4. *Shifts Arising from Changes in Technology:* An advance in technological knowledge shifts the aggregate-supply curve to the right. A decrease in the available technology (perhaps due to government regulation) shifts the aggregate-supply curve to the left.
5. *Shifts Arising from Changes in the Expected Price Level:* A decrease in the expected price level shifts the short-run aggregate-supply curve to the right. An increase in the expected price level shifts the short-run aggregate-supply curve to the left.

Two Causes of Economic Fluctuations

Now that we have introduced the model of aggregate demand and aggregate supply, we have the basic tools we need to analyze fluctuations in economic activity. In particular, we can use what we have learned about aggregate demand and aggregate supply to examine the two basic causes of short-run fluctuations: shifts in aggregate demand and shifts in aggregate supply.

To keep things simple, we assume the economy begins in long-run equilibrium, as shown in Figure 7. Output and the price level are determined in the long run by the intersection of the aggregate-demand curve and the long-run aggregate-supply curve, shown as point A in the figure. At this point, output is at its natural rate. Because the economy is always in a short-run equilibrium, the short-run aggregate-supply curve passes through this point as well, indicating that the expected price level has adjusted to this long-run equilibrium. That is, when an economy is in its long-run equilibrium, the expected price level must equal the actual price level so that the intersection of aggregate demand with short-run aggregate supply is the same as the intersection of aggregate demand with long-run aggregate supply.

The Effects of a Shift in Aggregate Demand

Suppose that a wave of pessimism suddenly overtakes the economy. The cause might be a scandal in the White House, a crash in the stock market, or the outbreak

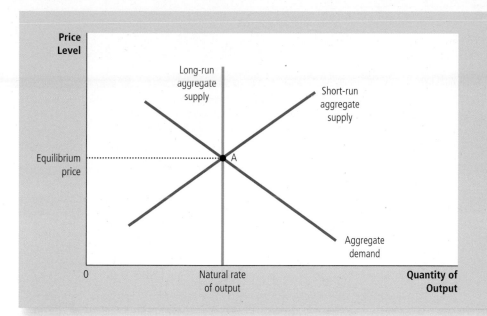

Figure **7**

The Long-Run Equilibrium

The long-run equilibrium of the economy is found where the aggregate-demand curve crosses the long-run aggregate-supply curve (point A). When the economy reaches this long-run equilibrium, the expected price level will have adjusted to equal the actual price level. As a result, the short-run aggregate-supply curve crosses this point as well.

of war overseas. Because of this event, many people lose confidence in the future and alter their plans. Households cut back on their spending and delay major purchases, and firms put off buying new equipment.

What is the macroeconomic impact of such a wave of pessimism? In answering this question, we can follow the three steps we used in Chapter 4 when analyzing supply and demand in specific markets. First, we determine whether the event affects aggregate demand or aggregate supply. Second, we decide in which direction the curve shifts. Third, we use the diagram of aggregate demand and aggregate supply to compare the initial and the new equilibrium. The new wrinkle is that we need to add a fourth step: We have to keep track of a new short-run equilibrium, a new long-run equilibrium, and the transition between them. Table 3 summarizes the four steps to analyzing economic fluctuations.

The first two steps are easy. First, because the wave of pessimism affects spending plans, it affects the aggregate-demand curve. Second, because households and firms now want to buy a smaller quantity of goods and services for any given price level, the event reduces aggregate demand. As Figure 8 shows, the aggregate-demand curve shifts to the left from AD_1 to AD_2.

Table **3**

1. Decide whether the event shifts the aggregate demand curve or the aggregate supply curve (or perhaps both).
2. Decide in which direction the curve shifts.
3. Use the diagram of aggregate demand and aggregate supply to determine the impact on output and the price level in the short run.
4. Use the diagram of aggregate demand and aggregate supply to analyze how the economy moves from its new short-run equilibrium to its long-run equilibrium.

Four Steps for Analyzing Macroeconomic Fluctuations

Figure **8**

A Contraction in Aggregate Demand

A fall in aggregate demand is represented with a leftward shift in the aggregate-demand curve from AD_1 to AD_2. In the short run, the economy moves from point A to point B. Output falls from Y_1 to Y_2, and the price level falls from P_1 to P_2. Over time, as the expected price level adjusts, the short-run aggregate-supply curve shifts to the right from AS_1 to AS_2, and the economy reaches point C, where the new aggregate-demand curve crosses the long-run aggregate-supply curve. In the long run, the price level falls to P_3, and output returns to its natural rate, Y_1.

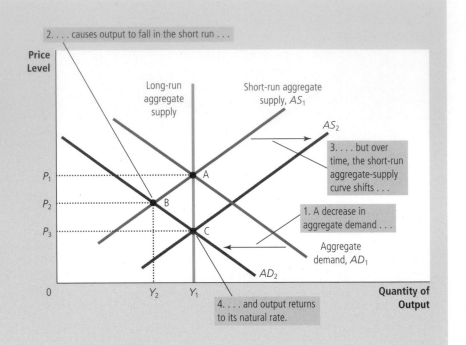

With this figure, we can perform step three: By comparing the initial and the new equilibrium, we can see the effects of the fall in aggregate demand. In the short run, the economy moves along the initial short-run aggregate-supply curve, AS_1, going from point A to point B. As the economy moves between these two points, output falls from Y_1 to Y_2, and the price level falls from P_1 to P_2. The falling level of output indicates that the economy is in a recession. Although not shown in the figure, firms respond to lower sales and production by reducing employment. Thus, the pessimism that caused the shift in aggregate demand is, to some extent, self-fulfilling: Pessimism about the future leads to falling incomes and rising unemployment.

Now comes step four—the transition from the short-run equilibrium to the long-run equilibrium. Because of the reduction in aggregate demand, the price level initially falls from P_1 to P_2. The price level is thus below the level that people were expecting (P_1) before the sudden fall in aggregate demand. People can be surprised in the short run, but they will not remain surprised. Over time, expectations catch up with this new reality, and the expected price level falls as well. The fall in the expected price level alters wages, prices, and perceptions, which in turn influences the position of the short-run aggregate-supply curve. For example, according to the sticky-wage theory, once workers and firms come to expect a lower level of prices, they start to strike bargains for lower nominal wages; the reduction in labor costs encourages firms to hire more workers and expands production at any given level of prices. Thus, the fall in the expected price level shifts the short-run aggregate-supply curve to the right from AS_1 to AS_2 in Figure 8. This shift allows the economy to approach point C, where the new aggregate-demand curve (AD_2) crosses the long-run aggregate-supply curve.

In the new long-run equilibrium, point C, output is back to its natural rate. The economy has corrected itself: The decline in output is reversed in the long

FYI

> ## Monetary Neutrality Revisited

According to classical economic theory, money is neutral. That is, changes in the quantity of money affect nominal variables such as the price level but not real variables such as output. Earlier in this chapter, we noted that most economists accept this conclusion as a description of how the economy works in the long run but not in the short run. With the model of aggregate demand and aggregate supply, we can illustrate this conclusion and explain it more fully.

Suppose that the Federal Reserve reduces the quantity of money in the economy. What effect does this change have? As we discussed, the money supply is one determinant of aggregate demand. The reduction in the money supply shifts the aggregate-demand curve to the left.

The analysis looks just like Figure 8. Even though the cause of the shift in aggregate demand is different, we would observe the same effects on output and the price level. In the short run, both output and the price level fall. The economy experiences a recession. But over time, the expected price level falls as well. Firms and workers respond to their new expectations by, for instance, agreeing to lower nominal wages. As they do so, the short-run aggregate-supply curve shifts to the right. Eventually, the economy finds itself back on the long-run aggregate-supply curve.

Figure 8 shows when money matters for real variables and when it does not. In the long run, money is neutral, as represented by the movement of the economy from point A to point C. But in the short run, a change in the money supply has real effects, as represented by the movement of the economy from point A to point B. An old saying summarizes the analysis: "Money is a veil, but when the veil flutters, real output sputters."

run, even without action by policymakers. Although the wave of pessimism has reduced aggregate demand, the price level has fallen sufficiently (to P_3) to offset the shift in the aggregate-demand curve, and people have come to expect this new lower price level as well. Thus, in the long run, the shift in aggregate demand is reflected fully in the price level and not at all in the level of output. In other words, the long-run effect of a shift in aggregate demand is a nominal change (the price level is lower) but not a real change (output is the same).

What should policymakers do when faced with a sudden fall in aggregate demand? In this analysis, we assumed they did nothing. Another possibility is that, as soon as the economy heads into recession (moving from point A to point B), policymakers could take action to increase aggregate demand. As we noted earlier, an increase in government spending or an increase in the money supply would increase the quantity of goods and services demanded at any price and, therefore, would shift the aggregate-demand curve to the right. If policymakers act with sufficient speed and precision, they can offset the initial shift in aggregate demand, return the aggregate-demand curve to AD_1, and bring the economy back to point A. If the policy is successful, the painful period of depressed output and employment can be reduced in length and severity. The next chapter discusses in more detail the ways in which monetary and fiscal policy influence aggregate demand, as well as some of the practical difficulties in using these policy instruments.

To sum up, this story about shifts in aggregate demand has three important lessons:

- In the short run, shifts in aggregate demand cause fluctuations in the economy's output of goods and services.

- In the long run, shifts in aggregate demand affect the overall price level but do not affect output.
- Policymakers who influence aggregate demand can potentially mitigate the severity of economic fluctuations.

Two Big Shifts in Aggregate Demand: The Great Depression and World War II

At the beginning of this chapter, we established three key facts about economic fluctuations by looking at data since 1965. Let's now take a longer look at U.S. economic history. Figure 9 shows data since 1900 on the percentage change in real GDP over the previous three years. In an average three-year period, real GDP grows about 10 percent—a bit more than 3 percent per year. The business cycle, however, causes fluctuations around this average. Two episodes jump out as being particularly significant: the large drop in real GDP in the early 1930s and the large increase in real GDP in the early 1940s. Both of these events are attributable to shifts in aggregate demand.

The economic calamity of the early 1930s is called the *Great Depression,* and it is by far the largest economic downturn in U.S. history. Real GDP fell by 27 percent from 1929 to 1933, and unemployment rose from 3 percent to 25 percent. At the same time, the price level fell by 22 percent over these four years. Many other countries experienced similar declines in output and prices during this period.

Figure 9

U.S. Real GDP Growth since 1900

Over the course of U.S. economic history, two fluctuations stand out as especially large. During the early 1930s, the economy went through the Great Depression, when the production of goods and services plummeted. During the early 1940s, the United States entered World War II, and the economy experienced rapidly rising production. Both of these events are usually explained by large shifts in aggregate demand.

Source: Louis D. Johnston and Samuel H. Williamson, "Annualized Growth Rate of Various Historical Economic Series." Economic History Services, November 2008, http://www.measuringworth.com/growth/index.php; Department of Commerce (Bureau of Economic Analysis).

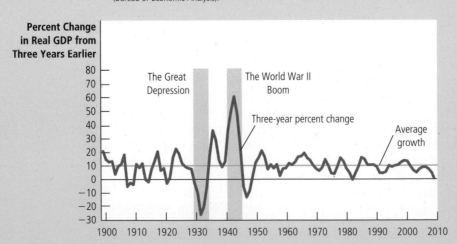

Economic historians continue to debate the causes of the Great Depression, but most explanations center on a large decline in aggregate demand. What caused aggregate demand to contract? Here is where the disagreement arises.

Many economists place primary blame on the decline in the money supply: From 1929 to 1933, the money supply fell by 28 percent. As you may recall from our discussion of the monetary system, this decline in the money supply was due to problems in the banking system. As households withdrew their money from financially shaky banks and bankers became more cautious and started holding greater reserves, the process of money creation under fractional-reserve banking went into reverse. The Fed, meanwhile, failed to offset this fall in the money multiplier with expansionary open-market operations. As a result, the money supply declined. Many economists blame the Fed's failure to act for the Great Depression's severity.

Other economists have suggested alternative reasons for the collapse in aggregate demand. For example, stock prices fell about 90 percent during this period, depressing household wealth and thereby consumer spending. In addition, the banking problems may have prevented some firms from obtaining the financing they wanted for investment projects, and this would have depressed investment spending. It is possible that all these forces may have acted together to contract aggregate demand during the Great Depression.

The second significant episode in Figure 9—the economic boom of the early 1940s—is easier to explain. The obvious cause of this event was World War II. As the United States entered the war overseas, the federal government had to devote more resources to the military. Government purchases of goods and services increased almost fivefold from 1939 to 1944. This huge expansion in aggregate demand almost doubled the economy's production of goods and services and led to a 20 percent increase in the price level (although widespread government price controls limited the rise in prices). Unemployment fell from 17 percent in 1939 to about 1 percent in 1944—the lowest level in U.S. history. ■

The outcome of a massive decrease in aggregate demand

The Recession of 2008–2009

In 2008 and 2009, the U.S. economy experienced a financial crisis and a severe downturn in economic activity. In many ways, it was the worst macroeconomic event in more than half a century.

The story of this downturn begins a few years earlier with a substantial boom in the housing market. The boom was, in part, fueled by low interest rates. In the aftermath of the recession of 2001, the Federal Reserve lowered interest rates to historically low levels. Low interest rates helped the economy recover, but by making it less expensive to get a mortgage and buy a home, they also contributed to a rise in housing prices.

In addition to low interest rates, various developments in the mortgage market made it easier for *subprime borrowers*—those borrowers with a higher risk of default based on their income and credit history—to get loans to buy homes. One development was *securitization*, the process by which a financial institution (specifically, a mortgage originator) makes loans and then (with the help of an investment bank) bundles them together into financial instruments called *mortgage-backed securities*. These mortgage-backed securities were then sold to other institutions (such as banks and insurance companies), which may not have fully appreciated the risks in these securities. Some economists blame inadequate regulation for these high-risk loans. Others blame misguided government policy: Some policies encouraged this high-risk lending to make the goal of homeownership more attainable for low-income families. Together, these many forces drove up housing demand and housing prices. From 1995 to 2006, average housing prices in the United States more than doubled.

The high price of housing, however, proved unsustainable. From 2006 to 2009, housing prices nationwide fell about 30 percent. Such price fluctuations should not necessarily be a problem in a market economy. After all, price movements are how markets equilibrate supply and demand. In this case, however, the price

· · · · · · · · · · · · · · · · in the **news**

> ## Modern Parallels to the Great Depression

As the economy sank in recession in 2008, some observers wondered whether we might see a downturn similar to the Great Depression. As of 2010, when this book was going to press, that scenario seemed unlikely. But the similarities between the events of 2008 and 2009 and those of the 1930s were too troubling to ignore. This article describes how things looked in the midst of the recent economic downturn.

But Have We Learned Enough?

BY N. GREGORY MANKIW

Like most economists, those at the International Monetary Fund are lowering their growth forecasts. The financial turmoil gripping Wall Street will probably spill over onto every other street in America. Most likely, current job losses are only the tip of an ugly iceberg.

But when Olivier Blanchard, the I.M.F.'s chief economist, was asked about the possibility of the world sinking into another Great Depression, he reassuringly replied that the chance was "nearly nil." He added, "We've learned a few things in 80 years."

Yes, we have. But have we learned what caused the Depression of the 1930s? Most important, have we learned enough to avoid doing the same thing again?

The Depression began, to a large extent, as a garden-variety downturn. The 1920s were a boom decade, and as it came to a close the Federal Reserve tried to rein in what might have been called the irrational exuberance of the era.

In 1928, the Fed maneuvered to drive up interest rates. So interest-sensitive sectors like construction slowed.

But things took a bad turn after the crash of October 1929. Lower stock prices made households poorer and discouraged consumer spending, which then made up three-quarters of the economy. (Today it's about two-thirds.)

According to the economic historian Christina D. Romer, a professor at the University of California, Berkeley, the great volatility of stock prices at the time also increased consumers' feelings of uncertainty, inducing them to put off purchases until the uncertainty was resolved. Spending on consumer durable goods like autos dropped precipitously in 1930.

Next came a series of bank panics. From 1930 to 1933, more than 9,000 banks were shuttered, imposing losses on depositors and shareholders of about $2.5 billion. As a share of the economy, that would be the equivalent of $340 billion today.

The banking panics put downward pressure on economic activity in two ways. First, they put fear into the hearts of depositors. Many people concluded that cash in their mattresses was wiser than accounts at local banks.

As they withdrew their funds, the banking system's normal lending and money creation went into reverse. The money supply collapsed, resulting in a 24 percent drop in the consumer price index from 1929 to 1933. This deflation pushed up the real burden of households' debts.

decline had two related repercussions that caused a sizable fall in aggregate demand.

The first repercussion was a substantial rise in mortgage defaults and home foreclosures. During the housing boom, many homeowners had bought their homes with mostly borrowed money and minimal down payments. When housing prices declined, these homeowners were *underwater* (they owed more on their mortgages than their homes were worth). Many of these homeowners stopped paying their loans. The banks servicing the mortgages responded to these defaults by taking the houses away in foreclosure procedures and then selling them off. The banks' goal was to recoup whatever they could from the bad loans. As you

Second, the disappearance of so many banks made credit hard to come by. Small businesses often rely on established relationships with local bankers when they need loans, either to tide them over in tough times or for business expansion. With so many of those relationships interrupted at the same time, the economy's ability to channel financial resources toward their best use was seriously impaired.

Together, these forces proved cataclysmic. Unemployment, which had been 3 percent in 1929, rose to 25 percent in 1933. Even during the worst recession since then, in 1982, the United States economy did not experience half that level of unemployment.

Policy makers in the 1930s responded vigorously as the situation deteriorated. But like a doctor facing a patient with a new disease and strange symptoms, they often acted in ways that, with the benefit of hindsight, appeared counterproductive.

Probably the most important source of recovery after 1933 was monetary expansion, eased by President Franklin D. Roosevelt's decision to abandon the gold standard and devalue the dollar. From 1933 to 1937, the money supply rose, stopping the deflation. Production in the economy grew about 10 percent a year, three times its normal rate.

Less successful were various market interventions. According to a study by the economists Harold L. Cole and Lee E. Ohanian, both of the University of California, Los Angeles, and the Federal Reserve Bank of Minneapolis, President Roosevelt made things worse when he encouraged the formation of cartels through the National Industrial Recovery Act of 1933. Similarly, they argue, the National Labor Relations Act of 1935 strengthened organized labor but weakened the recovery by impeding market forces.

Looking back at these events, it's hard to avoid seeing parallels to the current situation. Today, as then, uncertainty has consumers spooked. By some measures, stock market volatility in recent days has reached levels not seen since the 1930s. With volatility spiking, the University of Michigan's survey reading of consumer sentiment has been plunging.

Deflation across the economy is not a problem (yet), but deflation in the housing market is the source of many of our present difficulties. With so many homeowners owing more on their mortgages than their houses are worth, default is an unfortunate but often rational choice. Widespread foreclosures, however, only perpetuate the downward spiral of housing prices, further defaults and additional losses at financial institutions.

The Fed and the Treasury Department, intent on avoiding the early policy inaction that let the Depression unfold, have been working hard to keep credit flowing. But the financial situation they face is, arguably, more difficult than that of the 1930s. Then, the problem was largely a crisis of confidence and a shortage of liquidity. Today, the problem may be more a shortage of solvency, which is harder to solve.

What's next? Perhaps the most troubling study of the 1930s economy was written in 1988 by the economists Kathryn Dominguez, Ray Fair and Matthew Shapiro; it was called "Forecasting the Depression: Harvard Versus Yale." (Mr. Fair is an economics professor at Yale; Ms. Dominguez and Mr. Shapiro are at the University of Michigan.)

The three researchers show that the leading economists at the time, at competing forecasting services run by Harvard and Yale, were caught completely by surprise by the severity and length of the Great Depression. What's worse, despite many advances in the tools of economic analysis, modern economists armed with the data from the time would not have forecast much better. In other words, even if another Depression were around the corner, you shouldn't expect much advance warning from the economics profession.

Let me be clear: Like Mr. Blanchard at the I.M.F., I am not predicting another Great Depression. We have indeed learned a lot over the last 80 years. But you should take that economic forecast, like all others, with more than a single grain of salt.

Source: *New York Times*, October 26, 2008.

might have expected from your study of supply and demand, the increase in the number of homes for sale exacerbated the downward spiral of house prices. As house prices fell, spending on the construction of housing also collapsed.

A second repercussion was that the various financial institutions that owned mortgage-backed securities suffered huge losses. In essence, by borrowing large sums to buy high-risk mortgages, these companies had bet that house prices would keep rising; when this bet turned bad, they found themselves at or near the point of bankruptcy. Because of these large losses, many financial institutions did not have funds to loan out, and the ability of the financial system to channel resources to those who could best use them was impaired. Even creditworthy customers found themselves unable to borrow to finance investment spending.

As a result of all these events, the economy experienced a large contractionary shift in aggregate demand. Real GDP and employment both fell sharply. Real GDP declined by almost 4 percent between the fourth quarter of 2007 and the second quarter of 2009. The rate of unemployment rose from 4.4 percent in May 2007 to 10.1 percent in October 2009.

As the crisis unfolded, the U.S government responded in a variety of ways. Three policy actions—all aimed in part at returning aggregate demand to its previous level—are most noteworthy. First, the Fed cut its target for the federal funds rate from 5.25 percent in September 2007 to about zero in December 2008. The Federal Reserve also started buying mortgage-backed securities and other private loans in open-market operations. By purchasing these instruments from the banking system, the Fed provided banks with additional funds in the hope that the banks would makes loans more readily available.

Second, in an even more unusual move in October 2008, Congress appropriated $700 billion for the Treasury to use to rescue the financial system. The goal was to stem the financial crisis on Wall Street and make loans easier to obtain. Much of these funds were used for equity injections into banks. That is, the Treasury put funds into the banking system, which the banks could use to make loans; in exchange for these funds, the U.S. government became a part owner of these banks, at least temporarily.

Finally, when Barack Obama became president in January 2009, his first major initiative was a large increase in government spending. After a relatively brief congressional debate over the form of the legislation, the new president signed a $787 billion stimulus bill on February 17, 2009. This policy move is discussed more fully in the next chapter when we consider the impact of fiscal policy on aggregate demand.

As this book was going to press, the economy was starting to recover from the economic downturn. Real GDP was growing again, and unemployment had fallen to 9.5 percent in June 2010. Which, if any, of these many policy moves were most important for promoting this economic recovery? That is surely a question that macroeconomic historians will debate in the years to come. ■

The Effects of a Shift in Aggregate Supply

Imagine once again an economy in its long-run equilibrium. Now suppose that suddenly some firms experience an increase in their costs of production. For example, bad weather in farm states might destroy some crops, driving up the cost of producing food products. Or a war in the Middle East might interrupt the shipping of crude oil, driving up the cost of producing oil products.

To analyze the macroeconomic impact of such an increase in production costs, we follow the same four steps as we always do. First, which curve is affected? Because production costs affect the firms that supply goods and services, changes in production costs alter the position of the aggregate-supply curve. Second, in which direction does the curve shift? Because higher production costs make selling goods and services less profitable, firms now supply a smaller quantity of output for any given price level. Thus, as Figure 10 shows, the short-run aggregate-supply curve shifts to the left from AS_1 to AS_2. (Depending on the event, the long-run aggregate-supply curve might also shift. To keep things simple, however, we will assume that it does not.)

The figure allows us to perform step three of comparing the initial and the new equilibrium. In the short run, the economy goes from point A to point B, moving along the existing aggregate-demand curve. The output of the economy falls from Y_1 to Y_2, and the price level rises from P_1 to P_2. Because the economy is experiencing both *stagnation* (falling output) and *inflation* (rising prices), such an event is sometimes called **stagflation.**

Now consider step four—the transition from the short-run equilibrium to the long-run equilibrium. According to the sticky-wage theory, the key issue is how stagflation affects nominal wages. Firms and workers may at first respond to the higher level of prices by raising their expectations of the price level and setting higher nominal wages. In this case, firms' costs will rise yet again, and the short-run aggregate-supply curve will shift farther to the left, making the problem of stagflation even worse. This phenomenon of higher prices leading to higher wages, in turn leading to even higher prices, is sometimes called a *wage-price spiral.*

At some point, this spiral of ever-rising wages and prices will slow. The low level of output and employment will put downward pressure on workers' wages because workers have less bargaining power when unemployment is high. As nominal wages fall, producing goods and services becomes more profitable, and the short-run aggregate-supply curve shifts to the right. As it shifts back toward AS_1, the price level falls, and the quantity of output approaches its natural rate. In

stagflation
a period of falling output and rising prices

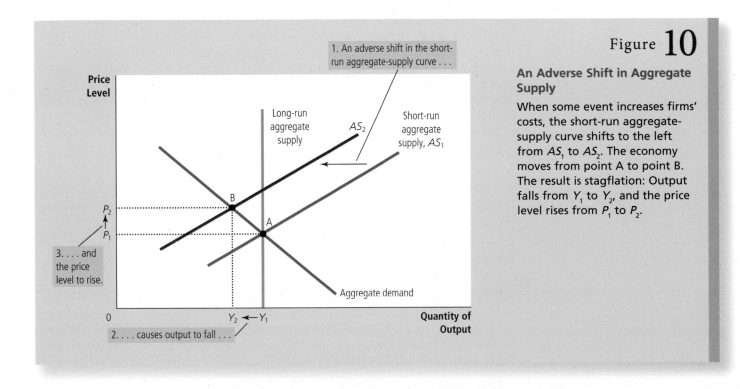

Figure **10**

An Adverse Shift in Aggregate Supply

When some event increases firms' costs, the short-run aggregate-supply curve shifts to the left from AS_1 to AS_2. The economy moves from point A to point B. The result is stagflation: Output falls from Y_1 to Y_2, and the price level rises from P_1 to P_2.

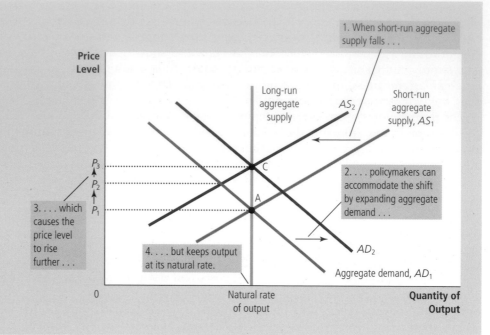

Figure **11**

Accommodating an Adverse Shift in Aggregate Supply
Faced with an adverse shift in aggregate supply from AS_1 to AS_2, policymakers who can influence aggregate demand might try to shift the aggregate-demand curve to the right from AD_1 to AD_2. The economy would move from point A to point C. This policy would prevent the supply shift from reducing output in the short run, but the price level would permanently rise from P_1 to P_3.

the long run, the economy returns to point A, where the aggregate-demand curve crosses the long-run aggregate-supply curve.

This transition back to the initial equilibrium assumes, however, that aggregate demand is held constant throughout the process. In the real world, that may not be the case. Policymakers who control monetary and fiscal policy might attempt to off-set some of the effects of the shift in the short-run aggregate-supply curve by shift-ing the aggregate-demand curve. This possibility is shown in Figure 11. In this case, changes in policy shift the aggregate-demand curve to the right from AD_1 to AD_2—exactly enough to prevent the shift in aggregate supply from affecting output. The economy moves directly from point A to point C. Output remains at its natural rate, and the price level rises from P_1 to P_3. In this case, policymakers are said to *accommodate* the shift in aggregate supply. An accommodative policy accepts a permanently higher level of prices to maintain a higher level of output and employment.

To sum up, this story about shifts in aggregate supply has two important lessons:

- Shifts in aggregate supply can cause stagflation—a combination of recession (falling output) and inflation (rising prices).
- Policymakers who can influence aggregate demand can potentially mitigate the adverse impact on output but only at the cost of exacerbating the problem of inflation.

 Oil and the Economy

Some of the largest economic fluctuations in the U.S. economy since 1970 have originated in the oil fields of the Middle East. Crude oil is a key input into the production of many goods and services, and much of the world's oil comes from Saudi Arabia, Kuwait, and other Middle Eastern countries. When some event (usually political in origin) reduces the supply of crude oil flowing from this region, the price of oil rises around the world. U.S. firms that produce gasoline, tires, and many other products experience rising costs, and they find it less profitable to supply their output of goods and services at any given price level. The result is a leftward shift in the aggregate-supply curve, which in turn leads to stagflation.

The first episode of this sort occurred in the mid-1970s. The countries with large oil reserves got together as members of OPEC, the Organization of Petroleum Exporting Countries. OPEC is a *cartel*—a group of sellers that attempts to thwart competition and reduce production to raise prices. And indeed, oil prices rose substantially. From 1973 to 1975, oil approximately doubled in price. Oil-importing countries around the world experienced simultaneous inflation and recession. The U.S. inflation rate as measured by the CPI exceeded 10 percent for the first time in decades. Unemployment rose from 4.9 percent in 1973 to 8.5 percent in 1975.

Almost the same thing happened a few years later. In the late 1970s, the OPEC countries again restricted the supply of oil to raise the price. From 1978 to 1981, the price of oil more than doubled. Once again, the result was

FYI

> ## The Origins of the Model of Aggregate Demand and Aggregate Supply

Now that we have a preliminary understanding of the model of aggregate demand and aggregate supply, it is worthwhile to step back from it and consider its history. How did this model of short-run fluctuations develop? The answer is that this model, to a large extent, is a by-product of the Great Depression of the 1930s. Economists and policymakers at the time were puzzled about what had caused this calamity and were uncertain about how to deal with it.

In 1936, economist John Maynard Keynes published a book titled *The General Theory of Employment, Interest, and Money*, which attempted to explain short-run economic fluctuations in general and the Great Depression in particular. Keynes's primary message was that recessions and depressions can occur because of inadequate aggregate demand for goods and services.

Keynes had long been a critic of classical economic theory—the theory we examined earlier in the book—because it could

John Maynard Keynes

explain only the long-run effects of policies. A few years before offering *The General Theory*, Keynes had written the following about classical economics:

> *The long run is a misleading guide to current affairs. In the long run we are all dead. Economists set themselves too easy, too useless a task if in tempestuous seasons they can only tell us when the storm is long past, the ocean will be flat.*

Keynes's message was aimed at policymakers as well as economists. As the world's economies suffered with high unemployment, Keynes advocated policies to increase aggregate demand, including government spending on public works.

In the next chapter, we examine in detail how policymakers can use the tools of monetary and fiscal policy to influence aggregate demand. The analysis in the next chapter, as well as in this one, owes much to the legacy of John Maynard Keynes.

Changes in Middle East oil production are one source of U.S. economic fluctuations.

stagflation. Inflation, which had subsided somewhat after the first OPEC event, again rose above 10 percent per year. But because the Fed was not willing to accommodate such a large rise in inflation, a recession was soon to follow. Unemployment rose from about 6 percent in 1978 and 1979 to about 10 percent a few years later.

The world market for oil can also be a source of favorable shifts in aggregate supply. In 1986, squabbling broke out among members of OPEC. Member countries reneged on their agreements to restrict oil production. In the world market for crude oil, prices fell by about half. This fall in oil prices reduced costs to U.S. firms, which now found it more profitable to supply goods and services at any given price level. As a result, the aggregate-supply curve shifted to the right. The U.S. economy experienced the opposite of stagflation: Output grew rapidly, unemployment fell, and the inflation rate reached its lowest level in many years.

In recent years, the world market for oil has not been as important a source of economic fluctuations. Part of the reason is that conservation efforts and changes in technology have reduced the economy's dependence on oil. The amount of oil used to produce a unit of real GDP has declined about 40 percent since the OPEC shocks of the 1970s. As a result, the economic impact of any change in oil prices is smaller today than it was in the past. ■

QUICK QUIZ   *Suppose that the election of a popular presidential candidate suddenly increases people's confidence in the future. Use the model of aggregate demand and aggregate supply to analyze the effect on the economy.*

Conclusion

This chapter has achieved two goals. First, we have discussed some of the important facts about short-run fluctuations in economic activity. Second, we have introduced a basic model to explain those fluctuations, called the model of aggregate demand and aggregate supply. We continue our study of this model in the next chapter to understand more fully what causes fluctuations in the economy and how policymakers might respond to these fluctuations.

SUMMARY

- All societies experience short-run economic fluctuations around long-run trends. These fluctuations are irregular and largely unpredictable. When recessions do occur, real GDP and other measures of income, spending, and production fall, and unemployment rises.

- Classical economic theory is based on the assumption that nominal variables such as the money supply and the price level do not

influence real variables such as output and employment. Most economists believe that this assumption is accurate in the long run but not in the short run. Economists analyze short-run economic fluctuations using the model of aggregate demand and aggregate supply. According to this model, the output of goods and services and the overall level of prices adjust to balance aggregate demand and aggregate supply.

- The aggregate-demand curve slopes downward for three reasons. The first is the wealth effect: A lower price level raises the real value of households' money holdings, which stimulates consumer spending. The second is the interest-rate effect: A lower price level reduces the quantity of money households demand; as households try to convert money into interest-bearing assets, interest rates fall, which stimulates investment spending. The third is the exchange-rate effect: As a lower price level reduces interest rates, the dollar depreciates in the market for foreign-currency exchange, which stimulates net exports.

- Any event or policy that raises consumption, investment, government purchases, or net exports at a given price level increases aggregate demand. Any event or policy that reduces consumption, investment, government purchases, or net exports at a given price level decreases aggregate demand.

- The long-run aggregate-supply curve is vertical. In the long run, the quantity of goods and services supplied depends on the economy's labor, capital, natural resources, and technology but not on the overall level of prices.

- Three theories have been proposed to explain the upward slope of the short-run aggregate-supply curve. According to the sticky-wage theory, an unexpected fall in the price level temporarily raises real wages, which induces firms to reduce employment and production. According to the sticky-price theory, an unexpected fall in the price level leaves some firms with prices that are temporarily too high, which reduces their sales and causes them to cut back production. According to the misperceptions theory, an unexpected fall in the price level leads suppliers to mistakenly believe that their relative prices have fallen, which induces them to reduce production. All three theories imply that output deviates from its natural rate when the actual price level deviates from the price level that people expected.

- Events that alter the economy's ability to produce output, such as changes in labor, capital, natural resources, or technology, shift the short-run aggregate-supply curve (and may shift the long-run aggregate-supply curve as well). In addition, the position of the short-run aggregate-supply curve depends on the expected price level.

- One possible cause of economic fluctuations is a shift in aggregate demand. When the aggregate-demand curve shifts to the left, for instance, output and prices fall in the short run. Over time, as a change in the expected price level causes wages, prices, and perceptions to adjust, the short-run aggregate-supply curve shifts to the right. This shift returns the economy to its natural rate of output at a new, lower price level.

- A second possible cause of economic fluctuations is a shift in aggregate supply. When the short-run aggregate-supply curve shifts to the left, the effect is falling output and rising prices—a combination called stagflation. Over time, as wages, prices, and perceptions adjust, the short-run aggregate-supply curve shifts back to the right, returning the price level and output to their original levels.

KEY CONCEPTS

recession, *p. 319*

depression, *p. 319*

model of aggregate demand and aggregate supply, *p. 325*

aggregate-demand curve, *p. 325*

aggregate-supply curve, *p. 326*

natural rate of output, *p. 333*

stagflation, *p. 349*

QUESTIONS FOR REVIEW

1. Name two macroeconomic variables that decline when the economy goes into a recession. Name one macroeconomic variable that rises during a recession.

2. Draw a diagram with aggregate demand, short-run aggregate supply, and long-run aggregate supply. Be careful to label the axes correctly.

3. List and explain the three reasons the aggregate-demand curve is downward sloping.
4. Explain why the long-run aggregate-supply curve is vertical.
5. List and explain the three theories for why the short-run aggregate-supply curve is upward sloping.
6. What might shift the aggregate-demand curve to the left? Use the model of aggregate demand and aggregate supply to trace through the short-run and long-run effects of such a shift on output and the price level.
7. What might shift the aggregate-supply curve to the left? Use the model of aggregate demand and aggregate supply to trace through the short-run and long-run effects of such a shift on output and the price level.

PROBLEMS AND APPLICATIONS

1. Suppose the economy is in a long-run equilibrium.
   a. Draw a diagram to illustrate the state of the economy. Be sure to show aggregate demand, short-run aggregate supply, and long-run aggregate supply.
   b. Now suppose that a stock-market crash causes aggregate demand to fall. Use your diagram to show what happens to output and the price level in the short run. What happens to the unemployment rate?
   c. Use the sticky-wage theory of aggregate supply to explain what will happen to output and the price level in the long run (assuming there is no change in policy). What role does the expected price level play in this adjustment? Be sure to illustrate your analysis in a graph.
2. Explain whether each of the following events will increase, decrease, or have no effect on long-run aggregate supply.
   a. The United States experiences a wave of immigration.
   b. Congress raises the minimum wage to $10 per hour.
   c. Intel invents a new and more powerful computer chip.
   d. A severe hurricane damages factories along the East Coast.
3. Suppose an economy is in long-run equilibrium.
   a. Use the model of aggregate demand and aggregate supply to illustrate the initial equilibrium (call it point A). Be sure to include both short-run and long-run aggregate supply.
   b. The central bank raises the money supply by 5 percent. Use your diagram to show what happens to output and the price level as the economy moves from the initial to the new short-run equilibrium (call it point B).
   c. Now show the new long-run equilibrium (call it point C). What causes the economy to move from point B to point C?
   d. According to the sticky-wage theory of aggregate supply, how do nominal wages at point A compare to nominal wages at point B? How do nominal wages at point A compare to nominal wages at point C?
   e. According to the sticky-wage theory of aggregate supply, how do real wages at point A compare to real wages at point B? How do real wages at point A compare to real wages at point C?
   f. Judging by the impact of the money supply on nominal and real wages, is this analysis consistent with the proposition that money has real effects in the short run but is neutral in the long run?
4. In 1939, with the U.S. economy not yet fully recovered from the Great Depression, President Roosevelt proclaimed that Thanksgiving would fall a week earlier than usual so that the shopping period before Christmas would be longer. Explain what President Roosevelt might have been trying to achieve, using the model of aggregate demand and aggregate supply.
5. Explain why the following statements are false.
   a. "The aggregate-demand curve slopes downward because it is the horizontal sum of the demand curves for individual goods."
   b. "The long-run aggregate-supply curve is vertical because economic forces do not affect long-run aggregate supply."

c. "If firms adjusted their prices every day, then the short-run aggregate-supply curve would be horizontal."

d. "Whenever the economy enters a recession, its long-run aggregate-supply curve shifts to the left."

6. For each of the three theories for the upward slope of the short-run aggregate-supply curve, carefully explain the following:

   a. How the economy recovers from a recession and returns to its long-run equilibrium without any policy intervention.

   b. What determines the speed of that recovery.

7. Suppose the Fed expands the money supply, but because the public expects this Fed action, it simultaneously raises its expectation of the price level. What will happen to output and the price level in the short run? Compare this result to the outcome if the Fed expanded the money supply but the public didn't change its expectation of the price level.

8. The economy begins in long-run equilibrium. Then one day, the president appoints a new chairman of the Federal Reserve. This new chairman is well-known for his view that inflation is not a major problem for an economy.

   a. How would this news affect the price level that people would expect to prevail?

   b. How would this change in the expected price level affect the nominal wage that workers and firms agree to in their new labor contracts?

   c. How would this change in the nominal wage affect the profitability of producing goods and services at any given price level?

   d. How does this change in profitability affect the short-run aggregate-supply curve?

   e. If aggregate demand is held constant, how does this shift in the aggregate-supply curve affect the price level and the quantity of output produced?

   f. Do you think this Fed chairman was a good appointment?

9. Explain whether each of the following events shifts the short-run aggregate-supply curve, the aggregate-demand curve, both, or neither. For each event that does shift a curve, draw a diagram to illustrate the effect on the economy.

   a. Households decide to save a larger share of their income.

   b. Florida orange groves suffer a prolonged period of below-freezing temperatures.

   c. Increased job opportunities overseas cause many people to leave the country.

10. For each of the following events, explain the short-run and long-run effects on output and the price level, assuming policymakers take no action.

    a. The stock market declines sharply, reducing consumers' wealth.

    b. The federal government increases spending on national defense.

    c. A technological improvement raises productivity.

    d. A recession overseas causes foreigners to buy fewer U.S. goods.

11. Suppose firms become very optimistic about future business conditions and invest heavily in new capital equipment.

    a. Draw an aggregate-demand/aggregate-supply diagram to show the short-run effect of this optimism on the economy. Label the new levels of prices and real output. Explain in words why the aggregate quantity of output *supplied* changes.

    b. Now use the diagram from part (a) to show the new long-run equilibrium of the economy. (For now, assume there is no change in the long-run aggregate-supply curve.) Explain in words why the aggregate quantity of output *demanded* changes between the short run and the long run.

    c. How might the investment boom affect the long-run aggregate-supply curve? Explain.

12. In economy A, all workers agree in advance on the nominal wages that their employers will pay them. In economy B, half of all workers have these nominal wage contracts, while the other half have indexed employment contracts, so their wages rise and fall automatically with the price level. According to the sticky-wage theory of aggregate supply, which economy has a more steeply sloped short-run aggregate-supply curve? In which economy would a 5 percent increase in the money supply have a larger impact on output? In which economy would it have a larger impact on the price level? Explain.

For further information on topics in this chapter, additional problems, applications, examples, online quizzes, and more, please visit our website at www.cengage.com/economics/mankiw.

The Influence of Monetary and Fiscal Policy on Aggregate Demand

16

Imagine that you are a member of the Federal Open Market Committee, the group at the Federal Reserve that sets monetary policy. You observe that the president and Congress have agreed to raise taxes. How should the Fed respond to this change in fiscal policy? Should it expand the money supply, contract the money supply, or leave the money supply the same?

To answer this question, you need to consider the impact of monetary and fiscal policy on the economy. In the preceding chapter, we used the model of aggregate demand and aggregate supply to explain short-run economic fluctuations. We saw that shifts in the aggregate-demand curve or the aggregate-supply curve cause fluctuations in the economy's overall output of goods and services and its overall level of prices. As we noted in the previous chapter, monetary and fiscal policy can each influence aggregate demand. Thus, a change in one of these policies can lead to short-run fluctuations in output and prices. Policymakers will want to anticipate this effect and, perhaps, adjust the other policy in response.

In this chapter, we examine in more detail how the government's policy tools influence the position of the aggregate-demand curve. These tools include monetary policy (the supply of money set by the central bank) and fiscal policy (the levels of government spending and taxation set by the president and Congress). We have previously discussed the long-run effects of these policies. In Chapters 7 and 8, we saw how fiscal policy affects saving, investment, and long-run economic growth. In Chapters 11 and 12, we saw how monetary policy influences the price level in the long run. We now see how these policy tools can shift the aggregate-demand curve and, in doing so, affect macroeconomic variables in the short run.

As we have already learned, many factors influence aggregate demand besides monetary and fiscal policy. In particular, desired spending by households and firms determines the overall demand for goods and services. When desired spending changes, aggregate demand shifts. If policymakers do not respond, such shifts in aggregate demand cause short-run fluctuations in output and employment. As a result, monetary and fiscal policymakers sometimes use the policy levers at their disposal to try to offset these shifts in aggregate demand and thereby stabilize the economy. Here we discuss the theory behind these policy actions and some of the difficulties that arise in using this theory in practice.

How Monetary Policy Influences Aggregate Demand

The aggregate-demand curve shows the total quantity of goods and services demanded in the economy for any price level. The preceding chapter discussed three reasons the aggregate-demand curve slopes downward:

- *The wealth effect:* A lower price level raises the real value of households' money holdings, which are part of their wealth. Higher real wealth stimulates consumer spending and thus increases the quantity of goods and services demanded.
- *The interest-rate effect:* A lower price level reduces the amount of money people want to hold. As people try to lend out their excess money holdings, the interest rate falls. The lower interest rate stimulates investment spending and thus increases the quantity of goods and services demanded.
- *The exchange-rate effect:* When a lower price level reduces the interest rate, investors move some of their funds overseas in search of higher returns. This movement of funds causes the real value of the domestic currency to fall in the market for foreign-currency exchange. Domestic goods become less expensive relative to foreign goods. This change in the real exchange rate stimulates spending on net exports and thus increases the quantity of goods and services demanded.

These three effects occur simultaneously to increase the quantity of goods and services demanded when the price level falls and to decrease it when the price level rises.

Although all three effects work together to explain the downward slope of the aggregate-demand curve, they are not of equal importance. Because money holdings are a small part of household wealth, the wealth effect is the least important of the three. In addition, because exports and imports represent only a small fraction of U.S. GDP, the exchange-rate effect is not large for the U.S. economy. (This effect is more important for smaller countries, which typically export and import a higher fraction of their GDP.) *For the U.S. economy, the most important reason for the downward slope of the aggregate demand curve is the interest-rate effect.*

To better understand aggregate demand, we now examine the short-run determination of interest rates in more detail. Here we develop the **theory of liquidity preference.** This theory of interest-rate determination will help explain the downward slope of the aggregate-demand curve, as well as how monetary and fiscal policy can shift this curve. By shedding new light on aggregate demand, the theory of liquidity preference expands our understanding of what causes short-run economic fluctuations and what policymakers can potentially do about them.

The Theory of Liquidity Preference

In his classic book *The General Theory of Employment, Interest, and Money,* John Maynard Keynes proposed the theory of liquidity preference to explain the factors that determine an economy's interest rate. The theory is, in essence, an application of supply and demand. According to Keynes, the interest rate adjusts to balance the supply of and demand for money.

You may recall that economists distinguish between two interest rates: The *nominal interest rate* is the interest rate as usually reported, and the *real interest rate* is the interest rate corrected for the effects of inflation. When there is no inflation, the two rates are the same. But when borrowers and lenders expect prices to rise over the course of the loan, they agree to a nominal interest rate that exceeds the real interest rate by the expected rate of inflation. The higher nominal interest rate compensates for the fact that they expect the loan to be repaid in less valuable dollars.

Which interest rate are we now trying to explain with the theory of liquidity preference? The answer is both. In the analysis that follows, we hold constant the expected rate of inflation. This assumption is reasonable for studying the economy in the short run, because expected inflation is typically stable over short periods of time. In this case, nominal and real interest rates differ by a constant. When the nominal interest rate rises or falls, the real interest rate that people expect to earn rises or falls as well. For the rest of this chapter, when we refer to changes in the interest rate, you should envision the real and nominal interest rates moving in the same direction.

Let's now develop the theory of liquidity preference by considering the supply and demand for money and how each depends on the interest rate.

Money Supply   The first piece of the theory of liquidity preference is the supply of money. As we first discussed in Chapter 11, the money supply in the U.S. economy is controlled by the Federal Reserve. The Fed alters the money supply primarily by changing the quantity of reserves in the banking system through the purchase and sale of government bonds in open-market operations. When the Fed buys government bonds, the dollars it pays for the bonds are typically deposited in banks, and these dollars are added to bank reserves. When the Fed sells government bonds, the dollars it receives for the bonds are withdrawn from the banking system, and bank reserves fall. These changes in bank reserves, in turn, lead to changes in banks' ability to make loans and create money. Thus, by buying and selling bonds in open-market operations, the Fed alters the quantity of money in the economy.

theory of liquidity preference
Keynes's theory that the interest rate adjusts to bring money supply and money demand into balance

In addition to open-market operations, the Fed can influence the money supply using a variety of other tools. One option is for the Fed to change how much it lends to banks. For example, a decrease in the discount rate (the interest rate at which banks can borrow reserves from the Fed) encourages more bank borrowing, which increases bank reserves and thereby the money supply. Conversely, an increase in the discount rate discourages bank borrowing, which decreases bank reserves and the money supply. The Fed also alters the money supply by changing reserve requirements (the amount of reserves banks must hold against deposits) and by changing the interest rate it pays banks on the reserves they are holding.

These details of monetary control are important for the implementation of Fed policy, but they are not crucial for the analysis in this chapter. Our goal here is to examine how changes in the money supply affect the aggregate demand for goods and services. For this purpose, we can ignore the details of how Fed policy is implemented and assume that the Fed controls the money supply directly. In other words, the quantity of money supplied in the economy is fixed at whatever level the Fed decides to set it.

Because the quantity of money supplied is fixed by Fed policy, it does not depend on other economic variables. In particular, it does not depend on the interest rate. Once the Fed has made its policy decision, the quantity of money supplied is the same, regardless of the prevailing interest rate. We represent a fixed money supply with a vertical supply curve, as in Figure 1.

Figure 1

Equilibrium in the Money Market

According to the theory of liquidity preference, the interest rate adjusts to bring the quantity of money supplied and the quantity of money demanded into balance. If the interest rate is above the equilibrium level (such as at r_1), the quantity of money people want to hold (M_1^d) is less than the quantity the Fed has created, and this surplus of money puts downward pressure on the interest rate. Conversely, if the interest rate is below the equilibrium level (such as at r_2), the quantity of money people want to hold (M_2^d) is greater than the quantity the Fed has created, and this shortage of money puts upward pressure on the interest rate. Thus, the forces of supply and demand in the market for money push the interest rate toward the equilibrium interest rate, at which people are content holding the quantity of money the Fed has created.

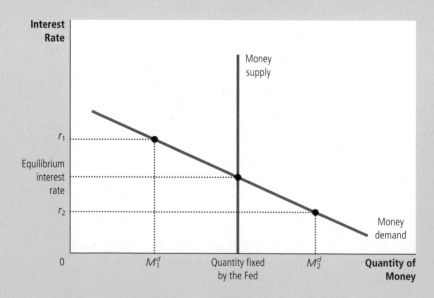

Money Demand   The second piece of the theory of liquidity preference is the demand for money. As a starting point for understanding money demand, recall that any asset's *liquidity* refers to the ease with which that asset can be converted into the economy's medium of exchange. Because money is the economy's medium of exchange, it is by definition the most liquid asset available. The liquidity of money explains the demand for it: People choose to hold money instead of other assets that offer higher rates of return because money can be used to buy goods and services.

Although many factors determine the quantity of money demanded, the one emphasized by the theory of liquidity preference is the interest rate. The reason is that the interest rate is the opportunity cost of holding money. That is, when you hold wealth as cash in your wallet, instead of as an interest-bearing bond, you lose the interest you could have earned. An increase in the interest rate raises the cost of holding money and, as a result, reduces the quantity of money demanded. A decrease in the interest rate reduces the cost of holding money and raises the quantity demanded. Thus, as shown in Figure 1, the money-demand curve slopes downward.

Equilibrium in the Money Market   According to the theory of liquidity preference, the interest rate adjusts to balance the supply and demand for money. There is one interest rate, called the *equilibrium interest rate,* at which the quantity of money demanded exactly balances the quantity of money supplied. If the interest rate is at any other level, people will try to adjust their portfolios of assets and, as a result, drive the interest rate toward the equilibrium.

For example, suppose that the interest rate is above the equilibrium level, such as r_1 in Figure 1. In this case, the quantity of money that people want to hold, M_1^d, is less than the quantity of money that the Fed has supplied. Those people who are holding the surplus of money will try to get rid of it by buying interest-bearing bonds or by depositing it in an interest-bearing bank account. Because bond issuers and banks prefer to pay lower interest rates, they respond to this surplus of money by lowering the interest rates they offer. As the interest rate falls, people become more willing to hold money until, at the equilibrium interest rate, people are happy to hold exactly the amount of money the Fed has supplied.

Conversely, at interest rates below the equilibrium level, such as r_2 in Figure 1, the quantity of money that people want to hold, M_2^d, is greater than the quantity of money that the Fed has supplied. As a result, people try to increase their holdings of money by reducing their holdings of bonds and other interest-bearing assets. As people cut back on their holdings of bonds, bond issuers find that they have to offer higher interest rates to attract buyers. Thus, the interest rate rises and approaches the equilibrium level.

The Downward Slope of the Aggregate-Demand Curve

Having seen how the theory of liquidity preference explains the economy's equilibrium interest rate, we now consider the theory's implications for the aggregate demand for goods and services. As a warm-up exercise, let's begin by using the theory to reexamine a topic we already understand—the interest-rate effect and the downward slope of the aggregate-demand curve. In particular, suppose that the overall level of prices in the economy rises. What happens to the interest rate

FYI

> ## Interest Rates in the Long Run and the Short Run

In an earlier chapter, we said that the interest rate adjusts to balance the supply of loanable funds (national saving) and the demand for loanable funds (desired investment). Here we just said that the interest rate adjusts to balance the supply of and demand for money. Can we reconcile these two theories?

To answer this question, we need to focus on three macroeconomic variables: the economy's output of goods and services, the interest rate, and the price level. According to the classical macroeconomic theory we developed earlier in the book, these variables are determined as follows:

1. *Output* is determined by the supplies of capital and labor and the available production technology for turning capital and labor into output. (We call this the natural rate of output.)
2. For any given level of output, the *interest rate* adjusts to balance the supply and demand for loanable funds.
3. Given output and the interest rate, the *price level* adjusts to balance the supply and demand for money. Changes in the supply of money lead to proportionate changes in the price level.

These are three of the essential propositions of classical economic theory. Most economists believe that these propositions do a good job of describing how the economy works *in the long run*.

Yet these propositions do not hold in the short run. As we discussed in the preceding chapter, many prices are slow to adjust to changes in the money supply; this fact is reflected in a short-run aggregate-supply curve that is upward sloping rather than vertical. As a result, *in the short run*, the overall price level cannot, by itself, move

to balance the supply of and demand for money. This stickiness of the price level requires the interest rate to move to bring the money market into equilibrium. These changes in the interest rate, in turn, affect the aggregate demand for goods and services. As aggregate demand fluctuates, the economy's output of goods and services moves away from the level determined by factor supplies and technology.

To think about the operation of the economy in the short run (day to day, week to week, month to month, or quarter to quarter), it is best to keep in mind the following logic:

1. The *price level* is stuck at some level (based on previously formed expectations) and, in the short run, is relatively unresponsive to changing economic conditions.
2. For any given (stuck) price level, the *interest rate* adjusts to balance the supply of and demand for money.
3. The interest rate that balances the money market influences the quantity of goods and services demanded and thus the level of *output*.

Notice that this precisely reverses the order of analysis used to study the economy in the long run.

The two different theories of the interest rate are useful for different purposes. When thinking about the long-run determinants of interest rates, it is best to keep in mind the loanable-funds theory, which highlights the importance of an economy's saving propensities and investment opportunities. By contrast, when thinking about the short-run determinants of interest rates, it is best to keep in mind the liquidity-preference theory, which highlights the importance of monetary policy.

that balances the supply and demand for money, and how does that change affect the quantity of goods and services demanded?

As we discussed in Chapter 12, the price level is one determinant of the quantity of money demanded. At higher prices, more money is exchanged every time a good or service is sold. As a result, people will choose to hold a larger quantity of money. That is, a higher price level increases the quantity of money demanded for any given interest rate. Thus, an increase in the price level from P_1 to P_2 shifts the money-demand curve to the right from MD_1 to MD_2, as shown in panel (a) of Figure 2.

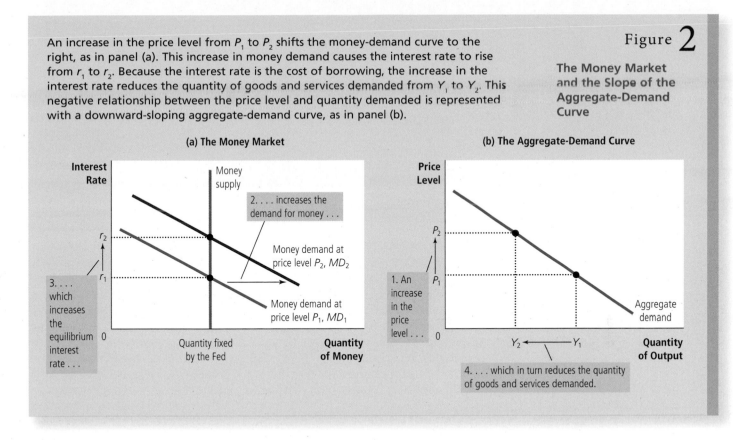

An increase in the price level from P_1 to P_2 shifts the money-demand curve to the right, as in panel (a). This increase in money demand causes the interest rate to rise from r_1 to r_2. Because the interest rate is the cost of borrowing, the increase in the interest rate reduces the quantity of goods and services demanded from Y_1 to Y_2. This negative relationship between the price level and quantity demanded is represented with a downward-sloping aggregate-demand curve, as in panel (b).

Figure **2**

The Money Market and the Slope of the Aggregate-Demand Curve

(a) The Money Market

(b) The Aggregate-Demand Curve

Notice how this shift in money demand affects the equilibrium in the money market. For a fixed money supply, the interest rate must rise to balance money supply and money demand. Because the higher price level has increased the amount of money people want to hold, it has shifted the money demand curve to the right. Yet the quantity of money supplied is unchanged, so the interest rate must rise from r_1 to r_2 to discourage the additional demand.

This increase in the interest rate has ramifications not only for the money market but also for the quantity of goods and services demanded, as shown in panel (b). At a higher interest rate, the cost of borrowing and the return to saving are greater. Fewer households choose to borrow to buy a new house, and those who do buy smaller houses, so the demand for residential investment falls. Fewer firms choose to borrow to build new factories and buy new equipment, so business investment falls. Thus, when the price level rises from P_1 to P_2, increasing money demand from MD_1 to MD_2 and raising the interest rate from r_1 to r_2, the quantity of goods and services demanded falls from Y_1 to Y_2.

This analysis of the interest-rate effect can be summarized in three steps: (1) A higher price level raises money demand. (2) Higher money demand leads to a higher interest rate. (3) A higher interest rate reduces the quantity of goods and services demanded. The same logic works in reverse: A lower price level reduces money demand, which leads to a lower interest rate, and this in turn increases the quantity of goods and services demanded. The result of this analysis is a negative relationship between the price level and the quantity of goods and services demanded, as illustrated by a downward-sloping aggregate-demand curve.

Changes in the Money Supply

So far, we have used the theory of liquidity preference to explain more fully how the total quantity of goods and services demanded in the economy changes as the price level changes. That is, we have examined movements along a downward-sloping aggregate-demand curve. The theory also sheds light, however, on some of the other events that alter the quantity of goods and services demanded. Whenever the quantity of goods and services demanded changes *for any given price level*, the aggregate-demand curve shifts.

One important variable that shifts the aggregate-demand curve is monetary policy. To see how monetary policy affects the economy in the short run, suppose that the Fed increases the money supply by buying government bonds in open-market operations. (Why the Fed might do this will become clear later, after we understand the effects of such a move.) Let's consider how this monetary injection influences the equilibrium interest rate for a given price level. This will tell us what the injection does to the position of the aggregate-demand curve.

As panel (a) of Figure 3 shows, an increase in the money supply shifts the money-supply curve to the right from MS_1 to MS_2. Because the money-demand curve has not changed, the interest rate falls from r_1 to r_2 to balance money supply and money demand. That is, the interest rate must fall to induce people to hold the additional money the Fed has created, restoring equilibrium in the money market.

Once again, the interest rate influences the quantity of goods and services demanded, as shown in panel (b) of Figure 3. The lower interest rate reduces the cost of borrowing and the return to saving. Households buy more and larger houses, stimulating the demand for residential investment. Firms spend more on

Figure 3

A Monetary Injection

In panel (a), an increase in the money supply from MS_1 to MS_2 reduces the equilibrium interest rate from r_1 to r_2. Because the interest rate is the cost of borrowing, the fall in the interest rate raises the quantity of goods and services demanded at a given price level from Y_1 to Y_2. Thus, in panel (b), the aggregate-demand curve shifts to the right from AD_1 to AD_2.

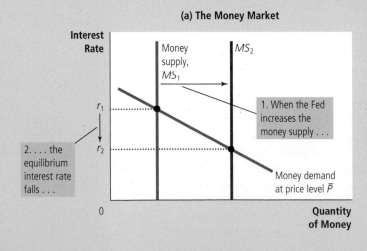

(a) The Money Market

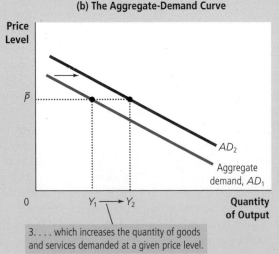

(b) The Aggregate-Demand Curve

new factories and new equipment, stimulating business investment. As a result, the quantity of goods and services demanded at a given price level, $\overline{P}$, rises from Y_1 to Y_2. Of course, there is nothing special about $\overline{P}$: The monetary injection raises the quantity of goods and services demanded at every price level. Thus, the entire aggregate-demand curve shifts to the right.

To sum up: *When the Fed increases the money supply, it lowers the interest rate and increases the quantity of goods and services demanded for any given price level, shifting the aggregate-demand curve to the right. Conversely, when the Fed contracts the money supply, it raises the interest rate and reduces the quantity of goods and services demanded for any given price level, shifting the aggregate-demand curve to the left.*

The Role of Interest-Rate Targets in Fed Policy

How does the Federal Reserve affect the economy? Our discussion here and earlier in the book has treated the money supply as the Fed's policy instrument. When the Fed buys government bonds in open-market operations, it increases the money supply and expands aggregate demand. When the Fed sells government bonds in open-market operations, it decreases the money supply and contracts aggregate demand.

Discussions of Fed policy often treat the interest rate, rather than the money supply, as the Fed's policy instrument. Indeed, in recent years, the Federal Reserve has conducted policy by setting a target for the *federal funds rate*—the interest rate that banks charge one another for short-term loans. This target is reevaluated every six weeks at meetings of the Federal Open Market Committee (FOMC). The FOMC has chosen to set a target for the federal funds rate, rather than for the money supply, as it has done at times in the past.

There are several related reasons for the Fed's decision to use the federal funds rate as its target. One is that the money supply is hard to measure with sufficient precision. Another is that money demand fluctuates over time. For any given money supply, fluctuations in money demand would lead to fluctuations in interest rates, aggregate demand, and output. By contrast, when the Fed announces a target for the federal funds rate, it essentially accommodates the day-to-day shifts in money demand by adjusting the money supply accordingly.

The Fed's decision to target an interest rate does not fundamentally alter our analysis of monetary policy. The theory of liquidity preference illustrates an important principle: *Monetary policy can be described either in terms of the money supply or in terms of the interest rate.* When the FOMC sets a target for the federal funds rate of, say, 6 percent, the Fed's bond traders are told: "Conduct whatever open-market operations are necessary to ensure that the equilibrium interest rate equals 6 percent." In other words, when the Fed sets a target for the interest rate, it commits itself to adjusting the money supply to make the equilibrium in the money market hit that target.

As a result, changes in monetary policy can be viewed either in terms of changing the interest rate target or in terms of changing the money supply. When you read in the newspaper that "the Fed has lowered the federal funds rate from 6 to 5 percent," you should understand that this occurs only because the Fed's bond traders are doing what it takes to make it happen. To lower the federal funds rate, the Fed's bond traders buy government bonds, and this purchase increases the money supply and lowers the equilibrium interest rate (just as in Figure 3). Similarly, when the FOMC raises the target for the federal funds rate, the bond traders sell government bonds, and this sale decreases the money supply and raises the equilibrium interest rate.

FYI

> ## The Zero Lower Bound

As we have just seen, monetary policy works through interest rates. This conclusion raises a question: What if the Fed's target interest rate has fallen as far as it can? In the recession of 2008 and 2009, the federal funds rate fell to about zero. What, if anything, can monetary policy do then to stimulate the economy?

Some economists describe this situation as a *liquidity trap.* According to the theory of liquidity preference, expansionary monetary policy works by reducing interest rates and stimulating investment spending. But if interest rates have already fallen almost to zero, then perhaps monetary policy is no longer effective. Nominal interest rates cannot fall below zero: Rather than making a loan at a negative nominal interest rate, a person would just hold cash. In this environment, expansionary monetary policy raises the supply of money, making the public's asset portfolio more liquid, but because interest rates can't fall any further, the extra liquidity might not have any effect. Aggregate demand, production, and employment may be "trapped" at low levels.

Other economists are skeptical about the relevance of liquidity traps and believe that a central bank continues to have tools to expand the economy, even after its interest rate target hits its lower bound of zero. One possibility is that the central bank could raise inflation expectations by committing itself to future monetary expansion. Even if nominal interest rates cannot fall any further, higher expected inflation can lower real interest rates by making them negative, which would stimulate investment spending.

A second possibility is that the central bank could conduct expansionary open-market operations with a larger variety of financial instruments than it normally uses. For example, it could buy mortgages and corporate debt and thereby lower the interest rates on these kinds of loans. The Federal Reserve actively pursued this last option during the downturn of 2008 and 2009.

Some economists have suggested that the possibility of hitting the zero lower bound for interest rates justifies setting the target rate of inflation well above zero. Under zero inflation, the real interest rate, like the nominal interest, can never fall below zero. But if the normal rate of inflation is, say, 4 percent, then the central bank can easily push the real interest rate to negative 4 percent by lowering the nominal interest rate toward zero. Thus, moderate inflation gives monetary policymakers more room to stimulate the economy when needed, reducing the risk of hitting up against the zero lower bound and having the economy fall into a liquidity trap.

The lessons from this analysis are simple: *Changes in monetary policy aimed at expanding aggregate demand can be described either as increasing the money supply or as lowering the interest rate. Changes in monetary policy aimed at contracting aggregate demand can be described either as decreasing the money supply or as raising the interest rate.*

CASE STUDY

Why the Fed Watches the Stock Market (and Vice Versa)

"The stock market has predicted nine out of the past five recessions." So quipped Paul Samuelson, the famed economist (and textbook author). Samuelson was surely right that the stock market is highly volatile and can give wrong signals about the economy. But fluctuations in stock prices are often a sign of broader economic developments. The economic boom of the 1990s, for example, appeared not only in rapid GDP growth and falling unemployment but also in rising stock prices, which increased about fourfold during this decade. Similarly, the deep recession of 2008 and 2009 was reflected in falling stock prices: From November 2007 to March 2009, the stock market lost about half its value.

How should the Fed respond to stock-market fluctuations? The Fed has no reason to care about stock prices in themselves, but it does have the job of monitoring and responding to developments in the overall economy, and the stock market is a piece of that puzzle. When the stock market booms, households become wealthier, and this increased wealth stimulates consumer spending. In addition, a rise in stock prices makes it more attractive for firms to sell new shares of stock, and this stimulates investment spending. For both reasons, a booming stock market expands the aggregate demand for goods and services.

As we discuss more fully later in the chapter, one of the Fed's goals is to stabilize aggregate demand, because greater stability in aggregate demand means greater stability in output and the price level. To promote stability, the Fed might respond to a stock-market boom by keeping the money supply lower and interest rates higher than it otherwise would. The contractionary effects of higher interest rates would offset the expansionary effects of higher stock prices. In fact, this analysis does describe Fed behavior: Real interest rates were kept high by historical standards during the stock-market boom of the late 1990s.

The opposite occurs when the stock market falls. Spending on consumption and investment tends to decline, depressing aggregate demand and pushing the economy toward recession. To stabilize aggregate demand, the Fed would increase the money supply and lower interest rates. And indeed, that is what it typically does. For example, on October 19, 1987, the stock market fell by 22.6 percent—one of the biggest one-day drops in history. The Fed responded to the market crash by increasing the money supply and lowering interest rates. The federal funds rate fell from 7.7 percent at the beginning of October to 6.6 percent at the end of the month. In part because of the Fed's quick action, the economy avoided a recession. Similarly, as we discussed in a case study in the preceding chapter, the Fed also reduced interest rates during the economic downturn and stock market decline of 2008 and 2009, but this time monetary policy was not sufficient to avert a deep recession.

While the Fed keeps an eye on the stock market, stock-market participants also keep an eye on the Fed. Because the Fed can influence interest rates and economic activity, it can alter the value of stocks. For example, when the Fed raises interest rates by reducing the money supply, it makes owning stocks less attractive for two reasons. First, a higher interest rate means that bonds, the alternative to stocks, are earning a higher return. Second, the Fed's tightening of monetary policy reduces the demand for goods and services, which reduces profits. As a result, stock prices often fall when the Fed raises interest rates. ■

QUICK QUIZ   *Use the theory of liquidity preference to explain how a decrease in the money supply affects the equilibrium interest rate. How does this change in monetary policy affect the aggregate-demand curve?*

How Fiscal Policy Influences Aggregate Demand

The government can influence the behavior of the economy not only with monetary policy but also with fiscal policy. **Fiscal policy** refers to the government's choices regarding the overall level of government purchases and taxes. Earlier in the book, we examined how fiscal policy influences saving, investment, and growth in the long run. In the short run, however, the primary effect of fiscal policy is on the aggregate demand for goods and services.

fiscal policy
the setting of the level of government spending and taxation by government policymakers

Changes in Government Purchases

When policymakers change the money supply or the level of taxes, they shift the aggregate-demand curve indirectly by influencing the spending decisions of firms or households. By contrast, when the government alters its own purchases of goods and services, it shifts the aggregate-demand curve directly.

Suppose, for instance, that the U.S. Department of Defense places a $20 billion order for new fighter planes with Boeing, the large aircraft manufacturer. This order raises the demand for the output produced by Boeing, which induces the company to hire more workers and increase production. Because Boeing is part of the economy, the increase in the demand for Boeing planes means an increase in the total quantity of goods and services demanded at each price level. As a result, the aggregate-demand curve shifts to the right.

By how much does this $20 billion order from the government shift the aggregate-demand curve? At first, one might guess that the aggregate-demand curve shifts to the right by exactly $20 billion. It turns out, however, that this is not the case. There are two macroeconomic effects that cause the size of the shift in aggregate demand to differ from the change in government purchases. The first—the multiplier effect—suggests the shift in aggregate demand could be *larger* than $20 billion. The second—the crowding-out effect—suggests the shift in aggregate demand could be *smaller* than $20 billion. We now discuss each of these effects in turn.

The Multiplier Effect

When the government buys $20 billion of goods from Boeing, that purchase has repercussions. The immediate impact of the higher demand from the government is to raise employment and profits at Boeing. Then, as the workers see higher earnings and the firm owners see higher profits, they respond to this increase in income by raising their own spending on consumer goods. As a result, the government purchase from Boeing raises the demand for the products of many other firms in the economy. Because each dollar spent by the government can raise the aggregate demand for goods and services by more than a dollar, government purchases are said to have a **multiplier effect** on aggregate demand.

multiplier effect
the additional shifts in aggregate demand that result when expansionary fiscal policy increases income and thereby increases consumer spending

This multiplier effect continues even after this first round. When consumer spending rises, the firms that produce these consumer goods hire more people and experience higher profits. Higher earnings and profits stimulate consumer spending once again and so on. Thus, there is positive feedback as higher demand leads to higher income, which in turn leads to even higher demand. Once all these effects are added together, the total impact on the quantity of goods and services demanded can be much larger than the initial impulse from higher government spending.

Figure 4 illustrates the multiplier effect. The increase in government purchases of $20 billion initially shifts the aggregate-demand curve to the right from AD_1 to AD_2 by exactly $20 billion. But when consumers respond by increasing their spending, the aggregate-demand curve shifts still further to AD_3.

This multiplier effect arising from the response of consumer spending can be strengthened by the response of investment to higher levels of demand. For instance, Boeing might respond to the higher demand for planes by deciding to buy more equipment or build another plant. In this case, higher government demand spurs higher demand for investment goods. This positive feedback from demand to investment is sometimes called the *investment accelerator*.

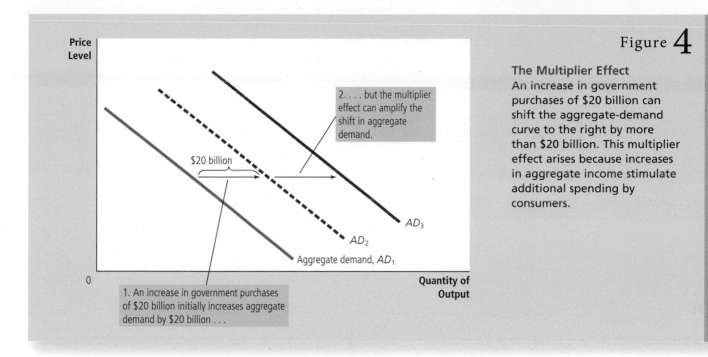

Figure **4**

The Multiplier Effect
An increase in government purchases of $20 billion can shift the aggregate-demand curve to the right by more than $20 billion. This multiplier effect arises because increases in aggregate income stimulate additional spending by consumers.

2. . . . but the multiplier effect can amplify the shift in aggregate demand.

$20 billion

AD_3

AD_2

Aggregate demand, AD_1

Quantity of Output

1. An increase in government purchases of $20 billion initially increases aggregate demand by $20 billion . . .

A Formula for the Spending Multiplier

Some simple algebra permits us to derive a formula for the size of the multiplier effect that arises when an increase in government purchases induces increases in consumer spending. An important number in this formula is the *marginal propensity to consume (MPC)*—the fraction of extra income that a household consumes rather than saves. For example, suppose that the marginal propensity to consume is ¾. This means that for every extra dollar that a household earns, the household spends $0.75 (¾ of the dollar) and saves $0.25. With an *MPC* of ¾, when the workers and owners of Boeing earn $20 billion from the government contract, they increase their consumer spending by ¾ × $20 billion, or $15 billion.

To gauge the impact on aggregate demand of a change in government purchases, we follow the effects step by step. The process begins when the government spends $20 billion, which implies that national income (earnings and profits) also rises by this amount. This increase in income in turn raises consumer spending by *MPC* × $20 billion, which in turn raises the income for the workers and owners of the firms that produce the consumption goods. This second increase in income again raises consumer spending, this time by *MPC* × (*MPC* × $20 billion). These feedback effects go on and on.

To find the total impact on the demand for goods and services, we add up all these effects:

Change in government purchases = $20 billion
First change in consumption   = *MPC* × $20 billion
Second change in consumption   = *MPC*² × $20 billion
Third change in consumption   = *MPC*³ × $20 billion
           ·   ·
           ·   ·
           ·   ·

Total change in demand
     = (1 + *MPC* + *MPC*² + *MPC*³ + . . .) × $20 billion.

Here "..." represents an infinite number of similar terms. Thus, we can write the multiplier as follows:

$$\text{Multiplier} = 1 + MPC + MPC^2 + MPC^3 + \ldots.$$

This multiplier tells us the demand for goods and services that each dollar of government purchases generates.

To simplify this equation for the multiplier, recall from math class that this expression is an infinite geometric series. For x between -1 and $+1$,

$$1 + x + x^2 + x^3 + \ldots = 1/(1 - x).$$

In our case, $x = MPC$. Thus,

$$\text{Multiplier} = 1/(1 - MPC).$$

For example, if MPC is ¾, the multiplier is $1/(1 - ¾)$, which is 4. In this case, the $20 billion of government spending generates $80 billion of demand for goods and services.

This formula for the multiplier shows an important conclusion: The size of the multiplier depends on the marginal propensity to consume. While an MPC of ¾ leads to a multiplier of 4, an MPC of ½ leads to a multiplier of only 2. Thus, a larger MPC means a larger multiplier. To see why this is true, remember that the multiplier arises because higher income induces greater spending on consumption. With a larger MPC, consumption responds more to a change in income, and so the multiplier is larger.

Other Applications of the Multiplier Effect

Because of the multiplier effect, a dollar of government purchases can generate more than a dollar of aggregate demand. The logic of the multiplier effect, however, is not restricted to changes in government purchases. Instead, it applies to any event that alters spending on any component of GDP—consumption, investment, government purchases, or net exports.

For example, suppose that a recession overseas reduces the demand for U.S. net exports by $10 billion. This reduced spending on U.S. goods and services depresses U.S. national income, which reduces spending by U.S. consumers. If the marginal propensity to consume is ¾ and the multiplier is 4, then the $10 billion fall in net exports means a $40 billion contraction in aggregate demand.

As another example, suppose that a stock-market boom increases households' wealth and stimulates their spending on goods and services by $20 billion. This extra consumer spending increases national income, which in turn generates even more consumer spending. If the marginal propensity to consume is ¾ and the multiplier is 4, then the initial impulse of $20 billion in consumer spending translates into an $80 billion increase in aggregate demand.

The multiplier is an important concept in macroeconomics because it shows how the economy can amplify the impact of changes in spending. A small initial change in consumption, investment, government purchases, or net exports can end up having a large effect on aggregate demand and, therefore, the economy's production of goods and services.

The Crowding-Out Effect

The multiplier effect seems to suggest that when the government buys $20 billion of planes from Boeing, the resulting expansion in aggregate demand is necessarily larger than $20 billion. Yet another effect works in the opposite direction. While an increase in government purchases stimulates the aggregate demand for goods and services, it also causes the interest rate to rise, which reduces investment spending and puts downward pressure on aggregate demand. The reduction in aggregate demand that results when a fiscal expansion raises the interest rate is called the **crowding-out effect.**

To see why crowding out occurs, let's consider what happens in the money market when the government buys planes from Boeing. As we have discussed, this increase in demand raises the incomes of the workers and owners of this firm (and because of the multiplier effect, of other firms as well). As incomes rise, households plan to buy more goods and services and, as a result, choose to hold more of their wealth in liquid form. That is, the increase in income caused by the fiscal expansion raises the demand for money.

The effect of the increase in money demand is shown in panel (a) of Figure 5. Because the Fed has not changed the money supply, the vertical supply curve remains the same. When the higher level of income shifts the money-demand curve to the right from MD_1 to MD_2, the interest rate must rise from r_1 to r_2 to keep supply and demand in balance.

crowding-out effect
the offset in aggregate demand that results when expansionary fiscal policy raises the interest rate and thereby reduces investment spending

Panel (a) shows the money market. When the government increases its purchases of goods and services, the resulting increase in income raises the demand for money from MD_1 to MD_2, and this causes the equilibrium interest rate to rise from r_1 to r_2. Panel (b) shows the effects on aggregate demand. The initial impact of the increase in government purchases shifts the aggregate-demand curve from AD_1 to AD_2. Yet because the interest rate is the cost of borrowing, the increase in the interest rate tends to reduce the quantity of goods and services demanded, particularly for investment goods. This crowding out of investment partially offsets the impact of the fiscal expansion on aggregate demand. In the end, the aggregate-demand curve shifts only to AD_3.

Figure **5**

The Crowding-Out Effect

(a) The Money Market

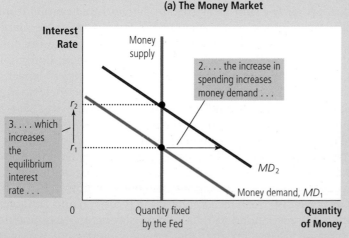

(b) The Shift in Aggregate Demand

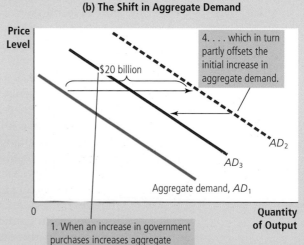

The increase in the interest rate, in turn, reduces the quantity of goods and services demanded. In particular, because borrowing is more expensive, the demand for residential and business investment goods declines. That is, as the increase in government purchases increases the demand for goods and services, it may also crowd out investment. This crowding-out effect partially offsets the impact of government purchases on aggregate demand, as illustrated in panel (b) of Figure 5. The increase in government purchases initially shifts the aggregate-demand curve from AD_1 to AD_2, but once crowding out takes place, the aggregate-demand curve drops back to AD_3.

To sum up: *When the government increases its purchases by $20 billion, the aggregate demand for goods and services could rise by more or less than $20 billion depending on the sizes of the multiplier and crowding-out effects.* The multiplier effect by itself makes the shift in aggregate demand greater than $20 billion. The crowding-out effect pushes the aggregate-demand curve in the opposite direction and, if large enough, could result in an aggregate-demand shift of less than $20 billion.

Changes in Taxes

The other important instrument of fiscal policy, besides the level of government purchases, is the level of taxation. When the government cuts personal income taxes, for instance, it increases households' take-home pay. Households will save some of this additional income, but they will also spend some of it on consumer goods. Because it increases consumer spending, the tax cut shifts the aggregate-demand curve to the right. Similarly, a tax increase depresses consumer spending and shifts the aggregate-demand curve to the left.

The size of the shift in aggregate demand resulting from a tax change is also affected by the multiplier and crowding-out effects. When the government cuts taxes and stimulates consumer spending, earnings and profits rise, which further stimulates consumer spending. This is the multiplier effect. At the same time, higher income leads to higher money demand, which tends to raise interest rates. Higher interest rates make borrowing more costly, which reduces investment spending. This is the crowding-out effect. Depending on the size of the multiplier and crowding-out effects, the shift in aggregate demand could be larger or smaller than the tax change that causes it.

In addition to the multiplier and crowding-out effects, there is another important determinant of the size of the shift in aggregate demand that results from a tax change: households' perceptions about whether the tax change is permanent or temporary. For example, suppose that the government announces a tax cut of $1,000 per household. In deciding how much of this $1,000 to spend, households must ask themselves how long this extra income will last. If households expect the tax cut to be permanent, they will view it as adding substantially to their financial resources and, therefore, increase their spending by a large amount. In this case, the tax cut will have a large impact on aggregate demand. By contrast, if households expect the tax change to be temporary, they will view it as adding only slightly to their financial resources and, therefore, will increase their spending by only a small amount. In this case, the tax cut will have a small impact on aggregate demand.

An extreme example of a temporary tax cut was the one announced in 1992. In that year, President George H. W. Bush faced a lingering recession and an upcoming reelection campaign. He responded to these circumstances by announcing a reduction in the amount of income tax that the federal government was withholding from workers' paychecks. Because legislated income tax rates did not change, however, every dollar of reduced withholding in 1992 meant an extra dollar of taxes due on April 15, 1993, when income tax returns for 1992 were to

FYI

> ## How Fiscal Policy Might Affect Aggregate Supply

So far, our discussion of fiscal policy has stressed how changes in government purchases and changes in taxes influence the quantity of goods and services demanded. Most economists believe that the short-run macroeconomic effects of fiscal policy work primarily through aggregate demand. Yet fiscal policy can potentially influence the quantity of goods and services supplied as well.

For instance, consider the effects of tax changes on aggregate supply. One of the *Ten Principles of Economics* in Chapter 1 is that people respond to incentives. When government policymakers cut tax rates, workers get to keep more of each dollar they earn, so they have a greater incentive to work and produce goods and services. If they respond to this incentive, the quantity of goods and services supplied will be greater at each price level, and the aggregate-supply curve will shift to the right.

Some economists, called *supply-siders*, have argued that the influence of tax cuts on aggregate supply is large. According to some supply-siders, the influence is so large that a cut in tax rates will stimulate enough additional production and income that tax revenue will actually increase. This is certainly a theoretical possibility, but most economists do not consider it the normal case. While the supply-side effects of taxes are important to consider, they are usually not large enough to cause tax revenue to rise when tax rates fall.

Like changes in taxes, changes in government purchases can also potentially affect aggregate supply. Suppose, for instance, that the government increases expenditure on a form of government-provided capital, such as roads. Roads are used by private businesses to make deliveries to their customers; an increase in the quantity of roads increases these businesses' productivity. Hence, when the government spends more on roads, it increases the quantity of goods and services supplied at any given price level and, thus, shifts the aggregate-supply curve to the right. This effect on aggregate supply is probably more important in the long run than in the short run, however, because it would take some time for the government to build the new roads and put them into use.

be filed. Thus, this "tax cut" actually represented only a short-term loan from the government. Not surprisingly, the impact of the policy on consumer spending and aggregate demand was relatively small.

QUICK QUIZ   *Suppose that the government reduces spending on highway construction by $10 billion. Which way does the aggregate-demand curve shift? Explain why the shift might be larger than $10 billion. Explain why the shift might be smaller than $10 billion.*

Using Policy to Stabilize the Economy

We have seen how monetary and fiscal policy can affect the economy's aggregate demand for goods and services. These theoretical insights raise some important policy questions: Should policymakers use these instruments to control aggregate demand and stabilize the economy? If so, when? If not, why not?

The Case for Active Stabilization Policy

Let's return to the question that began this chapter: When the president and Congress raise taxes, how should the Federal Reserve respond? As we have seen, the level of taxation is one determinant of the position of the aggregate-demand curve. When the government raises taxes, aggregate demand will fall, depressing production and employment in the short run. If the Federal Reserve wants to prevent this adverse effect of the fiscal policy, it can expand aggregate demand by increasing the money supply. A monetary expansion would reduce interest rates, stimulate investment spending, and expand aggregate demand. If monetary policy responds appropriately, the combined changes in monetary and fiscal policy could leave the aggregate demand for goods and services unaffected.

This analysis is exactly the sort followed by members of the Federal Open Market Committee. They know that monetary policy is an important determinant of aggregate demand. They also know that there are other important determinants as well, including fiscal policy set by the president and Congress. As a result, the Fed's Open Market Committee watches the debates over fiscal policy with a keen eye.

This response of monetary policy to the change in fiscal policy is an example of a more general phenomenon: the use of policy instruments to stabilize aggregate demand and, as a result, production and employment. Economic stabilization has been an explicit goal of U.S. policy since the Employment Act of 1946. This act states that "it is the continuing policy and responsibility of the federal government to . . . promote full employment and production." In essence, the government has chosen to hold itself accountable for short-run macroeconomic performance.

The Employment Act has two implications. The first, more modest, implication is that the government should avoid being a cause of economic fluctuations. Thus, most economists advise against large and sudden changes in monetary and fiscal policy, for such changes are likely to cause fluctuations in aggregate demand. Moreover, when large changes do occur, it is important that monetary and fiscal policymakers be aware of and respond to each others' actions.

The second, more ambitious, implication of the Employment Act is that the government should respond to changes in the private economy to stabilize aggregate demand. The act was passed not long after the publication of Keynes's *The General Theory of Employment, Interest, and Money,* which has been one of the most influential books ever written about economics. In it, Keynes emphasized the key role of aggregate demand in explaining short-run economic fluctuations. Keynes claimed that the government should actively stimulate aggregate demand when aggregate demand appeared insufficient to maintain production at its full-employment level.

Keynes (and his many followers) argued that aggregate demand fluctuates because of largely irrational waves of pessimism and optimism. He used the term "animal spirits" to refer to these arbitrary changes in attitude. When pessimism reigns, households reduce consumption spending, and firms reduce investment spending. The result is reduced aggregate demand, lower production, and higher unemployment. Conversely, when optimism reigns, households and firms increase spending. The result is higher aggregate demand, higher production, and inflationary pressure. Notice that these changes in attitude are, to some extent, self-fulfilling.

In principle, the government can adjust its monetary and fiscal policy in response to these waves of optimism and pessimism and, thereby, stabilize the economy. For example, when people are excessively pessimistic, the Fed can expand the money supply to lower interest rates and expand aggregate demand. When they are excessively optimistic, it can contract the money supply to raise interest rates and dampen aggregate demand. Former Fed Chairman William McChesney Martin described this view of monetary policy very simply: "The Federal Reserve's job is to take away the punch bowl just as the party gets going."

Keynesians in the White House

When a reporter in 1961 asked President John F. Kennedy why he advocated a tax cut, Kennedy replied, "To stimulate the economy. Don't you remember your Economics 101?" Kennedy's policy was, in fact, based on the analysis of fiscal policy we have developed in this chapter. His goal was to enact a tax cut, which would raise consumer spending, expand aggregate demand, and increase the economy's production and employment.

In choosing this policy, Kennedy was relying on his team of economic advisers. This team included such prominent economists as James Tobin and Robert Solow, who later would win Nobel Prizes for their contributions to economics. As students in the 1940s, these economists had closely studied John Maynard Keynes's *General Theory*, which then was only a few years old. When the Kennedy advisers proposed cutting taxes, they were putting Keynes's ideas into action.

Although tax changes can have a potent influence on aggregate demand, they have other effects as well. In particular, by changing the incentives that people face, taxes can alter the aggregate supply of goods and services. Part of the Kennedy proposal was an investment tax credit, which gives a tax break to firms that invest in new capital. Higher investment would not only stimulate aggregate demand immediately but also increase the economy's productive capacity over time. Thus, the short-run goal of increasing production through higher aggregate demand was coupled with a long-run goal of increasing production through higher aggregate supply. And indeed, when the tax cut Kennedy proposed was finally enacted in 1964, it helped usher in a period of robust economic growth.

Since the 1964 tax cut, policymakers have from time to time used fiscal policy as a tool for controlling aggregate demand. For example, when President Barack Obama moved into the Oval Office in 2009, he faced an economy in the midst of a recession. One of his first policy initiatives was a stimulus bill that included substantial increases in government spending. The accompanying In the News box discusses some of the debate over this policy initiative. ■

The Case against Active Stabilization Policy

Some economists argue that the government should avoid active use of monetary and fiscal policy to try to stabilize the economy. They claim that these policy instruments should be set to achieve long-run goals, such as rapid economic growth and low inflation, and that the economy should be left to deal with short-run fluctuations on its own. These economists may admit that monetary and fiscal policy can stabilize the economy in theory, but they doubt whether it can do so in practice.

The primary argument against active monetary and fiscal policy is that these policies affect the economy with a long lag. As we have seen, monetary policy works by changing interest rates, which in turn influence investment spending. But many firms make investment plans far in advance. Thus, most economists believe that it takes at least six months for changes in monetary policy to have much effect on output and employment. Moreover, once these effects occur, they can last for several years. Critics of stabilization policy argue that because of this lag, the Fed should not try to fine-tune the economy. They claim that the Fed often reacts too late to changing economic conditions and, as a result, ends up being a cause of rather than a cure for economic fluctuations. These critics advocate a passive monetary policy, such as slow and steady growth in the money supply.

in the news

How Large Is the Fiscal Policy Multiplier?

In the global economic downturn of 2008 and 2009, governments around the world turned to fiscal policy to prop up aggregate demand.

Much Ado about Multipliers

It is the biggest peacetime fiscal expansion in history. Across the globe countries have countered the recession by cutting taxes and by boosting government spending. The G20 group of economies, whose leaders meet this week in Pittsburgh, have introduced stimulus packages worth an average of 2% of GDP this year and 1.6% of GDP in 2010. Co-ordinated action on this scale might suggest a consensus about the effects of fiscal stimulus. But economists are in fact deeply divided about how well, or indeed whether, such stimulus works.

The debate hinges on the scale of the "fiscal multiplier". This measure, first formalised in 1931 by Richard Kahn, a student of John Maynard Keynes, captures how effectively tax cuts or increases in government spending stimulate output. A multiplier of one means that a $1 billion increase in government spending will increase a country's GDP by $1 billion.

The size of the multiplier is bound to vary according to economic conditions. For an economy operating at full capacity, the fiscal multiplier should be zero. Since there are no spare resources, any increase in government demand would just replace spending elsewhere. But in a recession, when workers and factories lie idle, a fiscal boost can increase overall demand. And if the initial stimulus triggers a cascade of expenditure among consumers and businesses, the multiplier can be well above one.

The multiplier is also likely to vary according to the type of fiscal action. Government spending on building a bridge may have a bigger multiplier than a tax cut if consumers save a portion of their tax windfall. A tax cut targeted at poorer people may have a bigger impact on spending than one for the affluent, since poorer folk tend to spend a higher share of their income.

Crucially, the overall size of the fiscal multiplier also depends on how people react to higher government borrowing. If the government's actions bolster confidence and revive animal spirits, the multiplier could rise as demand goes up and private investment is "crowded in." But if interest rates climb in response to government borrowing then some private investment that would otherwise have occurred could get "crowded out." And if consumers expect higher future taxes in order to finance new government borrowing, they could spend

Fiscal policy also works with a lag, but unlike the lag in monetary policy, the lag in fiscal policy is largely attributable to the political process. In the United States, most changes in government spending and taxes must go through congressional committees in both the House and the Senate, be passed by both legislative bodies, and then be signed by the president. Completing this process can take months or, in some cases, years. By the time the change in fiscal policy is passed and ready to implement, the condition of the economy may well have changed.

These lags in monetary and fiscal policy are a problem in part because economic forecasting is so imprecise. If forecasters could accurately predict the condition of the economy a year in advance, then monetary and fiscal policymakers could look ahead when making policy decisions. In this case, policymakers could stabilize the economy despite the lags they face. In practice, however, major recessions and depressions arrive without much advance warning. The best policymakers can do at any time is to respond to economic changes as they occur.

less today. All that would reduce the fiscal multiplier, potentially to below zero.

Different assumptions about the impact of higher government borrowing on interest rates and private spending explain wild variations in the estimates of multipliers from today's stimulus spending. Economists in the Obama administration, who assume that the federal funds rate stays constant for a four-year period, expect a multiplier of 1.6 for government purchases and 1.0 for tax cuts from America's fiscal stimulus. An alternative assessment by John Cogan, Tobias Cwik, John Taylor and Volker Wieland uses models in which interest rates and taxes rise more quickly in response to higher public borrowing. Their multipliers are much smaller. They think America's stimulus will boost GDP by only one-sixth as much as the Obama team expects.

When forward-looking models disagree so dramatically, careful analysis of previous fiscal stimuli ought to help settle the debate. Unfortunately, it is extremely tricky to isolate the impact of changes in fiscal policy. One approach is to use microeconomic case studies to examine consumer behaviour in response to specific tax rebates and cuts. These studies, largely based on tax changes in America, find that permanent cuts have a bigger impact on consumer spending than temporary ones and that consumers who find it hard to borrow, such as those close to their credit-card limit, tend to spend more of their tax windfall. But case studies do not measure the overall impact of tax cuts or spending increases on output.

An alternative approach is to try to tease out the statistical impact of changes in government spending or tax cuts on GDP. The difficulty here is to isolate the effects of fiscal-stimulus measures from the rises in social-security spending and falls in tax revenues that naturally accompany recessions. This empirical approach has narrowed the range of estimates in some areas. It has also yielded interesting cross-country comparisons. Multipliers are bigger in closed economies than open ones (because less of the stimulus leaks abroad via imports). They have traditionally been bigger in rich countries than emerging ones (where investors tend to take fright more quickly, pushing interest rates up). But overall economists find as big a range of multipliers from empirical estimates as they do from theoretical models.

To add to the confusion, the post-war experiences from which statistical analyses are drawn differ in vital respects from the current situation. Most of the evidence on multipliers for government spending is based on military outlays, but today's stimulus packages are heavily focused on infrastructure. Interest rates in many rich countries are now close to zero, which may increase the potency of, as well as the need for, fiscal stimulus. Because of the financial crisis relatively more people face borrowing constraints, which would increase the effectiveness of a tax cut. At the same time, highly indebted consumers may now be keen to cut their borrowing, leading to a lower multiplier. And investors today have more reason to be worried about rich countries' fiscal positions than those of emerging markets.

Add all this together and the truth is that economists are flying blind. They can make relative judgments with some confidence. Temporary tax cuts pack less punch than permanent ones, for instance. Fiscal multipliers will probably be lower in heavily indebted economies than in prudent ones. But policymakers looking for precise estimates are deluding themselves.

Source: *Economist*, September 24, 2009.

Automatic Stabilizers

All economists—both advocates and critics of stabilization policy—agree that the lags in implementation render policy less useful as a tool for short-run stabilization. The economy would be more stable, therefore, if policymakers could find a way to avoid some of these lags. In fact, they have. **Automatic stabilizers** are changes in fiscal policy that stimulate aggregate demand when the economy goes into a recession without policymakers having to take any deliberate action.

The most important automatic stabilizer is the tax system. When the economy goes into a recession, the amount of taxes collected by the government falls automatically because almost all taxes are closely tied to economic activity. The personal income tax depends on households' incomes, the payroll tax depends on workers' earnings, and the corporate income tax depends on firms' profits. Because incomes, earnings, and profits all fall in a recession, the government's tax revenue falls as well. This automatic tax cut stimulates aggregate demand and, thereby, reduces the magnitude of economic fluctuations.

automatic stabilizers

changes in fiscal policy that stimulate aggregate demand when the economy goes into a recession without policymakers having to take any deliberate action

Government spending also acts as an automatic stabilizer. In particular, when the economy goes into a recession and workers are laid off, more people apply for unemployment insurance benefits, welfare benefits, and other forms of income support. This automatic increase in government spending stimulates aggregate demand at exactly the time when aggregate demand is insufficient to maintain full employment. Indeed, when the unemployment insurance system was first enacted in the 1930s, economists who advocated this policy did so in part because of its power as an automatic stabilizer.

The automatic stabilizers in the U.S. economy are not sufficiently strong to prevent recessions completely. Nonetheless, without these automatic stabilizers, output and employment would probably be more volatile than they are. For this reason, many economists oppose a constitutional amendment that would require the federal government always to run a balanced budget, as some politicians have proposed. When the economy goes into a recession, taxes fall, government spending rises, and the government's budget moves toward deficit. If the government faced a strict balanced-budget rule, it would be forced to look for ways to raise taxes or cut spending in a recession. In other words, a strict balanced-budget rule would eliminate the automatic stabilizers inherent in our current system of taxes and government spending.

QUICK QUIZ   *Suppose a wave of negative "animal spirits" overruns the economy, and people become pessimistic about the future. What happens to aggregate demand? If the Fed wants to stabilize aggregate demand, how should it alter the money supply? If it does this, what happens to the interest rate? Why might the Fed choose not to respond in this way?*

in the news

> ## Offbeat Indicators

Because monetary and fiscal policy work with long lags, policymakers are constantly searching for clues about where the economy is heading. This article, written as the 2001 recession was just ending, describes some unusual ways economists monitor macroeconomic conditions.

Economic Numbers Befuddle Even the Best

BY GEORGE HAGER

Economists pore over scores of numbers every week, trying to sense when the recession is over. But quirky indicators and gut instinct might be almost as helpful—maybe even more so.

Is your dentist busy? Dentists say people put off appointments when times turn tough, then reschedule when the economy improves.

How far away do you have to park when you go to the mall? Fewer shoppers equal more parking spaces.

If you drive to work, has your commute time gotten shorter or longer?

Economist Michael Evans says a colleague with a pipeline into the garbage business swears by his own homegrown Chicago Trash index. Collections plunged after the Sept. 11 terror attacks, rebounded in October but then fell off again in mid-November. "Trash is a pretty good indicator of what people are buying," says Evans, an economist with Evans Carrol & Associates. "They've got to throw out the wrappings." . . .

What's actually happening is often clear only in hindsight. That's one reason the National Bureau of Economic Research waited until November to declare that a recession began last March—and why it took them until December 1992 to declare that the last recession had ended more than a year earlier, in March 1991.

"The data can fail you," says Allen Sinai, chief economist for Decision Economics. Sinai cautions that if numbers appear to be going up (or down), it's best to wait to see what happens over two or three months before drawing a conclusion—something hairtrigger financial markets routinely don't do.

"We have lots of false predictions of recoveries by (stock) markets that don't happen," he says.

Like a lot of economists, Sinai leaves the numbers with informal observations. These days, he's paying particular attention to what business executives say at meetings and cocktail parties because their mood—and their plans for investing and hiring—are key to a comeback.

Bad Times

Even the Federal Reserve, whose more than 200 economists monitor about every piece of the economy that can be measured, make room for anecdotes. Two weeks before every policy meeting, the Fed publishes its "beige book," a survey based on off-the-record conversations between officials at the Fed's 12 regional banks and local businesses.

The reports are peppered with quotes from unnamed business people ("Everybody's decided to go shopping again," someone told the Richmond Fed Bank last month) and the occasional odd detail that reveals just how far down the Fed inquisitors sometimes drill. Last March, the Dallas Fed Bank reported "healthy sales of singing gorillas" for Valentine's Day.

Good Times

Source: *USA Today*, December 26, 2001.

Conclusion

Before policymakers make any change in policy, they need to consider all the effects of their decisions. Earlier in the book, we examined classical models of the economy, which describe the long-run effects of monetary and fiscal policy. There we saw how fiscal policy influences saving, investment, and long-run growth and how monetary policy influences the price level and the inflation rate.

In this chapter, we examined the short-run effects of monetary and fiscal policy. We saw how these policy instruments can change the aggregate demand for goods and services and alter the economy's production and employment in the short run. When Congress reduces government spending to balance the budget, it needs to consider both the long-run effects on saving and growth and the short-run effects on aggregate demand and employment. When the Fed reduces the growth rate of the money supply, it must take into account the long-run effect on inflation as well as the short-run effect on production. In all parts of government, policymakers must keep in mind both long-run and short-run goals.

SUMMARY

- In developing a theory of short-run economic fluctuations, Keynes proposed the theory of liquidity preference to explain the determinants of the interest rate. According to this theory, the interest rate adjusts to balance the supply and demand for money.

- An increase in the price level raises money demand and increases the interest rate that brings the money market into equilibrium. Because the interest rate represents the cost of borrowing, a higher interest rate reduces investment and, thereby, the quantity of goods and services demanded. The downward-sloping aggregate-demand curve expresses this negative relationship between the price level and the quantity demanded.

- Policymakers can influence aggregate demand with monetary policy. An increase in the money supply reduces the equilibrium interest rate for any given price level. Because a lower interest rate stimulates investment spending, the aggregate-demand curve shifts to the right. Conversely, a decrease in the money supply raises the equilibrium interest rate for any given price level and shifts the aggregate-demand curve to the left.

- Policymakers can also influence aggregate demand with fiscal policy. An increase in government purchases or a cut in taxes shifts the aggregate-demand curve to the right. A decrease in government purchases or an increase in taxes shifts the aggregate-demand curve to the left.

- When the government alters spending or taxes, the resulting shift in aggregate demand can be larger or smaller than the fiscal change. The multiplier effect tends to amplify the effects of fiscal policy on aggregate demand. The crowding-out effect tends to dampen the effects of fiscal policy on aggregate demand.

- Because monetary and fiscal policy can influence aggregate demand, the government sometimes uses these policy instruments in an attempt to stabilize the economy. Economists disagree about how active the government should be in this effort. According to advocates of active stabilization policy, changes in attitudes by households and firms shift aggregate demand; if the government does not respond, the result is undesirable and unnecessary fluctuations in output and employment. According to critics of active stabilization policy, monetary and fiscal policy work with such long lags that attempts at stabilizing the economy often end up being destabilizing.

KEY CONCEPTS

theory of liquidity preference,
  p. 359

fiscal policy, *p. 367*
multiplier effect, *p. 368*

crowding-out effect, *p. 371*
automatic stabilizers, *p. 377*

QUESTIONS FOR REVIEW

1. What is the theory of liquidity preference? How does it help explain the downward slope of the aggregate-demand curve?
2. Use the theory of liquidity preference to explain how a decrease in the money supply affects the aggregate-demand curve.
3. The government spends $3 billion to buy police cars. Explain why aggregate demand might increase by more than $3 billion. Explain why aggregate demand might increase by less than $3 billion.

4. Suppose that survey measures of consumer confidence indicate a wave of pessimism is sweeping the country. If policymakers do nothing, what will happen to aggregate demand? What should the Fed do if it wants to stabilize aggregate demand? If the Fed does nothing, what might Congress do to stabilize aggregate demand?
5. Give an example of a government policy that acts as an automatic stabilizer. Explain why the policy has this effect.

PROBLEMS AND APPLICATIONS

1. Explain how each of the following developments would affect the supply of money, the demand for money, and the interest rate. Illustrate your answers with diagrams.
   a. The Fed's bond traders buy bonds in open-market operations.
   b. An increase in credit-card availability reduces the cash people hold.
   c. The Federal Reserve reduces banks' reserve requirements.
   d. Households decide to hold more money to use for holiday shopping.
   e. A wave of optimism boosts business investment and expands aggregate demand.
2. The Federal Reserve expands the money supply by 5 percent.
   a. Use the theory of liquidity preference to illustrate in a graph the impact of this policy on the interest rate.
   b. Use the model of aggregate demand and aggregate supply to illustrate the impact of this change in the interest rate on output and the price level in the short run.
   c. When the economy makes the transition from its short-run equilibrium to its long-run

equilibrium, what will happen to the price level?
   d. How will this change in the price level affect the demand for money and the equilibrium interest rate?
   e. Is this analysis consistent with the proposition that money has real effects in the short run but is neutral in the long run?
3. Suppose a computer virus disables the nation's automatic teller machines, making withdrawals from bank accounts less convenient. As a result, people want to keep more cash on hand, increasing the demand for money.
   a. Assume the Fed does not change the money supply. According to the theory of liquidity preference, what happens to the interest rate? What happens to aggregate demand?
   b. If instead the Fed wants to stabilize aggregate demand, how should it change the money supply?
   c. If it wants to accomplish this change in the money supply using open-market operations, what should it do?

4. Consider two policies—a tax cut that will last for only one year and a tax cut that is expected to be permanent. Which policy will stimulate greater spending by consumers? Which policy will have the greater impact on aggregate demand? Explain.

5. The economy is in a recession with high unemployment and low output.
   a. Draw a graph of aggregate demand and aggregate supply to illustrate the current situation. Be sure to include the aggregate-demand curve, the short-run aggregate-supply curve, and the long-run aggregate-supply curve.
   b. Identify an open-market operation that would restore the economy to its natural rate.
   c. Draw a graph of the money market to illustrate the effect of this open-market operation. Show the resulting change in the interest rate.
   d. Draw a graph similar to the one in part (a) to show the effect of the open-market operation on output and the price level. Explain in words why the policy has the effect that you have shown in the graph.

6. In the early 1980s, new legislation allowed banks to pay interest on checking deposits, which they could not do previously.
   a. If we define money to include checking deposits, what effect did this legislation have on money demand? Explain.
   b. If the Federal Reserve had maintained a constant money supply in the face of this change, what would have happened to the interest rate? What would have happened to aggregate demand and aggregate output?
   c. If the Federal Reserve had maintained a constant market interest rate (the interest rate on nonmonetary assets) in the face of this change, what change in the money supply would have been necessary? What would have happened to aggregate demand and aggregate output?

7. Suppose economists observe that an increase in government spending of $10 billion raises the total demand for goods and services by $30 billion.
   a. If these economists ignore the possibility of crowding out, what would they estimate the marginal propensity to consume (*MPC*) to be?
   b. Now suppose the economists allow for crowding out. Would their new estimate of the *MPC* be larger or smaller than their initial one?

8. Suppose the government reduces taxes by $20 billion, that there is no crowding out, and that the marginal propensity to consume is ¾.
   a. What is the initial effect of the tax reduction on aggregate demand?
   b. What additional effects follow this initial effect? What is the total effect of the tax cut on aggregate demand?
   c. How does the total effect of this $20 billion tax cut compare to the total effect of a $20 billion increase in government purchases? Why?
   d. Based on your answer to part (c), can you think of a way in which the government can increase aggregate demand without changing the government's budget deficit?

9. An economy is operating with output $400 billion below its natural rate, and fiscal policymakers want to close this recessionary gap. The central bank agrees to adjust the money supply to hold the interest rate constant, so there is no crowding out. The marginal propensity to consume is ⅘, and the price level is completely fixed in the short run. In what direction and by how much would government spending need to change to close the recessionary gap? Explain your thinking.

10. Suppose government spending increases. Would the effect on aggregate demand be larger if the Federal Reserve held the money supply constant in response or if the Fed were committed to maintaining a fixed interest rate? Explain.

11. In which of the following circumstances is expansionary fiscal policy more likely to lead to a short-run increase in investment? Explain.
    a. When the investment accelerator is large or when it is small?
    b. When the interest sensitivity of investment is large or when it is small?

12. For various reasons, fiscal policy changes automatically when output and employment fluctuate.
    a. Explain why tax revenue changes when the economy goes into a recession.
    b. Explain why government spending changes when the economy goes into a recession.
    c. If the government were to operate under a strict balanced-budget rule, what would it have to do in a recession? Would that make the recession more or less severe?

13. Some members of Congress have proposed a law that would make price stability the sole goal of monetary policy. Suppose such a law were passed.
    a. How would the Fed respond to an event that contracted aggregate demand?
    b. How would the Fed respond to an event that caused an adverse shift in short-run aggregate supply?

In each case, is there another monetary policy that would lead to greater stability in output?

For further information on topics in this chapter, additional problems, applications, examples, online quizzes, and more, please visit our website at www.cengage.com/economics/mankiw.

The Short-Run Trade-off between Inflation and Unemployment

Two closely watched indicators of economic performance are inflation and unemployment. When the Bureau of Labor Statistics releases data on these variables each month, policymakers are eager to hear the news. Some commentators have added together the inflation rate and the unemployment rate to produce a *misery index*, which purports to measure the health of the economy.

How are these two measures of economic performance related to each other? Earlier in the book, we discussed the long-run determinants of unemployment and the long-run determinants of inflation. We saw that the natural rate of unemployment depends on various features of the labor market, such as minimum-wage laws, the market power of unions, the role of efficiency wages, and the effectiveness of job search. By contrast, the inflation rate depends primarily on growth in the money supply, which a nation's central bank controls. In the long run, therefore, inflation and unemployment are largely unrelated problems.

In the short run, just the opposite is true. One of the *Ten Principles of Economics* discussed in Chapter 1 is that society faces a short-run trade-off between inflation and unemployment. If monetary and fiscal policymakers expand aggregate demand and move the economy up along the short-run aggregate-supply curve, they can expand output and lower unemployment for a while, but only at the cost of a more rapidly rising price level. If policymakers contract aggregate demand and move the economy down the short-run aggregate-supply curve, they can lower inflation, but only at the cost of temporarily lower output and higher unemployment.

In this chapter, we examine the inflation–unemployment trade-off more closely. The relationship between inflation and unemployment has attracted the attention of some of the most important economists of the last half century. The best way to understand this relationship is to see how thinking about it has evolved. As we will see, the history of thought regarding inflation and unemployment since the 1950s is inextricably connected to the history of the U.S. economy. These two histories will show why the trade-off between inflation and unemployment holds in the short run, why it does not hold in the long run, and what issues the trade-off raises for economic policymakers.

The Phillips Curve

Phillips curve

a curve that shows the short-run trade-off between inflation and unemployment

"Probably the single most important macroeconomic relationship is the Phillips curve." These are the words of economist George Akerlof from the lecture he gave when he received the Nobel Prize in 2001. The **Phillips curve** is the short-run relationship between inflation and unemployment. We begin our story with the discovery of the Phillips curve and its migration to America.

Origins of the Phillips Curve

In 1958, economist A. W. Phillips published an article in the British journal *Economica* that would make him famous. The article was titled "The Relationship between Unemployment and the Rate of Change of Money Wages in the United Kingdom, 1861–1957." In it, Phillips showed a negative correlation between the rate of unemployment and the rate of inflation. That is, Phillips showed that years with low unemployment tend to have high inflation, and years with high unemployment tend to have low inflation. (Phillips examined inflation in nominal wages rather than inflation in prices, but for our purposes, that distinction is not important. These two measures of inflation usually move together.) Phillips concluded that two important macroeconomic variables—inflation and unemployment—were linked in a way that economists had not previously appreciated.

Although Phillips's discovery was based on data for the United Kingdom, researchers quickly extended his finding to other countries. Two years after Phillips published his article, economists Paul Samuelson and Robert Solow published an article in the *American Economic Review* called "Analytics of Anti-Inflation Policy" in which they showed a similar negative correlation between inflation and unemployment in data for the United States. They reasoned that this correlation arose because low unemployment was associated with high aggregate

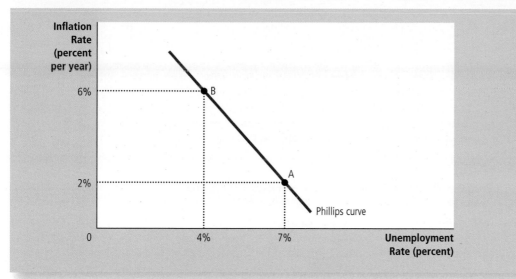

Figure **1**

The Phillips Curve
The Phillips curve illustrates a negative association between the inflation rate and the unemployment rate. At point A, inflation is low and unemployment is high. At point B, inflation is high and unemployment is low.

demand, which in turn puts upward pressure on wages and prices throughout the economy. Samuelson and Solow dubbed the negative association between inflation and unemployment the *Phillips curve*. Figure 1 shows an example of a Phillips curve like the one found by Samuelson and Solow.

As the title of their paper suggests, Samuelson and Solow were interested in the Phillips curve because they believed it held important lessons for policymakers. In particular, they suggested that the Phillips curve offers policymakers a menu of possible economic outcomes. By altering monetary and fiscal policy to influence aggregate demand, policymakers could choose any point on this curve. Point A offers high unemployment and low inflation. Point B offers low unemployment and high inflation. Policymakers might prefer both low inflation and low unemployment, but the historical data as summarized by the Phillips curve indicate that this combination is impossible. According to Samuelson and Solow, policymakers face a trade-off between inflation and unemployment, and the Phillips curve illustrates that trade-off.

Aggregate Demand, Aggregate Supply, and the Phillips Curve

The model of aggregate demand and aggregate supply provides an easy explanation for the menu of possible outcomes described by the Phillips curve. *The Phillips curve shows the combinations of inflation and unemployment that arise in the short run as shifts in the aggregate-demand curve move the economy along the short-run aggregate-supply curve.* As we saw in the preceding two chapters, an increase in the aggregate demand for goods and services leads, in the short run, to a larger output of goods and services and a higher price level. Larger output means greater employment and, thus, a lower rate of unemployment. In addition, a higher price level translates into a higher rate of inflation. Thus, shifts in aggregate demand push inflation and unemployment in opposite directions in the short run—a relationship illustrated by the Phillips curve.

To see more fully how this works, let's consider an example. To keep the numbers simple, imagine that the price level (as measured, for instance, by the consumer price index) equals 100 in the year 2020. Figure 2 shows two possible

Figure **2**

How the Phillips Curve Is Related to the Model of Aggregate Demand and Aggregate Supply

This figure assumes a price level of 100 for the year 2020 and charts possible outcomes for the year 2021. Panel (a) shows the model of aggregate demand and aggregate supply. If aggregate demand is low, the economy is at point A; output is low (15,000), and the price level is low (102). If aggregate demand is high, the economy is at point B; output is high (16,000), and the price level is high (106). Panel (b) shows the implications for the Phillips curve. Point A, which arises when aggregate demand is low, has high unemployment (7 percent) and low inflation (2 percent). Point B, which arises when aggregate demand is high, has low unemployment (4 percent) and high inflation (6 percent).

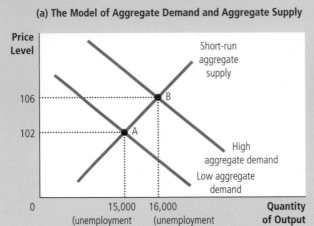

(a) The Model of Aggregate Demand and Aggregate Supply

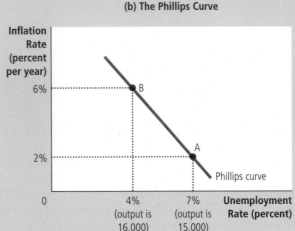

(b) The Phillips Curve

outcomes that might occur in the year 2021 depending of the strength of aggregate demand. One outcome occurs if aggregate demand is high, and the other occurs if aggregate demand is low. Panel (a) shows these two outcomes using the model of aggregate demand and aggregate supply. Panel (b) illustrates the same two outcomes using the Phillips curve.

Panel (a) of the figure shows what happens to output and the price level in the year 2021. If the aggregate demand for goods and services is low, the economy experiences outcome A. The economy produces output of 15,000, and the price level is 102. By contrast, if aggregate demand is high, the economy experiences outcome B. Output is 16,000, and the price level is 106. This is just an example of a familiar conclusion: Higher aggregate demand moves the economy to an equilibrium with higher output and a higher price level.

Panel (b) shows what these two possible outcomes mean for unemployment and inflation. Because firms need more workers when they produce a greater output of goods and services, unemployment is lower in outcome B than in outcome A. In this example, when output rises from 15,000 to 16,000, unemployment falls from 7 percent to 4 percent. Moreover, because the price level is higher at outcome B than at outcome A, the inflation rate (the percentage change in the price level from the previous year) is also higher. In particular, since the price level was 100 in the year 2020, outcome A has an inflation rate of 2 percent, and outcome B has an inflation rate of 6 percent. The two possible outcomes for the economy can be compared either in terms of output and the price level (using the model of aggregate demand and aggregate supply) or in terms of unemployment and inflation (using the Phillips curve).

Because monetary and fiscal policy can shift the aggregate-demand curve, they can move an economy along the Phillips curve. Increases in the money supply, increases in government spending, or cuts in taxes expand aggregate demand and move the economy to a point on the Phillips curve with lower unemployment and higher inflation. Decreases in the money supply, cuts in government spending, or increases in taxes contract aggregate demand and move the economy to a point on the Phillips curve with lower inflation and higher unemployment. In this sense, the Phillips curve offers policymakers a menu of combinations of inflation and unemployment.

QUICK QUIZ   *Draw the Phillips curve. Use the model of aggregate demand and aggregate supply to show how policy can move the economy from a point on this curve with high inflation to a point with low inflation.*

Shifts in the Phillips Curve: The Role of Expectations

The Phillips curve seems to offer policymakers a menu of possible inflation–unemployment outcomes. But does this menu of choices remain the same over time? Is the downward-sloping Phillips curve a stable relationship on which policymakers can rely? Economists took up these questions in the late 1960s, shortly after Samuelson and Solow had introduced the Phillips curve into the macroeconomic policy debate.

The Long-Run Phillips Curve

In 1968, economist Milton Friedman published a paper in the *American Economic Review* based on an address he had recently given as president of the American Economic Association. The paper, titled "The Role of Monetary Policy," contained sections on "What Monetary Policy Can Do" and "What Monetary Policy Cannot Do." Friedman argued that one thing monetary policy cannot do, other than for only a short time, is lower unemployment by raising inflation. At about the same time, another economist, Edmund Phelps, also published a paper denying the existence of a long-run trade-off between inflation and unemployment.

Friedman and Phelps based their conclusions on classical principles of macroeconomics. Classical theory points to growth in the money supply as the primary determinant of inflation. But classical theory also states that monetary growth does not affect real variables such as output and employment; it merely alters all prices and nominal incomes proportionately. In particular, monetary growth does not influence those factors that determine the economy's unemployment rate, such as the market power of unions, the role of efficiency wages, or the process of job search. Friedman and Phelps concluded that there is no reason to think that the rate of inflation would, in the long run, be related to the rate of unemployment.

Here, in his own words, is Friedman's view about what the Federal Reserve can hope to accomplish for the economy in the long run:

> The monetary authority controls nominal quantities—directly, the quantity of its own liabilities [currency plus bank reserves]. In principle, it can use this control to peg a nominal quantity—an exchange rate, the price level, the

nominal level of national income, the quantity of money by one definition or another—or to peg the change in a nominal quantity—the rate of inflation or deflation, the rate of growth or decline in nominal national income, the rate of growth of the quantity of money. It cannot use its control over nominal quantities to peg a real quantity—the real rate of interest, the rate of unemployment, the level of real national income, the real quantity of money, the rate of growth of real national income, or the rate of growth of the real quantity of money.

These views have important implications for the Phillips curve. In particular, they imply that monetary policymakers face a long-run Phillips curve that is vertical, as in Figure 3. If the Fed increases the money supply slowly, the inflation rate is low, and the economy finds itself at point A. If the Fed increases the money supply quickly, the inflation rate is high, and the economy finds itself at point B. In either case, the unemployment rate tends toward its normal level, called the *natural rate of unemployment*. The vertical long-run Phillips curve illustrates the conclusion that unemployment does not depend on money growth and inflation in the long run.

The vertical long-run Phillips curve is, in essence, one expression of the classical idea of monetary neutrality. Previously, we expressed monetary neutrality with a vertical long-run aggregate-supply curve. Figure 4 shows that the vertical long-run Phillips curve and the vertical long-run aggregate-supply curve are two sides of the same coin. In panel (a) of this figure, an increase in the money supply shifts the aggregate-demand curve to the right from AD_1 to AD_2. As a result of this shift, the long-run equilibrium moves from point A to point B. The price level rises from P_1 to P_2, but because the aggregate-supply curve is vertical, output remains the same. In panel (b), more rapid growth in the money supply raises the inflation rate by moving the economy from point A to point B. But because the Phillips curve is vertical, the rate of unemployment is the same at these two points. Thus, the vertical long-run aggregate-supply curve and the vertical long-run Phillips curve both imply that monetary policy influences nominal variables (the price level and the inflation rate) but not real variables (output and unemployment).

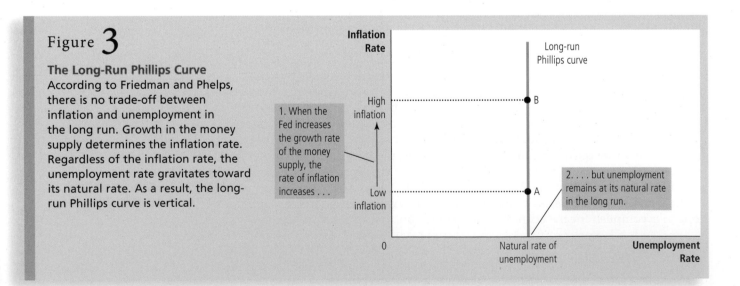

Figure 3

The Long-Run Phillips Curve
According to Friedman and Phelps, there is no trade-off between inflation and unemployment in the long run. Growth in the money supply determines the inflation rate. Regardless of the inflation rate, the unemployment rate gravitates toward its natural rate. As a result, the long-run Phillips curve is vertical.

Panel (a) shows the model of aggregate demand and aggregate supply with a vertical aggregate-supply curve. When expansionary monetary policy shifts the aggregate-demand curve to the right from AD_1 to AD_2, the equilibrium moves from point A to point B. The price level rises from P_1 to P_2, while output remains the same. Panel (b) shows the long-run Phillips curve, which is vertical at the natural rate of unemployment. In the long run, expansionary monetary policy moves the economy from lower inflation (point A) to higher inflation (point B) without changing the rate of unemployment.

Figure **4**

How the Long-Run Phillips Curve Is Related to the Model of Aggregate Demand and Aggregate Supply

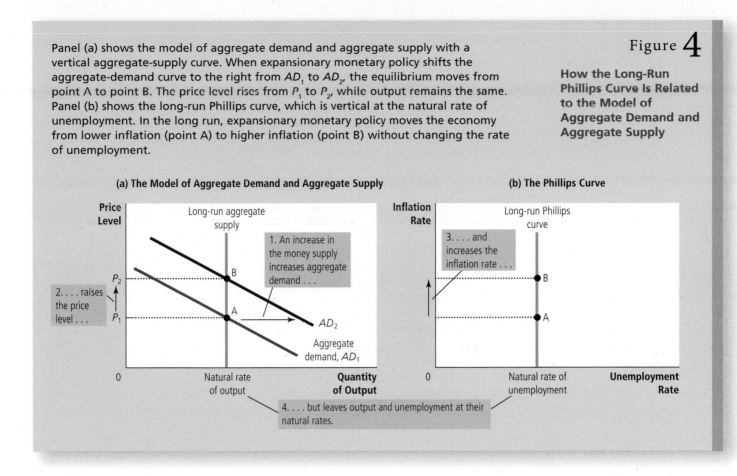

(a) The Model of Aggregate Demand and Aggregate Supply

(b) The Phillips Curve

Regardless of the monetary policy pursued by the Fed, output and unemployment are, in the long run, at their natural rates.

The Meaning of "Natural"

What is so "natural" about the natural rate of unemployment? Friedman and Phelps used this adjective to describe the unemployment rate toward which the economy gravitates in the long run. Yet the natural rate of unemployment is not necessarily the socially desirable rate of unemployment. Nor is the natural rate of unemployment constant over time.

For example, suppose that a newly formed union uses its market power to raise the real wages of some workers above the equilibrium level. The result is an excess supply of workers and, therefore, a higher natural rate of unemployment. This unemployment is natural not because it is good but because it is beyond the influence of monetary policy. More rapid money growth would reduce neither the market power of the union nor the level of unemployment; it would lead only to more inflation.

Although monetary policy cannot influence the natural rate of unemployment, other types of policy can. To reduce the natural rate of unemployment, policymakers should look to policies that improve the functioning of the labor market. Earlier in the book, we discussed how various labor-market policies, such as minimum-wage laws, collective-bargaining laws, unemployment insurance, and job-training programs, affect the natural rate of unemployment. A policy change that reduced the natural rate of unemployment would shift the long-run Phillips curve to the left. In addition, because lower unemployment means more workers are producing goods and services, the quantity of goods and services supplied would be larger at any given price level, and the long-run aggregate-supply curve would shift to the right. The economy could then enjoy lower unemployment and higher output for any given rate of money growth and inflation.

Reconciling Theory and Evidence

At first, the conclusion of Friedman and Phelps that there is no long-run trade-off between inflation and unemployment might not seem persuasive. Their argument was based on an appeal to *theory*, specifically classical theory's prediction of monetary neutrality. By contrast, the negative correlation between inflation and unemployment documented by Phillips, Samuelson, and Solow was based on actual *evidence* from the real world. Why should anyone believe that policymakers faced a vertical Phillips curve when the world seemed to offer a downward-sloping one? Shouldn't the findings of Phillips, Samuelson, and Solow lead us to reject monetary neutrality?

Friedman and Phelps were well aware of these questions, and they offered a way to reconcile classical macroeconomic theory with the finding of a downward-sloping Phillips curve in data from the United Kingdom and the United States. They claimed that a negative relationship between inflation and unemployment exists in the short run but that it cannot be used by policymakers as a menu of outcomes in the long run. Policymakers can pursue expansionary monetary policy to achieve lower unemployment for a while, but eventually, unemployment returns to its natural rate, and more expansionary monetary policy leads only to higher inflation.

Friedman's and Phelps's work was the basis of our discussion of the difference between the short-run and long-run aggregate-supply curves in Chapter 15. As you may recall, the long-run aggregate-supply curve is vertical, indicating that the price level does not influence quantity supplied in the long run. But the short-run aggregate-supply curve is upward sloping, indicating that an increase in the price level raises the quantity of goods and services that firms supply. According to the sticky-wage theory of aggregate supply, for instance, nominal wages are set in advance based on the price level that workers and firms expected to prevail. When prices come in higher than expected, firms have an incentive to increase production and employment; when prices are less than expected, firms reduce production and employment. Yet because the expected price level and nominal wages will eventually adjust, the positive relationship between the actual price level and quantity supplied exists only in the short run.

Friedman and Phelps applied this same logic to the Phillips curve. Just as the aggregate-supply curve slopes upward only in the short run, the trade-off between inflation and unemployment holds only in the short run. And just as the long-run aggregate-supply curve is vertical, the long-run Phillips curve is also vertical. Once again, expectations are the key for understanding how the short run and the long run are related.

Friedman and Phelps introduced a new variable into the analysis of the inflation–unemployment trade-off: *expected inflation*. Expected inflation measures how much people expect the overall price level to change. Because the expected price level affects nominal wages, expected inflation is one factor that determines the position of the short-run aggregate-supply curve. In the short run, the Fed can take expected inflation (and, thus, the short-run aggregate-supply curve) as already determined. When the money supply changes, the aggregate-demand curve shifts, and the economy moves along a given short-run aggregate-supply curve. In the short run, therefore, monetary changes lead to unexpected fluctuations in output, prices, unemployment, and inflation. In this way, Friedman and Phelps explained the downward-sloping Phillips curve that Phillips, Samuelson, and Solow had documented.

The Fed's ability to create unexpected inflation by increasing the money supply exists only in the short run. In the long run, people come to expect whatever inflation rate the Fed chooses to produce, and nominal wages will adjust to keep pace with inflation. As a result, the long-run aggregate-supply curve is vertical. Changes in aggregate demand, such as those due to changes in the money supply, affect neither the economy's output of goods and services nor the number of workers that firms need to hire to produce those goods and services. Friedman and Phelps concluded that unemployment returns to its natural rate in the long run.

The Short-Run Phillips Curve

The analysis of Friedman and Phelps can be summarized in the following equation:

$$\begin{array}{c}\text{Unemployment}\\\text{rate}\end{array} = \begin{array}{c}\text{Natural rate of}\\\text{unemployment}\end{array} - a \left(\begin{array}{c}\text{Actual}\\\text{inflation}\end{array} - \begin{array}{c}\text{Expected}\\\text{inflation}\end{array} \right).$$

This equation (which is, in essence, another expression of the aggregate-supply equation we have seen previously) relates the unemployment rate to the natural rate of unemployment, actual inflation, and expected inflation. In the short run, expected inflation is given, so higher actual inflation is associated with lower unemployment. (The variable a is a parameter that measures how much unemployment responds to unexpected inflation.) In the long run, people come to expect whatever inflation the Fed produces, so actual inflation equals expected inflation, and unemployment is at its natural rate.

This equation implies there can be no stable short-run Phillips curve. Each short-run Phillips curve reflects a particular expected rate of inflation. (To be precise, if you graph the equation, you'll find that the downward-sloping short-run Phillips curve intersects the vertical long-run Phillips curve at the expected rate of inflation.) When expected inflation changes, the short-run Phillips curve shifts.

According to Friedman and Phelps, it is dangerous to view the Phillips curve as a menu of options available to policymakers. To see why, imagine an economy that starts with low inflation, with an equally low rate of expected inflation, and with unemployment at its natural rate. In Figure 5, the economy is at point A. Now suppose that policymakers try to take advantage of the trade-off between inflation and unemployment by using monetary or fiscal policy to expand aggregate demand. In the short run, when expected inflation is given, the economy goes from point A to point B. Unemployment falls below its natural rate, and the actual inflation rate rises above expected inflation. As the economy moves from point A to point B, policymakers might think they have achieved permanently lower unemployment at the cost of higher inflation—a bargain that, if possible, might be worth making.

Figure 5

How Expected Inflation Shifts the Short-Run Phillips Curve
The higher the expected rate of inflation, the higher the short-run trade-off between inflation and unemployment. At point A, expected inflation and actual inflation are equal at a low rate, and unemployment is at its natural rate. If the Fed pursues an expansionary monetary policy, the economy moves from point A to point B in the short run. At point B, expected inflation is still low, but actual inflation is high. Unemployment is below its natural rate. In the long run, expected inflation rises, and the economy moves to point C. At point C, expected inflation and actual inflation are both high, and unemployment is back to its natural rate.

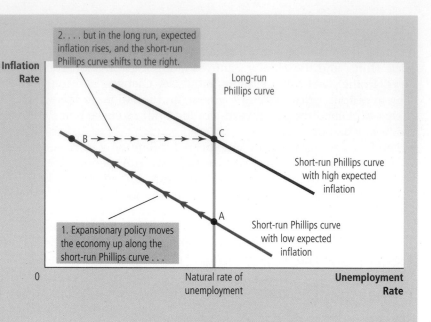

This situation, however, will not persist. Over time, people get used to this higher inflation rate, and they raise their expectations of inflation. When expected inflation rises, firms and workers start taking higher inflation into account when setting wages and prices. The short-run Phillips curve then shifts to the right, as shown in the figure. The economy ends up at point C, with higher inflation than at point A but with the same level of unemployment. Thus, Friedman and Phelps concluded that policymakers face only a temporary trade-off between inflation and unemployment. In the long run, expanding aggregate demand more rapidly will yield higher inflation without any reduction in unemployment.

The Natural Experiment for the Natural-Rate Hypothesis

Friedman and Phelps had made a bold prediction in 1968: If policymakers try to take advantage of the Phillips curve by choosing higher inflation to reduce unemployment, they will succeed at reducing unemployment only temporarily. This view—that unemployment eventually returns to its natural rate, regardless of the rate of inflation—is called the **natural-rate hypothesis.** A few years after Friedman and Phelps proposed this hypothesis, monetary and fiscal policymakers inadvertently created a natural experiment to test it. Their laboratory was the U.S. economy.

Before we see the outcome of this test, however, let's look at the data that Friedman and Phelps had when they made their prediction in 1968. Figure 6 shows the unemployment and inflation rates for the period from 1961 to 1968. These data trace out an almost perfect Phillips curve. As inflation rose over these eight years, unemployment fell. The economic data from this era seemed to confirm that policymakers faced a trade-off between inflation and unemployment.

The apparent success of the Phillips curve in the 1960s made the prediction of Friedman and Phelps all the bolder. In 1958, Phillips had suggested a negative

natural-rate hypothesis

the claim that unemployment eventually returns to its normal, or natural, rate, regardless of the rate of inflation

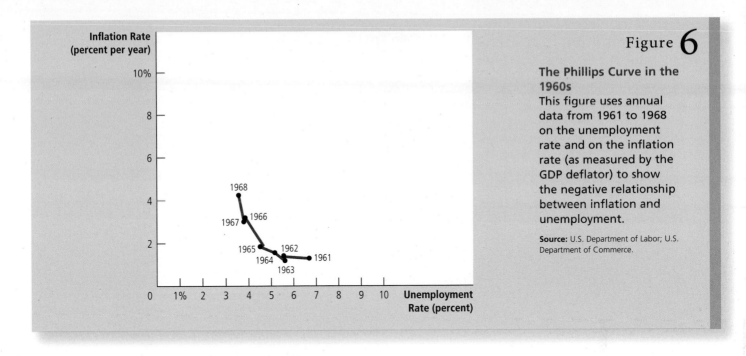

Figure **6**

The Phillips Curve in the 1960s
This figure uses annual data from 1961 to 1968 on the unemployment rate and on the inflation rate (as measured by the GDP deflator) to show the negative relationship between inflation and unemployment.

Source: U.S. Department of Labor; U.S. Department of Commerce.

association between inflation and unemployment. In 1960, Samuelson and Solow had shown it existed in U.S. data. Another decade of data had confirmed the relationship. To some economists at the time, it seemed ridiculous to claim that the historically reliable Phillips curve would start shifting once policymakers tried to take advantage of it.

In fact, that is exactly what happened. Beginning in the late 1960s, the government followed policies that expanded the aggregate demand for goods and services. In part, this expansion was due to fiscal policy: Government spending rose as the Vietnam War heated up. In part, it was due to monetary policy: Because the Fed was trying to hold down interest rates in the face of expansionary fiscal policy, the money supply (as measured by M2) rose about 13 percent per year during the period from 1970 to 1972, compared to 7 percent per year in the early 1960s. As a result, inflation stayed high (about 5 to 6 percent per year in the late 1960s and early 1970s, compared to about 1 to 2 percent per year in the early 1960s). But as Friedman and Phelps had predicted, unemployment did not stay low.

Figure 7 displays the history of inflation and unemployment from 1961 to 1973. It shows that the simple negative relationship between these two variables started to break down around 1970. In particular, as inflation remained high in the early 1970s, people's expectations of inflation caught up with reality, and the unemployment rate reverted to the 5 percent to 6 percent range that had prevailed in the early 1960s. Notice that the history illustrated in Figure 7 resembles the theory of a shifting short-run Phillips curve shown in Figure 5. By 1973, policymakers had learned that Friedman and Phelps were right: There is no trade-off between inflation and unemployment in the long run.

QUICK QUIZ *Draw the short-run Phillips curve and the long-run Phillips curve. Explain why they are different.*

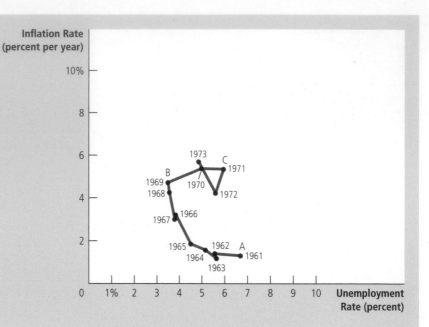

Figure 7

The Breakdown of the Phillips Curve
This figure shows annual data from 1961 to 1973 on the unemployment rate and on the inflation rate (as measured by the GDP deflator). The Phillips curve of the 1960s breaks down in the early 1970s, just as Friedman and Phelps had predicted. Notice that the points labeled A, B, and C in this figure correspond roughly to the points in Figure 5.

Source: U.S. Department of Labor; U.S. Department of Commerce.

Shifts in the Phillips Curve: The Role of Supply Shocks

Friedman and Phelps had suggested in 1968 that changes in expected inflation shift the short-run Phillips curve, and the experience of the early 1970s convinced most economists that Friedman and Phelps were right. Within a few years, however, the economics profession would turn its attention to a different source of shifts in the short-run Phillips curve: shocks to aggregate supply.

This time, the change in focus came not from two American economics professors but from a group of Arab sheiks. In 1974, the Organization of Petroleum Exporting Countries (OPEC) began to exert its market power as a cartel in the world oil market to increase its members' profits. The countries of OPEC, such as Saudi Arabia, Kuwait, and Iraq, restricted the amount of crude oil they pumped and sold on world markets. Within a few years, this reduction in supply caused the world price of oil to almost double.

A large increase in the world price of oil is an example of a supply shock. A **supply shock** is an event that directly affects firms' costs of production and thus the prices they charge; it shifts the economy's aggregate-supply curve and, as a result, the Phillips curve. For example, when an oil price increase raises the cost of producing gasoline, heating oil, tires, and many other products, it reduces the quantity of goods and services supplied at any given price level. As panel (a) of Figure 8 shows, this reduction in supply is represented by the leftward shift in the aggregate-supply curve from AS_1 to AS_2. Output falls from Y_1 to Y_2, and the price level rises from P_1 to P_2. The combination of falling output (stagnation) and rising prices (inflation) is sometimes called *stagflation*.

This shift in aggregate supply is associated with a similar shift in the short-run Phillips curve, shown in panel (b). Because firms need fewer workers to produce the smaller output, employment falls and unemployment rises. Because the price level is higher, the inflation rate—the percentage change in the price level from

supply shock
an event that directly alters firms' costs and prices, shifting the economy's aggregate-supply curve and thus the Phillips curve

Panel (a) shows the model of aggregate demand and aggregate supply. When the aggregate-supply curve shifts to the left from AS_1 to AS_2, the equilibrium moves from point A to point B. Output falls from Y_1 to Y_2, and the price level rises from P_1 to P_2. Panel (b) shows the short-run trade-off between inflation and unemployment. The adverse shift in aggregate supply moves the economy from a point with lower unemployment and lower inflation (point A) to a point with higher unemployment and higher inflation (point B). The short-run Phillips curve shifts to the right from PC_1 to PC_2. Policymakers now face a worse trade-off between inflation and unemployment.

Figure **8**

An Adverse Shock to Aggregate Supply

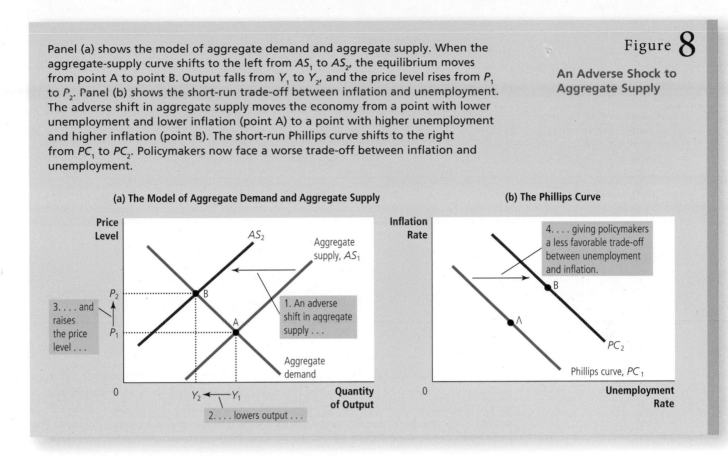

(a) The Model of Aggregate Demand and Aggregate Supply

(b) The Phillips Curve

the previous year—is also higher. Thus, the shift in aggregate supply leads to higher unemployment and higher inflation. The short-run trade-off between inflation and unemployment shifts to the right from PC_1 to PC_2.

Confronted with an adverse shift in aggregate supply, policymakers face a difficult choice between fighting inflation and fighting unemployment. If they contract aggregate demand to fight inflation, they will raise unemployment further. If they expand aggregate demand to fight unemployment, they will raise inflation further. In other words, policymakers face a less favorable trade-off between inflation and unemployment than they did before the shift in aggregate supply: They have to live with a higher rate of inflation for a given rate of unemployment, a higher rate of unemployment for a given rate of inflation, or some combination of higher unemployment and higher inflation.

Faced with such an adverse shift in the Phillips curve, policymakers will ask whether the shift is temporary or permanent. The answer depends on how people adjust their expectations of inflation. If people view the rise in inflation due to the supply shock as a temporary aberration, expected inflation will not change, and the Phillips curve will soon revert to its former position. But if people believe the shock will lead to a new era of higher inflation, then expected inflation will rise, and the Phillips curve will remain at its new, less desirable position.

In the United States during the 1970s, expected inflation did rise substantially. This rise in expected inflation was partly attributable to the Fed's decision to accommodate the supply shock with higher money growth. (Recall that policymakers are said to *accommodate* an adverse supply shock when they respond

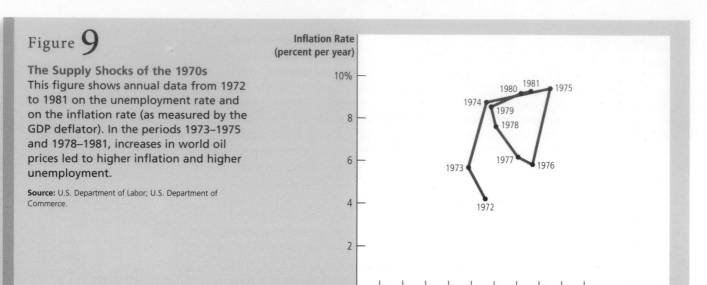

Figure **9**

The Supply Shocks of the 1970s
This figure shows annual data from 1972 to 1981 on the unemployment rate and on the inflation rate (as measured by the GDP deflator). In the periods 1973–1975 and 1978–1981, increases in world oil prices led to higher inflation and higher unemployment.

Source: U.S. Department of Labor; U.S. Department of Commerce.

to it by increasing aggregate demand in an effort to keep output from falling.) Because of this policy decision, the recession that resulted from the supply shock was smaller than it otherwise might have been, but the U.S. economy faced an unfavorable trade-off between inflation and unemployment for many years. The problem was compounded in 1979, when OPEC once again started to exert its market power, more than doubling the price of oil. Figure 9 shows inflation and unemployment in the U.S. economy during this period.

In 1980, after two OPEC supply shocks, the U.S. economy had an inflation rate of more than 9 percent and an unemployment rate of about 7 percent. This combination of inflation and unemployment was not at all near the trade-off that seemed possible in the 1960s. (In the 1960s, the Phillips curve suggested that an unemployment rate of 7 percent would be associated with an inflation rate of only 1 percent. Inflation of more than 9 percent was unthinkable.) With the misery index in 1980 near a historic high, the public was widely dissatisfied with the performance of the economy. Largely because of this dissatisfaction, President Jimmy Carter lost his bid for reelection in November 1980 and was replaced by Ronald Reagan. Something had to be done, and soon it would be.

QUICK QUIZ *Give an example of a favorable shock to aggregate supply. Use the model of aggregate demand and aggregate supply to explain the effects of such a shock. How does it affect the Phillips curve?*

The Cost of Reducing Inflation

In October 1979, as OPEC was imposing adverse supply shocks on the world's economies for the second time in a decade, Fed Chairman Paul Volcker decided that the time for action had come. Volcker had been appointed chairman by

President Carter only two months earlier, and he had taken the job knowing that inflation had reached unacceptable levels. As guardian of the nation's monetary system, he felt he had little choice but to pursue a policy of disinflation. *Disinflation* is a reduction in the rate of inflation, and it should not be confused with *deflation*, a reduction in the price level. To draw an analogy to a car's motion, disinflation is like slowing down, whereas deflation is like going in reverse. Chairman Volcker, along with many other Americans, wanted the economy's rising level of prices to slow down.

Volcker had no doubt that the Fed could reduce inflation through its ability to control the quantity of money. But what would be the short-run cost of disinflation? The answer to this question was much less certain.

The Sacrifice Ratio

To reduce the inflation rate, the Fed has to pursue contractionary monetary policy. Figure 10 shows some of the effects of such a decision. When the Fed slows the rate at which the money supply is growing, it contracts aggregate demand. The fall in aggregate demand, in turn, reduces the quantity of goods and services that firms produce, and this fall in production leads to a rise in unemployment. The economy begins at point A in the figure and moves along the short-run Phillips curve to point B, which has lower inflation and higher unemployment. Over time, as people come to understand that prices are rising more slowly, expected inflation falls, and the short-run Phillips curve shifts downward. The economy moves from point B to point C. Inflation is lower than it was initially at point A, and unemployment is back at its natural rate.

Thus, if a nation wants to reduce inflation, it must endure a period of high unemployment and low output. In Figure 10, this cost is represented by the movement of the economy through point B as it travels from point A to point C. The size of this cost depends on the slope of the Phillips curve and how quickly expectations of inflation adjust to the new monetary policy.

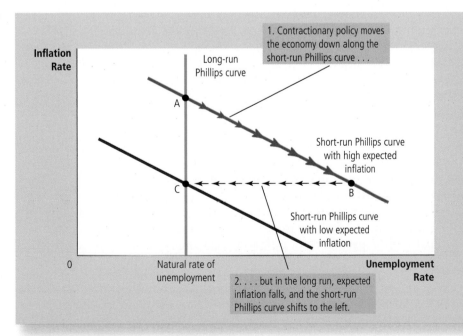

1. Contractionary policy moves the economy down along the short-run Phillips curve . . .

Long-run Phillips curve

Short-run Phillips curve with high expected inflation

Short-run Phillips curve with low expected inflation

Natural rate of unemployment

2. . . . but in the long run, expected inflation falls, and the short-run Phillips curve shifts to the left.

Figure 10

Disinflationary Monetary Policy in the Short Run and Long Run
When the Fed pursues contractionary monetary policy to reduce inflation, the economy moves along a short-run Phillips curve from point A to point B. Over time, expected inflation falls, and the short-run Phillips curve shifts downward. When the economy reaches point C, unemployment is back at its natural rate.

sacrifice ratio

the number of percentage points of annual output lost in the process of reducing inflation by 1 percentage point

Many studies have examined the data on inflation and unemployment to estimate the cost of reducing inflation. The findings of these studies are often summarized in a statistic called the **sacrifice ratio.** The sacrifice ratio is the number of percentage points of annual output lost in the process of reducing inflation by 1 percentage point. A typical estimate of the sacrifice ratio is 5. That is, for each percentage point that inflation is reduced, 5 percent of annual output must be sacrificed in the transition.

Such estimates surely must have made Paul Volcker apprehensive as he confronted the task of reducing inflation. Inflation was running at almost 10 percent per year. To reach moderate inflation of, say, 4 percent per year would mean reducing inflation by 6 percentage points. If each percentage point cost 5 percent of the economy's annual output, then reducing inflation by 6 percentage points would require sacrificing 30 percent of annual output.

According to studies of the Phillips curve and the cost of disinflation, this sacrifice could be paid in various ways. An immediate reduction in inflation would depress output by 30 percent for a single year, but that outcome was surely too harsh even for an inflation hawk like Paul Volcker. It would be better, many argued, to spread out the cost over several years. If the reduction in inflation took place over five years, for instance, then output would have to average only 6 percent below trend during that period to add up to a sacrifice of 30 percent. An even more gradual approach would be to reduce inflation slowly over a decade so that output would have to be only 3 percent below trend. Whatever path was chosen, however, it seemed that reducing inflation would not be easy.

Rational Expectations and the Possibility of Costless Disinflation

Just as Paul Volcker was pondering how costly reducing inflation might be, a group of economics professors was leading an intellectual revolution that would challenge the conventional wisdom on the sacrifice ratio. This group included such prominent economists as Robert Lucas, Thomas Sargent, and Robert Barro. Their revolution was based on a new approach to economic theory and policy called **rational expectations.** According to the theory of rational expectations, people optimally use all the information they have, including information about government policies, when forecasting the future.

rational expectations

the theory that people optimally use all the information they have, including information about government policies, when forecasting the future

This new approach has had profound implications for many areas of macroeconomics, but none is more important than its application to the trade-off between inflation and unemployment. As Friedman and Phelps had first emphasized, expected inflation is an important variable that explains why there is a trade-off between inflation and unemployment in the short run but not in the long run. How quickly the short-run trade-off disappears depends on how quickly people adjust their expectations of inflation. Proponents of rational expectations built on the Friedman-Phelps analysis to argue that when economic policies change, people adjust their expectations of inflation accordingly. The studies of inflation and unemployment that had tried to estimate the sacrifice ratio had failed to take account of the direct effect of the policy regime on expectations. As a result, estimates of the sacrifice ratio were, according to the rational-expectations theorists, unreliable guides for policy.

In a 1981 paper titled "The End of Four Big Inflations," Thomas Sargent described this new view as follows:

> An alternative "rational expectations" view denies that there is any inherent momentum to the present process of inflation. This view maintains that firms and workers have now come to expect high rates of inflation in the future and that they strike inflationary bargains in light of these expectations. However, it is held that people expect high rates of inflation in the future precisely because the government's current and prospective monetary and fiscal policies warrant those expectations. . . . An implication of this view is that inflation can be stopped much more quickly than advocates of the "momentum" view have indicated and that their estimates of the length of time and the costs of stopping inflation in terms of forgone output are erroneous. . . . This is not to say that it would be easy to eradicate inflation. On the contrary, it would require more than a few temporary restrictive fiscal and monetary actions. It would require a change in the policy regime. . . . How costly such a move would be in terms of forgone output and how long it would be in taking effect would depend partly on how resolute and evident the government's commitment was.

According to Sargent, the sacrifice ratio could be much smaller than suggested by previous estimates. Indeed, in the most extreme case, it could be zero: If the government made a credible commitment to a policy of low inflation, people would be rational enough to lower their expectations of inflation immediately. The short-run Phillips curve would shift downward, and the economy would reach low inflation quickly without the cost of temporarily high unemployment and low output.

The Volcker Disinflation

As we have seen, when Paul Volcker faced the prospect of reducing inflation from its peak of about 10 percent, the economics profession offered two conflicting predictions. One group of economists offered estimates of the sacrifice ratio and concluded that reducing inflation would have great cost in terms of lost output and high unemployment. Another group offered the theory of rational expectations and concluded that reducing inflation could be much less costly and, perhaps, could even have no cost at all. Who was right?

Figure 11 shows inflation and unemployment from 1979 to 1987. As you can see, Volcker did succeed at reducing inflation. Inflation came down from almost 10 percent in 1981 and 1982 to about 4 percent in 1983 and 1984. Credit for this reduction in inflation goes completely to monetary policy. Fiscal policy at this time was acting in the opposite direction: The increases in the budget deficit during the Reagan administration were expanding aggregate demand, which tends to raise inflation. The fall in inflation from 1981 to 1984 is attributable to the tough anti-inflation policies of Fed Chairman Paul Volcker.

The figure shows that the Volcker disinflation did come at the cost of high unemployment. In 1982 and 1983, the unemployment rate was about 10 percent— about 4 percentage points above its level when Paul Volcker was appointed Fed chairman. At the same time, the production of goods and services as measured by real GDP was well below its trend level. The Volcker disinflation produced a recession that was, at the time, the deepest United States had experienced since the Great Depression of the 1930s.

Does this episode refute the possibility of costless disinflation as suggested by the rational-expectations theorists? Some economists have argued that the

Figure **11**

The Volcker Disinflation
This figure shows annual data from 1979 to 1987 on the unemployment rate and on the inflation rate (as measured by the GDP deflator). The reduction in inflation during this period came at the cost of very high unemployment in 1982 and 1983. Note that the points labeled A, B, and C in this figure correspond roughly to the points in Figure 10.

Source: U.S. Department of Labor; U.S. Department of Commerce.

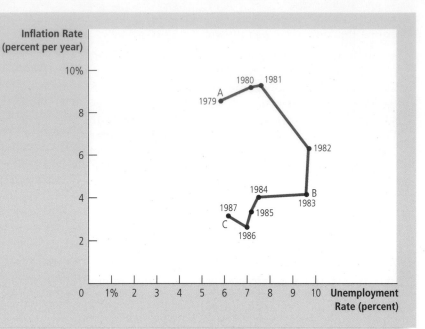

answer to this question is a resounding yes. Indeed, the pattern of disinflation shown in Figure 11 is similar to the pattern predicted in Figure 10. To make the transition from high inflation (point A in both figures) to low inflation (point C), the economy had to experience a painful period of high unemployment (point B).

Yet there are two reasons not to reject the conclusions of the rational-expectations theorists so quickly. First, even though the Volcker disinflation did impose a cost of temporarily high unemployment, the cost was not as large as many economists had predicted. Most estimates of the sacrifice ratio based on the Volcker disinflation are smaller than estimates that had been obtained from previous data. Perhaps Volcker's tough stand on inflation did have some direct effect on expectations, as the rational-expectations theorists claimed.

Second, and more important, even though Volcker announced that he would aim monetary policy to lower inflation, much of the public did not believe him. Because few people thought Volcker would reduce inflation as quickly as he did, expected inflation did not fall, and the short-run Phillips curve did not shift down as quickly as it might have. Some evidence for this hypothesis comes from the forecasts made by commercial forecasting firms: Their forecasts of inflation fell more slowly in the 1980s than did actual inflation. Thus, the Volcker disinflation does not necessarily refute the rational-expectations view that credible disinflation can be costless. It does show, however, that policymakers cannot count on people immediately believing them when they announce a policy of disinflation.

The Greenspan Era
Since the OPEC inflation of the 1970s and the Volcker disinflation of the 1980s, the U.S. economy has experienced relatively mild fluctuations in inflation and unemployment. Figure 12 shows inflation and unemployment from 1984 to 2005. This period is called the Greenspan era, after Alan Greenspan who in 1987 followed Paul Volcker as chairman of the Federal Reserve.

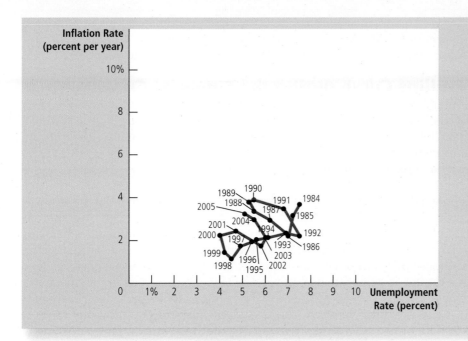

Figure 12

The Greenspan Era
This figure shows annual data from 1984 to 2005 on the unemployment rate and on the inflation rate (as measured by the GDP deflator). During most of this period, Alan Greenspan was chairman of the Federal Reserve. Fluctuations in inflation and unemployment were relatively small.

Source: U.S. Department of Labor; U.S. Department of Commerce.

This period began with a favorable supply shock. In 1986, OPEC members started arguing over production levels, and their long-standing agreement to restrict supply broke down. Oil prices fell by about half. As the figure shows, this favorable supply shock led to falling inflation and falling unemployment from 1984 to 1986.

Since then, the Fed has been careful to avoid repeating the policy mistakes of the 1960s, when excessive aggregate demand pushed unemployment below the natural rate and raised inflation. When unemployment fell and inflation rose in 1989 and 1990, the Fed raised interest rates and contracted aggregate demand, leading to a small recession in 1991 and 1992. Unemployment then rose above most estimates of the natural rate, and inflation fell once again.

The rest of the 1990s witnessed a period of economic prosperity. Inflation gradually drifted downward, approaching zero by the end of the decade. Unemployment also drifted downward, leading many observers to believe that the natural rate of unemployment had fallen. Part of the credit for this good economic performance goes to Alan Greenspan and his colleagues at the Federal Reserve, for low inflation can be achieved only with prudent monetary policy. But as the following case study discusses, good luck in the form of favorable supply shocks is also part of the story.

The economy, however, ran into problems in 2001. The end of the dot-com stock-market bubble, the 9/11 terrorist attacks, and corporate accounting scandals all depressed aggregate demand. Unemployment rose as the economy experienced its first recession in a decade. But a combination of expansionary monetary and fiscal policies helped end the downturn, and by early 2005, unemployment was close to most estimates of the natural rate.

In 2005 President Bush nominated Ben Bernanke to follow Alan Greenspan as the chairman of the Fed. Bernanke was sworn in on February 1, 2006. In 2009

Bernanke was reappointed by President Obama. At the time of his initial nomination, Bernanke said, "My first priority will be to maintain continuity with the policies and policy strategies established during the Greenspan years."

The Phillips Curve during the Financial Crisis

Ben Bernanke may have hoped to continue the policies of the Greenspan era and to enjoy the relative calm of those years, but his wishes would not be fulfilled. During his first few years on the job, the new Fed chairman faced some significant and daunting economic challenges.

As we have seen in previous chapters, the main challenge arose from problems in the housing market and financial system. From 1995 to 2006, the U.S. housing market boomed, and average U.S. house prices more than doubled. But this housing boom proved unsustainable, and from 2006 to 2009 house prices fell by about one third. This large fall led to declines in household wealth and difficulties in many financial institutions that had bet (through the purchase of mortgage-backed securities) that house prices would continue to rise. The resulting financial crisis resulted in a large decline in aggregate demand and a steep increase in unemployment.

We have already looked at the story of the crisis and the policy responses to it in many previous chapters, but Figure 13 shows the implications of these events for inflation and unemployment. As the decline in aggregate demand raised unemployment, it also reduced inflation. In essence, the economy rode the Phillips curve downward.

Policymakers used expansionary monetary and fiscal policy to try to reverse this move. The goal was to try to increase aggregate demand, thereby moving the economy back along the Phillips curve toward lower unemployment and somewhat higher inflation. One of the questions that policymakers faced was how much additional inflation they should aim for, a debate discussed in the accompanying In the News box. As this book was being written, it was unclear how

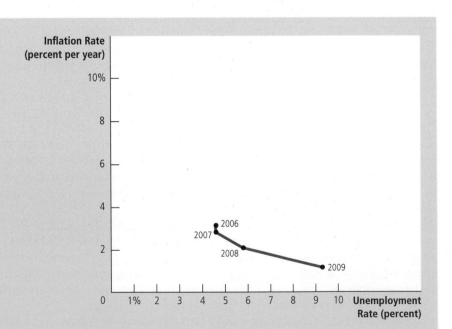

Figure **13**

The Phillips Curve during the Recession of 2008–2009
This figure shows annual data from 2006 to 2009 on the unemployment rate and on the inflation rate (as measured by the GDP deflator). A financial crisis caused aggregate demand to plummet, leading to much higher unemployment and pushing inflation down to a very low level.

Source: U.S. Department of Labor; U.S. Department of Commerce.

in the news

> ## Do We Need More Inflation?

In 2010, as the economy was struggling to recover from a deep recession, some people started wondering whether a bit more inflation would do the economy some good.

The Lure of Inflation's Siren Song

BY DAVID REILLY

Inflation is a tempting seductress, especially in an economy overburdened by debt and unemployment.

Why not, the thinking goes, keep the stimulus taps open longer than necessary to ensure a vigorous recovery by allowing inflation to overshoot targets for a year or two? Think of it as another dose of adrenaline helping unemployment fall faster and helping to erode budget deficits.

The problem: Once unleashed, inflation can't be easily contained, and sometimes the measures needed to do so can choke off growth.

So far, the Federal Reserve believes substantial slack in the economy makes inflation a distant prospect. Even if prices do rise, it has strong faith it can control them.

But there is a growing drumbeat of support for higher inflation. Olivier Blanchard, IMF chief economist, recently suggested central banks consider raising inflation targets

so they have more room to cut interest rates when crises hit. Some others argue employers and politicians are unwilling to address structural problems in the economy, leaving inflation as a more practical alternative.

Inflation can achieve what no congress can, fast reductions in fiscal deficits," Christian Broda, head of international research at Barclays Capital, wrote in a research note on Monday.

Mr. Broda estimated that letting inflation run at 5% for two years, compared with the Fed's 1.5% to 2% target for core inflation, would reduce the unemployment rate by three percentage points.

Of course, that is beguiling with consumers and the country as a whole struggling. And given tame inflation in the face of huge stimulus in recent years, the idea of runaway prices seems a distant threat, as the Fed said Tuesday.

But the risk that the central bank gets softer on inflation lies in its dual mandate to achieve both price stability and maximum employment. A desire to attack unemployment could lead to calls for letting inflation run up quietly, even if the target rate remains unchanged. After all, if

the economy really is recovering, zero interest rates could quickly become distortive.

Remember also that Fed Chairman Ben Bernanke's life study has been the Great Depression and how to avoid a repeat. Interestingly, that is at odds with the European Central Bank, whose view is heavily influenced by the hyperinflation of Germany's Weimar Republic.

Congress, which has attacked the Fed's independence, could also be an issue. It may push for inflation as an alternative to spending cuts or tax increases.

While attractive in the short-term, inflation would quickly be reflected in the cost of debt, hammering the value of fixed-income securities and pushing up the cost of borrowing. It could also hit the dollar and push commodity prices even higher. The experience of the 1970s shows how painful it can be to rein in inflation once unleashed.

So investors should be alert for any signs that the Fed is taking price stability for granted, or is willing to let inflation run above target. Heavy borrowers need to work through their problems to create a sustainable rebound.

Inflation would be a false fix.

Source: *The Wall Street Journal*, March 17, 2010.

quickly the economy would recover from this economic downturn and whether higher inflation, lower inflation, or perhaps even deflation was more likely.

QUICK QUIZ   *What is the sacrifice ratio? How might the credibility of the Fed's commitment to reduce inflation affect the sacrifice ratio?*

Conclusion

This chapter has examined how economists' thinking about inflation and unemployment has evolved. We have discussed the ideas of many of the best economists of the 20th century: from the Phillips curve of Phillips, Samuelson, and Solow, to the natural-rate hypothesis of Friedman and Phelps, to the rational-expectations theory of Lucas, Sargent, and Barro. Five members of this group have already won Nobel Prizes for their work in economics, and more may well be so honored in the years to come.

Although the trade-off between inflation and unemployment has generated much intellectual turmoil over the past half century, certain principles have developed that today command consensus. Here is how Milton Friedman expressed the relationship between inflation and unemployment in 1968:

> There is always a temporary tradeoff between inflation and unemployment; there is no permanent tradeoff. The temporary tradeoff comes not from inflation per se, but from unanticipated inflation, which generally means, from a rising rate of inflation. The widespread belief that there is a permanent tradeoff is a sophisticated version of the confusion between "high" and "rising" that we all recognize in simpler forms. A rising rate of inflation may reduce unemployment, a high rate will not.
>
> But how long, you will say, is "temporary"? . . . I can at most venture a personal judgment, based on some examination of the historical evidence, that the initial effects of a higher and unanticipated rate of inflation last for something like two to five years.

Today, almost a half century later, this statement still summarizes the view of most macroeconomists.

SUMMARY

- The Phillips curve describes a negative relationship between inflation and unemployment. By expanding aggregate demand, policymakers can choose a point on the Phillips curve with higher inflation and lower unemployment. By contracting aggregate demand, policymakers can choose a point on the Phillips curve with lower inflation and higher unemployment.

- The trade-off between inflation and unemployment described by the Phillips curve holds only in the short run. In the long run, expected inflation adjusts to changes in actual inflation, and the short-run Phillips curve shifts. As a result, the long-run Phillips curve is vertical at the natural rate of unemployment.

- The short-run Phillips curve also shifts because of shocks to aggregate supply. An adverse supply shock, such as an increase in world oil prices, gives policymakers a less favorable trade-off between inflation and unemployment. That is, after an adverse supply shock, policymakers have to accept a higher rate of inflation for any given rate of unemployment or a higher rate of unemployment for any given rate of inflation.

- When the Fed contracts growth in the money supply to reduce inflation, it moves the economy along the short-run Phillips curve, which results in temporarily high unemployment. The cost of disinflation depends on how quickly expectations of inflation fall. Some economists argue that a credible commitment to low inflation can reduce the cost of disinflation by inducing a quick adjustment of expectations.

KEY CONCEPTS

Phillips curve, *p. 386*
natural-rate hypothesis, *p. 394*

supply shock, *p. 396*
sacrifice ratio, *p. 400*

rational expectations, *p. 400*

QUESTIONS FOR REVIEW

1. Draw the short-run trade-off between inflation and unemployment. How might the Fed move the economy from one point on this curve to another?
2. Draw the long-run trade-off between inflation and unemployment. Explain how the short-run and long-run trade-offs are related.
3. What is "natural" about the natural rate of unemployment? Why might the natural rate of unemployment differ across countries?
4. Suppose a drought destroys farm crops and drives up the price of food. What is the effect on the short-run trade-off between inflation and unemployment?
5. The Fed decides to reduce inflation. Use the Phillips curve to show the short-run and long-run effects of this policy. How might the short-run costs be reduced?

PROBLEMS AND APPLICATIONS

1. Suppose the natural rate of unemployment is 6 percent. On one graph, draw two Phillips curves that describe the four situations listed here. Label the point that shows the position of the economy in each case.
   a. Actual inflation is 5 percent, and expected inflation is 3 percent.
   b. Actual inflation is 3 percent, and expected inflation is 5 percent.
   c. Actual inflation is 5 percent, and expected inflation is 5 percent.
   d. Actual inflation is 3 percent, and expected inflation is 3 percent.
2. Illustrate the effects of the following developments on both the short-run and long-run Phillips curves. Give the economic reasoning underlying your answers.
   a. A rise in the natural rate of unemployment
   b. A decline in the price of imported oil
   c. A rise in government spending
   d. A decline in expected inflation
3. Suppose that a fall in consumer spending causes a recession.
   a. Illustrate the immediate change in the economy using both an aggregate-supply/aggregate-demand diagram and a Phillips-curve diagram. On both graphs, label the initial long-run equilibrium as point

A and the resulting short-run equilibrium as point B. What happens to inflation and unemployment in the short run?
   b. Now suppose that over time expected inflation changes in the same direction that actual inflation changes. What happens to the position of the short-run Phillips curve? After the recession is over, does the economy face a better or worse set of inflation–unemployment combinations?
4. Suppose the economy is in a long-run equilibrium.
   a. Draw the economy's short-run and long-run Phillips curves.
   b. Suppose a wave of business pessimism reduces aggregate demand. Show the effect of this shock on your diagram from part (a). If the Fed undertakes expansionary monetary policy, can it return the economy to its original inflation rate and original unemployment rate?
   c. Now suppose the economy is back in long-run equilibrium, and then the price of imported oil rises. Show the effect of this shock with a new diagram like that in part (a). If the Fed undertakes expansionary monetary policy, can it return the economy to its original inflation rate and original unemployment rate? If the Fed undertakes contractionary monetary policy, can it return

the economy to its original inflation rate and original unemployment rate? Explain why this situation differs from that in part (b).

5. The inflation rate is 10 percent, and the central bank is considering slowing the rate of money growth to reduce inflation to 5 percent. Economist Milton believes that expectations of inflation change quickly in response to new policies, whereas economist James believes that expectations are very sluggish. Which economist is more likely to favor the proposed change in monetary policy? Why?

6. Suppose the Federal Reserve's policy is to maintain low and stable inflation by keeping unemployment at its natural rate. However, the Fed believes that the natural rate of unemployment is 4 percent when the actual natural rate is 5 percent. If the Fed based its policy decisions on its belief, what would happen to the economy? How might the Fed come to realize that its belief about the natural rate was mistaken?

7. Suppose the Federal Reserve announced that it would pursue contractionary monetary policy to reduce the inflation rate. Would the following conditions make the ensuing recession more or less severe? Explain.
   a. Wage contracts have short durations.
   b. There is little confidence in the Fed's determination to reduce inflation.
   c. Expectations of inflation adjust quickly to actual inflation.

8. Given the unpopularity of inflation, why don't elected leaders always support efforts to reduce inflation? Many economists believe that countries can reduce the cost of disinflation by letting their central banks make decisions about monetary policy without interference from politicians. Why might this be so?

9. As described in the chapter, the Federal Reserve in 2008 faced a decrease in aggregate demand caused by the housing and financial crises and a decrease in short-run aggregate supply caused by rising commodity prices.
   a. Starting from a long-run equilibrium, illustrate the effects of these two changes using both an aggregate-supply/aggregate-demand diagram and a Phillips-curve diagram. On both diagrams, label the initial long-run equilibrium as point A and the resulting short-run equilibrium as point B. For each of the following variables, state whether it rises or falls, or whether the impact is ambiguous: output, unemployment, the price level, the inflation rate.
   b. Suppose the Fed responds quickly to these shocks and adjusts monetary policy to keep unemployment and output at their natural rates. What action would it take? On the same set of graphs from part (a), show the results. Label the new equilibrium as point C.
   c. Why might the Fed choose not to pursue the course of action described in part (b)?

10. Suppose Federal Reserve policymakers accept the theory of the short-run Phillips curve and the natural-rate hypothesis and want to keep unemployment close to its natural rate. Unfortunately, because the natural rate of unemployment can change over time, they aren't certain about the value of the natural rate. What macroeconomic variables do you think they should look at when conducting monetary policy?

For further information on topics in this chapter, additional problems, applications, examples, online quizzes, and more, please visit our website at www.cengage.com/economics/mankiw.

PART VIII Final Thoughts

Six Debates over Macroeconomic Policy

18

I t is hard to open up the newspaper without finding some politician or editorial writer advocating a change in economic policy. The president should raise taxes to reduce the budget deficit, or he should stop worrying about the budget deficit. The Federal Reserve should cut interest rates to stimulate a flagging economy, or it should avoid such moves in order not to risk higher inflation. Congress should reform the tax system to promote faster economic growth, or it should reform the tax system to achieve a more equal distribution of income. Such economic issues are central to the continuing political debate in the United States and other countries around the world.

Previous chapters have developed the tools that economists use to analyze the behavior of the economy as a whole and the impact of policies on the economy. This final chapter considers six classic questions about macroeconomic policy. Economists have long debated these questions, and they will likely continue to do so for years to come. The knowledge you have accumulated in this course provides the foundation with which we can discuss these important, unsettled issues. It should help you choose a side in these debates or, at least, help you see why choosing a side is so difficult.

Should Monetary and Fiscal Policymakers Try to Stabilize the Economy?

In the preceding three chapters, we saw how changes in aggregate demand and aggregate supply can lead to short-run fluctuations in production and employment. We also saw how monetary and fiscal policy can shift aggregate demand and, thereby, influence these fluctuations. But even if policymakers *can* influence short-run economic fluctuations, does that mean they *should*? Our first debate concerns whether monetary and fiscal policymakers should use the tools at their disposal in an attempt to smooth the ups and downs of the business cycle.

Pro: Policymakers Should Try to Stabilize the Economy

Left on their own, economies tend to fluctuate. When households and firms become pessimistic, for instance, they cut back on spending, and this reduces the aggregate demand for goods and services. The fall in aggregate demand, in turn, reduces the production of goods and services. Firms lay off workers, and the unemployment rate rises. Real GDP and other measures of income fall. Rising unemployment and falling income help confirm the pessimism that initially generated the economic downturn.

Such a recession has no benefit for society—it represents a sheer waste of resources. Workers who lose their jobs because of declining aggregate demand would rather be working. Business owners whose factories are idle during a recession would rather be producing valuable goods and services and selling them at a profit.

There is no reason for society to suffer through the booms and busts of the business cycle. The development of macroeconomic theory has shown policymakers how to reduce the severity of economic fluctuations. By "leaning against the wind" of economic change, monetary and fiscal policy can stabilize aggregate demand and, thereby, production and employment. When aggregate demand is inadequate to ensure full employment, policymakers should boost government spending, cut taxes, and expand the money supply. When aggregate demand is excessive, risking higher inflation, policymakers should cut government spending, raise taxes, and reduce the money supply. Such policy actions put macroeconomic theory to its best use by leading to a more stable economy, which benefits everyone.

Con: Policymakers Should Not Try to Stabilize the Economy

Monetary and fiscal policy can be used to stabilize the economy in theory, but there are substantial obstacles to the use of such policies in practice.

One problem is that monetary and fiscal policy do not affect the economy immediately but instead work with a long lag. Monetary policy affects aggregate

demand primarily by changing interest rates, which in turn affect spending, particularly residential and business investment. But many households and firms set their spending plans in advance. As a result, it takes time for changes in interest rates to alter the aggregate demand for goods and services. Many studies indicate that changes in monetary policy have little effect on aggregate demand until about six months after the change is made.

Fiscal policy works with a lag because of the long political process that governs changes in spending and taxes. To make any change in fiscal policy, a bill must go through congressional committees, pass both the House and the Senate, and be signed by the president. It can take years to propose, pass, and implement a major change in fiscal policy.

Because of these long lags, policymakers who want to stabilize the economy need to look ahead to economic conditions that are likely to prevail when their actions will take effect. Unfortunately, economic forecasting is highly imprecise, in part because macroeconomics is such a primitive science and in part because the shocks that cause economic fluctuations are intrinsically unpredictable. Thus, when policymakers change monetary or fiscal policy, they must rely on educated guesses about future economic conditions.

Too often, policymakers trying to stabilize the economy do just the opposite. Economic conditions can easily change between the time a policy action begins and the time it takes effect. Because of this, policymakers can inadvertently exacerbate rather than mitigate the magnitude of economic fluctuations. Some economists have claimed that many of the major economic fluctuations in history, including the Great Depression of the 1930s, can be traced to destabilizing policy actions.

One of the first rules taught to physicians is "do no harm." The human body has natural restorative powers. Confronted with a sick patient and an uncertain diagnosis, often a doctor should do nothing but leave the patient's body to its own devices. Intervening in the absence of reliable knowledge merely risks making matters worse.

The same can be said about treating an ailing economy. It might be desirable if policymakers could eliminate all economic fluctuations, but that is not a realistic goal given the limits of macroeconomic knowledge and the inherent unpredictability of world events. Economic policymakers should refrain from intervening often with monetary and fiscal policy and be content if they do no harm.

QUICK QUIZ   *Explain why monetary and fiscal policy work with a lag. Why do these lags matter in the choice between active and passive policy?*

Should the Government Fight Recessions with Spending Hikes Rather Than Tax Cuts?

When George W. Bush became President in 2001, the economy was slipping into a recession. He responded by cutting tax rates. When Barack Obama became President in 2009, the economy was again in recession, the worst in many decades. He responded with a stimulus package that offered some tax reductions but also included substantial increases in government spending. The contrast between these two policies illustrates a second classic question of macroeconomics: Which instrument of fiscal policy—government spending or taxes—is better for reducing the severity of economic downturns?

Pro: The Government Should Fight Recessions with Spending Hikes

John Maynard Keynes transformed economics when he wrote *The General Theory of Employment, Interest and Money* in the midst of the Great Depression of 1930s, the worst economic downturn in U.S. history. Since then, economists have understood that the fundamental problem during recessions is inadequate aggregate demand. When firms are unable to sell a sufficient quantity of goods and services, they reduce production and employment. The key to ending recessions is to restore aggregate demand to a level consistent with full employment of the economy's labor force.

To be sure, monetary policy is the first line of defense against economic downturns. By increasing the money supply, the central bank reduces interest rates. Lower interest rates in turn reduce the cost of borrowing to finance investment projects, such as new factories and new housing. Increased spending on investment adds to aggregate demand and helps to restore normal levels of production and employment.

Fiscal policy, however, can provide an additional tool to combat recessions. When the government cuts taxes, it increases households' disposable income, which encourages them to increase spending on consumption. When the government buys goods and services, it adds directly to aggregate demand. Moreover, these fiscal actions can have multiplier effects: Higher aggregate demand leads to higher incomes, which in turn induces additional consumer spending and further increases in aggregate demand.

Fiscal policy is particularly useful when the tools of monetary policy lose their effectiveness. During the economic downturn of 2008 and 2009, for example, the Federal Reserve cut its target interest rate to almost zero. The Fed cannot reduce interest rates below zero, because people would hold onto their cash rather than lending it out at a negative interest rate. Thus, once interest rates are at zero, the

Roadside signs advertised the jobs created by the stimulus bill President Obama signed into law.

© AP PHOTO/AMY SANCETTA

Fed has lost its most powerful tool for stimulating the economy. In this circumstance, it is natural for the government to turn to fiscal policy—taxes and government spending—to prop up aggregate demand.

Traditional Keynesian analysis indicates that increases in government purchases are a more potent tool than decreases in taxes. When the government gives a dollar in tax cuts to a household, part of that dollar may be saved rather than spent. (That is especially true if households view the tax reduction as temporary rather than permanent.) The part of the dollar that is saved does not contribute to the aggregate demand for goods and services. By contrast, when the government spends a dollar buying a good or service, that dollar immediately and fully adds to aggregate demand.

In 2009, economists in the Obama administration used a conventional macroeconomic model to calculate the magnitude of these effects. According to their computer simulations, each dollar of tax cuts increases GDP by $0.99, whereas each dollar of government purchases increases GDP by $1.59. Thus, increases in government spending offer a bigger "bang for the buck" than decreases in taxes. For this reason, the policy response in 2009 featured fewer federal tax cuts and more increases in federal spending.

Policymakers focused on three kinds of spending. First, there was spending on "shovel-ready" projects. These were public works projects such as repairs to highways and bridges on which construction could begin immediately, putting the unemployed back to work. Second, there was federal aid to state and local governments. Because many of these governments are constitutionally required to run balanced budgets, falling tax revenues during recessions can make it necessary for them to lay off teachers, police, and other public workers; federal aid prevented that outcome or, at least, reduced its severity. Third, there were increased payments to the jobless through the unemployment insurance system. Because the unemployed are often financially stretched, they were thought to be likely to spend rather than save this extra income. Thus, these transfer payments were thought to contribute more to aggregate demand—and thereby production and employment—than tax cuts would. According to the macroeconomic model used by the Obama administration, the $800 billion stimulus package would create or save more than 3 million jobs by the end of the president's second year in office.

It is impossible to know for sure what effect the stimulus in fact had. Because we get only one run at history, we cannot observe the counterfactual—the same economy without the stimulus package. One thing is clear: While the economic downturn of 2008–2009 was severe, it could have been worse. As judged by the fall in GDP or rise in unemployment, it did not approach the magnitude of the Great Depression of the 1930s.

Con: The Government Should Fight Recessions with Tax Cuts

There is a long tradition of using tax policy to stimulate a moribund economy. President Kennedy proposed a tax reduction as one of his major economic initiatives; it eventually passed under President Johnson in 1964. President Reagan also signed into law significant tax cuts when he became president in 1981. Both of these tax reductions were soon followed by robust economic growth.

Tax cuts have important influence on both aggregate demand and aggregate supply. They increase aggregate demand by increasing households' disposable income, as emphasized in traditional Keynesian analysis. But they can also increase aggregate demand by altering incentives. For example, if the tax reductions take the form of an expanded investment tax credit, they can induce increased spending on investment goods. Because investment spending is the most volatile component of GDP over the business cycle, stimulating investment is a key to ending recessions. Policymakers can target it specifically with well-designed tax policy.

At the same time that tax cuts increase aggregate demand, they can also increase aggregate supply. When the government reduces marginal tax rates, workers keep a higher fraction of any income they earn. As a result, the unemployed have a greater incentive to search for jobs, and the employed have a greater incentive to work longer hours. Increased aggregate supply, along with the increased aggregate demand, means that the production of goods and services can expand without putting upward pressure on the rate of inflation.

There are various problems with increasing government spending during recessions. First of all, consumers understand that higher government spending, together with the government borrowing needed to finance it, will likely lead to higher taxes in the future. The anticipation of those future taxes will induce consumers to cut back spending today. Moreover, like most taxes, those in the future will likely cause a variety of deadweight losses. As businesses look ahead to a more highly distorted future economy, they may reduce their expectations of future profits and reduce investment spending today. Because of these various effects, government-spending multipliers may be smaller than is conventionally believed.

It is also far from clear whether the government can spend money both wisely and quickly. Large government spending projects often require years of planning, as policymakers and voters weigh the costs and benefits of the many alternative courses of action. By contrast, when unemployment soars during recessions, the need for additional aggregate demand is immediate. If the government increases spending quickly, it may end up buying things of little public value. But if it tries to be careful and deliberate in planning its expenditures, it may fail to increase aggregate demand in a timely fashion.

Tax cuts have the advantage of decentralizing spending decisions, rather than relying on a centralized and highly imperfect political process. Households spend their disposable income on things they value. Firms spend their investment dollars on projects they expect to be profitable. By contrast, when the government tries to spend large sums of money fast, subject to various political pressures, it may end up building "bridges to nowhere." Ill-conceived public projects may employ some workers, but they create little lasting value. Moreover, they will leave future generations of taxpayers with significant additional debts. In the end, the short-run benefits of additional aggregate demand from increased government spending may fail to compensate for the long-run costs.

QUICK QUIZ   *According to traditional Keynesian analysis, which has a larger impact on GDP—a dollar of tax cuts or a dollar of additional government spending? Why?*

Should Monetary Policy Be Made by Rule Rather Than by Discretion?

As we learned in the chapter on the monetary system, the Federal Open Market Committee sets monetary policy in the United States. The committee meets about every six weeks to evaluate the state of the economy. Based on this evaluation

CHAPTER 18 SIX DEBATES OVER MACROECONOMIC POLICY **417**

and forecasts of future economic conditions, it chooses whether to raise, lower, or leave unchanged the level of short-term interest rates. The Fed then adjusts the money supply to reach that interest-rate target, which will normally remain unchanged until the next meeting.

The Federal Open Market Committee operates with almost complete discretion over how to conduct monetary policy. The laws that created the Fed give the institution only vague recommendations about what goals it should pursue. A 1977 amendment to the 1913 Federal Reserve Act said the Fed "shall maintain long run growth of the monetary and credit aggregates commensurate with the economy's long run potential to increase production, so as to promote effectively the goals of maximum employment, stable prices, and moderate long-term interest rates." But the act does not specify how to weight these various goals, nor does it tell the Fed how to pursue whatever objective it might choose.

Some economists are critical of this institutional design. Our third debate over macroeconomic policy, therefore, focuses on whether the Federal Reserve should have its discretionary powers reduced and, instead, be committed to following a rule for how it conducts monetary policy.

Pro: Monetary Policy Should Be Made by Rule

Discretion in the conduct of monetary policy has two problems. The first is that it does not limit incompetence and abuse of power. When the government sends police into a community to maintain civic order, it gives them strict guidelines about how to carry out their job. Because police have great power, allowing them to exercise that power in whatever way they want would be dangerous. Yet when the government gives central bankers the authority to maintain economic order, it gives them few guidelines. Monetary policymakers are allowed undisciplined discretion.

As an example of the abuse of power, central bankers are sometimes tempted to use monetary policy to affect the outcome of elections. Suppose that the vote for the incumbent president is based on economic conditions at the time he or she is up for reelection. A central banker sympathetic to the incumbent might be tempted to pursue expansionary policies just before the election to stimulate production and employment, knowing that the resulting inflation will not show up until after the election. Thus, to the extent that central bankers ally themselves with politicians, discretionary policy can lead to economic fluctuations that reflect the electoral calendar. Economists call such fluctuations the *political business cycle*.

The second, subtler problem with discretionary monetary policy is that it might lead to more inflation than is desirable. Central bankers, knowing that there is no long-run trade-off between inflation and unemployment, often announce that their goal is zero inflation. Yet they rarely achieve price stability. Why? Perhaps it is because, once the public forms expectations of inflation, policymakers face a short-run trade-off between inflation and unemployment. They are tempted to renege on their announcement of price stability to achieve lower unemployment. This discrepancy between announcements (what policymakers *say* they are going to do) and actions (what they subsequently in fact do) is called the *time inconsistency of policy*. Because policymakers are so often time inconsistent, people are skeptical when central bankers announce their intentions to reduce the rate of inflation. As a result, people always expect more inflation than monetary policymakers claim they are trying to achieve. Higher expectations of inflation, in turn, shift the short-run Phillips curve upward, making the short-run trade-off between inflation and unemployment less favorable than it otherwise might be.

One way to avoid these two problems with discretionary policy is to commit the central bank to a policy rule. For example, suppose that Congress passed a law requiring the Fed to increase the money supply by exactly 3 percent per year. (Why 3 percent? Because real GDP grows on average about 3 percent per year and because money demand grows with real GDP, 3 percent growth in the money supply is roughly the rate necessary to produce long-run price stability.) Such a law would eliminate incompetence and abuse of power on the part of the Fed, and it would make the political business cycle impossible. In addition, policy could no longer be time inconsistent. People would now believe the Fed's announcement of low inflation because the Fed would be legally required to pursue a low-inflation monetary policy. With low expected inflation, the economy would face a more favorable short-run trade-off between inflation and unemployment.

Other rules for monetary policy are also possible. A more active rule might allow some feedback from the state of the economy to changes in monetary policy. For example, a more active rule might require the Fed to increase monetary growth by 1 percentage point for every percentage point that unemployment rises above its natural rate. Regardless of the precise form of the rule, committing the Fed to some rule would yield advantages by limiting incompetence, abuse of power, and time inconsistency in the conduct of monetary policy.

Con: Monetary Policy Should Not Be Made by Rule

There may be pitfalls with discretionary monetary policy, but there is also an important advantage to it: flexibility. The Fed has to confront various circumstances, not all of which can be foreseen. In the 1930s, banks failed in record numbers. In the 1970s, the price of oil skyrocketed around the world. In October 1987, the stock market fell by 22 percent in a single day. From 2007 to 2009, house prices dropped, home foreclosures soared, and the financial system experienced significant problems. The Fed must decide how to respond to these shocks to the economy. A designer of a policy rule could not possibly consider all the contingencies and specify in advance the right policy response. It is better to appoint good people to conduct monetary policy and then give them the freedom to do the best they can.

Moreover, the alleged problems with discretion are largely hypothetical. The practical importance of the political business cycle, for instance, is far from clear. In some cases, just the opposite seems to occur. For example, President Jimmy Carter appointed Paul Volcker to head the Federal Reserve in 1979. Nonetheless, in October of that year, Volcker switched to a contractionary monetary policy to combat the high rate of inflation that he had inherited from his predecessor. The predictable result of Volcker's decision was a recession, and the predictable result of the recession was a decline in Carter's popularity. Rather than using monetary policy to help the president who had appointed him, Volcker took actions he thought were in the national interest, even though they helped to ensure Carter's defeat by Ronald Reagan in the November 1980 election.

The practical importance of time inconsistency is also far from clear. Although most people are skeptical of central-bank announcements, central bankers can achieve credibility over time by backing up their words with actions. In the 1990s, the Fed achieved and maintained a low rate of inflation, despite the ever-present temptation to take advantage of the short-run trade-off between inflation and unemployment. This experience shows that low inflation does not require that the Fed be committed to a policy rule.

Any attempt to replace discretion with a rule must confront the difficult task of specifying a precise rule. Despite much research examining the costs

FYI

Inflation Targeting

Over the past few decades, many central banks around the world have adopted a policy called *inflation targeting*. Sometimes this takes the form of a central bank announcing its intentions regarding the inflation rate over the next few years. At other times it takes the form of a national law that specifies an inflation goal for the central bank.

Inflation targeting is not a commitment to an ironclad rule. In all the countries that have adopted inflation targeting, central banks are left with a fair amount of discretion. Inflation targets are usually set as a range—an inflation rate of 1 to 3 percent, for example—rather than a particular number. Thus, the central bank can choose where in the range it wants to be. Moreover, the central bank is sometimes allowed to adjust its target for inflation, at least temporarily, if some event (such as a shock to world oil prices) pushes inflation outside the target range.

Although inflation targeting leaves the central bank with some discretion, the policy does constrain how that discretion is used.

When a central bank is told simply to "do the right thing," it is hard to hold the central bank accountable, because people can argue forever about what the right thing is. By contrast, when a central bank has an inflation target, the public can more easily judge whether the central bank is meeting its goals. Inflation targeting does not tie the hands of the central bank, but it does increase the transparency and accountability of monetary policy. In a sense, inflation targeting is a compromise in the debate over rules versus discretion.

The Federal Reserve has not adopted an explicit policy of inflation targeting (although some commentators have suggested that it has an implicit inflation target of about 2 percent). One prominent advocate of inflation targeting is Ben Bernanke, a former economics professor who became Fed Chairman in 2006. It is possible, therefore, that the Federal Reserve may move toward inflation targeting in the future.

and benefits of alternative rules, economists have not reached consensus about what a good rule would be. Until there is consensus, society has little choice but to give central bankers discretion to conduct monetary policy as they see fit.

QUICK QUIZ *Give an example of a monetary policy rule. Why might your rule be better than discretionary policy? Why might it be worse?*

Should the Central Bank Aim for Zero Inflation?

One of the *Ten Principles of Economics* discussed in Chapter 1, and developed more fully in the chapter on money growth and inflation, is that prices rise when the government prints too much money. Another of the *Ten Principles of Economics* discussed in Chapter 1, and developed more fully in the preceding chapter, is that society faces a short-run trade-off between inflation and unemployment. Put together, these two principles raise a question for policymakers: How much inflation should the central bank be willing to tolerate? Our fourth debate is whether zero is the right target for the inflation rate.

Pro: The Central Bank Should Aim for Zero Inflation

Inflation confers no benefit on society, but it imposes several real costs. As we have discussed, economists have identified six costs of inflation:

- Shoeleather costs associated with reduced money holdings
- Menu costs associated with more frequent adjustment of prices
- Increased variability of relative prices
- Unintended changes in tax liabilities due to nonindexation of the tax code
- Confusion and inconvenience resulting from a changing unit of account
- Arbitrary redistributions of wealth associated with dollar-denominated debts

Some economists argue that these costs are small, at least for moderate rates of inflation, such as the 3 percent inflation experienced in the United States during the 1990s and 2000s. But other economists claim these costs can be substantial, even for moderate inflation. Moreover, there is no doubt that the public dislikes inflation. When inflation heats up, opinion polls identify inflation as one of the nation's leading problems.

The benefits of zero inflation have to be weighed against the costs of achieving it. Reducing inflation usually requires a period of high unemployment and low output, as illustrated by the short-run Phillips curve. But this disinflationary recession is only temporary. Once people come to understand that policymakers are aiming for zero inflation, expectations of inflation will fall, and the short-run trade-off will improve. Because expectations adjust, there is no trade-off between inflation and unemployment in the long run.

Reducing inflation is, therefore, a policy with temporary costs and permanent benefits. Once the disinflationary recession is over, the benefits of zero inflation would persist into the future. If policymakers are farsighted, they should be willing to incur the temporary costs for the permanent benefits. This is precisely the calculation made by Paul Volcker in the early 1980s, when he tightened monetary policy and reduced inflation from about 10 percent in 1980 to about 4 percent in 1983. Although in 1982 unemployment reached its highest level since the Great Depression, the economy eventually recovered from the recession, leaving a legacy of low inflation. Today, Volcker is considered a hero among central bankers.

Moreover, the costs of reducing inflation need not be as large as some economists claim. If the Fed announces a credible commitment to zero inflation, it can directly influence expectations of inflation. Such a change in expectations can improve the short-run trade-off between inflation and unemployment, allowing the economy to reach lower inflation at a reduced cost. The key to this strategy is credibility: People must believe that the Fed is actually going to carry through on its announced policy. Congress could help in this regard by passing legislation that makes price stability the Fed's primary goal. Such a law would make it less costly to achieve zero inflation without reducing any of the resulting benefits.

One advantage of a zero-inflation target is that zero provides a more natural focal point for policymakers than any other number. Suppose, for instance, that the Fed were to announce that it would keep inflation at 3 percent—the rate experienced during much of the previous two decades. Would the Fed really stick to that 3 percent target? If events inadvertently pushed inflation up to 4 or 5 percent, why wouldn't it just raise the target? There is, after all, nothing special about the number 3. By contrast, zero is the only number for the inflation rate at which the Fed can claim that it achieved price stability and fully eliminated the costs of inflation.

Con: The Central Bank Should Not Aim for Zero Inflation

Price stability may be desirable, but the benefits of zero inflation compared to moderate inflation are small, whereas the costs of reaching zero inflation are large. Estimates of the sacrifice ratio suggest that reducing inflation by 1 percentage point requires giving up about 5 percent of one year's output. Reducing inflation from, say, 4 percent to zero requires a loss of 20 percent of a year's output. People might dislike inflation of 4 percent, but it is not at all clear that they would (or should) be willing to pay 20 percent of a year's income to get rid of it.

The social costs of disinflation are even larger than this 20 percent figure suggests, for the lost income is not spread equitably over the population. When the economy goes into recession, all incomes do not fall proportionally. Instead, the fall in aggregate income is concentrated on those workers who lose their jobs. The vulnerable workers are often those with the least skills and experience. Hence, much of the cost of reducing inflation is borne by those who can least afford to pay it.

Economists can list several costs of inflation, but there is no professional consensus that these costs are substantial. The shoeleather costs, menu costs, and others that economists have identified do not seem great, at least for moderate rates of inflation. It is true that the public dislikes inflation, but the public may be misled into believing the inflation fallacy—the view that inflation erodes living standards. Economists understand that living standards depend on productivity, not monetary policy. Because inflation in nominal incomes goes hand in hand with inflation in prices, reducing inflation would not cause real incomes to rise more rapidly.

Moreover, policymakers can reduce many of the costs of inflation without actually reducing inflation. They can eliminate the problems associated with the nonindexed tax system by rewriting the tax laws to take account of the effects of inflation. They can also reduce the arbitrary redistributions of wealth between creditors and debtors caused by unexpected inflation by issuing indexed government bonds, as in fact the Clinton administration did in 1997. Such an act insulates holders of government debt from inflation. In addition, by setting an example, the policy might encourage private borrowers and lenders to write debt contracts indexed for inflation.

Reducing inflation might be desirable if it could be done at no cost, as some economists argue is possible. Yet this trick seems hard to carry out in practice. When economies reduce their rate of inflation, they almost always experience a period of high unemployment and low output. It is risky to believe that the central bank could achieve credibility so quickly as to make disinflation painless.

Indeed, a disinflationary recession can potentially leave permanent scars on the economy. Firms in all industries reduce their spending on new plants and equipment substantially during recessions, making investment the most volatile component of GDP. Even after the recession is over, the smaller stock of capital reduces productivity, incomes, and living standards below the levels they otherwise would have achieved. In addition, when workers become unemployed in recessions, they lose valuable job skills, permanently reducing their value as workers.

A little bit of inflation may even be a good thing. Some economists believe that inflation "greases the wheels" of the labor market. Because workers resist cuts in nominal wages, a fall in real wages is more easily accomplished with a rising price level. Inflation thus makes it easier for real wages to adjust to changes in labor market conditions.

········· in the **news**

> ### What Is the Optimal Inflation Rate?

In the aftermath of the financial crisis and recession of 2008–2009, economists started wondering whether higher inflation might be desirable.

Low-Inflation Doctrine Gets a Rethink, But Shift Is Unlikely

BY JON HILSENRATH

For the past quarter century, inflation has been a bogeyman that eats wealth and causes instability. But lately some smart people—including the chief economist at the International Monetary Fund and a senior Federal Reserve researcher—have been wondering aloud if a little more of it might actually be a good thing.

For several reasons, however, the idea isn't likely to gain traction any time soon.

The new argument for inflation goes like this: Low inflation and the low interest rates that accompany it leave central banks little room to maneuver when shocks hit. After Lehman Brothers collapsed in 2008, for example, the U.S. Federal Reserve quickly cut interest rates to near zero, but couldn't go any lower even though the economy needed a lot more stimulus.

Economists call this the "zero bound" problem. If inflation were a little higher to begin with, and thus interest rates were a little higher, the argument goes, the Fed would have had more room to cut interest rates and provided more juice to the economy.

Right now, the Fed and other big central banks have their sights set on inflation of around 2%. Economists had used a "Three Bears" approach to come up with this number—for a long time it seemed like it was not too hot and not too cold. But low and stable inflation could in theory mean something steady at a slightly higher rate.

IMF chief economist Olivier Blanchard, in a recent paper, said maybe the U.S. central bank's future inflation goal should be 4% instead. John Williams, head of the San Francisco Fed's research department, argued last year that higher targets might be needed to provide a cushion for future crises. . . .

There are other reasons some would welcome a little more inflation now. Governments in the U.S. and elsewhere, and many U.S. households, are sitting on mountains of debt. A little more inflation could in theory reduce the burden of servicing and paying that off, because while debt payments are often fixed, the revenue and income that households and governments generate to pay it off would rise with inflation.

But there are problems with the welcome-more-inflation argument.

The first is that it isn't yet clear that the "zero bound" on interest rates that Mr. Blanchard worries about is the economy's biggest problem. Thus addressing it might not be worth the costs that would be associated with higher inflation.

After the Fed pushed interest rates to near zero in December 2008, Chairman Ben Bernanke found alternatives to more interest-rate cuts: buying mortgage-backed securities and Treasury bonds and funneling credit to auto-loan, student-loan and credit-card markets. Those additional steps were no panacea, but they helped end the recession even if they didn't produce growth fast enough to bring unemployment down quickly. . . .

There is also a thornier problem. Suppose for a moment that Mr. Blanchard is right, and central banks around the world would be better prepared to fight future crises with

a little higher inflation. Getting from 2% to 4% could be a very messy process. Investors, businesses and households might well conclude a one-time shift to a higher inflation target actually means less commitment to stable inflation. Expectations of higher inflation could become a self-fulfilling prophecy. Instead of getting 4% inflation, central banks could end up with 5%, or 6% or 7%.

A higher inflation goal "would have a fairly immediate and disruptive effect" on markets, said Bruce Kasman, chief economist at J.P. Morgan Chase.

Mr. Bernanke has acknowledged the allure of a higher inflation goal. In written answers to lawmakers in December, he said a higher inflation target could in theory make it possible for the Fed to push inflation-adjusted interest rates lower, stimulating borrowing and economic growth.

But the opposite could happen, too. The prospect of higher inflation could cause interest rates to shoot up and make the burden of future borrowing even heavier. This is a particular problem for countries, like the U.S., that issue a lot of short-term debt and for people with adjustable-rate mortgages.

Mr. Bernanke concluded he didn't want to mess with people's fragile expectations. He said switching to a higher target would risk causing "the public to lose confidence in the central bank's willingness to resist further upward shifts in inflation, and so undermine the effectiveness of monetary policy going forward."

The 2% inflation goal that is so popular with central bankers around the world might not have been the ideal target in retrospect. But it looks like everybody is tied to it, for better or worse, for the foreseeable future.

Source: *The Wall Street Journal*, February 22, 2010.

In addition, inflation allows for the possibility of negative real interest rates. Nominal interest rates can never fall below zero, because lenders can always hold on to their money rather than lending it out at a negative return. If inflation is zero, real interest rates can never be negative as well. However, if inflation is positive, then a cut in nominal interest rates below the inflation rate produces negative real interest rates. Sometimes the economy may need negative real interest rates to provide sufficient stimulus to aggregate demand—an option ruled out by zero inflation.

In light of all these arguments, why should policymakers put the economy through a costly, inequitable disinflationary recession to achieve zero inflation? Economist Alan Blinder, who was once vice chairman of the Federal Reserve, argued in his book *Hard Heads, Soft Hearts* that policymakers should not make this choice:

> The costs that attend the low and moderate inflation rates experienced in the United States and in other industrial countries appear to be quite modest— more like a bad cold than a cancer on society. . . . As rational individuals, we do not volunteer for a lobotomy to cure a head cold. Yet, as a collectivity, we routinely prescribe the economic equivalent of lobotomy (high unemployment) as a cure for the inflationary cold.

Blinder concludes that it is better to learn to live with moderate inflation.

QUICK QUIZ   *Explain the costs and benefits of reducing inflation to zero. Which are temporary and which are permanent?*

Should the Government Balance Its Budget?

A persistent macroeconomic debate concerns the government's finances. Whenever the government spends more than it collects in tax revenue, it covers this budget deficit by issuing government debt. In our study of financial markets, we saw how budget deficits affect saving, investment, and interest rates. But how big a problem are budget deficits? Our fifth debate concerns whether fiscal policymakers should make balancing the government's budget a high priority.

Pro: The Government Should Balance Its Budget

The U.S. federal government is far more indebted today than it was two decades ago. In 1980, the federal debt was $710 billion; in 2009, it was $7.6 trillion. If we divide today's debt by the size of the population, we learn that each person's share of the government debt is about $25,000.

The most direct effect of the government debt is to place a burden on future generations of taxpayers. When these debts and accumulated interest come due, future taxpayers will face a difficult choice. They can choose some combination of higher taxes and less government spending to make resources available to pay off the debt and accumulated interest. Or, instead, they can delay the day of reckoning and put the government into even deeper debt by borrowing once again to pay off the old debt and interest. In essence, when the government runs a budget deficit and issues government debt, it allows current taxpayers to pass the bill for some of their government spending on to future taxpayers. Inheriting such a large debt cannot help but lower the living standard of future generations.

"What?!? My share of the government debt is $25,000?"

In addition to this direct effect, budget deficits have various macroeconomic effects. Because budget deficits represent *negative* public saving, they lower national saving (the sum of private and public saving). Reduced national saving causes real interest rates to rise and investment to fall. Reduced investment leads over time to a smaller stock of capital. A lower capital stock reduces labor productivity, real wages, and the economy's production of goods and services. Thus, when the government increases its debt, future generations are born into an economy with lower incomes as well as higher taxes.

There are, nevertheless, situations in which running a budget deficit is justifiable. Throughout history, the most common cause of increased government debt has been war. When a military conflict raises government spending temporarily, it is reasonable to finance this extra spending by borrowing. Otherwise, taxes during wartime would have to rise precipitously. Such high tax rates would greatly distort the incentives faced by those who are taxed, leading to large deadweight losses. In addition, such high tax rates would be unfair to current generations of taxpayers, who already have to make the sacrifice of fighting the war.

Similarly, it is reasonable to allow a budget deficit during a temporary downturn in economic activity. When the economy goes into a recession, tax revenue falls automatically because the income tax and the payroll tax are levied on measures of income. If the government tried to balance its budget during a recession, it would have to raise taxes or cut spending at a time of high unemployment. Such a policy would tend to depress aggregate demand at precisely the time it needed to be stimulated and, therefore, would tend to increase the magnitude of economic fluctuations.

Yet not all budget deficits can be justified by appealing to war or recession. U.S. government debt as a percentage of GDP increased from 26 percent in 1980 to 50 percent in 1995. During this period, the United States experienced neither a major military conflict nor a major economic downturn. Yet the government consistently ran a sizable budget deficit, largely because the president and Congress found it easier to increase government spending than to increase taxes.

The budget deficits of the first decade of the 2000s can, perhaps, be rationalized by the wars in Iraq and Afghanistan and the effects of the recessions in 2001 and 2008–2009. But it is imperative that this deficit not signal a return to the unsustainable fiscal policy of an earlier era. As the economy recovers from the most recent recession and unemployment returns to its natural rate, the government should bring spending in line with tax revenue. Compared to the alternative of ongoing budget deficits, a balanced budget means greater national saving, investment, and economic growth. It means that future college graduates will enter a more prosperous economy.

Con: The Government Should Not Balance Its Budget

The problem of government debt is often exaggerated. Although the government debt does represent a tax burden on younger generations, it is not large compared to the average person's lifetime income. The debt of the U.S. federal government is about $25,000 per person. A person who works 40 years for $50,000 a year will earn $2 million over his lifetime. His share of the government debt represents about 1 percent of his lifetime resources.

Moreover, it is misleading to view the effects of budget deficits in isolation. The budget deficit is just one piece of a large picture of how the government chooses to raise and spend money. In making these decisions over fiscal policy, policymakers affect different generations of taxpayers in many ways. The government's budget deficit or surplus should be considered together with these other policies.

For example, suppose the government reduces the budget deficit by cutting spending on public investments, such as education. Does this policy make younger generations better off? The government debt will be smaller when they enter the labor force, which means a smaller tax burden. Yet if they are less educated than they could be, their productivity and incomes will be lower. Many estimates of the return to schooling (the increase in a worker's wage that results from an additional year in school) find that it is quite large. Reducing the budget deficit rather than funding more education spending could, all things considered, make future generations worse off.

Single-minded concern about the budget deficit is also dangerous because it draws attention away from various other policies that redistribute income across generations. For example, in the 1960s and 1970s, the U.S. federal government raised Social Security benefits for the elderly. It financed this higher spending by increasing the payroll tax on the working-age population. This policy redistributed income away from younger generations toward older generations, even though it did not affect the government debt. Thus, the budget deficit is only a small part of the larger issue of how government policy affects the welfare of different generations.

To some extent, forward-looking parents can reverse the adverse effects of government debt. The parent can offset the impact simply by saving and leaving a larger bequest. The bequest would enhance the children's ability to bear the burden of future taxes. Some economists claim that people do in fact behave this way. If this were true, higher private saving by parents would offset the public dissaving of budget deficits, and deficits would not affect the economy. Most economists doubt that parents are so farsighted, but some people probably do act this way, and anyone could. Deficits give people the opportunity to consume at the expense of their children, but deficits do not require them to do so. If the government debt were actually a great problem facing future generations, some parents would help to solve it.

Critics of budget deficits sometimes assert that the government debt cannot continue to rise forever, but in fact, it can. Just as a bank evaluating a loan application would compare a person's debts to his income, we should judge the burden of the government debt relative to the size of the nation's income. Population growth and technological progress cause the total income of the U.S. economy to grow over time. As a result, the nation's ability to pay the interest on the government debt grows over time as well. As long as the government debt grows more slowly than the nation's income, there is nothing to prevent the government debt from growing forever.

Some numbers can put this into perspective. The real output of the U.S. economy grows on average about 3 percent per year. If the inflation rate is 2 percent per year, then nominal income grows at a rate of 5 percent per year. The government debt, therefore, can rise by 5 percent per year without increasing the ratio of debt to income. In 2009, the federal government debt was $7.6 trillion; 5 percent of this figure is $380 billion. As long as the federal budget deficit is smaller than $380 billion, the policy is sustainable.

To be sure, very large budget deficits cannot persist forever. In 2010, the federal budget deficit was about $1.5 trillion, but this astonishing number was driven by extraordinary circumstances: a major financial crisis, a deep economic downturn, and the policy responses to these events. No one suggests that a deficit of this magnitude can continue. But zero is the wrong target for fiscal policymakers. As long as the deficit is only moderate in size, there will never be a day of reckoning that forces the budget deficits to end or the economy to collapse.

QUICK QUIZ *Explain how reducing a government budget deficit makes future generations better off. What fiscal policy might improve the lives of future generations more than reducing a government budget deficit?*

in the news

> ### Dealing with Debt and Deficits

In 2010, the state government of California faced a fiscal crisis. Was it a sign of things to come for the U.S. federal government?

The Californization of Washington

BY DAVID WESSEL

California's economy is large, rich and vibrant. It accounts for more than $1 of every $7 of goods and services produced in the U.S. and is bigger than all but seven countries. California has less taxpayer-backed state debt per person than Massachusetts and less as a percentage of its economy than New York, according to rating agency Standard & Poor's.

By such measures, California, though hit hard by the recession and housing bust, would seem an unlikely candidate for a government that might not pay its debts.

But it is, the result of a dysfunctional political system that combines well-financed referendums, super-majorities in the legislature and politicians unable to grapple with fundamental issues. Talk, now fading, is that only a constitutional convention can fix things.

The future, it's often said, arrives in California first. Is Washington next?. . .

Today's big budget deficit is not the problem. It is swollen by following the textbook prescription in a deep recession in which the Federal Reserve has cut interest rates to zero. The government-borrowing surge has been matched by a decline in private borrowing.

But this won't last. The recent past is reassuring, falsely so. Over the past 40 years, the U.S. government has expanded benefits and avoided massive tax increases by cutting

defense spending and borrowing heavily with ease. That is no longer feasible. When deficits grew uncomfortably large, congressional and White House deal makers emerged to alter course. They always muddle through, the markets and the public concluded.

Today, the deficits projected are bigger than ever, baby boomers are beginning to retire, health-care costs keep rising and, surely, we're closer to the day when Asian governments grow reluctant to lend ever-greater sums to the U.S. Treasury at low interest rates.

The Congressional Budget Office projects current policies would take the deficit from today's 10% of gross domestic product to over 20% by 2020 and over 40% by 2080. Yet today's politics appear more toxic, and the ranks of congressional leaders

Should the Tax Laws Be Reformed to Encourage Saving?

A nation's standard of living depends on its ability to produce goods and services. This was one of the *Ten Principles of Economics* in Chapter 1. As we saw in the chapter on production and growth, a nation's productive capability, in turn, is determined largely by how much it saves and invests for the future. Our sixth debate is whether policymakers should reform the tax laws to encourage greater saving and investment.

Pro: The Tax Laws Should Be Reformed to Encourage Saving

A nation's saving rate is a key determinant of its long-run economic prosperity. When the saving rate is higher, more resources are available for investment in new plant and equipment. A larger stock of plant and equipment, in turn, raises labor productivity, wages, and incomes. It is, therefore, no surprise that with the skill and desire to fashion compromises instead of talking points are depleted.

So what happens? One possibility is a political miracle: A sudden attack of leadership or bipartisanship, perhaps the rise of another Ross Perot to galvanize public angst about deficits. Another is a plunge in the U.S. dollar or spike in bond-market interest rates that spurs government belt-tightening, perhaps forcing spending cuts and tax increases before the economy is strong enough to take them.

It could be worse. "A far worse situation would be for interest rates to stay low while we accumulated unprecedented amounts of debt only to respond very suddenly when financial markets or foreign lenders decide that the U.S. is not a good credit risk," Leonard Burman of Syracuse University and economists from the Urban Institute told a recent conference at the University of Southern California. "That could produce a catastrophic financial meltdown, similar to the one triggered by the bursting of the housing market boom, but with one important difference. . . . The [U.S.] government will not be able to borrow to deal with its effects."

Imagine this plausible scenario: Public confidence in government continues to decline.

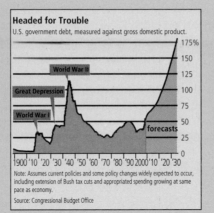

Headed for Trouble
U.S. government debt, measured against gross domestic product.

Note: Assumes current policies and some policy changes widely expected to occur, including extension of Bush tax cuts and appropriated spending growing at same pace as economy.

Source: Congressional Budget Office

Unemployment remains high. Americans demand more government services, more benefits and lower taxes. Politicians, seeking re-election, go along. . . .

In this scenario, even deficit-fearing politicians avoid taking on the long-term deficit. Mr. Burman imagines a White House political adviser saying: "Mr. President, if you raise taxes or cut popular programs, you or your party will be defeated in the polls and the bad guys will take over. The bad guys do not share your priorities and they do not care about the deficit.

Therefore, you cannot effectively deal with the deficit."

The challenge isn't coming up with options. The CBO has a book full of them, ranging from raising the retirement age to taxing carbon. It's arithmetically possible to eliminate the deficit exclusively by cutting spending. Wisconsin Republican Rep. Paul Ryan's Roadmap does. But there's no political majority for those proposals. It's arithmetically possible to eliminate the deficit by raising taxes, but the resulting tax rates would be politically and economically devastating. The challenge is fashioning a compromise that both solves the problem and is politically viable.

In August 1982, President Ronald Reagan went on TV to defend a package of spending cuts and tax increases that undid some of his earlier tax cuts: "Do we tell . . . Americans to give up hope, that their ship of state lies dead in the water because those entrusted with manning that ship can't agree on which sail to raise? We're within sight of the safe port of economic recovery. Do we make port or go aground on the shoals of selfishness, partisanship, and just plain bullheadedness?"

Good question.

Source: *The Wall Street Journal*, March 4, 2010.

---

international data show a strong correlation between national saving rates and measures of economic well-being.

Another of the *Ten Principles of Economics* presented in Chapter 1 is that people respond to incentives. This lesson should apply to people's decisions about how much to save. If a nation's laws make saving attractive, people will save a higher fraction of their incomes, and this higher saving will lead to a more prosperous future.

Unfortunately, the U.S. tax system discourages saving by taxing the return to saving quite heavily. For example, consider a 25-year-old worker who saves $1,000 of her income to have a more comfortable retirement at the age of 70. If she buys a bond that pays an interest rate of 10 percent, the $1,000 will accumulate at the end of 45 years to $72,900 in the absence of taxes on interest. But suppose she faces a marginal tax rate on interest income of 40 percent, which is typical of many workers once federal and state income taxes are added together. In this case, her after-tax interest rate is only 6 percent, and the $1,000 will accumulate at the end of 45 years to only $13,800. That is, accumulated over this long span of time, the tax rate on interest income reduces the benefit of saving $1,000 from $72,900 to $13,800—or by about 80 percent.

The tax code further discourages saving by taxing some forms of capital income twice. Suppose a person uses some of his saving to buy stock in a corporation.

When the corporation earns a profit from its capital investments, it first pays tax on this profit in the form of the corporate income tax. If the corporation pays out the rest of the profit to the stockholder in the form of dividends, the stockholder pays tax on this income a second time in the form of the individual income tax. This double taxation substantially reduces the return to the stockholder, thereby reducing the incentive to save.

The tax laws again discourage saving if a person wants to leave his accumulated wealth to his children (or anyone else) rather than consuming it during his lifetime. Parents can bequeath some money to their children tax-free, but if the bequest becomes large, the inheritance tax rate can be as high as 55 percent. To a large extent, concern about national saving is motivated by a desire to ensure economic prosperity for future generations. It is odd, therefore, that the tax laws discourage the most direct way in which one generation can help the next.

In addition to the tax code, many other policies and institutions in our society reduce the incentive for households to save. Some government benefits, such as welfare and Medicaid, are means-tested; that is, the benefits are reduced for those who in the past have been prudent enough to save some of their income. Colleges and universities grant financial aid as a function of the wealth of the students and their parents. Such a policy is like a tax on wealth and, as such, discourages students and parents from saving.

There are various ways in which the tax code could provide an incentive to save, or at least reduce the disincentive that households now face. Already the tax laws give preferential treatment to some types of retirement saving. When a taxpayer puts income into an Individual Retirement Account (IRA), for instance, that income and the interest it earns are not taxed until the funds are withdrawn at retirement. The tax code gives a similar tax advantage to retirement accounts that go by other names, such as 401(k), 403(b), Keogh plan, and profit-sharing plans. There are, however, limits to who is eligible to use these plans and, for those who are eligible, limits on the amount that can be put in them. Moreover, because there are penalties for withdrawal before retirement age, these retirement plans provide little incentive for other types of saving, such as saving to buy a house or pay for college. A small step to encourage greater saving would be to expand the ability of households to use such tax-advantaged savings accounts.

A more comprehensive approach would be to reconsider the entire basis by which the government collects revenue. The centerpiece of the U.S. tax system is the income tax. A dollar earned is taxed the same whether it is spent or saved. An alternative advocated by many economists is a consumption tax. Under a consumption tax, a household pays taxes only on the basis of what it spends. Income that is saved is exempt from taxation until the saving is later withdrawn and spent on consumption goods. In essence, a consumption tax puts all saving automatically into a tax-advantaged savings account, much like an IRA. A switch from income to consumption taxation would greatly increase the incentive to save.

Con: The Tax Laws Should Not Be Reformed to Encourage Saving

Increasing saving may be desirable, but it is not the only goal of tax policy. Policymakers also must be sure to distribute the tax burden fairly. The problem with proposals to increase the incentive to save is that they increase the tax burden on those who can least afford it.

It is undeniable that high-income households save a greater fraction of their income than low-income households. As a result, any tax change that favors people who save will also tend to favor people with high income. Policies such as tax-advantaged retirement accounts may seem appealing, but they lead to a less egalitarian society. By reducing the tax burden on the wealthy who can take advantage of these accounts, they force the government to raise the tax burden on the poor.

Moreover, tax policies designed to encourage saving may not be effective at achieving that goal. Economic theory does not give a clear prediction about whether a higher rate of return would increase saving. The outcome depends on the relative size of two conflicting forces, called the *substitution effect* and the *income effect*. On the one hand, a higher rate of return raises the benefit of saving: Each dollar saved today produces more consumption in the future. This substitution effect tends to increase saving. On the other hand, a higher rate of return lowers the need for saving: A household has to save less to achieve any target level of consumption in the future. This income effect tends to reduce saving. If the substitution and income effects approximately cancel each other, as some studies suggest, then saving will not change when lower taxation of capital income raises the rate of return.

There are ways to increase national saving other than by giving tax breaks to the rich. National saving is the sum of private and public saving. Instead of trying to alter the tax code to encourage greater private saving, policymakers can simply raise public saving by reducing the budget deficit, perhaps by raising taxes on the wealthy. This offers a direct way of raising national saving and increasing prosperity for future generations.

Indeed, once public saving is taken into account, tax provisions to encourage saving might backfire. Tax changes that reduce the taxation of capital income reduce government revenue and, thereby, lead to a larger budget deficit. To increase national saving, such a change in the tax code must stimulate private saving by more than the decline in public saving. If this is not the case, so-called saving incentives can potentially make matters worse.

QUICK QUIZ *Give three examples of how our society discourages saving. What are the drawbacks of eliminating these disincentives?*

Conclusion

This chapter has considered six classic debates over macroeconomic policy. For each, it began with a controversial proposition and then offered the arguments pro and con. If you find it hard to choose a side in these debates, you may find some comfort in the fact that you are not alone. The study of economics does not always make it easy to choose among alternative policies. Indeed, by clarifying the inevitable trade-offs that policymakers face, it can make the choice more difficult.

Difficult choices, however, have no right to seem easy. When you hear politicians or commentators proposing something that sounds too good to be true, it probably is. If they sound like they are offering you a free lunch, you should look for the hidden price tag. Few if any policies come with benefits but no costs. By helping you see through the fog of rhetoric so common in political discourse, the study of economics should make you a better participant in our national debates.

SUMMARY

- Advocates of active monetary and fiscal policy view the economy as inherently unstable and believe that policy can manage aggregate demand to offset the inherent instability. Critics of active monetary and fiscal policy emphasize that policy affects the economy with a lag and that our ability to forecast future economic conditions is poor. As a result, attempts to stabilize the economy can end up being destabilizing.

- Advocates of increased government spending to fight recessions argue that because tax cuts may be saved rather than spent, direct government spending does more to increase aggregate demand, which is key to promoting production and employment. Critics of spending hikes argue that tax cuts can expand both aggregate demand and aggregate supply and that hasty increases in government spending may lead to wasteful public projects.

- Advocates of rules for monetary policy argue that discretionary policy can suffer from incompetence, the abuse of power, and time inconsistency. Critics of rules for monetary policy argue that discretionary policy is more flexible in responding to changing economic circumstances.

- Advocates of a zero-inflation target emphasize that inflation has many costs and few if any benefits. Moreover, the cost of eliminating inflation—depressed output and employment—is only temporary. Even this cost can be reduced if the central bank announces a credible plan to reduce inflation, thereby directly lowering expectations of inflation. Critics of a zero-inflation target claim that moderate inflation imposes only small costs on society, whereas the recession necessary to reduce inflation is quite costly. The critics also point out several ways in which moderate inflation may be helpful to an economy.

- Advocates of a balanced government budget argue that budget deficits impose an unjustifiable burden on future generations by raising their taxes and lowering their incomes. Critics of a balanced government budget argue that the deficit is only one small piece of fiscal policy. Single-minded concern about the budget deficit can obscure the many ways in which policy, including various spending programs, affects different generations.

- Advocates of tax incentives for saving point out that our society discourages saving in many ways, such as by heavily taxing capital income and by reducing benefits for those who have accumulated wealth. They endorse reforming the tax laws to encourage saving, perhaps by switching from an income tax to a consumption tax. Critics of tax incentives for saving argue that many proposed changes to stimulate saving would primarily benefit the wealthy, who do not need a tax break. They also argue that such changes might have only a small effect on private saving. Raising public saving by decreasing the government's budget deficit would provide a more direct and equitable way to increase national saving.

QUESTIONS FOR REVIEW

1. What causes the lags in the effect of monetary and fiscal policy on aggregate demand? What are the implications of these lags for the debate over active versus passive policy?
2. According to traditional Keynesian analysis, why does a tax cut have a smaller effect on GDP than a similarly sized increase in government spending? Why might the opposite be the case?
3. What might motivate a central banker to cause a political business cycle? What does the political business cycle imply for the debate over policy rules?
4. Explain how credibility might affect the cost of reducing inflation.
5. Why are some economists against a target of zero inflation?
6. Explain two ways in which a government budget deficit hurts a future worker.
7. What are two situations in which most economists view a budget deficit as justifiable?

8. Give an example of how the government might hurt young generations, even while reducing the government debt they inherit.
9. Some economists say that the government can continue running a budget deficit forever. How is that possible?

10. Some income from capital is taxed twice. Explain.
11. Give an example, other than tax policy, of how our society discourages saving.
12. What adverse effect might be caused by tax incentives to raise saving?

PROBLEMS AND APPLICATIONS

1. The chapter suggests that the economy, like the human body, has "natural restorative powers."
   a. Illustrate the short-run effect of a fall in aggregate demand using an aggregate-demand/aggregate-supply diagram. What happens to total output, income, and employment?
   b. If the government does not use stabilization policy, what happens to the economy over time? Illustrate this adjustment on your diagram. Does it generally occur in a matter of months or a matter of years?
   c. Do you think the "natural restorative powers" of the economy mean that policymakers should be passive in response to the business cycle?
2. Policymakers who want to stabilize the economy must decide how much to change the money supply, government spending, or taxes. Why is it difficult for policymakers to choose the appropriate strength of their actions?
3. The problem of time inconsistency applies to fiscal policy as well as to monetary policy. Suppose the government announced a reduction in taxes on income from capital investments, like new factories.
   a. If investors believed that capital taxes would remain low, how would the government's action affect the level of investment?
   b. After investors have responded to the announced tax reduction, does the government have an incentive to renege on its policy? Explain.
   c. Given your answer to part (b), would investors believe the government's announcement? What can the government do to increase the credibility of announced policy changes?
   d. Explain why this situation is similar to the time inconsistency problem faced by monetary policymakers.

4. Chapter 2 explains the difference between positive analysis and normative analysis. In the debate about whether the central bank should aim for zero inflation, which areas of disagreement involve positive statements and which involve normative judgments?
5. Why are the benefits of reducing inflation permanent and the costs temporary? Why are the costs of increasing inflation permanent and the benefits temporary? Use Phillips-curve diagrams in your answer.
6. Suppose the federal government cuts taxes and increases spending, raising the budget deficit to 12 percent of GDP. If nominal GDP is rising 5 percent per year, are such budget deficits sustainable forever? Explain. If budget deficits of this size are maintained for twenty years, what is likely to happen to your taxes and your children's taxes in the future? Can you personally do something today to offset this future effect?
7. Explain how each of the following policies redistributes income across generations. Is the redistribution from young to old or from old to young?
   a. An increase in the budget deficit
   b. More generous subsidies for education loans
   c. Greater investments in highways and bridges
   d. An increase in Social Security benefits
8. The chapter says that budget deficits reduce the income of future generations but can boost output and income during a recession. Explain how both of these statements can be true.
9. What is the fundamental trade-off that society faces if it chooses to save more? How might the government increase national saving?
10. Suppose the government reduced the tax rate on income from savings and raised taxes on labor income to avoid increasing the budget deficit.

a. Who would benefit from this tax change most directly?

b. What would happen to the capital stock over time? What would happen to the capital available to each worker? What would happen to productivity? What would happen to wages?

c. In light of your answer to part (b), how might the long-run distributional effects differ from the answer you gave in part (a)?

For further information on topics in this chapter, additional problems, applications, examples, online quizzes, and more, please visit our website at www .cengage.com/economics/mankiw.

glossary

a

absolute advantage the ability to produce a good using fewer inputs than another producer

aggregate-demand curve a curve that shows the quantity of goods and services that households, firms, the government, and customers abroad want to buy at each price level

aggregate-supply curve a curve that shows the quantity of goods and services that firms choose to produce and sell at each price level

appreciation an increase in the value of a currency as measured by the amount of foreign currency it can buy

automatic stabilizers changes in fiscal policy that stimulate aggregate demand when the economy goes into a recession without policymakers having to take any deliberate action

b

balanced trade a situation in which exports equal imports

bank capital the resources a bank's owners have put into the institution

bond a certificate of indebtedness

business cycle fluctuations in economic activity, such as employment and production

c

capital flight a large and sudden reduction in the demand for assets located in a country

capital requirement a government regulation specifying a minimum amount of bank capital

catch-up effect the property whereby countries that start off poor tend to grow more rapidly than countries that start off rich

central bank an institution designed to oversee the banking system and regulate the quantity of money in the economy

circular-flow diagram a visual model of the economy that shows how dollars flow through markets among households and firms

classical dichotomy the theoretical separation of nominal and real variables

closed economy an economy that does not interact with other economies in the world

collective bargaining the process by which unions and firms agree on the terms of employment

commodity money money that takes the form of a commodity with intrinsic value

comparative advantage the ability to produce a good at a lower opportunity cost than another producer

complements two goods for which an increase in the price of one leads to a decrease in the demand for the other

compounding the accumulation of a sum of money in, say, a bank account, where the interest earned remains in the account to earn additional interest in the future

consumer price index (CPI) a measure of the overall cost of the goods and services bought by a typical consumer

consumption spending by households on goods and services, with the exception of purchases of new housing

crowding out a decrease in investment that results from government borrowing

crowding-out effect the offset in aggregate demand that results when expansionary fiscal policy raises the interest rate and thereby reduces investment spending

currency the paper bills and coins in the hands of the public

cyclical unemployment the deviation of unemployment from its natural rate

d

demand curve a graph of the relationship between the price of a good and the quantity demanded

demand deposits balances in bank accounts that depositors can access on demand by writing a check

demand schedule a table that shows the relationship between the price of a good and the quantity demanded

depreciation a decrease in the value of a currency as measured by the amount of foreign currency it can buy

depression a severe recession

diminishing returns the property whereby the benefit from an extra unit of an input declines as the quantity of the input increases

discount rate the interest rate on the loans that the Fed makes to banks

discouraged workers individuals who would like to work but have given up looking for a job

diversification the reduction of risk achieved by replacing a single risk with a large number of smaller, unrelated risks

e

economics the study of how society manages its scarce resources

efficient markets hypothesis the theory that asset prices reflect all publicly available information about the value of an asset

equilibrium a situation in which the market price has reached the level at which quantity supplied equals quantity demanded

equilibrium price the price that balances quantity supplied and quantity demanded

equilibrium quantity the quantity supplied and the quantity demanded at the equilibrium price

excludability the property of a good whereby a person can be prevented from using it

exports goods produced domestically and sold abroad

f

federal funds rate the interest rate at which banks make overnight loans to one another

Federal Reserve (Fed) the central bank of the United States

fiat money money without intrinsic value that is used as money because of government decree

finance the field that studies how people make decisions regarding the allocation of resources over time and the handling of risk

financial intermediaries financial institutions through which savers can indirectly provide funds to borrowers

financial markets financial institutions through which savers can directly provide funds to borrowers

financial system the group of institutions in the economy that help to match one person's saving with another person's investment

firm-specific risk risk that affects only a single company

fiscal policy the setting of the level of government spending and taxation by government policymakers

Fisher effect the one-for-one adjustment of the nominal interest rate to the inflation rate

fractional-reserve banking a banking system in which banks hold only a fraction of deposits as reserves

frictional unemployment unemployment that results because it takes time for workers to search for the jobs that best suit their tastes and skills

fundamental analysis the study of a company's accounting statements and future prospects to determine its value

future value the amount of money in the future that an amount of money today will yield, given prevailing interest rates

g

GDP deflator a measure of the price level calculated as the ratio of nominal GDP to real GDP times 100

government purchases spending on goods and services by local, state, and federal governments

gross domestic product (GDP) the market value of all final goods and services produced within a country in a given period of time

i

imports goods produced abroad and sold domestically

incentive something that induces a person to act

income elasticity of demand a measure of how much the quantity demanded of a good responds to a change in consumers' income, computed as the percentage change in quantity demanded divided by the percentage change in income

indexation the automatic correction by law or contract of a dollar amount for the effects of inflation

inflation an increase in the overall level of prices in the economy

inflation rate the percentage change in the price index from the preceding period

inflation tax the revenue the government raises by creating money

informational efficiency the description of asset prices that rationally reflect all available information

investment spending on capital equipment, inventories, and structures, including household purchases of new housing

j

job search the process by which workers find appropriate jobs given their tastes and skills

l

labor force the total number of workers, including both the employed and the unemployed

labor-force participation rate the percentage of the adult population that is in the labor force

law of demand the claim that, other things equal, the quantity demanded of a good falls when the price of the good rises

law of supply the claim that, other things equal, the quantity supplied of a good rises when the price of the good rises

law of supply and demand the claim that the price of any good adjusts to bring the quantity supplied and the quantity demanded for that good into balance

leverage the use of borrowed money to supplement existing funds for purposes of investment

leverage ratio the ratio of assets to bank capital

liquidity the ease with which an asset can be converted into the economy's medium of exchange

m

macroeconomics the study of economy-wide phenomena, including inflation, unemployment, and economic growth

marginal changes small incremental adjustments to a plan of action

market a group of buyers and sellers of a particular good or service

market economy an economy that allocates resources through the decentralized decisions of many firms and households as they interact in markets for goods and services

market failure a situation in which a market left on its own fails to allocate resources efficiently

market for loanable funds the market in which those who want to save supply funds and those who want to borrow to invest demand funds

market power the ability of a single economic actor (or small group of actors) to have a substantial influence on market prices

market risk risk that affects all companies in the stock market

medium of exchange an item that buyers give to sellers when they want to purchase goods and services

menu costs the costs of changing prices

microeconomics the study of how households and firms make decisions and how they interact in markets

model of aggregate demand and aggregate supply the model that most economists use to explain short-run fluctuations in economic activity around its long-run trend

monetary neutrality the proposition that changes in the money supply do not affect real variables

monetary policy the setting of the money supply by policymakers in the central bank

money the set of assets in an economy that people regularly use to buy goods and services from other people

money multiplier the amount of money the banking system generates with each dollar of reserves

money supply the quantity of money available in the economy

multiplier effect the additional shifts in aggregate demand that result when expansionary fiscal policy increases income and thereby increases consumer spending

mutual fund an institution that sells shares to the public and uses the proceeds to buy a portfolio of stocks and bonds

n

national saving (saving) the total income in the economy that remains after paying for consumption and government purchases

natural rate of output the production of goods and services that an economy achieves in the long run when unemployment is at its normal rate

natural rate of unemployment the normal rate of unemployment around which the unemployment rate fluctuates

natural resources the inputs into the production of goods and services that are provided by nature, such as land, rivers, and mineral deposits

natural-rate hypothesis the claim that unemployment eventually returns to its normal, or natural, rate, regardless of the rate of inflation

net capital outflow the purchase of foreign assets by domestic residents minus the purchase of domestic assets by foreigners

net exports spending on domestically produced goods by foreigners (exports) minus spending on foreign goods by domestic residents (imports)

nominal exchange rate the rate at which a person can trade the currency of one country for the currency of another

nominal GDP the production of goods and services valued at current prices

nominal interest rate the interest rate as usually reported without a correction for the effects of inflation

nominal variables variables measured in monetary units

normative statements claims that attempt to prescribe how the world should be

o

open economy an economy that interacts freely with other economies around the world

open-market operations the purchase and sale of U.S. government bonds by the Fed

opportunity cost whatever must be given up to obtain some item

p

Phillips curve a curve that shows the short-run trade-off between inflation and unemployment

physical capital the stock of equipment and structures that are used to produce goods and services

positive statements claims that attempt to describe the world as it is

present value the amount of money today that would be needed, using prevailing interest rates, to produce a given future amount of money

private saving the income that households have left after paying for taxes and consumption

producer price index a measure of the cost of a basket of goods and services bought by firms

production possibilities frontier a graph that shows the combinations of output that the economy can possibly produce given the available factors of production and the available production technology

productivity the quantity of goods and services produced from each unit of labor input

property rights the ability of an individual to own and exercise control over scarce resources

public saving the tax revenue that the government has left after paying for its spending

purchasing-power parity a theory of exchange rates whereby a unit of any given currency should be able to buy the same quantity of goods in all countries

q

quantity demanded the amount of a good that buyers are willing and able to purchase

quantity equation the equation $M \times V = P \times Y$ relates the quantity of money, the velocity of money, and the dollar value of the economy's output of goods and services

quantity supplied the amount of a good that sellers are willing and able to sell

quantity theory of money a theory asserting that the quantity of money available determines the price level and that the growth rate in the quantity of money available determines the inflation rate

r

random walk the path of a variable whose changes are impossible to predict

rational expectations the theory that people optimally use all the information they have, including information about government policies, when forecasting the future

rational people people who systematically and purposefully do the best they can to achieve their objectives

real exchange rate the rate at which a person can trade the goods and services of one country for the goods and services of another

real GDP the production of goods and services valued at constant prices

real interest rate the interest rate corrected for the effects of inflation

real variables variables measured in physical units

recession a period of declining real incomes and rising unemployment

reserve ratio the fraction of deposits that banks hold as reserves

reserve requirements regulations on the minimum amount of reserves that banks must hold against deposits

reserves deposits that banks have received but have not loaned out

risk aversion a dislike of uncertainty

s

sacrifice ratio the number of percentage points of annual output lost in the process of reducing inflation by 1 percentage point

scarcity the limited nature of society's resources

shoeleather costs the resources wasted when inflation encourages people to reduce their money holdings

shortage a situation in which quantity demanded is greater than quantity supplied

stagflation a period of falling output and rising prices

stock a claim to partial ownership in a firm

store of value an item that people can use to transfer purchasing power from the present to the future

structural unemployment unemployment that results because the number of jobs available in some labor markets is insufficient to provide a job for everyone who wants one

substitutes two goods for which an increase in the price of one leads to an increase in the demand for the other

supply curve a graph of the relationship between the price of a good and the quantity supplied

supply schedule a table that shows the relationship between the price of a good and the quantity supplied

supply shock an event that directly alters firms' costs and prices, shifting the economy's aggregate-supply curve and thus the Phillips curve

surplus a situation in which quantity supplied is greater than quantity demanded

t

technological knowledge society's understanding of the best ways to produce goods and services

theory of liquidity preference Keynes's theory that the interest rate adjusts to bring money supply and money demand into balance

trade balance the value of a nation's exports minus the value of its imports; also called net exports

trade deficit an excess of imports over exports

trade policy a government policy that directly influences the quantity of goods and services that a country imports or exports

trade surplus an excess of exports over imports

u

unemployment insurance a government program that partially protects workers' incomes when they become unemployed

unemployment rate the percentage of the labor force that is unemployed

unit of account the yardstick people use to post prices and record debts

v

velocity of money the rate at which money changes hands

index

SUGGESTIONS *for* SUMMER READIN...

IF YOU ENJOYED THE ECONOMICS COURSE THAT YOU ... JUST FINISHED, YOU MIGHT LIKE TO READ MORE ABOUT ... ECONOMIC ISSUES IN THE FOLLOWING BOOKS.

• • •

YORAM BAUMAN AND GRADY KLEIN

The Cartoon Introduction to Economics

(New York: Hill and Wang, 2010)

Basic economic principles, with humor.

• • •

NARIMAN BEHRAVESH

Spin-Free Economics

(New York: McGraw-Hill, 2008)

A straightforward guide to major economic policy debates.

• • •

WILLIAM BREIT AND BARRY T. HIRSCH

Lives of the Laureates

(Cambridge, MA: MIT Press, 2009)

Twenty-three winners of the Nobel Prize in Economics offer autobiographical essays about their life and work.

• • •

BRYAN CAPLAN

The Myth of the Rational Voter: Why Democracies Choose Bad Policies

(Princeton, NJ: Princeton University Press, 2008)

An economist asks why elected leaders often fail to follow the policies that economists recommend.

• • •

PAUL COLLIER

The Bottom Billion: Why the Poorest Countries Are Failing and What Can Be Done About It

(New York: Oxford University Press, 2007)

A former research director at the World Bank offers his insights into how to help the world's poor.

• • •

AVINASH DIXIT AND BARRY NALEBUFF

Thinking Strategically: The Competitive Edge in Business, Politics, and Everyday Life

(New York: Norton, 1991)

This introduction to game theory discusses how all people—from corporate executives to criminals under arrest—should and do make strategic decisions.

• • •